Manual of Standard Tibetan

Manual of Standard Tibetan

Language and Civilization

Introduction to Standard Tibetan (Spoken and Written)
Followed by an Appendix on Classical Literary Tibetan

by
Nicolas Tournadre and Sangda Dorje

Translated by Charles Ramble
Foreword by Matthew Kapstein

Snow Lion Publications
Ithaca, New York
Boulder, Colorado

Snow Lion Publications
P.O.Box 6483
Ithaca, NY 14851 USA
(607) 273-8519
www.snowlionpub.com

Printed in Canada on acid-free recycled paper.

ISBN 1-55939-189-8

Table of Contents

Lessons

Foreword

When I began to study the Tibetan language, during a visit to Nepal in 1970, suitable texts for beginners were few and far between. At first I located a tattered copy of the Rev. Bruce Hannah's ancient Tibetan grammar in a used book stand, and found to my dismay that the good pastor's illustrations of the language were entirely drawn from missionary translations of Bible stories. Not exactly the thing for a late-sixties dharma bum! A local shopkeeper, no doubt very much amused by my efforts to communicate on this basis, took pity and provided me with a small textbook published in the Punjab, that taught me how to order tea using a level of speech suitable only for small children, household domestics, and Khampa hillbillies. This proved to be quite adequate for the *chang*-stalls of Bodh Nath, but little more. Finally, I had the good fortune to borrow a copy of George Roerich's *Textbook of Colloquial Tibetan* and, given the general absence of technology in Kathmandu at the time, eagerly set about transcribing the entire book by hand. Though by no means ideal, the exercise proved to be a useful apprenticeship. It was only after I returned to the United States the following year that I was able to avail myself of the texts by Chang and Shefts, and by Goldstein and Nornang, works that marked the first efforts to adapt modern methods of language pedagogy to the requirements of Tibetan language instruction.

In the three decades that have passed since, a substantial number of contributions both to Tibetan linguistics and to Tibetan language teaching have thoroughly transformed the lay of the land, and the would-be learner of Tibetan, far from having to struggle to gain access to the merest crumb, is now more likely to suffer from an embarrassment of riches. For those who are finding it difficult to make up their minds about which course to use, I do not hesitate to recommend Nicolas Tournadre and Sangda Dorje's excellent *Manual of Standard Tibetan.* Their collaboration represents the confluence of linguistic analysis of the first order with the stylistic sensibilities of a leading contemporary master of Tibetan composition. Both share a keen appreciation of an approach in which the learning of language and of culture must inform one another, with the result that this is one of those rare language textbooks that is a pleasure to read.

The *Manual of Standard Tibetan* emphasizes Modern colloquial Tibetan as spoken in and around Lhasa, but adhering to a register that is widely used and understood. The student who masters it should have little difficulty communicating in most communities where Tibetan is spoken. The rudiments of the literary language are also thoroughly introduced, making it possible to make rapid progress in either Classical Tibetan or Modern Literary Tibetan during the second year of study. The cultural background incorporated in the entertaining dialogues and texts given throughout the book will prove invaluable to all who wish to enter the rich and endlessly fascinating sphere of Tibetan Civilization, whether they do so as scholars, casual visitors, or in connection with work in development or in commerce.

It is often said that learning a language begins one's exploration of an entire new world. Rare, however, is the language course that succeeds in conveying the sense of excitement and discovery thus promised. In the *Manual of Standard Tibetan* you will find yourself transported to monastery courtyards and to nomad camps; and, though Tibetan remains always a challenging language, requiring discipline and effort to learn, the rough journey in this case turns out to be a genuine delight.

Matthew T. Kapstein
The University of Chicago
June 2002

Welcoming the English edition

The original idea of a manual of the Tibetan language, and its first dialogues, were developed between 1993 and 1995 by the teaching team at the Tibetan Section of INALCO: the Venerable Dakpo Rinpoche, Ngawang Dakpa, Heather Stoddard and Nicolas Tournadre. The actual writing of the Manual, with its detailed linguistic commentaries and its cultural annotations, was undertaken by Nicolas Tournadre and Sangda Dorje, whose scholarship in Modern and Classical Tibetan are internationally recognized. These two authors have achieved the remarkable feat of producing the first manual of Tibetan in which the structures and idioms of the vernacular language are analyzed and placed within the living context of Tibet today.

The Tibetan Section of INALCO is delighted to welcome the publication of this English edition, joining the second French edition.

Heather Stoddard
Director of the Tibetan Section
Institut National des Langues et Civilisations Orientales,
Paris.

Supplementary materials for the Manual on the web

The Tibetan and Himalayan Digital Library of the University of Virginia hosts a website (www.thdl.org) providing supplementary materials for the *Manual of Standard Tibetan*, as well as a broad variety of other curricular materials for learning Spoken and Literary Tibetan. From the home page, go to Education: Languages: Tibetan. The site will ultimately include videos of many of the dialogues in the Manual, video recordings of each chapter's vocabulary, supplementary drills and exercises, and testing procedures. It is constantly updated as new materials become available, so we invite everyone to consult it regularly, and teachers to consider participating by offering their own materials.

Acknowledgments for the French Edition

This Manual would not have been possible without the collaboration of the teaching staff at the Tibetan section of INALCO (l'Institut National des Langues et Civilizations Orientales).

We would therefore first of all like to thank Heather Stoddard, the director of the section, who not only took part in the formulation of the Manual and the selection of illustrations, but also read and corrected a preliminary draft and made numerous valuable suggestions. We are very grateful to Mr. Ngawang Dakpa and the Ven. Dakpo Rinpoche (Jhampa Gyatso), who edited parts of the text and helped to formulate the content of the work. There is no doubt that this book would never have seen the light of day without their precious help.

We are grateful to Clause Hagège for his foreword. Our sincerest thanks are due to Samten Karmay, Fernand Meyer, Tenzin Samphel and Françoise Robin, who read and corrected the manuscript and offered very helpful suggestions.

Anne-Marie Blondeau generously made available to us the thematic Tibetan-French dictionary that she had developed within the framework of URA (Research Unit) 1229 of the CNRS "Langues et cultures de l'aire tibétaine" (Languages and Cultures of the Tibetan Region).

We are indebted to Martine Mazaudon and Boyd Michailovsky for their linguistic expertise and their unfailing support and encouragement over the past ten years, and also to the laboratory of LACITO (CNRS), which has financed Nicolas Tournadre's research trips to Tibet, Ladakh and Bhutan since 1986.

We would like to express our gratitude to colleagues living in Tibet: Konchok Jiatso and Thupten Wangpo, both at the Tibetan Academy of Social Science, for helping us in the course of our linguistic research; to Tibet University, which appointed Sangda Dorje to teach Tibetan at INALCO in Paris for two years; and to Kesang Gyurme, previously professor at the Nationalities University in Beijing, who taught Tibetan at INALCO in 1989.

Very many thanks are due to Christophe Gigaudaut for preparing the maps, for the page-setting of the Manual and for developing the Tibetan font, to Jean-Marc Eldin who was responsible for the typesetting and lay-out of the Second French Edition and also to Laurent Venot (LACITO) for recording the CDs; to Ngawang Dakpa, Choepel Lama and Namgyel and Rigdzin Wangmo for lending us their voices; to Tenzin Lodrup for recording songs from Kham; to Philippe Dufourg for his contribution on Tibetan crafts; to Gérard Muguet, Lodreu Zangpo, Pierre Jutier, Karen Léotoing and Jhampa Jigme for all the help they have given us, especially in developing the illustrations and symbols.

And finally, we wish to thank the students at INALCO whose questions have helped to refine our teaching of this language.

Nicolas Tournadre and Sangda Dorje
Paris and Lhasa, November 2002

Acknowledgments for the English edition

This book is an English translation of the second French edition of Nicolas Tournadre and Sangda Dorje's *Manuel de tibétain standard* (Paris, l'Asiathèque, 2003). The second French edition, and this English edition, incorporate many improvements over the original version, including new recordings, additional summary tables, more detailed linguistic and cultural commentary, and information about Tibetan dialects. Various people have contributed to the production of this Manual, and we would like to express our gratitude to them here:

- Charles Ramble: It would have been hard to find anyone better suited to the task of translating this Manual into English than Charles Ramble, currently lecturer in Tibetan and Himalayan Studies at Oxford University. Aside from being an internationally recognized anthropologist, he has a remarkable knowledge of both Spoken and Literary Tibetan. Furthermore, having lived in France, he also has an excellent knowledge of French language and culture. I am deeply grateful to him for his meticulous translation.
- Matthew Kapstein for writing the foreword and offering support.
- Christophe Gigaudaut who produced the maps and improved the typesetting, and Jean-Marc Eldin who finalized the lay-out.
- Boyd Michailovky and Nancy Caplow who commented on linguistic aspects of the manuscript.
- David Germano for his encouragement and his support.
- The University of Virginia and the U.S. Department of Education International Research and Studies Program for their strong financial support, notably for funding field trips to Tibet by Nicolas Tournadre between 2000 and 2002.
- Travis McCauley, who was responsible for making the recordings presented on the accompanying CDs.
- Wangdu, Dedrön n, Yeshe Dorje, and Chris Walker, whose voices can be heard on the recordings.
- Alison Joyner, who translated much of the introduction and some of the earlier lessons.
- Marc Lieberman, who supported our project and put us in contact with Snow Lion Publications.
- Steven Rhodes of Snow Lion who patiently corrected the final version of the manuscript.

NT and SD
Paris and Lhasa, April 2003

སློབ་དེབ་ཀྱི་དམིགས་ཡུལ། CD I • Tr. 2

༄། དེང་སང་འཛམ་གླིང་ཐོག་བོད་ཀྱི་རིག་གནས་ལ་དོ་སྣང་བྱེད་མཁན་ཇེ་མང་ཇེ་མང་དུ་འགྲོ་བཞིན་ཡོད་པས། བོད་ཀྱི་རིག་གནས་ཐད་འཚོལ་བསྡུ་དང་ཞིབ་འཇུག་བྱེད་པའི་སྒོ་མོ་འབྱེད་པ་ལ་མེད་དུ་མི་རུང་བའི་ལྡེ་མིག་དང་པོ་དེ་ནི་བོད་ཀྱི་སྐད་ཡིག་ཁོ་ན་ཡིན། དེས་ན་ད་ལྟའི་ཆར་བོད་ཀྱི་སྐད་ཡིག་སྦྱོང་མཁན་མཚོ་བཞི་གླིང་ལྔར་ཁྱབ་པ་ཀུན་གྱི་མཐོང་ཆོས་སུ་གྱུར་པས། བོད་ཀྱི་སྐད་ཡིག་སློབ་སྦྱོང་བྱེད་པའི་སློབ་དེབ་ཀྱི་དགོས་མཁོ་ཇེ་ཆེར་འགྲོ་བཞིན་པར་བརྟེན། ང་ཚོས་སློབ་དེབ་འདི་གསར་རྩོམ་ཞུས་པ་ཡིན། བོད་ཀྱི་སྐད་ཡིག་ལ་ཡིག་རྩོམ་དང་ཁ་སྐད་བར་ལ་ཁྱད་པར་ངེས་ཅན་ཡོད་ཁར་ཤར་ནུབ་དང་ལྷོ་བྱང་བར་གྱི་ཡུལ་སྐད་ལའང་ཁྱད་པར་ཆེན་པོ་ཡོད་པས་ང་ཚོའི་སློབ་དེབ་འདིར་དེང་དུས་སྤྱོད་པའི་ལྷ་སའི་སྐད་གཙོ་བོར་བཟུང་སྟེ་སྤྱི་སྐད་ཅིག་ཏུ་གྲུབ་པའི་འབད་བརྩོན་ཅི་ནུས་བྱས་པ་ཡིན་པས་སློབ་དེབ་འདི་བཞིན་བོད་སྐད་ཡིག་སྦྱོང་མཁན་རྣམས་ཀྱི་གྲོགས་པོ་བཟང་པོ་ཞིག་ཏུ་འགྱུར་བའི་སྨོན་འདུན་ཞུ་རྒྱུ་བཅས།

ལྷ་སར་ ༡༩༩༧ ལོའི་ཟླ་བ་ ༩ པར།

རྡོ་དགོན་གསང་བདག་རྡོ་རྗེ་དང་ཉི་སྐུ་ཟླ་ཡིས།

The Aims of This Manual

Interest in Tibet is currently increasing throughout the world. The indispensable key to the study and research of Tibetan culture is the spoken and written language. For some time now it has been possible to find students of Tibetan on all five continents, and the need for manuals of language instruction has therefore become all the more urgent. The present work is our contribution to meeting this demand. Literary Tibetan is significantly different from the spoken language, and there are marked variations in dialect from east to west and north to south. In this Manual we have therefore concentrated on presenting the standard spoken language, which is based on the dialect of Lhasa. It is our hope that this book will be a close companion to students of the Tibetan language.

Dhogonpa Sangda Dorje
and Nicolas Tournadre,
Lhasa, September 1997.

Preface

Tibetan Civilization is rich and fascinating. Over the years both nomads and settled peoples of the high plateau have developed a culture that in many respects has a universal appeal. Apart from Tibetan Buddhist philosophy, the medicine, astrology, iconography, architecture, poetry, grammar and music of the Land of the Snows have all gained a reputation which extends far beyond the Himalayas. The impact of Tibetan Civilization has for centuries been felt in Central Asia. It has been influential in China, Mongolia, Buryatia, Nepal, northern India, and even in the European part of Russia, particularly in Kalmykia.

It is worth drawing attention to several little-known facts about Tibetan language and literature. Many Buddhist texts have survived only in Tibetan, while their Chinese and Indian versions have been lost. Tibetan language offers a route to Buddhism and an entry point to understanding this religious philosophy. Tibetan literature is extremely rich in this area, whether it be indigenous to Tibet, or coming from translations from Sanskrit or Chinese. Lamas, the keepers of a living tradition, continue to explain and elaborate these texts.

Whether lay or religious, the body of Tibetan literature is vast and the majority of texts have not yet been translated. It also manifests striking originality, a world rich in symbolism, and a poetic tradition of remarkable beauty. The Epic of Gesar, celebrated throughout Central Asia and rivalling Gilgamesh as one of the greatest epics of the world, is written in Tibetan. Modern Tibetan literature, although barely known, is very much alive. Contemporary texts, particularly poems and short stories, abound.

Finally, Tibet is at a crossroads between the Indian, Chinese and Mongol cultures. At the same time, besides Buddhism, it has seen the development of a religion unique to the area, Bön.

To sample these literary treasures or even just to address a monk, a yogin perched in a cave at 5,000 meters altitude or a Tibetan trader, or to talk to a nomad letting fly his sling over the turquoise lakes, you have to be able to speak the language of Milaräpa and Gesar, the vehicle of this culture.

This Manual is for all those who want to learn spoken and written Tibetan.

Note

Tibetan contains a number of particular difficulties, mainly at the level of syntax[1] and semantics. One of the fundamental features of Tibetan verbs is that they distinguish systematically between intentional and unintentional actions. Moreover, the ubiquity of agentive (or "ergative") constructions in which it is the agent, not the object, that is marked, sometimes creates the disconcerting impression that it is an entirely "passive" language. For example, the sentence "Lobzang drank the tea" would be translated into Tibetan as lōpsang-ki' cha̲ tūng-song, which means literally "By Lobzang drank tea".

Generally speaking, Tibetan syntax is very different from that of European languages, though it does bear certain resemblances to the syntax of Hindi, Mongol, Japanese and Korean. The word order "subject-object-verb", which pertains also in subordinate clauses, often means that to understand a sentence we have to turn it "inside-out", and work backwards from the end. This being said, Tibetan syntax is completely logical and accessible once a certain number of new rules and novel ideas have been taken on board.[2] This entails making a certain terminological investment, which will be quickly recouped in the form of easier progress and more thorough comprehension. The grammatical information has been presented as simply as possible in order to make the language accessible to anyone who has a reasonable grasp of English grammar.

Regarding pronunciation, the Manual uses a very readable transcription that employs no special signs, and which can be used without any knowledge of IPA (the International Phonetic Alphabet).

The problems presented by Tibetan (other than syntax) fall into two main categories: those relating to the oral and to the literary language. As far as oral Tibetan is concerned, the phonetic system and the system of auxiliary verbs are relatively complicated, but the main obstacles can be overcome by working through the exercises provided in each lesson, and by means of regular practice. For written Tibetan, the absence of any separation between words, as well as a very archaic spelling (comparable to that of English or French) make reading hard going at the beginning, but the difficulties are relatively minor and by no means insurmountable.

And finally, the good news: Tibetan verbs involve no agreement in gender, number or person (except the first person in certain cases). Furthermore, the declension of nouns is very easy: cases are formed by association with suffixes, and the basic term remains unchanged.

---

1. Students often find that even though they may recognise every word in a sentence they still have no idea of the overall meaning. What they often lack is a grasp of the structures that underlie the organization of the sentence. We may well imagine the confusion of unprepared readers on being presented with a dozen or so subordinate clauses in a row or, even worse, "nested" inside one another like Russian dolls.

2. The familiar concepts of subject, object, transitivity, conjugation, declension and so on are not always very relevant in Tibetan, and don't always help us to grasp the peculiarity and genius of the language. Nevertheless, to simplify matters, the Manual will use these terms throughout, with appropriate modifications wherever necessary.

Abbreviations

*	grammatically incorrect formulation
abl.	ablative case
abs. or Ø	absolutive case
adj.	adjective
adv.	adverb
arch.	archaic
art.	article
aux.	auxiliary
caus.	causative verb
Chin.	Chinese
co.	connective, conjunction
dat.	dative case
dem.	demonstrative
det.	determinant
dial.	dialectal
ego.	egophoric
el.	elegant style
erg.	ergative case
excl.	exclusive
exp.	expressive particle
fem.	feminine
fig.	figurative
gen.	genitive case
H	honorific
h	humilific
HH	high honorific
hH	reciprocal honorific
idiom.	idiomatic
incl.	inclusive
interr.	interrogative
inv.	non-volitional verb
L	literary language
lit.	literally
loc.	locative
masc.	masculine
mod.	modal verb
Mong.	Mongol
n.	noun
pr.n.	proper noun
NEG.	negation
obl.	oblique case
part.	particle
f.i.p.	final interrogative particle
pl.	plural
post.	postposition
pres.	present
pron.	pronoun
interr. pron.	interrogative pronoun
quant.	quantifier
res.	resultative verb
NP.	noun phrase
VP.	verb phrase
ST.	Standard Tibetan
v.	verb
vol.	volitional verb
(1)	present-future stem
(2)	past stem
(3)	imperative stem
[A]	participant in the absolutive case
T.A.C.	Tibetan Autonomous County
T.A.P.	Tibetan Autonomous Prefecture
T.A.R.	Tibetan Autonomous Region
Tr.	track (CD)
[D]	participant in the dative case
[E]	participant in the agentive (or "ergative") case

N.B.: Bracketed words in the Tibetan text represent literary variants.

Introduction

1. The Tibetan language

Tibetan belongs to the Tibeto-Burman family of languages. This group encompasses about two hundred and fifty languages, spoken mainly in the Himalayas, on the Tibetan plateau and in the vicinity of the Mekong and the Salween. Within this linguistic family there are only two ancient literary languages: Burmese (12th century) and Tibetan (7th century). While very different, the common parentage of these two languages means that they share certain characteristics of phonology, syntax and vocabulary.

The Tibeto-Burman group of languages is part of the Sino-Tibetan superfamily, which compares in size and diversity with the Indo-European family.[3] Apart from Tibeto-Burman, the Sino-Tibetan family includes the Karen and Chinese languages (comprising most importantly the languages of Wu, Xiang, Hakka, Mandarin, and Min). These groups of languages are however only distantly related.

With the exception of Burmese, Tibetan, both in terms of syntax and vocabulary, is entirely different from the other major languages of the region: Chinese, Hindi, Nepali, the Turkish languages (Uigur, Kazakh, Tatar, etc.) and Mongolian.

Tibetan in its various dialects is spoken over an area the size of Western Europe, stretching from Baltistan (Pakistan) in the west, to Sichuan (China) in the east. To the north, the linguistic range of Tibetan extends beyond Lake Kokonor (in the province of Qinghai, China). Its southern limits are the southern slopes of the Himalaya, encompassing the independent state of Bhutan, Sikkim (India), the high valleys of Mustang and Dölpo, and Solukhumbu (Nepal), the region of Everest inhabited by the Sherpas of Nepal.

The language presented in this Manual

The language presented here is "Standard Tibetan" སྤྱི་སྐད་ *spyi-skad* /cīkä'/.[4] It corresponds to the language spoken in Central Tibet in the region of Lhasa, as well as among the diaspora community. This language is a variety of the "Central Tibetan"[5] དབུས་སྐད་ *dbus-skad* /ǖkä'/,

---

3. Remember that this Indo-European family includes such disparate languages as English, Greek, Russian, Persian, Hindi, French, Swedish, etc.

4. The literal translation of this term is "common language". We also come across the term "unified language" (*gcig 'gyur skad*). Here we use "Standard Tibetan" (*spyi skad*), the term increasingly widely used. Strictly however, it would be more accurate to speak of "language in the process of standardization". There is in fact neither a genuine academy of the Tibetan language, nor the political will to round off the process of standardization, which is nevertheless taking place naturally.

5. There are several varieties of "Central Tibetan". There are peculiarities and linguistic variations between each valley, even between different villages in Central Tibet. However these differences are minimal and do not hinder communication. In this Manual the terms "Standard Tibetan" and "Central Tibetan" will be used interchangeably. In 1999, an important book called *Collective Work on the Common Tibetan Language* was published in Beijing, with the participation of many prominent scholars from all the regions of Tibet. This is the first major recognition of Standard Tibetan based on Lhasa dialect.

spoken around Lhasa, which has become the *lingua franca* among Tibetans. It allows Tibetans living in other regions of Tibet (Amdo, Kham, Ngari, etc), and indeed those residing in China, India, Nepal, Bhutan, Europe and North America, to communicate with one another whatever their native dialect ཡུལ་སྐད་ *yul-skad* /yü̱:kä'/.[6] The general term བོད་སྐད་ *bod-skad* /phö̱kä'/, "Tibetan language",[7] is also sometimes used to describe the *lingua franca*, as are ཁ་སྐད་ *kha-skad* /khākä'/ spoken language or ཕལ་སྐད་ *phal-skad* /phā:kä'/ "ordinary language" – which differentiates it from Literary Tibetan ཡིག་སྐད་ *yig-skad* /yi̱kkä'/.

The term "Lhasa language" ལྷ་སའི་སྐད་ *lha-sa 'i-skad* /lhāsä: kā̈'/, often used to describe Standard Tibetan, will be avoided here as it has too narrow a meaning to be accurate. The language spoken in Tibet's capital includes peculiarities not found in villages just outside.

Conversely, a knowledge of Central or Standard Tibetan allows a clear understanding of the dialect གཙང་སྐད་ *gtsang-skad* /tsāngkä'/ spoken in the province of Tsang, of which the main town is Zhikatse. On the basis of this similarity, the term དབུས་གཙང་སྐད་ *dbus-gtsang skad*, /ǖtsang kā̈'/,is sometimes used to refer to this group of dialects.

It is possible to write Standard Spoken Tibetan and preserve the orthography inherited from Literary Tibetan. For the rare words not found in the literary language a new orthography is adopted. This is the written language presented in the Manual.

Literary Tibetan

There is however another form of Tibetan used by educated people: Literary Tibetan, ཡིག་སྐད་ *yig-skad* /yi̱kkä'/ or ཡིག་རྩོམ་བོད་ཡིག་ *yig-rtsom bod-yig* /yi̱ktsom phö̱yi'/. This is considered more prestigious and is common to scholars of all regions of Tibet, as well as the countries where Vajrayana Buddhism is established. Literary and Standard (or Central) Tibetan share the same basic grammar and are very similar lexically, to the extent that with a knowledge of one it is possible to read the other without too much difficulty.[8]

---

6. It should be noted that some intellectuals from Amdo and even from Kham are reluctant to learn the current "Standard Tibetan", based on Central Tibetan. They would prefer a common language not entirely derived from the latter. Unfortunately such a language does not exist. When Amdowas or Khampas meet natives of Tsang or Central Tibet they have no other option, if they don't know "Standard Spoken Tibetan", but to converse in Chinese or English (depending on the country in which they find themselves), or indeed to write in Literary Tibetan, which is common to all Tibet but is not a spoken language. At Tibetology conferences throughout the world (in China, Europe, India and the United States), speakers normally use Standard Tibetan whatever their dialect of origin.

7. This usage has the disadvantage of being used also to describe the other dialects.

8. Many Tibetans, as well as some non-Tibetans consider that only Literary Tibetan has a true grammar. Educated Tibetans are mildly disparaging of their spoken language, which they consider "vulgar" or "ordinary" (Tib. *phal-skad*). Only classical Literary Tibetan is well regarded enough to be "blessed" with a grammar. Linguists oppose such claims as false, and for non-specialists, it is worth stressing that Standard Spoken Tibetan does indeed possess a grammar. While fundamentally similar to that of literature, the grammar of the spoken language contains certain peculiarities. Examples include the working of auxiliaries and the way in which they are used with different connectives, or evidentials (or "mediatory moods", see the Glossary) which are one of the characteristics unique to the oral language.
The literary and oral registers are better regarded as two poles. Some works in Literary Tibetan reveal the influence of the spoken language, while the reverse is also true: letters written in the vernacular contain literary features. The difference between the two registers is greater than in the case of spoken and literary *English*.

In contrast to Standard or Central Tibetan, Literary Tibetan is not normally used for conversation. However, some lamas or lay intellectuals use a form of expression which is virtually Literary Tibetan, referred to as the "speech of the learned" མཁས་པའི་ཁ་སྐད་ *mkhas-pa'i kha-skad* /khāpä: khākä'/. There is therefore a real diglossia in their speech.

It is possible to identify in Literary Tibetan, depending on period and region, different types, styles and registers, each belonging to one of three broad categories: Old Tibetan (7th to 11th century), Classical Literary Tibetan (12th to 19th century) and Modern Literary Tibetan[9] (20th century). It should be noted that Modern Literary Tibetan is still very conservative[10] in its grammar, such that a non-specialist can read texts going back as far as the 12th century and even beyond. In its vocabulary, on the other hand, Modern Literary Tibetan has a large stock of neologisms, relating mainly to technical inventions.

The current manual focuses on Standard Spoken Tibetan and its written form. Literary Tibetan is briefly presented in Appendix 1, where the main differences from the spoken form are noted.

There are nevertheless some words in standard Tibetan which do not have a literary form, or where the pronunciation is notably different from that in Literary Tibetan. In these cases, a spelling which reflects Standard Tibetan is given, followed in brackets by the Literary Tibetan word.

The language of Dharma

The term ཆོས་སྐད་ *chos-skad* /chōkä'/, "language of Dharma", refers to the language of the religion and philosophy. However this does not mean that liturgical and philosophical languages have a separate grammar. Chōkä' is in fact pure Literary Tibetan, using a philosophical terminology that is specific to Dharma. Classical Tibetan is used as the liturgical language outside the Tibetan-speaking world in Mongolia and in the Russian Federation in Buriatia, Tuva and in Kalmykia. It is also sometimes used by various ethnic groups of Nepal such as Tamangs, Manangis, Lepchas, Gurungs, etc.

Oral teachings are normally given in the vernacular language, usually Spoken Standard Tibetan, fully complemented with quotations in Literary Tibetan.[11]

---

9. Modern Literary Tibetan includes the language of journalism *(gsar-shog gi skad-yig)*, as well as modern biographies *(rnam-thar)*, scientific texts and novels.

10. To this extent, Tibetan is comparable to Hebrew or Persian. By contrast, other languages such as French, English and Chinese have evolved much more rapidly. In these languages, writings from the fifteenth century are effectively accessible only to specialists.

11. It is sometimes said that some lama has been giving teachings in a Kham or Amdo dialect. In fact this happens when lamas are at home but it is rare, when they teach Dharma outside their native region. In that case they use the Standard Spoken language mixed with Literary Tibetan, and pronounce the words with an accent of their native dialect. We wouldn't say that a native of Cardiff or Aberystwyth was speaking Gaelic if he was conversing in English with a Welsh accent.

The term chōkä' is sometimes also used for political reasons in order to avoid mentioning the word "Tibetan", which refers to a nation and may therefore be less than ideal in a religious context. Finally, one occasionally hears the term chōkä' used to refer to the common language spoken in large monasteries that house monks of diverse regional provenance.

Levels of language

As in Literary Tibetan, there are several registers of politeness in Spoken Tibetan. The basic difference is between a form of polite speech ཞེ་ས་ *zhe-sa* /shesa/ and ordinary speech, སྐད་དཀྱུས་མ་ *skad dkyus-ma* /kā' kyūma/. The polite form means using honorific (H) expressions for the 2nd and 3rd persons and humilific (h) expressions for the 1st person. ཞེ་ས་ /shesa/ is expressed mainly through personal pronouns, nouns, verbs and their auxiliaries. In this Manual, the honorific is identified with a capital H and the humilific term with a small h. The honorific forms are only specified when they are used in everyday speech.[12]

Slang and "secret languages"

In Tibet, as in most other parts of the world, there are cryptic language codes corresponding to "argots", slang usages or languages of guilds, known as ལོགས་སྐད་ *logs skad* /lokkä'/. In Lhasa, certain artisanal associations, such as carpenters, use special argots. In cities, too, some youth sub-cultures have also developed their own sociolects.

The term /lokkä'/ has a secondary meaning of "isolated" language, usually a Tibeto-Burman language that is close to, but mutually incomprehensible with, Tibetan. These languages are sometimes also referred to as "secret languages" གསང་བའི་སྐད་ *gsang ba'i skad* /sāngwä kā' / or "languages of the Dakinis (celestial goddesses)" མཁའ་ འགྲོ་མའི་ སྐད་ *mkha'-'gro ma'i skad* /khāndromä kā'/.

An example of this is the language of Basum, which is spoken in Kongpo about four hundred kilometers from Lhasa by fewer than three thousand people. There are some twenty "isolated" languages spoken on the high plateau by populations that are either Tibetan or else have been assimilated to Tibetan culture.

The main Tibetan dialects

There are dozens of Tibetan dialects spread over five countries: China, Bhutan, Nepal India and Pakistan. The Tibetan dialects are derived from Old Tibetan and are closely related to Literary Tibetan.

The term *dialects* is used in the present work, though there is no mutual understanding between some of the dialects and they might as well be called *languages*. The main reason why

---

12. For further details, see also Appendix 3, which deals with the honorific register.

we speak of dialects is that they traditionally share Classical Tibetan as their literary language[13]. The expression "Tibetan dialects" to denote closely related languages that share a common literary language is analogous to the traditional terms of "Arabic dialects" or "Chinese dialects". We will list below the main dialects and their location within each country (see also the map of the dialects, on plate II).

in China:

- དབུས་སྐད་ *dbus skad* /ǖkä'/ in Lhasa Prefecture, Tibetan Autonomous Region.
- གཙང་སྐད་ *gtsang skad* /tsāngkä'/ in Zhikatse Prefecture, T.A.R.
- ཀོང་པོའི་སྐད་ *kong-po'i skad* /kōngpö: kā̃'/ in Nyingthri Prefecture, T.A.R.
- སྟོད་སྐད་ *stod skad* /tökä'/ in Ngari Prefecture, T.A.R, and in Nepal.
- ལྷོ་ཁའི་སྐད་ *lho-kha'i skad* /lhōkä: kā̃'/ in Lhokha Prefecture, T.A.R.
- ཧོར་སྐད་ *hor-skad* /hōrkä'/ in Nagchu Prefecture, T.A.R.
- ཁམས་སྐད་ *khams-skad* /khāmkä'/. Kham dialects are spoken in Chamdo Prefecture (T.A.R.), Kandze T.A.P. (Sichuan), in Yushu T.A.P. (Qinghai), and Dechen T.A.P. (Yunnan). Some Kham dialects are also spoken in Gannan Prefecture (Gansu, Choni County) and even in Ngari Prefecture (T.A.R., Gertse County).
- ཨ་མདོའི་སྐད་ *a-mdo'i skad* /āmtö: kā̃'/. Amdo dialects are spoken around Kokonor Lake, in Tshochang T.A.P., North of the Lake, (Qinghai, Haibei), Tsholho T.A.P., South of the Lake (Qinghai, Hainan), Tshonup T.A.P., West of the Lake (Qinghai, Haixi), in Tshoshar Prefecture, East of the Lake (Qinghai, Haidong). They are also spoken in Golok T.A.P. (Qinghai, guoluo), to the south of the Yellow River, in Malho T.A.P. (Qinghai Huangnan), in Kanlho T.A.P. (Gansu, Gannan) in Ngapa T.A.P. (Sichuan, Aba). Amdo dialects are also spoken by some nomads (*drogpa*) of Kandze Prefecture.

in Bhutan:

- རྫོང་ཁ་ *rdzong-kha* /tso̱ngka/ or འབྲུག་སྐད་ *'brug skad* /tru̱kkä'/, Dzongkha (lit: "the language of the fortresses"), the national language of Bhutan is spoken in the twenty districts of Bhutan, but only in eight districts as a native language: Thimphu, Paro, Punakha, Wangdi Phodra, Garsa, Hâ, Dhakarna and Chukha (for more details, see Driem, 1998.)

In Bhutan, one finds other Tibetan dialects such as:

- ཁྱོད་ཅ་ང་ཅ་ཁ་ *khyod-ca nga-ca kha* /khyȫcha nga̱cha khā/ is spoken in Lhüntsi and Monggar districts.
- ལ་ཁ་ *la-kha* /la̱ka/. Lakha is spoken in Wangdi Phodra district.

13. The only exception is the Balti dialect. Balti people in Pakistan were Buddhists until their conversion to Islam in the sixteenth century. Before that date, they also used Classical Tibetan as their literary language.

- མེ་རག་སག་སྟེང་འབྲོག་སྐད་ *me-rag sag-steng 'brog skad* /me̱ra' sākteng tro̱kkä'/. This dialect is spoken by yakherds in Trashigang district. It is called འབྲོག་ཁ་ /bjo̱kha/ in Dzongkha.
- དུར་གྱི་འབྲོག་སྐད་ *dur-gyi 'brog-skad* /thu̱rki tro̱kkä'/. This dialect referred locally as Brokkat is spoken by yakherds in Bhumthang district.

in Nepal:

- ཤར་པའི་སྐད་ *shar-pa'i skad* /shārpä: kǟ'/. The Sherpa dialect is found in the area near the Jhomolangma and the Ghangchendzönga ridges mainly in the following districts Solo-khumbu, Taplejung, Sankhuwa-Sabha, Dolakha and Sindupalchok. It is also spoken in the Tibetan Autonomous Region in Dram County.
- གདོལ་པོའི་སྐད་ *gdol-po'i skad* /tö̱:pö: kǟ'/.The Dölpo dialect is found in Dolpa district.
- གློ་སྐད་ *glo skad* /lōkä'/. The Lokä or Mustangi dialect is found in Mustang district.
- གྲོགས་པའི་སྒོ་ལའི་སྐད་ *grogs pa'i sgo la'i skad* /thro̱kpä ko̱lä: kǟ'/. The Dhrogpai Gola dialect is spoken in Taplejung district.

in India:

- འབྲས་ལྗོངས་སྐད་ *'bras-ljongs skad* /trä̱ncong kǟ'/. The Dränjong dialect or Sikkimese is spoken in the state of Sikkim.
- ལ་དྭགས་སྐད་ *la-dwags skad* /la̱ta' kǟ'/. Ladakhi is spoken in Ladakh district and Zangskar Tehsil of Kargil district in the state of Jammu and Kashmir.
- པུ་རིག་སྐད་ *pu-rig skad* /pūri' kǟ'/. Purik dialect is spoken in Kargil Tehsil of Ladakh district in the state of Jammu and Kashmir.
- སྤི་ཏིའི་སྐད་ *spiti'i skad* /pīti: kǟ'/. Spiti dialect is spoken in the district of Lahul and Spiti in the state of Himachal Pradesh.
- ལ་ཧུལ་སྐད་ *la-hul skad* /la̱hü: kǟ'/ or གར་ཞྭ་སྐད་ *gar-shwa skad* /kha̱rsha kǟ'/.

  The Lahuli dialect locally called Gharsha dialect is spoken in the district of Lahul and Spiti (Himachal Pradesh).
- ཉམ་སྐད་ *nyam skad* /nya̱m kǟ'/. Nyamkat dialect is located in the district of Upper Kinnaur (Himachal Pradesh).

in Pakistan:

- སྦལ་ཏིའི་སྐད་ *sbal-ti'i skad* /pä̱:ti: kǟ'/. Balti dialect is spoken in Baltistan and Ghanche districts in the Northern Areas of Pakistan.

It is possible to regroup the dialects in the following groups:[14]

14. This is a tentative classification. For some dialects such as Sherpa or Mustangi, further research is needed to establish their affiliation.

The Ü-Tsang group: Ü, Lhokha, Kongpo, Tsang, Tö.

The Tö subgroup of Ü-Tsang includes dialects from Ngari and Zhikatse Prefectures in the T.A.R. as well as various dialects spoken in northwestern Nepal (Limi, Mugu, Dolpo, Mustangi and Nubri) and northeastern Nepal (Lhomi, Dhrogpai Gola and Walungchung Gola).

The Kham-Hor group: Central Kham (Derge and Chamdo area), Southern Kham (Dechen area), Northeastern Kham (Yüshu, Nangchen area), Northeastern Kham (Thewo, Choni), and Hor (Nagchu area).

The Amdo group: North Kokonor Amdo (Kangtsa, Chilen, etc.), West Kokonor Amdo (Dulan, Nagormo, etc.), Southeast Kokonor Amdo (Chentsa, Thrika, Hualong, etc.), South Gansu Amdo (Labrang, Luchu, etc.), Golok Amdo (Machen, Matö, Gade, etc.), Ngapa Amdo (Ngapa, Dzorge, Dzamthang, etc.) and Kandze area Amdo spoken by some *drogpa* tribes.

The Dzongkha-Sikkimese group: Dzongkha, Lakha, Chochangacha, Sikkhimese, Merak Sakteng Drogpa, Dur Drogpa.

The Ladakhi-Balti group: Ladakhi, Balti, Purik.

The Lahul-Spiti group: Lahul, Spiti, Nyamkat.

The Sherpa-Jirel group: Solu Sherpa, Khumbu Sherpa, Jirel (all spoken in northeastern Nepal).

The Kyirong-Kagate group: Kyirong (spoken in Kyirong County, T.A.R.), and Kagate, Tsum, Langtang, and Yolmo (sometimes called Helambu Sherpa), all spoken in northeastern Nepal[15].

Mutual comprehension is generally good between the dialects of the Ü-Tsang group and Standard Tibetan. On the other hand, with the dialects of the other groups, communication is severely limited if their speakers know absolutely no Standard or Literary Tibetan: Of these the furthest removed from Central Tibetan are the dialects of Ladakh, Balti and Amdo, which did not develop tones.

Nomad-pastoralists, from whichever region (Ngari, Nagchu, Kham, etc.) have a particular speech referred to as འབྲོག་སྐད་ *'brog skad* /tr̠okkä'/, as distinct from the speech of sedentary agriculturalists, which is described as རོང་སྐད་ *rong skad* /r̠ongkä'/.[16]

15. I am grateful to Roland Bielmeier who provided valuable information on dialects of Nepal and Pakistan. (personal communication, February 2003).

16. The word *rong-pa* refers to farming communities in the low-lying valleys, as opposed to the nomads. Tibetans in Nepal use the term to denote the ethnic groups of the middle hills.

Amongst the populations bordering Tibet, many people speak Tibetan. Two examples are the populations of Gyarong རྒྱལ་རོང་ *rgyal-rong* /kyä̱:rong/ and Minyak མི་ཉག་ *mi-nyag* /mi̱nyak/ in Sichuan.[17]

It should be noted finally that within the Tibetan-speaking world, most educated people in the cities speak at least one or even two languages apart from their native Tibetan language: Chinese, Hindi-Urdu, Nepali or English depending on the country where they live.

2. Pronunciation and transcription

Phonological transcription[18] of Tibetan words will be provided up to Lesson 20. Before tackling the alphabet, it would be a good idea to get to grips with the Tibetan phonological system, and we shall therefore begin with a brief presentation of the pronunciation of sounds. For further details, refer to the basics of phonology given in Appendix 2.

The 28 consonants in Tibetan are: k, ky, ', p, t, tr, ts, c, s, r, sh, l, m, n , ng, ny, w, y and the aspirates kh, khy, ph, th, thr, tsh, ch, rh, lh, h. The eight vowels are: a, ä, e, o, ö, u, ü, i.

Each of these sounds will now be presented.

The consonants

We suggest that you make use of the CD when reading the explanations given here.

All the sounds presented here are illustrated in Appendix 2 with corresponding recordings.

• /k/ with a high tone[19] is pronounced like the *k* of *poker* or *skull*; with a low tone like the *g* of *gasp* and, in other cases, somewhere between a *k* and a *g*. Thus /kā/ is pronounced *ka*, while /ka̱/ is pronounced *ga*, and /ka/ falls somewhere between *ka* and *ga*. At the end of a word (and sometimes within a word), the pronunciation of the *k* is very weak, corresponding to a barely audible glottal stop.[20]

• /kh/ corresponds to an aspirated k, rather like the *c* of *cull* or *curb*. Aspiration involves breathing out sharply while uttering the consonant.

17. The inhabitants of both Gyarong and Minyak consider themselves as Tibetans and they usually speak Tibetan. However, in neither case is the native language a Tibetan dialect, although Tibetan is used by both as the literary language.

18. Phonetic transcription of Tibetan words would be very complex and unreadable for non-specialists. The system used in this Manual is therefore both a simple and largely phonological one that will enable readers to know the pronunciation of words and to predict their contextual variations by means of standard keyboard signs.

19. High and low tones are indicated by a line above and below the vowel respectively. Further information on tones is provided below.

20. The glottal stop will be indicated by an apostrophe.

- /'/ The apostrophe[21] corresponds to a glottal stop. The sound is produced by starting to say a *k* but stopping abruptly before expelling the air. Sometimes this is heard just as a tone or a lengthening of the preceding vowel. The effect is similar to the ending of the word *what* spoken in a South London accent [wo'], or in the middle of the American exclamation "uh-oh!"

- /ky/ with a high tone corresponds to a slightly "moist" *k*, i.e., as if it were followed by a short *i*. Thus /kyu/ is pronounced like the *cu* in *cute*. In other cases (when in an unstressed position), /ky/ is pronounced somewhere between *ky* and *gy*.

- /khy/ is pronounced like /ky/, but aspirated and always voiceless.

- /tr/ is very similar to the English *tr,* particularly when followed by rounded vowels such as /o, u/. When it is followed by non-rounded vowels, the pronunciation differs from English in that the lips are drawn back. When it carries a high tone, /tr/ is pronounced like the *tr* in *metropolitan*; when it carries a low tone, it is pronounced like the *dr* in English *drew,* and in other cases somewhere between a *tr* and a *dr*.

- /thr/ is pronounced similarly to /tr/, but aspirated and always voiceless, as in *true*.

- /t/ is pronounced with a high tone like the *t* in *stop,* with a low tone like the *d* in *debt,* and in other cases somewhere between *t* and *d*.

- /th/ is similar to *t* but aspirated. It corresponds roughly to the *t* of *top*.

- /p/ with a high tone is pronounced like the *p* in *spit* or *depot*, and with a low tone like the *b* in *bit*; and in other cases it falls somewhere between *p* and *b*.

- /ph/ is pronounced like *p*, but aspirated. It corresponds to the *p* in *pit* or *pot*.

- /c/ with a high tone is similar to the *ch* of *chair*, or the Italian *ciao,* but with less aspiration and more "moist". With a low tone /c/ is similar to the *j* of *journey* but, again, more "moist". The rest of the time it is pronounced somewhere between *ch* and *j*.

- /ch/ is pronounced like the *ch* in *chair*.

---

21. In certain rare cases, the apostrophe appears after a nasal to indicate a falling tone.

- /ts/ with a high tone is pronounced like the *ts* of *patsy*, or the *z* in *Mozart*, and with a low tone like the *dz* in *adze.*

- /tsh/ is pronounced like *ts*, but aspirated.

- /sh/ corresponds to the *sh* of *show*, but is "moistened". It is equivalent to the Chinese sound *xi* in pinyin transcription.

- /r/ can be pronounced in two different ways. The first corresponds to a rolled *r,* similar to that in the Spanish *cara* or Russian *gora* or the British rolled *r*. The second is quite close to the English *r* in *raw*, but pronounced with the lips drawn back (and not rounded). It is virtually the same as the Chinese pinyin *r* in *rou*. At the end of a word or syllable, the *ra* is barely audible and most of the time becomes a lengthening of the preceding vowel, similar to the *r* of *better*.

- /rh/ is approximately like the *s* in *sugar*, but lightly aspirated, with the point of the tongue curled back, touching the alveolar ridge (upper gums) and the lips retracted. This sound is noted in the transcription as /rh/ for two reasons: first, because it is written in Tibetan as an h with an r subjoined. Secondly, because at the beginning of the second syllable, the sound is normally pronounced as an /r/.

- /s/ is similar to the *s* of *sit*.

- /l/ is similar to the *l* of *lap* or *low*. At the end of a word or syllable, the *l* is barely pronounced and normally becomes a lengthening of the preceding vowel.

- /lh/ corresponds to a heavily-aspirated *l*.

- /h/ corresponds to the *h* in *holy* or *hello*.

- /m/ corresponds to the *m* of *me*.

- /n/ corresponds to the *n* of *nut*. At the end of a word, the sound is lightly pronounced and generally becomes a nasalization of the preceding voewel, similar, though a little more pronounced, than the *n* in the French *main* or *sain*.

- /ny/ is equivalent to the *neu* of *neutral*.

- /ng/ is equivalent to the *ng* of *king* or *song*. In some English dialects, the nasal velar also occurs within a word, as in "singer". In Tibetan, this sound appears not only at the end of a word or syllable, but also at the beginning – contrary to most European languages. At the end of the word or syllable, /ng/ also nasalizes the preceding vowel. Thus the pronunciation of /la̱ng/, /te̱ng/ and /lo̱ng/ is quite similar to that of the French words *langue*, *dingue* and *longue*.

- /w/ corresponds to the *w* in *we*.

- /y/ corresponds to the *y* of *year* or *young*.

Vowels

The eight Tibetan vowels /a, e, ä, o, ö, u, ü, i/ are relatively straightforward, the vowel system being similar to that in French and German.

- /a/ is an open central vowel, similar to the *a* in *am* or *ram*. Apart from when it is stressed, it tends to be pronounced like a central vowel *a,* similar to the English article *a*.
- /ä/ corresponds to the vowel sound in *share,* or the *è* of the French *père.*
- /e/ corresponds to *é* of the French *été* or the *ee* of the German *See*. When the vowel is followed by a consonant (closed syllable), it is pronounced like an /ä/.
- /ö/ corresponds to the sound *eu* in French or the German *ö*.
- /o/ corresponds to the sound *o* in the word *so.* When the syllable is closed, the sound is normally pronouced more openly, as in *sock.*
- /u/ corresponds to the sound *oo* in the word *cool* or the *u* in *rune.*
- /ü/ corresponds to the sound *u* in the French word *rue,* or the *ü* in the German *Bücher*.
- /i/ corresponds to the *ee* in *see*.

Tones

Phonologically, standard Tibetan has only two tones: high and low. The tone is only important for the first syllable of a word. Thus, for polysyllabic words, the tone will be marked only for the first syllable, while the following syllables are atonal. To the extent that there is only one tone per word, and it falls on the first syllable, tones can be a good criterion for distinguishing words in Standard Tibetan.

It is important to be able to hear the tones, since this makes it possible to distinguish between a large number of words. In the transcription, the high and low tones are marked by a bar respectively above and below the vowel.

Ex.: /nga̱/ "I", /ngā/ "five" or "drum", /la̱ng/ "to get up", /lāng/ "to lift up", /sä̱'/ "to eat", /sǟ'/ "to kill"(past tense), /sha̱mo/ "hat", /shāmo/ "mushroom", etc.

Tone contour

In monosyllabic words, high and low tones are pronounced with different "contours" or "shapes" (flat or modulated), depending on the final consonant of the syllable. We can distinguish four types: high flat, high falling, low flat (rising) and low rising-falling.

While the level of tones (high or low) is essential for understanding and producing sounds, the contours are secondary and can be ignored without hindering communication. Thus, the following paragraphs are for information only, and can be skipped by readers without impeding the process of learning the language.

The high tone is flat or slightly falling if the syllable ends with a vowel or with the nasals (n, m, ng). For example: /sā/ "earth", /chāng/ "beer", /chū/ "water", /sāng/ "scales (for weighing)", /khām/ "piece".

- The high tone is falling[22] if the syllable ends with the consonant p, a glottal stop ', or the nasals n', m', ng'. For example: /sǟ'/ "to kill", /shū'/ "strength", /thāp/ "hearth, stove", /khām'/ "Kham" (a region of Tibet), /sāng'/ "to become enlightened".
- The low tone is flat (slightly rising)[23] if the syllable ends in a vowel or with the nasals (n, m, ng). For example: /nga̱/ "I", /sa̱/ "to eat", /la̱ng/ "to get up", /kha̱ng/ "full, one".
- The low tone is rising followed by a short fall[24] if the syllable ends with the consonants p or ' or with the nasals (n', m', ng').[25] For example: /shu̱'/ "to sit down" /sä̱'/ "to eat"(past tense), /la̱ng'/ "to get up (past tense)", /kha̱ng'/ "snow".

Note: After the final nasals *n, m, ng,* the apostrophe is used to indicate a modulated tone rather than a glottal stop. This comes from an *s*[26] (*yang-'jug*) which was formerly pronounced, but which is now only written. Thus /khām'/ "Kham, Eastern Tibet" /sāng'/ "fumigation", /sūng'/ "to say"(H) are pronounced with a sharply falling high tone.

Aspiration

Aspiration can only occur at the beginning of a word, on a high or a low tone. It never occurs in the middle of a word.

It is nevertheless possible to distinguish many words according to aspiration, by comparing the following two series: /p, t, tr, ky, k, ts, c, l, r/ and /ph, th, thr, khy, kh, tsh, ch, lh, rh/.

---

22. The fall is very abrupt: 52.
23. Slightly rising: 12.
24. The configuration is 132.
25. After nasals, the apostrophe denotes a tone: see above.
26. Less frequently, it can be a *da drag*, or adjoined *d:* see the following section.

The relationship between tone, aspiration and voicing

It is important to note the following rule: aspirated consonants are always voiceless while **non-aspirated consonants** are **voiceless when they carry a high tone** but **voiced with a low tone.**

Aspiration is strong with a high tone and weaker with a low tone. In the case of a low tone, a difference in voicing goes with the difference between aspirated and non-aspirated sounds: aspirated voiceless versus non-aspirated voiced.

Finally, it should be noted that a non-aspirated high tone is pronounced higher than an aspirated high tone.

Ex.: **(high tone):** /kāngpa/ "leg, foot", /khāngpa/ "house", /tā/ "horse", /thā/ "end", /tsōkpa/ "dirty", /tshōkpa/ "group, association", /pākpa/ "skin", /phākpa/ "pig",
(low tone): /ta̱/ "arrow", /tha̱/ "now", /pu̱/ "insect", /phu̱/ "son", /ce̱'/ "to forget", /che̱'/ "to do", /ca̱/ "rainbow", /cha̱/ "bird", /ko̱/ "head", /kho̱/ "to hear".

The combined oppositions of aspiration and tone allow the following series to be identified; it is important to be able to hear the differences and to train yourself to reproduce them:

nonaspirated high tone (voiceless) versus **aspirated high** tone (voiceless).

nonaspirated low tone (voiced) versus **aspirated low** tone (voiceless).

Ex.: /tā/ "horse"; /thā/ "end"; /tha̱/ "now"; /ta̱/ "arrow"
/tāng/ "to send"; /thāng/ "plain"; /tha̱ng/ "and"; /ta̱ng/ "tune"
/pū/ "hair"; /phū/ "bottom"; /phu̱/ "son"; /pu̱/ "insect"
/cā/ "letter ca"; /chā/ "pair"; /cha̱/ "bird"; /ca̱/ "rainbow"
/pār/ "photo"; /phār/ "over there"; /pha̱r/ "between"; /pa̱r/ "to be lit"
/kō/ "yak hide"; /khō/ "he"; /kho̱/ "to understand"; /ko̱/ "head"

Geminates

There are sometimes double letters in phonological notation. These are not pronounced as double or long. Double letters in Tibetan only change the length of the preceding vowels (compare English *fiber* and *fibber*) and the tone contour, both of which can be overlooked in the early stages of learning Tibetan.

Thus the words /lāppa/ "instruction"; /lāpa/ "employee" are pronounced identically, except for lengthening of the vowel and a lightly falling tone on the first syllable of /lāppa/.

Stress

In Tibetan, the stress normally falls on the first syllable of polysyllabic words,[27] but the accentuation is weak and not very noticeable (by contrast with English, Italian or Russian). Accentuation therefore poses little problem in Tibetan. Nevertheless, it is worth noting that grammatical suffixes (plural, case, conjunctions, nominalization, etc.) are generally atonal and attached to the preceding word. This has implications for the segmentation of phrases, rhythm and intonation.

Tibetan poetry relies entirely on metre and doesn't rhyme, and in this context stress is therefore essential.

Summary of the essential rules of pronunciation

- 1. Tones are only distinctive for the first syllable of words.
- 2.With a low tone, nonaspirated initial consonants are voiced (or are partially voiced): p =[b], k = [g], t = [d] tr = [dr], ts = [dz].
- 3. Aspirated consonants are always voiceless.
- 4. There is no aspiration in the second syllable.
- 5. The consonants /k, p, r, l/ "weaken" at the end of a syllable or word, and are sometimes barely pronounced.
- 6. The final nasals /ng, n/ are weakly pronounced and cause a nasalization of the preceding vowel.

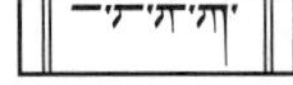

Exercises

1) Practice pronouncing and listening to the differences between the following words:

/kā/, /kyā/, /cā/, /trā/, /tā/

/kō/, /kyō/, /cō/, /trō/, /tō/

/kū/, /kyū/, /cū/, /trū/, /tū/

/kī/, /kyī/, /cī/, /trī/, /tī/

/kē/, /kyē/, /cē/, /trē/, /tē/

27. As opposed to French, for example, where the weak stress falls on the last syllable.

2) Do the same with the aspirated series:

/khā/, /khyā/, /chā/, /thrā/, /thā/

/khō/, /khyō/, /chō/, /thrō/, /thō/

/khū/, /khyū/, /chū/, /thrū/, /thū/

/khī/, /khyī/, /chī/, /thrī/, /thī/

/khē/, /khyē/, /chē/, /thrē/, /thē/

3) Do the same with the nasal series:

/na̱/, /nga̱/, /nya̱/

/no̱/, /ngo̱/, /nyo̱/

/nü/, /ngü/, /nyü/

/ne̱/, /nge̱/, /nye̱/

/ni̱/, /ngi̱/, /nyi̱/

4) Learn to pronounce the high/low tones, and to hear the difference between them:

/na̱/, /nā/, /ma̱/, /mā/, /nga̱/, /ngā/, /nya̱/, /nyā/

/ya/, /yā/, /sa̱/, /sā/, /sha̱/, /shā/, /la̱/, /lā/,

/wa̱/, /wā/.

5) Learn to pronounce the high and low tones and aspirated sounds by differentiating the following series. Repeat the same exercise with each of the four different vowels:

/kā/, /khā/, /kha̱/, /ka̱/

/kyā/, /khyā/, /khya̱/, /kya̱/

/cā/, /chā/, /cha̱/, /ca̱/

/trā, /thrā/, /thra̱/, /tra̱/

/pā/, /phā/, /pha̱/, /pa̱/

/tsā/, /tshā/, /tsha̱/, /tsa̱/.

6) Learn to pronounce and hear the difference between the following series, with and without glottal stops:

/āra/, /āra'/; /tā/, /tā'/; /thū/, /thū'/; /ra̱/, /ra̱'/; /chā/, /chā'/; /lo̱/, /lo̱'/; /lō/, /lō'/; /shu̱/, /shu̱'/; /shī/, shī'/; /lhā/, lhā'/; /sā/, sā'/; /sa̱/, /sa̱'/; /sō/, /sō'/; /khā/, /khā'/; /kü/, /kü'/; /thō/, /thō'/; /nā/, /nā'/; /cī/, /cī'/; /chā/, /chā'/; /mā/, /mā'/; /mi̱/, /mī'/; /tshō/, /tshō'/; /tso̱/, /tso̱'/; /ri̱/, /ri̱'/; /lū/, /lū'/; /shā/, /shā'/; /sho̱/, /sho̱'/; /yā/, /yā'/; /yō/, /yō'/; /yū/, /yū'/; /me̱/, /me̱'/.

7) Pronounce clearly the high and low tones in the following pairs:

/nga̱/ "I", /ngā/ "five" or "drum"; /sā/ "earth", /sa̱/ "to eat"; /na̱ng/ "in", /nāng/ "to give"; /la̱ng/ "to get up", /lāng/ "to lift up"; /nyä̱:/ "to lie down", /nyǟ:/ "to lay down"; /nye̱'/ "to hit", /nyē'/ "to find"; /sō/ "tooth", /so̱/ "to make"; /sä̱'/ "to eat", /sǟ'/ "to kill"; /ma̱/ "mother", *negation*, /mā/ "wound"; /se̱r/ "to say", /sēr/ "gold"; /rä̱:/ "to be torn", /rǟ:/ "to tear"; /la̱/ "pass", /lā/ "to rent"; /sha̱mo/ "hat", /shāmo/ "mushroom"; /shu̱'/ "to sit down", /shū'/ "strength"; /sho̱kpa/ "morning", /shōkpa/ "wing"; /tha̱/ "now", /thā/ "end, edge"; /tha̱ngpo/ "first", /thāngpo/ "in good health"; /thö̱n/ "meaning", /thȫn/ "to go out"; /cha̱ng/ "north", /chāng/ "beer"; /shi̱ka/ "estate", /shīka/ "temperament".

8) Pronounce clearly the aspirated sounds in the following pairs:

High tone: /kāngpa/ "leg, foot", /khāngpa/ "house"; /kāwa/ "pillar", /khāwa/ "snow"; /tā/ "horse", /thā/ "end"; /tsōkpa/ "dirty", /tshōkpa/ "group, association"; /pākpa/ "skin", /phākpa/ "pig"; /kā'/ "to stop", /khā'/ "sort"; /pū/ "hair", /phū/ "bottom"; /cǟ'/ "to cut", /chǟ'/ "to be cut"; /cā'/ "to break", /chā'/ "to be broken"; /tōngpa/ "empty", /thōngpa/ "to see"; /pār/ "photo", /phār/ "over there"; /cū/ "ten", /chū/ "water"; /tsē/ "summit", /tshē/ "life"; /tsā/ "vein, grass", /tshā/ "salt"; /tsām/ "just, about", /tshām/ "limit"; /lā/ "to rent, soul", /lhā/ "divinity"; /lō/ "lung", /lhō/ "south"; /lūng/ "air"; /lhūng/ "to fall".

Low tone: /ta̱/ "arrow", /tha̱/ "now"; /ka̱/ "to like", /kha̱/ "letter *ga*"; /pu̱/ "insect", /phu̱/ "son"; /ce̱'/ "to forget", /che̱'/ "to do"; /ca̱/ "rainbow", /cha̱/ "bird"; /pa̱r/ "to be lit", /pha̱r/ "between"; /cü̱'/ "to grasp", /chü̱'/ "policy, strategy"; /ko̱/ "head", /kho̱/ "to listen".

3. Tibetan writing

The Tibetan alphabet consists of thirty letters corresponding to consonants[28] which are pronounced with the vowel *a* by default. The vowels *i*, *u*, *e* and *o* are marked as accents (diacritical signs) written above or below these letters. Written Tibetan བོད་ཡིག་ *bod-yig* /phö̱yi'/[29] is derived from Devanagari writing (more specifically from the Gupta variant of this, once used in northern India), and bears some similarities to written Burmese and other alphabets of Southeast Asia, which also derive from Devanagari. It was created in the seventh century, during the First Diffusion of Buddhism in Tibet. According to Tibetan tradition, King Songtsän Gampo (*Srong-btsan sGam-po*), an emanation of the bodhisattva Avalokiteśvara, dispatched to India his minister Thönmi Sambhota, himself an emanation of the bodhisattva Mañjusri, with the aim of establishing a permanent alphabet, which would allow the translation of Buddhist texts in particular. This story does not rule out the possibility that a writing system could have existed in Tibet before the seventh century, but it is from this date that written Tibetan began to flourish on the high plateau.

The Tibetan alphabet CD I • Tr. 3-4 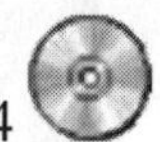

Table 1
The thirty consonants and their pronunciation གསལ་བྱེད་སུམ་ཅུ།

ཀ	kā	ཁ	khā	ག	kha̱	ང	nga̱
ཅ	cā	ཆ	chā	ཇ	cha̱	ཉ	nya̱
ཏ	tā	ཐ	thā	ད	tha̱	ན	na̱
པ	pā	ཕ	phā	བ	pha̱	མ	ma̱
ཙ	tsā	ཚ	tshā	ཛ	tsha̱	ཝ	wa̱
ཞ	sha̱	ཟ	sa̱	འ	a̱	ཡ	ya̱
ར	ra̱	ལ	la̱	ཤ	shā	ས	sā
ཧ	hā	ཨ	ā				

28. These thirty letters include two vowels and two semi-vowels. The vowel a̱ is in fact a consonant by origin, as revealed by its pronunciation as a glottal fricative [ɦ] or nasal in certain contexts (see the appendix on phonology).

29. The term *bod-yig* means primarily "written Tibetan", but by extension it refers also to "Tibetan literature". The word "alphabet" in Tibetan is like our own (alpha-beta), formed from the first two letters: *ka-kha*.

The four diacritic vowels དབྱངས་བཞི།

ཨི	i	ཨུ	u	ཨེ	e	ཨོ	o

These are called respectively གི་གུ་ *gi-gu* /khi̱ku/, ཞབས་ཀྱུ་ *zhabs-kyu* /sha̱pkyu/, འགྲེང་བུ་ *'greng-bu* /tre̱ngpu/, ན་རོ་ *na-ro* /na̱ro/.

Ex.: མི་ mì, ཕུ་ phù, མེ་ mè, ལོ་ lò

How to write the letters of the Tibetan alphabet

ཀ	ཁ	ག
ང	ཅ	ཆ
ཇ	ཉ	ཏ
ཐ	ད	ན
པ	ཕ	བ
མ	ཙ	ཚ
ཛ	ཝ	ཞ
ཟ	འ	ཡ
ར	ལ	ཤ
ས	ཧ	ཨ

Notes on the alphabet

Unlike the Greek, Hebrew or Arabic alphabets, Tibetan letters, apart from the vowels, do not have a name. Each letter, however, has a precise symbolism in Tibetan Buddhism. The alphabet is read by pronouncing each letter with the vowel A, which is implicit. Following the Indian tradition, the letters come in an order reflecting the phonology of the language; they are presented by series according to their locus of articulation. For the first four series (ka, ca, ta, pa), the order follows the progress of articulation from the back of the mouth (velars) to the edge of the lips (labials), via the palate (palatals) and teeth (dentals), after which there is the series of affricates (sounds consisting of an plosive followed by a fricative).

1) ཀ kā velars 2) ཅ cā palatals 3) ཏ tā dentals 4) པ pā labials 5) ཙ tsā affricates (dentals).

The remaining letters do not correspond to a clear phonological order.Regarding the first five series, we note that the first letter of each series is voiced with a high tone, the second is also a high tone but aspirated, the third is a low tone lightly aspirated,[30] and the fourth is a nasal corresponding to the place of articulation of the three preceding letters.

The vowel markers are written above and below the consonants.

The I, the E and the O are written above the letter, while the U is written below. The A is not marked, but is implicit. When the Tibetan language was first written as this alphabet of thirty letters, there were no tones.[31] Over time, the convergence of voiced and voiceless consonants has created tonal oppositions. As we have seen, Standard Tibetan has two tones important enough to identify and distinguish. However, **tones are not marked with special signs**, and must be deduced from the radical letter. Most radicals are associated with a distinct high or low tone. The nine original voiced consonants ག་kha̲, ཇ་cha̲, ད་tha̲, བ་pha̲[32], ཛ་tsha̲, འ་ a̲[33], ཞ་ sha̲, ཟ་ sa̲, ཝ་ wa̲, are always pronounced with a low tone, whereas fourteen sounds, the voiceless ཀ་kā, ཁ་khā, ཅ་cā, ཆ་chā, ཏ་tā, ཐ་thā, པ་pā, ཕ་phā, ཙ་tsā, ཚ་tshā, ཤ་shā, ས་sā, ཧ་ hā and the vowel ཨ་ ā, always carry a high tone.

However, seven letters that usually carry a low tone shift to a high tone when they figure in certain combinations (when they are prefixed or superscribed): these are the four nasals ང་nga̲, ཉ་ nya̲, ན་ na̲, མ་ma̲, and the letters ཡ་ya̲, ར་ ra̲, ལ་la̲.

---

30. This sound corresponds to an old voiced consonant which is still pronounced as such in many dialects. The Wylie transliteration therefore writes a voiced consonant *g, j, d, b.* See the table on the following page.

31. The dialects of Ladakh, Baltistan and Amdo have never developed a tonal system.

32. This consonant is an exception to the general rule insofar as it carries a high tone when it appears with certain combinations involving a prefixed letter.

33. The letter *'a chung* yields a low tone but also generates a labialization in front of back vowels *a, o.* Thus /o̲ma/ "milk" is usually pronounced [wo̲ma].

Transliteration and phonological transcription

Table 2

The thirty consonants: transliteration and pronunciation

ཀ	*ka*	kā	ཁ	*kha*	khā	ག	*ga*	kha̲	ང	*nga*	nga̲
ཅ	*ca*	cā	ཆ	*cha*	chā	ཇ	*ja*	cha̲	ཉ	*nya*	nya̲
ཏ	*ta*	tā	ཐ	*tha*	thā	ད	*da*	tha̲	ན	*na*	na̲
པ	*pa*	pā	ཕ	*pha*	phā	བ	*ba*	pha̲	མ	*ma*	ma̲
ཙ	*tsa*	tsā	ཚ	*tsha*	tshā	ཛ	*dza*	tsha̲	ཝ	*wa*	wa̲
ཞ	*zha*	sha̲	ཟ	*za*	sa̲	འ	*'a*	a̲	ཡ	*ya*	ya̲
ར	*ra*	ra̲	ལ	*la*	la̲	ཤ	*sha*	shā	ས	*sa*	sā
ཧ	*ha*	hā	ཨ	*a*	ā						

The four vowels

ཨི	*i*	ī	ཨུ	*u*	ū	ཨེ	*e*	ē	ཨོ	*o*	ō

Transliteration

In European, Japanese, and Chinese works that deal with Tibetan culture, or whenever (for typographical reasons) the Tibetan script can't be used, a system of romanized transliteration may be employed.

The principle of transliteration is that each letter of the Tibetan alphabet corresponds to one or more Roman letters. While transliteration enables the reader to recognize the Tibetan spelling of a word and, to a certain extent, its archaic pronunciation, it gives *no straightforward indication of how it is pronounced* in Modern Central Tibetan.[34] It may be noted that while spelling is standard throughout the Tibetan-speaking world (Ü, Tsang, Tö Ngari, Ladakh, Amdo, Kham, Bhutan, etc.), texts are read with different pronunciation according to the regional provenance of the reader.

34. There are numerous differences between Central Tibetan and Old Tibetan (which provided the basis for the current system of spelling), especially in the case of consonant clusters. As far as the pronunciation of individual letters is concerned, however, the only difference lies in the fact that the voiced plosives of Old Tibetan have produced low tones, while voiceless plosives have produced high tones. It is interesting to note that the spelling of Modern Tibetan is at least as archaic as that of modern French and in some cases, English. Tibetan spelling represents the way in which the language was pronounced around the eighth century, whereas that of English corresponds to its pronunciation around the fifteenth. Certain archaic dialects of Baltistan, Ladakh and Amdo have retained a pronunciation close to the written form.

This Manual will make use of the Wylie system of transliteration (the simplest and most commonly used), presented in Table 2. Transliterated renderings will be presented **in italics.** Transliteration of polysyllabic words will use the following conventions:

- Syllables within a word will be linked by a hyphen. Grammatical morphemes (case markers and connectives) attached to words will be preceded by the sign +. For example: *dge-rgan+gyis* "by the teacher".
- The letter *y* preceded by a prefix will be distinguished from the subscript *y* by a full stop after the prefix. For example: གཡག་ *g.yag* "yak" and གྱར་ *gyar* "to be separated".

Phonological transcription

The transcription that figures in this Manual **in roman letters** (and sometimes between oblique strokes) reproduces the pronunciation of Standard Tibetan or Central Tibetan.[35] This is the transcription that was presented in the last chapter. Although it gives no indication of the spelling of words, it is all the more useful insofar as spelling is often very far removed from pronunciation. However, by applying a few simple rules, you will be able to deduce the pronunciation from the orthographic presentation. Note that there are certain exceptions (see Appendix 1, section 2.1). Moreover, there are a few rare words in the spoken language with no written form.[36] The literary pronunciation of words will be indicated by the sign (L).

Note: When there is a slight disparity between current and literary pronunciation, in the absence of a written Standard form, the word will be written in Literary Tibetan, but the transcription will reproduce the colloquial form.[37]

• The following convention will be used for the transcription of polysyllabic words: syllables of the same word will be joined without any hyphen, while grammatical morphemes (case markers and connectives) attached to the word will be preceded by a hyphen. For example: ke̱kän-ki' "by the teacher".

---

35. It also makes it possible to grasp the pronunciation of Tibetan in the province of Tsang, which is very close to that of Central Tibet, and certain basic rules of correspondence make it possible to shift from one to the other. By contrast, the phonological systems that obtain in Ladakh, Zangskar, Ngari, Amdo, Kham and Bhutan (in the case of Dzongkha) are different from the one presented here. For example, in Amdo and Kham, there are sounds such as [x] (the Spanish jota) and [ʁ], the French or German *r*, [ʒ] (the French *j*) and [z] (the English *z*). These sounds are all *absent* in Standard Tibetan (ST). In Dzongkha there are also sounds such as [ptç] (*pch* in English) and [bdʒ] (*bj*), which are also absent in ST. Since all these dialects share the same literary language, the way in which texts are read varies considerably according to the regional provenance of the speaker. The fact that the same letter can be pronounced in several different ways is not a unique feature of Tibetan. The same is true of Latin and the Romance languages derived from it. For example, *ch* is pronounced as [ʃ] in French (as in *Chine*) but [k] in Italian (as in *chiuso*) and [tʃ] *ch* in spanish (as in *China*); *g* is pronounced [ʒ] in French (as in *gens*), [x] in Spanish (as in *gente*) and [dʒ] in Italian (as in *giorno*). The same phenomenon may be observed in Chinese, where the pronunciation of a single character varies from one dialect to another.

36. By contrast, a number of words from Literary Tibetan are not used in the colloquial language.

37. The literary pronunciation can always be deduced from the spelling.

Orthography of Tibetan words within the English text

When presenting Tibetan words in scientific publications in English (or other languages), most authors use Wylie transliteration which renders the Tibetan orthography but does not provide the actual pronunciation in Standard Tibetan. For non-specialists, a transcription system of the pronunciation is more appropriate. However, until now there is a considerable variation between the various authors. For the sake of standardization, we propose in this Manual a system of phonetic transcription that is simple and directly derived from the Wylie transliteration. It is presented in Appendix 7. It will be used to transcribe the Tibetan words that occur in the lessons as well as on the maps [38].

The syllable

The thirty basic letters of the alphabet may be combined to produce other sounds. Certain letters may be "stacked up" within a syllable, which is the main unit when reading.

Syllables ཚིག་འབྲུ་ /tshīngtru/[39] are easy to identify in written Tibetan: each syllable is marked off from its neighbours by an intersyllabic dot ་ called ཚེག་ /tshā'/. Thus the syllables, which are connected to one another by these dots, are strung together like beads on a thread without any spaces between words or even, in many cases, between clauses.

A syllable may contain from one to seven letters

The simplest syllable consists of a single radical letter, while the most complex comprises seven letters in the following combination: a prefix, a superscript, a radical, a subscript, a vowel-accent, a first suffix and a second suffix.[40] Even if there is theoretically a very large set of possibilities, the actual number of complex syllables is relatively limited.[41]

A full list of possible combinations is provided in Appendix 6.

---

38. The problem of multiple renderings is due not only to constant variation (sometimes even on the part of the same author) but often to a lack of consistency. For example, these renderings rarely distinguish the pronunciation of the *g* in words such as *dga'-ldan* and *gangs-ljongs*; in fact the first is a low-toned voiced velar whereas the second is a slightly aspirated low-toned voiceless velar. In this Manual they will be presented respectively as *gandän* and *ghangjong.* The letter *k* represents high-toned velars (always voiceless) that appear for example in the words *khang-bdag* and *rkang-gling,* which will be rendered respectively as *khangdak* and *kangling.*

39. The term *tshig 'bru* literally means "word grain or unit". Other expressions are also sometimes used, such as *tsheg-bar* which literally means "[that which is] between the dots", and *tsheg-khyim* "household [of letters between] the dots", as well as *yig-'bru* "seed letter". The latter is also used in tantric rituals: the "seed syllable" enables the practitioner to produce the divinity in the course of the "generation" phase of meditation.

40. This Manual will use the usual terminology of "first suffix" and "second suffix". These should, however, be regarded as syllable-finals, and not as suffixes in the usual sense of the term.

41. For example, of the radicals that can take superscripts and subscripts (that is, all except *'a, ya, la, a*) only *ka, ga, pa, ba, ma* and *tsa* can have both at once. And even among these, only certain combinations of superscripts and subscripts are possible. The consonant *k* takes three superscripts: *rk, sk* and *lk*, and all four subscripts: *kr, ky, kl* and *kw*, but the combinations *lky, rkr* and *lkr* are never encountered. Certain prefixes and subscripts are also incompatible; for example, although *k* may be prefixed by the letter *ba,* the combination *blka* does not exist.

Syllabic structure in detail

A syllable consists of:

- a radical letter མིང་གཞི་ (*ming-gzhi*), corresponding to one of the thirty consonants.

And possibly:

- a vowel accent (or diacritical mark) དབྱངས་ (*dbyangs*) placed above or below the basic consonant. There are four vowel accents, and the A is implied by default.
- a superscribed letter མགོ་ཅན་ (*mgo-can)* placed immediately above the radical. There are three superscribed consonants.
- a subscribed letter འདོགས་ཅན་ (*'dogs-can)* placed immediately below the radical. There are four subscribed consonants.
- a prefixed letter སྔོན་འཇུག་ (*sngon-'jug)* placed immediately before the radical letter. There are five prefixed consonants.
- a first suffix རྗེས་འཇུག་ (*rjes-'jug)* placed immediately after the radical. There are ten first suffixes.
- a second suffix ཡང་འཇུག་ (*yang-'jug)* placed immediately after the first suffixed consonant. There are two second suffixes.

The principles of spelling

The traditional Tibetan procedure for learning to read involves spelling out loud (*sbyor klog*) over the course of weeks or even months before coming to the stage of word pronunciation (*bsdus klog*). Young Tibetans spell entire texts aloud, and only begin to read directly when they have thoroughly mastered the technique of spelling.

As a general rule, when a syllable contains several letters, they are spelled out in the following order: prefix, superscript, radical, subscript, vowel, first suffix, second suffix.[42] In other words, the letters are spelled out horizontally from left to right and vertically from top to bottom (except in the case of superscribed vowels, which are pronounced after the subscribed consonant).

The simple radical

In many cases, the simple radical, with or without a vowel, is sufficient to constitute a word, as the following examples illustrate:

ས་ sa /sā/ "earth", "place", ར་ra /ra̲/ "goat", ལ་la /la̲/ "pass", ཇ་ ja /cha̲/ "tea", ཆ་ cha /chā/ "pair", ན་ na /na̲/ "to be ill", མ་ ma /ma̲/ "negation", ཟ་ za /sa̲/ "to eat", ཤ་ sha /shā/ "meat", ང་nga /nga̲/ "I", ཉ་ nya /nya̲/ "fish", ཁ་kha /khā/ "mouth".

---

42. These various letters are described in the next section, which deals with the syllable.

སོ་so /sō/ "tooth", སུ་ su /sū/ "who", ཁོ་kho /khō/ "he", ཉོ་ nyo /nyo̱/ "to buy", མི་mi /mi̱/ "man", མེ་me /me̱/ "fire", ཞོ་ zho /sho̱/ "yogurt", ཤི་ shi /shī/ "to die", རི་ri /ri̱/ "mountain", ལོ་ lo /lo̱/ "year", རེ་ re /re̱/ "each", རོ་ro /ro̱/ "corpse".

Spelling a simple consonant and a vowel accent entails pronouncing the consonant followed by the name of the vowel.

Ex.: སོ་ sā na̱ro sō, ལོ་ la̱ na̱ro lo̱, ཕུ་ pha̱ sha̱pkyu phu̱, སུ་ sā sha̱pkyu sū, རི་ ra̱ khi̱ku ri̱,
མི་ma̱ khi̱ku mi̱, མེ་ma̱ tre̱ngpu me̱, ཐེ་tha̱ tre̱ngpu the̱.

Subscripts, superscripts

There are four subscribed and three superscribed consonants. Certain letters involve ligatures or *sandhi* when they are combined, and in this case the shape of the letters is modified.

The four subscribed consonants འདོགས་ཅན་བཞི་/to̱kcän shi̱/

These are: ཡ་ya̱, ར་ ra̱, ལ་ la̱, ཝ་ wa̱.

When these letters are subscribed, their shape is more or less modified as follows:

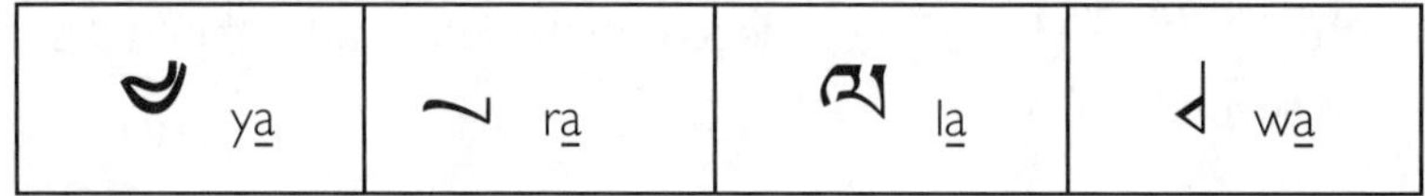

They are known respectively as ཡ་བཏགས་ ya̱ta' ("attached" ya̱), ར་བཏགས་, ra̱ta' ("attached" ra̱), ལ་བཏགས་ la̱ta' ("attached" la̱), ཝ་ཟུར་ wa̱sur ("corner" wa).

• The 7 consonants that may be combined with a subscript *ya* are:

ཀྱ་	kyā	ཁྱ་	khyā	གྱ་	khya̱	ང་	—
ཅ་	—	ཆ་	—	ཇ་	—	ཉ་	—
ཏ་	—	ཐ་	—	ད་	—	ན་	—
པྱ་	cā	ཕྱ་	chā	བྱ་	cha̱	མྱ་	nya̱
ཙ་	—	ཚ་	—	ཛ་	—	ཝ་	—
ཞ་	—	ཟ་	—	འ་	—	ཡ་	—
ར་	—	ལ་	—	ཤ་	—	ས་	—
ཧ་	—	ཨ་	—				

The seven letters with a subscript *ya* all produce palatal consonants viz, palatal plosives ky; palatal affricates c ("ch"); and the palatal nasal ny (like the "nio" of "onion").

On rare occasions you may encounter the combination ཧྱ་ hyā, which is used to transcribe words from other languages, especially Sanskrit.

To spell a syllable containing a subscribed letter, first pronounce the radical, then the subscript followed by the sound བཏགས་/tā'/ (which means "attached"), and then conclude with the result of the combination.

Ex.: ཀྱ་ kā ya̱ta' kyā, ཁྱ་ khā ya̱ta' khyā, གྱ་ kha̱ ya̱ta' khya̱, པྱ་ pā ya̱ta' cā, ཕྱ་ phā ya̱ta' chā, བྱ་ pha̱ ya̱ta' cha̱, མྱ་ ma̱ ya̱ta' nya̱, ཁ་ཡ་བཏགས་ཁྱ་གི་གུ་ཁྱི་ khā ya̱ta' khyā khi̱ku khyī.

• The 13 consonants with a subscript *ra*:

ཀྲ་	trā	ཁྲ་	thrā	གྲ་	thra̱	ང་	—
ཅ་	—	ཆ་	—	ཇ་	—	ཉ་	—
ཏྲ་	trā	ཐྲ་	thrā	དྲ་	thra̱	ན་	—
པྲ་	trā	ཕྲ་	thrā	བྲ་	thra̱	མྲ་	mā
ཙ་	—	ཚ་	—	ཛ་	—	ཝ་	—
ཞ་	—	ཟ་	—	འ་	—	ཡ་	—
ར་	—	ལ་	—	ཤྲ་	shā	སྲ་	sā
ཧྲ་	rhā	ཨ་	—				

The subscript *ra* produces a significant change in the pronunciation of the radical letters. The velars *ka, kha, ga,* the dentals *ta, tha, da*, the labials *pa, pha, ba* and the fricative *sa* (in certain cases) become the retroflex plosives /tr/. The *ha,* too, is modified, and is pronounced as a retroflex fricative /rh/, but this sound occurs in only a few words. The subscript *ra* does not alter the pronunciation of the radicals *sha, ma* (but generates a high tone on mā).

The radical *sa* with a subscript *ra* is always pronounced sā when reading. In conversational Tibetan, however, there are two ways of pronouncing the combination depending on the word involved: /s/ or /tr/.[43] Another pronunciation, /rh/, appears in certain dialects (Tsang, Hor, Amdo, Ladakhi, etc.).

Ex.: སྲིད་གཞུང་ sīshung, སྲུ་མོ་ sōmo, སྲད་ sā̃', སྲན་མ་ trā̃nma, sā̃nma (L); སྲབ་ trāp, sāp (L); སྲབ་པོ་ trāppo, sāppo (L); མེ་སྲེག་ me̱tra', me̱se' (L); སྲམ་ trām, sām (L); སྲུང་trūng, sūng (L).

A combination containing a subscript *ra* is spelled by pronouncing the radical, followed by ra̱ta', and finally the outcome of the combination.

ཀྲ་ kā ra̱ta' trā; ཁྲ་ khā ra̱ta' thrā; གྲ་ kha̱ ra̱ta' thra̱; ཏྲ་ tā ra̱ta' trā; ཐྲ་ thā ra̱ta' thrā; དྲ་tha̱ ra̱ta' thra̱; པྲ་ pā ra̱ta' trā; ཕྲ་ phā ra̱ta' thrā; བྲ་ pha̱ ra̱ta' thra̱; མྲ་ ma̱ ra̱ta' mā; ཤྲ་ shrā ra̱ta' shā; སྲ་ sā ra̱ta' sā; ཧྲ་ hā ra̱ta' rhā.

43. This variant appears in colloquial Tibetan, but is not pronounced when reading.

Note: In exceptional cases, the combination br is pronounced /pr/ and not /tr/, when it appears in the second syllable of certain words: བླ་བྲང་ *bla-brang* /lāprang/,[44] ཨ་བྲ་ *a-bra* /āpra/, ལྷོ་བྲག་ *lho-brag* /lhōpra'/, ལྷ་བྲིས་པ་ *lha-bris-pa* /lhāpripa/.

• The 6 consonants with a subscript *la:*

ཀླ་	lā	ཁ་	—	གླ་	lā	ང་	—
ཅ་	—	ཆ་	—	ཇ་	—	ཉ་	—
ཏ་	—	ཐ་	—	ད་	—	ན་	—
པ་	—	ཕ་	—	བླ་	lā	མ་	—
ཙ་	—	ཚ་	—	ཛ་	—	ཝ་	—
ཞ་	—	ཟླ་	ta̱	འ་	—	ཡ་	—
རླ་	lā	ལ་	—	ཤ་	—	སླ་	lā
ཧ་	—	ཨ་	—				

The combinations that contain a subscript *la* all produce the sound lā with the exception of ཟླ་ *zla* which is pronounced ta̱.

Spelling out a combination comprising a radical and a subscript *la* entails first of all pronouncing the consonant, then la̱(p)ta', and finally the result of the combination, as follows:

ཀླ་ kā la̱ta' lā, གླ་ kha̱ la̱ta' lā, བླ་ pha̱ la̱ta' lā, རླ་ ra̱ la̱ta' lā, སླ་ sā la̱ta' lā, ཟླ་ sa̱ la̱ta' ta̱.

Note: When occurring as a second syllable in some words, ཟླ་ *zla* produces a nasalization and is pronounced nta̱. See Appendix 1, section 1.1.

• The 16 consonants with a subscript *wa:*

ཀྭ་	kā	ཁྭ་	khā	གྭ་	kha̱	ང་	—
ཅྭ་	cā	ཆ་	—	ཇ་	—	ཉྭ་	nya̱
ཏྭ་	tā	ཐ་	—	དྭ་	tha̱	ན་	—
པ་	—	ཕ་	—	བ་	—	མ་	—
ཙྭ་	tsā	ཚྭ་	tshā	ཛ་	—	ཝ་	—
ཞྭ་	sha̱	ཟྭ་	sa̱	འ་	—	ཡ་	—
རྭ་	ra̱	ལྭ་	la̱	ཤྭ་	shā	སྭ་	sā
ཧྭ་	hā	ཨ་	—				

In some words, the subscript *wa* is attached to a subscript *ra*. This is illustrated by the syllable གྲྭ་ thra̱ in གྲྭ་ཚང་ thra̱tsang "monastic college" or སློབ་གྲྭ་ lōptra "school".

44. It is as if there were a "resyllabification" going on. For example, the *b* which belongs to the second syllable *brang* is treated in the spoken language as if it were the final consonant of the first syllable. In Standard Spoken Tibetan, the pronunciation /pr/ never occurs at the beginning of a word.

Nowadays the wa̱sur (lit. "corner *wa*") does not change the sound of the radical to which it is attached, and consequently even scholars frequently forget to write it. In the past it probably corresponded to a labialization resulting in a slight lengthening, but these features have vanished and the wa̱sur is now just a vestigial spelling. However, it is currently used in the transcription of foreign words such as *swa-sti* and *tun-hwang* (i.e., Dunhuang).

To spell out the combination of a consonant with a subscript wa̱sur, first pronounce the radical, then wa̱sur, and finally the overall result:

Ex.: ཚྭ་ tshā wa̱sur tshā, རྭ་ ra̱ wa̱sur ra̱.

• The subscript *'a chung*

In the case of certain rare modern Tibetan words, as well as a few loanwords and mantras, the *'a chung* appears as a subscribed letter. The subscript *'a chung* has the effect of lengthening the vowel.

Ex.: པཱ་ལགས། pā:la'

Table 3

Pronunciation of the subscribed letters འདོགས་ཅན་གྱི་རེའུ་མིག་

combinations with a subscript "ya"							
ཀྱ་	ཁྱ་	གྱ་	པྱ་	ཕྱ་	བྱ་	མྱ་	
kyā	khyā	khya̱	cā	chā	cha̱	nya̱	
combinations with a subscript "ra"							
ཀྲ་	ཁྲ་	གྲ་	ཏྲ་	ཐྲ་	དྲ་		
trā	thrā	thra̱	trā*[45]	thrā*	thra̱		
པྲ་	ཕྲ་	བྲ་	མྲ་	ཤྲ་	སྲ་	ཧྲ་	
trā	thrā	thra̱	mā	shā*[46]	sā	rhā	
combinations with a subscript "la"							
ཀླ་	གླ་	བླ་	རླ་	སླ་	ཟླ་		
lā	lā	lā	lā	lā	ta̱		
combinations with a subscript "wa"							
ཀྭ་	ཁྭ་	གྭ་	ཅྭ་	ཉྭ་	ཏྭ་	དྭ་	ཙྭ་
kā	khā	kha̱	cā	nya̱	tā	tha̱	tsā
ཚྭ་	ཞྭ་	ཟྭ་	རྭ་	ལྭ་	ཤྭ་	སྭ་	ཧྭ་
tshā	sha̱	sa̱	ra̱	la̱	shā	sā	hā

The three superscribed consonants མགོ་ཅན་གསུམ་ /ko̱cän sūm/:

ར ra̱ ལ la̱ ས sā

They are known as ར་མགོ་ ra̱nko ("head" ra), ལ་མགོ། la̱nko ("head" la), ས་མགོ། sānko ("head" sa).

---

45. Combinations followed by an asterisk are used only in mantras or foreign loanwords.

46. This combination is spelled shā, but it is pronounced shrā in mantras.

The three superscribed letters *ra, la* and *sa* have two effects:

- They raise the tone of the nasals
- They cause the low-toned consonants kha̱, cha̱, tha̱, pha̱, tsha̱ to lose their aspiration, so that they are pronounced ka̱, ca̱, ta̱, pa̱, tsa̱ . This alteration is often accompanied by partial or complete voicing, that is, the consonants become closer to the corresponding voiced sounds:[ga̱, dʑa̱, da̱, ba̱, dza̱.]

Note: Even though the letters may be partly or wholly voiced, this will not be indicated in the transcription, which will be as follows: ka̱, ca̱, ta̱, pa̱, tsa̱, since it is only the low tone and the lack of aspiration that are relevant. As a general rule, speakers of European languages at first have difficulty in picking up the tones and hear them instead as the corresponding voiced sounds:[ga̱, dʑa̱, da̱, ba̱, dza̱]. By contrast, speakers of Standard Tibetan perceive a low tone and a lack of aspiration. The fact that the sound is more or less voiced (between ka̱ and ga̱, ta̱ and da̱, pa̱ and ba̱), or even completely voiced, is not a determining factor. Indeed, Tibetan speakers have difficulty in distinguishing between "brick" and "prig", "gut" and "cut", "battle" and "paddle", and so forth.

Historically, the superscribed letters were pronounced in Central Tibet, and their disappearance resulted in the emergence of tones. In some Amdo dialects, and especially in those of Baltistan and Ladakh, the superscripts are still pronounced, or else have left phonetic traces. These dialects have never developed tones.

To spell combinations involving superscribed consonants, begin with the top letter and then go on to the one below followed by བཏགས་/tā'/ (meaning "attached"), and finally the result of the combination.

- The 12 consonants with a superscript *ra*:

In Central Tibetan, while the superscribed *ra* has no effect on the actual pronunciation of the radical, it does modify tone and aspiration.[47]

རྐ་	kā	ཁ་	—	རྒ་	ka̱	རྔ་	ngā
ཅ་	—	ཆ་	—	རྗ་	ca̱	རྙ་	nyā
རྟ་	tā	ཐ་	—	རྡ་	ta̱	རྣ་	nā
པ་	—	ཕ་	—	རྦ་	pa̱	རྨ་	mā
རྩ་	tsā	ཚ་	—	རྫ་	tsa̱	ཝ་	—
ཞ་	—	ཟ་	—	འ་	—	ཡ་	—
ར་	—	ལ་	—	ཤ་	—	ས་	—
ཧ་	—	ཨ་	—				

Ex. of spellings: རྐ་ ra̱ kāta' kā, རྔ་ ra̱ nga̱ta' ngā.

Note: In some rare cases, the superscript *r* of the second syllable of a word is pronounced.

47. It may be noted in passing that in certain Amdo dialects and in Ladakhi the superscript *ra* is in fact pronounced.

Ex.: ཀ་རྒྱུག་ ka-rgyug /kārkyu'/ "tent pole", མི་རྒོད་ mi-rgod /mi̲rkö'/ "yeti",
ང་རྒྱལ་nga-rgyal /nga̲rkyä:/ "pride, aggression", རྡོ་རྗེ་ rdo-rje /to̲rce/ "vajra" (first name).

• The 10 consonants with a superscript *la*:

The superscript *la* has much the same effect on pronunciation as the superscript *ra,* in that it primarily alters tone or aspiration.[48]

ལྐ་	kā	ཁ་	—	ལྒ་	ka̲	ལྔ་	ngā
ལྕ་	cā	ཆ་	—	ལྗ་	ca̲	ཉ་	—
ལྟ་	tā	ཐ་	—	ལྡ་	ta̲	ན་	—
ལྤ་	pā	ཕ་	—	ལྦ་	pa̲	མ་	—
ཙ་	—	ཚ་	—	ཛ་	—	ཝ་	—
ཞ་	—	ཟ་	—	འ་	—	ཡ་	—
ར་	—	ལ་	—	ཤ་	—	ས་	—
ལྷ	lhā	ཨ་	—				

Ex. of spellings: ལྟ་ la̲ tāta' tā, ལྷ la̲ hāta' lhā

Note: In some rare cases, the superscript *l* of the second syllable of a word produces a nasal n or m. This occurs in the combinations *lt, ld.* See Appendix 1.

Ex.: ད་ལྟ་ *da-lta* /tha̲nta/ "now", དགའ་ལྡན་*dga'-ldan* /ka̲ntän/ "Gandän (monastery)"

• The 11 consonants with a superscript *sa*:

The effect of the superscript *sa* is, likewise, essentially on tone or aspiration.[49]

སྐ་	kā	ཁ་	—	སྒ་	ka̲	སྔ་	ngā
ཅ་	—	ཆ་	—	ཇ་	—	སྙ་	nyā
སྟ་	tā	ཐ་	—	སྡ་	ta̲	སྣ་	nā
སྤ་	pā	ཕ་	—	སྦ་	pa̲	སྨ་	mā
སྩ་	tsā	ཚ་	—	ཛ་	—	ཝ་	—
ཞ་	—	ཟ་	—	འ་	—	ཡ་	—
ར་	—	ལ་	—	ཤ་	—	ས་	—
ཧ་	—	ཨ་	—				

Ex. of spellings: སྣ་ sā na̲ta' nā, སྤ་ sā pha̲ta' pa̲.

48. In Ladakhi and Balti the superscript *la* is still pronounced as l.

49. However, in certain dialects such as those of Ladakh and Baltistan, the "s" is clearly heard (for example *stag* [stak]), while in Amdo it may be pronounced as a fricative or an aspirate, for example *sta* [ştak] or [htak].

Table 4

Pronunciation of superscribed letters མགོ་ཅན་གྱི་རེའུ་མིག

Simple letters	Letters with superscripts
compatible radicals	*with superscript "ra"*
	(pronunciation identical)
ཀ་ ཏ་ ཙ་ kā tā tsā	རྐ་ རྟ་ རྩ་ kā tā tsā
	(loss of aspiration)
ག་ ཇ་ ད་ བ་ ཛ་ kha̲ cha̲ tha̲ pha̲ tsha̲	རྒ་ རྗ་ རྡ་ རྦ་ རྫ་ ka̲ ca̲ ta̲ pa̲ tsa̲
	(shift to high tone)
ང་ ཉ་ ན་ མ་ nga̲ nya̲ na̲ ma̲	རྔ་ རྙ་ རྣ་ རྨ་ ngā nyā nā mā

compatible radicals	*with superscript "la"*	
	(pronunciation identical)	
ཀ་ ཅ་ ཏ་ པ་ kā cā tā pā	ལྐ་ ལྕ་ ལྟ་ ལྤ་ kā cā tā pā	
	(loss of aspiration)	
ག་ ཇ་ ད་ བ་ kha̲ cha̲ tha̲ pha̲	ལྒ་ ལྗ་ ལྡ་ ལྦ་ ka̲ ca̲ ta̲ pa̲	
	(shift to high tone)	
ང ཧ་ nga̲ hā	ལྔ་ ngā	ལྷ་ lhā

compatible radicals	*with superscript "sa"*
	(pronunciation identical)
ཀ་ ཏ་ པ་ ཙ་ kā tā pā tsā	སྐ་ སྟ་ སྤ་ སྩ་ kā tā pā tsā
	(loss of aspiration)
ག་ ད་ བ་ kha̲ tha̲ pha̲	སྒ་ སྡ་ སྦ་ ka̲ ta̲ pa̲
	(shift to high tone)
ང་ ཉ་ ན་ མ་ nga nya na ma	སྔ་ སྙ་ སྣ་ སྨ་ ngā nyā nā mā

It is possible to associate a superscript *(ra, sa)* and a subscript *(ra, ya)*. The number of such combinations is in fact very limited as appears from the Table 5 below.

Table 5

Pronunciation of stacked letters (subscripts and superscripts) བརྩེགས་ཡིག

radical with superscript "ra" and subscript "ya"
རྐྱ་ kyā རྒྱ་ kya̱ རྙ་ nyā
radical with superscript "sa" and subscript "ya"
སྐྱ་ kyā སྒྱ་ kya̱ སྤྱ་ cā སྦྱ་ ca̱ སྨྱ་ nyā
radical with superscript "sa" and subscript "ra"
སྐྲ་ trā སྒྲ་ tra̱ སྤྲ་ trā སྦྲ་ tra̱ སྨྲ་ mā

The ten "first suffixes" རྗེས་འཇུག /ce̱ncu'/:

ག kha̱, ང nga̱, ད tha̱, ན na̱, བ pha̱, མ ma̱, འ a̱, ར ra̱, ལ la̱, ས sā are the ten consonants that may figure as "first suffixes". There are very few final consonants by comparison with radicals. This situation is confirmed by the traditional presentation of the alphabet, inasmuch as only one third of the letters may appear at the end of a syllable or a word, whereas any of the thirty may feature as an initial or "radical" *(ming-gzhi)*.

It should be remembered that none of these letters is voiced, and that the pronunciation of some of them varies according to the context (see the discussion of phonology in Appendix 2, and listen to the CD).

- ག: k or '

Ex.: སོག་པོ་ sog-po /sōkpo/ "Mongol", ཐུག་པ་ thug-pa /thūkpa/ "noodles",
ལག་པ་ lag-pa /la̱kpa/ "hand", ལུག་ lug /lu̱'/ "sheep", དུག་ lug /thu̱'/ "poison".

- ང: ng. This usually causes a nasalization of the preceding vowel.

Ex.: མིང་ ming /mi̱ng/ "name", རང་ rang /ra̱ng/ "self, really".

- ན: n. In general, the *n* causes a nasalization of the preceding vowel, and also has the effect of an *umlaut* on the vowels /a, o, u/ which become respectively /ä, ö, ü/.

Ex.: ཡིན་ yin /yi̱n/ "I am", ལན་ lan /lä̱n/ "reply, message", ཡོན་ཏན་ yon-tan /yö̱ntän/ "qualities, excellence".

• མ: m

Ex.: ལམ་ lam /l̲am/ "way, road", དོམ་ dom /thom/ "bear", ཡུམ་ yum /y̲um/ "mother"(H).

• བ: p

Ex.: ཁབ་ khab /khāp/ "needle", ཐོབ་ཐང་ thob-thang /thōptang/ "right, share", དེབ་ deb /thep/ "book".

• ད / ས: are not pronounced.

They do, however, create the effect of an *umlaut* on the vowels /a, o, u/ which become respectively /ä, ö, ü/. At the end of a word, they produce a glottal stop (') Ex.: འོད་ཟེར *'od-zer* /ö̲ser/ "sunray", དུས་ཚོད *dus-tshod* /thü̲tsö'/ "time", ལུས་ *lus* /lü̲'/ "body".

Note: The fact that the final *s* and *d* become silent is precisely analogous to what happens in French. In the case of the latter, too, the dental plosives *t, d* and *s* are commonly not pronounced at the end of a word, even though they are still written. Compare the following French, English and Tibetan examples:

French: bere*t,* pie*d*, ni*d*, ta*s*, pa*s***.**

American English: Arkansa*s*, bere*t*.

Tibetan: འོད *od* /ö̲'/ "light", རེད་ re*d* /re̲'/ "to be", ལས་ la*s* /lä̲'/ "karma", རས ra*s* /rä̲'/ "cotton", "cloth".

• ར: is either pronounced r or produces a lengthening of the vowel (marked as:)

Ex.: མར mar /mar/ (or ma:), "butter; below", སེར་པོ་ ser-po /sērpo/ (or sē:po) "yellow", ཕོར་པ་ phor-pa /phōrpa/ (or phō:pa) "(wooden) bowl".

• ལ: produces a lengthening (marked as:) and has the effect of an *umlaut* on the preceding vowels, /a, o, u/ which become respectively /ä, ö, ü/. When a speaker is articulating carefully in a literary register, the /l/ may be heard.

Ex.: ཕ་ཡུལ་ pha-yul /phāyü:/ (or phāyül) "native land", བལ་པོ་ bal-po /phä̲:po/ (or phä̲lpo) "Nepalese", ཤེལ shel /shē:/ (or shēl) "crystal", རིལ་བུ་ ril-bu /ri̲:pu/ (or ri̲lpu) "pill".

• འ: the presence of this suffix has no effect on pronunciation.[50]

Ex.: མེ་མདའ་ me-mda' /me̲nta/ "gun", ནམ་མཁའ་ nam-mkha' /na̲mka/ "sky".

---

50. After consulting the *lotsawa* (the great translators of Buddhist texts) King Trisong Detsän issued an edict aimed at reforming spelling. Previously, most words ending in a vowel carried a final 'a. For example, "mountain" was written རིའ *ri'*.

The letter འ *'a chung* may carry a vowel.

As a suffix, the letter འ may carry the vowel *i* or *u* (and in rare cases *e* or *o*). In this case the syllable contains two vowels, which are written as follows:

ཨའི་ /ä:/ ཨིའི་ /i:/ ཨུའི་ /ü:/ ཨེའི་ /e:/ ཨོའི་ /ö:/ ཨའོ /ao/, etc.

ཨའུ་ /au/ ཨེའུ་ /eu/ ཨིའུ་ /iu/ ཨོའུ་ /ou/ ཨུའུ་ /u:/

The addition of the vowel *i* results in a lengthening in the case of all preceding vowels, and moreover has the effect of an *umlaut* on /a,o,u/, which become respectively /ä, ö, ü/.

Ex.: བྱིའུ་ /chiu̱/ "fledgling, little bird", གའུ་ /khau̱/ "amulet box", སུའི་ /sǖ:/ "whose", ཁོང་ཚོའི་ /khōngtsö̱:/ "their", ལེའུ་ /leu̱/ "chapter supplementary", ཤེས་པར་བྱའོ་ /shē'-par-cha̱o/ "Should be known" (L).

The two secondary suffixes ཡང་འཇུག /ya̱ngcu'/**:**

These suffixes are ས sā and ད tha̱.[51]

The suffix ས appears after the first suffixes ག kha̱, ང nga̱, བ pha̱, མ ma̱. Although it never alters the pronunciation of the preceding consonant, when it is appended to nasals it transforms the flat tone into a contour tone. For example, compare ཁམ་ *kham* /khām/ "piece" and ཁམས་ *khams* /khām'/ (the name of an eastern Tibetan region), or གང་ *gang* /kha̱ng/ "full" and གངས་*gangs* /kha̱ng'/[52] "snow", གསང་ *gsang* /sāng/ "secret" and བསངས་ *bsangs* /sāng'/ "to purify (past)", ལང་ *lang* /la̱ng/ "to rise (present)" and ལངས་ *langs* /la̱ng'/ "to rise (past)" (see the description of the tones in section 2).

The archaic suffix ད known as ད་དྲག་ *da-drag* corresponds to an appendage that may appear in certain words: གྱུརད་ *gyur(d)* /kyu̱r/ "to be transformed", བསྐོརད་ *bskor(d)* /kōr/ "to turn", བསྟནད་ *bstan(d)* /tǟn'/ "to teach".

The letter gradually disappeared from the tenth century onward, following a decree of King Rälpachän aimed at simplifying the conventions of spelling. However, even though it is invisible, it still exerts an influence in both speaking and writing. In the former case it may have an effect on the tone. For example ཕྱིན་ *phyin* is not pronounced /chīn/ but /chīn'/, with a falling tone, because it used originally to be written ཕྱིནད་ *phyin(d)*. In writing, it affects the spelling of particles and suffixes to the extent that these agree not with the last letter of the preceding syllable but with the *da-drag*.

Ex.: བསྟན་ཀྱང་ "even though it had been shown that…" *bstan(d)+kyang* /tǟn'-kyang/ and not **bstan+yang;* /tǟn'-yang/, བསྐོར་ཅིང་ "while turning, as he/she was turning" *bskor(d)+cing*

---

51. Traditionally, the suffix *d* is generally presented before the suffix *s*. This order has been reversed here because the former, which was used in Old Tibetan, has disappeared in the classical language.

52. Remember that after a nasal, the apostrophe indicates not a glottal stop but a falling tone.

/kōr-cing/ and not **bskor+zhing* /kōr-shing/. The *da-drag* is already obsolete in Classical Tibetan, and no longer figures in modern dictionaries.

To spell a word containing one or two suffixes, say them after the radical letter and pronounce the overall result.

Ex.: ཁང་ kha̲ nga̲ kha̲ng, ཁངས་ kha̲ nga̲ sā kha̲ng'.

Table 6

Pronunciation of vowels and suffixed letters

དབྱངས་དང་རྗེས་འཇུག་ཡང་འཇུག་བཅས་ཀྱི་རེའུ་མིག

Suffixes	ཨ་ a	ཨི་ i	ཨུ་ u	ཨེ་ e	ཨོ་ o
—ག་	ཨག་ a'/ak#[53]	ཨིག་ i'/ik#	ཨུག་ u'/uk#	ཨེག་ e'/ek#	ཨོག་ o'/ok#
—ང་	ཨང་ ang	ཨིང་ ing	ཨུང་ ung	ཨེང་ eng	ཨོང་ ong
—ད་	ཨད་ ä'/ä #	ཨིད་ i'/i #	ཨུད་ ü'/ü #	ཨེད་ e'/e #	ཨོད་ ö'/ö #
—ན་	ཨན་ än	ཨིན་ in	ཨུན་ ün	ཨེན་ en	ཨོན་ ön
—བ་	ཨབ་ ap	ཨིབ་ ip	ཨུབ་ up	ཨེབ་ ep	ཨོབ་ op
—མ་	ཨམ་ am	ཨིམ་ im	ཨུམ་ um	ཨེམ་ em	ཨོམ་ om
—འ་	ཨའ་ a:				
—འི་	ཨའི་ ä:	ཨིའི་ i:	ཨུའི་ ü:	ཨེའི་ e:	ཨོའི་ ö:
—འུ་	ཨའུ་ au	ཨིའུ་ iu		ཨེའུ་ eu	
—ར་	ཨར་ a:/ar*	ཨིར་ i:/ir*	ཨུར་ u:/ur*	ཨེར་ e:/er*	ཨོར་ o:/or*
—ལ་	ཨལ་ ä:/äl*	ཨིལ་ i:/il*	ཨུལ་ ü:/ül*	ཨེལ་ e:/el*	ཨོལ་ ö:/öl*
—ས་	ཨས་ ä'/ä #	ཨིས་ i'/i #	ཨུས་ ü' /ü #	ཨེས་ e'/e #	ཨོས་ ö'/ö #
—གས་	ཨགས་ a'/ak#	ཨིགས་ i'/ik#	ཨུགས་ u'/uk#	ཨེགས་ e'/ek#	ཨོགས་ o'/ok#
—ངས་	ཨངས་ ang'	ཨིངས་ ing'	ཨུངས་ ung'	ཨེངས་ eng'	ཨོངས་ ong'
—བས་	ཨབས་ ap	ཨིབས་ ip	ཨུབས་ up	ཨེབས་ ep	ཨོབས་ op
—མས་	ཨམས་ am'	ཨིམས་ im'	ཨུམས་ um'	ཨེམས་ em'	ཨོམས་ om'

53. The # sign indicates a pronunciation that is used in certain contexts, notably when the suffix appears at the end of the first syllable of a word. The asterisk signifies a very formal, rather literary pronunciation.

The five prefixes སྔོན་འཇུག /ngōncu'/:

The five consonants that can immediately precede the radical in a syllable are:

ག kha̲ ད tha̲ བ pha̲ མ ma̲ འ a̲

- The prefix ག kha̲ may occur before the letters ཅ་cā, ཉ་ nya̲, ཏ་tā, ད་tha̲, ན་na̲, ཙ་tsā, ཞ་sha̲, ཟ་ sa̲, ཤ་ shā, ས་ sā, ཡ་ ya̲.

- The prefix ད tha̲ may appear before the letters ཀ་kā, ག་ kha̲, ང་nga̲, པ་pā, བ་ pha̲, མ་ ma̲.

- The prefix བ pha̲ may appear before the letters ཀ་kā, ག་kha̲, ང་nga̲, ཅ་cā, ཇ་cha̲, ཉ་ nya̲, ཏ་ tā, ད་ tha̲, ན་ na̲, ཙ་ tsā, ཛ་ tsha̲, ཞ་ sha̲, ཤ་ shā, ས་ sā, ཟ་sa̲.

- The prefix མ ma̲ may appear before the letters ཁ་khā, ག་ kha̲, ང་nga̲, ཆ་ chā, ཇ་ cha̲, ཉ་nya̲, ཐ་ thā, ད་ tha̲, ན་ na̲, ཚ་ tshā, ཛ་ tsha̲.

- The prefix འ a̲ may appear before the letters ཁ་khā, ག kha̲, ཆ་ chā, ཇ་ cha̲, ཐ་ thā, ད་ tha̲, ཕ་ phā, བ་ pha̲, ཚ་ tshā, ཛ་ tsha̲.

The five prefixes are usually **silent**[54] but they play a crucial role in the production of tones and the neutralization of aspiration: when they carry a prefix, the five radicals ག kha̲, ཇ cha̲, ད tha̲, བ pha̲, ཛ tsha̲ lose their aspiration and are pronounced respectively: ka̲, ca̲, ta̲, pa̲, tsa̲.[55]

Ex.: འདུག་ tu̲', འཇའ་ ca̲, མཛོད་ tsö̲'.

When the four nasal consonants carry a prefix, they shift to a high tone: ང nga̲, ཉ nya̲, ན na̲, མ ma̲ are pronounced respectively: ngā, nyā, nā, mā.

Ex.: སྔ་ ngā, སྨ་ mā, དམའ་ mā, སྣ་ nā, གཉའ་ nyā.

When ཡ ya̲ is prefixed it shifts to a high tone /yā/.

Ex.: གཡག་ yā'

- Pronunciation of prefixes in exceptional cases:

As we have seen, the five prefixes are not pronounced, and only have an effect on tone and aspiration. However, *the prefixes of the second syllable* within certain words may be pronounced. Those most likely to be pronounced are: མ ma̲ and འ a̲, which produce a nasalization between the syllables: *n*, *m* or *ng*. The other prefixes only affect pronunciation in rare cases.

- In certain words the prefix ག kha̲ produces the sound /k/ or even the sound /p/.

---

54. These prefixes are the vestiges of an ancient pronunciation that is still preserved in several dialects (particularly in Amdo). Even in Central Tibetan they are still pronounced in certain words (see below).

55. Remember that while non-Tibetan-speakers generally perceive these sounds as being voiced rather than voiceless, for Central Tibetans the important feature is that the consonant is unaspirated and carries a low tone. The fact that it is more or less voiced is regarded as a secondary feature!

Ex.: བཅུ་གསུམ་ cu-gsum /cūksum/ "thirteen", ཨ་གསར་ a-gsar /āksar/ "infatuation", ས་གདན་ sa-gdan /sāptän/ "rug", ཁ་གཅོད་kha-gcod /khāpcö'/ "lid".

• The prefix བ pha̲ produces the sound /p/.

Ex.: བློ་བཟང་ blo-bzang /lōpsang/[56] (first name), བཅོ་བརྒྱད་bco-brgyad /cōpkyä/ '"eighteen", བཞི་བཅུ་bzhi-bcu /shi̲pcu/ "forty", བཅུ་བདུན་ bcu-bdun /cūptün/ "seventeen".

• The prefix ད tha̲ modifies pronunciation only in དབའ *dba'*, དབྱ་ *dbya* and དབྲ་*dbra*. In all three cases, the combination *db* is not pronounced but produces a high tone.

དབའ་ is pronounced /wā/ with the vowel A, whereas in the case of other vowels the semi-vowel (or glide) *w* disappears, leaving དབོ་ /ō/,དབེ་ /ē/, དབུ་ /ū/, དབི་ /ī/. དབྲ་ is pronounced /rā/ and དབྱ་ as /yā/.

Ex.: དབང་ /wāng/ "power", དབུ་ /ū/ "head (H)", དབོར་/ōr/ "to transport, to shift", དབེན་ /ēn/ "remote place", དབྲལ་ /rā̈:/ "to tear", དབྱར་ཁ་ /yārka/ "summer", དབྱིན་ཇི་ /yīnci/[57] "English", དབྱེ་བ་ /yēwa/ "difference", དབྱིབས་ /yīp/ "shape".

• The prefixes མ ma̲ and འ a̲ often produce a nasal sound /m, n or ng/.[58]

Ex.: མི་འདུག་ mi̲ntu' "there is not", རྒྱུ་མཚན་ kyu̲mtsän "reason", etc.

When spelling out a syllable that contains a prefix, the prefix in question is followed by the syllable འོག་ /o'/. Thus in the case of the syllable དཀར་ in which the prefix is the ད, the spelling is: ད་འོག་ཀ་ར་དཀར་ tha̲o' kā ra̲ kār. (It may be mentioned in passing that in Kham and Amdo the procedure is different: while the prefix is not marked, the suffix is followed by བཞག་/sha'/. Thus the same word would be spelled: ད་ཀ་ར་བཞག་དཀར་tha̲ kā ra̲-sha̲' kār.)

Ex.: བཞི་ pha̲o sha̲ khi̲ku = shi̲, དབུ་ tha̲o wa̲ sha̲pkyu = ū

Note: The radical letter (*ming-gzhi*) is easy to identify within a syllable, insofar as it is the letter that takes the vowel and the affixes (i.e., the superscripts and subscripts).

Ex.: བཟོས bzos /sö̲'/ "to make" (past), དགེ་འདུན་ dge-'dun /ke̲ntün/ "monastic community, monk", བསྐོར bskor /kōr/ "to turn", སྒྲུབ་ /thru̲p/ "to be fulfilled", འགྲོ་ 'gro /tro̲/ "to go", འཇིག་རྟེན་ 'jig-rten /ci̲kten/ "the world", སྟག་ stag /tā'/ "tiger".

When the vowel is an A (i.e., implied by default), and there is neither a superscript nor a subscript on the radical, there is chance of ambiguity. The problem may be circumvented by following these rules concerning the identification of the radical:

---

56. This may also be pronounced lōsang.

57. The semi-vowel y sometimes disappears before an i. For example, /yīnci/ is also pronounced /īnci/.

58. See also Appendix 1.

a) In a two-letter syllable, the radical is *the first*.

Ex.: མང་ ma̱ng, དག་ tha̱', དང་ tha̱ng, དམ་ tha̱m, དན་ thä̱n, གང་khang.

b) In a syllable of three letters where there is no suffix ས *sa*, the radical is the second.

Ex.: དགའ་ ka̱, མངའ་ ngā, བསང་ sāng, བཟང sa̱ng.

c) In a syllable of three letters with the suffix ས *sa*, there are two possibilities. In most cases, the radical is the first:

Ex.: གངས་ kha̱ng', བབས་ pha̱p.

However, where the first letter could qualify as a prefix, the radical may be the second:

མངས་ can be read as either /ma̱ng'/ or /ngä̱'/; དབས་ can be read as either /tha̱p/ or /wā̈'/; དངས་ can be read as either /tha̱ng'/ or /ngā̈'/; དགས་ can be read as either /tha̱'/ or /kä̱'/.

Words that carry this ambiguity are rare (there are fewer than ten), and their structure may be deduced from the context. The ambiguity is sometimes disposed of altogether by adding a wa̱sur to the radical: དྭགས can only be read as /tha̱'/.

d) In a syllable of four letters, the radical is always the second:

Ex.: དམངས māng', བསངས་ sāng', བདམས ta̱m'.

Table 7

Pronunciation of Prefixed Letters (with simple radicals)

མིང་གཞི་ལ་སྦྱར་བའི་སྔོན་འཇུག་གི་རེའུ་མིག་

Prefix ག	identical pronunciation གཅ—' གཏ—' གཙ—' གཞ—' གཟ—' གཤ—' གས—' cā tā tsā sha̱ sa̱ shā sā
	modified pronunciation གད—'(loss of aspiration.) གཉ—' གན—' གཡ—'(shift to high tone) ta̱ nyā nā yā
Prefix ད	identical pronunciation དཀ—' དཔ—' kā pā
	modified pronunciation དག—'(loss of aspiration) དང—' དམ—' དབ—'(shift to high tone) ka̱ ngā mā wā
Prefix བ	identical pronunciation བཀ—' བཅ—' བཏ—' བཙ—' བཞ—' བཟ—' བཤ—' བས—' kā cā tā tsā sha̱ sa̱ shā sā
	modified pronunciation བག—' བད—' (loss of aspiration) ka̱ ta̱
Prefix མ	identical pronunciation མཁ—' མཆ—' མཐ—' མཚ—' khā chā thā tshā
	loss of aspiration མག—' མཇ—' མད—' མཛ—' ka̱ ca̱ ta̱ tsa̱
	shift to high tone མང—' མཉ—' མན—' ngā nyā nā
Prefix འ	identical pronunciation འཁ—' འཆ—' འཐ—' འཕ—' འཚ—' khā chā thā phā tshā
	loss of aspiration འག—' འཇ—' འད—' འབ—' འཛ—' ka̱ ca̱ ta̱ pa̱ tsa̱

Table 8

Pronunciation of prefixed letters with stacked consonants

འདོགས་ཅན་དང་མགོ་ཅན་བརྩེགས་ཡིག་བཅས་ལ་སྦྱར་བའི་སྔོན་འཇུག་གི་རེའུ་མིག

Prefix								
Prefix ད	དཀྱ—'	དགྱ—'	དཔྱ—'	དབྱ—'	དམྱ—'			
	kyā	kya̱	cā	yā	nyā			
	དཀྲ—'	དགྲ—'	དཔྲ—'	དབྲ—'				
	trā	tra̱	trā	rā				
Prefix བ	བརྐ—'	བརྒ—'	བརྔ—'	བརྗ—'	བརྙ—'	བརྟ—'	བརྡ—'	བརྣ—'
	kā	ka̱	ngā	ca̱	nyā	tā	ta̱	nā
	བལྟ—'	བལྡ—'						
	tā	ta̱						
	བསྐ—'	བསྒ—'	བསྔ—'	བསྙ—'	བསྟ—'	བསྡ—'	བསྣ—'	བསྩ—'
	kā	ka̱	ngā	nyā	tā	ta̱	nā	tsā
	བཀྱ—'	བགྱ—'	བཀྲ—'	བགྲ—'	བསྲ—'			
	kyā	kya̱	trā	tra̱	sā			
	བཀླ—'	བགླ—'	བརླ—'	བསླ—'	བཟླ—'			
	lā	lā	lā	lā	ta̱			
	བརྐྱ—'	བརྒྱ—'	བསྐྱ—'	བསྒྱ—'	བསྐྲ—'	བསྒྲ—'		
	kyā	kya̱	kyā	kya̱	trā	tra̱		
Prefix མ	མཁྱ—'	མགྱ—'	མཁྲ—'	མགྲ—'				
	khyā	kya̱	thrā	tra̱				
Prefix འ	འཁྱ—'	འགྱ—'	འཕྱ—'	འབྱ—'				
	khyā	kya̱	chā	ca̱				
	འཁྲ—'	འགྲ—'	འདྲ—'	འཕྲ—'	འབྲ—'			
	thrā	tra̱	tra̱	thrā	tra̱			

Combinations used for transliterating Sanskrit:

- The 6 reversed letters ལོག་པ་དྲུག་:

These letters are marginal, and don't feature in the basic alphabet of thirty letters. They correspond to the retroflexes in the Sanskrit alphabet, and are used principally to transcribe text or mantras. In transliteration they appear as capitals or, in certain conventions, as lower-case letters with a diacritical dot beneath them.

ཊ་	ཋ་	ཌ་	ཎ་	ཥ་	ཀྵ་
Ta trā	*Tha* thrā	*Da* thra̲	*Na* nā	*Sha* khā/shā	*kSha* khyā

The Sanskrit sounds corresponding to *Na* (nasal retroflex), *kSha* and *Sha* do not exist in Tibetan, and are respectively pronounced: na̲, khā (or shā), khyā.

Ex.: མ་ཎི་ /ma̲Ni/ "jewel" is pronounced simply /ma̲ni/ and not with a retroflex n as /ma̲Ni/.

The three retroflexes *T, Th* and *D* are phonetically interchangeable with the combinations *kr, khr* and *gr.* In Modern Tibetan, they are used only to represent the retroflex sounds of certain loanwords. For example, མོ་ཊ་ /mo̲tra/, "car", borrowed from the English *motor* (the English *t* is treated as a retroflex by Tibetans) and "dollar", which is written ཌོ་ལར་*Do-lar* /thro̲lar/.

To spell combinations that contain a reversed letter, pronounce the letter followed by lo' (meaning "reversed"), and then the result of the combination.

Ex.: ཌ་tha̲ lo' thra̲.

- The five subscript *ha* or "thick" consonants མཐུག་པོ་ལྔ་:

The following combinations, which contain a subscript *ha,* are used primarily for transcribing text or mantras from Sanskrit. These borrowed sounds do not belong to the Tibetan phonological system.

གྷ་	ཛྷ་	དྷ་	བྷ་	ཌྷ་
gha gha̲	*dzha* dzha̲	*dha* dha̲	*bha* bha̲	*Dha* drha̲

In contemporary usage they are employed in the transcription of foreign names: *bhom-bhe* "Bombay" or *dha-ram-sa-la* "Dharamsala". To spell out these combinations, begin with the top consonant followed by hāta', and finally the overall combination.

Ex. of spellings: དྷ་ tha̲ hāta' dha̲, བྷ་ pha̲ hāta' bha̲.

And finally, there is the combination ཧྥ་ *hph*, pronounced fā, to transcribe the sound f, which doesn't exist in Tibetan but does appear in Chinese and English words.

Words

In ancient Literary Tibetan, words are usually monosyllabic, whereas words of two syllables are most common in Modern Central Tibetan.

Compound words

Some polysyllabic words cannot be analysed. For example, the words ཞི་མི་ *zhi-mi* /shi̱mi/ "cat", མེ་ལོང་ *me-long* /me̱long/ "mirror", སྟ་རེ་ *sta-re*/tāre/ "axe", རི་མོ་ *ri-mo* /ri̱mo/ "drawing", and ཚ་ལུ་མ་ *tsha-lu-ma* /tshāluma/ "orange" cannot be broken down into syllables with an independent meaning (or if they can, then the syllables have nothing to do with the overall meaning of the word in question). In many cases, however, words may be analysed, so that each syllable has a meaning that contributes to the general sense. This is true for example of the words:

དམག་མི་ *dmag-mi* /mā'mi/ "soldier" (lit.: "war man"), གངས་རི་ *gangs-ri* /kha̱ngri/ "snow-capped mountain" (lit.: "snow-mountain"), མེ་རོ་ *me-ro* /me̱ro/ "embers" (lit.: "fire corpse"), དངུལ་ཁང་ *dngul-khang* /ngǖ:kang/ "bank" (lit.: "money house"), གནམ་གྲུ་ *gnam-gru* /nāmtru/ "aeroplane" (lit.: "sky ship"), ཆུ་ཚོད་ *chu-tshod* /chūtsö'/ "hour, watch" (lit.: "water measure"[59]), བཞི་བཅུ་ *bzhi-bcu* /shīpcu/ "forty" (lit.: "four-ten").

Even though each syllable constitutes a semantic unit, it is important to think of these compositions as integral words, and not just as a juxtaposition of two distinct words. For example, from a semantic point of view, the etymology is by no means always obvious (as in the case of "fire corpse" or "water measure"); and from a phonological perspective, these words function as a unit, since they carry only one tone. The pronunciation of a word is therefore not the result of treating the component syllables in isolation. For example: བཞི་བཅུ་ shi̱pcu "forty" is not the same as བཞི་shi̱+ བཅུ་ cū.

Spelling aloud of compound words

When a word consists of several syllables, each of the latter is pronounced to give the intermediary result, and then the overall combination is pronounced at the end.

Ex.: བཞི་བཅུ་ pha̱o sha̱ khi̱ku shi̱ / pha̱o cā sha̱pkyu cū=shi̱pcu

Phonology of syllables within a word

It should be remembered that it is only the first syllable of a word that carries a tone. Syllables within a word **carry neither tone nor aspiration**.[60] Furthermore the syllables བ་ pha̱ and བོ་ pho̱ (including when followed by a case particle) are pronounced respectively wa and wo when they do not appear at the beginning of a word.

Ex.: ཟླ་བ་ ta̱wa (and not ta̱pha̱) "moon", སློབ་གྲྭ་བ་ lōptrawa "student", ཟླ་བོ་ ta̱wo "spouse", ལྷོད་ལྷོད་ lhōlö' (and not lhōlhö') "relaxed".

---

59. The etymology refers to the ancient water clock.

60. Even if Tibetan spelling uses an aspirated consonant.

Isolating words when reading

Since written Tibetan does not separate words from one another by blanks or any other sign, before acquiring a substantial vocabulary it is not always easy to identify them and separate them off from one another. The task may be made easier by picking out grammatical particles such as plurals, conjunctions and case markers, which always follow the words with which they are associated, and therefore indicate where they end.

At the beginning, when reading and trying to recognize words, you may encounter certain ambiguities: a syllable could be identified as the second syllable of a previous word or as the first syllable of the word that follows. These problems are solved to a large extent by context and with experience. The interpretation you choose has certain obvious consequences for meaning and pronunciation: the existence of tone (and perhaps aspiration) when the syllable is the first in a word, or their absence when the syllable occurs later. (For more details see Appendix 8.)

Summary of rules concerning the pronunciation of letters

In the pronunciation of Modern Central Tibetan, the radicals, subscripts, first suffixes and vowels play a crucial part, whereas the prefixes and superscripts have only a minimal influence. In other words, everything that precedes the radical is generally of secondary importance from the point of view of pronunciation.

• With the exception of the *wa*, the subscript consonants alter the pronunciation of the radical:

The subscript *ra* produces the series of retroflexes: /tra/ (etc.).

The subscript *ya* produces the series of palatal plosives: /kya/ (etc.) /ca/ (etc.) and /nya/.

Combinations involving the letter *la* are pronounced /la/ at the expense of the radical (except in the case of zl).

• The three superscript consonants *ra*, *sa* and *la*, as well as the prefixed consonants *ga*, *ba*, *ma* and *'a* (i.e., all but *da*) affect only the tone and aspiration of the radical.

• Tones are not marked by special signs, but must be deduced from the radicals and affixes. It is important to distinguish between the following sets:

Table 9

Phonological oppositions in Tibetan[61] CD I • Tr. 5-7

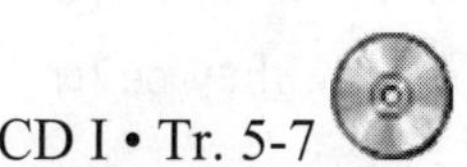

high unaspirated		high aspirated		low aspirated		low unaspirated			
ཀ་	kā	ཁ་	khā	ག་	kha̲	འག་	(N)ka̲	རྒ་	ka̲
ཀྱ་	kyā	ཁྱ་	khyā	གྱ་	khya̲	འགྱ་	(N)kya̲	རྒྱ་	kya̲
ཅ་/པྱ་	cā	ཆ་/ཕྱ་	chā	ཇ/བྱ་	cha̲	འཇ་/འབྱ་	(N)ca̲	རྗ་	ca̲
ཀྲ་/པྲ་	trā	ཁྲ་/ཕྲ་	thrā	གྲ་/དྲ་/བྲ་	thra̲	འགྲ་/འདྲ་/འབྲ་	(N)tra̲	སྒྲ	tra̲
ཏ་	tā	ཐ་	thā	ད་	tha̲	འད་/ཟླ་	(N)ta̲	རྡ་	ta̲
པ་	pā	ཕ་	phā	བ་	pha̲	འབའ་	(N)pa̲	རྦ་	pa̲
ཙ་	tsā	ཚ་	tshā	ཛ་	tsha̲	འཛ་	(N)tsa̲	རྫ་	tsa̲
ཤ་	shā	ཧྲ་	rhā					ཞ་	sha̲
ཀླ་	lā	ལྷ་	lhā					ལ་	la̲
ཨ་	ā	ཧ་	hā					འ་	a̲
རྔ་	ngā							ང་	nga̲
རྙ་	nyā							ཉ་	nya̲
རྣ་	nā							ན་	na̲
རྨ་	mā							མ	ma̲
ས་	sā							ཟ་	sa̲
དབྲའ་	rā							ར་	ra̲
དབྱའ་	yā							ཡ་	ya̲
དབའ་	wā							ཝ་	wa̲

Punctuation

This Manual will use three punctuation marks taken from Literary Tibetan (see the Appendices): the simple bar: ། known as རྐྱང་ཤད་ *rkyang-shad* or ཚེག་རིང་ *tsheg-ring* which courresponds more or less to a comma or a full stop; the double bar:༎ called ཉིས་ཤད་ *nyis-shad*, which usually marks the end of a section and can be represented by a full stop; and the sign ༄ called ཡིག་འགོ་ *yig-'go* or དབུ་འཁྱུད་ *dbu-'khyud,* which marks the beginning of a text or of a page (see Appendix 1, section 2.6).

---

61. In this table, it would of course be possible to give orthographic variations with prefixes or superscripts for unaspirated and aspirated high tones and unaspirated low tones that would be equivalent in phonetic terms. See also the list of homophones in Table 10 in Appendix 6.

Note: While the phoneme /rh/ is associated with /r/ from a phonological point of view, it is included in this series because it is phonetically close to /sh/.

The fourth column, corresponding to unaspirated consonants before low-tone vowels, has two variations: one prenazalized, marked with a N in brackets, and the other with no prenasalization. The brackets indicate that certain speakers (especially younger people) do not pronounce the prenasalizations.

Question marks and brackets will be used in the exercises. These two punctuation marks have been borrowed from European languages, and although they are used in some modern works, they never occur in classical texts.

Using the dictionary

Dictionary entries follow the alphabetical order of the thirty letters of the alphabet and the five vowels *a, i, u, e, o.*

To find a word in the dictionary, begin by locating the *radical letter* of the first syllable according to alphabetical order.

Then, if relevant, look for the *initial consonant cluster* (subscript, superscript and prefix), according to the procedure outlined below, then the *vowel* and finally the *suffixes*.

To summarize:

1) Radical letter or initial consonant cluster (see below)

2) Vowel

3) Suffixed letter(s)

Note: The subscript *wa* is to be found in dictionaries *after* the vowels: a, i, u, e, o, w.

If the word is polysyllabic, the order of appearance of the second and following syllables follows the same principles.

As for the *initial consonants in a syllable,* entries in the dictionary are classified under each radical according to the following system:

1) Radicals without superscripts or prefixes

a) without subscripts, b) with subscripts.

The following sequence illustrates the order of appearance in the dictionary.

Ex.: ག་རེ་ གངས་ གི་ གིས་ གུར་ གེ་སར་ གོ་ གྭ་ གྱུང་ གྲུར་ གྲང་མོ་ གྲངས་ གླ་ གླང་

2) Radicals with prefixes (but without superscripts)

a) without subscripts, b) with subscripts.

Ex.: དགའ་ དགུ་ དགེ་བ་ དགོས་ དགྲ་ བགམས་ བགེགས་ མགུར་ མགྱོགས་

3) Radicals with superscripts (but without prefixes)

a) without subscripts, b) with subscripts.

Ex.: རྐན་ རྐོད་པོ་ རྐྱ་ རྐྱ་མ་ ལྐང་བུ་ སྐ་ སྐུག་ སྐོར་མོ་ སྐྱུར་ སྐྲ་

4) Radicals with superscripts and prefixed by the letter B

a) without subscripts, b) with subscripts.

Ex.: བཀལ་ བརྒྱ་ བསྒོམས་ བསྒྱུར་ བསྒྲགས་ བསྒྲིགས་

By making frequent use of the dictionary you will become familiar with the order without having to memorize these rules.

Since the vocabulary of Literary Tibetan is different from that of Spoken Tibetan, make sure to choose a dictionary that suits your purposes. For the spoken language, the most complete dictionaries are Melvyn Goldstein's *New Tibetan-English Dictionary of Modern Tibetan* and *English-Tibetan Dictionary of Modern Tibetan* (see Bibliography). For Literary Tibetan, there are the *Tibetan-English Dictionary* of Sarat Chandra Das, H.A. Jäschke's *Tibetan-English Dictionary* and George Roerich's *Tibetan-Russian-English Dictionary with Sanskrit Equivalents.* From the first year on you may find it helpful to consult the *Large Tibetan-Tibetan-Chinese Dictionary (Bod-rgya tshig-mdzod chen-mo).*

The different styles of writing

The many styles of writing Tibetan may be grouped into two main categories: "capital letters" དབུ་ཅན་ ūcän (lit. "with a head"),[62] used mainly for the purposes of printing, and དབུ་མེད། ūme' (lit. "without a head"), which includes the various cursive and ornamental styles.

The first of these – which is the one we shall use in this Manual – is standard throughout the various countries and regions of Tibetan culture, from Amdo to Bhutan, Ladakh to Kham and in the liturgical texts of the Mongols, Buryats and Kalmyks. The cursive script, by contrast, varies considerably from one region to another. Central Tibetan cursive is slightly different from that of Kham or Bhutan. In Amdo it is very little used at all, and people tend to write in ūcän.

Among the most important cursive styles are ཚུགས་ཡིག་ tshū'yi', འབྲུ་ཚ་ tru̱tsa, the usual handwriting style འཁྱུག་ཡིག་ khyū'yi', and the decorative ལཉྫ་ lä̱ntsa, which is used for Sanskrit.

The structure and pagination of traditional books

Until the 1950s, there were hardly any books in Tibet apart from the traditional *pecha* (*dpe-cha*), consisting of unbound rectangular pages block-printed or handwritten on both sides. Usually, the front of the page (recto) bears a sign (*dbu-khyud*), and the first line is indented. The page number is written in letters in a vertical strip in the left-hand margin (usually on the recto face). The corresponding place on the verso side often carries an abridged title of the work. In Tibetan, the recto side is called *gong-ma*, "upper", while the verso side is called *'og-ma,* "lower".

---

62. In Amdo and Kham, the terms ཡིག་དཀར་ "white letters" and ཡིག་ནག་ "black letters" are used instead of ūcän and ūme'.

Cursive and ornamental styles

འཁྱུག་ཡིག་ khyū'yi' **style**

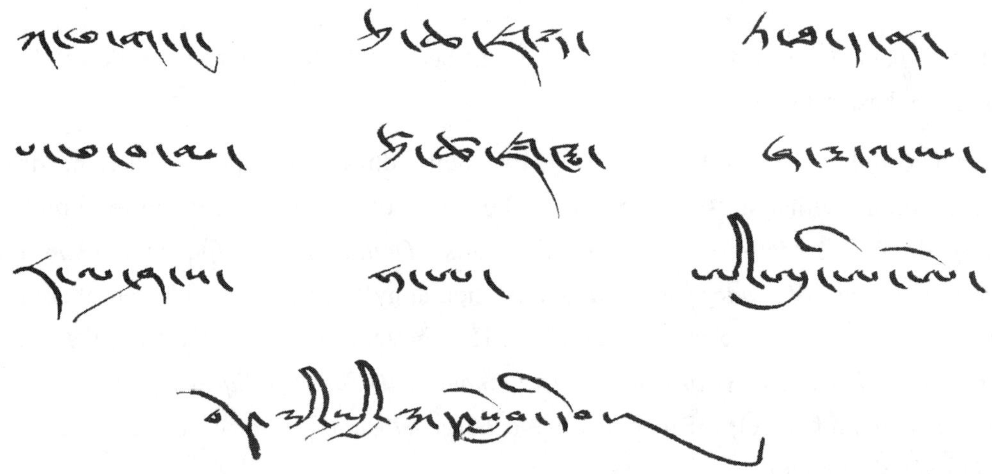

ཀ་ཁ་ག་ང་ ཅ་ཆ་ཇ་ཉ་ ཏ་ཐ་ད་ན་

པ་ཕ་བ་མ་ ཙ་ཚ་ཛ་ཝ་ ཞ་ཟ་འ་ཡ་

ར་ལ་ཤ་ས་ ཧ་ཨ་ ཨི་ཨུ་ཨེ་ཨོ་

[illegible]

འབྲུ་ཚ་ tru̲tsa **style**

ཀ་ཁ་ག་ང་ ཅ་ཆ་ཇ་ཉ་ ཏ་ཐ་ད་ན་

པ་ཕ་བ་མ་ ཙ་ཚ་ཛ་ཝ་ ཞ་ཟ་འ་ཡ་

ར་ལ་ཤ་ས་ ཧ་ཨ་ ཨི་ཨུ་ཨེ་ཨོ་

[illegible]

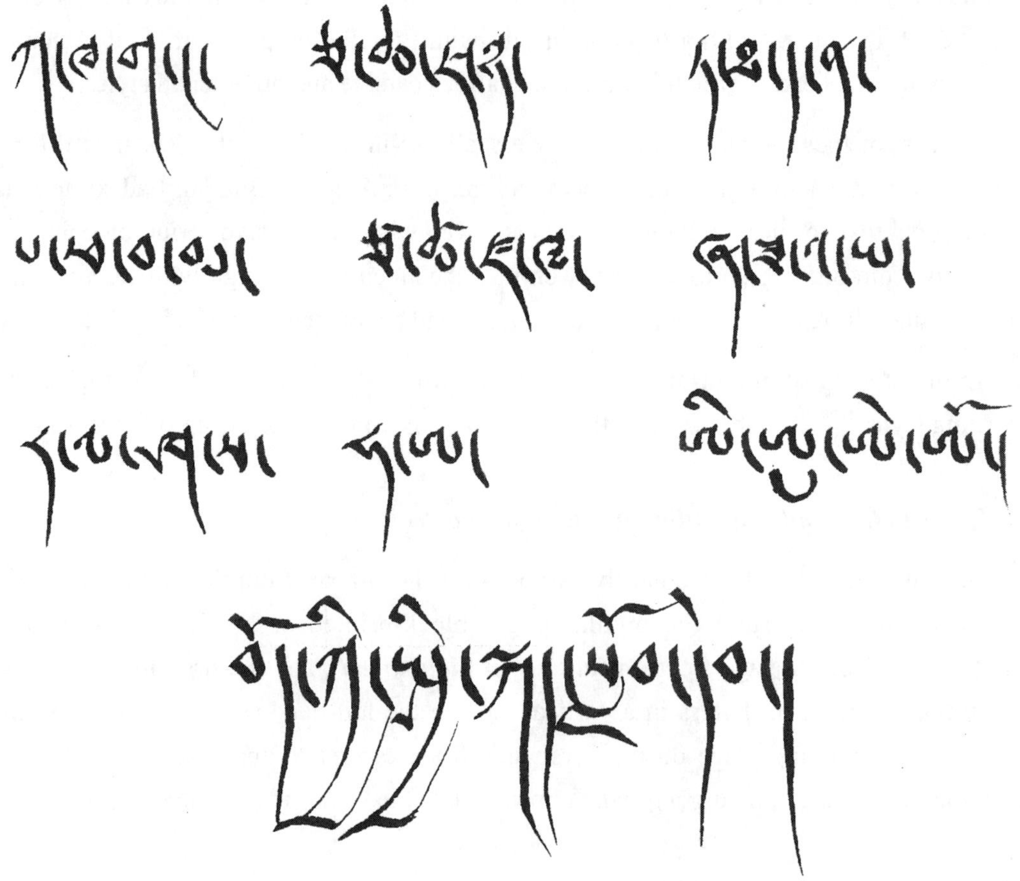

ཚུགས་ཐུང་ tshū'thung **style** (one of the forms of ཚུགས་ཡིག་ tshū'yi')

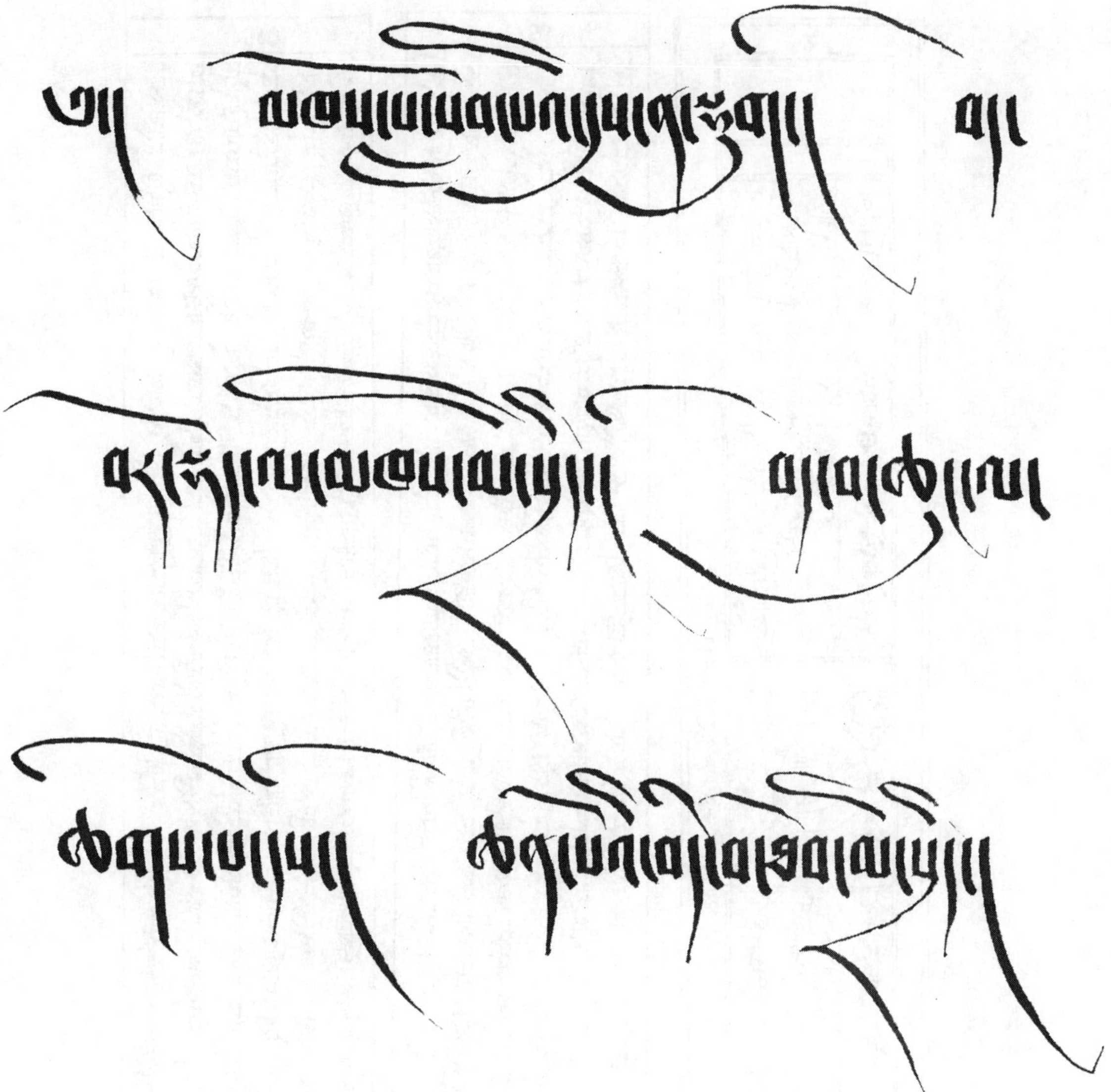

ལནྡྷ་ lä̱ntsa **style**

Kalachakra mantra

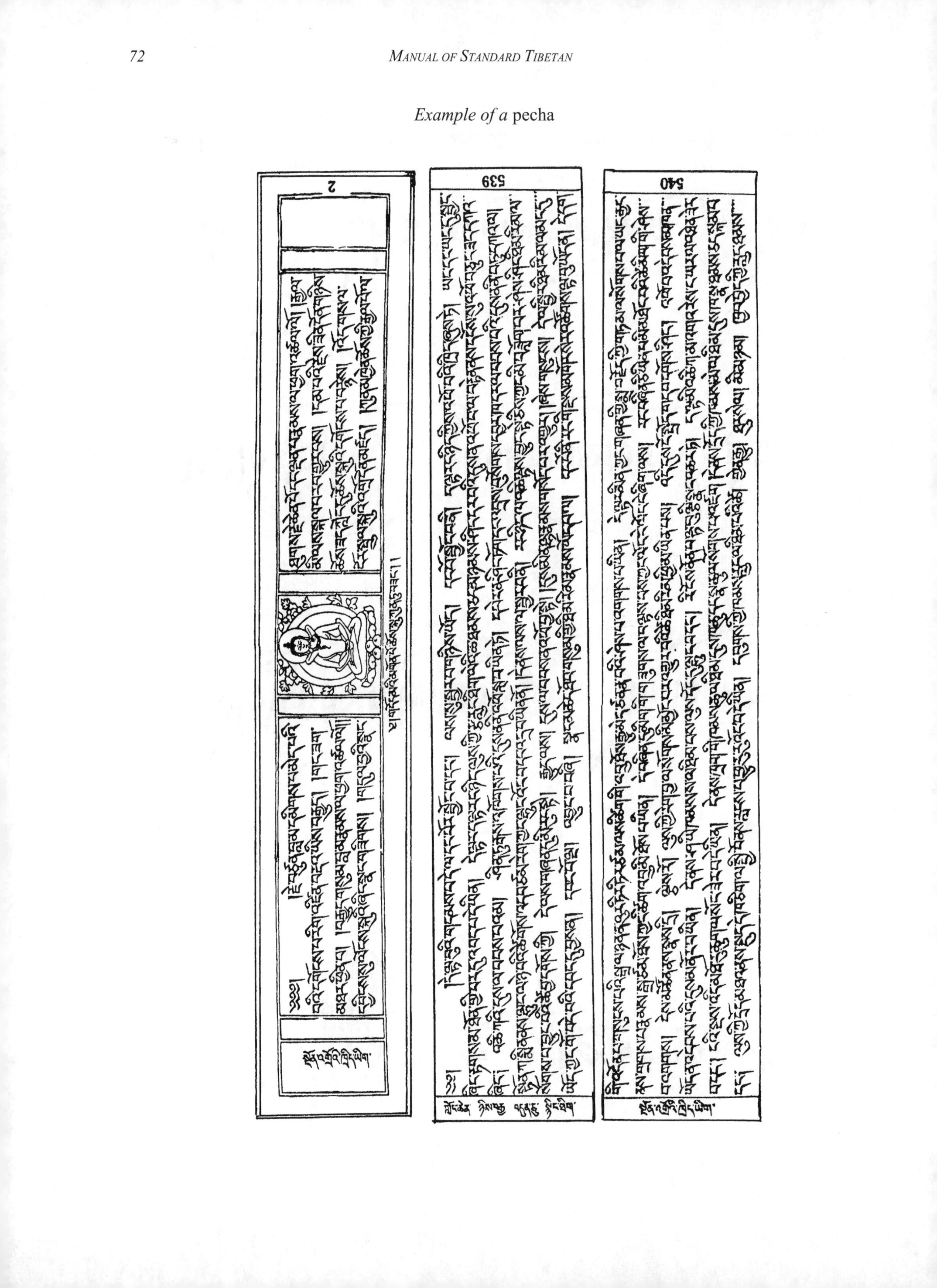

Example of a pecha

The volume number is also shown in the margin by a letter of the Tibetan alphabet: from *ka* (1) to *a* (30), then from *ki* (31) to *i* (60), from *ku* (61) to *u* (90), from *ke* (91) to *e* (120) and finally from *ko* (121) to *o* (150). These cardinal numbers may be transformed into ordinal numbers by adding the suffix *pa.* Thus *ka-pa* signifies "volume 1", and *khi-par* "in volume 32".

The exact organization and structure of the text depends on the genre of literature involved, but the following layout is fairly typical of all genres:

- Title page
- Invocation
- The text proper
- A colophon at the end which contains the name of the author and perhaps the sponsor and the scribe, as well as the place and circumstances of the text's production. Most *pecha* deal with traditional subjects (Buddhism, philosophy, religious biography, medicine, grammar, history, etc.), but in recent decades have also tended to be concerned with more modern issues. Nevertheless, most books (including religious works) – both in Tibet proper as well as in the diaspora community – are now produced in European format. Western-style books are called thep (*deb*).

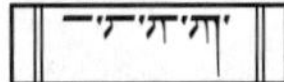

Exercises:

1. Practice writing the letters of the Tibetan alphabet.

2. Read aloud the letters of the alphabet and visualize them.

3. Pronounce the letters of the alphabet with special attention to the tones.

4. Read the following words and write them out in phonological transcription:

ཁ་ "mouth", ང་ "I", ཆ་ "pair", ཇ་ "tea", ཉ་ "fish", ད་ "now", ན་ "to be ill", བ་ "cow", མ་ "mother", ཚ་ "salt", ར་ "goat", ལ་ "pass", ཤ་ "meat", ས་ "place", ཟ་ "to eat", མི་ "man", རི་ "mountain", ཤི་ "to die", ངུ་ "to weep", ཆུ་ "water", ཨུ་ "breath", བུ་ "son", ཤུ་ "whistle", སུ་ "who", དེ་ "that", མེ་ "fire", ཚེ་ "life", ཁོ་ "he", ངོ་ "face", ཉོ་ "to buy", ཕོ་ "male", མོ་ "female", ཞོ་ "yogurt", ཟོ་ "to make", རོ་ "corpse", ལོ་ "year", ཤོ་ "dice", སོ་ "tooth".

5. Spell out and pronounce the following words:

– with a subscript or a superscript:

རྔ་ *rnga* /ngā/ "drum", རྟ་ *rta* /tā/ "horse", རྨ་ *rma* /mā/ "wound", རྩ་ *rtsa* /tsā/ "grass", ལྔ་ *lnga* /ngā/ "five", ལྟ་ *lta* /tā/ "to look", བྱ་ *bya* /cha̱/ "bird", ཀླུ་ *klu* /lū/ "naga, serpent-spirit", ཁྲོ་ *khro* /thrō/ "cauldron".

– with a subscript and a superscript:

སྐྲ་ *skra* /trā/ "hair", སྒྲོ་ *sgro* /tro̱/ "feather", སྐྱེ་ *skye* /kyē/ "to be born", སྒྲ་ *sgra* /tra̱/ "sound", སྨྱོ་ *smyo* /nyō/ "to be mad".

– with a prefix, a subscript and a superscript:

བརྒྱ་ *brgya* /kya̱/ "hundred", བསྒྲོ་ *bsgro* /tro̱/ "to discuss".

– with a prefix, a subscript, a superscript and a suffix:

བརྒྱད་ *brgyad* /kyä̱'/ "eight", བརྒྱབ *brgyab* /kya̱p/ "to do".

– with a prefix, a subscript, a superscript and two suffixes:

བསྒྲིབས་ *bsgrib* /tri̱p/ "to veil", བསྒྲིགས་ *bsgrigs* /tri̱'/ "to arrange", བསྒྲེངས་ *bsgrengs* /tre̱ng'/ "to train", བསྒྲུབས་ *bsgrubs* /tru̱p/ "to accomplish".

6. Look up the words listed in Exercise 5 in the dictionary.

7. Spell out the following words: CD I • Tr. 8 

རོགས་པ། སློབ་གྲྭ་པ། དགེ་རྒན། བཀྲ་ཤིས། སྐུ་མདུན། ཆ། ཆུ། དབྱར་ཁ། གྲུབ་འབྲས། དབྲལ། དབང་པོ།

8. Transliterate the words given in Exercise 7 and look them up in the dictionary.

9. Spell out the combinations given in Table 10 of Appendix 6.

10. Select any text and spell out all the syllables until you can do so without hesitation. It is only from this moment onward that you can begin to read directly.

11. Read the following words, being careful to distinguish high and low tones: CD I • Tr.9

ང་། ལྔ་། ས། ཟ། ནང་། གནང་། ལང་། བསླང་། ཉལ། སྙལ། ཉེས། བརྙེད། སོ། ཟོ། བཟས། བསད། མ། རྨ། ཟེར། གསེར། རལ། དབྲལ། ལ། ཟླ། ཤ་མོ། ཞྭ་མོ། བཞུགས། ཤུགས། ཚོགས་པ། སོགས་པ། སོར། ཚོར། ད། མཐའ། ཐང་པོ། དང་པོ། དོན། ཐོན། བྱང་། ཆང་།

12. Write out the words in Exercise 11 in phonological transcription.

13. Read the following series, being careful to distinguish high and low tones and aspiration. CD I • Tr. 10 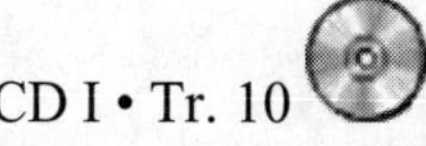

ཏ།　མཐའ།　ད།　མདའ།　　བཏང་།　ཐང་།　དང་།　མདངས།　　སྤྱུ།　ཕྱུ།　བྱུ།　འབྱུ།
ཅ།　ཆ།　བྱ།　འཇའ།　　པར།　ཕར།　བར།　འབར།　　ཀོ།　ཁོ།　གོ　མགོ
གཏད།　ཐད།　དད།　བསྟད།

First Part

THE LESSONS

The Manual includes 41 lessons, organized as follows: First, the grammar aims presented in the lesson are summarized in a frame. This is followed by the Tibetan text, comprising a dialogue or short narrative. A phonetic transcription is included for the texts through Lesson 20, to aid the student in reading and pronunciation. Recordings of all the texts are provided on the accompanying CD. Each text is followed by a list of new vocabulary, the grammatical lessons, and relevant exercises. Some chapters include comments on elements of Tibetan civilization.

"What's this?"

ti̲ kha̲re rä̲'

Grammar aims བརྡ་སྤྲོད་རིག་པའི་དམིགས་ཚད།

- Word order.
- The verb "to be" རེད་ re̲'.
- The demonstratives འདི་ ti̲ དེ་ the̲ ཕ་གི་ phāki.
- The interrogative pronoun ག་རེ་ kha̲re.
- The honorific.

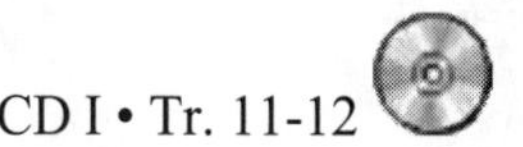
CD I • Tr. 11-12

1.1 Dialogue དྲི་བ་དྲིས་ལན། (thri̲wa thri̲län)

༄༅། །ས་བཀྲ་ལ་ལྟ་དུས།།

"Looking at the map"

ཉི་མ་ ཿ nyi̲ma	འདི་ ti̲	ག་རེ་ kha̲re	རེད། rä̲'	What's this?
ཟླ་བ་ ཿ ta̲wa	འདི་ ti̲	བོད་ phö̲'	རེད། re̲'	This is Tibet
ཉི་མ་ ཿ nyi̲ma	འདི་ ti̲	ལྷ་ས་ lhāsa	རེད། re̲'	This is Lhasa
ཟླ་བ་ ཿ ta̲wa	དེ་ the̲	གཞིས་ཀ་རྩེ་ shi̲katse	རེད་པས། re̲'-pä'	Is that Zhikatse?
ཉི་མ་ ཿ nyi̲ma	ལགས་རེད་ la̲' re̲'	གཞིས་ཀ་རྩེ་ shi̲katse	རེད། re̲'	Yes, that's Zhikatse

ཀ་ཁ་ག་ང་

1.2 Vocabulary ཚིག་གསར། *(*tshīksar*)*

འདི་ ti̲	(det. pron.) this, this one, *proximal dem.*
དེ་ the̲	(det. pron.) that, that one, *medial dem.*
ཕ་གི་ phāki	(det. pron.) that, that one over there *distal dem.*
འདའི tä̲: འདིར་ ti̲r (L)	(adv.) here
དེར་ the̲r	(adv.) there
ཕ་གའི་ phākä ཕ་གིར་ phākir (L)	(adv.) over there
ག་རེ་ kha̲re	(interr. pron.) what?
བོད་པ་ phö̲'pa	(n., adj.) Tibetan (person)
པས་ pä'	(part.) *final interrogative particle*
ལགས་ la̲'	(part.) mark of politeness, after names or before "yes" and "no"
དེབ་ the̲p ཕྱག་དེབ་ chā'tep (H)	(n.) book (Western style)
དཔེ་ཆ་ pēca ཕྱག་དཔེ་ (H) chā'pe	(n.) *pecha,* Tibetan-style book
སྨྱུ་གུ་ nyūku ཕྱག་སྨྱུག་ chā'nyu' (H)	(n.) pen
སྨྱུག་མ་ nyūkma (H)	(n.) bamboo
དཀར་ཡོལ་ kāryö: ཞལ་དཀར་ shä̲:kar (H)	(n.) cup
ཕོར་པ་ phōrpa	(n.) wooden bowl
ས་བཀྲ་ sāptra	(n.) map
ཇ་ cha̲ གསོལ་ཇ་ sȫ:ca (H)	(n.) tea
ཆང་ chāng མཆོད་ཆང་ chȫ:cang (H)	(n.) *chang,* local beer usually made from barley
ཉི་མ་ nyi̲ma	(n.) sun, day
ཟླ་བ་ ta̲wa	(n.) moon, month
འཛམ་གླིང་ tsa̲mling	(n.) world
ཤོག་གུ་ shū'ku ཕྱག་ཤོག་ chāksho' (H)	(n.) paper
སྣག་ཚ་ nāktsa ཕྱག་སྣག་ chā'na' (H)	(n.) ink
སློབ་ཚན་ lōptsän	(n.) lesson
རེད་ re̲' (rä̲' with interrogative pronouns)	(aux.) to be

Proper nouns

བོད་ phö'	Tibet
གཞིས་ཀ་རྩེ་ shi̱katse	Zhikatse, Tibet's second city
ལྷ་ས་ lhāsa / lhā̃:sa[63]	Lhasa, capital of Tibet
ཉི་མ་ nyi̱ma	Nyima
ཟླ་བ་ ta̱wa	Dawa

1.3 Remarks འགྲེལ་བཤད། (tre̱:shä')

1.3.1 Word order

In both Spoken and Literary Tibetan, **the verb always comes last in a clause.** This applies to the verb not only in the main clause but also in subordinate clauses (relative, causal, complementary, etc.). The simple sentence may be broken down into three components: a subject noun phrase, an object noun phrase and the verb complex (or predicate).[64]

Usual word order is "subject – object – verb" (SOV). However, the object may precede the subject (OSV) in order to give special emphasis to the latter, or in the case of certain questions. The emphasis is accompanied by a particular stress on the element that is being emphasized, and by a rising intonation.

Compare:

འདི་	དེབ་	རེད།	དེབ་	འདི་	རེད།
ti̱	the̱p	re̱'	the̱p	ti̱	re̱'
this	book	to be	book	this	to be
"This is a book"			"It's this book."		

The only indispensable element in the sentence is the verb; the subject and object may be implied or omitted. The verb exhibits **no agreement** in terms of:

– gender

– number

– person

63. This variant represents the way in which the people of Lhasa themselves pronounce the word.

64. Even though the notions of "subject" and "object" are not really appropriate in the case of languages such as Tibetan, these terms have been retained in this book for the sake of convenience.

There is no distinction between the active and the passive voice. The neutrality of the verb and its lack of orientation mean that passive transformations are impossible.

It is only the case particles that make it possible to distinguish between the agent and the person or thing that is acted upon.[65]

1.3.2 The auxiliary verb རེད་ re̱' *and its negation* མ་རེད་ ma̱re'

The auxiliary re̱' is similar to the verb "to be" in English. It can function either as an autonomous linking verb (or "copula"), or as the auxiliary of another verb. This is comparable to the English "to be" or the French "être", which are both copulas (e.g., "he is mad", "il est fou") and auxiliaries (e.g., "he is working", "il est arrivé"). Likewise, in the following Tibetan sentences re̱'is a copula in the first and an auxiliary (associated with nominalizer *pa*) in the second:

a)	ཁོང་སྨྱོན་པ་རེད།	khōng nyȫnpa re̱'	"he is mad"
b)	ཁོང་ཕེབས་པ་རེད།	khōng phēp-pare'	"he came" (literally, "he is come")

As a copula, re̱' expresses the nature or the essential quality of the subject. Note that re̱' « to be » is used to express people's age (see also 6.4), just as in English.

The verb རེད་ re̱' is generally pronounced rä̱' (with a more open vowel) in sentences that have an interrogative pronoun. However, the Tibetan spelling remains unaffected.

Questions are constructed by using the final interrogative particle པས་ pä (see Lesson 2): རེད་པས། re̱'-pä' "is it?", མ་རེད་པས། ma̱re'-pä' "isn't it?"

Like other auxiliaries, the verb re̱' and its negation ma̱re' are used to signify "yes" and "no". They may be preceded by the polite marker ལགས་ la'.

1.3.3 The demonstratives འདི་ ṯi, དེ་ the̱, ཕ་གི་ phāki

The demonstratives function both as adjectives and as pronouns. As adjectives, they always come after the noun (or after the noun phrase), and carry a case or plural marker as appropriate.

Ex.:	འདི་ག་རེ་རེད།	ṯi kha̱re rä̱'	"What is this?" ("This is what?")
	ཤོག་གུ་འདི་ག་རེ་རེད།	shūkku ṯi kha̱re rä̱'	"What is this paper?"
	ཤོག་གུ་འདི་ཚོ་ག་རེ་རེད།	shūkku ṯintso kha̱re rä̱'	"What are these papers?"

The demonstratives འདི་ ṯi *(proximal),* དེ་ the̱ *(medial)* and ཕ་གི་ phāki *(distal)* denote three degrees of removal: nearby, distant and far-off, corresponding to the English expressions "here", "there" and "over there".

---

65. The neutrality of Tibetan verbs can be illustrated by comparison with nouns, which are intrinsically neither active nor passive. Thus the sentences "Lobzang corrected the book" or "The book was corrected by Lobzang" might be rendered as "(there was) a correction (of) the book *by* Lobzang".

The demonstratives ti̲, the̲ and phāki function as pronouns and adjectives. When used as adjectives, demonstratives always come after the noun (or after the noun phrase); they are given a case particle and, where appropriate, a plural particle.

The demonstratives ti̲ and the̲ are employed not only to draw attention to something/ point out/ show something (deictic function), but also to refer to elements previously mentioned (anaphoric function) in a text or conversation. The expression phāki, however, is used only to indicate spatial distance.

The demonstrative ti̲ is linked to the present moment; the̲, on the other hand, is associated with the past or the future, and with the notions of "the beyond" and the invisible.

Ex.:			
	ངས་དེ་ཞུས་པ་ཡིན།	nga̲ä' the̲ shü̲'-payin	"I said that"
	ངས་འདི་ཞུ་གི་ཡིན།	nga̲ä' ti̲ shu̲-kiyin	"I'll say this"
	ལོ་འདི་	lo̲ ti̲	"this year" (present)
	ལོ་དེ་	lo̲ the̲	"that year" (past or future)
	དེབ་འདི་	the̲p ti̲	"this book"
	དེབ་དེ་	the̲p the̲	"that book"
	དེབ་ཕ་གི་	the̲p phāki	"that book over there"

The demonstratives འདི་ ti̲, དེ་ the̲, ཕ་གི་ phāki are used to form the adverbs འདིར་ ti̲r, དེར་ the̲r, ཕ་གིར་ phākir "here, there, over there". In the spoken language they have undergone a small variation in their pronunciation འདའི་ tä: (འདིར་), ཕ་གའི་ phākä: (ཕ་གིར་)

1.4 Exercises སྦྱོང་ཚན། (co̲ngtsän)

1.4.1 Translate into Tibetan:

1. What's this?
2. This is a book.
3. What's that?
4. That's a pecha.
5. Is this tea?
6. It's chang.
7. What's that over there?
8. That's Lhasa over there.

1.4.2 Transliterate the dialogue at the beginning of this lesson.

1.4.3 Translate into English:

༡) འདི་ག་རེ་རེད།

༢) འདི་དཀར་ཡོལ་རེད་པས།

༣) དེ་ཆང་རེད།

༤) ཕ་གི་དཔེ་ཆ་རེད་པས།

༥) འདི་ས་བཀྲ་རེད་པས།

༦) འདི་ཉི་མ་རེད།

༧) འདི་འཛམ་གླིང་རེད།

༨) ཕ་གི་ཟླ་བ་རེད་པས།

༩) ཕ་གི་ཟླ་བ་རེད།

1.4.4 Read the sentences in the preceding exercise and mark the high and low tones as follows:

འདི་˳ དཀ˚ར་ཡོལ་ རེ˳ད་པས།

1.4.5 Complete the following sentences using words you have learned:

༡) འདི་ ( ) རེད་པས།

༢) འདི་ ( ) རེད།

༣) ཕ་གི་ ( ) རེད་པས།

༤) ཕ་གི་ ( ) རེད།

༥) དེ་ ( ) རེད་པས།

༦) དེ་ ( ) རེད།

"Who's that ?"

ཁོང་སུ་རེད།

khōng sū rä̱'

Grammar aims བརྡ་སྤྲོད་རིག་པའི་དམིགས་ཚད།

- the interrogative particles ངས་ ngä' གས་ kä' པས་ pä'.
- the plural marker ཚོ་ tshō.
- gender
- the interrogative pronoun སུ་ sū.

CD I • Tr. 13-14

2.1 Dialogue དྲི་བ་དྲིས་ལན། *(thri̱wa thri̱län)*

ཉི་མ་ཿ	ཁོང་ khōng	སུ་ sū	རེད། rä̱'	Who's that?
ཟླ་བ་ཿ	ཁོང་ khōng	བློ་བཟང་ lōsang	རེད། re̱'	That's Lobzang.
ཉི་མ་ཿ	ཚེ་རིང་ tshēring	སུ་ sū	རེད། rä̱'	Who's Tshering?
ཟླ་བ་ཿ	ཚེ་རིང་ tshēring	ཁོང་ khōng	རེད། re̱'	That's Tshering.
ཉི་མ་ཿ	ཁོང་ཚོ་ khōngtso	སུ་ sū	རེད། rä̱'	Who are they?
ཟླ་བ་ཿ	ཁོང་ཚོ་ khōngts	སླབ་གྲྭ་བ་(སློབ་གྲྭ་བ་) lāptrawa	རེད། re̱'	They're students.
ཉི་མཿ	བློ་བཟང་ lōsang	དགེ་རྒན་ ke̱kän	རེད་པས། re̱'-pä'	Is Lobzang a teacher?

ཟླ་བ་ཿ	དགེ་རྒན་	མ་རེད།	
	ke̱kän	ma̱re'	No, (he) isn't a teacher.
	སླབ་གྲྭ་བ་(སློབ་གྲྭ་བ་)	རེད།	
	lāptrawa	re̱'	He's a student.

ཀ་ཁ་ག་ང་

2.2 Vocabulary ཚིག་གསར། *(tshīksar)*

ཁོང་ khōng (H)	(pron.) he, she
ཁོང་ཚོ་ khōngtso (H)	(pron.) they (masc. and fem.)
ཁོ་ khō	(pron.) he
ཁོ་རང་ཚོ་ khōrangtso	(pron.) they
མོ་ mo̱	(pron.) she
ཚོ་ tshō /-tso	(part.) *plural marker*
འདི་ཚོ་ ti̱(n)tso	(det., pron.) these, *proximal dem.*
དེ་ཚོ་ the̱(n)tso	(det., pron.) those, *medial dem.*
ཕ་ཚོ་ phātso	(det., pron.) those (over there), *distal dem.*
སུ་ sū	(interr. pron.) who?
མ་ ma̱	(part.) *negation*
སླབ་གྲྭ་བ་ lāptrawa སློབ་གྲྭ་བ་ lōptrawa (L)	(n.) student, pupil
སླབ་གྲྭ་ lāptra སློབ་གྲྭ་ lōptra (L)	(n.) school
དགེ་རྒན་ ke̱kän རྒན་ལགས་ kä̱nla'(H)	(n.) master, teacher
རྒན་ལགས་ kä̱nla' (H)	(n.) Sir (term of address)
བླ་མ་ lāma	(n.) lama, teacher, master
གྲྭ་པ་ thra̱pa དགེ་འདུན་པ་ ke̱ntünpa (H)	(n.) monk
སྐུ་ཞོག་ kūsho' (H) སྐུ་ཞབས་ kūshap (L, H)	(n.) Sir; Venerable (of monks)
ཆོས་ལགས་ chō̱la' (H)	(n.) Venerable (of nuns)
ཨ་ནི་ āni[66] རྗེ་བཙུན་མ་ ce̱tsünma (H)	(n.) nun
འབྲོག་པ་ tro̱kpa	(n.) nomad, pastoralist

66. This word is also used to mean "paternal aunt".

དྲུང་ཡིག་ thru̲ngyi'	(n.) secretary
ཞིང་པ་ shi̲ngpa	(n.) farmer
ཚགས་པར་ tshākpar	(n.) newspaper
ཞྭ་མོ་ sha̲mo དབུ་ཞྭ་ ūsha (H)	(n.) hat
ཀུབ་ཀྱག་ kūpkya' ཞབས་ཀྱག་ sha̲pkya (H)	(n.) chair
ཅོག་ཙེ་ *or* ལྕོག་ཙེ་ cōktse གསོལ་ཅོག་ sō:co' (H)	(n.) table
འཛིན་གྲྭ་ tsi̲ntra	(n.) class

Proper nouns

བློ་བཟང་ lō(p)sang	Lobzang[67]
ཚེ་རིང་ tshēring	Tshering

2.3 Remarks འགྲེལ་བཤད། (tre̲:shä')

2.3.1 *The final interrogative particles* པས་ -pä', ངས་-ngä' གས་ -kä'

Interrogative sentences end with a **final interrogative particle** (f.i.p.),[68] the precise form of which is determined by the last letter of the preceding auxiliary.[69]

after ང་ nga	>	ངས་ ngä'
after ག་ kha̲	>	གས་ kä'
in all other cases	>	པས pä'

Ex.: ཡིན་པས་ yi̲n-pä', རེད་པས་ re̲'-pä', ཡོད་པས་ yö̲'-pä', སོང་ངས་ sōng-ngä', མྱོང་ངས་ nyo̲ng-ngä', བྱུང་ངས་ chu̲ng-ngä', འདུག་གས་ tu̲'-kä'.

Final interrogative particles are not used with the copulas and auxiliaries mentioned above when a sentence already contains an interrogative pronoun (such as kha̲re "what", sū "who", etc.).

67. Tibetan names often consist of two juxtaposed names. In Central and Western Tibet and in Khams names usually consist of four syllables, whereas in Amdo they tend to have three. People of aristocratic origin may also use a family name, and nomads too often make use of clan names. Among farming communities, there seems to be a historical trend whereby clan names are disappearing and individuals are identified instead by the name of the household in which they were born. In the vast majority of cases, Tibetan personal names have an obvious meaning. Thus Lobzang means "Excellent Mind", Tshering means "Long Life", Nyima means "Sun", Dawa "Moon" and Lhagpa "Mercury"; the last three also denote the days of the week Sunday, Monday and Wednesday respectively, and are applied to people as appropriate to the day on which they were born. Dorje means "Vajra" or "Diamond" , Thubtän "Buddhist Doctrine", Rinchen Kyi "Precious-Joyous", Dhöndrup Gyäl "Victorious One Who Achieves His Aims", and so forth. While the majority of names are gender-neutral, there are a few that are either specifically masculine (e.g., Dorje) or feminine (e.g., Drölkar).

68. Tibetan final interrogative particles may be compared to Burmese /'la/ and Chinese /ma/.

69. From a historical point of view, the interrogative particles *ngas* and *gas* probably correspond to variants of the particle *pas*. The phonological assimilation rule is explained in Appendix 1, section 1.

However, with the verb yi̱n, a final interrogative particle pa is sometimes used. If there is no interrogative pronoun in the question, the sentence ends with yi̱n-pä', the interrogative form of the verb yi̱n; if the question does contain an interrogative pronoun, the sentence ends in yi̱n-pa or yi̱n.

Ex.: ཁྱེད་རང་དགེ་རྒན་ཡིན་པས་ khyērang ke̱kän yi̱n-pä' "Are you a teacher?"
སུ་ཡིན་པ་ sū yi̱n-pa = སུ་ཡིན་ sū yi̱n "Who are you?"

Interrogative pronouns are usually placed directly before the verb. The pronoun kha̱re means both "what" and "which", and corresponds to the literary forms ཅི་ cī and གང་kha̱ng (it is in fact derived from the latter). The interrogative pronouns kha̱re "what" and sū "who" may be doubled (ག་རེ་ག་རེ་ kha̱re kha̱re, སུ་སུ་ sūsu) to elicit an enumeration in the reply or to mean "what types of…?" or "what kinds of…?"

2.3.2 *Number and the plural marker* ཚོ་ tshō /-tso

Number is never marked on verbs, adjectives or the majority of nouns. Plurality is usually implied either by context, or by quantifiers such as མང་པོ་ ma̱ngpo "many", ཚང་མ་ tshāngma "all", ཁ་ཤས་ khāshä' "some, certain", གཉིས་ nyī' "two", etc.

However, there is a plural marker ཚོ་-tso,[70] which appears with demonstratives and personal pronouns: འདི་ཚོ་ ti̱tso "these", དེ་ཚོ་ the̱tso "those", ཕ་ཚོ་ phātso "those, those over there", ཁོང་ཚོ་ khōngtso "they", etc.

The marker -tso by itself is used with nouns denoting people only when the people in question are specified/defined: ཨ་མ་ཚོ་ āma-tso "the mothers", དགེ་རྒན་ཚོ་ ke̱kän-tso "the teachers", སློབ་གྲྭ་བ་ཚོ་ lōptrawa-tso "the students", etc. (but not *mothers, *teachers, etc.). The non-specific plural is not marked with the plural particle: ཨ་མ་ āma "mothers", དགེ་རྒན་ke̱kän "teachers".

This suffix is not used with animals or inanimate objects: * ལུག་ཚོ་ lu̱'-tso "[the] sheep", * ཅོག་ཙེ་ཚོ་ cōktse-tso "[the] tables", * ཐང་ཀ་ཚོ་ thāngka-tso "[the] *thangka*s".

Consequently, unambiguous renderings of the plural / indications of plurality require the use of demonstratives: ལུག་དེ་ཚོ་ lu̱' the̱tso "those sheep", ཅོག་ཙེ་དེ་ཚོ་ cōktse the̱tso "those tables".

Number is only marked once per noun or noun phrase; the marker, which is placed at the end of the group, is therefore never redundant.

Ex.: བུ་མོ་ཆུང་ཆུང་དེ་ཚོ་ phu̱mo chūncung the̱tso "those little girls"
གངས་རི་མཐོ་པོ་དེ་ཚོ་ kha̱ngri thōpo the̱tso "those high snow-mountains"
ཨ་མ་གཞོན་པ་ཚོ་ āma shö̱npa-tso "the young mothers"
རོགས་པ་གཞན་པ་ཚོ་'' ro̱kpa shä̱nta'-tso "the other companions"

N.B.: the following demonstratives also occur in conversation:

70. When the marker is not accentuated it is pronounced without aspiration: -tso.

འདི་ཀྱང་ t̲ikyä' "these" (nearby), དེ་ཀྱང་ the̲kyä' "those" (distant)
འདི་ཀྱང་འདི་ t̲ikyä' t̲i "all these", དེ་ཀྱང་དེ་ the̲kyä' the̲ "all those"

These last two expressions are used to make a selection from a group.

Ex.: དེབ་འདི་ཀྱང་འདི་ the̲p t̲ikyä' t̲i "all these books" (and not the others)

2.3.3 Gender

Grammatical gender (masculine, feminine, neuter) **does not exist in Tibetan**.

Articles, demonstratives, adjectives and verbs are therefore invariable with respect to gender. Male and female sex are, however, sometimes marked within the lexicon (by distinct words) or else by means of suffixes (pa or po for the male and ma or mo for the female) in the case of certain pronouns and substantives denoting animate beings.

Ex.: གཡག་ yā' "yak" (male), འབྲི་ tr̲i "yak-cow", རྟ་ tā "horse" (generic), རྒོད་མ་ kö̲ma "mare", བུ་ phu̲ "boy", བུ་མོ་ phu̲mo "girl", ཁམས་པ་ khāmpa "man from Kham", ཁམས་མོ་ khāmmo "woman from Kham", རྣལ་འབྱོར་པ་ nä̲:corpa "yogin", རྣལ་འབྱོར་མ་ nä̲:corma "yogini", མཛོ་ tso̲ "yak/cow hybrid", མཛོ་མོ་ tso̲mo "female dzo"

N.B.: some pronouns make no distinction between "he" and "she":

ཁོང་ཕྱུག་པོ་རེད། khōng chūkpo re̲' "He/she is rich."

2.4 Exercises སྦྱོང་ཚན།

2.4.1 Translate into Tibetan:

1. This isn't a chair, it's a table.
2. This is a pecha, it isn't a book.
3. These are nuns, they aren't monks!
4. Who is the teacher?
5. Is he a lama?
6. No, he's a monk.
7. Are those nomads over there?
8. No, those are farmers.
9. He is a secretary.
10. She is a teacher.

2.4.2 Transliterate the dialogue at the beginning of this lesson.

2.4.3 *Translate into English:*

༡) འདི་ཚོ་སུ་རེད།
༢) འདི་ཚོ་གྲྭ་པ་རེད།
༣) ཕ་ཚོ་སུ་རེད།
༤) ཕ་ཚོ་སློབ་གྲྭ་བ་རེད།
༥) ཕ་གི་སུ་རེད།
༦) ཕ་གི་བློ་བཟང་རེད།
༧) དེ་ཚོ་དེབ་རེད་པས། དེབ་མ་རེད། དཔེ་ཆ་རེད།
༨) འདི་རྐུབ་ཀྱག་རེད་པས། རྐུབ་ཀྱག་མ་རེད། ཅོག་ཙེ་རེད།
༩) དགེ་རྒན་དེ་ཚོ་སུ་རེད།
༡༠) འདི་ཇ་རེད་པས། ཇ་མ་རེད། ཆང་རེད།
༡༡) ཕ་གི་དཀར་ཡོལ་རེད་པས། དཀར་ཡོལ་མ་རེད། ཕོར་པ་རེད།

2.4.4 *Read the sentences above and mark the high and low tones.*

2.4.5 *With the use of your dictionary, find ten words containing the following honorific prefixes:* phyag *"hand"*, dbu *"head"*, ljags *"tongue"*, thugs *"mind"*, sku *"body"*.

2.4.6 *Give the plural of the following words using the markers* ྌཚོ་ *or* དེ་ཚོ་*:*

སྨྱུག་གུ་ དཀར་ཡོལ་ སློབ་ཚན་ ཁོང་ འབྲོག་པ་ སློབ་གྲྭ་

"The telephone"

Grammar aims བརྡ་སྤྲོད་རིག་པའི་དམིགས་ཚད།

- personal pronouns.
- the verb ཡིན་ yin and "egophoric" verbs.
- the rule of anticipation.
- the place of adjectives.
- the existential verb འདུག་ tu'.

ཁ་པར།

khāpar

CD I • Tr. 15-16

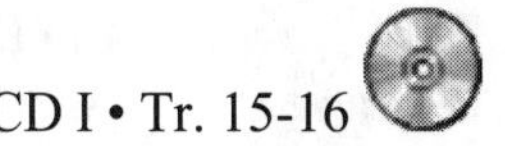

3.1 Dialogue དྲི་བ་དྲིས་ལན།

༄།། ཁྲིར་ཁྲིར་ཁྲིར་ཁྲིར།།

"Dring! Dring!..."

བློ་བཟང་ ༔ ལོའོ་(ལགས་)
lo:

རྡོ་རྗེ་ ༔ བཀྲ་ཤིས་བདེ་ལེགས།
trāshi' tele'

བློ་བཟང་ ༔ བཀྲ་ཤིས་བདེ་ལེགས།
trāshi' tele'

རྡོ་རྗེ་ ༔ ཐུབ་བསྟན་ལགས་ ཡིན་པས།
thūptän-la' yin-pä

བློ་བཟང་ ༔ ལགས་མན་(མིན་) ཁྱེད་རང་ སུ་ ཡིན་པ།
la' män, khyērang sū yin-pa

རྡོ་རྗེ་ ༔ ང་ རྡོ་རྗེ་ ཡིན། ཁྱེད་རང་ སུ་ ཡིན་ན་(ནམ)།
nga torce yin, khyērang sū yin-na

བློ་བཟང་ ༔ ཨ་ལའི། དགོངས་དག རྡོ་རྗེ་ལགས་ ང་ བློ་བཟང་ ཡིན།
ālä: kongta' torce-la', nga lōsang yin,

སྐུ་གཟུགས་ བདེ་པོ་ ཡིན་པས།
kūsu' tepo yin-pä

རྡོ་རྗེ་ ༔	ལགས་ཡིན། la̲' yi̲n,	ཐུབ་བསྟན་ལགས་ thūptän-la'		འདུག་གས། tu̲'-kä'
བློ་བཟང་ ༔	ལགས་ la̲'	མི་འདུག mi̲ntu'		
རྡོ་རྗེ་ ༔	འོ་ན་ o̲na	ཐུགས་རྗེ་ཆེ་ thūkce chē,	རྗེས་མར་མཇལ་ཡོང་། ce̲mar cä̲:-yong	
བློ་བཟང་ ༔	རྗེས་མར་མཇལ་ཡོང་། ce̲mar cä̲:-yong			

Translation

Lobzang — Hello?
Dorje — Hello (formal)
Lobzang — Hello (formal)
Dorje — Is that Thubtän?
Lobzang — No, who are you?
Dorje — I'm Dorje, and you?
Lobzang — Ah, sorry, Dorje, I'm Lobzang. How are you?
Dorje — I'm fine, thanks. Is Thubtän there?
Lobzang — No, he isn't.
Dorje — Well, thanks. See you later.
Lobzang — Bye, see you later.

ཀ་ཁ་ག་ང་

3.2 Vocabulary ཚིག་གསར།

རང་ ra̲ng	(pron.) same, you
ན na/ ནམ་ nam (L)	(part.) *final interrogative particle*
ཨ་ལའི་ ālä:	(exp.) ah!
འོ་ན་ o̲na	(exp.) well, well then
མི་ mi̲	(n.) man, person
ལམ་ཁག་ la̲mka' ལམ་ la̲m (L)	(n.) road, path, way
སེམས་ sēm' ཐུགས། thū' (H)	(n.) mind, spirit
གཟུགས་པོ་ su̲kpo སྐུ་གཟུགས་ kūsu' (H)	(n.) body
དགོངས་དག་ ko̲ngta'	(n.) sorry
ཐུགས་རྗེ་ཆེ་ thūkce chē	(n.) thank you
ལྡེ་མིག་ te̲mi' ཕྱག་ལྡེ་ chānte (H)	(n.) key

ཁ་པར་ khāpar ཞལ་པར་ shä̱:par (H)	(n.) telephone
རྗེས་མར་ ce̱mar	(adv.) later, afterwards
རིང་པོ་ ri̱ngpo	(adj.) long
ཐུང་ཐུང་ thūngtung	(adj.) short
གཟུགས་པོ་རིང་པོ་ su̱kpo ri̱ngpo	(adj.) tall
གཟུགས་པོ་ཆུང་ཆུང་ su̱kpo chūngcung	(adj.) short
ཆུང་ཆུང་ chūngcung	(adj.) small
ཆེན་པོ་ chēnpo	(adj.) big
བདེ་པོ་ te̱po	(adj.) well, fine
དཀར་པོ་ kārpo	(adj.) white
ནག་པོ་ na̱kpo	(adj.) black
རྗེས་མ་ ce̱ma	(adj.) next, following
བཀྲ་ཤིས་བདེ་ལེགས་ trāshi te̱le'	(idiom.) hello, greetings
རྗེས་མར་མཇལ་ཡོང་ ce̱mar cä̱:yong	(idiom.) see you later
སྐུ་གཟུགས་བདེ་པོ་ཡིན་པས་ kūsu' te̱po yi̱n pä'	(idiom.) how are you?
ཡིན་ yi̱n	(aux.) to be, *egophoric*
མན་ mä̱n མིན་ mi̱n (L)	(aux.) not to be, *egophoric*
འདུག་ tu̱'	(aux.) there is, to have, to be, *testimonial*
མི་འདུག་ mi̱ntu'	(aux.) there isn't, not to have, not to be, *testimonial*
མི་ mi̱	(aux.) *negation*

Proper nouns

ཐུབ་བསྟན་ thūptän	Thubtän
རྡོ་རྗེ་ to̱rce	Dorje

Personal pronouns

1st person	2nd person	3rd person
ང་ nga̱ "I"	ཁྱེད་རང་ khyērang "you" (H) ཁྱོད་ khyȫ' "you" རང་ ra̱ng "you"	ཁོང་ khōng "he", "she" (H) མོ་ mo̱ "she" ཁོ་ khō "he"
ང་ཚོ་ nga̱(n)tso "we" ང་གཉིས་ nga̱nyi' "we two"	ཁྱེད་རང་ཚོ་ khyērangtso "you" (H) ཁྱེད་རྣམ་ཚོ་ khyēnamtso "you" (HH) ཁྱོད་རང་ཚོ་ khyȫrangtso "you" (pl.) ཁྱོད་རང་གཉིས་ khyȫrangtso "you two" ཁྱེད་རང་གཉིས་ khyērangnyi' "you two" (H)	ཁོང་ཚོ་ khōngtso "they" (H) ཁོང་རྣམ་ཚོ་ khōngnamtso "they" (HH) ཁོ་རང་ཚོ་ khōrangtso "they" ཁོ་གཉིས་ khūnyi' "those two" ཁོང་གཉིས་ khōngnyi' "those two" (H)

༣༣

3.3 Remarks འགྲེལ་བཤད།

3.3.1 Personal pronouns

There are three registers of personal pronouns: ordinary, honorific and high honorific. In Literary Tibetan, as well as in some dialects (Tsang), a humilific form (*bdag*) is used for the first person. This form is not used in Standard Spoken Tibetan.

In Literary Tibetan and in certain dialects (including Kham and Mustang), there are distinct forms for the **exclusive** ("us, not including you") and **inclusive** ("us, including you") first person plural. This opposition, too, is absent in Standard Tibetan.

For the second person, it is safest to use the honorific form ཁྱེད་རང་ khyērang / ཁྱེད་རང་ཚོ་ khyērangtso and ཁོང་ / ཁོང་ཚོ་ khōng/khōngtso. The ordinary forms རང་ ra̱ng "you", ཁོ་ khō "he", ཁོ་རང་ khōrang "he" and མོ་ mo̱ or མོ་རང་ mo̱rang "she" imply familiarity. The forms ཁྱོད་ khyȫ' and ཁྱོད་

རང་ཚོ་ khyōrangtso "you" carry pejorative connotations in Standard Tibetan, whereas they are the normal terms in Literary Tibetan and certain dialects (Kham, Hor, Amdo).

In Standard Tibetan and many other dialects, as well as in Literary Tibetan, there is a special dual form for both personal pronouns and demonstratives: ང་གཉིས་ nga̱nyi' "we two", ཁྱེད་རང་གཉིས་ khyērangnyi' "you two", ཁོ་གཉིས་ khūnyi' "the two of them" དེ་གཉིས་ the̱nyi' "those two".

3.3.2 *"Egophoric"* (rang ngos) *auxiliary verbs*

Certain auxiliary verbs are associated only with **the first person** (singular or plural), irrespective of the function of that person in the sentence, i.e., as subject, object or complement. The use of an "egophoric"[71] auxiliary expresses the speaker's knowledge or personal intention, often directly implied in the event that is being described. Whereas this type of auxiliary does not occur in Classical Literary Tibetan, it plays an important role in the spoken language. The egophoric auxiliaries (and copulas) are:

ཡིན་ yi̱n, ཡོད་ yö̱', བྱུང་ chu̱ng, མྱོང་-nyong, དགོས་ ko'.

In contrast, all the remaining auxiliaries are neutral with respect to person:

རེད་re̱', འདུག་tu̱', ཡོད་རེད་yo̱:re', སོང་-song, བཞག་-sha'

Ex.:		
ང་རྡོ་རྗེ་ཡིན།	nga̱ to̱rce yi̱n	"I am Dorje."
ང་དགའ་པོ་བྱུང་།	nga̱ ka̱po chu̱ng	"I was happy."
ངར་དེབ་མང་པོ་ཡོད།	ngar the̱p ma̱ngpo yö̱'	"I have many books."
ང་ནག་ཆུར་འགྲོ་མྱོང་།	nga̱ na̱kcur tro̱-nyong	"I have been (lit. gone) to Nagchu."
ཡི་གེ་མང་པོ་བཏང་པ་ཡིན།	yi̱ke ma̱ngpo tāng-payin	"[I] sent many letters."

In all the above sentences, it is possible to dispense with the pronoun nga̱, "I", in view of the fact that the first person is indicated by the auxiliary (or the copula).

In the following sentences, the egophorics do not agree with the subject but with a complement:

ལྡེ་མིག་འདི་ངའི་ཡིན།	te̱mi' ti̱ ngä̱: yi̱n	"This key is mine!"
ཁོང་ངའི་ནང་ལ་ཕེབས་ཀྱི་ཡོད།	khōng ngä̱: na̱ng-la phēp-kiyö'	"He [generally] comes to my place."
ངའི་བུ་མོ་སློབ་གྲྭ་ལ་འགྲོ་གི་ཡོད།	ngä̱: phu̱mo lāptra-la tro̱-kiyö'	"My daughter goes to school." (cf. English "I've got my daughter in school.")
ཁོང་གིས་ངར་ཡི་གེ་བཏང་བྱུང་།	khōng-ki' ngar yi̱ke tāng-cung	"He sent me a letter."

71. Etymologically, "egophoric" signifies "bearer of 'I' or 'ego'".

འདི་ཁྱེད་རང་གི་གསོལ་ཇ་ཡིན། ṯi khyērang-ki sō̈:ca yi̱n — “This is your tea (the tea that I made for you or that I intend you should drink).”

When the first person appears as an oblique complement (other than as a subject or object), the use of an egophoric auxiliary usually stresses the personal intention or the certainty of the speaker. Where there is no such emphasis, egophoric auxiliaries may always be replaced by neutral auxiliaries. For example, some of the above sentences may be rephrased as follows:

ལྡེ་མིག་འདི་ངའི་རེད། ṯemi' ṯi ngä̱: re̱' — “This key is mine.”

ངའི་བུ་མོ་སློབ་གྲྭ་ལ་འགྲོ་གི་ཡོད་རེད། ngä̱: phu̱mo lāptra-la tro̱-kiyo:re'
“My daughter goes to school.”

འདི་ཁྱེད་རང་གི་ཇ་རེད། ṯi khyērang-ki cha̱ re'
“This is your tea (this is the tea that’s yours).”

Whereas egophoric auxiliaries need not always be used with the first person, it is incorrect to use egophorics in statements that neither contain the first person nor express the speaker’s personal involvement.

Finally, it should be noted that egophoric forms are used only when an auxiliary verb occurs in the main clause, but usually not in subordinate clauses.

For the time being, the important thing to remember is that the auxiliary ཡིན་ yin is used mainly for the first person, whereas the auxiliary རེད་ re̱' is used for the second and third persons.

3.3.3 The existential verb འདུག་ *tu̱' and its negation* མི་འདུག་ *mi̱ntu'*

The verb tu̱', which depending on context may mean “to have” or “there is” or “to be”, implies that the speaker is or has been a direct witness to whatever he or she is asserting. The verb will be described in detail in Lesson 6.

3.3.4 The rule of anticipation

In the case of interrogative sentences that directly concern the person being addressed (that is, sentences containing second-person pronouns), the questioner must anticipate an answer containing an “I” or a “we” by making advance use of an egophoric auxiliary in the question itself.

Ex.: — ཁྱེད་རང་བདེ་པོ་ཡིན་པས། khyērang ṯepo yi̱n-pä — “Are you well?”
— ང་རང་བདེ་པོ་ཡིན་/ མིན། nga̱rang ṯepo yi̱n/ mi̱n — “I’m well / not well.”

This exchange might be rendered literally in English as "Am you well?", since the anticipated reply, whether positive or negative, is "I am well/ not well".

The rule of anticipation operates in a similar way, but with a reverse result, when the speaker is asking a question about him– or herself. In this case, since the reply will of course contain a "you", the rule requires that the first person be represented by a neutral, not egophoric, auxiliary.

Ex.: — ང་སྨྱོན་པ་རེད་པས། nga̱ nyō̄npa re̱'-pä' "Am I mad?"
— ཁྱེད་རང་སྨྱོན་པ་(མ་)རེད། khyērang nyō̄npa (ma) re̱' "You are (not) mad!"

A more literal English rendering of this exchange would be:

— "Are I mad?"
— "You are(n't) mad."

This "anticipatory mood" is a distinctive feature of Tibetan. It appears not only in Standard Tibetan but in all other Tibetan dialects too, though not in the classical literary language.

3.3.4 The place of adjectives

In the spoken language, adjectives always come after the nouns they describe, and may be followed by determinants such as articles and quantifiers: N. + Adj. + Art.

Although adjectives are invariable they have a long and a short form, a subject which will be addressed in Lesson 17.

Constructions involving an attributive adjective bear a superficial resemblance to constructions with a predicate adjective.

སྙུ་གུ་ནག་པོ་རེད། nyūku na̱kpo re̱' "The pen is black", or "(This) is a black pen"

The ambiguity may be avoided by using a demonstrative. Compare:

སྙུ་གུ་འདི་ནག་པོ་རེད། nyūku ti̱ na̱kpo re̱' "This pen is black."
འདི་སྙུ་གུ་ནག་པོ་རེད། ti̱ nyūku na̱kpo re̱' "This is a black pen."

3.4 Exercises སྦྱོང་ཚན།

3.4.1 Translate into Tibetan:

1. This key is big.
2. Who is this great lama?
3. What is this little book?
4. Is there any tea?
5. There isn't any paper.
6. Is Nyima there?
7. There are no big cups.
8. Is Dorje well?
9. Lobzang is short.

3.4.2 Transliterate the dialogue at the beginning of this lesson.

3.4.3 Translate into English:

༡) དཀར་ཡོལ་འདི་ཆུང་ཆུང་རེད།
༢) དེབ་འདི་ཚོ་ཆེན་པོ་རེད།
༣) སྣག་ཚ་ནག་པོ་མི་འདུག
༤) ཅོག་ཙེ་འདི་རིང་པོ་རེད།
༥) ཞྭ་མོ་དེ་ཚོ་ནག་པོ་རེད།
༦) རྐུབ་ཀྱག་འདུག་གས།
༧) འཇམ་གླིང་ཆུང་ཆུང་རེད།
༨) ཤོག་གུ་དཀར་པོ་མི་འདུག་གས།
༩) ལམ་ཁག་འདི་ཐུང་ཐུང་རེད།

3.4.4 Read the above sentences and mark the high and low tones.

3.4.5 Rewrite the sentences in Exercise 3.4.3 in the honorific form.

3.4.6 Complete the following sentences with affirmative or interrogative auxiliaries as appropriate: ཡིན་; ཡིན་པས་; རེད་ or རེད་པས་:

༡) ཁྱེད་རང་དྲུང་ཡིག་ ( )?
༢) ཁྱེད་རང་ཚོ་སློབ་གྲྭ་བ་ ( )?
༣) ཁོང་ཚོ་དགེ་རྒན་ ( )?
༤) ང་རང་ཚོ་འགྲོགས་པ་ ( )!
༥) ང་རང་དགེ་རྒན་ ( )?
༦) ཁོང་ཚོ་བདེ་པོ་ ( )?
༧) ང་བདེ་པོ་ ( )!
༨) ཁྱེད་རང་རྡོ་རྗེ་ལགས་ ( )?
༩) མ་རེད། རྡོ་རྗེ་ལགས་ཁོང་ ( )!
༡༠) ཁོང་གཟུགས་པོ་རིང་པོ་ ( )?
༡༡) ཁོང་གཟུགས་པོ་ཆུང་ཆུང་ ( )!

"Come in!"

ཡར་ཕེབས།

yar phēp

Grammar aims བརྡ་སྤྲོད་རིག་པའི་དམིགས་ཚད།

- General presentation of cases.
- The genitive case: གི་ -ki and its variants.
- The absolutive case.
- The imperative mood with the verb alone.

CD I • Tr. 17-18

4.1 Dialogue དྲི་བ་དྲིས་ལན།

སྒྲོལ་དཀར་ ཿ	འདི་ ངའི་ ཁང་པ་ རེད། ཡར་ཕེབས།
trö̱:kar	ti̱ ngä̱: khāngpa re̱', ya̱r phēp
བློ་བཟང་ ཿ	ཁོང་ སུ་ རེད།
lōsang	khōng sū rä̱'
སྒྲོལ་དཀར་ ཿ	ངའི་ པ་ལགས་ རེད། པ་ལགས། ཁོང་ ངའི་ གྲོགས་པོ་ བློ་བཟང་ལགས་ རེད། བཀྲ་ཤིས་ལགས་ཀྱི་ བུ་ རེད།
	ngä̱: pāla' re', pāla', khōng ngä̱: thro̱kpo lōsang-la' re̱', trāshi-la'-ki phu̱ re̱'
པ་པ་ ཿ	ཡར་ཕེབས། བཞུགས་གདན་འཛགས།
papa	ya̱r phēp, shu̱tänca'
བློ་བཟང་ ཿ	ཐུགས་རྗེ་ཆེ།
	thūkce chē
སྒྲོལ་དཀར་ ཿ	འདི་ ངའི་ ཨ་མ་ལགས་ རེད།
	ti̱ ngä̱: āma-la' re̱'
ཨ་མ་ ཿ	ཕྱག་ཕེབས་གནང་བྱུང་།
ama	chāpe' nāng-cung
བློ་བཟང་ ཿ	བཀྲ་ཤིས་བདེ་ལེགས།
	trāshi te̱le'

Translation

Drölkar	—	This is our house. Come in!
Lobzang	—	Who is it?
Drölkar	—	It's my father. Father, this is my friend Lobzang. (He)'s Trashi's son.
Father	—	Come in, sit down.
Lobzang	—	Thank you.
Drölkar	—	This is my mother.
Mother	—	Welcome.
Lobzang	—	How do you do?

ཀ་ཁ་ག་ང་

4.2 Vocabulary ཚིག་གསར།

ཁང་པ་ khāngpa གཟིམ་ཤག་ s̱imsha' (H)	(n.) house
ཞིང་ཁ་ shi̱ngka	(n.) field
སྡུག་བསྔལ་ tu̱'ngä:	(n.) suffering
བདེ་བ་ te̱wa	(n.) happiness
པ་ཕ་ pāpa པཱ་ལགས་ pāla' (H)	(n.) father
ཨ་མ་ āma ཨ་མ་ལགས་ āma-la' (H)	(n.) mother
དཔོན་པོ་ pö̃npo	(n.) leader, master, boss
གྲོགས་པོ་ thro̱kpo	(n.) friend (masc.)
གྲོགས་མོ་ thro̱kmo	(n.) friend (fem.)
བུ་ phu̱ སྲས་ sä̃'(H)	(n.) son
བུ་མོ་ phu̱mo སྲས་མོ་ sä̃mo (H)	(n.) daughter
སྤུ་གུ་ pūku ཕྲུ་གུ་ thrūku (L) ཨ་བ་ āwa (H)	(n.) child
རྙིང་པ་ nyīngpa	(adj.) old (object)
གསར་པ་ sārpa	(adj.) new
ལས་སླ་པོ་ lä̱' lāpo	(adj.) easy
དཀའ་ལས་ཁག་པོ་ kālä' khākpo	(adj.) difficult
ཡར་ ya̱r	(adj.) upwards
མར་ ma̱r	(adj.) downwards
འགྲོ་ tro̱(1) / ཕྱིན་ chīn (2) / རྒྱུགས་kyu̱' (3) [72]	(v.) [vol., A] to go

72. Remember that the numbers in brackets correspond to the forms of the present-future (1), the past (2) and the imperative (3). Literary Tibetan uses certain verb forms that have disappeared from the spoken language. As we shall see later, "inflected" verbs of this sort are rather uncommon in Standard Tibetan. When the infinitive of a verb that has several forms in oral Tibetan is cited, the present-future form will be given. Contrary to usual practice, the form in which infinitives are cited here will not contain the nominalizing particle *pa,* since this adds nothing to the reader's understanding.

ཕེབས་ phēp (H)	(v.) [vol., A] to go, to come
ཡོང་ yo̱ng (1, 2) / ཤོག་ shō' (3)	(v.) [vol., A] to come
ཡར་ཤོག་ ya̱r shō' ཡར་ཕེབས་ ya̱r phēp (H)	(v.) [vol., A] come in!
བསྡད་ tä̱' (1, 2) / སྡོད་ tö̱' (3)	(v.) [vol., A] to stay, sit
བཞུགས་ shu̱' (H)	(v.) [vol., A] to stay, sit
མར་བསྡད་ ma̱r tä̱' མར་བཞུགས་ ma̱r shu̱' (H)	(v.) [vol., A] to sit down
བཞུགས་གདན་འཇགས་ shu̱tänca' (HH)	(idiom.) please take a seat
ཕྱག་ཕེབས་གནང་བྱུང་ chā'pe' nāngcung	(idiom.) welcome!

Proper nouns

སྒྲོལ་དཀར་ trö̱:kar	Drölkar
བཀྲ་ཤིས་ trāshi'	Trashi

4.3 Remarks འགྲེལ་བཤད།

4.3.1 General remarks on cases

Both the spoken and literary languages contain case-marking particles that specify the function of a noun within a sentence.

There are six cases: the absolutive (unmarked), the agentive *gis,* the genitive *gi,* the oblique *la,* the ablative *nas* and the associative *dang.* The following lessons will discuss each one in turn.

In English, these cases are represented by prepositions such as "to", "of", "in", "by", or "for", or else are not translated at all.

The system of cases in Tibetan is quite distinct from that of European languages such as Latin, Greek, German and Russian, for a number of reasons:

• First of all, contrary to the case of these languages, the form of **the noun itself remains invariable.**[73] Instead, it makes use of particles or **suffixes that vary in form.** For example, some Tibetan case suffixes vary according to the final letter (or sound) of the preceding word.

• Literary Tibetan and to a lesser extent the spoken language show some features of agglutinative morphology. That is, the case suffixes and the other grammatical suffixes are added on in a series. For example, the plural is marked by a suffix distinct from case (unlike Latin or Russian, where they are blended together with each other and often with the noun stem). In the following

73. There are no exceptions to this rule in the written language, and very few in Spoken Tibetan.

sentences in Literary Tibetan, the head nouns *lus* "body" and *mkhas-pa* "learned" are followed by three suffixes including a plural marker and then a case marker (genitive or agentive):

མཁས་པ་རྣམས་ཀྱིས་ཀྱང་	མ་གཟིགས་
khāpa-nam-kyi'-kyang	ma si'
learned-*plural-agentive-additive*	*negation* see (H)
"Even the learned ones have not seen (it)."	

ལུས་ཅན་དག་གི་	ལས་
lü'-cän-ta'-ki	lä'
body-*possession suffix-plural-genitive*	karma
"The karma of those who have a body…"	

• Cases markers in Tibetan have a range of functions that are not confined to the noun, but *also relate to the verb.* Thus all case markers have two basic functions: a **case-related function** and a **connective function**[74] (See the discussion on the ablative case in Lesson 9, and Appendix 1, section 3.3). When they follow a noun or noun phrase, they mark case, indicating the role of that noun or noun phrase in the clause or sentence. When the same forms are used after a verb or a clause, they serve as a connective function, indicating how two clauses are related (e.g., co-ordination, subordination, etc.).

The following are the main case-related and connective functions:

གིས -ki', the **agentive** case, traditionally referred to as བྱེད་སྒྲ་ /chetra/, literally "agent-sound", indicates the agent of the action ("by"), the instrument ("with"), the cause ("because of", "by"), and the manner ("with"); this form also marks causal subordinate clauses, in which case it may be translated by "since", "because", etc.

གི་ -ki, the **genitive** case, traditionally referred to as འབྲེལ་སྒྲ་ /tre:tra/, literally "link-sound", designates the complement of the noun, and is translated by "of"; this form may also correspond to the conjunction "but" (L), when it is used to link clauses.

---

74. Our presentation of case does not reflect the Tibetan grammatical tradition which is based on Sanskrit, a sacred language for Tibetans (Sanskrit is an Indo-European language entirely different in its structures from the Tibeto-Burman languages). The Tibetan tradition usually mentions eight cases corresponding to the eight Sanskrit cases in the following order: 1st case: *ngo-bo-tsam* 'absolutive' (Ø), 2nd case: *las-su bya-ba* 'accusative' (*la* or its variants), 3rd case: *byed-sgra* 'agentive' or 'instrumental' (*gis* and its variants), 4th case: *dgos-ched* 'dative' (*la* or its variants), 5th case: *'byung-khungs* 'ablative' (*nas* or *las*), 6th case: *'brel-sgra* 'genitive' (*gi* or its variants), 7th case: *gnas-gzhi* 'locative' (*la* or its variants), 8th case: *'bod-sgra* 'vocative' (Ø).

ལ་ -la, the **oblique** (or dative-locative) case, traditionally referred to as ལ་དོན་ /la̲tön/ literally "meaning of 'to'", indicates the person or goal to which an action is directed, as well as place and direction, and corresponds to the English prepositions "to", "at" or "in"; this form may also mark a subordinate purpose clause, where it is translated as "to" or "in order to".

Ø the **absolutive** case, traditionally referred to as ངོ་བོ་ཙམ་ /ngo̲wotsam/, literally "just the essence", or "the meaning in essence", is the unmarked case. It denotes the patient, i.e., the person or thing that undergoes the action (in the case of transitive verbs), and the single participant (in the case of intransitive verbs).

ནས་ -nä', the **ablative** case, traditionally referred to as འབྱུང་ཁུངས་ཀྱི་སྒྲ་ /cu̲ngkung-ki tra̲/, literally "sound of the source", indicates provenance ("from"); this form also marks causal or temporal subordinate clauses, where it may be translated by "because" or "after", or simply by "and". Another ablative marker ལས་ -lä' is also used in Literary Tibetan. However, this form is restricted to the use as a comparative marker in the spoken language.

དང་ -tang, the **associative** case, traditionally referred to as དང་སྒྲ་ /tha̲ngtra/[75], literally "sound of 'with'", has the sense of "with", "against" or "from"; when it links clauses, this form may also mean simply "and", and may function as a temporal connective meaning "as soon as" (literary).

• There is no agreement on the basis of function within the elements of a noun group or noun phrase: **the case marker appears just once, at the end of the noun phrase**, and there is consequently no redundancy.

For example, if the noun is not followed by any qualification such as adjectives, demonstratives and so forth, the case particle is suffixed directly:

དཔོན་པོས་ pōnpö' "by the leader" (agentive)
དཔོན་པོ་ལ་ pōnpo-la "to the leader" (dative)

But if the noun is qualified, the final element of the noun group is followed by a case particle:

དཔོན་པོ་ཆེན་པོ་འདི་གཉིས་ཀྱིས་ pōnpo chēnpo ti̲nyi'-ki' "by these two great leaders"
དཔོན་པོ་ཆེན་པོ་འདི་གཉིས་ལ་ pōnpo chēnpo ti̲ nyi̲'-la "to these two great leaders"

The case may be omitted in the literary language (mainly in order to preserve the metre in poetic writing) as well as in the spoken language, in circumstances that will be discussed below.

75. In traditional grammars, *dang* is not considered to be a case (*rnam-dbye*) but a particle (*tshig-phrad*). See Lesson 9.3.3 and Appendix 1, section 3.3 for an explanation of why it is treated as a case in this Manual.

4.3.2 The genitive གི་

Traditional grammars refer to this marker as *'brel-sgra* (lit. link sound, relation sound), and it is commonly translated in English as "of".

The genitive has several variant forms depending on the final letter of the preceding word. These variants are: གི་ *gi*, གྱི་ *gyi*, ཀྱི་ *kyi*, འི་ *'i:*

- after a vowel and འ *'a* > འི་ *'i* /:/
- after ག *g*, ང *ng* > གི་ *gi* /khi̲/Δ[76]
- after ད *d*, བ *b*, ས *s* and the *da-drag* ད *d* > ཀྱི་ *kyi* /kyī/Δ
- after ན *n*, མ *m*, ར *r*, ལ *l* > གྱི་ *gyi* /khyi̲/Δ

In Classical Tibetan, vowels and the letter 'a may be followed by the variant ཡི་ yi /yi/; this is especially true in poetry, to suit the requirements of the metre.

The three particles གི་/khi̲/, ཀྱི་ /kyī/, གྱི་ /khyi̲/ are pronounced in exactly the same way in conversation, as an unstressed syllable: /-ki/. The addition of the variant 'i to the vowel produces a lengthening of the latter in speech; in the case of /a, u, o/, the result is equivalent to the addition of an umlaut: a+'i > /ä:/, u+'i > /ü:/, o+'i /ö/, e+ 'i > /e:/, i+'i > /i:/.

Ex.:

ཉི་མ་ /nyi̲ma/ "sun"	>	ཉི་མའི་ /nyi̲mä:/
རི་མོ་ /ri̲mo/ "water"	>	རི་མོའི་ /ri̲mö:/
ཆུ་ /chū/ "water"	>	ཆུའི་ /chǖ:/
མི་ /mi̲/ "man, person"	>	མིའི་ /mi̲:/
མེ་ /me̲/ "fire"	>	མེའི་ /me̲:/
མདའ་ /ta̲/ "arrow"	>	མདའི་ /tä̲:/
དགེ་རྒན་ /ke̲kän/ "teacher"	>	དགེ་རྒན་གྱི་ /ke̲kän-ki/
རྒན་ལགས་ /kä̲nla'/ "teacher (H)"	>	རྒན་ལགས་ཀྱི་/kä̲nla'-ki/
དྲུང་ཡིག་ /thru̲ngyi'/ "secretary"	>	དྲུང་ཡིག་གི་ /thru̲ngyi'-ki/

The genitive is used not only to form noun complements, possessive pronouns and adjectives, but also relative clauses. In this case, it may be translated by a relative pronoun such as "that", "who", "where", etc. The complement that is marked by the genitive always precedes the noun to which it refers.

Ex.:

ངའི་གྲོགས་པོ་	ngä̲: thro̲kpo	"my friend" (lit. "the friend of me")
ཁོང་གི་ཕྱག་སྨྱུག་	khōng-ki chā'nyu'	"his pen" (lit.: the pen of him)
བཀྲ་ཤིས་ལགས་ཀྱི་བུ་	trāshi'-la'-ki phu̲	"Tashi's son"
བླ་མའི་སློབ་མ་	lāmä: lōpma	"the lama's disciple"

76. Pronunciations followed by the symbol Δ correspond to a literary register or an accentuated reading of the particle. Because case particles are unstressed when read under normal conditions, their tone and aspiration are irrelevant.

གཞུང་གི་ལས་བྱེད་པ་	shu̱ng-ki lä̱cepa	"government civil servant"
དགེ་རྒན་གྱི་དེབ་	ke̱kän-ki the̱p	"the teacher's book"
དེབ་ནང་ལ་ཡོད་པའི་པར་	the̱p na̱ng-la yö̱'-pä: pār	"the photo that's in the book"

4.3.3 The absolutive case

The absolutive is marked by the absence of any overt case particle: it is morphologically void.[77] Because it lacks a formal mark, the absolutive in Tibetan isn't always easy to identify at first. Remember that a case marker is always to be found at the end of any noun group (or phrase).

The absolutive indicates the grammatical **role of patient.** This role typically refers to the animate or inanimate participant that undergoes or suffers a given action performed by an agent (in the case of transitive verbs),[78] or a single participant in a process (in the case of intransitive verbs).

In syntactic or relational terms, it designates both the object of a transitive verb and the subject of an intransitive verb.

Ex.: ཇ་འཐུངས་ cha̱ thūng' "Drink the tea", ཇ་ཚ་པོ་འདུག་ cha̱ tshāpo tu̱' "The tea is hot"

In both these examples, the "tea" (cha̱) is in the absolutive case. However, in the first sentence it is a direct object, while in the second it is the subject of the verb. By contrast, the subject of a transitive verb is marked by the agentive case (see Lesson 8).

4.3.4 The imperative with the verb alone

The imperative mood may be formed by means of a verb without an auxiliary. In most cases, as we shall see (Lesson 9), verbs in the imperative mood are followed by "jussive" particles (see Lesson 19). Moreover, some verbs have a special form (an inflection) to mark the imperative.

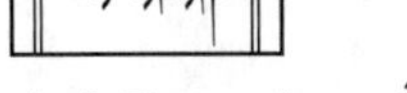

4.4 Exercises སྦྱོང་ཚན།

4.4.1 Translate into Tibetan:

1. There are some old books.
2. This is my cup.
3. That's your hat.
4. That's his new girlfriend.

---

77. Unlike the other cases which are overtly marked by a particle, the absolutive is not distinguished by any formal marker.

78. The role of patient also includes the experiencer of an emotion.

5. That small boy is hers.
6. This lesson is easy.
7. That's our field over there.
8. Isn't that man your friend?
9. Is this the key to the house?
10. This person is their mother.

4.4.2 Transliterate the dialogue at the beginning of this lesson.

4.4.3 Translate into English:

༡) མི་གསར་པ་འདི་སུ་རེད།

༢) ཁྱེད་རང་གི་གྲོགས་པོ་རེད་པས།

༣) ཕྲུ་གུ་དེ་ཚོ་བཀྲ་ཤིས་ལགས་ཀྱི་རེད།

༤) ཁོང་ང་རང་གི་གྲོགས་པོ་སྙིང་པ་རེད།

༥) སློབ་ཚན་འདི་དཀའ་ལས་ཁག་པོ་རེད།

༦) འདི་ངའི་སྨྱུ་གུ་མ་རེད།

༧) འདི་ཁོང་གི་ཕྱག་སྨྱུག་རེད།

༨) ལམ་ཁག་པ་གི་གསར་པ་རེད།

4.4.4 Make a phonological transcription of the sentences in the last exercise.

4.4.5 Complete the sentences using the appropriate form of the genitive.

༡) མོ་རང་ང་( )བུ་མོ་རེད།

༢) འདི་ཁྱེད་རང་( )དབུ་ཞྭ་རེད་པས།

༣) དེ་ཚོ་ཟླ་མ་( )ཞིང་ཁ་རེད།

༤) འདི་པ་ལགས་( )སྨྱུ་གུ་རེད།

༥) ཁོང་( )ཁང་པ་གསར་པ་དེ་རེད།

༦) འདི་དགེ་རྒན་( )དེབ་རེད།

༧) འདི་བོད་( )ས་བཀྲ་རེད།

༨) པ་གི་རྡོ་རྗེ་ལགས་( )གཟིམ་ཤག་རེད།

༩) ཇ་འདི་སུ་( )རེད།

“I have many books”

Grammar aims བརྡ་སྤྲོད་རིག་པའི་དམིགས་ཚད།

- The oblique case ལ་ -la.
- Evidential moods.
- The connective ཡང་ ya̲ng “also”.
- The existential verbs ཡོད་རེད་ yo̲:re’ and ཡོད་ yö̲’.

དེབ་མང་པོ་ཡོད།

the̲p ma̲ngpo yö̲’

CD I • Tr. 19-20

5.1 Dialogue དྲི་བ་དྲིས་ལན།

ལྷ་བཟང་ ཿ དེབ་ཡོད་པས།

སྒྲོལ་དཀར་ ཿ དེབ་མང་པོ་ཡོད།

ལྷ་བཟང་ ཿ བོད་ཡིག་རེད་པས།

སྒྲོལ་དཀར་ ཿ མང་ཆེ་བ་བོད་ཡིག་རེད། ད་དུང་རྒྱ་ཡིག་དང་དབྱིན་ཇིའི་ཡི་གེ་ཡའི་(ཡང་) ཡོད།

ལྷ་བཟང་ ཿ དེབ་འདི་ག་རེ་རེད།

སྒྲོལ་དཀར་ ཿ འདི་ཨ་མེ་རི་ཀའི་དུས་དེབ་རེད།

ལྷ་བཟང་ ཿ ཨ་མེ་རི་ཀར་གཡག་དང་འབྲི་རྒོད་ཡོད་རེད་པས།

སྒྲོལ་དཀར་ ཿ གཡག་ཡོད་མ་རེད། ཡིན་ནའི་(ཡིན་ན་ཡང་) འབྲི་རྒོད་ཡོད་རེད། རྟ་དང་ལུག་དང་བ་ཕྱུགས་ཡའི་(ཀྱང་) ཡོད་རེད།

ལྷ་བཟང་ ཿ རི་མཐོ་པོ་ཡོད་རེད་པས།

སྒྲོལ་དཀར་ ཿ ཡོད་རེད།

ལྷ་བཟང་ ཿ ལ་དྭགས་ལ་གཡག་འདུག་གས།

སྒྲོལ་དཀར་ ཿ ལ་དྭགས་ལ་གཡག་འདུག ད་དུང་ཟངས་དཀར་དང་འབྲས་ལྗོངས་དང་འབྲུག་ཡུལ་ལ་འདུག བོད་རིགས་ཀྱི་ལུང་པ་མང་ཆེ་བ་ལ་ཡོད་རེད།

ལྷ་བཟང་ ཿ ལ་དྭགས་ལ་ར་དང་། ལུག་དང་། བོང་གུ་(བོང་བུ་) ལ་སོགས་པ་འདུག་གས།

སྒྲོལ་དཀར་ ཿ འདུག མང་པོ་འདུག

Pronunciation

- the̱p yö̱'-pä'

- the̱p ma̱ngpo yö̱'

- phö̱yi' re̱' pä'

- ma̱ng chēwa phö̱yi' re', tha̱tung kya̱yi'-tang yīnci: yi̱ke yä̱: yö̱'

- the̱p ti̱ kha̱re rä̱'

- ti̱ āmerikä: thü̱tep re̱'

- āmerikar ya'-tang cha̱kö' yo̱:re'-pä'

- yā' yo̱:mare' yi̱n-nä: cha̱kö' yo̱:re', tā-tang lu̱'-tang pha̱cu' yä̱: yo̱:re'

- ri̱ thōpo yo̱:re'-pä'

- yo̱:re'

- la̱ta'-la yā' tu̱'-kä'

- la̱ta'-la yā' tu̱' tha̱tung sa̱ngkar-tang trä̱ncong-tang tru̱'yü:-la tu̱'. phö̱ri'-ki lu̱ngpa ma̱ng chēwa-la yo̱:re'

- la̱ta' ra̱-tang lu̱'-tang pho̱ngku la̱sokpa tu̱'-kä'

- tu̱' ma̱ngpo tu̱'

Translation

Lobzang — Have you got any books?
Drölkar — Yes, I have many books.
Lobzang — Are they in Tibetan?
Drölkar — Most are in Tibetan, but I also have some in Chinese and in English.
Lobzang — What's this book?
Drölkar — This is an American magazine.
Lobzang — Are there yaks and vultures in America?
Drölkar — There aren't any yaks, but there are vultures. There are also horses, sheep and cows.
Lobzang — Are there any high mountains?
Drölkar — Yes, there are.
Lobzang — And in Ladakh, are there yaks?
Drölkar — Yes, there are in Ladakh, and in Zangskar, Sikkim and Bhutan, too, as well as in most of the regions inhabited by ethnic Tibetans.
Lobzang — In Ladakh, are there goats, sheep, donkeys and so on?
Drölkar — Yes, plenty.

║ ཀ་ཁ་ག་ང་ ║

5.2 Vocabulary ཚིག་གསར།

ཡི་གེ་ yi̱ke   ཕྱག་བྲིས་ chā'ri' (H) — (n.) letter, mail[79]

དུས་དེབ་ thü̱tep — (n.) magazine

བོད་ཡིག་ phö̱yi' — (n.) Tibetan (written)

བོད་སྐད་ phö̱kä' — (n.) Tibetan (oral)

བོད་རིགས་ phö̱ri' — (n.) Tibetan (ethnic group)

རྒྱ་ཡིག་ kya̱yi' — (n.) Chinese (written)

དབྱིན་ཇི་ yīnci — (n.) English

ལུང་པ་ lu̱ngpa — (n.) country, valley

ཕ་ཡུལ་ phāyü̱: — (n.) natal land

ར་ ra̱ — (n.) goat

ལུག་ lu̱' — (n.) sheep

རྟ་ tā   ཆིབས་པ་ chīppa (H) — (n.) horse

བྱ་རྒོད་ cha̱kö' — (n.) vulture

བོང་ཀུ་ phu̱ngku   བོང་བུ་ pho̱ngpu (L)[80] — (n.) donkey

གཡག་ yā' — (n.) yak

མཛོ་ tso̱ — (n.) *dzo,* yak-cow crossbreed

བ་ཕྱུགས་ pha̱cu' — (n.) cow

མང་ཆེ་བ་ ma̱ng chēwa — (n.) most, the majority

ད་དུང་ tha̱tung — (n.) still, furthermore, yet

རི་ ri̱ — (n.) hill, mountain

མང་པོ་ ma̱ngpo — (adj., adv.) many

ཉུང་ཉུང་ nyu̱ngnyung — (adj., adv.) few

མཐོ་པོ་ thōpo   མཐོན་པོ་ thōnpo (L) — (adj.) high

དམའ་པོ་ māpo — (adj.) low

སྙན་པོ་ nyānpo — (adj.) pleasant to hear, interesting

སྙིང་རྗེ་པོ་ nyīng ce̱po — (adj.) pretty, nice

---

79. The non-honorific form denotes both a letter of the alphabet as well as a postal letter. The honorific form, however, refers only to the latter.

80. The difference in pronunciation between the familiar and literary registers is explained in Appendix 1, section 1.

ཡག་པོ་ yakpo	(adj.) good
སྡུག་ཅག tukca'	(adj.) bad, wicked
ཡིན་ནའི་ yinnä: ཡིན་ན་ཡང་ yinnayang (L)	(adv.) but
ལ་སོགས་པ་ lasokpa	(locution) *et cetera,* and so forth
ཡའི་ (y)ä ཡང་ yang (L)	(co.) also
དང་ -tang	(co.) and
ཡོད་ yö'	(aux.) to have, *egophoric*
མེད་ me'	(aux.) not to have, *egophoric*
ཡོད་རེད་ yo:re'	(aux.) there is/ are, to have, *assertive*
ཡོད་མ་རེད་ yo:mare'	(aux.) there isn't/ aren't, not to have, *assertive*

Proper nouns

རྒྱ་ནག་ kyana'	China
རྒྱ་གར་ kyakar	India
འབྲུག་ཡུལ་ tru'yü:	Bhutan
ལ་དྭགས་ lata'	Ladakh (India)
ཟངས་དཀར་ sangkar	Zangskar (India)
འབྲས་ལྗོངས་ träncong	Sikkim (India)
ཡུ་རོབ་ yurop	Europe, European
ཨ་མེ་རི་ཀ་ āmerika	America, American

5.3 Remarks on grammar འགྲེལ་བཤད།

5.3.1 The oblique case ལ་ -la

The oblique particle *la* has two main case-related functions: as the locative and as the dative. In Spoken Tibetan there are two variants,[81] depending on the final letter of the preceding word. These markers are: ལ་ la, –ར་ – r:

- After vowels or འ *'a* > –ར་ – *r* /-r/
- After all endings (consonants or vowels) > ལ་ *la* /la/

81. In Literary Tibetan, there are seven forms. See Appendix 1, section 3.3.

In the conversational register, the particle la is sometimes pronounced ལ་ཡ་/laya/ or even ཡ་/ya/. Note also that the variant -r is rarely used with monosyllabic words for the dative (except in the case of personal pronouns, as well as demonstrative and interrogative adjectives).

Thus རི་ལ་ri̲-la "to the mountain" is used in preference to རིར་ ri̲-r, and བུ་ལ་ phu̲-la "to the boy" in preference to བུར་ phu̲-r.

• The locative is used to mark complements of place (with or without movement) or time (date, time), and is generally translated by English "at", "to", "in" or "on".

Ex.: ལ་དྭགས་ལ་	la̲ta'-la	"to/ in Ladakh"
ཨ་མེ་རི་ཀར་	āmerikar	"to/ in America"
རྒྱ་གར་ལ་	kya̲kar-la	"to/ in India"
ཆུ་ཚོད་གཉིས་པར་	chūtsö' nyīpar	"at two o'clock"
ཚེས་པ་བཅོ་ལྔར་	tshēpa cōngar	"on the fifth [of the month]"
དགུན་ཁར་	ku̲nkar	"in winter"

• The dative is used to indicate the grammatical role of **goal**, i.e., the person or thing to which the action is directed, or the owner of something in possessive constructions. This particle corresponds to English "to", or else is not translated at all. It is also used to form adverbs.

Ex.: ཁོང་གིས་བློ་བཟང་ལ་ཡི་གེ་བཏང་སོང་། khōng-ki' lōpsang-la yi̲ke tāng-song
"He sent a letter to Lobzang."

ཁོང་ལ་དངུལ་ཡོད་རེད། khōng-la ngü̲: yo̲:re' "He has money."

གསལ་པོ་ sā̃:po "clear" > གསལ་པོར་ sā̃:por "clearly"

As we have just seen, possessive constructions in Tibetan are formed with the dative: Subject (dat.) + Object (abs.) + Verb. This structure follows the pattern: [to X there is Y], and may be translated literally as "to him there is money".[82] It has exactly the same form as constructions of existence.

Thus the sentence སློབ་གྲྭ་ལ་དེབ་འདུག་ lāptra-la the̲p tu̲'may mean both "There are books at the school" and "The school has books".

N.B.: Be careful not to confuse this construction with the genitive:

སློབ་གྲྭའི་དེབ་འདུག་ lāpträ: the̲p tu̲' "There are (some of) the school's books."

82. The same structure is used in Russian, Hebrew and numerous other languages that lack a lexical verb "to have".

5.3.2 Evidential moods

These moods are conveyed by auxiliary verbs (or by copulas), and have the function of specifying **the source of information** on which a statement is based. There are basically four moods:[83] egophoric, testimonial, assertive and inferential. These four moods are used with any statement that conveys an information.

The assertive auxiliary verbs re̱' and yo̱:re' specify that the information being transmitted may be **a general truth** or **a specific fact,** and is something that is considered by the speaker to be **certain.** In general, the assertive implies that the speaker is letting it be known that while the assertion is certain, he or she has not personally witnessed it. Typically, the information has been obtained second-hand from some other source (reported speech, a book, the radio, etc.) or else forms a part of the speaker's general knowledge.

However, it may happen that even though the speaker can personally testify to the validity of the assertion, he or she may use the assertive in order to present the statement as an objective or well-known fact.

N.B.: The assertive mood should not be confused with the marker of reported speech, which may be used in combination with any of the four moods (see Lesson 15) and implies a measure of uncertainty (cf. "it would seem that…").

Testimonial or "sensorial" auxiliaries such as tu̱' signify that the speaker has **personally observed** the fact or event he or she is reporting. The evidence is usually derived from the senses, most commonly sight or hearing, but occasionally also from the other three, as in the case of a pain suffered by the speaker.[84] In other words, the speaker is, or has been, a direct witness to what he or she is describing. Thus in Lesson 5, the use of the testimonial tu̱' suggests that Drölkar has actually been to Ladakh and witnessed the things she is talking about. The assertive and testimonial moods could be described as respectively objective and subjective, but as far as the speaker is concerned they are equally certain.

The egophoric mood is linked to **personal knowledge** or intention on the speaker's part, and has been described above (see 3.4).

Finally, the inferential mood (see 10.4) indicates that the basis of the speaker's assertion is an **inference or a conclusion that is being drawn** from the traces or the present results of a past action.

N.B.: Auxiliary verbs almost always come after the main clause, at the end of the sentence. On rare occasions they may be placed after subordinate clauses.

---

83. These moods are essential in Central Tibetan, and appear in different forms in several other Tibetan dialects (Dzongkha, Ladakhi, Kham, Amdo, Sherpa, etc.). However, they are practically nonexistent in Literary Tibetan.

84. Or by the original source of the assertion in the case of reported speech.

5.3.3 The connective ཡང་ ya̲ng *"also"*

In Spoken Tibetan, ཡང་ ya̲ng is pronounced ཡའི་ (y) ä̲:. In Literary Tibetan, this connective has three possible forms, depending on the last letter of the preceding syllable.

- after the consonants ང་ ན་ མ་ ར་ ལ་ > ཡང་ ya̲ng
- after the consonants ག་ ད་ བ་ ས་ and the da-drag > ཀྱང་ kyāng
- after vowels and འ་ > འང་ a̲ng / ཡང་ya̲ng

It also appears in the expression ཡིན་ན་ཡང་yi̲nnayang, meaning "but, nevertheless", and pronounced ཡིན་ནའི་ yi̲nnä: in Spoken Tibetan.

5.3.4 The existential verbs ཡོད་རེད་ yo̲:re' *and* ཡོད་ yö̲'

These are generally translated by the verbs "to have" or "there is/ are", or "to be". The assertive verb yo̲:re' indicates information that is certain (see 5.3.2) and is used for the second and third persons singular and plural. The egophoric verb yö̲' refers to information that directly concerns the speaker (see 5.3.2) and is used only with the first person singular and plural. Its application will be described in detail in Lesson 6.

5.4 Exercises སྦྱོང་ཚན།

5.4.1 Translate into English:

༡) བོད་ལ་རི་མཐོ་པོ་མང་པོ་ཡོད་རེད།

༢) མི་དེ་ཚོར་སྡུག་བསྔལ་མང་པོ་ཡོད་རེད།

༣) ལུང་པ་དེར་གཡག་མང་པོ་འདུག

༤) ཅོག་ཙེ་འདི་དམའ་པོ་རེད།

༥) སྐད་འདི་སྙན་པོ་འདུག

༦) རི་ཕ་གི་མཐོ་པོ་འདུག

༧) བློ་བཟང་གི་གྲོགས་མོ་སྙིང་རྗེ་པོ་འདུག

༨) ཁོང་ལ་ཨ་ལྷ་འདུག

5.4.2 Rewrite the above sentences, first in the interrogative, then in the negative.

5.4.3 Read the sentences in 5.4.1 and mark the high and low tones.

5.4.4 Translate into Tibetan:

1. This teacher has many students.
2. There aren't many schools in Tibet.
3. Are there any white yaks?
4. Are there any vultures in Europe?
5. This monk has many *pecha*.
6. Have you got any tea?
7. The white house is pretty.

5.4.5 Complete the sentences using the appropriate form of the oblique: ལ་ or ར་:

༡) ཁོང་ལྷ་ས་(   )ཡོད་རེད།

༢) ཁྱེད་རང་(   )སྨྱུ་གུ་ཡོད་པས།

༣) འབྲོག་པ་(   )ལུག་མང་པོ་འདུག

༤) གཞིས་ཀ་རྩེ་(   )བཀྲ་ཤིས་ལྷུན་པོ་དགོན་པ་ཡོད་རེད།

༥) ཁོང་གི་ཨ་མ་བོད་(   )ཡོད་རེད།

༦) བློ་བཟང་(   )གྲོགས་པོ་གསར་པ་མང་པོ་འདུག

5.5 Civilization རིག་གཞུང་།

The main cities and towns of Tibetan culture.[85]

ལྷ་ས་ lhāsa	Lhasa (T.A.R.)
རྩེ་ཐང་ tsētang	Tsethang (T.A.R.)
ཆབ་མདོ་ chāmto	Chamdo (T.A.R.)
སྐྱེ་རྒུ་མདོ་ kyēkunto	Kyegundo (Qinghai)
དར་རྩེ་མདོ་ thartsento	Dhartsendo (Sichuan)
རྨ་ཆེན་ mācen	Machen (Qinghai)
རེབ་ཀོང་ repkong	Rebkong (Gansu)
རྔ་པ་ ngāpa	Ngapa (Sichuan)
གླེ་ or སླེ་ lē	Leh (Ladakh, India)
བཀའ་བློན་སྤུག་ kālönpu'	Kalimpong (India)

85. In some cases, even though Tibetan culture may not be the dominant one, it occupies an important place. This is particularly true of towns that are not located in Tibet, such as Thimpu (the capital of Bhutan) and Darjeeling (India).

གློ་སྨོན་ཐང་ lōmöntang'	Lo-Mönthang (Mustang, Nepal)
ཉིང་ཁྲི་ nyintri	Nyingthri (T.A.R.)
དྷ་རམ་ས་ལ་ tharamsala	Dharamsala (India)
གཞིས་ཀ་རྩེ་ shikatse	Zhikatse (T.A.R.)
རྒྱལ་རྩེ་ kyantse	Gyantse (T.A.R.)
ནག་ཆུ་ nakcu	Nagchu (T.A.R.)
འབའ་ཐང་ patang	Bathang (Sichuan)
ཆབ་ཆ་ chāpca	Chabcha (Qinghai)
སྡེ་དགེ་ terke	Derge (Sichuan)
བླ་བྲང་ lāprang	Labrang (Gansu)
རྡོ་རྗེ་གླིང་ torceling	Darjeeling or Dorjeling (India)
སྒང་ཏོག་ kangto'	Gangtok (Sikkim, India)
ཐིམ་ཕུ་ thīmpu	Thimphu (Bhutan)

"Family photo"

ནང་མིའི་པར།

na̱ngmi: pār

Grammar aims བརྡ་སྤྲོད་རིག་པའི་དམིགས་ཚད།

- The singular indefinite article; ཅིག་ cī'.
- The importance of the situation in communication.
- The essential and existential verbs རེད་ re', ཡོད་རེད་ yo̱:re', འདུག་tu̱'.
- The interrogative pronoun ག་པར་ kha̱par.

CD I • Tr. 21-22

6.1 Dialogue དྲི་བ་དྲིས་ལན།

བློ་བཟང་ཿ ཨོ། ཕ་གའི་(ཕ་གིར་) པར་ཅིག་འདུག

སྒྲོལ་དཀར་ཿ ཕ་གི་ངའི་པར་རེད།

བློ་བཟང་ཿ པར་གཞན་དག་ཡོད་པས།

སྒྲོལ་དཀར་ཿ ང་ཚོའི་ནང་མིའི་པར་ཡོད།

བློ་བཟང་ཿ ག་པར་ཡོད་རེད།

སྒྲོལ་དཀར་ཿ ཕ་གའི་(ཕ་གིར་) ཡོད་རེད།

བློ་བཟང་ཿ འདི་སུ་རེད།

སྒྲོལ་དཀར་ཿ མི་གཞོན་གཞོན་དེ་ངའི་ཇོ་ལགས་རེད། འདི་ངའི་འོག་མ་རེད། འོ། འདི་ངའི་རྨོ་ལགས་རེད་བཞག

བློ་བཟང་ཿ ཁྱེད་རང་ལ་པར་ཆས་ཡོད་པས།

སྒྲོལ་དཀར་ཿ ངར་པར་ཆས་མེད། སྤོ་ལགས་ལ་ཡོད་རེད།

Pronunciation

- ō, phākä: pār ci' tu̱'

- phāki ngä̱: pār re̱'

- pār shä̱nta' yö̱'-pä'

- nga̱tsö: na̱ngmi: pār yö̱'

- kha̱par yo̱:rä'

- phākä: yo̱:re'

- ti̱ sū rä̱'

- mi̱ shö̱nshön the̱ ngä̱: cho̱la' re̱' ti̱ ngä̱: o̱kma re'. ō, ti̱ ngä̱: mōla' re̱'-sha'

- khyērang-la pārcä' yö̱'-pä'

- nga̱-r pārcä' me̱', pōla'-la yo̱:re'

Translation

Lobzang — Oh, there's a photo over there.
Drölkar — It's a photo of me.
Lobzang — Have you got any other photos?
Drölkar — I have photos of my family.
Lobzang — Where are they?
Drölkar — [They're] over there.
(looking at the photos)
Lobzang — Who's this?
Drölkar — This young man is my elder brother; this is my little sister. Look! This is Grandmother.
Lobzang — Have you got a camera?
Drölkar — I haven't got a camera, but my Grandfather has one.

ཀ་ཁ་ག་ང་

6.2 Vocabulary ཚིག་གསར།

ཅིག་ cī' (L) ཞིག་ (ཤིག་)	(art.) a, one
པར་ pār སྐུ་པར་ kūpar(H)	(n.) photo
རི་མོ་ ri̱mo	(n.) drawing
པར་ཆས་ pārcä'	(n.) camera
ནང་མི་ na̱ngmi	(n.) family, family member
ག་པར་ kha̱par	(interr. pron.) where?
གཅིག་ cī'	(adj.) one
གཞན་དག་ shä̱nta'	(adj.) other, another

གཞོན་གཞོན་ shö̱nshön	(adj.) young
རྒན་འཁོགས་ kǟ̱nko' བགྲེས་སྒོང་ tre̱song (H)	(adj.) old, elderly (person)
སྔན་མ་ ngǟnma སྔོན་མ་ ngȫma (L) སྔ་མ་ ngāma (L)	(adv., adj.) before, past, previous(ly)
རེད་བཞག་ re̱'-sha'	(aux.) to be, *revelatory mood*

The main kinship terms

སྤུན་སྐྱ་ pīnkya' སྐུ་མཆེད་ kūmce' (H)	relative, sibling, cousin
རྨོ་མོ་ mōmo རྨོ་ལགས་ mōla' (H)	grandmother, elderly woman
སྤོ་བོ་ pōwo སྤོ་ལགས་ pōla' (H)	grandfather, elderly man
ཚ་བོ་ tshāwo སྐུ་ཚ་ kūtsa (H)	nephew, grandson
ཚ་མོ་ tshāmo སྐུ་ཚ་ kūtsa (H)	niece, granddaughter
ཨ་མ་ āma ཨ་མ་ལགས་ āma-la' (H)	mother
ཡུམ་ yu̱m (H)	mother (of someone else)
པ་པ་ pāpa པ་ལགས་ pāla' (H)	father
ཡབ་ ya̱p (H)	father (of someone else)
སྤུ་གུ་ pūku ཕྲུ་གུ་ thrūku (L) ཨ་ཝ་ āwa (H)	child
བུ་ phu̱ སྲས་ sǟ' (H)	son
བུ་མོ་ phu̱mo སྲས་མོ་ sǟmo (H)	daughter
ཕ་གཅིག་མ་གཅིག་ phāci' ma̱ci'	brother/sister (same parents)
ཨ་ལྕག་ āca' ཨ་ཅེ āce (L)	elder sister, wife, Madam
ཅོ་ཅོག་ cōco' ཇོ་ལགས་ cho̱la'(H)	elder brother
འོག་མ་ o̱kma ཨོ་ལགས་ ōla' (H)	younger brother/sister
གཅུང་མོ་ cūngmo (L)	younger sister
གཅུང་པོ་ cūngpo (L)	younger brother
གཅེན་པོ་ cēnpo (L)	elder brother
གཅེན་མོ་ cēnmo (L)	elder sister
ཨ་ནེ་ āni	paternal aunt
སྲུ་མོ་ sūmo	maternal aunt
ཨ་ཁུ་ āku	paternal uncle
ཨ་ཞང་ āshang	maternal uncle
མནའ་མ་ nāma བག་མ་ pha̱kma	bride, daughter-in-law
མག་པ་ ma̱kpa སྐུ་བག་ kūpa' (H)	groom, son-in-law
ཟླ་བོ་ ta̱wo སྐུ་ཟླ་ kūnta (H)	husband, wife, spouse

6.3 Remarks འགྲེལ་བཤད།

6.3.1 The singular indefinite article ཅིག་ cī'

Articles are not generally used in Tibetan.

Ex.: According to the context or the situation, སྨྱུ་གུ་ཡོད་པས། nyūku yö̱'-pä' may mean "Have you got a/ the/ any pen(s)?"

However, this statement ought to be slightly modified: first, as we saw earlier, the use of the plural marker -tso implies that the (human) noun so qualified is definite, and that it should be preceded in the English translation by the use of the (plural) definite article 'the'. Secondly, Tibetan does indeed have a singular indefinite article cī' that is placed after the noun, but this is used only when the noun is specific:

Ex.: དགེ་རྒན་ཅིག་ ke̱kän cī' "a (certain) teacher", སློབ་གྲྭ་བ་ཅིག་ lōptrawa cī' "a (certain) student"
but not when the noun is generic:

Ex.: ཁོང་དགེ་རྒན་རེད་ khōng ke̱kän re' "he is a teacher", but ཁོང་དགེ་རྒན་ཅིག་རེད། khōng ke̱kän cī' re̱'
"He's one (of the) teacher(s)"

The form of the indefinite article ཅིག་ cī' "a" should not be confused with that of the cardinal number "one" གཅིག་ cī', although the pronunciation of the two is the same. In Literary Tibetan, the indefinite article has three variants –ཅིག་, ཞིག་, ཤིག་– depending on the final letter of the preceding word.

• after ག *g*, ད *d*, བ *b*, and the da-drag	>	ཅིག་ *cig*	/cī'/
• after vowels and འ *'a*, ང *ng* ན *n*, མ *m*, ར *r*, ལ *l*	>	ཞིག་ *zhig*	/shi̱'/
• after ས *s*	>	ཤིག་ *shig*	/shī'/

In the spoken language, only the form ཅིག་cī' is used.

Finally, the demonstrative དེ་the̱ is often used in much the same way as a (specific) definite article in the European languages.

Ex.:	དེབ་གསར་པ་དེ་ག་པར་འདུག	the̱p sārpa the̱ kha̱par to'	"Where is that/ the new book?"
	བློ་བཟང་གི་སྤུན་སྐྱ་དེ་ཁོང་རེད།	lōsang-ki pīnkya' the̱ khōng re̱'	"He's the brother of Lobzang."

6.3.2 The importance of situation and context

In languages in general, statements are rooted in a given situation or context. Tibetan is particularly sensitive to situation and environment, as well as the sources of information on which a speaker's assertions are based. It would be therefore appropriate to speak of a "situational grammar". For example, we have seen the use of evidential or "mediatory" auxiliaries (see 5.4) which reveal whether or not the speaker directly witnessed whatever he or she is stating to be the case.

When a statement cannot be immediately associated with a concrete situation of communication, Tibetans tend not to accept it or to find it strange. One consequence of this attitude is a reluctance to present verbs in a series of conjugations. For example, when the verb "to be" is "mechanically" conjugated – "I am a student", "you are a student", etc., Tibetan speakers will accept the first person without any trouble but often stop short at the second, since the absence of a marked intonation makes it difficult for them to imagine a situation in which they would be telling someone, "You're a student!" since the addressee is obviously in a better position than they are to know this.

6.3.3 Essential and existential verbs

Tibetan has several stative verbs or copulas corresponding to the verbs "to be" and "to have" in European languages. Two main categories may be distinguished: essential copulas, which denote an essential quality of the person or thing; and existential copulas, which express the existence of a phenomenon or a characteristic with the implication of an evaluation by the speaker.[86] Furthermore, these "essential" and "existential" stative verbs are associated with various evidential moods, as we shall see presently.

Note that they may be used for both the present and the past.[87]

A) The essential copulas: རེད་ re̱', ཡིན་ yi̱n, རེད་བཞག་re̱'-sha'

These express the nature or essence of the subject (equative meaning), or else an inherent quality of it (attributive meaning). They differ only in terms of the evidential mood that they convey (assertive, egophoric, testimonial, etc.).

• The "assertive" copula རེད་ re̱' and its negation མ་རེད་ ma̱re'.

The copula re̱' is usually translated by the verb "to be", and corresponds to an objective assertion or affirmation (see 5.4). The attribute of the subject, which immediately precedes the verb, may be a substantive (equative meaning) or an adjective (attributive meaning). Age is also expressed with the use of re̱'.

Ex.:		
འདི་ཐུབ་བསྟན་རེད།	ti̱ thūptän re̱'	"This is Thubtän."
ཁོང་འབྲོག་པ་མ་རེད།	khōng tro̱kpa ma̱re'	"He isn't a nomad."
ཉི་མ་ལོ་བདུན་རེད།	nyi̱ma lo̱ tü̱n re̱'	"Nyima is seven."
མོ་རང་སྙིང་རྗེ་པོ་རེད།	mo̱rang nyīngcepo re̱'	"She's pretty."
ཁོ་རང་སྨྱོན་པ་ མ་རེད།	khōrang nyōnpa ma̱re'	"He isn't mad."
ཁོང་སེམས་བཟང་པོ་རེད།	khōng sēm' sa̱ngpo re̱'	"He's kind."

In rare cases, re̱' may also be used to express an essential property or an inalienable possession of the subject, in which case it corresponds to the English "to have".

86. The distinction between existential and essential is similar to the difference between the verbs *ser* and *estar* in Spanish.

87. The present and the past have the same form, with the meaning depending on the context. However, as we shall see in Lesson 10.4, this applies only to the past imperfective: for the perfective past, there are specific forms.

Ex.:	ཁོང་ཡོན་ཏན་ཆེན་པོ་རེད།	khōng yo̱ntän chēnpo re'	"He has great qualities."
	མོ་རང་མིག་ཆུང་ཆུང་རེད།	mo̱rang mī'[88] chūngcung re'	"She has small eyes."
	ཁོང་ཨ་མཆོག་ཆེན་པོ་རེད།	khōng āmco' chēnpo re̱'	"He has big ears."

• The "egophoric" copula: ཡིན yi̱n and its negation མིན་ mä̱n.

The copula yi̱n functions as an essential stative verb, normally associated with the first person (see 3.4), and is generally translated by "I am". The attribute of the subject may be a substantive (equative sense) or an adjective (attributive sense).

Ex.:	ང་ཐུབ་བསྟན་ཡིན།	nga̱ thūptän yin	"I am Thubtän."
	ང་འབྲོག་པ་ཡིན།	nga̱ tro̱kpa yi̱n	"I am a nomad."
	ང་བདེ་པོ་ཡིན།	nga̱ te̱po yi̱n	"I am fine."

In rare cases, they may express an intention or an insistence on the part of the speaker.

Ex.:	ཁྱེད་རང་གི་ཇ་ཡིན།	khyērang cha̱ yi̱n	"It's your tea [that I'm intending to give you]."
	དེ་ངའི་ལྡེ་མིག་ཡིན།	the̱ ngä̱: te̱mi' yi̱n	"That's my key."

• The "revelatory" copula རེད་བཞག re̱'-sha' and its negation རེད་མི་འདུག re̱'-mi̱ntu'.

The copula re'-sha' functions like an essential stative verb, implying that the speaker has just discovered or become aware of whatever he or she is asserting. It may often be translated by the verb "to be" preceded by some exclamation such as "Why!" or "Hey!"

Ex.:	ཐུབ་བསྟན་རེད་བཞག	thūptän re̱'-sha'	"Hey! It's Thubtän."
	འབྲོག་པ་རེད་མི་འདུག	tro̱kpa re̱'-mi̱ntu'	"No, he isn't a nomad."
	སྨྱོན་པ་རེད་བཞག	nyō̱npa re̱'-sha'	"Why, he's mad! [I've just realized it]"

B) The existential copulas འདུག་tu̱', ཡོད་རེད་yo̱:re' ཡོད་yö̱'

These verbs express existence, location, or a circumstantial feature of the subject, often implying an evaluation on the speaker's part. These various stative verbs differ only in terms of the evidential mood that they convey (assertive, testimonial, egophoric, etc.).

• The "assertive" copula ཡོད་རེད་ yo̱:re' and its negation ཡོད་མ་རེད་ yo̱:mare'.

There are two other ways of writing ཡོད་རེད་ yo̱:re', but the pronunciation is the same in each case: ཡོག་རེད་ or ཡོའོ་རེད་, as well as a literary form ཡོད་པ་རེད་ yö̱pare'.[89] The negative form of the auxiliary is ཡོད་མ་རེད་ yo̱:mare', for which there are also two other written forms: ཡོག་མ་རེད་and ཡོའོ་མ་རེད་ yo̱:mare', as well as a literary form ཡོད་པ་མ་རེད་ yö̱pa ma̱re'.

---

88. Note that *mig* is pronounced with a high tone. It is an exceptional case since the radical *m* does not have any prefixed or subscribed letter.

89. The variant *yod-red* has been retained here because it is the one most commonly used in contemporary writing. Moreover, the spelling is based on the etymology of the expression: *yod-red* is in fact derived from *yod-pa-red,* whereas the forms *yog-red* and *yo'o-red* are purely phonetic.

The copula yo̱:re' implies a definite assertion or affirmation by the speaker. According to the context, it may be translated as "there is/are" (existential sense) or "to be at (a certain location)" (situational sense), or by the verb "to have" (possessive sense).

Ex.:	བོད་ལ་གནམ་གྲུ་ཡོད་རེད།	phö̱'-la nāmtru yo̱:re' "There are aeroplanes in Tibet."
	ཐུབ་བསྟན་འདའི་(འདིར་)ཡོད་རེད།	thūptän tä̱: yo̱:re' "Thubtän is here."
	ཁོང་ལ་དེབ་མང་པོ་ཡོད་རེད།	khōng-la the̱p ma̱ngpo yo̱:re' "He has many books."
	ཚེ་རིང་ལ་མོ་ཊ་ཡོད་རེད།	tshēring-la mo̱tra yo̱:re' "Tshering has a car."
	སྔན་མ་བོད་ལ་གནམ་གྲུ་ཡོད་མ་རེད།	ngā̄ma phö̱'-la nāmtru yo̱:mare' "In the past, there were no aeroplanes in Tibet."
	དེ་དུས་ཚེ་རིང་ལ་མོ་ཊ་ཡོད་རེད།	the̱tü' tshēring-la mo̱tra yo̱:re' "At that time, Tshering had a car."

Remember that constructions expressing possession are identical to existential constructions.

The copula yo̱:re' may also be translated by some form of the verb "to be" (attributive sense). This requires that the attribute of the subject that precedes the verb should be a qualifying adjective.

Ex.:	འདི་སྙིང་རྗེ་པོ་ཡོད་རེད།	ti̱ nyīngcepo yo̱:re'	"This is pretty."
	འདི་གསལ་པོ་ཡོད་རེད།	ti̱ sā̄:po yo̱:re'	"This is clear."
	འདི་ཚ་པོ་ཡོད་རེད།	ti̱ tshāpo yo̱:re'	"This is hot."

It may not, however, be used with a noun: * ཁོང་རྒྱ་མི་ཡོད་རེད། khōng kya̱mi yo̱:re' "He is Chinese".

• The testimonial copula: འདུག tu̱' and its negation མི་འདུག mi̱ntu'

This copula indicates a past or present testimony on the speaker's part. In English, it is translated by the same expressions as for yo̱:re', i.e., according to context as "there is/are" (existential sense), "to be at" (situational sense), "to have" (possessive sense), or by the verb "to be" (attributive sense). The latter applies only when the verb is preceded by a qualifying adjective. Thus the only difference between tu̱' and yo̱:re' lies in the different evidential moods they express (these moods have been described above). The translation of the following phrases would therefore be exactly the same as those given above:

Ex.:	བོད་ལ་གནམ་གྲུ་འདུག	phö̱'-la nāmtru tu̱'	"There are aeroplanes in Tibet."
	ཐུབ་བསྟན་འདའི་(འདིར་) འདུག	thūptän tä̱: tu̱'	"Thubtän is here."
	ཁོང་ལ་དེབ་མང་པོ་འདུག	khōng-la the̱p ma̱ngpo tu̱'	"He has many books."
	འདི་སྙིང་རྗེ་པོ་འདུག	ti̱ nyīngcepo tu'	"This is pretty."

འདི་གསལ་པོ་འདུག	ti̱ sä:po tu̱'	"This is clear."
འདི་ཚ་པོ་འདུག	ti̱ tshāpo tu̱'	"This is hot."

However, exactly as in the case of the assertive copula, it is impossible to say: * ཁོང་རྒྱ་མི་འདུག khōng kya̱mi tu̱' "He is Chinese".

• The "egophoric" copula ཡོད་ yö̱' and its negation མེད་ me̱'

This copula is always associated with the first person, and is generally translated as "I have" (possessive sense), or as "I am (at)" (locative sense). In certain rare cases, it may also indicate a personal or intimate acquaintance by the speaker, and should accordingly be translated by the verb "to be".

Ex.:	དེབ་མང་པོ་ཡོད།	the̱p ma̱ngpo yö̱'	"I have many books."
	རྒྱ་ནག་ལ་ཡོད།	kya̱na'-la yö̱'	"I am in China."
	ཇ་འདི་ཞིམ་པོ་ཡོད།	cha̱ ti̱ shi̱mpo yö̱'	"This tea is good (in my opinion)."

The copulas

affirmative	interrogative (without pronoun)	interrogative (with pronoun)	negative	negative interrogative
ཡིན་ yi̱n	ཡིན་པས་ yi̱n-pä'	ཡིན་ / ཡིན་པ་ yi̱n/ yi̱n-pa	མིན་ mä̱n	མིན་པས་ mä̱n-pä'
རེད་ re̱'	རེད་པས་ re̱'-pä'	རེད་ rä̱'	མ་རེད་ ma̱re'	མ་རེད་པས་ ma̱re'-pä'
རེད་བཞག་ re̱'-sha'	རེད་འདུག་གས་ re̱'-tu̱'-kä'	རེད་འདུག་ rä̱'-to'	རེད་མི་འདུག་ re̱'-mi̱ntu'	རེད་མི་འདུག་གས་ re̱'-mi̱ntu'-kä'
ཡོད་ yö̱'	ཡོད་པས་ yö̱'-pä'	ཡོད་ yö̱'	མེད་ me̱'	མེད་པས་ me̱'-pä'
འདུག་ tu̱'	འདུག་གས་ tu̱'-kä'	འདུག་ to̱'	མི་འདུག་ mi̱ntu'	མི་འདུག་གས་ mi̱ntu'-kä'
ཡོད་རེད་ yo̱:re'	ཡོད་རེད་པས་ yo̱:re'-pä'	ཡོད་རེད་ yo̱:rä'	ཡོད་མ་རེད་ yo̱:mare'	ཡོད་མ་རེད་པས yo̱:mare'-pä'

Remark: When used with interrogative pronouns, the copulas (and the corresponding auxiliaries) རེད་ re̱', ཡོད་རེད་ yo̱:re', འདུག་ tu̱' are pronounced with an opened vowel རེད་ rä̱', ཡོད་རེད་ yo̱:rä', འདུག་ to̱'. However, this small phonetic variation is not traditionally recorded in Tibetan orthography.

Ex.:	འདི་ག་རེ་རེད།	ti̱ kha̱re rä̱'	"What is it?"
	མི་ག་ཚོད་འདུག	mi̱ kha̱tsö' to̱'	"How many people are there?"

6.4 Exercises སྦྱོང་ཚན།

6.4.1 Translate into English:

༡) སེམས་ག་པར་འདུག

༢) ཁྱེད་རང་གི་ནང་མི་ག་པར་ཡོད།

༣) ང་རང་ཚོའི་ལྡེ་མིག་ག་པར་འདུག

༤) པ་གིར་ཁང་པ་ཆེན་པོ་ཅིག་འདུག

༥) པ་གིར་མི་ཅིག་འདུག

6.4.2 Replace the indefinite article with the form required in literary usage.

༡) མི་ཅིག

༢) རི་མོ་ཅིག

༣) པར་ཆས་ཅིག

༤) རི་ཅིག

༥) དེབ་ཅིག

༦) ཁང་པ་ཆེན་པོ་ཅིག

༧) དགེ་རྒན་ཅིག

༨) གཡག་ཅིག

༩) བྱ་རྒོད་ཅིག

༡༠) དཀར་ཡོལ་ཅིག

༡༡) ཚགས་པར་ཅིག

༡༢) ལམ་ཁག་ཐུང་ཐུང་ཅིག

6.4.3 Translate into Tibetan:

1. It's his (paternal) uncle.
2. He is in Zhikatse.
3. He used to be in Lhasa.
4. In the past, were there many monks in Tibet?
5. Yes, there were many.
6. Dorje used to be a teacher.

6.4.4 Rewrite these sentences in the testimonial mood:

༡) རྒྱ་ནག་ལ་མི་མང་པོ་ཡོད་རེད།

༢) རྒྱ་གར་ལ་ཡང་མི་མང་པོ་ཡོད་རེད་པས།

༣) ཁོང་ལ་གཡག་མང་པོ་ཡོད་རེད།

༤) བོད་ལ་ཁང་པ་མཐོ་པོ་ཡོད་རེད་པས།

༥) སྒོ་ལགས་ལ་པར་ཆས་ཡོད་མ་རེད།

"Where did you go ?"

ག་པར་ཕེབས་པ།

Grammar aims བརྡ་སྤྲོད་རིག་པའི་དམིགས་ཚད།

- Word order and postpositions.
- The past tense auxiliaries: པ་རེད་ pare', པ་ཡིན་ payin, སོང་ song.
- The essential and existential verbs "to be" "to have" in the past.
- The cardinal and ordinal numbers.

CD I • Tr. 23-24

7.1 Dialogue དྲི་བ་དྲིས་ལན།

ཟླ་བ་ཿ ཁྱེད་རང་ཁའི་ས་(ཁ་སང་)ག་པར་ཕེབས་པ།

ཉི་མ་ཿ ཁའི་ས་(ཁ་སང་)གླིང་གར་ཕྱིན་པ་ཡིན།

ཟླ་བ་ཿ སུ་མཉམ་པོ་ཕེབས་པ།

ཉི་མ་ཿ སྤུ་གུ་ཚོ་(ཕྲུ་གུ་ཚོ་)མཉམ་པོ་ཕྱིན་པ་ཡིན།

ཟླ་བ་ཿ སྒྲོལ་དཀར་ལགས་ཕེབས་སོང་ངས།

ཉི་མ་ཿ ཁོང་ནང་ལ་བཞུགས་སོང་།

ཟླ་བ་ཿ ཨ་མ་ལགས་ནང་ལ་བཞུགས་པ་རེད་པས།

ཉི་མ་ཿ མ་རེད། གླིང་སྐོར་ལ་ཕེབས་པ་རེད།

ཟླ་བ་ཿ གླིང་ག་དེའི་ནང་ལ་ག་རེ་འདུག

ཉི་མ་ཿ གླིང་གའི་ནང་ལ་མེ་ཏོག་དང་ཆུ་འཛིང་མང་པོ་འདུག ཆུའི་ནང་ལ་ཉ་མང་པོ་འདུག ཉ་དེ་ཚོ་སྙིང་རྗེ་པོ་ཞེ་དྲགས་འདུག

Pronunciation

- khyērang khāsa kha̱par phēp-pa
- khāsa līngkar chīn-payin
- sū nyāmpo phēp-pa
- pūku-tso nyāmpo chīn-payin
- trö̱:kar-la' phēp-song-ngä'
- khōng na̱ng-la shu̱'-song
- āmala' na̱ng-la shu̱'-pare'-pä'
- ma̱re', līngkor-la phēp-pare'
- līngka the̱: na̱ng-la kha̱re to̱ '
- līngkä: na̱ng-la me̱to'-tang chūtsing ma̱ngpo tu̱', chū: na̱ng-la nya̱ ma̱ngpo tu̱'. nya̱ the̱tso nyīng ce̱po she̱tra' tu̱'.

Translation

Dawa	—	Where did you go yesterday?
Nyima	—	Yesterday, I went to the park.
Dawa	—	Who did you go with?
Nyima	—	I went with the children.
Dawa	—	Has Drölkar come?
Nyima	—	She stayed at home.
Dawa	—	Did [your] mother stay at home?
Nyima	—	No, she went on a circumambulation of the Lingkor.
Dawa	—	What was in the park?
Nyima	—	In the park there were flowers and many ponds. In the water, there were lots of fish. Those fish were very lovely.

ཀ་ཁ་ག་ང་

7.2 Vocabulary ཚིག་གསར།

ཆུ་ chū ཆབ་ chāp (H)	(n.) water
ཉ་ nya̱	(n.) fish
འབུ་ pu̱	(n.) insect
གླིང་ག་ līngka བཞུགས་གླིང་ shu̱kling (H)	(n.) park
གླིང་སྐོར་ līngkor	(n.) circular pilgrimage route
མེ་ཏོག་ me̱to'	(n.) flower
ཆུ་འཛིང་ chūtsin	(n.) pond, reservoir
ཕྱི་ལོགས་ chīlo'	(n.) outside

ནང་ལོགས་ nanglo'	(n.) inside
ནང་ལ་ nang-la	(n.) at home
ནང་ nang	(post.) in
འོག་ o'	(post.) under
སྒང་ kang	(post.) on
གཡོན་ yōn	(post.) left
གཡས་ yā'	(post.) right
མདུན་ tün	(post.) in front of
རྒྱབ་ kyap	(post.) behind
འཁྲིས་ thrī'	(post.) near, beside
སྐོར་ kōr	(post.) concerning, about
ལྗང་ཁུ་ cangku	(adj.) green
སྔོན་པོ་ ngōnpo	(adj.) blue, green (grass, crops)
དམར་པོ་ mārpo	(adj.) red
སེར་པོ་ sērpo	(adj.) yellow
ཁའི་ས་ khāsa ཁ་སང་ khāsang (L)	(adv.) yesterday
མཉམ་པོ་ nyāmpo ལྷན་རྒྱས་ lhānkyä' (H)	(adv.) with
ཞེ་དྲགས་ shetra'	(adv.) very
ཉལ་ nyä: གཟིམ་ sim (H)	(v.) [vol., A] to sleep, lie down
སྐྱེ་ kyē འཁྲུངས་ thrūng' (H)	(v.) [inv., A] to be born
སོང་ song	(aux.) *testimonial past*
པ་ཡིན་ payin	(aux.) *volitional egophoric past*
པ་རེད་ pare'	(aux.) *assertive past*

7.3 Remarks འགྲེལ་བཤད།

7.3.1 Word order and postpositions

As we have seen above, basic word order in Tibetan is Subject-Object-Verb. As is often the case in languages with this SOV word order, there are no prepositions but postpositions. The head nouns of relative clauses are usually placed after the relative clause. Moreover, the main clause, which goes at the end of the statement, is always placed after the subordinate clause (object, causal, etc.). The main information is therefore almost always deferred to the end of the sentence.

Word order within a noun phrase is as follows: the substantive head comes first, followed by the qualifying adjective, the article (or demonstrative adjective), the plural marker and the case. The case particle takes last place in the the noun phrase (although it may happen that the case marker is followed by the topicaliser *ni*).

Noun + [Adj. + Det.+ Pl.] + Case

Ex.: བུ་མོ་ སྙིང་རྗེ་པོ་ དེ་ཚོར་
phu̲mo nyīngcepo the̲tso+r "to those pretty girls"
girl pretty those+Dative

In Tibetan, then, there are no prepositions but only postpositions: the equivalents of "in", "on", "with", and so on all follow the noun to which they relate. We don't say "in the water" but "water in"; not "on the table" but "table on".

Postpositions are always followed by a case particle, usually the locative case (but also sometimes other cases such as the genitive or the ablative). They also command the genitive, which is inserted between the noun group and the postposition. The structure of the prepositional phrase is therefore:

Noun[90] + [Gen.: ཀི་] + Postposition + Loc. ལ་

E.g., "water of inside-in", which would correspond to the English word order "in [the inside of] the water".

Note: The postpositions are all clearly derived from substantives. They generally require that the preceding noun (or noun group) be followed by a genitive particle. While the genitive is always used when the preceding word ends in a vowel, its use is optional with certain post-positions when the preceding word ends in a consonant. This is particularly the case with: ནང་ na̲ng "in", སྒང་ ka̲ng "on", རྒྱབ་ kya̲p "behind", མདུན་ tü̲n "in front of".

Ex.: གླིང་ཀའི་ ནང་ལ
līngkä: na̲ng-la "in the park"
park+Gen. in+Loc.

དེབ་(ཀྱི་) ནང་ལ་
the̲p-(ki) na̲ng-la "in the book"
book +Gen. in+Loc.

Ex.: ཅོག་ཙེའི་འོག་ལ་ cōktse: o̲'-la "under the table", འཛམ་གླིང་ནང་ལ་ tsa̲mling na̲ng-la "in the world", སློབ་ཚན་ནང་ལ་ lōptsän na̲ng-la "in the lesson", སློབ་གྲྭའི་འཁྲིས་ལ་ lāpträ: thrī'-la "next to the school"

90. Or noun phrase.

7.3.2. The past tense

The past tense[91] is formed by placing after the verb the expressions པ་རེད་ pare' (assertive), པ་ཡིན་ payin (intentional egophoric) or སོང་ song (testimonial).

In English these forms can be translated by the past or sometimes by the present perfect.

The forms པ་ཡིན་ payin/ པ་རེད་ pare' are composed of the suffix པ་ pa followed by the essential copula རེད་ re' or ཡིན་ yin. The intentional form payin may only be used with volitional[92] verbs in the first person.

In interrogative sentences which contain no interrogative pronoun (where, who, why, what, etc.), the egophoric form པ་ཡིན་ payin is replaced by པས་ pä'; in sentences where there is an interrogative pronoun, པ་ཡིན་ payin is replaced by པ་ pa.

The auxiliary པ་རེད་ pare' is used in narratives and stories, which is why it is sometimes described as the "narrative past". The various forms are presented in the following table.

Ex.:			
ང་	ནང་ལ་	བསྡད་པ་ཡིན་	
nga	nang-la	tä'-payin	"I stayed at home"
I	in+Loc.	stay-Past + egophoric	
ཉི་མ་	ནང་ལ་	བསྡད་པ་རེད་	
nyima	nang-la	tä'-pare'	"Nyima stayed at home"
Nyima	home + Loc.	stay-Past + assertive	
ཉི་མ་	ནང་ལ་	བསྡད་སོང་	
nyima	nang-la	tä'-song	"Nyima stayed at home"
Nyima	home + Loc.	stay-Past + testimonial	

Table: the past tense

affirmative	interrogative (without pronouns)	interrogative (with pronouns)	negative	negative interrogative
པ་ཡིན་ payin	པ་ཡིན་པས་/payin-pä པས་ pä'	པ་ pa	མ་+ V Δ ma + V	མ་+ V + པས་ ma + V + pä'
སོང་ song	སོང་ངས་ song-ngä'	སོང་ song	མ་སོང་ masong	མ་སོང་ངས་ masong-ngä'
པ་རེད་ pare'	པ་རེད་པས་ pare'-pä'	པ་རེད་ parä'	མ་+ V པ་རེད་ Δ ma + V pare'	མ་ V པ་རེད་པས་ ma + V pare'-pä'

---

91. As we shall see in Lesson 10.4, this is the perfective past.

92. I.e., verbs in which it is implied that the subject has control over the action. This class of verbs is described in Lesson 8.

N.B.: The negative forms that are marked in the table with a Δ: མ་ma+V or མ་ma +V+པ་རེད་ pare', as well as the corresponding negative interrogative forms, are rarely used, and other forms are usually preferred (see the perfect tense-aspect in Lesson 10). The simple past forms may be used to emphasize the subject's refusal to perform the action: "I / he didn't go (even though I/he was supposed to)".

Ex.: ཉི་མ་ མ་ཕྱིན་པ་རེད་
nyi̱ma ma̱ chīn-pa-re' "Nyima did not go"

ང་ མ་ཕྱིན་
nga̱ ma̱ chīn "I did not go"

7.3.3 The essential and existential verbs "to be" and "to have" in the past

The forms of the imperfective are equivalent to those of the present (see 6.3). For the perfective[93] past however, there are special forms. The following full verbs are used in the construction of the (perfective) past: ཆགས་ chā' "to become", བྱེད་ che̱' "to do", བསྡད་ tä̱' "to stay", བྱུང་chu̱ng "to happen, to obtain". All these verbs correspond to the (perfective) past tense of the verbs ཡིན་ "to be" and ཡོད་ "to have". For the sake of convenience, we may distinguish between essential and existential statements.

A) Essential statements

• When the complement of the subject is a substantive (equative meaning), Tibetan uses the verb: བྱེད་che̱' "to do" (in the past stem[94]: བྱས་ chä̱') or the verb ཆགས་chā' followed by past auxiliaries (in association with the various evidential moods: assertive, testimonial, egophoric).

Ex.: ཁོང་སྨྱོན་པ་ཆགས་པ་རེད། khōng nyōnpa chā'-pare' "He became crazy." (assertive)
ཁོང་སྨྱོན་པ་ཆགས་སོང་། khōng nyōnpa chā'-song "He became crazy." (testimonial)
ཁོང་ཨེམ་ཆི་བྱས་པ་རེད། khōng āmci chä̱'-pare' "He became a doctor."
ང་ཨེམ་ཆི་བྱས་པ་ཡིན། nga̱ āmci chä̱'-payin "I became a doctor."

Note: In the case of the imperfective past, the same form as the present is used:

Ex.: དེ་དུས་ཁོང་ཨེམ་ཆི་རེད། the̱tü' khōng āmci re' "He was a doctor" (lit. "at that time he is a doctor").

B) Existential statements

• Possession and existence are constructed with the use of the verb བྱུང་ chu̱ng in the (perfective) past tense (in association with the various evidential moods: assertive, testimonial, egophoric).

---

93. The notions of perfective and imperfective aspects are explained in 10.4. Here we need only bear in mind that the imperfective past forms are equivalent to the present.

94. About the verb stems, see Lesson 10.

Ex.: མོ་རང་ལ་མཚེ་མ་བྱུང་པ་རེད། morang-la tshēma chung-pare' "She had twins."
ཁོང་ལ་དངུལ་བྱུང་པ་རེད། khōng-la ngū: chung-pare' "He got some money."
སྙོག་ཁྲ་བྱུང་པ་རེད། nyōktra chung-pare' "There were some problems."
སྙོག་ཁྲ་བྱུང་སོང་། nyōktra chung-song "He had (or, there were) problems." (testimonial)
ངར་སྙོག་ཁྲ་བྱུང་། nga: nyōktra chung "I had problems." (egophoric)

• When the complement of the subject is an adjective, the verb བྱུང་ chung in the (perfective) past is also used (in association with the various evidential moods: assertive, testimonial, egophoric).

Ex.: ལས་སླ་པོ་བྱུང་པ་རེད། lä' lāpo chung-pare' "It was easy."
སྐྱིད་པོ་བྱུང་སོང་། kyīppo chung-song "It was pleasant." (testimonial)
སྐྱིད་པོ་བྱུང་། kyīppo chung "It was pleasant (for me)." (egophoric)

• To convey a locative meaning, the verb བསྡད་ tä' "to stay", or its honorific བཞུགས་ shu' is used in the (perfective) past (in association with the various evidential moods: assertive, testimonial, egophoric).

Ex.: ཁོང་ལྷ་སར་ལོ་གསུམ་བཞུགས་པ་རེད། khōng lhāsar lo sūm shu'-pare'
"He has been in Lhasa for three years." (lit. stayed)
ང་ལྷ་སར་ལོ་གསུམ་བསྡད་པ་ཡིན། nga lhāsar lo sūm tä'-payin
"I have been in Lhasa for three years." (lit. stayed)

Note: In the case of the imperfective past, the same form as the present is used:

Ex.: དེ་དུས་ཁོང་ལྷ་སར་ཡོད་རེད། thetü' khōng lhāsar yo:re'
"At that time he was in Lhasa." (lit. is in Lhasa)

7.3.4 The cardinal and ordinal numbers

Numbers come after the noun. Unlike Burmese, Chinese and several other Asian languages, Tibetan has no classifiers.

༠ ལྐད་ཀོར་ lākor "zero"	༡ གཅིག་ cī' "one"	༢ གཉིས་ nyī' "two"	༣ གསུམ་ sūm "three"	༤ བཞི shi "four"
༥ ལྔ་ ngā "five"	༦ དྲུག thru' "six"	༧ བདུན་ tün "seven"	༨ བརྒྱད་ kyä' "eight"	༩ དགུ ku "nine"

༡༠ བཅུ་ cū "ten"

༡༡ བཅུ་གཅིག་ cūci' "eleven"

༡༢ བཅུ་གཉིས་ cūnyi' "twelve"

༡༣ ༡༣ བཅུ་གསུམ་ cūksum "thirteen"

༡༤ བཅུ་བཞི་ cūpshi "fourteen"

༡༥ བཅོ་ལྔ་ cō̃nga "fifteen"

༡༦ བཅུ་དྲུག་ cūtru' "sixteen"

༡༧ བཅུ་བདུན་ cūptün "seventeen"

༡༨ བཅོ་བརྒྱད་ cōpkyä' "eighteen"

༡༩ བཅུ་དགུ་ cūrku "nineteen"

Between 20 and 90, each set of ten makes use of a special particle:

ཙ་	སོ་	ཞེ་	ང་	རེ་	དོན་	གྱ་	གོ་
tsā (20)	sō (30)	she̲ (40)	nga̲ (50)	re̲ (60)	thö̲n (70)	khya̲ (80)	kho̲ (90)

Remembering these particles is made easier by the fact that, with the exception of tsā, they are all derived from the term for the set of ten in question. For example, sō, the particle for the thirties, is derived from sūm "three". The same is true of the forties, where she̲ is a modification of shi̲ "four", and so on.

༢༠ ཉི་ཤུ་ nyi̲shu "20".

༢༡ ཉི་ཤུ་རྩ་གཅིག་ nyi̲shu tsāci' "21" > ༢༩ ཉི་ཤུ་རྩ་དགུ་ nyi̲shu tsāku "29"

༣༠ སུམ་ཅུ་ sūmcu "30"

༣༡ སུམ་ཅུ་སོ་གཅིག་ sūmcu sōci' "31" > ༣༩ སུམ་ཅུ་སོ་དགུ sūmcu sōku "39"

༤༠ བཞི་བཅུ་ shi̲pcu "40"

༤༡ བཞི་བཅུ་ཞེ་གཅིག་ shi̲pcu she̲ci' "41" > ༤༩ བཞི་བཅུ་ཞེ་དགུ་ shi̲pcu she̲ku "49"

༥༠ ལྔ་བཅུ་ ngāpcu "50"

༥༡ ལྔ་བཅུ་ང་གཅིག་ ngāpcu nga̲ci' "51" > ༥༩ ལྔ་བཅུ་ང་དགུ་ ngāpcu nga̲ku "59"

༦༠ དྲུག་ཅུ་ thru̲kcu "60"

༦༡ དྲུག་ཅུ་རེ་གཅིག་ thru̲kcu re̲ci' "61" > ༦༩ དྲུག་ཅུ་རེ་དགུ thru̲kcu re̲ku "69"

༧༠ བདུན་ཅུ་ tü̲ncu "70"

༧༡ བདུན་ཅུ་དོན་གཅིག་ tü̲ncu thö̲nci' "71" > ༧༩ བདུན་ཅུ་དོན་དགུ་ tü̲ncu thö̲nku "79"

༨༠ བརྒྱད་ཅུ་ kyä̲cu "80"

༨༡ བརྒྱད་ཅུ་གྱ་གཅིག་ kyä̲cu khya̲ci' "81" > ༨༩ བརྒྱད་ཅུ་གྱ་དགུ་ kyä̲cu khya̲ku "89"

༩༠ དགུ་བཅུ་ ku̲pcu "90"

༩༡ དགུ་བཅུ་གོ་གཅིག་ ku̲pcu kho̲ci' "91" > ༩༩ དགུ་བཅུ་གོ་དགུ་ ku̲pcu kho̲ku "99"

བརྒྱ་ kya̱ "hundred": ཆིག་བརྒྱ་ chīkkya "one hundred", ཉིས་བརྒྱ་ nyi̱kya "two hundred", སུམ་བརྒྱ་ sūmkya "three hundred".

Between 100 and 199, the number "hundred" is followed by the connective དང་ tha̱ng (-tang) "and"[95].

Ex: བརྒྱ་དང་ལྔ་བཅུ་ kya̱-tang ngāpcu "150"

སྟོང་ tōng "thousand": ཆིག་སྟོང་ chīktong "one thousand", ཉིས་སྟོང་ nyi̱tong "two thousand", སུམ་སྟོང་ sūmtong "three thousand".

ཁྲི་ thrī "ten thousand": ཆིག་ཁྲི་ chīktri "one myriad", ཉིས་ཁྲི་ nyi̱tri "twenty thousand (two myriad)", སུམ་ཁྲི་ sūmtri "thirty thousand".

འབུམ་ pu̱m "a hundred thousand": ཆིག་འབུམ chīkpum "one (unit of a) hundred thousand", ཉིས་འབུམ་ nyi̱pum "two hundred thousand", སུམ་འབུམ་ sūmpum "three hundred thousand".

After "million", the numbers are treated as substantives and must be followed (not preceded) by the number of units.

ས་ཡ་ sāya "million": ས་ཡ་གཅིག་ sāya cī' "one million", ས་ཡ་གཉིས་ sāya nyī' "two million", etc.

བྱེ་བ་ che̱wa "ten million": བྱེ་བ་གཅིག་ che̱wa cī' "(one unit of) ten million", བྱེ་བ་གཉིས་ che̱wa nyī' "twenty million", etc.

དུང་ཕྱུར་ thu̱ngcur "hundred million": དུང་ཕྱུར་གཅིག་ thu̱ngcur cī' "one (unit of a) hundred million", དུང་ཕྱུར་གཉིས་ thu̱ngcur nyi' "two hundred million", དུང་ཕྱུར་བཅུ་ thu̱ngcur cū' "one billion".

From a hundred up to a hundred thousand, units may be placed afterwards, and the number is therefore treated syntactically as a substantive. In the case of "thousand", the suffix ཕྲག་ thra' is added.

Ex.: སྟོང་ཕྲག་གཉིས་ tōngtra' nyī' "two thousand", ཁྲི་གསུམ་ thrī sūm "thirty thousand"
འབུམ་གསུམ་ pu̱m sūm "three hundred thousand"

From one hundred up, when there is a zero in the tens, hundreds or any higher column, as in 108 or 1015, the column name (10, 100, etc.) is followed by མེད་ me' "without". This expression is optional.

Ex: ཆིག་སྟོང་བཞི་བརྒྱ་བཅུ་མེད་བདུན་ chīktong shi̱pkya (cūme') tü̱n "1407"
ཆིག་སྟོང་བརྒྱ་མེད་བཅུ་དྲུག chīktong (kya̱me') cūtru' "1016"

Note: The numbers 1, 2, 3 and 10 are spelled differently according to the other numbers with which they are combined, as in the case of 15 (10+5), 18 (10+8), 20 (2x10), 30 (3x10), etc.

95. Between 200 and 999 *dang* is optional and usually dropped.

The written variants represent a formalization, from the classical period, of different pronunciations of the numbers in question.

བཅུ་ bcu /cū/ > བཅོ་/cō̃/ in བཅོ་ལྔ་ /cō̃nga/ "15" and /cō/ in བཅོ་བརྒྱད་ /cōpkyä'/ "18"

བཅུ་ bcu /cū/ > ཤུ་ /shū/ in ཉི་ཤུ་ /nyi̱shu/ "20"

བཅུ་ bcu /cū/ > ཅུ་ /cū/ in སུམ་ཅུ་ /sūmcu/ "30" and in དྲུག་ཅུ་ /thru̱kcu/ "60", etc.

གཅིག་ gcig /ci'/ > ཆིག་ /chi'/ in ཆིག་སྟོང་/chīktong/ "1000"

གཉིས་ gnyis /nyī'/ > ཉི་ /nyi̱/ in ཉི་ཤུ་ /nyi̱shu/ "20"

གཉིས་ gnyis /nyī'/ > ཉིས་ /nyi̱'/ in ཉིས་སྟོང /nyi̱tong/ "2000"

གསུམ་ gsum /sūm/ > སུམ་ /sūm/ in སུམ་ཅུ་ /sūmcu/ "30"

Note that round tens and hundreds may be followed by ཐམ་པ་ thāmpa.

Ex.: བརྒྱ་ཐམ་པ་ kya̱ thāmpa "a hundred", སུམ་ཅུ་ཐམ་པ་ sūmcu thāmpa "thirty".

Ordinal numbers present no difficulties. With the exception of "first", which has a special radical, they are formed simply by adding the suffix pa.

Ex.: དང་པོ་ tha̱ngpo "first", གཉིས་པ་ nyīpa "second", གསུམ་པ་ sūmpa "third", བཅུ་པ་ cūpa "tenth", བཅུ་གཅིག་པ་ cūcikpa "eleventh", etc.

The percentages and fractions are formed by using the word ཆ་ cha "part". Thus

Ex.:			
One hundred percent	བརྒྱ་ཆ་བརྒྱ་	kya̱ca kya̱	"100%"
Fifty percent	བརྒྱ་ཆ་ལྔ་བཅུ་	kya̱ca ngāpcu	"50%"
One third	གསུམ་ཆ་གཅིག་	sūmca cī'	"1/3"
Three quarters	བཞི་ཆ་གསུམ་	shi̱ca sūm	"3/4"

7.4 Exercises སྦྱོང་ཚན།

7.4.1 Rewrite the dialogue at the beginning of this lesson in the non-honorific register.

7.4.2 Translate into Tibetan:

1. The field is behind the house.
2. The key is on the table.
3. The camera is on the chair.
4. They are at school.
5. There are two schools.

8. The teacher is fifty-nine years old.
9. The school is beside the road.
10. Bhutan is next to Tibet.
11. Lobsang has six horses.
12. Nyima has twenty dzo.

6. They have thirty yaks.
7. Dawa is twenty-two years old.
13. There are insects on the flower.

7.4.3 Complete the sentences using the appropriate form: སོང་, *པ་*, པས་ *or* སོང་ངས་.

༡) རྒན་ལགས་གླིང་གར་ཕེབས་ ( )?
༢) ཁོང་རྒྱ་གར་ལ་ཕྱིན་ ( )!
༣) ཁྱེད་རང་ཁ་ས་ག་པར་ཕེབས་ ( )?
༤) ཉི་མ་སློབ་གྲྭར་ཕེབས་ ( )?
༥) ཁ་ས་ཁོ་ག་པར་ཕྱིན་ ( )?
༦) ཁྱེད་རང་གླིང་གར་སུ་མཉམ་པོ་ཕེབས་ ( )?
༧) ཁྱེད་རང་ཁ་ས་ག་པར་བཞུགས་ ( )?
༨) ཁ་ས་ཁྱེད་རང་གླིང་གར་ཕེབས་ ( )?

7.4.4. Rewrite the following sentences in the assertive mode (using the auxiliaries yo:re' *and* pare' *as appropriate).*

༡) ཁོང་གི་ནང་ལ་སྤུ་གུ་མང་པོ་འདུག
༢) ཟླ་བ་ལགས་སློབ་གྲྭར་ཕེབས་སོང་།
༣) བོད་ལ་གཡག་མང་པོ་འདུག
༤) བོད་ལ་རྟ་ཡང་མང་པོ་འདུག་གས།
༥) ཁོང་ལྷ་སར་མི་འདུག་གས།
༦) ཤོག་གུའི་མེ་ཏོག་དེ་ཚོ་སྙིང་རྗེ་པོ་འདུག

7.4.5 Write out these numbers in full in Tibetan:

༡༢ ༢༩ ༣༥ ༤༢ ༥༧ ༦༨ ༧༡ ༨༣

༩༢ ༡༠༨ ༡༩༥༩ ༢༡༣༨ ༥༧༦༠ ༡༥༩༣༡

7.4.6 Translate into English:

ང་བོད་ལ་སྐྱེས་པ་རེད། ཁྱེད་རང་ག་པར་འཁྲུངས་པ་རེད། འདི་ཁོང་གི་པར་ཆས་རེད། བློ་བཟང་ཨ་མེ་རི་ཀར་སྐྱེས་པ་རེད། སྒྲོལ་དཀར་ལགས་རྒྱ་ནག་ལ་འཁྲུངས་པ་རེད། ཁྱེད་རང་རྒྱ་གར་ལ་སྐྱེས་པ་རེད་པས། རྒྱ་ནག་ལ་མི་དུང་ཕྱུར་བཅུ་གཉིས་ཡོད་རེད། ལྷ་སར་མི་འབུམ་གཉིས་ཡོད་རེད།

"Invitation to a meal"

གསོལ་ཚིགས་བཏང་བ།

Grammar aims བརྡ་སྤྲོད་རིག་པའི་དམིགས་ཚད།

- Classes of verbs.
- The agentive case གིས་ -ki'.
- The future auxiliaries: གི་རེད་ -kire', གི་ཡིན་ -kiyin.
- The future forms of the verbs "to be" and "to have".
- The past tense receptive egophoric auxiliary: བྱུང་ -cung.
- The interrogative pronoun ག་གི་ kha̱ki.

CD I • Tr. 25-26 

8.1 Dialogue དྲི་བ་དྲིས་ལན།

ཨ་མ་ ཿ ཞལ་ལག་མཉེས་པོ་གནང་སོ

བློ་བཟང་ ཿ ཐུགས་རྗེ་ཆེ། དེ་འདྲའི་བྲོ་བ་ཆེ་བ་ལ་ཨ། ཁྱེད་རང་གིས་བཟོས་གནང་པས།

ཨ་མ་ ཿ ངས་སྣེ་ཁ་གཅིག་བཟོས་པ་ཡིན།

བློ་བཟང་ ཿ ག་གི་བཟོས་གནང་པ།

ཨ་མ་ ཿ འདི་ངས་བཟོས་པ་ཡིན། འདི་ཚོ་བུ་མོས་བཟོས་པ་རེད།

བློ་བཟང་ ཿ དངོས་གནས་སྦྲོ་པོ་ཞེ་དྲགས་འདུག

ཨ་མ་ ཿ ཞལ་ལག་ཡག་པོ་བྱུང་མ་སོང་། དགོངས་པ་མ་ཚོམས། ཁྱེད་རང་ག་རེར་མཉེས་པོ་ཡོད།

བློ་བཟང་ ཿ ཤ་བག་ལེབ། ཤ་མོག་མོག ཤ་འབྲས། ད་དུང་ཕྱུར་ར་(ཕྱུར་བ་)མོག་མོག་ཡའི་(ཡང་)དགའ་པོ་ཡོད།

ཨ་མ་ ཿ འོ་ན་སང་ཉིན་ཕྱུར་ར་མོག་མོག་བཟོ་གི་ཡིན་ད།

བུ་མོ་ ཿ སྤུ་མོ་ལགས་སང་ཉིན་ཕེབས་ཀྱི་རེད་པས།

ཨ་མ་ ཿ ཁའི་ས་(ཁ་སང་)ཕེབས་བྱུང་། སང་ཉིན་ཕེབས་ཀྱི་མ་རེད།

བུ་མོ་ ཿ ཨ་ཁུ་ལགས་མཇལ་བྱུང་ངས།

ཨ་མ་ ཿ མཇལ་བྱུང་།

བློ་བཟང་ ཿ ང་དགོངས་པ་ཞུ་གི་ཡིན། ཐུགས་རྗེ་ཆེ། དེ་རིང་སྐྱིད་པོ་ཞེ་དྲགས་བྱུང་། མགྱོགས་པོ་མཇལ་ཡོང་།

Pronunciation

- shä̱:la' nyēpo nāngko

- thūkce chē the̱nträ: thro̱wa chēwala a ! khyērang-ki' sö̱' nāng-pä'

- ngä̱' nēka cī' sö̱'-payin

- kha̱ki sö̱' nāng-pa

- ti̱ ngä̱' sö̱'-payin, ti̱ntso phu̱mö' sö̱'-pare'

- ngȫnä', trōpo she̱tra' tu̱'

- shä̱:la' ya̱kpo chu̱ng-masong, ko̱ngpa ma tshōm, khyērang kha̱rer nyēpo yö̱'

- shā pha̱klep shā mo̱mo' shāmträ', tha̱tung chūrra mo̱mo' yä̱: ka̱po yö̱'

- o̱na sāngnyin chūrra mo̱mo' so̱-kiyin-ta

- sōmo-la' sāngnyin phēp-kire'-pä'

- khǟsa phēp-cung, sāngnyin phēp-kimare'

- āku-la' cä̱:-cung-ngä'

- cä̱:-cung

- nga̱ ko̱ngpa shu̱-kiyin thūkce chē, the̱ring kyīpo she̱tra' chu̱ng, kyo̱kpo cä̱:-yong

Translation

Mother — Bon appetit!
Lobzang — Thanks, it's very good (lit. "such a great taste!"). Was it you who made it?
Mother — I made one of the dishes.
Lobzang — Which one did you make?
Mother — I made this one, and my daughter made these.
Lobzang — It's really excellent!
Mother — The meal wasn't good – our apologies. What [kind of food] do you like?
Lobzang — Bread with meat stuffing, meat momos, and meat stew with rice [and potatoes]; I also like cheese momos.
Mother — Well then, tomorrow I shall make cheese momos.
Daughter — Will our aunt come tomorrow?
Mother — She came yesterday. She won't come tomorrow.
Daughter — Did you see (lit. meet) our uncle?
Mother — Yes, I saw him.
Lobzang — I shall take my leave, thank you. I've had a very pleasant day (lit. today was very pleasant [for me]). See you soon!

ཀ་ཁ་ག་ང་

8.2 Vocabulary ཚིག་གསར།

ག་གི་ kha̱ki (interr. pron.) which?

ལ་ཡ་ la-a (part.) *interjection after an adjective*

ད་ tha̱ — (part.) *expressive particle*

མ་བྱན་ ma̱cän — (n.) cook

སྤང་ཀོ་ pāngko སྤྲང་པོ་ trāngpo (L) — (n.) beggar

ཨེམ་ཆི་ āmci, ēmci — (n.) doctor

ནད་གཡོག་ nä̱yo' — (n.) nurse

བག་ལེབ་ pha̱'lep བཞེས་བག་ she̱pa'(H) — (n.) bread

ཕྱུར་བ་ chūrra ཞིབ་ཕྱུར་ shi̱pcur (H) — (n.) cheese

ཤ་ shā གསོལ་དཀྲུམ་ sȫ:trum (H) — (n.) meat

མོག་མོག mo̱'mo' བཞེས་མོག་ she̱mo' (H) — (n.) *momo,* meat ravioli or dumplings

རྩམ་པ་ tsāmpa གསོལ་ཞིབ་ sȫ:ship (H) — (n.) *tsampa,* roasted barley flour

འབྲས་ trä̱' བཞེས་འབྲས་ she̱nträ' (H) — (n.) rice

ཤ་བག་ལེབ་ shāpa'lep — (n.) bread with meat stuffing

ཐུག་པ་ thūkpa བཞེས་ཐུག་ she̱tu' (H) — (n.) noodles, noodle soup

ཤ་འབྲས་ shāmträ' — (n.) meat stew with rice [and potatoes]

ཁ་ལག་ khāla' ཞལ་ལག་ shä̱:la' (H) — (n.) meal, food

གསོལ་ཚིགས་ sȫ:tsi' (H) — (n.) meal

སྣེ་ཁ་ nēka — (n.) sort, kind

བྲོ་བ་ thro̱wa ལྗགས་བྲོ་ ca̱ktro (H) — (n.) taste

འབྲི་དེབ་ tri̱tep — (n.) exercise book

སྨན་ mǟn གསོལ་སྨན་ sȫ:män (H) — (n.) medicine

ཚིག་ tshī' — (n.) word

ཚིག་མཛོད་ tshīntsö' — (n.) dictionary

ཚིག་གྲུབ་ tshīktrup — (n.) sentence

ཆེ་བ་ chēwa — (adj.) very big, bigger[96]

ཆུང་བ་ chūngwa — (adj.) very small, aller

མགྱོགས་པོ་ kyo̱kpo སྟོལ་པོ་ tsȫ:po (H) — (adj., adv.) fast, quickly

ག་ལེ་ག་ལེ་ kha̱le kha̱le — (adj., adv.) slow, slowly

སྐྱིད་པོ་ kyīpo སྤྲོ་པོ་ trōpo (H) — (adj.) pleasant, happy

ཞིམ་པོ་ shi̱mpo སྤྲོ་པོ་ trōpo (H) — (adj.) delicious

ཞལ་ལག་མཉེས་པོ་གནང་གོ་ shä̱la' nyēpo nāngko — (idiom.) *bon appetit*

དགོངས་པ་མ་ཚོམས་ ko̱ngpa ma̱ tshōm — (idiom.) excuse me

---

96. See Lesson 17. When followed by a suffix (comparative, superlative, etc.), the short form of the adjective must be used.

སང་ཉིན་ sāngnyin	(adv.) tomorrow
དེ་རིང་ the̱ring	(adv.) today
དེ་འདྲ་ the̱ntra	(adv.) so, such, thus
དངོས་ནས་ ngȫnä'	(adv.) really
དགའ་པོ་ ka̱po མཉེས་པོ་ nyēpo (H)	(adj.) happy
དགའ་ ka̱ མཉེས་ nyē' (H)	(v.) [inv., AD] to like
བཟོ་ so̱ (1) / བཟོས་ sö̱' (2,3)	(v.) [vol., EA] to make, to do
ཐུག་ thū' མཇལ་ cä̱: (H)	(v.) [inv., EA] to meet
སྤྲད་ trǟ' གནང་ nāng (H)	(v.) [vol., EA] to give, pass
སྟེར་ tēr	(v.) [vol. EA] to make a gift of
གསོལ་རས་+ གནང་ sȫ:rä' nāng (H)	(v.) [vol., EA] to make a gift of
ཁ་ལག་+ བཟོ་ khāla' so̱	(v.) [vol., E] to prepare a meal
བྱུང་ chu̱ng	(v.) [inv., A] to occur, happen – (aux.) *receptive*
ཆགས་ chā'	(v.) [inv., A] to become
ཞུ་ shu̱(1) / ཞུས་ shü̱' (2-3) (h)	(v.) [vol., EA] to take (v.) - [vol., EDA] to say, ask, – *verbalizer*
ཕུལ་ phǖ: (h)	(v.) - [vol., EDA] to offer, give, – *verbalizer*[97]
འབྲི་ tri̱' (1) / བྲིས་ thri̱'(2,3)	(v.) [vol., EA] to write
ཀློག་ lō' ལྗགས་ཀློག་གནང་ ca̱lo' nāng (H)	(v.) [vol., EA] to read
བྱེད་ che̱' (1,3) / བྱས་ chä̱' (2)	(v.) - [vol., EA] to do, act, – *verbalizer*
གནང་ nāng (H)	(v.) - [vol., EDA] to give, do, – *verbalizer*
བཏང་ tāng	(v.) - [vol., EDA] to send, - [vol., EA] to let by, – *verbalizer*
དགོངས་པ་+ ཞུ་ ko̱ngpa shu̱ (h)	(v.) - [vol., E] to take leave

---

97. In Literary Tibetan, certain verbs such as *phul, klog, btang, etc.* have several variants according to tense, but these have become invariable in the spoken language. See Appendix 1, section 10.

༡༢༢

8.3 Remarks on grammar འགྲེལ་བཤད།

8.3.1 Classes of verbs

Tibetan verbs fall into two main classes: **volitional verbs** and **non-volitional verbs.** The first group are concerned with controllable actions, and are compatible with intentional auxiliaries such as -payin (see 10.4) and "jussive" suffixes that convey an order or a suggestion (such as -ta or sh). Moreover, these verbs sometimes have a special inflected form for the imperative.

The verbs in the second class imply non-controllable processes which do not depend on the subject's volition, and are compatible with neither intentional auxiliaries nor imperative markers. With non-volitional verbs, non-intentional auxiliaries such as -cung or -song must be used. In this Manual, volitional verbs are marked as "[vol.]", while non-volitional verbs are identified as "[inv.]"

Ex. of volitional verbs:

བལྟས་པ་ཡིན། tā̃'-payin "I looked." ལྟོས་ཤིག tō̃'-sh "Look!"

ཉལ་པ་ཡིན། nyä̱:-payin "I went to bed." ཉོལ་ཤིག nyö̱:-sh "Go to bed! Lie down!"

Ex. of non-volitional verbs:

མཐོང་བྱུང་། thōng-cung "I saw." དྲག་བྱུང་། thra'-cung "I recovered."

Thus the following forms are incorrect because they combine a non-volitional verb with an intentional auxiliary: * མཐོང་པ་ཡིན། thōng-payin, * དྲག་པ་ཡིན་ thra'-payin; so, too, are the following imperatives:[98] * མཐོང་ཤིག thōng-sh, * དྲག་ཤིག thra'-sh.

The grammar of European languages does not make the opposition volitional / non-volitional. However in their vocabulary, they do differentiate between *hear, see* (non-volitional) and *listen, look* (volitional).

As in other languages, a distinction is made between **transitive verbs** (or polyvalent verbs)[99] and **intransitive verbs** (or monovalent verbs). Transitive verbs require an object, whereas intransitive verbs do not.

Ex.: ལྟ་ tā "to look" and མཐོང་ thōng "to see" are transitive whereas ཉལ་ nyä̱: "to go to bed, to lie down" and དྲག་ /thra'/ "to recover (from an illness)" are intransitive.

In this Manual, whether a verb is transitive or intransitive will be indicated indirectly: for each verb, the case required for the subject and, where relevant, for the direct or indirect object

---

98. With some non-volitional verbs which imply a certain degree of control, such as "lose" or "fall asleep", the imperative forms are also possible.

99. In order to avoid the linguistically problematic notion of "subject" in Tibetan, verbs may be defined according to their valency, e.g., the number of participants they require. See the Glossary of linguistic terms.

will be specified. Thus if an object is required, the verb must be a transitive one (see 8.3.2 below, "The ergative construction", as well as section 9.3).

There are, then, altogether four basic classes of verbs: non-volitional intransitive, volitional intransitive, non-volitional transitive and volitional transitive.

In the case of transitive verbs, a distinction may be made between those which require two participants (bivalent verbs) and those which require three (trivalent verbs).

Summary of the four categories

	Volitional བྱ་ཚིག་རང་དབང་ཅན་	*Non-volitional* བྱ་ཚིག་གཞན་དབང་ཅན་
Transitive བྱ་ཚིག་ཐ་དད་པ་	ལྟ་ /tā/ "look" ཉན་/nyä̱n/ "listen" བཟོ་/so̱/ "make"	མཐོང་ /thōng/ "see" གོ་ /kho̱/ "hear" ཧ་གོ་ /hā kho̱/ "understand"
Intransitive བྱ་ཚིག་ཐ་མི་དད་པ་	ཉལ་ /nyä̱:/ "lie down" ལང་ /la̱ng/ "get up" འགྲོ་ /tro̱/ "go"	ན་ /na̱/ "be sick" ཤི་ /shī/ "die" དྲག་ /thra̱'/ "recover"

8.3.2 The agentive གིས་ /-ki'/

Traditional grammars refer to this mark as *byed-sgra* (lit. agent-sound). The agentive is formed by adding an '*s*' to the genitive. The variants follow the same pattern as in the case of the genitive: གིས་ gis, གྱིས་ gyis, ཀྱིས་ kyis, ས་ s.

- after vowels and འ *'a* > ས་ *s* /-'/
- after ག *g*, ང *ng* > གིས་ *gis* /khi̱'/Δ
- after ད *d*, བ *b*, ས *s* and the *da-drag* > ཀྱིས་ *kyis* /kyī'/Δ
- after ན *n* མ *m*, ར *r*, ལ *l* > གྱིས་ *gyis* /khyi̱'/Δ[100]

In Classical Tibetan, vowels may also be followed by the variant ཡིས་ *yis* /yi'/, or even by the more archaic form འིས *'i s* /-'/.

In conversation, the three particles གིས /khi̱'/, ཀྱིས/kyī'/, གྱིས་/khyi̱'/ are pronounced in exactly the same way, as an unstressed syllable: /-ki'/. Remember that adding the variant '*s*' produces a glottal stop (or a modulated tone) in the pronunciation, and that in the case of /a, u, o/, an umlaut

100. Pronunciations followed by the symbol Δ correspond to a literary register or an accentuated reading of the particle. Because case particles are unstressed when read under normal conditions, their tone and aspiration are irrelevant.

is effectively added: a+s > /ä'/, u+s > /ü'/, o+s > /ö'/. The vowels /e,i/ do not change: e+ s > /e'/, i+s > /i'/.

Ex.: ཉི་མ་ /nyi̲ma/ "sun" > ཉི་མས་ /nyi̲mä'/
རི་མོ་ /ri̲mo/ "drawing" > རི་མོས་ /ri̲mö'/
ཆུ་ /chū/ "water" > ཆུས་ /chǖ'/
མི་ /mi̲/ "man, person" > མིས་ /mi̲'/
མེ་ /me̲/ "fire" > མེས་/me̲'/.
མདའ་/ta̲/ "arrow" > མདས་ /tä̲'/.
དགེ་རྒན་ /ke̲kän/ "teacher" > དགེ་རྒན་གྱིས་ /ke̲kän-ki'/
རྒན་ལགས་ /kä̲nla'/ "teacher (H)" > རྒན་ལགས་ཀྱིས་/kä̲nla'-ki'/
དྲུང་ཡིག་ /thru̲ngyi'/ "secretary" > དྲུང་ཡིག་གིས་/thru̲ngyi'-ki'/

• The agentive particle has two case-related functions: the ergative and the instrumental:[101] The ergative function is used to mark the grammatical **role of agent.** In transitive clauses, this role typically matches the semantic agent or causer who performs an action on a patient, but also includes the agent of "mental" and "verbal" actions and the perceiver of a sensation. However, it does not refer to the experiencer of an emotion, which is marked as the patient (the absolutive or zero case). In syntactic or relational terms, the agentive particle generally marks the **subject of transitive verbs** governing an ergative construction. Most transitive verbs require an ergative construction but some non-volitional transitive verbs require other constructions (affective or possessive, see Lesson 9.3).

Ergative constructions may seem strange at first, to the extent that they work in the opposite way to accusative constructions in European languages (except Basque). However, even though ergative constructions are not familiar to speakers of European languages, they are as logical as accusative constructions. As discussed in Chapter 4, the main point is that all languages need a mechanism or device to distinguish "who does what to whom", or, in other words, to distinguish between the subject and the object of a transitive verb. In accusative European languages, as well as in Chinese, it is not the subject that is marked, but the object, either by using a distinct accusative case marker (as in Latin and Russian), or by opposition in the sentence, i.e., being placed after the verb (as in French, English and Chinese)[102]. In English, for example, word

101. In traditional grammars, the first is referred to as the particle of "the main agent" *(byed-pa-po gtso-bo),* while the second is referred to as the particle of "the secondary agent" *(byed-pa-po phal-ba).*

102. We may compare the same transitive statement in five different languages, which all operate according to an accusative model.

Latin:	ego	ill+**um**	libr+**um**	legi
Russian:	ja	èt+**u**	knig+**u**	procël
	I + Nomin.	this + Accus.	book + Accus.	read (past)
Chinese:	wo	kan-guo	zhe+ben	shu
French:	j'ai	lu	ce	livre
English:	I	read	this	book

order is used to distinguish between 'the *policeman* killed the *fugitive*' and 'the *fugitive* killed the *policeman*'.

Tibetan chooses to mark not the object, but subject of the transitive verb, by using a distinct case marker – the ergative. It is called བྱེད་སྒྲ་གཙོ་བོ་ *byed sgra gtso bo* "main ergative" in the traditional grammars.

A subject that is marked by the ergative is almost always a human or other animate. The object lacks an overt formal marker (Ø); in linguistic terminology this is known as the "absolutive", and in traditional Tibetan grammars as ངོ་བོ་ཙམ་ *ngo-bo-tsam,* "just (the word) in the absolute".

Here are some examples:

S (erg.)	O (abs.)	V(ergative construction)	
ངས་	དེབ་	བལྟས་པ་ཡིན།	
nga-s	*deb* + ∅	*bltas-payin*	"I read the book."
ngä'	thep	tā̃'-payin	
I + Erg.	book + Abs.	read-past	

In Basque, the only ergative language of Europe, the structure is similar:

S (erg.)	O (abs.)	V
ni-k	liburu-a-∅	irakurri d-u-t
I + Erg.	Book-def + Abs.	Read Abs-Aux-Erg

བླ་མས་	གསོལ་ཇ་	མཆོད་སོང་།	
lāmä'	sō̃:ca	chō̃'-song	"The lama drank the tea."
lama + Erg.	tea (H) + Abs.	drink (H)-past	
ཚེ་རིང་གིས་	རྟ་	ཉོས་པ་རེད།	
tshēring-ki'	tā	nyö̱'-pare'	"Tshering bought the horse."
Tshering+Erg.	horse + Abs.	buy -past	

Verbs that take the ergative construction will be identified as: E(rgative) A(bsolutive).

Ex.: ཉོ "to buy" [vol., EA]

It should be noted that there is also an **indirect ergative** in which the subject is in the ergative and the object in the dative (indirect object).

S (erg.)	O (dat.)	V (mixed construction)	
ཚེ་རིང་གིས་	རྟ་ལ་	བལྟས་པ་རེད།	
tshēring-ki'	tā-la	tā̃'-pare'	"Tshering looked at the horse."
Tshering + Erg.	horse+Dat.	look-past	

Verbs governing this type of construction will be identified as: E(rgative) D(ative).

Ex.: ལྟ "to look (at)" [vol., ED]

This construction appears mainly with compound verbs (which usually have three syllables), such as དོ་སྣང་བྱེད་ tho̱nang che̱' "to be interested (in)", གཟབ་གཟབ་བྱེད་ sa̱psap che̱' "to be careful (of)", ཁ་པར་བཏང་ khāpar tāng "to make a phone call (to)", ཡིད་ཆེས་བྱེད་ yi̱ce' che̱' "to have faith (in)".

The ergative also appears with verbs involving three participants (ditransitive):

S (erg.)	O indirect (dat.)	O (abs.)	V
ང་ཚོས་	ཁོང་ལ་	ཕྱག་དེབ་ཅིག་	ཕུལ་པ་ཡིན།
nga̱tsö'	khōng-la	chātep cī'	phū̃:-payin
we + Erg.	he + Dat.	book a + Abs.	give (h)-past

"We gave him a book."

Verbs that take this type of construction will be noted as: E(rgative) D(ative) A(bsolutive).

Ex.: ཕུལ་ "to offer" [vol., EDA]

In exceptional cases, the ergative may also be used to mark the agent of volitional intransitive verbs, especially verbs of movement (see Lesson 27). The effect of the ergative in this case is to emphasize the agent or his/her volition.

• The instrumental is used to convey three main meanings: the instrument or implement; the manner; the cause. It may be used either with an agent (explicit or implicit) or without one.

Ex.: སྨན་ འདི་ཚོ་ རྩ་སྨན་གྱིས་ བཟོས་པ་རེད།
mā̃n ti̱tso tsāmän-ki' sö̱'-pare'
"These medicines are made with medicinal herbs."

ཁོས་ རི་མོ་ འདི་ ས་སྨུག་གིས་ བྲིས་སོང་།
khō̃' ri̱mo ti̱ sānyu'-ki' thri̱'-song
"He drew this picture with chalk."

ལུག་རྫིས་ ཁྱི་ དབྱུག་པས་ བརྡུངས་སོང་།
lu̱ktsi' khyī yūkpä' tu̱ng-song
"The shepherd hit the dog with a stick."

ཁོ་ སྨན་གྱིས་ དྲག་སོང་།
khō mā̃n-ki' thra̱'-song
"He got better thanks to the medicine."

8.3.3 Future auxiliaries

The future is formed by placing after the verb the particles: གི་རེད་ kire' (assertive) or གི་ཡིན་ kiyin (intentional egophoric). These are composed by adding the essential copula re' or yin to the suffix གི་ ki. In written Tibetan, གི་ki has several possible variants according to the final consonant of the preceding syllable. The pattern of these variants is the same as in the case of the genitive (see 4.3.2) except for vowels and the letter *'a*:

• after vowels and འ *'a,* ག *g,* ང *ng* > གི་ *gi* /khi̠/

• after ད *d,* བ *b,* ས *s* and the *second crypted suffix* ད *d* > ཀྱི་ *kyi* /kyī/

• after ན་*n,* མ་*m,* ར་*r,* ལ་ *l* > གྱི་ *gyi* /kyi̠/

In Spoken Tibetan, the suffix is pronounced ki in all cases.

The intentional form kiyin may be used only with volitional verbs in the first person. In interrogative sentences, the egophoric form གི་ཡིན་ kiyin is replaced by གས་ kä' if the statement contains no interrogative pronoun, and by ག ka otherwise.

The different forms are given in the following table:

The future auxiliaries

affirmative	interrogative (without pronoun)	interrogative (with pronoun)	negative	negative interrogative
གི་ཡིན་	གི་ཡིན་པས་ kiyin-pä'	ག་	གི་མིན་	གི་མིན་པས་
kiyin	གས་ kä'	ka	kimän	kimän-pä'
གི་རེད་	གི་རེད་པས་	གི་རེད་	གི་མ་རེད་	གི་མ་རེད་པས་
kire'	kire'-pä'	kire'	kimare'	kimare'-pä'

Ex.: སང་ཉིན་མོག་མོག་བཟོ་གི་ཡིན། sāngnyin mo̠mo' so̠-kiyin "Tomorrow I shall make momos."
སང་ཉིན་མོག་མོག་བཟོ་གི་རེད། sāngnyin mo̠mo' so̠-kire' "Tomorrow he/she will make momos."

8.3.4 The future forms of the verbs "to be" and "to have"

The copulas yö̠', tu̠', yo̠:re', etc. are not used in future constructions. Instead, the future forms of the full verbs ཆགས་ chā' "to become", བྱེད་ che̠' "to do", ཡོང་yo̠ng "to come"[103] and བསྡད་ tä̠' "to stay" are used. A distinction may be made between essential and existential statements.

A) Essential statements

• When the complement of the subject is a substantive (equative sense), Tibetan uses the following verbs: ཆགས་ཀྱི་རེད་chā'-kire' or བྱེད་ཀྱི་རེད་ che̠'-kire'.

Ex.: ཁོང་ཨེམ་ཆི་བྱེད་ཀྱི་རེད། khōng āmci che̠'-kire' "He/she will be a doctor."
མོ་རང་ནད་གཡོག་ཆགས་ཀྱི་རེད། mo̠rang nä̠yo' chā'-kire' "She will be a nurse."

• When the complement of the subject is an adjective, the following verbs are used: ཆགས་ཀྱི་རེད་chā'-kire' or ཡོང་གི་རེད་yo̠ng-kire'.

103. Note that *yong* may also mean "to be appropriate".

Ex.:	ལས་སླ་པོ་ཡོང་གི་རེད།	lä̱' lāpo yo̱ng-kire'	"It will be easy."
	སྐྱིད་པོ་ཆགས་ཀྱི་རེད།	kyīppo chā'-kire'	"It will be pleasant."

• If the gradual process of the future is to be stressed, the form ཆགས་ཡོང་གི་རེད་ is also used:

Ex.:	སྔོན་པོ་ཆགས་ཡོང་གི་རེད་	ngōnpo chā' yo̱ng-kire'	"It will turn blue."

B) Existential statements

A distinction may be made between expressions of situation, of existence and of possession.

• The verb "to be" in the sense of "to be located at" (situational sense) is translated by the future of the verb "to stay" བསྡད་ tä̱', or its honorific form བཞུགས་shu̱':

Ex.:	ང་ནང་ལ་བསྡད་ཀྱི་ཡིན།	nga̱ na̱ng-la tä̱'-kiyin	"I shall be (or stay) at home."
	ཁོང་རྒྱལ་སར་བཞུགས་ཀྱི་རེད།	khōng kyä̱:sar shu̱'-kire'	"He will be (or stay) in the capital."

• Possession and existence are expressed by using the future form of the verb ཡོང་ yo̱ng.

Ex.:	མོ་ལ་མཚེ་མ་ཡོང་གི་རེད།	mo̱la tshēma yo̱ng-kire'	"She will have twins."
	ཁོང་ལ་དངུལ་ཡོང་གི་རེད།	khōng-la ngǖ: yo̱ng-kire'	"He will have money."
	ཉོག་ཁྲ་ཡོང་གི་མ་རེད།	nyōktra yo̱ng-kimare'	"He won't have any problems."

8.3.5 The receptive egophoric past tense auxiliary བྱུང་ chu̱ng/-cung

The "receptive" auxiliary -cung is used only in the past tense. This auxiliary is associated with the first-person pronoun, whether this be the subject ("I"), the object ("me"), the indirect ("to me") or an adverbial ("at my place", etc.).

Ex.:	ང་ན་བྱུང་།	nga̱ na̱-cung	"I fell ill."
	ཁོས་ང་ལ་ཁ་པར་བཏང་བྱུང་།	khȫ' nga̱-la khāpar tāng-cung	"He phoned me."
	ཨ་ཁུ་ལགས་མཇལ་བྱུང་།	āku-la' cä̱: -cung	"I met our uncle."
	ཁོང་ངའི་རྩ་ལ་ཕེབས་བྱུང་།	khōng ngä̱:tsā-la phēp-cung	"He came to my place."

8.4 Exercises སྦྱོང་ཚན།

8.4.1 Fill in the brackets using the appropriate future form གི་རེད། གི་རེད་པས། གི་ཡིན། ག *or* གས། *(remember to use the proper form of the suffix* གི་*):*

༡) སང་ཉིན་ང་པོ་ཏ་ལར་འགྲོ་ ( )!
༢) ཁོང་སང་ཉིན་སློབ་གྲྭར་ཕེབས་ ( )?
༣) ཁྱེད་རང་སང་ཉིན་གླིང་ཀར་ཕེབས་ ( )?
༤) བློ་བཟང་ཨ་མེ་རི་ཀར་བཞུགས་ ( )?
༥) སང་ཉིན་མོ་རང་མོག་མོག་བཟོ་ ( )!
༦) ངས་ཡི་གེ་འབྲི་ ( )!
༧) ཁྱེད་རང་གཟིམ་ཤག་ལ་བཞུགས་ ( )?
༨) ཁོང་གིས་ཕྱག་བྲིས་གནང་ ( )?
༩) ང་ལྷ་སར་བསྡད་ ( )!
༡༠) ཁྱེད་རང་སང་ཉིན་ག་པར་ཕེབས་ ( )?
༡༡) དེབ་འདི་སུ་ལ་སྤྲད་ ( )?

8.4.2 Rewrite sentences 1-9 from Exercise 8.4.1 in the negative.

8.4.3 Complete the sentences using the appropriate form of the genitive or the agentive.

༡) འདི་སུ་ ( ) བཟོས་པ་རེད།
༢) འདི་རྡོ་རྗེ་ལགས་ ( ) བཟོས་གནང་པ་རེད།
༣) འདི་ཁྱེད་རང་ ( ) བཟོས་གནང་པས།
༤) འདི་ཁྱེད་རང་ ( ) དེབ་རེད་པས།
༥) ང་ ( ) ཁོང་ལ་ཕྱག་དེབ་ཅིག་ཕུལ་པ་ཡིན།
༦) ཁོང་ ( ) ང་ལ་མེ་ཏོག་གནང་བྱུང་།
༧) དཀར་ཡོལ་འདི་སུ་ ( ) རེད།
༨) ལམ་ཁག་གངས་ ( ) འགག་པ་རེད།

8.4.4 Translate into English:

༡) སྨྱུ་གུ་དང་སྣག་ཚ་སྤྲད་བྱུང་།
༢) ངས་ཁོང་ལ་ཞུས་པ་ཡིན།
༣) ཟླ་བ་ལགས་ཀྱིས་ང་ལ་ཕྱག་བྲིས་ཅིག་གནང་བྱུང་།
༤) ང་དགའ་པོ་ཞེ་དྲགས་བྱུང་།
༥) སྐྱིད་པོ་བྱུང་སོང་ངས།
༦) ཁོང་ལྡི་ལིར་ཕེབས་ཀྱི་རེད་པས།

8.4.5 Translate into Tibetan:

1. The cook made bread with meat stuffing.
2. I met your mother.
3. The doctor gave me some medicine.
4. His older brother loves chang.
5. My younger sister gave me a pen.
6. He wrote three words.

"What's your name?"

ཁྱེད་རང་གི་མཚན་ལ་ག་རེ་ཞུ་གི་ཡོད།

Grammar aims བརྡ་སྤྲོད་རིག་པའི་དམིགས་ཚད།

- Verb constructions: ergative, affective and possessive.
- The ablative case ནས་ -nä'.
- The associative case དང་ -tang.
- The present auxiliaries: གི་ཡོད་རེད་ -kiyo:re', གི་འདུག་ -kitu', གི་ཡོད་ -kiyö'.
- The interrogative pronouns ག་ནས་ kha̲nä' and ག་ཚོད་ kha̲tsö'.

CD I • Tr. 27-28 

9.1 Dialogue དྲི་བ་དྲིས་ལན།

ཟླ་ཟང་ ៖ རྡོ་རྗེ་ལགས། ཕྱག་ཕེབས་གནང་བྱུང་།

རྡོ་རྗེ་ ៖ ལགས་ཡོད། སྐུ་དཀྱིལ་གསལ་དྲགས།

ཟླ་བཟང་ ៖ ཁོང་ཚོ་ག་ནས་ཕེབས་པ་རེད།

རྡོ་རྗེ་ ៖ ཁོང་ཚོ་རྒྱལ་ཁབ་འདྲ་མི་འདྲ་ནས་ཕེབས་པ་རེད།

ཟླ་བཟང་ ៖ རྡོ་རྗེ་ལགས། ཁོང་ག་ནས་རེད། དབྱིན་ཇི་ནས་རེད་པས།

རྡོ་རྗེ་ ៖ མ་རེད། ཁོང་ཨ་མེ་རི་ཀ་ནས་རེད།

ཟླ་བཟང་ ៖ ཁྱེད་རང་གི་མཚན་ལ་ག་རེ་ཞུ་གི་ཡོད།

འཇོར་ཌོན་ ៖ ངའི་མིང་ལ་འཇོར་ཌོན་ཟེར་གྱི་ཡོད།

ཟླ་བཟང་ ៖ བཀྲ་ཤིས་བདེ་ལེགས། ངའི་མིང་ལ་ཟླ་བཟང་ཟེར་གྱི་ཡོད། ཁོང་ཚོ་ག་ནས་ཡིན་ན།

རྡོ་རྗེ་ ៖ ཁོང་ཚོ་ཕ་རན་སི་ནས་རེད། མཚན་ལ་མ་རི་དང་ཀ་རོ་ལིན་ཞུ་གི་ཡོད་རེད། ཁོང་གཉིས་ཉི་ཧོང་ནས་རེད། མཚན་ལ་ཡུ་ཀོ་དང་མ་ཀོ་ཧོ་ཞུ་གི་ཡོད་རེད། ཁོང་འཇར་མན་ནས་རེད། མཚན་ལ་ཏན་སི། ཁོང་རྒྱ་མི་རེད་ཧོང་ཀོང་ནས་རེད་མཚན་ལ་ལྷང་ཞུ་གི་ཡོད་རེད། ཁོང་གཉིས་ཨུ་རུ་སུ་ནས་རེད། མ་ཤ་དང་ཏ་ཤ་ཞུ་གི་ཡོད་རེད། ཁོང་ཚོ་བལ་ཡུལ་དང་རྒྱ་གར་ནས་རེད། མཚན་ལ་ར་མེ་ཤེ་དང་སུ་ནི་ཏ་ཞུ་གི་ཡོད་རེད། ཁོང་ཚོ་འབྲུག་ཡུལ་དང་སོག་ཡུལ་ནས་རེད། ཁོང་ཚོར་བོད་པའི་མིང་ཡོད་རེད། མཚན་ལ་ལྷག་པ་སྐྱབས་དང་དག་དབང་རྡོ་རྗེ་ཞུ་གི་ཡོད་རེད།

ཟླ་བཟང་ ៖ བོད་ལ་ཉི་མ་ག་ཚད་(ག་ཚོད་)བཞུགས་ཀྱི་རེད།

རྡོ་རྗེ་ ៖ བདུན་ཕྲག་གཅིག་ཙ་(ཙམ་) བཞུགས་ཀྱི་རེད།

Pronunciation

- to̱rce-la', chā'pe' nāng-cung,
- la̱' yö̱', kūkyi: sā̱:tang
- khōngtso kha̱nä' phēp-parä'
- khōngtso kyä̱:kap tra̱mintra-nä' phēp-pare'
- to̱rce'-la', khōng kha̱nä' rä̱', yīnci-nä' re̱'-pä'
- ma̱re', khōng āmerika-nä' re̱'
- khyērang-ki tshā̱n-la kha̱re shu̱-kiyö'
- ngä̱: mi̱ng-la co̱:n se̱r-kiyö'
- trāshi te̱le', ngä̱: mi̱ng-la lōsang se̱r-kiyö'
- khōngtso kha̱nä' yi̱n-na
- khōngtso phāränsi-nä' re̱', tshän-la mari-tang kārolin shu̱-kiyo:re'. khūnyi' nyi̱hong-nä' re̱' tshā̱n-la yu̱ko-tang ma̱koto shu̱-kiyo:re', khōng ca̱rmän-nä' re̱', tshän-la hānsi, khōng kya̱mi re̱' hōngkong-nä' re', tshā̱n-la wa̱ng shu̱-kiyo:re', khūnyi' ūrusu-nä' re̱', ma̱sha-tang tānya shu̱-kiyo:re'. khōngtso phä̱:yü:-tang kya̱kar-nä' re̱' tshā̱n-la ra̱mesh-tang sūnita shu̱-kiyo:re'. khōngtso tru̱'yü:- tang sō'yü:- nä' re̱' khōngtso-r phö̱pä: mi̱ng yo̱:re' lhākpakyap-tang nga̱wang to̱rce shu̱-kiyo:re'
- phö̱'-la nyi̱ma kha̱tsö' shu̱'-kirä'
- tü̱ntra' cī'-ts shu̱'-kire'

Translation

Lobzang — Dorje, welcome.
Dorje — Thanks, how are you? (Is the mandala of your body clear?)
Lobzang — Where are they from?
Dorje — They are (have come) from various countries.
Lobzang — Tell me Dorje, where's he from? Is he from England?
Dorje — No, he's from America.
Lobzang — What's your name?
John — My name's John.
Lobzang — How do you do, my name's Lobzang. And where are they from?
Dorje — They're French, and they're called Marie and Caroline. They're Japanese and they're called Yuko and Makoto. He's German, and he's called Hans. He's Chinese; he comes from Hong Kong and he's called Wang. They come from Russia and they're called Masha and Tania. Those come from India and Nepal. They're called Ramesh and Sunita. They come from Bhutan and Mongolia, and they have Tibetan names: Lhakpa Gyap and Ngawang Dorje.
Lobzang — How long (how many days) are they going to stay in Tibet?
Dorje — About a week.

ཀ་ཁ་ག་ང་

9.2 Vocabulary ཚིག་གསར།

མིང་ mi̱ng མཚན་ tshā̃n (H)	(n.) name
རྒྱལ་ཁབ་ kyä̱:kap	(n.) state, country
བདུན་ཕྲག་ tü̱ntra'	(n.) week
ག་ནས་ kha̱nä'	(pron.) from where?
ག་ཚད་ kha̱tsä' ག་ཚོད་ kha̱tsö' (L)	(pron.) how much, how many?
ཙ་ ts/ ཙམ་ tsām (L)	(part.) about
བར་དུ་ pha̱rtu	(post.) up to
འདྲ་མི་འདྲ་ tra̱mintra	(adj.) various
སྐུ་དཀྱིལ་གསལ་དྭངས་ kūkyi: sā̃:tang	(idiom.) how are you?
ཟེར་ se̱r ཞུ་ shu̱ (h)	(v.) [inv., DA] to call, to be called, named
ཞེད་ she̱'	(v.) [inv., AD] to be afraid

Names of countries:

Country		*Inhabitants*	
རྒྱ་ནག་ kya̱na'	China	རྒྱ་མི་ kya̱mi	Chinese
ཀྲུང་གོ་ trūngko	PRC	ཀྲུང་གོའི་མི་ trūngkö: mi̱	member of the PRC
རྒྱ་གར་ kya̱kar	India	རྒྱ་གར་བ་ kya̱karra	Indian
སོག་ཡུལ་ sō'yu̱:	Mongolia	སོག་པོ་ sōkpo	Mongol
བལ་ཡུལ་ phä̱:yü:	Nepal	བལ་པོ་ phä̱:po	Nepalese
འབྲུག་ཡུལ་ tru̱'yü:	Bhutan	འབྲུག་པ་ tru̱kpa	Bhutanese
ཏ་ཟིག་ tāsi'	Persia, Iran	ཏ་ཟིག་གི་མི་ tāsi'ki mi̱	Iranian
ཨུ་རུ་སུ་ ūrusu	Russia	ཨུ་རུ་སུའི་མི་ ūrusü: mi̱	Russia
འབར་མ་ pa̱rma	Burma, Myanmar	འབར་མའི་མི་ pa̱rmä: mi̱	Burmese
པ་ཀི་སི་ཏན་ pākisitän	Pakistan	པ་ཀི་སི་ཏན་གྱི་མི་ pākisitänki mi̱	Pakistani
ཉི་ཧོང་ nyi̱hong	Japan	ཉི་ཧོང་གི་མི་ nyi̱hongki mi̱	Japanese
ཨི་ཏ་ལི་ ītali	Italy	ཨི་ཏ་ལིའི་མི་ ītali: mi̱	Italian
སུད་སི་ sū̃si	Switzerland	སུད་སིའི་མི་ sū̃si: mi̱	Swiss
འཇར་མན་ ca̱rmän	Germany	འཇར་མན་གྱི་མི་ ca̱rmänki mi̱	German
ཕ་རན་སི་ phāränsi	France	ཕ་རན་སིའི་མི་ phāränsi: mi̱	French

དབྱིན་ཇི་ yīnci	England	དབྱིན་ཇིའི་མི་ yīnci: mi̱	English
ཨ་མེ་རི་ཀ་ āmerika	America	ཨ་མེ་རི་ཀ་པ་ āmerikawa	American[104]

The spelling of country names that have no standard written form reproduces the English or Chinese pronunciation.

Some languages:

རྒྱ་གར་སྐད་ kya̱kar kā̃'	Hindi	རྒྱ་སྐད་ kya̱kä'	Chinese
བལ་པོའི་སྐད་ phä̱:pö: kā̃'	Nepali	སོག་པོའི་སྐད་ sōkpö: kā̃'	Mongol
འབྲུག་པའི་སྐད་ tru̱kpä: kā̃'	Bhutanese	འབར་མའི་སྐད་ pa̱rmä: kā̃'	Burmese
ཏ་ཟིག་གི་སྐད་ tāsi'-ki kā̃'	Persian	ཉི་ཧོང་སྐད་ nyi̱hong kā̃'	Japanese
ཨུ་རུ་སུའི་སྐད་ ūrusü: kā̃'	Russian	ཨ་རབ་སྐད་ ārap kā̃'	Arabic
དབྱིན་ཇིའི་སྐད་ īnci: kā̃'	English	སེ་པན་སྐད་ sēpän kā̃'	Spanish
ཕ་རན་སིའི་སྐད་ phārānsi: kā̃'	French	འཇར་མན་སྐད་ ca̱rmän kā̃'	German
ཨི་ཏ་ལིའི་སྐད་ ītali: kā̃'	Italian		

9.3 Remarks འགྲེལ་བཤད།

9.3.1 Verb constructions

The ergative construction (see 8.4) is used by the following class of verbs:

A) All volitional transitive verbs:

- Verbs of action (e.g., བཟོ་ so̱ "to make"), verbs of speech (e.g., ལབ་ la̱p "to speak"), etc.
- Several verbs that are formed with the use of the transitive verbalizers[105] བཏང་ tāng "to send" (e.g., བསམ་བློ་བཏང་ sāmlo tāng "to think, reflect"), བྱེད་ che̱' "to do" (e.g., སེམས་ཁྲལ་བྱེད་ sēmträ: che̱' "to worry", གཟབ་གཟབ་བྱེད་ sa̱psap che̱' "to be careful"), etc.

B) Non-volitional transitive verbs:

- Certain verbs of perception (e.g., མཐོང་ thōng "to see", གོ་ kho̱ "to hear").
- Certain psychological verbs (e.g., བསམ་ sām "to think", བརྗེད་ ce̱' "to forget").

Verbs that require the particle ki' will be referred to as "ergative verbs".

---

104. The abbreviated form ཨ་རི་ āri is often used.

105. Verbalizers are "meaning-free" verbs such as "to do" which are combined with nouns to create a wide range of verbs. See Lesson 14.

Unlike volitional transitive verbs, which only govern ergative constructions, non-volitional transitive verbs may take several different kinds of constructions. Depending on the circumstances, non-volitional transitive verbs may require: the *ergative* construction, the *affective* construction and the *possessive* construction.

With non-volitional verbs, **ergative constructions** are identical to what we have already seen for volitional verbs: the subject is in the ergative case, while the object is in the absolutive.

S (Erg.)	O (Abs.)	V(ergative construction)
ཚེ་རིང་གིས་	རྟ་	མཐོང་པ་རེད།
tshēring-ki'	tā	thōng-pare'

"Tshering saw the horse."

Verbs that govern this type of construction will be identified as: inv(oluntary), E(rgative) A(bsolutive).

Ex.: མཐོང་ "to see" [inv., EA]

In **affective constructions,** the subject is in the absolutive and the object in the dative. The construction is governed mainly by verbs of feeling such as དགའ་ ka̲ "to like", ཞེད་ she̲' "to be afraid", ཚིག་པ་ཟ་ tshīkpa sa̲ "to get angry", ཧ་ལས་ hā lä̲' "to be amazed", etc.

S (Abs.)	O (Dat.)	V (affective construction)
ཚེ་རིང་	རྟ་ལ་	ཞེད་པ་རེད།
tshēring	tā-la	she̲'-pare'

"Tshering was afraid of the horse."

Verbs that govern this sort of construction will be identified as: inv(oluntary), A(bsolutive) D(ative).

Ex.: ཞེད་ "to be afraid" [inv., AD]

In **possessive constructions,** the subject is in the dative and the object in the absolutive. They are governed mainly by verbs relating to belonging or acquisition, such as ཐོབ་ thōp "to get", རག་ ra̲' "to find, acquire", སྐྱེ་ kyē' "to be born", རྨི་ལམ་བཏང་ mīlam tāng "to dream", etc.

S (Dat.)	O (Abs.)	V (possessive construction)
ཚེ་རིང་ལ་	རྟ་	བརྙེད་པ་རེད།
tshēring-la	tā	nyē'-pare'

"Tshering found the horse."

Verbs governing this kind of construction will be identified as: inv(oluntary), D(ative) A(bsolutive).

Ex.: བརྙེད་ "to find" [inv., DA]

9.3.2 *The ablative* ནས་ -nä'

• This invariable case-particle indicates spatial or temporal provenance.

Ex.:	ལྷ་ས་ནས་ཆབ་མདོ་བར་དུ།	lhāsa-nä' chāmto pha̱rtu	"from Lhasa to Chamdo"
	ཆུ་ཚོད་གསུམ་པ་ནས་ལྔ་པ་བར་དུ།	chūtsö' sūmpa-nä' ngāpa pha̱rtu	"from three to five o'clock"

N.B.: The ablative is often associated with verbs indicating acquisition, such as བརྙེད་ nyē' "to find", ཉོ་ nyo̱ "to buy", ཐོབ་ thōp "to obtain", གཡར་ yār "to borrow", རག་ ra̱' "to get, find", and verbs of movement such as འགྲོ་ tro̱ "to go".

Ex.:	ཁྲོམ་ནས་ཉོས་པ་རེད།	thrōm-nä' nyö̱'-pare'	"bought from the market"
	ལམ་ཁག་ནས་བརྙེད་བྱུང་།	la̱mka'-nä' nyē'-cung	"I found it on [lit. from] the road"
	འདི་ནས་འགྲོ།	ti̱-nä' tro̱	"go through [lit. from] here"

• When it follows an animate being, the ablative may also assume the role of the ergative, and thus becomes a marker for the **agent of the action.** Used in this way, it is the same as the agentive case. While this usage is common in Literary Tibetan, it is rare in the spoken language.

Ex.: རིན་པོ་ཆེ་ནས་བཀའ་སློབ་གནང་སོང་། ri̱npoche-nä' kālop nāng song
"Rinpoche[106] gave a teaching."

གཞུང་ནས་ཁོང་ལ་ཕོགས་ག་ཚོད་རྒྱག་གི་འདུག shūng-nä' khōng-la phō' kha̱tsö' kya̱'-kitu'
"What (lit. how much) salary does the government give him?"

• The particle -nä' may be used in the composition of postpositions and adverbs.

Ex.: ཐོག་ནས་ thō'-nä' adverbalizer, "in an X way", སྒོ་ནས་ ko̱-nä' adverbalizer "in an X way", ཁྱོན་ནས་ khyōn-nä' "absolutely (not)", ཙ་བ་ནས་ tsāwa-nä' "absolutely (not)", etc.

As in the other cases, the particle -nä' may function as a **subordinating conjunction.** When used in this way it means "after", "then", "because", or it may be used to form gerundives (see 14.4).

9.3.3 *The associative case* དང་ tha̱ng/ -tang.

• This particle, which we have met earlier, is used mainly as a coordinating conjunction (or connective) meaning "and"; however, it also corresponds to a case, the **associative**, which is generally translated as "with" or "against", or else is not translated at all. In the spoken language, this case-related function is little used (for the literary language, see section 3.3 in Appendix 1).

106. A title, accorded to certain lamas, meaning "precious".

• The particle -tang is usually unstressed, and attached to the preceding word. However, on certain occasions it is stressed, in which case it is pronounced: tha̱ng.

Contrary to normal practice in the European languages and in Chinese, Tibetan inserts a pause (when one is required) *after,* not before, the conjunction. In fact, the particle -tang is often followed by a punctuation mark, the *kyang-shad,* which indicates a pause.

Ex.: པ་ལགས་དང་། ཨ་ཁུ་དང་། ཨ་ནེ། pāla'-tang āku-tang āni "the father, the uncle and the aunt"

To reproduce the Tibetan rhythm, we would have to say: "the father and… the uncle and… the aunt".

• The conjunction -tang is distributive with respect to case and number. This means that the noun group which precedes it has no number or case marker: these markers appear only once, at the end of the whole group. Thus in the following examples, the plural marker appears only once.

Ex.: ཨ་མ་དང་སྤུ་གུ་ཚོ། āma-tang pūkutso "the mother and the children"
(Tibetan would not say: ཨ་མ་ཚོ་དང་སྤུ་གུ་ཚོ་ āmatso-tang pūkutso.)

In the following examples, the case marker appears only once:

Ex.: བུ་དང་བུ་མོ་ཚོར་ལག་རྟགས་སྤྲད་པ་རེད། phu̱-tang phu̱motso-r la̱kta' trǟ'-pare'
"(They) gave presents to the boys and (to the) girls."
ཚེ་རིང་དང་བློ་བཟང་གིས་ཨ་རག་བཏུངས་སོང་། tshēring-tang lōsang-ki' āra' tūng'-song
"Tshering and Lobzang drank some alcohol."

• In the spoken language, the associative case applies to a very limited number of verbs. Furthermore, it may sometimes be replaced by other cases such as the absolutive or the oblique. Here are some verbs that still take this case in oral usage:

མཐུན་པོ་ thūnpo "to get on with", འགལ་ kä̱: "to break (a law)", བརྗེ་ ce̱' "to exchange (for)" ནོར་ no̱r "to mistake (for)", ཁག་ཁག་བྱེད་ khā'ka' che̱' "to separate (from)", and certain adverbial constructions: མཉམ་པོ་ nyāmpo "with", etc.

Ex.: རྩམ་པ་དང་བརྗེ་གི་ཡོད། tsāmpa-tang ce̱'-kiyö'
"I exchange it for tsampa."

ཚེ་རིང་བློ་བཟང་དང་མཐུན་པོ་འདུག tshēring lōsang-tang thūnpo tu̱'
"Tshering gets on well with Lobzang."

ངས་མོ་དང་ཁག་ཁག་བྱེད་ཀྱི་ཡིན། ngä̱' mo̱-tang khā'ka' che̱'-kiyin
"I'm going to separate from her."

9.3.4 Present tense auxiliaries

The present tense is formed by placing after the verb the particles: གི་ཡོད་རེད་ kiyo:re' (assertive), གི་འདུག kitu' (testimonial) and གི་ཡོད་ kiyö' (egophoric). These are formed by adding an existential copula to the suffix གི་. The resulting auxiliaries have the same evidential value as the existential copulas. In modern conversational usage, the form གི་འདུག་ kitu' is often abbreviated to གིས་ ki'.

In English, these forms may be translated either by the progressive or the simple present depending on the context.

The various forms are presented in the following table:

The present tense auxiliaries

affirmative	interrogative (without pronouns)	interrogative (with pronouns)	negative	negative interrogative
གི་ཡོད་ kiyö'	གི་ཡོད་པས་ kiyö'-pä'	གི་ཡོད་ kiyö'	གི་མེད་ kime'	གི་མེད་པས་ kime'-pä'
གི་འདུག་/གིས kitu'/ki'	གི་འདུག་གས་ kitu'-kä'	གི་འདུག་ kito'	གི་མི་འདུག་ kimintu'	གི་མི་འདུག་གས་ kimintu'-kä'
གི་ཡོད་རེད་ kiyo:re'	གི་ཡོད་རེད་པས་ kiyo:re'-pä'	གི་ཡོད་རེད་ kiyo:rä:	གི་ཡོད་མ་རེད་ kiyo:mare'	གི་ཡོད་མ་རེད་པས་ kiyo:mare'-pä'

Ex.: ང་ཁ་ལག་བཟོ་གི་ཡོད། nga̲ khāla' so̲-kiyö'

"I am preparing the meal." or "I prepare the meal." (egophoric)

ང་ཡི་གེ་འབྲི་གི་ཡོད། nga̲ yi̲ke tri̲-kiyö'

"I am writing a letter." or "I write letters." (egophoric)

བློ་བཟང་ཁ་ལག་བཟོ་གི་ཡོད་རེད། lōsang- khāla' so̲ kiyo:re'

"Lobzang prepares food." or "Lobzang is preparing food." (assertive)

བློ་བཟང་ཁ་ལག་བཟོ་གི (འདུག) lōsang- khāla' so̲-kitu'

"Lobzang is preparing food." or "Lobzang prepares food." (testimonial)

རྡོ་རྗེ་ཡི་གེ་འབྲི་གི་ཡོད་རེད། to̲rce yi̲ke tri̲-kiyo:re'

"Dorje writes letters." or "Dorje is writing a letter." (assertive)

རྡོ་རྗེ་ཡི་གེ་འབྲི་གི (འདུག) to̲rce yi̲ke tri̲-kitu'

"Dorje is writing a letter." or "Dorje writes letters." (testimonial)

9.4 Exercises སྦྱོང་ཚན།

9.4.1 Complete the following sentences with the use of present auxiliaries.

༡) ཁྱེད་རང་ག་རེ་གནང་ (   )?

༢) ང་ཡི་གེ་འབྲི་ (   )!

༣) རྡོ་རྗེ་ག་རེ་བྱེད་ (   )?

༤) ཁོང་ཡི་གེ་འབྲི་ (   )!

༥) རྡོ་རྗེ་ཡི་གེ་འབྲི་ (   )?

༦) ཁྱེད་རང་ག་པར་བཞུགས་ (   )?

༧) ང་བྲེ་ཞིང་ལ་བསྡད་ (   )!

༨) ཁྱེད་རང་གཞིས་ཀ་རྩེར་བཞུགས་ (   )?

9.4.2 Rewrite the following sentences in the testimonial mood (using the auxiliaries song, kitu' *or* tu' *as appropriate).*

༡) ཁོང་གིས་ཡི་གེ་བྲིས་པ་རེད།

༢) ཨ་མས་མོག་མོག་བཟོས་པ་རེད་པས།

༣) སྒྲོལ་དཀར་ག་རེ་བྱེད་ཀྱི་ཡོད་རེད།

༤) བླ་མའི་སྐུ་པར་ག་པར་ཡོད་རེད།

༥) རྡོ་རྗེ་གླིང་ཀར་ཕྱིན་པ་རེད།

༦) ཉི་མ་ལགས་ག་པར་བཞུགས་ཀྱི་ཡོད་རེད།

༧) བོད་ལ་བྱ་རྒོད་ཡོད་མ་རེད་པས།

༨) ཁོས་ག་རེ་བྱས་པ་རེད།

༩) ཨ་མ་ལགས་ཞིང་ཁར་ཕེབས་པ་རེད།

9.4.3 Translate into Tibetan:

1. Tomorrow my son will not go to school.
2. She gave the teacher flowers.
3. The teacher gave me a book.
4. I love momos.
5. Nyima prepared the meal.
6. It's really delicious.

9.4.4 Rewrite the sentences following the example given:

ཁོང་ག་ནས་ཕེབས་པ་རེད།(པེ་ཅིང་) > ཁོང་པེ་ཅིང་ནས་ཕེབས་པ་རེད།

༡) སྒྲོལ་དཀར་པ་གིར་ཉི་མ་ག་ཚོད་བསྡད་པ་རེད།(བདུན་ཕྲག་ཅིག)

༢) ཉི་མ་ག་པར་ཕྱིན་སོང་།(གླིང་ཀ་)

༣) བློ་བཟང་ག་ནས་ཡོང་པ་རེད།(བལ་ཡུལ་)

༤) ཨ་མས་ཁ་ལག་ག་རེ་བཟོས་སོང་།(ཤ་འབྲས་)

༥) མོག་མོག་འདི་ཚོ་སུས་བཟོས་པ་རེད།(ང་)

9.4.5 Translate into English:

ཁྱེད་ རང་ ག་ པར་ ཕེབས་ ག ང་ ཡར་ འགྲོ་ གི་ ཡིན། ཁྱེད་ རང་ ག་ ནས་ ཡིན་ པ། ང་ གཞིས་ ཀ་ རྩེ་ ནས་ ཡིན། སྐུ་ གཟུགས་ བདེ་ པོ་ ཡིན་ པས། བདེ་ པོ་ ཡིན། ཐུགས་ རྗེ་ ཆེ། ཁྱེད་ རང་ ག་ ནས་ ཕེབས་ པ། ང་ རྒྱ་ གར་ ནས་ ཡོང་ པ་ ཡིན། ཁྱེད་ རང་ ལ་ པར་ ག་ ཚོད་ ཡོད། ངར་ པར་ གསུམ་ ཡོད།

9.4.6 Complete the following sentences by inserting the appropriate case particles in the brackets.

༡) ངའི་གྲོགས་པོ་ (   ) ཤ་འབྲས་ (   ) དགའ་པོ་ཡོད་རེད།

༢) བློ་བཟང་ (   ) པར་ཆས་ཅིག་ (   ) འདུག

༣) ཁྱེད་རང་གི་མིང་ (   ) ག་རེ་ (   ) ཟེར་གྱི་ཡོད།

༤) སྒྲོལ་དཀར་ (   ) གཡག་ (   ) ཞེད་སོང་།

༥) ཐུབ་བསྟན་ (   ) ཡི་གེ་ (   ) བྲིས་སོང་།

"What are you doing these days?"

དེང་སང་ག་རེ་བྱེད་ཀྱི་ཡོད།

Grammar aims བརྡ་སྤྲོད་རིག་པའི་དམིགས་ཚད།

- The notion of verb aspect.
- Verb inflection.
- Auxiliary verbs and the system of tenses.
- The past (perfect) tense auxiliaries: ཡོད་ -yö̱'; བཞག་-sha' (or འདུག་-tu̱'), ཡོད་རེད་ -yo̱:re'.
- The interrogative pronoun ག་དུས་ kha̱tü'.
- Alternative interrogative forms.

CD I • Tr. 29-30 

10.1 Dialogue དྲི་བ་དྲིས་ལན།

རྡོ་རྗེ་ ཿ	བློ་བཟང་ལགས་བཞུགས་འདུག་གས།
སྒྲོལ་དཀར་ ཿ	ལགས་བཞུགས་བཞག ཡར་ཆིབས་སྒྱུར་གནང་གོ བློ་བཟང་ལགས། འདའི་(འདིར་)ཅིག་ཕེབས་སོང་།
བློ་བཟང་ ཿ	ཨོ། རྡོ་རྗེ་རེད་པ། བདེ་པོ་ཡིན་པས།
རྡོ་རྗེ་ ཿ	བདེ་པོ་ཡིན། ཁྱེད་རང་།
བློ་བཟང་ ཿ	བདེ་ཐག་ཆོད། དེང་སང་ག་རེ་བྱེད་ཀྱི་ཡོད།
རྡོ་རྗེ་ ཿ	སླབ་གྲྭར་(སློབ་གྲྭར་)འགྲོ་གི་ཡོད།
བློ་བཟང་ ཿ	གུང་སང་ག་དུས་རེད།
རྡོ་རྗེ་ ཿ	ཟླ་བ་རྗེས་མ་རེད།
སྒྲོལ་དཀར་ ཿ	གསོལ་ཇ་བཀྲུག་ག། ཁོ་ཕི་བཀྲུག་ག།
རྡོ་རྗེ་ ཿ	གསོལ་ཇ་གང་ཞུ་གི་ཡིན།
བློ་བཟང་ ཿ	ཆང་འཐུང་གི་མན་(མིན་)པས།
རྡོ་རྗེ་ ཿ	ལགས་མན། ཆང་འཐུང་གི་མན་(མིན་)།
བློ་བཟང་ ཿ	ཨ་མ་ལགས་མཆོད་ཆང་མཆོད་ཀྱི་རེད་པས།
རྡོ་རྗེ་ ཿ	ཁྲིན་ནས་མཆོད་ཀྱི་མ་རེད།

Pronunciation

- lōsang-la shu̱'-tu'-kä'

- la' shu̱'-sha' ya̱r chīpkyur nāngko, lōsang-la' tä̱: cī' phēp-song

- ō to̱rce re̱'-wa, te̱po yi̱npä

- te̱po yi̱n, khyērang?

- te̱ thākcö' the̱ngsang kha̱re che̱'-kiyö'

- lāptrar tro̱-kiyö'

- khu̱ngsang kha̱tü' rä̱'

- ta̱wa ce̱mar re̱'

- sȫ:ca kyā'-ka khōpi kyā'-ka

- sȫ:ca kha̱ng shu̱-kiyin

- chāng thūng-kimä̱n-pä

- la̱' mä̱n, chāng thūng-kimän

- āmala' chȫcang chȫ'-kire'-pä'

- khyȫnä' chȫ'-kimare'

Translation

Dorje	—	Is Lobzang there (lit.: has he stayed)?
Drölkar	—	Yes, he's here. Please come in. Lobzang, someone's come!
Lobzang	—	Oh, it's Dorje, isn't it? How are you?
Dorje	—	Fine, and you?
Lobzang	—	Very well indeed. What are you doing these days?
Dorje	—	I'm going to school.
Lobzang	—	When are the holidays?
Dorje	—	Next month.
Drölkar	—	Shall I bring some tea or coffee?
Dorje	—	I'll have a cup of tea.
Lobzang	—	Won't you have some *chang?*
Dorje	—	No thanks, I won't have any *chang*.
Lobzang	—	Will your mother have some *chang*?
Dorje	—	No, she never drinks

ཀ་ཁ་ག་ང་

10.2 Vocabulary ཚིག་གསར།

གུང་སང་ khu̱ngsang གུང་སེང་ khu̱ngseng (L)	(n.) holidays, vacation
བདེ་ཐག་ཆོད་ te̱ thākcö'	(n.) very well indeed
དེང་སང་ the̱nsang	(n.) these days
ཁོ་ཕི་ khōpi	(n.) coffee

ལས་ཀ་ la̲ka ཕྱག་ལས་ chā'lä' (H) — (n.) work
ཁང་ kha̲ng — (class.) one, a unit
ཅིག་ cī' — (pron.) someone
ག་དུས་ kha̲tü' — (pron. interr.) when?
ག་ -ka — (part.) *"alternative" particle*
འདི་ ta̲: འདིར་ ti̲r (L) — (adv.) here
ཁྱོན་ནས་ khyōnnä' — (adv.) not at all, never. (+ neg.)
ཐག་ཆོད་ thā'cö' — (suff.) very, really[107]
ཡར་ཆིབས་སྐྱུར་གནང་གོ་ ya̲r chīpkyur nāng-ko (HH) — (idiom.) come in!
རེད་པ་ re̲'-pa, re̲'-wa — (aux.) isn't it, isn't that so?
ཟ་ sa̲ (1) / བཟས་ sa̲' (2) / ཟོས་ so̲ (3) — (v.) [vol., EA] to eat
འཐུང་(1) thūng / བཏུངས་tūng'(2) / འཐུངས་thūng'(3) — (v.) [vol., EA] to drink
མཆོད་ chō' (H) — (v.) [vol., EA] to eat, drink
ལེན་ le̲n བཞེས་ she̲' (H) — (v.) [vol., EA] to take
བཀྱག་ kyā' — (v.) [vol., EA] to bring
སློབ་སྦྱོང་ + བྱེད་ lōpcong che̲' — (v.) [vol., EA] to study
ལས་ཀ་ + བྱེད་ la̲ka che̲' — (v.) [vol., E] to work
སྦྱངས་ ca̲ng' — (v.) [vol., EA] to learn
བསླབས་ lāp — (v.) [vol., EA] to teach

10.3 Remarks འགྲེལ་བཤད།

10.3.1 The notion of verb aspect

The notion of aspect is essential for learning the system of verb "tenses" in most of the world's languages. In view of the importance of aspect in Tibetan, it may be good to have a working definition of the term, following a reminder of what we mean by "tense".

Tense is defined most immediately with respect to the moment of speech utterance. Whatever precedes this moment is the past; everything that coincides with it is the present; and whatever follows it is the future.

Aspect is concerned primarily with whether the action has or has not been completed with respect to a given point of reference (past, present or future). According to the chosen perspective, the process is regarded as **perfective,** that is completed, or else as **imperfective,** meaning that it is still going on or is a habitual event. (In either case the point of reference need not be the

107. This is an adjectival suffix. The category is dealt with in Lesson 17.

present.) This explains why, in many languages, the imperfective bears a strong resemblance to the present: both the present and the imperfective past are non-completed.[108] The action is regarded as still going on, and is seen as being incomplete from a given point of reference (respectively, the present and the future). In Tibetan, the present and the imperfective past are identical, whereas the perfective past is entirely different (see Lesson 6.4).

Only context makes it possible to distinguish between the present and the past imperfective. For example, the sentences below convey a present meaning.

Ex.: རྒྱལ་མཚན་ལགས་ཨེམ་ཆི་རེད། kyä̱ntsän-la' ēmci re̱'
"Gyäntshän is a doctor."

ཁོང་ཉམས་ལེན་མང་པོ་བྱེད་ཀྱི་ཡོད་རེད། khōng nya̱mlen ma̱ngpo che̱'-kiyo:re'
"He practices a lot."[109]

ཁོང་ལྷ་སར་ཡོད་རེད། khōng lhāsar yo̱:re'
"He is in Lhasa."

ཚེ་རིང་དཔེ་མཛོད་ཁང་ནང་ལ་ལས་ཀ་བྱེད་ཀྱི་ཡོད་རེད། tshēring pēntsökang na̱ng-la lä̱ka che̱'-ki yo:re'
"Tshering works in the library."

However, if each of these sentences were preceded by དེ་དུས་ the̱tü' ("at that time") or སྔན་མ་ ngā̱ma, they would correspond to the past imperfective (without any transformation of the verb).

Ex.: དེ་དུས་རྒྱལ་མཚན་ལགས་ཨེམ་ཆི་རེད།
the̱tü' kyä̱ntsän ēmci re̱'
"At that time, Gyäntshän was a doctor." (same as: Gyäntshän is a doctor)

དེ་དུས་ཁོང་ལྷ་སར་ཡོད་རེད།
the̱tü' khōng lhāsar yo̱:re'
"At that time he was in Lhasa." (same as: is in Lhasa)

དེ་དུས་ཁོང་ཉམས་ལེན་མང་པོ་བྱེད་ཀྱི་ཡོད་རེད།
the̱tü' khōng nya̱mlen ma̱ngpo che̱'-kiyore'
"At that time, he used to practice a lot." (same as: He practices a lot)

སྔན་མ་ཚེ་རིང་དཔེ་མཛོད་ཁང་ནང་ལ་ལས་ཀ་བྱེད་ཀྱི་ཡོད་རེད།
ngā̱ma tshēring pēntsökang na̱ng-la lä̱ka che̱'-ki yo̱:re'
"Before, Tshering worked / used to work in the library."

"Perfective" means that an action is regarded as being finished (from a present, past or even future point of reference).[110]

---

108. In English for example, the progressive formed with the present participle "ing" and the auxiliary "be" corresponds to an imperfective aspect. The progressive past, present and future are all formed with the same present participle. I.e.: was practic-**ing**, is practic-**ing** and will be practic-**ing**.

109. In the present and the future, the mark for the agent is often left out. See the "remarks" section in Lesson 12.

110. More precisely, with the imperfective aspect, no limit of the process is overstepped or reached, while with the

The last two examples become in the perfective past:

Ex.: ཁོང་གིས་ཉམས་ལེན་མང་པོ་བྱས་པ་རེད། khōng-ki' nya̱mlen ma̱ngpo chä̱'-pare'
"He practiced a lot."

ཚེ་རིང་གིས་དཔེ་མཛོད་ཁང་ནང་ལ་ལས་ཀ་བྱས་པ་རེད། tshēring-ki' pēntsökang na̱ng-la lä̱ka chä̱'-pare'
"Tshering worked in the library."

• The perfective aspect may be subdivided into perfect and aorist (or non-perfect). The perfect signifies that the effects of an action performed in the past are still relevant at the moment the statement is made, while in the case of the aorist, the past action being referred to bears no relationship to the present moment.[111]

In Tibetan, as in English, there is a grammatical opposition between aorist and perfect.

In English, the aorist is marked by the preterite while the perfect is marked by the "present perfect".[112]

Ex.: ཁ་ལག་བཙོས་ཡོད། khāla' sö̱'-yö'
"I've prepared the meal." (it's ready, we can eat)

ཁ་ལག་བཙོས་པ་ཡིན། khāla' sö̱'-payin
"I prepared the meal." (last time, some time ago, etc.)

The perfect aspect will be described in detail below in 10.3.3.

10.3.2 Verb inflection

In Classical Tibetan many verbs have up to four different root forms (see Appendix 1). Spoken Tibetan makes indiscriminate use of verb stem forms that correspond to the "future" and the "present" in Literary Tibetan, and at the most only distinguishes between two tenses: the **past** and the **present-future**. While some verbs also have a distinctive imperative stem, in most cases this stem resembles either the present-future or the past. Very often, the verb is quite simply **invariable** (see Appendix 1, section 3.6).

---

perfective the final limit (or sometimes the initial limit) has been reached. The above definition is based on D. Cohen's theory in *l'Aspect verbal* (1989). Let us quote here also Comrie's definition of these aspects: "The imperfective pays essential attention to the internal structure of the situation". "Perfectivity indicates the view of a situation as a single whole" Comrie (1987: 16).

The French imparfait, Spanish imperfecto, Russian imperfective (nesoveršennyj vid), the English progressive all bear the basic features of the imperfective, while the French passé composé, the Russian perfective (soveršennyj vid), the Spanish preterito all bear the basic features of the perfective. The English preterite however is neutral and may be translated depending on the context either by perfective or imperfective forms in other languages.

111. The opposition between the perfect and the aorist in Tibetan corresponds to the oppostion we find in literary French between the passé composé and the passé simple; in English between the present perfect and the preterite, and in Spanish between the preterite and the passado compuesto "composed past".

112. In Tibetan, however, this opposition is not as pervasive as in English. The simple past perfective may convey both perfect and aorist meanings in the absence of specific perfect form.

The large number of invariable verbs means that inflection is practically obsolete in the spoken language. Tenses are formed by using a system of auxiliaries. In this Manual, the present-future stem form will be marked by the number (1), the past by (2) and the imperative by (3).

10.3.3 The perfect auxiliaries

ཡོད་རེད་ yo̱:re', བཞག sha̱' (or འདུག་tu̱') and ཡོད་ yö̱' are directly connected to the past tense form of the main verb. These auxiliaries respectively represent the three evidential moods: assertive, inferential and egophoric.

Ex.: ཁང་པ་གསར་པ་མང་པོ་བརྒྱབ་ཡོད་རེད། khāngpa sārpa ma̱ngpo kya̱p yo̱:re'
"Many new houses have been built."

ཁང་པ་གསར་པ་མང་པོ་བརྒྱབ་བཞག khāngpa sārpa ma̱ngpo kya̱p-sha'
"Look! Many new houses have been built."

ངས་ཇ་བཟོས་ཡོད། ngä̱' cha̱ sö̱'-yö̱'
"I've made the tea."

The range of the perfect forms is presented in the following table:

The perfect tense auxiliaries

affirmative	interrogative (without pronouns)	interrogative (with pronouns)	negative	negative interrogative
ཡོད་ yö̱'	ཡོད་པས་ yö̱'-pä'	ཡོད་ yö̱'	མེད་ me̱'	མེད་པས་ me̱'-pä'
བཞག་ / འདུག་ sha̱'/tu̱'	འདུག་གས་ tu̱'-kä'	འདུག་ to̱'	མི་འདུག་ mi̱ntu'	མི་འདུག་གས་ mi̱ntu'-kä'
ཡོད་རེད་ yo̱:re'	ཡོད་རེད་པས་ yo̱:re'-pä'	ཡོད་རེད་ yo̱:rä'	ཡོད་མ་རེད་ yo̱:mare'	ཡོད་མ་རེད་པས་ yo̱:mare'-pä'

• The inferential perfect.

The auxiliary བཞག *bzhag* /sha̱'/ is sometimes spelled *shag* ཤག་ /shā'/, but here we shall use the former spelling for etymological reasons: the word is derived from the verb *bzhag*, which means "to put, leave".

As a general rule, the use of the form -sha' (or its variant tu̱') implies that the speaker is making an "inference" or a deduction in discovering the result or the enduring traces of a past action. Most of the time, the inferential mode may be translated into English by adding "Look!", "My!" or "Why!" to the beginning of a statement in the past tense. In the example given above, it's *upon discovering* a construction site in a sector of Lhasa that the speaker says "Why, they've built a lot of new houses!" In certain contexts, the form -sha' may have another, purely resultative connotation: the speaker may use it to emphasize the enduring presence of a past action, even if he or she has been able to see not just these traces but the entirety of the action that is being described.

Ex.: བློ་བཟང་ལགས་འདིར་བཞུགས་བཞག "Lobzang is here (lit. has stayed here)."

In this statement, the speaker has just discovered Lobzang's presence either by seeing him directly or from various clues (his hat, for example). Alternatively, he might have been aware of his presence for some time but is emphasizing the fact that he is *still* around.

• The assertive perfect

The assertive perfect refers to a past action or event with current relevance. Its evidential function is to convey certainty though the speaker does not claim to have personally witnessed the event.

Ex.: ཁང་པ་གསར་པ་མང་པོ་བརྒྱབ་ཡོད་རེད། khāngpa sārpa ma̲ngpo kya̲p yo̲:re'
"Many new houses have been built."

• The egophoric perfect

Unlike the inferential perfect (and to a certain extent the assertive perfect), the egophoric perfect auxiliary is not widely used. The use of this auxiliary is a complex matter, and it is restricted to a small class of volitional verbs. For example, with the non-volitional verbs ན་ na "to be sick" or མཐོང་ thong "to see", the egophoric perfect aspect may not be used. Even some volitional verbs such as ཟ་ "eat", བལྟ་ "look" are not compatible with the egophoric perfect. In this case, one must instead use the perfective forms.

Ex.: ང་ན་བྱུང་། nga̲ na̲-cung "I fell ill, I have fallen ill."
and not * ང་ན་ཡོད།

ངས་མཐོང་བྱུང་། nga̲' thōng-cung "I saw, I have seen."
and not * ངས་མཐོང་ཡོད།

ངས་ཁ་ལག་བཟས་པ་ཡིན། nga̲' khāla' sa̲'-payin "I ate, I have eaten the food."
and not * ངས་ཁ་ལག་བཟས་ཡོད།

ང་ཕྱིན་པ་ཡིན། nga̲ chīn-payin "I have gone (there)."
and not * ང་ཕྱིན་ཡོད།

However with some volitional verbs[113] such as བཟོ་ "prepare", འབྲི་ "write", སྡོད་ "stay", etc. the egophoric aspect frequently occurs.

Ex.: ངས་ཁ་ལག་བཟོས་ཡོད། nga̲' khāla' so̲' yö' "I have prepared the food." (the food is here, ready)
ངས་ཡི་གེ་བྲིས་ཡོད། nga̲' yi̲ke thri̲'-yö' "I have written the letter." (the letter is here)

113. In most cases, the compatibility of the perfect depends on whether the object of the transitive verb (or the subject of an intransitive verb) exists objectively after the completion of the action and is still present.

ང་ནང་ལ་བསྡད་ཡོད། nga̲ na̲ng-la tä̲'-yö' "I have stayed at home." (I am still there)

Note: The negative forms of the egophoric and assertive perfect auxiliaries are more widely used than the affirmative forms. They are often even preferred to the simple perfective, and may occur with non-volitional verbs. Thus, negation in the past tense blurs the distinction between the perfect and perfective aspects.

For example, ང་ཕྱིན་མེད། "I haven't gone" is more commonly heard than ང་མ་ཕྱིན།, and similarly, ཁོང་ཕེབས་ཡོད་མ་རེད། "He hasn't gone" rather than ཁོང་མ་ཕེབས་པ་རེད།.

Nevertheless, perfective forms may be used to emphasize the subject's refusal to perform the action: ང་(ངས་)མ་ཕྱིན། "I didn't go (even though I was supposed to)."[114].[deontic modality]

10.3.4 Auxiliary verbs and the system of tenses

Tense-aspects are formed by combining two kinds of marker: verb inflection, as described above, and the use of a system of final auxiliaries. In view of the large number of invariable verbs, oral Tibetan makes extensive use of these auxiliaries. The latter indicate both the **tense-aspect** and the **evidential nature** of a given statement, which thereby reveals the source of information from which its authority is derived.

As far as tense-aspect is concerned, Tibetan distinguishes: future, present (similar to the imperfective past), perfective past and perfect.

Reminder: auxiliaries usually go after the main verb, i.e., at the end of the sentence and only rarely within subordinate clauses.

The system of auxiliary verbs is summarized in Table 3 of Appendix 6.

10.3.5 Auxiliary verbs and evidential modalities

Auxiliaries have the same evidential categories as copulas (see 5.3 and 6.3): testimonial, assertive, egophoric and inferential.

A) The assertive

The assertive corresponds to a definite item of information, or else a historical or general truth (see Lesson 5.3). This mood may be used in all the tenses: future གི་རེད་, present གི་ཡོད་རེད་ and past པ་རེད་. Note that the present includes forms similar to the future that denote a habitual state of affairs or a general truth (see Lesson 24.3).

Ex.: གངས་བཏང་གི་རེད། kha̲ng' tāng-kire' "It's going to snow."

---

114. The ergative case is sometimes used with intransitive volitional verbs in order to put an emphasis on the subject. (see Lesson 12).

གངས་བཏང་པ་རེད།	khang' tāng-pare'	"It's snowed." or "it snowed." (a definite fact)

ལྷ་སར་གངས་མང་པོ་བཏང་གི་ཡོད་མ་རེད། lhāsar khang' mangpo tāng-kiyo:mare'
"In Lhasa, it doesn't snow much." (general fact)

ཁོས་རི་མོ་སྙིང་རྗེ་པོ་ཅིག་བྲིས་པ་རེད། khō' rimo nyīng cepo cī' thri'-pare'
"He drew a pretty picture." (definite fact).

༡༩༦༩ ལོར་མིས་ཟླ་བའི་སྟེང་ལ་གོམ་པ་བརྒྱབ་པ་རེད།
chīktōng kupkya thrukcu reku lor mi' tawä: kang-la kompa kyap-pare'
"In 1969, man walked on the moon." (historical fact)

B) The testimonial

The testimonial specifies that the speaker is personally a witness to what he or she is stating to be the case. The authority is usually visual, but may also be aural or derived from any of the other senses (touch, smell or taste). This mood appears only in the present with གི་འདུག་ and in the past with སོང་. It does not appear in future constructions because of the impossibility of witnessing what hasn't already happened!

Ex.: གངས་བཏང་སོང་། khang' tāng-song "It snowed." (I saw it snowing)
གངས་བཏང་གི་འདུག khang' tāng-kitu' "It's snowing." (I can see it snowing)
རི་མོ་སྙིང་རྗེ་པོ་ཅིག་བྲིས་སོང་། rimo nyīng cepo cī' thri'-song
"He drew a pretty picture." (I saw him drawing it)

With volitional verbs and most non-volitional verbs, the testimonial mood is used *essentially for the second and third persons* (singular and plural), except in special instances of self-observation (looking in the mirror, dreaming, watching a video recording of oneself, etc.) or performing involuntary actions.

Ex.: ང་ནོར་བུ་གླིང་ཀར་འགྲོ་གི་འདུག nga norpu līngkar tro-kitu'
"I'm going to the Norbu lingka." (I see myself going there in a dream, in a film, etc.)
ངས་ཤ་བཟས་སོང་། ngä' shā sä'-song "(Dammit) I've eaten meat."
ངས་འབུ་བསད་སོང་། ngä' pu sā'-song "I've killed an insect." (accidentally)

These sentences are usually constructed with intentional auxiliaries.

On the other hand, when the testimonial mood is associated with certain non-volitional verb forms, particularly of perception (such as གོ་ kho to hear, མཐོང་ thōng to see, ན་ na to be ill, etc.) and affect (such as དགའ་ ka love, ཞེད་ she' fear), it appears naturally with the first person, and more rarely with the second and third (in which case reported or inferential speech is preferred). The perception of *certain feelings or sensations is accessible only to the speaker.* We refer to this as the endopathic function of the testimonial mood.

Ex.: ང་ན་གི་འདུག nga na-kitu' "I'm ill, I'm in pain." (I feel it)
ངས་དྲན་གྱི་འདུག ngä' thrän-kitu' "I remember!" (I can testify to it)

ང་གྲོད་ཁོག་ལྟོགས་ཀྱི་འདུག	nga̲ thrö̲ko' tō'-kitu'	"I'm hungry." (I feel hunger)
*ཁོ་ན་གི་འདུག	khō na̲-kitu'	
*ཁོ་གྲོད་ཁོག་ལྟོགས་ཀྱི་འདུག	khō thrö̲ko' tō'-kitu'	

The last two sentences are normally not acceptable because the speaker cannot have direct access to this sort of information – that is, he cannot perceive the state of pain or hunger experienced by the sufferer.[115] The two sentences would be correctly expressed, using the inferential mood (explained immediately below), as:

ཁོ་ན་བཞག	khō na̲-sha'	"He's ill, he's in pain."
ཁོ་གྲོད་ཁོག་ལྟོགས་བཞག	khō thrö̲ko' tō'-sha'	"He's hungry."

The statement in each case corresponds to an inference based on an observation of the sufferer's symptoms.

C) The inferential

The inferential mood བཞག་ implies that the authority for what is said is derived from the enduring traces or results of a past action. Even if the speaker has not taken part in the event being described, he or she considers it to be definitely factual.

Ex.: གངས་བཏང་བཞག — kha̲ng' tāng-sha'
"Look, it's snowed!" (I can see the traces)

རི་མོ་སྙིང་རྗེ་པོ་ཅིག་བྲིས་བཞག — ri̲mo nyīng ce̲po cī' thri̲'-sha'
"He's drawn a pretty picture." (I've just come across it)

དར་ལྕོགས་གསར་པ་མང་པོ་བཙུགས་བཞག — tha̲rco' sārpa ma̲ngpo tsū'-sha'
"They've put up a lot of prayer-flags."

སྤོས་མང་པོ་སྤར་བཞག — pō' ma̲ngpo pār-sha' "(Look!) they've burned a lot of incense." (we can smell it, and see the ash)

The inferential is rarely used with the first person. However, it may be used when the subject has not been aware of performing the action and only later has discovered he actually did it.

Ex.: ངས་འབུ་བསད་བཞག — ngä̲' pu̲ sā̲'-sha' "Why, I've killed an insect."

D) The egophoric

Remember that the term "egophoric" refers to auxiliaries that are used only with the first person, whatever the role of the latter may be in a given sentence (subject, object, indirect object,

115. The Japanese language has similar restrictions regarding the endopathic function.

complement). The final auxiliaries include several kinds of egophorics: intentional, receptive, habitual, experiential (see Lesson 15) and allocentric (see Lesson 23).

• Intentional egophoric

These imply that the subject-speaker is performing an action **deliberately** and may be used only with volitional (or controllable) verbs. The intentional auxiliaries are: གི་ཡིན་ -kiyin(future), གི་ཡོད་ -kiyö' (present), པ་ཡིན་ -payin (perfective), ཡོད་-yö' (perfect).

Ex.:			
	ངས་རྩམ་པ་ཉོ་གི་ཡིན།	ngä' tsāmpa nyo-kiyin	"I'll buy some tsampa."
	ངས་རྩམ་པ་ཉོས་ཡོད།	ngä' tsāmpa nyö'-yö'	"I've bought some tsampa." (perfect)
	ངས་རྩམ་པ་ཉོས་པ་ཡིན།	ngä' tsāmpa nyö'-payin	"I bought some tsampa." (perfective)
	ང་ནོར་བུ་གླིང་ཁར་འགྲོ་གི་ཡོད།	nga norpu lĩngkar tro-kiyö'	"I go (*or* I am going) to the Norbu lingkha palace." (now or habitually)
	ངས་ཤ་བཟས་པ་ཡིན།	ngä' shā sä'-payin	"I ate some meat."
	ངས་འབུ་བསད་པ་ཡིན།།	ngä' pu sā'- payin	"I've killed an insect." (intentionally)

• The receptive egophoric

The "receptive" (non-intentional) auxiliary བྱུང་ chung, which is used only in the perfective past, implies that the subject-speaker has undergone the action, perceived it (involuntarily) or has been the recipient of it. This auxiliary is associated with the first person pronoun, whether as a subject ("I"), direct object ("me"), indirect object ("to me") or adverbial ("at my place", etc.). It may also signify that the action is directed (actually or metaphorically) towards the speaker. Thus we can't say: * ངས་བརྐྱགས་བྱུང་། "I've lost (it)" but rather ངས་བརླགས་སོང་། since the verb "to lose" implies a "distancing" from the speaker.

Ex.:			
	ང་ན་བྱུང་།	nga na-cung	"**I** fell ill."
	ཁོས་ང་ལ་ཁ་པར་བཏང་བྱུང་།	khö' nga-la khāpar tāng-cung	"He phoned **me.**"
	ངས་འཇའ་གསུམ་མཐོང་བྱུང་།	ngä' ca sūm thōng-cung	"**I** saw three rainbows."
	ཁོང་གིས་ང་སྨན་ཁང་ལ་ཁྲིད་བྱུང་།	khōng-ki' nga mänkang-la thrī'-cung "He took **me** to the hospital."	

It is sometimes possible to replace the receptive egophoric auxiliary by the testimonial as shown below, with a subtle distinction in their meaning.

Ex.:			
	ངས་ཧ་གོ་བྱུང་།	ngä hā kho-cung	"**I** understood." or "I have understood."
	ངས་ཧ་གོ་སོང་།	ngä hā kho-song	"**I** have understood." (just right now)

The use of cung indicates that the verbal action (or process) may have happened some time before the moment of speech, while the use of the testimonial song suggests that it has just happened just now.

• The habitual egophoric

The auxiliary གི་ཡོད kiyö' is used with reference to habitual facts that involve the speaker:

Ex.:	ང་ན་གི་མེད།	nga̱ na̱-kime' "I'm never ill."
	སྔན་མ་ང་ཡག་པོ་མཐོང་གི་ཡོད།	ngā̃ma nga̱ ya̱kpo thōng-kiyö' "Previously, I used to see well."
	ངའི་བུ་མོ་སློབ་གྲྭ་ལ་འགྲོ་གི་ཡོད།	ngä̱: phu̱mo lāptrar tro̱-kiyö' "My daughter goes to school."
	ཁོང་ངའི་ནང་ལ་ཡང་སེ་ཕེབས་ཀྱི་ཡོད།	khōng ngä̱: na̱ng-la ya̱ngse phē'-kiyö' "He often comes to my place."

10.3.6 Questions with alternative interrogative

Questions involving alternatives, such as "Would you like this or that?", are formed by placing the final interrogative particle ག -ka (for the future) and པ -pa (for the past) after each of the alternative sentences.

Ex.:	གསོལ་ཇ་བཀུག་ག ཁོ་ཕི་བཀུག་ག	sō̃:ca kyā'-ka khōpi kyā'-ka "Shall I bring you tea or coffee?"
	ཆམ་ཆམ་ལ་ཕེབས་ག་ ནང་ལ་བཞུགས་ག	chāmcam-la phēp-ka na̱ng-la shu̱'-ka "Will you go for a stroll or will you stay in?"

This formulation is sometimes referred to as a **consultative construction.**

10.4 Exercises སྦྱོང་ཚན།

10.4.1 Rewrite the following sentences in the inferential perfect.

༡) ཨ་མས་མོག་མོག་བཟོས་པ་རེད།

༢) རྡོ་རྗེས་ཁ་ལག་མང་པོ་བཟས་པ་རེད།

༣) ཁོས་ཆང་བཏུངས་པ་རེད།

༤) ཁོང་གིས་ཡི་གེ་བྲིས་པ་རེད་པས།

༥) རྡོ་རྗེ་གླིང་ཁར་ཕྱིན་པ་རེད།

10.4.2 Rewrite the above sentences in the negative.

10.4.3 Translate into Tibetan:

1. How are you? Please sit down, have some tea.
2. I won't have any tea. I'll drink some chang.
3. Are you working a lot these days? — No, I'm not working much.
4. Have you eaten? — Yes, I've eaten, thank you.

10.4.4 Answer the following questions in the negative, as follows:

ཁྱེད་རང་མོག་མོག་བཟོ་གས། > ང་མོག་མོག་བཟོ་གི་མིན།

༡) ཁོང་ཚོས་ཆང་བཏུངས་སོང་ངས། > …………………………...

༢) རྡོ་རྗེ་སློབ་གྲྭར་འགྲོ་གི་ཡོད་རེད་པས། > …………………………...

༣) ཁ་ས་ཁྱེད་རང་ཆང་བཏུངས་པས། > …………………………...

༤) ལྷ་བཟང་ལགས་གསོལ་ཇ་མཆོད་ཀྱི་རེད་པས། > …………………………...

༥) ཆུའི་ནང་ལ་ཉ་འདུག་གས། > …………………………...

༦) སྒྲོལ་མ་ལགས་ཀྱིས་ཞལ་ལག་བཟོས་གནང་འདུག་གས། > …………………………...

༧) ཁྱེད་རང་དེང་སང་གླིང་གར་ཕེབས་ཀྱི་ཡོད་པས། > …………………………...

"Pilgrimage"

གནས་མཇལ།

Grammar aims བརྡ་སྤྲོད་རིག་པའི་དམིགས་ཚད།

- The auxiliaries of probability
  - ཡོད་པ་འདྲ་ yö̱patra, ཡོད་ཀྱི་རེད་ yö̱kire', ཡོད་ས་རེད་ yö̱sare'.
  - ཡིན་པ་འདྲ་ yi̱npatra, ཡིན་ཀྱི་རེད་ yi̱nkire', ཡིན་ས་རེད་ yi̱nsare'.
- Nominalizing suffixes
- The nominalizers ཡག་ -ya' and རྒྱུ་ -kyu.
- The connective:V+ ཙང་ -tsang "because".
- Presentations of secondary verbs.
- The modal verbs ཐུབ་ thūp, སིད་ sī' "to be able"

༄། ལུང་པ་རེ་རེར་སྐད་ལུགས་རེ་རེ། བླ་མ་རེ་རེར་ཆོས་ལུགས་རེ་རེ།།
"Each valley has its dialect, each lama has his religion." (proverb)

CD I • Tr. 31-32 

11.1 Dialogue དྲི་བ་དྲིས་ལན།

ལྷ་བཟང་ ཿ རྡོ་རྗེ་ལགས་ཟླ་བ་སྟོན་མ་ (སྟོ་མ་) ཁྱེད་རང་ག་པར་ཕེབས་པ།
རྡོ་རྗེ་ ཿ ང་གནས་མཇལ་ལ་ཕྱིན་པ་ཡིན།
ལྷ་བཟང་ ཿ གཙང་གནས་ལ་ཕེབས་པ། ལྷོ་གནས་ལ་ཕེབས་པ།
རྡོ་རྗེ་ ཿ དུས་ཚོད་མང་པོ་མེད་ཙང་གཙང་གནས་དང་ལྷོ་གནས་ལ་འགྲོ་ཐུབ་མ་བྱུང་།
ལྷ་བཟང་ ཿ འོ་ན་ག་པར་ཕེབས་པ།
རྡོ་རྗེ་ ཿ ལྷ་ས་དང་ལྷ་སའི་ཉེ་སྐོར་ལ་ཕྱིན་པ་ཡིན།
ལྷ་བཟང་ ཿ དབུས་ཁུལ་ལ་མཇལ་རྒྱུ་མང་པོ་ཡོད་པ་འདྲ།
རྡོ་རྗེ་ ཿ མང་ པོ་ ཞེ་ དྲགས་ འདུག གཙོ་ བོ་ ལྷ་ སའི་ ཇོ་ ཁང་ དང་ སེ་ ར། འབྲས་ སྤུངས། དགའ་ ལྡན་ དང་ རྩེ་ པོ་ བྲང་། ནོར་ བུ་ གླིང་ ཁ། ད་ ག་ ནང་ བཞིན་ ལྷ་ སའི་ ཉེ་ འདབས་ ལ་ དགོན་ པ་ ཚུང་ ཚུང་ མང་ པོ་ མཇལ་ ཡག་(རྒྱུ) འདུག
ལྷ་བཟང་ ཿ དགའ་ལྡན་ལ་ག་འདྲས་ཟེ་ཕེབས་པ།
རྡོ་རྗེ་ ཿ གྲོགས་པོའི་མོ་ཊའི་ནང་ལ་ཕྱིན་པ་ཡིན།

Pronunciation

- to̱rce-la' ta̱wa nga̿ma khyērang kha̱par phēp-pa

- nga̱ na̿ncä:-la chīn-payin

- tsāngnä'-la phēp-pa, lhōnä' la phēp-pa

- thṳ̈tsö' ma̱ngpo me̱'-tsang, tsāngnä'-tang lhōnä' tro̱ thūp-macung

- o̱na kha̱par phēp-pa

- lhāsa-tang lhāsä: nye̱kor-la chīn-payin

- ü̿ khü̿:-la cä̱:-kyu ma̱ngpo yö̱patra

- ma̱ngpo she̱tra' tu̱', tsōwo lhāsä: chö̱:kang, sēra, trä̱pung, ka̱ntän-tang tsē phōtrang no̱rpu līngka tha̱ka na̱ngshing, lhāsä: nye̱ntap-la ko̱mpa chūngcung ma̱ngpo cä̱:-ya̱' (kyu̱) tu̱'

- ka̱ntän-la kha̱nträs phēp-pa

- thro̱kpö: mo̱trä: na̱ng-la chīn-payin

Translation

Lobzang — Dorje, where did you go last month?
Dorje — I went on pilgrimage.
Lobzang — The Tsang pilgrimage or the Lhokha pilgrimage?
Dorje — Because I didn't have much time, I couldn't go to either Tsang or Lhokha.
Lobzang — So where did you go?
Dorje — I went to Lhasa and the area around Lhasa.
Lobzang — There must be a lot of places to visit in Central Tibet.
Dorje — Very many indeed! Mainly, the Jhokhang[116] of Lhasa, the monasteries of Sera, Gandän and Dräpung, the Potala Palace and the gardens of the Norbu lingkha. There are also many small monasteries to visit in the Lhasa surroundings.
Lobzang — How did you go to Gandän?
Dorje — I went in [my] friend's car.

ཀ་ཁ་ག་ང་

11.2 Vocabulary ཚིག་གསར།

གཙོ་བོ་ tsōwo	(adj.) main
ད་ག་ནང་བཞིན་ tha̱ka na̱ngshin	(adv.) in the same way
གནས་མཇལ་ na̿ncä:	(n.) pilgrimage

116. The main temple of Lhasa is generally written as "Jokhang". This corresponds to the Tibetan spelling of the word rather than to its pronunciation. The spelling used here is intended to represent the pronunciation.

As a general rule, the spelling of Tibetan words in European writing varies not only from one language to another, but also from one writer to another within the same language. Moreover, the conventions themselves are often not based on a consistent logic. Thus the conventional spelling "Jokhang" is based on Tibetan orthography, while renderings such as "losar", "yak", "Bharkor" are derived from the pronunciation (the orthography is respectively lo-gsar, g.yag, bar-skor). In this Manual, the spelling of Tibetan names follows their pronunciation, according to the rules set out in Appendix 7.

གནས་རི་ nāri	(n.) sacred mountain
དུས་ཚོད་ thü̱tsö'	(n.) time
ཉེ་སྐོར་ nye̱kor	(n.) surroundings
ཉེ་འདབས་ nye̱ntap	(n.) vicinity, environs
དགོན་པ་ ko̱npa, ko̱mpa	(n.) monastery
ཕོ་བྲང་ phōtrang	(n.) palace
མོ་ཊ་ mo̱tra ཕེབས་ཁྲོ་ phēptro (H)	(n.) car
རླངས་འཁོར་ lāngkor (L)	(n.) car
ཡག་ ya̱'	(part.) *nominalizer*
ཀྱུ kyu̱	(part.) *nominalizer*
ག་འདྲས་ཟེ་ kha̱nträs	(pron.) how?
ཙང་ tsāng/ -tsang	(co.) because
ཡོད་པ་འདྲ་ yö̱patra	(aux.) there probably is/are
ཐུབ་ thūp	(v. mod.) to be able

Proper nouns

ལྷོ་གནས་ lhōnä'	Lhokha pilgrimage
གཙང་གནས་ tsāngnä'	Tsang pilgrimage
རྩེ་ཕོ་བྲང་ tsē phōtrang	"Summit Palace", another name of the Potala, residence of the Dalai Lamas
ནོར་བུ་གླིང་ཁ་ no̱rpu lingka	Norbu lingkha, summer palace of the Dalai Lamas
ཇོ་ཁང་ chö̱:kang	Jhokhang (main temple of Lhasa)
དབུས་ཁུལ་ ū' khū:	Region of Central Tibet
སེ་ར་ sēra	Sera, a major monastery north of Lhasa
འབྲས་སྤུངས་ trä̱pung'	Dräpung, major monastery west of Lhasa
དགའ་ལྡན་ ka̱ntän	Gandän, major monastery 30 km east of Lhasa

11.3 Remarks འགྲེལ་བཤད།

11.3.1 Auxiliaries of probability

In addition to final auxiliary verbs that convey various tenses and evidential moods, there is also a set of "epistemic" final copulas and auxiliaries that express different degrees of **certainty or probability**. These correspond to the epistemic adverbs of European languages, such as "perhaps", "probably", "apparently" and to modal verbs such as "must", "may", "can", etc. A distinction may be drawn between, on the one hand, stative verbs or copulas that figure as independent verbs and, on the other hand, auxiliary verbs that (like evidential auxiliaries) go at the end of the sentence after the main verb. These auxiliaries are also associated with different tense-aspects, and for the most part involve the same verbs as the evidential auxiliaries, but combined in a different way (see Table 6 of Appendix 6, which summarizes the use of these auxiliaries in relation to tense-aspect).

A) Epistemic copulas

Tibetan contains an important set of epistemic stative verbs (or copulas). These do not vary according to tense-aspect. As in the case of declarative stative verbs, a distinction is drawn between existential and essential epistemic copulas. The former are derived from the verb yö̱' and the latter from the verb yi̱n.

• The existential copulas:

	ཡོད་པ་འདྲ་ yö̱patra	ཡོད་ཀྱི་རེད་ yö̱kire'	ཡོད་ས་རེད་ yö̱sare'
and the negatives:	མེད་པ་འདྲ་ me̱patra	ཡོད་ཀྱི་མ་རེད་ yö̱kimare'	ཡོད་ས་མ་རེད་ yö̱samare'

• The essential copulas:

	ཡིན་པ་འདྲ་ yi̱npatra	ཡིན་ཀྱི་རེད་ yi̱nkire'	ཡིན་ས་རེད་ yi̱nsare'
and the negatives:	མིན་པ་འདྲ་ mä̱npatra	ཡིན་ཀྱི་མ་རེད་ yi̱nkimare'	ཡིན་ས་མ་རེད་ yi̱nsamare'

These copulas express a high degree of probability and according to the context may be translated by the use of adverbs such as "surely", "probably" or the modal verb "must".

Ex.:	མི་མང་པོ་ཡོད་པ་འདྲ།	mi̱ ma̱ngpo yö̱patra	"There must be a lot of people."
	འབྲོག་པ་ཡོད་ཀྱི་རེད།	tro̱kpa yö̱kire'	"There must be some nomads."
	ཁོང་རྒྱ་མི་ཡིན་གྱི་རེད།	khōng kya̱mi yi̱nkire'	"He must be Chinese."

There is a slight difference between the auxiliaries formed with འདྲ་ tra̱ and those formed with རེད་ re̱'. The former suggests that the speaker's inference is based on his direct observation of the evidence, while the latter indicates that the speaker's inference is based on logic or on factual information not borne out by observation.

Other auxiliaries such as ཡོད་འགྲོ་ ' yö̱tro, པ་ཡོད་ payö', ཨ་ཡོད་ ayö' are presented in Lessons 18, 28 and 29.

B) The epistemic auxiliaries

These auxiliaries are effectively similar to copulas and may also be translated by the same devices. How they are used depends on the tense of the verb.

See the tables in Appendix 6.

Ex.:	འགྲིག་གི་ཡོད་པ་འདྲ།	tri̱'-kiyöpatra	"It must be all right."
	ཁོང་ཕེབས་ཀྱི་ཡོད་ས་རེད།	khōng phēp-kiyösare'	"He will probably come."
	སྐྱག་རྫུན་བཤད་ཀྱི་ཡོད་ཀྱི་རེད་	kyāktsün shä'-kiyökire'	"[he/she] probably lies."

11.3.2 Nominalizers

In Tibetan, any verb may be followed by a nominalizing suffix or "nominalizer". Nominalization converts a verb or even an entire clause into a noun (or rather a noun phrase). It is an important and complex feature of Tibetan grammar.

The commonest suffixes are: པ་ pā; རྒྱུ་ kyu̱;, མཁན་ khān, ས་ sā, སྟངས་ tāng, ཚུལ་ tshǖ:, སྟོལ་ sȫ:, ཡག་ ya̱' (*L) and འགྱོག་ nkyo̱' (*L)[117].

Most of these suffixes are used for three main purposes:

- They form **nominal clauses**[118] functioning like any noun phrase as subject, object, complement, etc. The nominalized verb (or the proposition) becomes the head of the noun phrase: i.e., it operates as a *noun* and may be followed by a demonstrative and a case marker (see 11.3.3 below and Lessons 18, 20, 25, 40).
- They form **relative clauses**[119] functioning as modifiers of noun phrases like an adjective (see Lesson 26).
- Finally, it may be noted that most of these nominalizers may combine with final auxiliary verbs to form **inflectional endings**: པ་ཡིན pā+yi̱n (see Lesson 7.3.2), མཁན་ཡིན་ khān+yi̱n (see Lesson 20.3.1), རྒྱུ་ཡིན kyu̱ + yin and ཡག་ཡིན ya̱'+yi̱n (see Lesson 28.3.1), etc.

11.3.3 The nominalizers ཡག་ ya' *and* རྒྱུ་ kyu

The suffixes ya' and kyu are associated only with the present-future form of the verb.

Ex.: ཞུ་ཡག་ shu̱-ya' but not * ཞུས་ཡག་shu̱'-ya'
ཟ་ཡག་sa̱-ya' but not * བཟས་ཡག་ sä̱'-ya'
བལྟ་ཡག་ tā-ya' but not * བལྟས་ཡག་ tǟ'ya'

The suffix ཡག་ -ya', which is sometimes spelled ཡས་ -yä', does not occur in Literary Tibetan, which instead uses the nominalizer པ་ pa. The form རྒྱུ་ -kyu, on the other hand, is used both in Spoken Tibetan and in the literary language.

- The functions of ཡག་ ya'

Verbs followed by the nominalizer ya' indicate the present, future or imperfective past depending on the context. Furthermore, they often convey a sense of obligation (deontic sense).

The nominalizer ya' is used to form nominal and relative clauses. A distinction needs to be made between two functions:

---

117. All these nominalizers are used in Literary Tibetan with the exception of ya' and nkyo'. The latter is used exclusively in a familiar register, and despite the frequency of its occurrence doesn't figure in grammars. The spelling given here is purely phonetic. All the other suffixes are clearly derived from nouns and have kept a grammatical role linked with their original meaning.

118. In English, nominal clauses correspond to *that*-clauses, *ing*-clauses and infinitive clauses. See 11.3.3.

119. In English, relative clauses are introduced by *wh*-pronouns or *that* (including zero-*that*). See 26. 3.1.

The nominalizer indicates the **grammatical patient** of the verbal action (the object of a transitive verb or the subject of an intransitive verb) in the present and future.[120]

འབྲི་ཡག་ "that (which) needs to be written, that (which) one writes", འབུལ་ཡག་ (L.: འབུལ་ཡག་) "that (which) is to be offered, that (which) one offers", མཇལ་ཡག་ "that (which) is to be visited, that one visits", བཟོ་ཡག་ "that (which) is to be built, that (which) one builds".

Ex.: དཀར་ཡོལ་བཀྲུ་ཡག་དེ་ཚོ་ག་པར་ཡོད་རེད། "Where are the cups to be washed?"
ཅ་ལག་ཁྱེར་ཡག་དེ་ཚོ་ཕ་གིར་འདུག "The things (that have) to be taken are over there."
ཕྱག་དེབ་ཕུལ་ཡག་(འབུལ་ཡག་)འདི་ཁྱེར་ཡོད་པས། "Have you brought the book that we're going to present?"

The suffix also operates as a neutral nominalizer: it nominalizes the **entire clause.**

In this case, the suffix is not oriented towards any grammatical role and nominalizes the entire clause. From a syntactic point of view, the nominalized verb functions as a head noun and may be translated in English by a verb in the infinitive, by an *ing*- clause, a *that*- clause or even by a noun: འབྲི་ཡག་ "(the fact of) writing", ཕུལ་ཡག (L.: འབུལ་ཡག) "(the fact of) offering", མཇལ་ཡག་ "(the fact of) visiting", བཟོ་ཡག་ "(the fact of) constructing, construction".

Ex.: དེབ་ཁྱེར་ཡག་བརྗེད་བཞག "I've forgotten to bring the book."
སློབ་སྦྱོང་བྱེད་ཡག་དེ་གལ་ཆེན་པོ་རེད། "Studying is very important."
དགོན་པ་ཆུང་ཆུང་མང་པོ་མཇལ་ཡག་འདུག "There are many small monasteries to visit."

Only the syntactic context allows one to distinguish between the neutral nominalizer and the patient-centered nominalizer.

• The functions of རྒྱུ་ kyu

Verbs followed by the nominalizer -kyu correspond to the future or the imperfective, often with a sense of obligation. The functions of the nominalizer -kyu are analogous to those of -ya', though it has more formal, and rather literary, overtones.

Ex.: དེབ་ཁྱེར་རྒྱུ་བརྗེད་བཞག "I've forgotten to bring the book."
དགོན་པ་ཆུང་ཆུང་མང་པོ་མཇལ་རྒྱུ་འདུག "There are many small monasteries to visit."

11.3.4 The conjunction ཙང་ -tsang *"because", "since", "for"*

This very common conjunction is suffixed directly to the verb or to certain auxiliaries. It appears in the following combinations: ཡིན་ཙང་ yi̱n-tsang, ཡོད་ཙང་ yö̱'-tsang. However, the following combinations are incorrect: *རེད་ཙང་ re̱'-tsang, *ཡོད་རེད་ཙང་ yo̱:re'-tsang, *འདུག་ཙང་ tu̱'-tsang.

Ex.: དུས་ཚོད་མང་པོ་མེད་ཙང་ང་འགྲོ་ཐུབ་ཀྱི་མ་རེད།

"Since I haven't got much time I won't be able to go there."

---

120. From a syntactic point of view, the nominalized verb functions here as a head noun or as a modifier of the head noun and may often be translated in English by using a relative clause (see also Lesson 26) as the examples show.

ངས་རྒྱ་གར་སྐད་ཡག་པོ་མ་ཤེས་ཙང་དཀའ་ལས་ཁག་པོ་བྱེད་ས་རེད།
"That may be difficult because I don't speak Hindi well."
ད་རེས་ང་ཡུ་རོབ་ལ་འགྲོ་ཡག་ཐེངས་དང་པོ་ཡིན་ཙང་རྒྱུས་ཞེ་དྲགས་མེད།
"I'm not very sure, as this is the first time I've been to Europe."

11.3.5 Secondary verbs

There are about twenty or so "secondary" verbs that go between the principal and auxiliary verb: **principal** V + **secondary** V + AUX.

Most of these verbs are **modal verbs**

དགོས་ ko' "to need, want, have to", ཐུབ་ thūp "to be able", སིད་ sī' "to be possible", ཆོག་ chō' "to be allowed", ཤེས་ shē' "to know", ནུས་ nü' "to dare", འདོད་ tö' "to want, wish", སྙིང་འདོད་ nyīngtö' "to wish", བསམ་ sām "to think", རྩིས་ tsī' "to intend, plan".

There are also a number of "tense-aspect" verbs:

ཚར་tshār "to finish", བསྡད་ tä' "to stay", རན་ rän "to be time to", འགྲོའ་(གྲབས་) tro: "to be about to", ཆོག་ཆོག་ chō'co' "to be ready to", ལོང་ long "to have the time to", as well as the directional verbs ཡོང་ yong "to come"(action towards) and འགྲོ་ tro "to go" (action away from).

As in English, the modal verbs are defective[121] insofar as they are not compatible with certain auxiliary verbs. Their compatibility will be examined as they are introduced in the course of the lessons.

11.3.6 The modal verbs ཐུབ་ thūp "to be able", "can", སིད་ sī' "to be possible", "may".

When combined with modal verbs, the main verb must be in the present-future. The past form is incorrect.

Ex.: རྙོག་དྲ་ཡོང་སིད་ཀྱི་རེད། "There may be problems (later)."
མོ་ལགས་ལང་ཐུབ་ཀྱི་མི་འདུག "This grandmother can't get up."
ས་ཁུལ་དེར་འགྲོ་ཐུབ་མ་བྱུང་། "I couldn't go to that area."
(In this case it would be incorrect to say * ས་ཁུལ་དེར་ཕྱིན་ཐུབ་མ་བྱུང་།)

ཐུབ་ thūp is compatible with most non-intentional auxiliaries: ཐུབ་ཀྱི་རེད་ thūp-kire', ཐུབ་ཀྱི་ཡོད་རེད་ thūp-kiyo:re', ཐུབ་ཀྱི་ཡོད་thūp-kiyö', ཐུབ་བྱུང་thūp-cung, ཐུབ་སོང་thūp-song, ཐུབ་པ་རེད་thūp-pare', ཐུབ་བཞག་thūp-sha', ཐུབ་ཡོད་རེད་ thūp-yo:re'. It is usually incompatible with the following egophoric auxiliaries *ཐུབ་ཡོད་ thūp-yö, *ཐུབ་པ་ཡིན་thūp-payin *ཐུབ་ཀྱི་ཡིན་thūp-kiyin. The compatibility of སིད་ sī' with auxiliary verbs is relatively restricted. As a rule, only the forms སིད་ཀྱི་རེད་ sī'-kire' and སིད་པ་རེད་ sī'-pare' are encountered.

---

121. For example, the modal verbs have no infinitives (*to can, *to may, *to must), and they cannot be conjugated (*he cans, *he mays, *he musts).

–་༡་ཀ་ག་

11.4 Exercises སྦྱོང་ཚན།

11.4.1 Translate into English:

༡) ཁྱེད་རང་ཁ་ས་ག་རེ་གནང་པ།
༢) ཁྱེད་རང་སློབ་གྲྭར་ཕེབས་པས།
༣) ཁོང་ཚོ་གནས་མཇལ་ལ་ཕེབས་པ་རེད།
༤) ཁོ་རྒྱ་གར་ལ་ག་འདྲས་ཟེ་ཕྱིན་པ་རེད།
༥) ཟླ་བ་རྒྱ་ནག་ལ་སློབ་སྦྱོང་བྱེད་ཀྱི་ཡོད་རེད།
༦) ཁོང་ནང་ལ་བཞུགས་མི་འདུག ག་པར་ཐེག་པ་རེད།
༧) རྡོ་རྗེ་ལ་ལས་ཀ་མང་པོ་ཡོད་ཀྱི་རེད།
༨) ཁ་ལག་ཟ་ཡག་འདུག་གས།
༩) དེབ་ལྷ་ཡག་ཡོད་པས།
༡༠) ལམ་ཁག་ཡག་པོ་མེད་ཙང་འགྲོ་ཐུབ་ཀྱི་མ་རེད།
༡༡) བློ་བཟང་གི་ནང་ལ་དཔེ་ཆ་མང་པོ་ཡོད་ཀྱི་རེད།

11.4.2 Reply to these questions as follows:

Q: ཁྱེད་རང་དགོན་པར་ཕེབས་པས། R: དགོན་པར་འགྲོ་ཐུབ་མ་བྱུང་།

༡) ཁོང་གིས་ཞལ་ལག་བཟོས་གནང་སོང་ངས།
༢) ཁོང་ཚོ་ཟླ་ཉིན་བོད་ལ་ཕེབས་སོང་ངས།
༣) བློ་བཟང་གིས་ལས་ཀ་བྱས་ཡོད་རེད་པས།
༤) ཁྱེད་རང་ཞལ་ལག་མཆོད་པས།

11.4.3 Translate into Tibetan:

1. The lama has a nice car.
2. When will you leave for India?
3. There are many monasteries to visit over there.
4. Have you got some time?
5. In Tibet there are sacred mountains.
6. How will you travel to Peking?
7. How many months will you stay there?
8. Did the teacher have a camera?

11.5 Civilization རིག་གཞུང་།

The main mountains of Tibet

གངས་ཏི་སེ་ khang' tīse	Kailash
ཇོ་མོ་གླང་མ་ chomo lāngma	Jhomo langma (Everest)
གཉན་ཆེན་ཐང་ལྷ་ nyāncen thāngla	Nyänchen thangla
ཡར་ལྷ་ཤམ་པོ་ yarla shāmpo	Yarla shampo
རྨ་ཆེན་སྤོམ་ར་ mācen pōmra	Machen pomra
ཨ་མྱེས་རྨ་ཆེན་ āmnye' mācen	Amnye machen
ཇོ་མོ་ལྷ་རི་ chomo lhāri	Jhomo lhari
ཤིས་ཤ་སྤང་མ་ shīsha pāngma	Shisha pangma
གདང་ལ་ tangla	Dangla
གངས་ཆེན་མཛོད་ལྔ་ khangcen tsönga	Ghangchen dzönga (Kanchenjunga)
གངས་དཀར་རི་བོ་ khangkar riwo	Ghongkar riwo

Pilgrimage

The main lakes of Tibet

ཡར་འབྲོག་གཡུ་མཚོ་ ya̲:mtro yūmtso	Yamdro yumtsho
མཚོ་སྔོན་པོ་ tshō ngȫnpo	The Blue Lake, Qinghai (Chin.), Kokonor (Mong.)
མཚོ་མ་ཕམ་ tshō ma̲pam	Manasarowar
གནམ་མཚོ་ཕྱུག་མོ་ nāmtso chūkmo	Namtsho, Heaven Lake
ལྷ་མོའི་བླ་མཚོ་ lhāmö: lātso	Lhamo latsho

The main rivers of Tibet

Some of the greatest rivers of Asia rise in Tibet and cross much of the high plateau (for example the Mekong, of which more than a thousand kilometers are in Tibet).

ཡར་ཀླུངས་གཙང་པོ་ ya̲rlung tsāngpo	Brahmaputra
རྟ་མཆོག་ཁ་འབབ་ tāco' khāpap	alternative name of the Brahmaputra
སེང་གེ་ཁ་འབབ་ sēnge khāpap	Indus (Chin. Shiquanhe)
གླང་ཆེན་ཁ་འབབ་ lāngcen khāpap	Sutlej (Chin. Xiangquanhe)
རྨ་ཆུ་ mācu	Yellow River (Chin. Huanghe)
རྫ་ཆུ་ tsa̲cu / ཟླ་ཆུ་ ta̲cu	Mekong (Chin. Lancangjiang)
འབྲི་ཆུ་ tri̲cu	Blue River (Chin. Changjiang)
རྒྱ་མོ་རྔུལ་ཆུ་ kya̲mo ngǖcu	Salween (Chin. Nüjiang)
སྐྱིད་ཆུ་ kyīcu	Kyichu ("River of Happiness") or ལྷ་སའི་གཙང་པོ་ Lhasa River

"The football match"

རྐང་རྩེད་སྤོ་ལོ།

Grammar aims བརྗོད་སྒྲིག་རིག་པའི་དམིགས་ཚད།

- The complement of verbs of motion: གར་-ka:.
- The time.
- Omitting the ergative case.
- Omitting the subject.
- The various meanings of གཅིག་ cï'.

CD I • Tr. 33-34

12.1a Dialogue དྲི་བ་དྲིས་ལན།

ཐུབ་བསྟན་ ༔ ག་པར་འགྲོ་ག

བསམ་གཏན་ ༔ སྤོ་ལོ་བལྟ་གར་འགྲོ་གི་ཡིན།

ཐུབ་བསྟན་ ༔ ག་པར་ཡོད་རེད།

བསམ་གཏན་ ༔ སྤོ་གླིང་ཁར།

ཐུབ་བསྟན་ ༔ ཁ་གཏད་སུ་དང་སུ་རེད།

བསམ་གཏན་ ༔ ང་ཚོའི་སླབ་གྲྭ་(སློབ་གྲྭ་)དང་གྲོང་ཁྱེར་ལྷ་སའི་རུ་ཁག་རེད།

ཐུབ་བསྟན་ ༔ ཨོ། བྱས་ན་ལྟད་མོ་ཆེན་པོ་ཡོད་རེད། ཆུ་ཚོད་ག་ཚོད་ལ་འགོ་ཚུགས་ཀྱི་རེད།

བསམ་གཏན་ ༔ ཆུ་ཚོད་གཉིས་པར་ཚུགས་ཀྱི་རེད།

ཐུབ་བསྟན་ ༔ བྱས་ན་བྲེལ་བ་མི་འདུག

བསམ་གཏན་ ༔ ཛ་གང་འཕྱུང་གར་འགྲོ

ཐུབ་བསྟན་ ༔ འོང་རེད།

བསམ་གཏན་ ༔ ཁྱེད་རང་གི་རྐང་ག་རིལ་(རྐང་འཁོར་) ག་པར་བཞག་ཡོད།

ཐུབ་བསྟན་ ༔ སྨན་རྩིས་ཁང་གི་མདུན་ལ་བཞག་ཡོད།

བསམ་གཏན་ ༔ ཐ་མག་ཉོ་གི་ཡིན། དངུལ་གཅིག་གཡར་ད་(དང་)།

ཐུབ་བསྟན་ ༔ ཡིན་ད་ཡིན། འདའི་(འདིར) ཡོད།

བསམ་གཏན་ ༔ ད་ཆུ་ཚོད་གཉིས་པ་ཟིན་པར་སྐར་མ་་བཅུ་རེད། ང་གཉིས་མགྱོགས་པོ་འགྲོ

Pronunciation

- kha̲par tro̲-ka ?
- pōlo tā-kar tro̲-kiyin
- kha̲par yo̲:rä' ?
- pōlingkar
- khāptä' sū-tang sū rä̲'
- nga̲tsö: lāptra-tang thro̲ngkyer lhāsä: ru̲ka' re̲'
- o̲ chä̲'-na tǟmo chēnpo yo̲:re' chūtsö' kha̲tsö'-la ko̲ tshū'-kirä'
- chūtsö' nyīpar tshū'-kire'
- chä̲'-na thre̲lla mi̲ntu'
- cha̲ kha̲ng tūng-kar tro̲
- o̲ng re̲'
- khyērang-ki tāngkari: kha̲par sha̲'-yö'
- mǟntsikang-ki tü̲n-la sha̲'-yö'
- thāma' nyo̲-kiyin ngǖ: cī' yār-ta
- yi̲n-ta yi̲n, tä̲:-yö'
- tha̲ chūtsö' nyīpa si̲mpar kārma cū re̲' nga̲nyi' kyo̲kpo tro̲

Translation

Thubtän — Where are you going?
Samtän — I'm going to watch a football match.
Thubtän — Where?
Samtän — At the Polingkha Stadium.
Thubtän — Who's playing who? (The opponents are who and who?)
Samtän — Our school and the Lhasa city team.
Thubtän — Ah, that's going to be a big show! What time does it start?
Samtän — It starts at two o'clock.
Thubtän — So we have time (there's no hurry).
Samtän — Let's go and have some tea.
Thubtän — Sure.
Samtän — Where have you left your bike?
Thubtän — I've left it in front of the traditional medicine hospital.
Samtän — I'll go and buy some cigarettes. Lend me a bit of money.
Thubtän — Yes, of course.
Samtän — It's ten to two – let's go quickly!

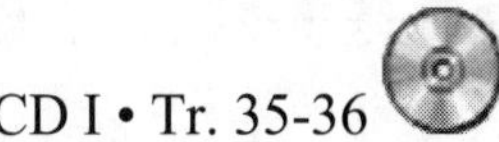

CD I • Tr. 35-36

12.1b Text རྩོམ་ཡིག

ངའི་གྲོགས་པོ་རྡོ་རྗེ།

༄། བུ་རྡོ་རྗེ་ལོ་བརྒྱད་རེད། ཁོང་གི་ནང་གྲོང་གསེབ་ལ་ཡོད་རེད། ད་ལྟ་ཁོང་ལྷ་སར་ཁོང་གི་ཨ་ཁུ་ལགས་ཀྱི་ཁང་པར་བསྡད་ཡོད་རེད། ཁོང་ལྷ་སར་སླེབས་ནས་ལོ་གཅིག་ཕྱིན་པ་རེད། ཁོང་སློབ་གྲྭར་འགྲོ་གི་ཡོད་རེད། དབྱར་ཁ་དང་དགུན་ཁ་གུང་སང་ཟླ་བ་གཅིག་ཙ་ཡོད་རེད། གུང་སང་ལ་ཁོང་གྲོང་གསེབ་ལ་པ་ལགས་དང་ཨ་མ་ལགས་མཇལ་གར་འགྲོ་གི་ཡོད་རེད།།

Translation

"My friend Dorje"

The boy Dorje is eight years old. His home is in the countryside. Now he stays at his uncle's home in Lhasa. It's been one year since he came to Lhasa. He goes to school. In summer and winter there is a holiday of about one month. During the holiday he goes to meet his father and mother.

ཀ་ཁ་ག་ང་

12.2 Vocabulary ཚིག་གསར།

གཞུང་ཚབ་ཁང་ shu̲ngtsapkang	(n.) embassy
དངུལ་ཁང་ ngǖ:kang	(n.) bank
ཆང་ཁང་ chāngkang	(n.) bar
དཔེ་མཛོད་ཁང་ pēntsökang	(n.) library
སྦྲག་ཁང་ tra̲kkang	(n.) post office
འདུ་ཁང་ tu̲kang	(n.) assembly hall of a monastery
སྨན་ཁང་ mǟnkang	(n.) hospital
མགྲོན་ཁང་ trö̲nkang	(n.) hotel
པར་ཁང་ pārkang	(n.) printers
ཚོང་ཁང་ tshōngkang	(n.) shop, store
ཇ་ཁང་ cha̲kang	(n.) teashop
འགྲེམ་སྟོན་ཁང་ tre̲mtönkang	(n.) museum
སྐྲ་ཁང་ trākang སྐྲ་བཞར་ཁང་ trāsharkang (L)	(n.) hairdresser
ལྷ་ཁང་ lhākang	(n.) shrine, chapel
ཟློས་གར་ཁང་ tö̲karkang	(n.) theatre
ཁྲིམས་ཁང་ thrīmkang	(n.) courthouse
གློག་བརྙན་ཁང་ lō'nyänkang	(n.) cinema
ཟ་ཁང་ sa̲kang	(n.) restaurant.
གློག་ཁང་ lōkkang	(n.) hydroelectric plant

སློབ་གྲྭ་འབྲིང་བ་ lōptra tri̲ngnga (n.) secondary school
སློབ་གྲྭ་ཆེན་མོ་ lōptra chēnmo (n.) university
སློབ་གྲྭ་ཆུང་ཆུང་ lōptra chūngcung (n.) primary school
ཀང་ག་རིལ་ kāngkari:, tāngkari ཀང་འཁོར་ kāngkor (L) (n.) bicycle
སྦག་སྦག་ pa̲kpa' (n.) motor cycle
ཐ་མག་ thāma' བཞེས་ཐག་ she̲ta' (H) (n.) cigarette, tobacco
ཀང་རྩེད་སྤོ་ལོ་ kāngtse pōlo (n.) football
སྤོ་ལོ་ pōlo (n.) ball
དངུལ་ ngǖ: ཕྱག་དངུལ་ chā'ngü: (H) (n.) money, silver
སྐར་མ་ kārma (n.) star, minute
སྐར་ཆ་ kārca (n.) second
ཕྱེད་ཀ་ chēka (n.) half
ཆུ་ཚོད་ chūtsö' ཕྱག་ཚོད་ chā'tsö'(H) (n.) hour, watch
ལྟད་མོ་ tǟmo གཟིགས་མོ་ si̲kmo (H) (n.) show, performance
རུ་ཁག་ ru̲ka' (n.) team, brigade
ལྟ་བ་ tāwa (n.) doctrine, vision
ཁ་གཏད་ khāptä' (n.) opponent, adversary
ཟིན་པར sinpar (n.) to (*telling time*)
བྲེལ་བ་ thre̲lla ཐུགས་བྲེལ་ thūktre: (H) (n.) urgent business
གྲོང་ཁྱེར་ thro̲ngkyer (n.) town, city
ལྟ་ tā (1) / བལྟས་ tǟ' (2) / ལྟོས་ tȫ' (3) (v.) – [vol., ED] to look at
– [vol., EA] to read

ཉོ་ nyo̲ (1) / ཉོས་ nyö̲' (2,3) (v.) [vol., EA] to buy
གཟིགས་ si̲' (H) (v.) – [vol., EA] to buy
– [vol., ED] to look at
– [inv., EA] to see

འཚོང་ tshōng (1) / བཙོང་ tsōng(2,3) (v.) [vol., EA] to sell
བཞག་ sha̲' (v.) [vol., EA] to put, place
གཡར་ yār (v.) [vol., EDA] to lend, borrow
གཡར་གནང་ yār nāng (H) (v.) [vol. EDA] to lend, borrow
འགོ་ཚུགས་ ko̲ tshū' (v.) [inv., A] to begin
འགོ་བཙུགས་ ko̲ tsū' དབུ་བཙུགས་ ū tsū' (H) (v.) [vol., EA] to begin
ཚར་ tshār (v.) [vol., EA] to end
བྱས་ན་ chä̲'-na (idiom.) and so

Proper nouns

སྤོ་གླིང་ཁ་ pōlingka "Polingkha" Stadium
སྨན་རྩིས་ཁང་ mǟntsikang Mäntsikhang, hospital of traditional medicine in Lhasa

༡༢༣

12.3 Remarks འགྲེལ་བཤད།

12.3.1 The suffix ཀར་ -kar

This verb suffix, which may be spelled either ཀག་ -ka' or ཀར་ -kar, occurs only in Spoken Tibetan. It is used to introduce the complement of a verb of motion. The verb to which this suffix is attached must be in the present-future stem. It is translated by the English infinitive. We must therefore say ལྟ་ཀར་ tā-kar, "to watch", and not *བལྟས་ཀར་ tā̃'-kar. In Literary Tibetan, this suffix is replaced by the forms པར་ pār and བར་wa̱.

Ex.: སྤོ་ལོ་ལྟ་ཀར་འགྲོ་གི་ཡིན།

pōlo tā-kar tro̱ ki-kiyin

"I'm going to watch the soccer match."

ཁོང་ཁྲོམ་ལ་བཞེས་ཚལ་གཟིགས་ཀར་ཕེབས་སོང་།

khōng thrōm-la she̱tsä: si̱'-kar phēp-song

"He has gone to buy vegetables in the market (H)."

ཟླ་བ་ཁྱེད་རང་མཇལ་ཀར་བཅར་གྱི་རེད།

ta̱wa khyērang cä̱:-kar cār-kire'

"Dawa will come to see you (H)."

12.3.2 Time

When telling time, complete hours are expressed by means of ordinal numbers. "It's one o'clock" in Tibetan literally means "It's the first hour", and "It's two o'clock" means "It's the second hour", and so on. However, when minutes are involved, cardinal numbers are used, except in the case of one o'clock.

ཆུ་ཚོད་ག་ཚོད་རེད། chūtsö' kha̱tsö' rä̱'	"What's the time?"
ཆུ་ཚོད་དང་པོ་རེད། chūtsö' tha̱ngpo re̱'	"It's one o'clock."
ཆུ་ཚོད་དང་པོ་དང་ཕྱེད་ཀ་རེད།	"It's half past one."
ཆུ་ཚོད་གཉིས་པ་ཟིན་པར་སྐར་མ་བཅོ་ལྔ་རེད།	"It's a quarter to two."
ཆུ་ཚོད་གཉིས་པ་ཏག་ཏག་རེད།	"It's exactly two o'clock."
ཆུ་ཚོད་གཉིས་དང་སྐར་མ་བཅོ་ལྔ་རེད།	"It's a quarter past two."
ཆུ་ཚོད་གཉིས་དང་ཕྱེད་ཀ་རེད།	"It's half past two."
ཕྱག་ཚོད་ག་ཚོད་ལ་ཕེབས་ཀྱི་རེད།	"At what time will he come?"
ཆུ་ཚོད་ལྔ་པ་དྲུག་པ་ལ་ཕེབས་ཀྱི་རེད།	"He'll come at five or six o'clock."

12.3.3 Omitting the ergative

The particle ki' must be used with "ergative" verbs[122] in the perfective past. However, the particle is often omitted in the present (or past imperfective) and future.

Ex.: རང་ག་རེ་བྱེད་ཀྱི་ཡོད། ra̲ng kha̲re che̲'-kiyö'
"What are you doing?"

ཨ་མ་ལགས་མཆོད་ཆང་མཆོད་ཀྱི་རེད་པས། āma-la' chō̄cang chō̄'-kire'-pä'
"Will your mother have some beer?"

However, it reappears if the speaker is either stressing the agent or if the latter is being contrastively emphasized.

Ex.: ཁོང་གསོལ་ཇ་བཟོ་གི་ཡོད་རེད། khōng sō̄:ca so̲-kiyo:re'
"He's making tea."

ཁོང་གིས་གསོལ་ཇ་བཟོ་གི་ཡོད་རེད། khōng-ki' sō̄:ca so̲-kiyo:re'
"He's making the tea." (I'm making momos)

In cases where the ergative marker is omitted, the agentive function is simply indicated by word order: the grammatical agent[123] comes first, while the patient figures just before the verb.

Ex.: ང་ཁྱེད་རང་དྲན་གྱིས། nga̲ khyērang thra̲n-ki' "I remember you."[124]
ཁྱེད་རང་ང་དྲན་གྱི་འདུག་གས། khyērang nga̲ thra̲n-kitu'-kä' "Do you remember me?"

In both these examples the agentive particle could of course be inserted; this would have the effect of emphasizing the agent.

ངས་ཁྱེད་རང་དྲན་གྱིས། ngä̲' khyērang thra̲n-ki' "*I* remember you."

When the agent is shifted to occupy the position just before the verb, it usually carries a case marker.

ཁྱེད་རང་ངས་དྲན་གྱིས། khyērang ngä̲' thra̲n-ki "You, I remember."

The ergative marker is not usually used with volitional intransitive verbs (notably verbs of motion), but it may appear with verbs in this category if the subject is being emphatically contrasted with another.

Ex.: ང་གནས་མཇལ་ལ་ཕྱིན་པ་ཡིན། nga̲ nä̃ncä:-la chīn-payin
"I went on a pilgrimage."

ངས་གནས་མཇལ་ལ་ཕྱིན་པ་ཡིན། ngä̲' nä̃ncä:-la chīn-payin
"*I* went on a pilgrimage." (They went trading)

---

122. See Lesson 8.

123. I.e., the subject of a transitive ergative verb.

124. This is also the usual way of saying "I miss you!"

By contrast, it should be remembered that the ergative never occurs with non-volitional intransitive verbs.

• The functions of agent and possessor

When the agent (marked with the ergative) and the possessor of an object (marked with the genitive) refer to the same person in a single sentence (in which case they are coreferential), in most cases only the possessor is mentioned. For example, in the following sentence, the owner of the bicycle and the agent of the verb "to put" are the same person, and therefore only the genitive case appears, without the agentive.

Ex.: ཁྱེད་རང་གི་རྐང་གა་རིལ་ ག་པར་བཞག་ཡོད། "Where did (you) put your bicycle?"

The use of the ergative instead of the genitive is possible, but this would place the stress on the action and not on ownership.

Ex.: ཁྱེད་རང་གིས་རྐང་ག་རིལ་ ག་པར་བཞག་ཡོད། "Where did you put (the/ your) bicycle?"

The use of both agent and possessor would be very odd:

? ཁྱེད་རང་གིས་ཁྱེད་རང་གི་རྐང་ག་རིལ་ག་པར་བཞག་ཡོད།

12.3.4 Omitting the subject

In both Spoken and Literary Tibetan, the subject is often omitted. In the preceding lessons we have encountered numerous sentences without any subject being specified.

Ex.: ཁོང་ནས་མཆོད་ཀྱི་མ་རེད། "(She) never drinks."
དབྱིན་ཇི་ནས་རེད་པས། "Is (he) from England?"

It is often the case that the auxiliary or the interrogative particle indicates whether the subject is the first, second or third person, but in many instances context is our only clue. Thus in another context the last sentence might mean "Am I from England?"

12.3.5 The pronoun གཅིག་ *cī' "someone, something"*

The number cī' "one" has several meanings. We have already come across (in Lesson 10) the pronominal use of cī'. It means both "someone" and "something". On the other hand, in certain contexts, cī' means "once" or "a little".

Ex.: འདིར་གཅིག་ཕེབས་སོང་། "Someone came here."
དངུལ་གཅིག་གཡར་དང་། "Lend me a little money."
ང་རང་ཁོ་དང་གཅིག་འཛིང་གི་ཡིན། "I'm going to have a bit of a quarrel with him."

12.4 Exercises སྦྱོང་ཚན།

12.4.1 Translate into English:

༄༅། ད་ལྟ་ཆུ་ཚོད་ག་ཚོད་རེད། ཆུ་ཚོད་ལྔ་དང་ཕྱེད་ཀ་རེད། ཆུ་ཚོད་ག་ཚོད་ལ་ཐེབས་ག ཆུ་ཚོད་དགུ་པ་ཟིན་པར་སྐར་མ་བཅུ་ལ་ཡོང་གི་ཡིན། ཁྱེད་རང་གློག་བརྙན་གཟིགས་ཡག་ལ་མཉེས་པོ་ཡོད་པས། དེབ་འདི་སུས་ཉོས་པ་རེད། དེབ་འདི་ངས་ཉོས་པ་ཡིན། བཀྲ་ཤིས་ལགས་ཕྱག་ལས་གནང་གར་ཐེབས་སོང་ངས། ཕྱག་ལས་གནང་གར་ཐེབས་མ་སོང་། གཟིགས་མོ་གཟིགས་གར་ཐེབས་སོང་། ང་པོ་ལོ་བལྟ་ཡག་ལ་དགའ་པོ་ཡོད། སྒྲོལ་མ་ལགས་གསོལ་ཀྲུམ་གཟིགས་གར་ཐེབས་སོང་ངས། ཁྱེད་རང་ལ་དངུལ་ག་ཚོད་ཡོད།

12.4.2 Translate into Tibetan:

1. They are in the restaurant.
2. Dorje has gone to the bank.
3. I went to have (lit. drink) some tea.
4. Nyima stayed in hospital.
5. Behind the hospital there is a library.
6. They bought some tsampa (ground roasted barley).
7. Now it's half past four; we have to get up!
8. Will you come to the show? What time is the show? At a quarter to nine.
9. There are many hotels in Lhasa.
10. Where is the post office?

12.4.3 Read and translate Text 12.1.b of this lesson.

12.4.4 Insert the appropriate verb suffix ཡག་(ལ་) or གར་.

༡) ཁོང་གློག་བརྙན་ལྟ་ ( ) ཕྱིན་པ་རེད།

༢) རྡོ་རྗེ་པོ་ལོ་ལྟ་ ( ) དགའ་པོ་ཡོད་རེད།

༣) ཁོང་གར་རོལ་གཞོན་ ( ) དགའ་པོ་ཡོད་རེད།

༤) གནམ་གྲུའི་སྟ་སེ་ཉོ་ ( ) ལས་སླ་པོ་མི་འདུག

༥) ཕྱི་རྒྱལ་གྱི་མི་དེ་ཚོ་རི་འཛེགས་ ( ) དགའ་པོ་ཡོད་པ་འདྲ།

༦) བཀྲ་ཤིས་མར་ཉོ་ ( ) ཕྱིན་སོང་།

༧) ཁོང་ཚོ་བླ་མ་མཇལ་ ( ) ཐེབས་སོང་།

༨) རྡོ་རྗེ་རྒྱ་གར་ལ་སྤྱུན་སྐྱུ་ཐུག་ ( ) ཕྱིན་པ་རེད།

12.4.5 Write a phonological transcription of Text 12.1b.

"Arriving at the Airport"
གནམ་གྲུ་འབབ་ཐང་ལ་སླེབས་པ།

Grammar aims བརྡ་སྤྲོད་རིག་པའི་དམིགས་ཚད།

- The conditional.
- The imperative suffix རོགས་གནང་ ro'nang.
- The construction V+ འགྲོའོ་+ Aux. "about to", "have just".

CD I • Tr. 37-38

13.1 Dialogue དྲི་བ་དྲིས་ལན།

བློ་བཟང་ ༔	གཟིགས་ད་(དང་)། དེ་འདྲའི་མཛེས་པོ།
མི་ཤེལ་ ༔	ད་ག་རང་། ཧི་མ་ལ་ཡའི་རི་རྒྱུད་ཡིན་པ་འདྲ།
བློ་བཟང་ ༔	ལགས་རེད། རྫོ་ཁའི་གནམ་ཐང་ལ་སླེབས་འགྲོའོ་(གྲབས་)ཡོད་རེད།
མི་ཤེལ་ ༔	ཨོ། སླེབས་སོང་།
གནམ་གྲུ་ཁ་ལོ་པ་ ༔	ག་ལེ་ཕེབས་གོ
མི་ཤེལ་དང་བློ་བཟང་ ༔	ཐུགས་རྗེ་ཆེ། ག་ལེ་བཞུགས།
མཐའ་སྲུང་དམག་ ༔	སྐུ་ཤོག་(སྐུ་ཞབས་) ཕྱག་ཕེབས་གནང་བྱུང་། ག་ནས་ཕེབས་པ། ཁྱེད་རང་གི་ཕྱག་ཁྱེར་ག་པར་ཡོད།
མི་ཤེལ་ ༔	པ་རན་སི་ནས་ཡོང་པ་ཡིན། ལག་ཁྱེར་འདུའི་(འདིར་)ཡོད།
མཐའ་སྲུང་དམག་ ༔	ཐུགས་རྗེ་ཆེ། ག་ལེ་ཕེབས།
མི་ཤེལ་ ༔	ལགས་སོ། ག་ལེ་བཞུགས།
འགག་སྲུ་ ༔	སྐུ་ཤོག་ཕྱག་ཕེབས་གནང་། ཕྱག་ཁྱེར་ངར་བསྟན་རོགས་གནང་། སྐུ་ཆས་ལ་ལྟ་ཙ་(ཙམ་) བྱས་ན་འགྲིག་གི་རེད་པས།
མི་ཤེལ་ ༔	ཡིན་ད་ཡིན། ངའི་ཅ་ལག་ཚང་མ་འདུའི་(འདིར་)ཡོད། གཟིགས་རོགས་གནང་།
འགག་སྲུ་ ༔	ཐུགས་ཆེ། ད་ཁ་བསྐྱོན་རོགས་གནང་།

Pronunciation

- si'-ta tinträ' tsepo !

- thaka rang hīmalayä: rikyü' yinpatra

- la' re' lhōkä: nāmtang-la lēp tro:-yo:re'

- ō lēp-song

- khale phēp-ko

- thūkce chē khale shu'

- kūsho', chā'pe' nāng-cung

- khanä' phēp-pa. khyērang-ki chākkyer khapar yö'

- phāransi-nä' yong-payin la'kyer tä: yö'

- thūkce chē khale phēp

- la'-so khale shu'

- kūsho' chāpe' nāng chākkyer ngar tān-ro'nang kūcä'-la tā-ts chä'-na tri'-kire'-pä'

- yin-ta yin ngä: cāla' tshāngma tä: yö'. si'-ro'nang

- thūkce chē. tha, khā kyōn-ro'nang.

Translation

Lobzang	—	Look, It's so beautiful!
Michel	—	Isn't it just! That's probably the Himalayan Range.
Lobzang	—	Yes, we're about to arrive at Lhokha Airport.
Michel	—	Oh! We've arrived.
Pilot	—	Goodbye.
Michel and Lobzang	—	Thank you, goodbye (lit. stay slowly).
Frontier policeman	—	Welcome. Where have you come from? (Where's) your passport, please?
Michel	—	I've come from France. Here's my passport.
Frontier policeman	—	Thank you, goodbye.
Michel	—	Lovely, thank you.
Customs official	—	Welcome, gentlemen. Show me your passports, please. May I take a look at your luggage please? (If I take a brief look at your luggage will that be all right?)
Michel	—	Certainly, all my things are in here! Please take a look.
Customs official	—	Thank you. Now close them please.

ཀ་ཁ་ག་ང་

13.2 Vocabulary ཚིག་གསར།

སྐུ་ཞོག་ kūsho' སྐུ་ཞབས་ kūshap (L) — (n.) sir

སྐུ་ངོ་ kūngo — (n.) Your Excellency

ལས་བྱེད་པ་ lä̱cepa	(n.) official, civil servant
ཁ་ལོ་པ་ khālopa	(n.) driver, pilot
དམག་མི་ mā'mi	(n.) soldier
ལག་ཁྱེར་ la̱kkyer ཕྱག་ཁྱེར chākkyer (H)	(n.) permit, passport
རི་རྒྱུད་ ri̱kyü'	(n.) mountain range
གནམ་གྲུ་འབབ་ཐང་ nāmtru pa̱ptang	(n.) airport
གནམ་ཐང་ nāmtang	(n.) airport
འབབ་ཚུགས་ pa̱ptsu'	(n.) station
སྒོ་ ko̱ གཟིམ་སྒོ་ si̱mko (H)	(n.) door
རྒྱུད་ kyü̱'	(n.) chain, range, *tantra*
ཅ་ལག་ cāla' སྐུ་ཆས་ kūcä' (H)	(n.) things, belongings
གནམ་གྲུ་ nāmtru	(n.) aeroplane
རི་ལི་ ri̱li མེ་འཁོར་ me̱kor (L)	(n.) train
གྲུ་གཟིངས་ thru̱sing'	(n.) boat
ཐད་ཕུར་གནམ་གྲུ་ thā̱pur nāmtru	(n.) helicopter
སྤྱི་སྤྱོད་རླངས་འཁོར་ cī̱cö' lāngkor	(n.) bus
མཛེས་པོ་ tse̱po	(adj.) beautiful
མདོག་ཉེས་ to̱'nye'	(adj.) ugly
ད་ག་རང་ tha̱ka ra̱ng	(adv.) really, absolutely
ཡིན་ད་ཡིན་ yi̱n-ta-yi̱n	(adv.) of course, certainly
གལ་སྲིད་ khä̱si'	(co.) if
ཚང་མ་ tshāngma	(quant.) all
འགྲོ་ tro̱: གྲབས་ thra̱p (L)	(aux.) to be about to
རོགས་གནང་ ro'nang (H)	(aux.) *imperative*
སླེབས་ lēp	(v.) [inv., A] to arrive
འགྲིག་ tri̱'	(v.) [inv., A] to be all right
བསྟན་ tā̱n	(v.) [vol., EA] to show
རྒྱག་(1) kya̱'/ བརྒྱབ་ (2) kya̱p/ རྒྱོབ་kyo̱p(3)	(v.) [vol., EA] – to make, do – *verbalizer*
བསྐྱོན་ kyōn (H)	(v.) [vol., EA] – to make, do – *verbalizer*
ཁ་ཕྱེ་ khā chē ཞལ་ཕྱེ་shä̱: chē (H)	(v.) [vol., EA] to open (objects)
ཁ་རྒྱག་ khā kya̱' ཁ་བསྐྱོན་ khā kyōn (H)	(v.) [vol., EA] to close (objects)
སྒོ་ཕྱེ་ ko̱ chē གཟིམ་སྒོ་ཕྱེ་ si̱mko chē (H)	(v.) [vol., EA] to open (a door)
སྒོ་རྒྱག་ ko̱ kya̱' གཟིམ་སྒོ་བསྐྱོན་ si̱mko kyōn (H)	(v.) [vol., EA] to close (a door)
ག་ལེ་ཕེབས་ kha̱le phēp	(idiom.) goodbye (to someone leaving)
ག་ལེ་ཞུགས་ kha̱le shu̱'	(idiom.) goodbye (to someone staying)

Proper nouns

ཧི་མ་ལ་ཡ་ hīmalaya	Himalaya

༡༣༣

13.3 Remarks འགྲེལ་བཤད།

13.3.1 The conditional

Tibetan has no specific verb mood to express the conditional. The conditional is formed by adding the particle ན་ -na “if” to the verb in the subordinate clause or to its auxiliary. The particle -na is combined with auxiliaries in the following cases: ཡོད་ན་ yö̱'-na, འདུག་ན་ tu̱'-na, ཡིན་ན་ yi̱n-na, but the following combinations are incorrect: *རེད་ན་ re̱'-na and *ཡོད་རེད་ན་ yo̱:re'-na.

The protasis (the “if” clause) may be preceded by the expression གལ་སྲིད་ khä̱:si'. There are basically three types of constructions, corresponding respectively to the present, past and “future” conditional.

• The **present conditional** expresses a situation that has not occurred, but that remains a possibility at the time the statement is made; or else a pure hypothesis, about the likelihood of which the statement has nothing to say. In this case the verb in the subordinate clause appears in the past tense optionally followed by the past auxiliary པ་ཡིན་[125] and the main clause verb is in the future tense. The structure may be represented as follows:

གལ་སྲིད་ […] V (past) + ན་ […], V + AUX (future)

གལ་སྲིད་ […] V (past) + པ་ཡིན་ན་ […], V + AUX (future)

These constructions, which translate both the conditional and indicative moods of English, are by far the most commonly used in Tibetan to formulate conditionals. They are also sometimes used to express past and future conditionals.

Ex.: ཁྱི་རིལ་ཚང་མ་བཟས་ན་གྲོད་ཁོག་ན་གི་རེད། chi̱ri: tshāngma sä̱'-na thrö̱ko' na̱-kire'
“If he ate all the sweets, he would have a stomach ache.”

ཁྱི་རིལ་ཚང་མ་བཟས་པ་ཡིན་ན་གྲོད་ཁོག་ན་གི་རེད། chi̱ri: tshāngma sä̱'-payin-na thrö̱ko' na̱-kire'
“If he ate all the sweets, he would have a stomach ache.”

སྒམ་ལ་སྒོ་ལྕགས་བརྒྱབ་ན་ཅ་ལག་བརླག་གི་མ་རེད། ka̱m-la ko̱ca' kya̱p-na cāla' lā'-kimare'
“If you close the box with a padlock, the things won’t be lost.”

ཁྱེད་རང་གིས་མོ་ཊ་བཙོང་ན་ངས་ཉོ་གི་ཡིན། “If you were to sell your car, I’d buy it.”

---

125. The auxiliary *pa-yin* may be used with any verb class (volitional or non-volitional), although sometimes other auxiliaries such as *byung-na* or *song-na* may also be used. There is a slight difference between the two constructions: when the verb is followed by the auxiliary *pa-yin*, it can indicate a mere hypothesis, a general statement which is not linked to the ongoing situation.

On the other hand, the present conditional is often used to translate polite requests with the verb “can” or “may” (lit. would it be all right if…).

Ex.: འདི་འདྲས་བྱས་ན་འགྲིག་གི་རེད་པས། “May I do that?”
ཁྱེད་རང་དོ་དགོངས་འདིར་གཟིམ་ན་འགྲིག་གི་རེད། “You can sleep here tonight.”

Finally, there is another construction involving the present conditional: The subordinated conditional clause is followed by the perfect auxiliary. The meaning differs from the above construction only in terms of verb aspect.

གལ་སྲིད་ […] V (past) + ཡོད་ན་ […], V + AUX (future)

Ex.: བྱི་རིལ་ཚང་མ་བཟས་ཡོད་ན་གྲོད་ཁོག་ན་གི་རེད། chi̱ri: tshāngma sä̱'-yö'-na thrö̱ko' na̱-ki:re'
“If he has eaten all the sweets, he will have a stomach ache.”

• The **past conditional** expresses a possibility that could have been envisaged in the past, but that did not actually occur. The verb in the subordinate clause is usually in the past tense-aspect (perfect or perfective); the main verb is usually in the past and is followed by the perfect auxiliary or auxiliaries of probability.[126]

གལ་སྲིད་ […] V (past) + ཡོད་ན་ […] V + ཡོད་རེད་ / པ་ཡོད་

གལ་སྲིད་ […] V (past) + པ་ཡིན་ན་ […] V + ཡོད་རེད་ / པ་ཡོད་

Ex.: བྱི་རིལ་ཚང་མ་བཟས་ཡོད་ན་གྲོད་ཁོག་ན་ཡོད་རེད། chi̱ri: tshāngma sä̱'-yö'-na thrö̱ko' na̱-yo:re'
“If (he) had eaten all the sweets, he would have had a stomach ache.”

The perfective is also sometimes used:
བྱི་རིལ་ཚང་མ་བཟས་པ་ཡིན་ན་གྲོད་ཁོག་ན་ཡོད་རེད། chi̱ri: tshāngma sä̱'-payin-na thrö̱ko' na̱-yo:re'
idem.

Ex.: སྒམ་ལ་སྒོ་ལྕགས་བརྒྱབ་ཡོད་ན་ཅ་ལག་བརླག་ཡོད་མ་རེད། ka̱m-la ko̱ca' kya̱p-na cāla' lā'-yo:mare'
“If the box had been padlocked, the things wouldn’t have been lost.”

Or: སྒམ་ལ་སྒོ་ལྕགས་བརྒྱབ་ཡོད་ན་ཅ་ལག་བརླག་པ་མེད། ka̱m-la ko̱ca' kya̱p-na cāla' lā'-pame' idem.

Ex.: ཁྱེད་རང་གིས་མོ་ཊ་བཙོང་ཡོད་ན་ངས་ཉོས་ཡོད་རེད། “If you’d sold your car, I’d have bought it.”

Or: ཁྱེད་རང་གིས་མོ་ཊ་བཙོང་ཡོད་ན་ངས་ཉོས་པ་ཡོད། idem.

• The **future conditional** expresses a future possibility. In this case, the verbs of the subordinate and main clauses are both in the future. This construction is not very commonly used, and it is usually replaced by the present conditional.

---

126. The auxiliaries -payö' / patu' are discussed in Lesson 28.

གལ་སྲིད་ […] V (present-future) + AUX (future) + ན་ […] V + AUX (future)

Ex.: ཁྱེད་རང་གིས་མོ་ཊ་ཚོང་གི་ཡིན་ན་ངས་ཉོ་གི་ཡིན། "If you sell (lit. will sell) your car, I'll buy it."

13.3.2 The imperative suffix རོགས་གནང་ ro'nang

This suffix may be attached to any volitional verb, preferably an honorific one, to formulate a request or a polite command.

Ex.:			
	གཟིགས་རོགས་གནང་།	si̱'-ro'nang	"Look." or "Buy."
	ཁ་བརྒྱུན་རོགས་གནང་།	khā kyön-ro'nang	"Close it."
	ཕེབས་རོགས་གནང་།	phēp-ro'nang	"Come."

13.3.3 The constructions "to be about to" and "to have just".

These two constructions are expressed by placing འགྲོའོ་tro̱:, which is derived from the literary form གྲབས་thra̱p, after the main verb.

To say "to be about to", Tibetan uses the existential auxiliaries yo̱re', tu̱', yö̱': འགྲོའོ་ཡོད་ tro̱:-yö' (ego), འགྲོའོ་འདུག་ tro̱:-tu', འགྲོའོ་ཡོད་རེད་ tro̱:-yo:re'.

"To have just" is expressed by using the essential auxiliaries re̱' or yi̱n: འགྲོའོ་ཡིན་ tro̱:-yin (ego), འགྲོའོ་རེད་ tro̱:-re'.

And finally, the verb འགྲོའོ་tro̱: (or its literary form གྲབས་thra̱p) may be followed by the verb "to do" བྱེད་ che̱' to mean "all but" or "almost".

Ex.:		
	ཁྱེད་རང་ཞལ་ལག་མཆོད་འགྲོའོ་ཡོད་པས།	"Are you about to eat?"
	ཁོང་ཆུ་འདིའི་ནང་ལ་ཤི་འགྲོའོ་བྱས་པ་རེད།	"He almost died in this river."
	གནམ་ཐང་ལ་སླེབས་འགྲོའོ་ཡོད་རེད།	"We're about to arrive at the airport."
	ང་འབྲུག་ཡུལ་ནས་ཡོང་འགྲོའོ་ཡིན།	"I've just come from Bhutan."

13.4 Exercises སྦྱོང་ཚན།

13.4.1 Translate into English:

༡) པ་གི་སློ་བཟང་ལགས་ཡིན་པ་འདྲ། མ་རེད། པ་གི་རྡོ་རྗེ་རེད།

༢) འདི་རྡོ་རྗེའི་ཡི་གེ་ཡིན་པ་འདྲ། ལགས་རེད། འདི་ཁོང་གིས་བྲིས་པ་རེད།

༣) ཀན་ལགས་ལྷ་སར་སླེབས་འགྲོའོ་ཡོད་རེད་པས། ལགས་རེད་སླེབས་འགྲོའོ་ཡོད་རེད།

༤) ཁྱེད་རང་གི་ཕྱག་དེབ་དེ་ངར་ཅིག་བསྟན་རོགས་གནང་།

༥) གཉིས་དང་བདུན་བསྡོམས་པས་དགུ་རེད།

༦) བཞི་བཅུ་ཞེ་ལྔ་དང་བཅུ་བསྡོམས་པས་ང་བཅུ་ང་ལྔ་རེད།

༧) བཅུ་ནས་གཅིག་འཐེན་པས་དགུ་རེད།

༨) དྲུག་ཅུ་རེ་བཞི་ནས་སུམ་ཅུ་སོ་ལྔ་འཐེན་པས་ཉི་ཤུ་རྩ་དགུ་རེད།

༩) བདུན་ཅུ་དོན་བརྒྱད་ནས་བཅོ་ལྔ་འཐེན་པས་དྲུག་ཅུ་རེ་གསུམ་རེད།

༡༠) གསུམ་དང་ལྔ་བསྡོམས་པས་བརྒྱད་རེད།

13.4.2 Rewrite the sentences according to the example given.

ཁྱེད་རང་བོད་ལ་ཕེབས་རོགས་གནང་། > བོད་ལ་ཕེབས་ན་ཡག་པོ་ཡོད་རེད།

༡) རྒྱ་ཁོལ་མ་མཆོད་རོགས་གནང་། > …………………………...

༢) བོད་སྐད་སློབ་སྦྱོང་གནང་རོགས་གནང་། > …………………………...

༣) ཞིང་ཏོག་མང་པོ་མཆོད་རོགས་གནང་། > …………………………...

13.4.3 Complete the following sentences using the appropriate auxiliaries.

༡) ད་ལྟ་མིག་མིག་མ་བཟས་ན་གྲོད་ཁོག་ལྟོགས་( )།

༢) ཁྱེད་རང་གི་ཁང་པ་ཚོང་གི་ཡིན་ན་ངས་ཉོ་( )།

༣) ཁྱེད་རང་ཕྱུག་ལས་ལ་མ་ཕེབས་ན་ང་ཡང་འགྲོ་( )།

༤) ཐུ་པོ་ཕྱིན་ཡོད་ན་སླེབས་( )།

༥) སློབ་སྦྱོང་མ་བྱས་ན་ཡོན་ཏན་ཤེས་( )།

༦) ང་དེ་དུས་སློབ་སྦྱོང་ཡག་པོ་བྱས་ཡོད་ན་ད་ལྟ་མཁས་པ་ཆགས་( )།

13.4.4 Complete the following sentences using the appropriate auxiliaries.

༡) ཁོང་ད་ལྟ་རང་བོད་ནས་ཕེབས་འགྲོའོ་( )།

༢) ཁོང་གཉིས་བདུན་ཕྲག་སྔོན་མ་ཚང་ས་བརྒྱབ་འགྲོའོ་( )།

༣) སྐར་མ་ལྔ་སྒུགས་རོགས་གནང་།རྐན་ལགས་ཕེབས་འགྲོའོ་( )།

༤) ང་ཁྱེད་རང་ནང་ལ་ཡོང་འགྲོའོ་( )།

13.4.5 Translate into Tibetan:

1. The pilot of the aeroplane is Tibetan.
2. They've just arrived at the station.
3. There are some helicopters at the airport.

4. There are a lot of soldiers on the train.
5. If you haven't got a permit, you won't be able to go there.
6. If you go to Gandän monastery, you'll meet his brother.

13.5 Civilization རིག་གཞུང་།

Administrative Tibet

Situated in the southwest of the People's Republic of China, the Tibet Autonomous Region, the Tibetan Autonomous Prefectures and the Tibetan Autonomous Counties comprise a vast territory of over 2 200 000 km^2. The Tibetan Autonomous Prefectures are located within the Chinese provinces of Qinghai, Sichuan, Gansu and Yunnan.

The Tibet Autonomous Region

- བོད་རང་སྐྱོང་ལྗོངས་ phö̱' ra̱ngkyong co̱ng (*Chin.* xizang zizhiqu)

  1 138 400 km^2 (excluding NEFA or Arunachal Pradesh, a border region under Indian control but claimed by the PRC). Apart from Standard Tibetan, the dialects spoken in the T.A.R. include those of Ü, Tsang, Tö Ngari and Kham. (དབུས་སྐད། ǖkä', གཙང་སྐད། tsāngkä', སྟོད་སྐད་ tōkä', ཁམས་སྐད། khāmkä').

  The T.A.R. is subdivided into six prefectures and one municipality: Lhasa Municipality ལྷ་ས་གྲོང་ཁྱེར་(lhāsa thro̱ngkyer), Zhikatse Prefecture གཞིས་ཀ་རྩེ་ས་ཁུལ་(shi̱katse sākü:), Lhokha Prefecture ལྷོ་ཁ་ས་ཁུལ་ (lhōka sākü:), Chamdo Prefecture ཆབ་མདོ་ས་ཁུལ་ (chāmto sākü:), Nagchu Prefecture ནག་ཆུ་ས་ཁུལ་(na̱kcu sākü:), Ngari Prefecture མངའ་རིས་ས་ཁུལ་ (ngāri' sākü:), and Nyingthri Prefecture ཉིང་ཁྲི་ས་ཁུལ་(nyi̱ntri sākü:)

The Chinese province of Qinghai (མཚོ་སྔོན། tshō ngō̱n)

The Tibetan areas of Qinghai cover a total of 723 600 km^2.

- Golok Tibetan Autonomous Prefecture

  མགོ་ལོག་བོད་རིགས་རང་སྐྱོང་ཁུལ་ ko̱lo' phö̱ri' ra̱ngkyong khǖ: (*Chin.* guoluo zangzu zizhizhou). Various Amdo dialects (ཨ་མདོ་སྐད་ āmto kä') are spoken in this area.

- Kyegundo Tibetan Autonomous Prefecture

  སྐྱེ་དགུ་མདོ་(ཡུས་ཤུ་) བོད་རིགས་རང་སྐྱོང་ཁུལ། kyēkunto (*or* yu̱shu) phö̱ri' ra̱ngkyong khǖ: (*Chin.* yushu zangzu zijizhou). Various Kham dialects (ཁམས་སྐད་ khāmkä') are spoken.

- Tibetan Autonomous Prefecture of the South of the Yellow River

  རྨ་ལྷོ་བོད་རིགས་རང་སྐྱོང་ཁུལ་ mā lhō phö̱ri' ra̱ngkyong khǖ: (*Chin.* huangnan zangzu zizhizhou). Various Amdo dialects (ཨ་མདོ་སྐད་ āmto kä') are spoken in this area.

• Tibetan Autonomous Prefecture of North of the Lake (Kokonor)

མཚོ་བྱང་བོད་རིགས་རང་སྐྱོང་ཁུལ tshō cha̱ng phö̱ri' ra̱ngkyong khǖ:. (*Chin.* haibei zangzu zizhizhou). Various Amdo dialects (ཨ་མདོ་སྐད་ āmto kä') are spoken in this area.

• Mongol and Tibetan Autonomous Prefecture of the West of the Lake (Kokonor)

མཚོ་ནུབ་བོད་རིགས་དང་སོག་རིགས་རང་སྐྱོང་ཁུལ། tshō nu̱p phö̱ri'-tang sō'ri' ra̱ngkyong khǖ:. (*Chin.* haixi mengguzu zangzu zizhizhou). Various Amdo dialects (ཨ་མདོ་སྐད་ āmto kä') are spoken in this area.

• Mongol and Tibetan Autonomous Prefecture of the South of the Lake (Kokonor)

མཚོ་ལྷོ་བོད་རིགས་རང་སྐྱོང་ཁུལ། tshō lhō phö̱ri' ra̱ngkyong khǖ:. (*Chin.* hainan zangzu zizhizhou). Various Amdo dialects (ཨ་མདོ་སྐད་ āmto kä') are spoken in this area.

This province also contains a number of Tibetan townships (བོད་རིགས་གྲོང་ཚོ་ phöri' thro̱ngtso, *Chin.* zangzu xiang) attached to Chinese counties or autonomous counties of other nationalities (Hui, Salar, Tu).

• Region East of the Lake (Kokonor)

མཚོ་ཤར་ཁུལ། tshō shār khǖ:. (*Chin.* Haidong). Although this area, around the city of Xining, has a population of some 200,000 Tibetans as well as a number of other ethnic groups, it has no autonomous status. Various Amdo dialects (ཨ་མདོ་སྐད་ āmto kä') are spoken in this area.

The Chinese Province of Gansu (ཀན་སུའུ་ kānsu)

The Tibetan areas of Gansu cover a total of 45 625 km^2.

• The Tibetan Autonomous Prefecture of the South of Gansu.

ཀན་ལྷོ་བོད་རིགས་རང་སྐྱོན་ཁུལ། kān lhō phö̱ri' ra̱ngkyong khǖ: (*Chin.* gannan zangzu zizhizhou). (39 825 km^2). Various Amdo dialects (ཨ་མདོ་སྐད་ āmto kä') are spoken in this area.

• The Tibet Autonomous County of Pari

དཔལ་རིས་བོད་རིགས་རང་སྐྱོང་རྫོང་། pā:ri' phö̱ri' ra̱ngkyong tso̱ng: (*Chin.* tianzhu zangzu zizhixian) (5 800 km^2). Amdo dialect (ཨ་མདོ་སྐད་ āmto kä') is spoken in this area.

This province also contains a number of Tibetan townships (བོད་རིགས་གྲོང་ཚོ་ phöri' thro̱ngtso, *Chin.* zangzu xiang) attached to Chinese counties.

The Chinese Province of Sichuan (སི་ཁྲོན་ sītrön)

The Tibetan areas of Sichuan cover a total of 247 530 km^2.

• Ngapa Tibetan Autonomous Prefecture.

རྔ་པ་(རྔ་བ)བོད་རིགས་རང་སྐྱོང་ཁུལ། ngāpa phö̱ri' ra̱ngkyong khǖ: (*Chin*. aba zangzu zizhizhou) (83 201 km^2). Dialects of Amdo (ཨ་མདོ་སྐད་ āmto kǟ') and Kham (ཁམས་སྐད་ khāmkä') as well as Gyälrong language (རྒྱལ་རོང་སྐད་ kyä̱:rong kǟ') are spoken in this area.

• Kanze Tibetan Autonomous Prefecture

དཀར་མཛེས་བོད་རིགས་རང་སྐྱོང་ཁུལ kāntse phö̱ri' ra̱ngkyong khǖ: (*Chin*. ganzi zangzu zizhizhou) (151 082 km^2). Dialects of Kham (ཁམས་སྐད་ khāmkä') as well as Gyälrong language (རྒྱལ་རོང་སྐད་ kyä̱:rong kǟ') are spoken in this area.

• Mili Tibetan Autonomous County

སྨི་ལི་བོད་རིགས་རང་སྐྱོང་རྫོང་། mīli phö̱ri' ra̱ngkyong tso̱ng (*Chin*. muli zangzu zizhixian). (13 246 km^2). Various Kham dialects (ཁམས་སྐད་ khāmkä') are spoken in this area.

This province also contains Tibetan townships attached to Chinese counties, and an autonomous county of the Yi nationality.

The Chinese province of Yunnan (ཡུན་ནན་yu̱nnän)

• Dechen Tibetan Autonomous Prefecture

བདེ་ཆེན་བོད་རིགས་རང་སྐྱོང་ཁུལ། te̱cen phö̱ri' ra̱ngkyong khǖ: (*Chin*. diqing zangzu zizhizhou) (23 870 km^2). Various Kham dialects (ཁམས་སྐད་ khāmkä') are spoken in this area.

(See map *Tibetan administrative areas*)

"The Banagzhöl Area"
སྦ་ནག་ཞོལ།

Grammar aims བརྡ་སྤྲོད་རིག་པའི་དམིགས་ཚད།

- The verbalizers བྱེད་che' རྒྱག་ kya̲' བཏང་tāng.
- The connective ནས་-nä'.
- The construction V+ པ་ད་ག -pataka.

CD I • Tr. 39-40 

14.1 Dialogue དྲི་བ་དྲིས་ལན།

བློ་བཟང་ ཿ རིག་ཞོག སྦ་ནག་ཞོལ་བར་དུ་ག་ཚོད་བྱེད་ག
རིག་ཞོག་ ཿ སྐོར་མོ་བདུན།
བློ་བཟང་ ཿ འོ་ཡོང་ང་།
མི་ཤེལ་ ཿ སླེབས་འགྲོའི་(གྲབས་)ཡོད་རེད་པས།
བློ་བཟང་ ཿ སླེབས་འགྲོའི་འདུག ཐག་ཉེ་པོ་རེད།
མི་ཤེལ་ ཿ ད་ག་པར་རེད།
བློ་བཟང་ ཿ འདའི་(འདིར་)རེད། ངའི་ཨ་ནེའི་ཁང་པ་འདི་རེད།
མི་ཤེལ་ ཿ ལགས་སོ། འདའི་སྐོར་མོ་བདུན་ཡོད།
རིག་ཞོག་ ཿ ཐུགས་ཆེ་གནང་། བཞུགས་གདན་འཇགས་གོ
ཨ་ནེ་ ཿ ཕྱག་ཕེབས་གནང་བྱུང་།
བློ་བཟང་ ཿ ལགས་ཡོད། ཨ་ནེ་ལགས་སྐུ་གཟུགས་བདེ་པོ་ཡིན་པས།
ཨ་ནེ་ ཿ བདེ་པོ་ཡིན།
བློ་བཟང་ ཿ ངའི་གྲོགས་པོ་མི་ཤེལ་རེད། ཁོང་པ་རན་སི་ནས་རེད། བོད་སྐད་དང་བོད་ཀྱི་ཤེས་རིག་སློབ་སྦྱོང་
གནང་གི་ཡོད་རེད། ང་གཉིས་ཉི་མ་ཁ་ཤས་བསྡད་ས་ཡོད་པས།
ཨ་ནེ་ ཿ བཞུགས་ས་ཡོད། ཨ་ལའི། ཡར་ཕེབས། ཁོང་ལྷ་སར་ཕེབས་ནས་ག་ཚོད་ཐད་(ཕྱིན་)སོང་།
བློ་བཟང་ ཿ སླེབས་པ་ད་ག་རེད། ང་གཉིས་གཟའ་ཉི་མ་བར་དུ་བསྡད་ན་འགྲིག་གི་རེད་པས།
ཨ་ནེ་ ཿ འགྲིག་གི་རེད།

Pronunciation

- ri̱ksho, pa̱nakshö: pha̱rtu kha̱tsö' che̱'-ka
- ko̱rmo tü̱n
- o̱ yo̱ng-nga
- lēp tro̱: yo̱:re'-pä'
- lēp tro̱ tu̱' thā' nye̱po re̱'
- tha̱ kha̱par rä̱'
- tä̱: re̱' ngä̱: āni: khāngpa ti̱ re̱'
- la̱'-so tä̱: ko̱rmo tü̱n yö̱'
- thūkce nāng shu̱tänca-ko
- chāpe' nāng-cung
- la̱' yö̱' āni-la' kūsu' te̱po yi̱n-pä'
- te̱po yi̱n
- ngä̱: tro̱kpo mi̱she: khōng phāränsi-nä' re̱' pho̱kä'-tang phö̱'-ki she̱ri' lōpcong nāng-kiyo:re'. nga̱nyi' nyi̱ma khāshä' tä̱'-sa yö̱'-pä'
- shu̱'-sa yö̱' ālä ya̱r phēp. khōng lhāsar phēp-nä' kha̱tsö' thā̱'-song
- lēp-pataka re̱' nga̱nyi' sa̱ nyi̱ma pha̱rtu tä̱'-na tri̱'-kire'-pä'
- tri'-kire'

Translation

Lobzang — *Rickshaw*! How much is it (lit. will you make it) up to Banagzhöl?
The *rickshaw* — Seven *gormo.*
Lobzang — That's fine.
Michel — Are we about to arrive?
Lobzang — Yes, we're nearly there, it's very close.
Michel — Where is it?
Lobzang — It's here. Here's my aunt's house.
Michel — Well then, here's seven *gormo.*
The *rickshaw* — Thanks, goodbye!
Aunt — Welcome!
Lobzang — Thank you. How are you, Auntie?
Aunt — I'm fine.
Lobzang — This is my friend Michel. He's French. He's studying Tibetan language and culture. Have you got a room where we can stay for a few days?
Aunt — Yes, I have a room. But come in! How long has he been in Lhasa? (lit. since he arrived how much [time] has passed)
Lobzang — He's just arrived. Can we stay until Sunday (lit. if we stay will that be all right)?
Aunt — Yes, that will be fine.

ཀ་ཁ་ག་ང་

14.2 Vocabulary ཚིག་གསར།

སྒོར་མོ་ ko̲rmo	(n.) *gormo*, currency unit
རིག་ཤོག་ ri̲ksho' སའན་ལུན་ sānlün (ch.)	(n.) *rickshaw*
པ་ད་ཀ་ pataka	(aux.) just
ས་ sā	(n.) earth, place
བསྡད་ས་ tä̲'-sa བཞུགས་ས་ shu̲'-sa (H)	(n.) room, place
གཟའ་ sa̲	(n.) planet
གཟའ་ཉི་མ་ sa̲ nyi̲ma	(n.) Sunday
གཟའ་ཟླ་བ་ sa̲ ta̲wa	(n.) Monday
གཟའ་མིག་དམར་ sa̲ mīkmar	(n.) Tuesday
གཟའ་ལྷག་པ་ sa̲ lhākpa	(n.) Wednesday
གཟའ་ཕུར་བུ་ sa̲ phūrpu	(n.) Thursday
གཟའ་པ་སངས་ sa̲ pāsang	(n.) Friday
གཟའ་སྤེན་པ་ sa̲ pēnpa	(n.) Saturday
ཟླ་བ་དང་པོ་ ta̲wa tha̲ngpo	(n.) January
ཟླ་བ་གཉིས་པ་ ta̲wa nyīpa	(n.) February
ཟླ་བ་གསུམ་པ་ ta̲wa sūmpa	(n.) March
ཟླ་བ་བཞི་པ་ ta̲wa shi̲pa	(n.) April
ཟླ་བ་ལྔ་པ་ ta̲wa ngāpa	(n.) May
ཟླ་བ་དྲུག་པ་ ta̲wa thru̲kpa	(n.) June
ཟླ་བ་བདུན་པ་ ta̲wa tü̲npa	(n.) July
ཟླ་བ་བརྒྱད་པ་ ta̲wa kyä̲pa	(n.) August
ཟླ་བ་དགུ་པ་ ta̲wa ku̲pa	(n.) September
ཟླ་བ་བཅུ་པ་ ta̲wa cūpa	(n.) October
ཟླ་བ་བཅུ་གཅིག་པ་ ta̲wa cūkcikpa	(n.) November
ཟླ་བ་བཅུ་གཉིས་པ་ ta̲wa cūnyipa	(n.) December
བོད་ཟླ་ phö̲nta	(n.) month (lunar calendar)
སྤྱི་ཟླ་ cīnta	(n.) month (international calendar)
སྤྱི་ལོ་ cīlo	(n.) year (international calendar)
ཚེས་པ་ tshēpa	(n.) date
ཆང་ས་ chāngsa ཁྲུང་ས་ thrūngsa(H)	(n.) marriage
བསམ་བློ་ sāmlo དགོངས་པ་ ko̲ngpa (H)	(n.) thought, idea
ཐག་ཉེ་པོ་ thā' nye̲po	(adj.) close, near
ཐག་རིང་པོ་ thā' ri̲ngpo	(adj.) far, distant
ཁ་ཤས་ khāshä'	(adj.) some, several
བསམས་sām'	(v.) [inv., EA] to think
བསམ་བློ་ + བཏང་ sāmlo tāng	(v.) [vol., E] to think, ponder

དགོངས་པ་ + བཞེས་ ko̱ngpa she̱' (H)	(v.) [vol., E] to think, ponder
ཆང་ས་ + རྒྱག་ chāngsa kya̱'	(v.) [vol., E] to marry
པར་ + རྒྱག་ pār kya̱'	(v.) [vol., ED] to photograph
བཞུགས་གདན་འཇགས་གོ་ shu̱ktänca'-ko	(idiom.) goodbye!
ཡོང་ང་ yo̱ngnga	(idiom.) all right, fine
ཐུགས་རྗེ་གནང་ thūkce nāng	(idiom.) thank you

Proper nouns

མི་ཞེལ་ mi̱she:	Michel
མིག་དམར་ mīkmar	Mars
ལྷག་པ་ lhākpa	Mercury
ཕུར་བུ་ phūrpu	Jupiter
པ་སངས་ pāsang	Venus
སྤེན་པ་ pēnpa	Saturn

༡༤༣

14.3 Remarks འགྲེལ་བཤད།

14.3.1 Compound verbs and verbalizers

In Spoken Tibetan, compound verbs are more common than simple verbs (verbs comprising only one syllable). For the most part, these consist of a noun and a "verbalizer". Verbalizers (Tibetan: *bya-tshig stong-pa*) are verbs that do not convey a specific meaning or else mean "to do" in a general sense. Compound verbs of this sort generally comprise two or three syllables, but some contain up to five.

The **three basic verbalizers** are: བྱེད་che̱' / གནང་nāng (H) "to do, act", རྒྱག་ kya̱' / བསྐྱོན་ kyōn (H) "to make" and བཏང་tāng / བཏང་གནང་tāng-nāng (H) "to send, do".[127]

Other verbalizers – some of them used only rarely – include: བཟོ་so̱ "to make", ཞུ་ shu̱ (h) "to say, to take",བཞེས་ she̱' "to take", བསླངས་ lāng' "to lift", ལང་ la̱ng "to get up", འགྲོ་ tro̱ "to go", ཤོར་ shōr "to let go",ཐེབས་ thēp "to be caught or hit", འཁོར་ khōr "to circulate", etc.

• The choice of verbalizer is determined partly by whether the verb is volitional or non-volitional. The verbalizers shōr, tro̱, la̱ng and thēp are used in the formation of non-volitional verbs.

Ex.:	མགོ་སྐོར་བཏང་	"to deceive"	མགོ་འཁོར་ཐེབས་	"to be deceived"
	ཁོང་ཁྲོ་བསླངས་	"to make angry"	ཁོང་ཁྲོ་ལང་	"to get angry"

127. Losang Thonden, *Modern Tibetan Language* (1986), volume 2, provides a substantial list of compound verbs involving these three verbalizers.

ཡར་རྒྱས་བཏང་	"to improve"	ཡར་རྒྱས་འགྲོ་	"to be improved"
མེ་མདའ་རྒྱག་	"to shoot"	མེ་མདའ་ཐེབས་	"to be hit (by a bullet)"
མིག་ཆུ་བཏང་	"to shed tears"	མིག་ཆུ་ཤོར་	"to burst into tears"
ཏུག་དྲི་བཏང་	"to fart (intentionally)"	ཏུག་དྲི་ཤོར་	"to fart (accidentally)"
གཅིན་པ་བཏང་	"to urinate (intentionally)"	གཅིན་པ་ཤོར་	"to wet oneself "
བསམ་བློ་བཏང་	"to ponder"	བསམ་བློ་འཁོར་	"to have an idea"
སྐྱུག་པ་སྐྱུག་	"to (make oneself) vomit"	སྐྱུག་པ་ཤོར་	"to vomit"

• The honorifics of compound verbs are formed by putting both the verbalizer and the preceding noun in the honorific.

Ex.: ཆང་ས་རྒྱག་ "to marry" — ཁྲུང་ས་བསྐྱོན་ "to marry" (H)
ལས་ཀ་བྱེད་ "to work" — ཕྱག་ལས་གནང་ "to work" (H)

• Compound verbs retain a certain syntactic flexibility: the noun can be separated from the verbalizer by an adverb or a negation, and may also be marked by a complement:

Ex.: བསམ་བློ་མང་པོ་བཏང་དགོས་རེད། "(We) have to give it a lot of thought."
བུ་མོས་གཞས་སྙན་པོ་ཞིག་བཏང་སོང་། "The girl sang a lovely song."
གཟབ་གཟབ་མ་བྱས་ན་ཉེན་ཁ་འདུག "If you're not careful, it's risky."

• The semantics of a verb offer no clue as to the verbalizer that should be used. As a general rule, compound verbs take only one verbalizer.

Ex.: ལས་ཀ་བྱེད་ "to work" but not *ལས་ཀ་བཏང་ or *ལས་ཀ་རྒྱག་
ཆང་ས་རྒྱག་ "to marry" but not *ཆང་ས་བྱེད་ or *ཆང་ས་བཏང་

In certain cases, however, there is a choice of which verbalizer may be used:

Ex.: བེད་སྤྱོད་བཏང་ or བེད་སྤྱོད་བྱེད་ "to use"; འགུལ་སྐྱོད་བརྒྱབ་ or འགུལ་སྐྱོད་བྱེད་ "to move"

In some exceptional instances, different verbalizers may be used, yielding a different meaning in each case.

Ex.: སྐད་བཏང་ "to call" but སྐད་རྒྱག་ "to shout"
མེ་རྒྱག་ "to set fire" but མེ་བཏང་ "to light, make a fire"
ལན་རྒྱག་ "to reply" but ལན་བཏང་ "to send a message"

• Like all verbs, verbalizers must be followed by auxiliaries. Here is a list of the "conjugations" (in all the tense-aspects and moods) with the auxiliaries we have encountered so far. Knowing all these forms will enable you to conjugate most verbs in Standard Tibetan.

Verbalizer བཏང	Verbalizer རྒྱག་	Verbalizer བྱེད་
བཏང་(གཏོང་)གི་ཡིན།	རྒྱག་གི་ཡིན།	བྱེད་ཀྱི་ཡིན།
བཏང་(གཏོང་)གི་རེད།	རྒྱག་གི་རེད།	བྱེད་ཀྱི་རེད།
བཏང་(གཏོང་)གི་ཡོད།	རྒྱག་གི་ཡོད།	བྱེད་ཀྱི་ཡོད།
བཏང་(གཏོང་)གི་འདུག	རྒྱག་གི་འདུག	བྱེད་ཀྱི་འདུག
བཏང་(གཏོང་)གི་ཡོད་རེད།	རྒྱག་གི་ཡོད་རེད།	བྱེད་ཀྱི་ཡོད་རེད།
བཏང་པ་ཡིན།	བརྒྱབ་པ་ཡིན།	བྱས་པ་ཡིན།
བཏང་བྱུང་།	བརྒྱབ་བྱུང་།	བྱས་བྱུང་།
བཏང་སོང་།	བརྒྱབ་སོང་།	བྱས་སོང་།
བཏང་པ་རེད།	བརྒྱབ་པ་རེད།	བྱས་པ་རེད།
བཏང་ཡོད།	བརྒྱབ་ཡོད།	བྱས་ཡོད།
བཏང་བཞག	བརྒྱབ་བཞག	བྱས་བཞག
བཏང་ཡོད་རེད།	བརྒྱབ་ཡོད་རེད།	བྱས་ཡོད་རེད།

Note: The egophoric auxiliaries and the perfect auxiliaries are not compatible with all verbs. For example, for a verb such as སྐད་བཏང་ "to call", depending on context it is possible to use either the intentional auxiliary or the receptive auxiliary: སྐད་བཏང་པ་ཡིན། "I called", སྐད་བཏང་བྱུང་།"I was called, (someone) called me". On the other hand, for a non-volitional verb such as རྨི་ལམ་བཏང་། "to dream", the intentional auxiliary is incorrect * རྨི་ལམ་བཏང་པ་ཡིན། and instead the receptive auxiliary must be used རྨི་ལམ་བཏང་བྱུང་།.

• Some verbs can take a complement in the form of a direct or an indirect object, whereas others cannot. The verbalizer gives no indication as to whether a verb is "transitive" or "intransitive". The following verbs all take an object:

Ex.: ཁོས་(རྒྱ་སྐད་)སློབ་སྦྱོང་བྱས་པ་རེད། "He studied (Chinese)."
ཁོས་(གློག་ལས་འཕྲུལ་འཁོར་)བེད་སྤྱོད་བྱས་པ་རེད། "He used (the computer)."
དགེ་རྒན་གྱིས་(སློབ་མ་)སྐད་བཏང་སོང་། "The teacher called (the student)."
ང་ལ་(ཁྱེད་རང་)རྨི་ལམ་བཏང་བྱུང་། "I dreamed (about you)."
དགེ་རྒན་གྱིས་(གནས་ཚུལ་)ངོ་སྤྲོད་ཞུས་སོང་། "The teacher presented (the situation)."
ཁོང་གིས་(ཆོས་)ཉམས་ལེན་ཞེ་པོ་ཅིག་བྱེད་ཀྱི་འདུག་ག "He practices (the Dharma) a lot!"

Unlike the verb "to study", the verb "to work" is not transitive, and one can not say: *ཁོས་(ཤིང་) ལས་ཀ་བྱས་པ་རེད། "He worked the wood."

Note: Several "intransitive" compound verbs take an ergative construction, whereas in the case of "simple" verbs this construction occurs only with transitive verbs. This may be explained by the fact that the noun that precedes the verbalizer can be analyzed as an "internal" object. In other words, the verbalizer acts as if it were an autonomous transitive verb.

14.3.2 The connective ནས་ nä̲' / -nä'

This particle, which is the same as that used to form the ablative case, is placed after the verb in a temporal or causal subordinate clause to link it with a following clause. It is always placed *directly* after the verb, and may not be preceded by an auxiliary. The marker -nä' is translated, according to the context, by the conjunctions "and" or "then", or else by "after" or "since".

Ex.: ཁ་ལག་བཟས་ནས་ཡོང་གི་ཡིན། "I'll come after I've eaten."

ལྷ་སར་ཕེབས་ནས་ག་ཚོད་ཕྱིན་སོང་། "How long has he been in Lhasa?"

(lit. since he came to Lhasa how much [time] has passed)

སྔ་པོ་ལང་ནས་སློབ་གྲྭར་འགྲོ་གི་ཡོད། "I get up early and go to school."

14.3.3 The construction V (past) + པ་དག་ -pataka

The expression -pataka is derived from the form པ་དེ་ག་ -pateka, which consists of the nominalizer པ་ and the demonstrative དེ་ག་ "just that" or "just there". This expression, which is always attached to a verb in the past tense, means "to have just" or "as soon as". In Literary Tibetan, it is replaced by མ་ཐག་ -matha' or པ་དང་ -patang.

Ex.: ཁ་ལག་བཟས་པ་དག་ཡོང་པ་ཡིན། "I came as soon as I'd eaten."

ཚེ་རིང་སླེབས་པ་དག་རེད། "Tshering has just arrived."

ང་ཚོ་སྦྲ་གུར་ནང་ལ་སླེབས་པ་དག་ཇ་ཚ་པོ་''བཏུངས་''པ་ཡིན།

"As soon as we got into the tent, we drank some hot tea."

ཇོ་ཁང་གཟིམ་སྒོ་ཕྱེ་པ་དག་རེད། "The Jhokhang has just been opened."

14.4 Exercises སྦྱོང་ཚན།

14.4.1 Translate into English:

ཁོང་རྒྱ་གར་ལ་ཕྱིན་འགྲོའི་རེད་པས། ལགས་རེད། ཁོང་ཕྱིན་ནས་ཉི་མ་མང་པོ་ཕྱིན་མ་སོང་། ཁོང་གི་ཁང་པ་རྙིང་པ་རེད་
པས།མ་རེད། ཁོང་ཁང་པ་བརྒྱབ་འགྲོའི་རེད། ཁྱེད་རང་འདིར་ཕེབས་འགྲོའི་ཡིན་པས། ལགས་ཡིན། ང་སླེབས་
ནས་ཟླ་བ་གཅིག་ཕྱིན་སོང་། དགོན་པ་འདི་ཞིག་གསོ་བྱས་འགྲོའི་རེད་པས། ལགས་རེད། ཞིག་གསོ་བྱས་ནས་ཞེ་དྲགས་
ཕྱིན་མ་སོང་། ཁྱེད་རང་འདིར་ཕེབས་ནས་སྐར་མ་ག་ཚོད་ཕྱིན་སོང་། ང་ད་ལྟ་སླེབས་པ་དག་ཡིན། ང་ཚོ་ཁ་ལག་བཟས་
པ་དག་ཁྲོམ་ལ་འགྲོ་གི་ཡིན།

14.4.2 Learn the "conjugations" of the three basic verbalizers བཏང་ tāng, བྱེད་ che̱' *and* རྒྱག་ kya̱' *(see section 14.3.1). Conjugate the verbs* སློབ་སྦྱོང་བྱེད་ *"to study",* སྒོ་རྒྱག་ *"to close",* ཆང་ས་རྒྱག་ *"to marry" and* བསམ་བློ་བཏང་ *"to ponder" in all the tense-aspects and moods that have been covered so far.*

14.4.3 Rewrite the following sentences in the honorific:

༡) བློ་བཟང་བཟོ་གྲྭའི་ནང་ལ་ལས་ཀ་བྱེད་ཀྱི་ཡོད་རེད།

༢) རྡོ་རྗེ་མོ་ཊ་བཏང་གི་ཡོད་རེད།

༣) ཁོ་ཆང་ས་བརྒྱབ་པ་རེད།

༤) ཁོས་ཁང་པ་གསར་པ་བརྒྱབ་པ་རེད།

༥) ཁོ་སློབ་གྲྭ་ཆེན་མོའི་ནང་ལ་སློབ་སྦྱོང་བྱེད་ཀྱི་ཡོད་རེད

༦) ཁོས་བསམ་བློ་བཏང་སོང་།

༧) རྡོ་རྗེས་པར་བརྒྱབ་སོང་།

14.4.4 Translate into Tibetan:

1. She is going to study Tibetan at the university from May to September.
2. Drölkar got married in February.
3. Lobzang photographed the monastery.
4. Trashi came on the 11th of June.
5. Do you work on Sundays?
6. He will be in Peking from April to October.
7. They went to China to take photos.
8. He met Dorje in Delhi in November.
9. She'll come back to Lhasa in July.

14.5 Civilization རིག་གཞུང་།

Tibetan astrology and the lunar calendar.

In Tibet, astrology and divination are still an important part of everyday life. Tibetans often prefer to mention their natal sign rather than their year of birth according to the international calendar, and traditional festivals are situated in terms of the lunar calendar. Astrologers are still frequently consulted for weddings and for the appropriate form of funerals (see Lesson 35.5). Almanacs, or *loto* (*lo-tho*), containing correspondences between the international and native calendars, are regularly used.

Tibetan astrology[128] involves five elements and twelve animals:

ཤིང་shīng "wood", མེ་me̱ "fire", ས་sā "earth", ལྕགས་cā' "iron", ཆུ་chū "water".

Each of these elements may be associated with a masculine ཕོ་phō or feminine མོ་ mo̱ gender. The twelve animals are:

ཡོས་ yö̱' "hare", འབྲུག་ tru̱' "dragon", སྦྲུལ་ trü̱: "snake", རྟ་tā "horse", ལུག་ lu̱' "sheep", སྤྲེལ་ trē: "monkey", བྱ་ cha̱ "bird", ཁྱི་ khyī "dog", ཕག་ phā' "pig", བྱི་ chi̱ "rat", གླང་ lāng "ox", སྟག་ tā' "tiger".

For the calendar, Tibetans use a cycle of twelve years corresponding to the list of twelve animals. In association with each of the five elements they constitute a major cycle of sixty years.

For example: མེ་ཡོས་ལོ་ me̱ yö̱' lo̱ "fire hare year", ས་འབྲུག་ལོ་ sā tru̱' lo̱ "earth dragon year", ས་སྦྲུལ་ལོ་ sā trü̱: lo̱ "earth snake year", ལྕགས་རྟ་ལོ་cā' tā lo̱ "iron horse year", etc.

Year	*animal*	*element*
2000	Dragon	Iron
2001	Snake	Iron
2002	Horse	Water
2003	Sheep	Water
2004	Monkey	Wood
2005	Bird	Wood
2006	Dog	Fire
2007	Pig	Fire
2008	Rat	Earth
2009	Ox	Earth
2010	Tiger	Iron
2011	Hare	Iron
2012	Dragon	Water

A Tibetan month usually contains thirty lunar days. The first day of the month corresponds to the new moon, and the fifteenth day to the full moon. The Tibetan New Year (see Lesson 36) shifts between the beginning of February and the beginning of March depending on the year.

ཁྱེད་རང་གི་ལོ་རྟགས་ག་རེ་རེད། khyērang-ki lo̱pta' kha̱re rä̱' "What is your (animal) birth sign?"

128. Tibet has two astrological systems: naktsi (*nag-rtsis*), also called jungtsi (*'byung-rtsis*), which is of Chinese origin and used mainly for divination, and kartsi (*dkar-rtsis*), also spelled *skar-rtsis*, which comes from India and is used for calendrical computation. The influence of divination and rituals in the Bön religion has also undoubtedly played an important part in the development of Tibetan astrology.

"Lobzang's house"

བློ་བཟང་གི་ཁང་པ།

Grammar aims བརྡ་སྤྲོད་རིག་པའི་དམིགས་ཚད།

- Reported speech.
- The experiential auxiliary མྱོང་ nyo̲ng.

CD I • Tr. 41-42

15.1 Dialogue དྲི་བ་དྲིས་ལན།

ཟླ་བ་ ཿ བློ་བཟང་གི་ཁང་པ་ག་པར་ཡོད་རེད།

ཉི་མ་ ཿ ལྷ་སའི་སྐྱིད་ཆུ་ཕར་ཕྱོགས་ཀྱི་གྲོང་གསེབ་ལ་ཡོད་རེད།

ཟླ་བ་ ཿ གྲིབ་ལ་ཡོད་རེད་པས།

ཉི་མ་ ཿ ལགས་རེད།

ཟླ་བ་ ཿ གྲིབ་ལ་མི་ཚང་ག་ཚོད་ཡོད་རེད།

ཉི་མ་ ཿ མི་ཚང་ཐེམ་པ་ཉི་ཤུ་ལྷག་ཙ་(ལྷག་ཙམ་)ཡོད་རེད་ཟ (ཟེར་གྱི་འདུག)

ཟླ་བ་ ཿ ཕ་གིར་ཚོང་ཁང་ཡོད་རེད་པས།

ཉི་མ་ ཿ ཆུང་ཆུང་གཅིག་ཡོད་རེད།

ཟླ་བ་ ཿ སླབ་གྲྭ་(སློབ་གྲྭ་)ཡོད་རེད་པས།

ཉི་མ་ ཿ ལགས་ཡོད་རེད། དམངས་བཙུགས་སླབ་གྲྭ་(སློབ་གྲྭ་)གཅིག་ཡོད་རེད།

ཟླ་བ་ ཿ དགོན་པ་ཡོད་རེད་པས།

ཉི་མ་ ཿ ཡོད་རེད། ཚེ་མཆོག་གླིང་དགོན་པ་ཟེར་གྱི་རེད།

ཟླ་བ་ ཿ ཁྱེད་རང་ཕེབས་མྱོང་ངས་།

ཉི་མ་ ཿ འགྲོ་མྱོང་།

Pronunciation

- lōpsang-ki khāngpa kha̱par yo̱:rä'
- lhāsä: kyīcu phāco'-ki thro̱ngsep-la yo̱:re'
- thri̱p-la yo̱:re'-pä'
- la̱' re̱'
- thri̱p-la mi̱tsang kha̱tsö' yo̱:rä'
- mi̱tsang thēmpa nyi̱shu lhākts yo̱:re'-sa
- phākä: tshōngkang yo̱:re'-pä'
- chūngcung cī' yo̱:re'
- lāptra yo̱:re'-pä'
- la̱' yo̱:re' māngtsu' lāptra cī' yo̱:re'
- ko̱mpa yo̱:re'-pä'
- yo̱:re' tsēco'ling kompa se̱r-kire'
- khyērang phēp-nyong-ngä'
- tro̱-nyong

Home of a well-to-do Tibetan family

Translation

Dawa — Where's Lobzang's house?
Nyima — It's in a village on the other side of the Lhasa River.
Dawa — Is it in Dhrip?
Nyima — Yes.
Dawa — How many families are there in Dhrip?
Nyima — There are said to be more than twenty households.
Dawa — Is there a shop over there?
Nyima — There's a small one.
Dawa — Is there a school?
Nyima — Yes, there's a community school.
Dawa — Is there a monastery?
Nyima — Yes, there's Tshechogling Monastery.
Dawa — Have you ever been (lit. gone) there?
Nyima — Yes, I've been there.

ཀ་ཁ་ག་ང་

15.2 Vocabulary ཚིག་གསར།

ལྷག་ཙ་ lhākts ལྷག་ཙམ་ lhāktsam (L)	(adv.) a little more
མི་ཚང་ mi̱tsang	(n.) family
ཐེམ་པ་ thēmpa	(n.) household
ཁྱིམ་ཚང་ khyīmtsang	(n.) family
ཚོང་པ་ tshōngpa	(n.) shopkeeper, businessman
ཚུར་ tshūr	(n.) towards oneself, this way, hither
ཕར་ phār	(n.) away, thither
ཁྱིམ་མཚེས་ khyīmtse'	(n.) neighbour
ཕྱོགས་ chō'	(n.) direction, side
གྲོང་གསེབ་ thro̱ngsep	(n.) village
དམངས་བཙུགས་སློབ་གྲྭ་ māngtsu' lāptra	(n.) community school
ཆུ་ chū	(n.) river, stream
གཙང་པོ་ tsāngpo	(n.) river
ཟ་ sa̱ ཟེར་ se̱r (L)	(aux.) it is said, *hearsay, end of quotation*
ཟེ་ s	(part.) *end of quotation*
མྱོང་ nyo̱ng མྱངས་ nya̱ng'	(v.) [vol. EA] to taste, try (aux.) *experiential*
ཟེར་གྱི་ཟ་ se̱rkisa	(idiom.) it seems that X has said, *hearsay*

Proper nouns

གྲིབ་ thri̱p	Dhrip (*name of a village*)
སྐྱིད་ཆུ་ kyīcu	Kyichu, "Happy River"
ཚེ་མཆོག་གླིང་ tshēco'ling	Tshechogling (*name of a monastery*)

༡༡༡

15.3 Remarks འགྲེལ་བཤད།

15.3.1 Reported speech.

Reported speech is indicated by the marker ཟེ་ /s/ which corresponds to closing quotation marks. This marker /s/, derived from the verb ཟེར་ /se̲r/ "to say", is used for both direct and indirect speech.[129] There is a special form ཟ་/sa/ to convey hearsay. The distinguishing feature of reported speech in Tibetan is that it is inserted between the author of the quotation and the verb of speech. When Tibetans read or quote a text, they often conclude the citation with an /s/ to make it clear that these were not their own words.

• Direct speech

Reported speech begins by first mentioning the source (the speaker) and then, where applicable, the intended recipient (the addressee), respectively in the ergative and dative cases. The quotation is concluded by the sound /-s/, which corresponds to closing quotation marks, followed immediately by a verb of speech. Direct speech reproduces a statement in the original words. Note that quotation marks are actually used in certain modern writings, whereas traditional Tibetan literature uses no punctuation at all.

source + གིས་ [+goal + ལ་]: "citation" + ཟེ་ + verb of speech

Ex.: རྒན་ལགས་ཀྱིས་སློབ་གྲྭ་བ་ཚོར་ང་ལམ་སང་ཚུར་ཡོང་གི་ཡིན་ཟེ་གསུངས་སོང་།

kä̲nla'-ki' lāptrawa-tsor nga̲ la̲msang tshūr yo̲ng-kiyin-s sūng-song

The teacher said to the students, "I'll come back immediately."

ཁོང་གིས་ ང་ཨེམ་ཆི་ཡིན་ཟེ་ལབ་སོང་།

khōng-ki' nga̲ āmci yi̲n-s la̲p-song

He said, "I'm a doctor."

ཁོང་གིས་ དཔལ་ལྡན་ཨེམ་ཆི་རེད་ཟེ་ལབ་སོང་།

khōng-ki' pǟntän āmci re̲'-s la̲p-song

He said, "Pändän is a doctor." or He said that Pändän was a doctor.[130]

ཁོང་གིས་ང་ལ་ ཁྱེད་རང་ཨེམ་ཆི་མ་རེད་ཟེ་གསུང་བྱུང་།

khōng-ki' nga̲la khyērang āmci ma̲re'-s sūng-cung

He said to me, "You're not a doctor!"

---

129. These categories are not always relevant. For certain statements there is only one type of discourse, and they may therefore be translated into European languages by either direct or reported speech. However, as we shall see below, it is sometimes possible to distinguish between direct and "hybrid" indirect speech.

130. In this case only one form of reported speech is possible.

དོན་གྲུབ་ཀྱིས་ང་ལ་ཡི་གེ་འབྱོར་མ་བྱུང་ཟེ་ལབ་པ་རེད།
tho̱ntrup-ki' nga̱-la yi̱ke co̱r macung-s la̱p-pare'
Dhöndrup said, "I didn't receive the letter."

ཚེ་རིང་གིས་ངས་ཡི་གེ་བཏང་པ་ཡིན་ཟེ་ལན་བརྒྱབ་སོང་།
tshēring-ki' ngä̱' yi̱ke tāng-payin-s lä̱n kya̱p-song.
Tshering replied, "I sent the letter."

• "Hybrid" reported speech.

If it happens that the source of a quotation is the same person as someone who is mentioned in it, or else is the actual speaker, Tibetans prefer to substitute "hybrid" reported speech for direct speech. For example, in the statement "He said 'I'm a doctor'", the two pronouns "he" and "I" refer to the same person (and are therefore "coreferential"). The same is true of the statement "He said to me, 'You're not a doctor!'" in which the pronouns "me" and "you" are coreferential. In such cases, Tibetan generally uses a particular form of reported speech that has the following features:

— A. The pronouns[131] of the original quotation and the register (honorific, humilific or ordinary) are **reformulated** to suit the speaker's current situation. This is similar to the reported speech of European languages.

— B. By contrast, when the first person pronoun "I", "me", etc. appears in the original citation, the **egophoric** auxiliary (*yin, byung*, etc.) that is associated with it is preserved in the "hybrid" reported speech.

— C. Once a sentence has been transformed into reported speech, if it contains coreferential nouns or pronouns one of the two forms is **dropped.**

"quotation + AUX (ego)" + ཟེ་ + verb of speech

For example, the sentence "He said, 'I'm a doctor'" is transformed into the hypothetical stage A): * ཁོང་གིས་ཁོང་ཨེམ་ཆི་ཡིན་ཟེ་ལབ་སོང་། khōng-ki' khōng āmci yi̱n-s la̱p-song. Following the rule set out in B), the sentence preserves the egophoric auxiliary yi̱n; and as a result of eliminating the first pronoun, we end up with: ཁོང་ཨེམ་ཆི་ཡིན་ཟེ་ལབ་སོང་། khōng āmci yi̱n-s la̱p-song "He said he was a doctor."

Here are some other examples of indirect reported speech:

Ex.: ཁོང་གིས་ང་ཨེམ་ཆི་མ་རེད་ཟེ་གསུང་བྱུང་། khōng-ki' nga̱ āmci ma̱re'-s sūng-cung
"He told me I wasn't a doctor."

---

131. The pronouns "I" and "you" and, more generally, the "deictics", that is, words connected to the statement like the adverbs "here" and "now", as well as demonstratives such as "that" which can only be interpreted in relation to the context of the dialogue.

དོན་གྲུབ་ཀྱིས་ཡི་གེ་འབྱོར་མ་འབྱུང་ཟེ་ལབ་པ་རེད། thöntrup-ki' nga-la yike cor-macung-s lap-pare'
"Dhöndrup said he hadn't received a letter."

Note: In this case, the subject could also be in the dative.

Ex.: རྒན་ལགས་ལམ་སང་ཚུར་ཕེབས་ཀྱི་ཡིན་ཟེ་གསུངས་སོང་།kãnla'-ki' lamsang tshūr phē'-kiyin-s sūng-song
"The teacher said he would come back immediately."
ཚེ་རིང་གིས་ཡི་གེ་བཏང་པ་ཡིན་ཟེ་ལན་བརྒྱབ་སོང་། tshēring yike tāng-payin-s län kyap-song
"Tshering replied that he'd sent the letter."

• "Hearsay" is formulated directly without introducing a speaker, citing and closing the assertion with the marker ཟ་ -sa "it is said that", or ཟེར་གྱི་ཟ་-serkisa. "X is said to have said that…", "X allegedly said that…"

Ex.: ཁོང་ཨེམ་ཆི་རེད་ཟ། khōng āmci re'-sa
"They say he's a doctor."
བོད་ལ་གསེར་མང་པོ་ཡོད་རེད་ཟ། phö'-la sēr mangpo yo:re'-sa
"There's said to be a lot of gold in Tibet."
བཀྲ་ཤིས་ལགས་རྒྱ་གར་ལ་ཕེབས་པ་རེད་ཟེར་གྱི་ཟ། trāshi'-la' kyakar-la phē'-pare serkisa
"Apparently he said that Trashi had gone to India."

15.3.2 The experiential auxiliary མྱོང་ nyong

This signifies that the subject has already, at least once, experienced the action to which nyong refers. The verb preceding the auxiliary nyong must be in the present tense. When nyong isn't followed by anything, the implication is egophoric. In this case, it is used with the first person, which may be either the subject or the direct or indirect object. In other cases, nyong again becomes a full verb and must be followed by an assertive past auxiliary: ཡོད་རེད། yo:re', པ་རེད། pare'. In English it may be translated by "has/have ever…"

Ex.: ང་འབྲུག་ཡུལ་ལ་འགྲོ་མྱོང་། nga tru'yü:-la tro-nyong
"I've been (lit. gone) to Bhutan."

ཁོས་ང་བརྡུངས་མྱོང་། khō' nga tung-nyong
"He has (previously) hit me."

ཁོང་ངའི་རྩ་ལ་ཕེབས་མྱོང་། khōng ngä: tsā-la phē'-nyong
"He's been (lit. come) to my place."

ཁོང་འབྲུག་ཡུལ་ལ་ཕེབས་མྱོང་ཡོད་རེད། khōng tru'yü:-la phēp-nyong-yo:re'
"He has been (lit. gone) to Bhutan."

15.4 Exercises སྦྱོང་ཚན།

15.4.1 Translate into Tibetan:

1. He's never eaten momos.
2. She has drunk Tibetan tea.
3. I have been (lit. gone) to India.
4. I've never done anything like that.
5. This nomad has never been in (lit. got into) a car.
6. He has travelled by aeroplane.
7. Dorje said there was no problem.
8. They say the road isn't good.

15.4.2 Change the following sentences into indirect speech.

༡) ཁོང་གིས་ང་ཟླ་བ་གཉིས་པའི་ནང་ལ་བོད་ལ་འགྲོ་གི་ཡིན་ཟེ་གསུང་བྱུང་།

༢) ཁོང་གིས་ངས་ཡི་གེ་ཤེས་ཀྱི་མེད་ཟེ་གསུང་གྱི་འདུག

༣) རྡོ་རྗེ་ངས་ཕ་གིར་ཕྱིན་པ་ཡིན་ཟེར་ལབ་སོང་།

༤) བཀྲ་ཤིས་ཀྱིས་ངས་ཁ་ལག་བཟོས་པ་ཡིན་ཟེ་ལབ་སོང་།

15.4.3 Translate into English:

༡) ཁྱེད་རང་བོད་ཇ་འཐུང་མྱོང་ངས།

༢) ཁོང་གིས་གཡག་མཐོང་མ་མྱོང་ཟེ་གསུངས་སོང་།

༣) ང་རང་ཚོ་གངས་རིན་པོ་ཆེ་ལ་འགྲོ་མྱོང་།

༤) སློ་བཟང་ལས་ཀ་བྱས་ནས་ཁྲོམ་ལ་ཕྱིན་པ་རེད།

༥) ཁ་ལག་བཟས་ནས་ལས་ཀ་བྱེད་གར་ཕྱིན་སོང་།

༦) ཁོང་མཆོད་ཆང་བཞེས་ནས་གཟིམ་གར་ཕེབས་སོང་།

༧) སྐྱིད་མོ་བསྐྱས་ནས་ཇ་ཁང་ལ་ཕྱིན་པ་རེད།

༨) ཁོང་བལ་ཡུལ་ལ་ཕེབས་ཐུབ་ཀྱི་མ་རེད་ཟེ་གསུང་གིས།

"Lobzang's house"
(continued)

བློ་བཟང་གི་ཁང་པ།

སྔ་མའི་འཕྲོས།

Grammar aims བརྡ་སྤྲོད་རིག་པའི་དམིགས་ཚད།

- The modal verb དགོས་ ko̱ "to have to".
- The interrogative pronoun "why".

༄། །མིས་རྒྱུ་བཟོས་པ་ལས། རྒྱུས་མི་བཟོས་པ་མིན།།

"It's not the fortune that makes the man, but the man that makes the fortune." (proverb)

CD I • Tr. 43-44 

16.1 Dialogue དྲི་བ་དྲིས་ལན།

སྒྲོལ་དཀར་ ༔ བཀྲ་ཤིས་ལགས། གཟིགས་ད་(དང་)། བུ་དང་ཕྱི་རྒྱལ་ཅིག་ཡོང་གིས། (ཡོང་གི་འདུག)

བཀྲ་ཤིས་ ༔ ཨ་ལའི།

བློ་བཟང་ ༔ བཀྲ་ཤིས་བདེ་ལེགས། པཱ་ལགས། ཁོང་ངའི་གྲོགས་པོ་མི་ཤེལ་རེད།

བཀྲ་ཤིས་ ༔ ཕྱག་ཕེབས་གནང་བྱུང་། བཞུགས་ད། བོད་སྐད་མཁྱེན་གྱི་ཡོད་པས།

མི་ཤེལ་ ༔ ལགས། ཤེན་(ཤེས་)གི་ཡོད།

བཀྲ་ཤིས་ ༔ ངའི་མིང་ལ་བཀྲ་ཤིས་ཟེར་གྱི་ཡོད། འདི་ངའི་ཨྰ་མོ་ཡིན། མིང་ལ་སྒྲོལ་དཀར་ཟ་(ཟེར་)འདི་ངའི་བུ་ཆུང་བ་ཡིན། ཁྱེད་རང་ག་ནས་ཡིན་པ།

མི་ཤེལ་ ༔ དཔལ་རི་སི་ནས་ཡིན།

བཀྲ་ཤིས་ ༔ དཔལ་རི་སི་རྒྱལ་ས་རེད་པ།

མི་ཤེལ་ ༔ ལགས་རེད་པ་རན་སིའི་རྒྱལ་ས་རེད། འདི་ནས་ལྷ་ས་ཐག་རིང་པོ་རེད་པས།

བཀྲ་ཤིས་ ༔ མ་རེད། རྐང་ཐང་ལ་ཆུ་ཚོད་ཅིག་ཙ་(ཙམ)རེད། ཨ་ནི། ལྷ་ས་ནས་དཔལ་རི་སི་བར་དུ་གནམ་གྲུའི་ནང་ལ་ཆུ་ཚོད་ག་ཚོད་འགྲོ་དགོས་རེད།

མི་ཤེལ་ ༔ ཆུ་ཚོད་བཅུ་གཉིས་འགྲོ་དགོས་རེད།

བཀྲ་ཤིས་ ༔ ཨ་ཙི། ཐག་རིང་པོ་ཞེ་པོ་ཅིག་རེད། འདི་ང་ཚོའི་ཁང་པ་རེད། པ་རན་སིར་ཁང་པ་འདི་འདྲས་ཡོད་ཀྱི་མ་རེད།

Pronunciation

- trāshi'-la' si̱'-ta phu̱-tang chīkyä: cī' yo̱ng-ki'
- ālä'
- trāshi te̱le' pāla' khōng ngä̱: thro̱kpo mi̱she: re̱'
- chāpe' nāng-cung shu̱'-ta phö̱kä' khyēn-kiyö'-pä'
- la̱' shēn-kiyö'
- ngä̱: mi̱ng-la trāshi' se̱r-kiyö'. ti̱ ngä̱: ta̱wo yin. mi̱ng-la trö̱:kar sa̱. ti̱ ngä̱: phu̱ chūngwa yi̱n khyērang kha̱nä' yi̱n-pa
- pā̱ris-nä' yi̱n
- pā̱ris kyä̱:sa re̱'-wa
- la̱' re̱' phāransi: kyä̱:sa re̱'
- ti̱nä' lhāsa thā' ri̱ngpo re̱'-pä'
- ma̱-re' kāngtang-la chūtsö' cī'-ts re' āni lhāsa-nä' pā̱ris pha̱rtu kha̱tsö' tro̱ ko̱rä'
- chūtsö' cūnyi' tro̱ ko̱re'
- ātsi thā' ri̱ngpo she̱poci' re̱'. ti̱ ngatsö: khāngpa re̱', phārānsir khāngpa ti̱nträ' yö̱'-kimare'

Translation

Drölkar — Look Trashi, our son and a foreigner are coming!
Trashi — Aha.
Lobzang — Hello Dad. This is my friend Michel.
Trashi — Welcome. Have a seat. Do you speak Tibetan?
Michel — Yes, I do.
Trashi — My name's Trashi. This is my wife. She's called Drölkar. He's my youngest son. Where are you from?
Michel — I come from Paris.
Trashi — It's a capital city, isn't it?
Michel — Yes, it's the capital of France. Is Lhasa far from here?
Trashi — No, ten minutes on foot. How long does it take (lit. does one have to go) by plane from Lhasa to Paris?
Michel — It takes (lit. one has to go) twelve hours .
Trashi — Wow! That's really far! Here's our house. There can't be any houses like this in France!

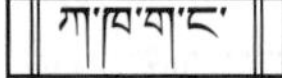

16.2 Vocabulary ཚིག་གསར།

ཕྱི་རྒྱལ་ chīkyä: (n.) foreigner
རྐང་ཐང་ kāngtang (n.) on foot
རྒྱལ་ས་ kyä̱:sa (n.) capital

ཨ་ཙི་ ātsi	(part.) wow, fancy that!
ཨ་ཚ་ ātsa	(part.) ouch (that's hot)!
ཨ་ཆུ་ ācu	(part.) ouch (that's cold)!
ཨ་རོ་ āro	(part.) oh! ow!
ཨ་མ་མ་ āmama	(part.) good heavens!
ཨ་ནི་ āni དེ་ནས་ thenä' (L)	(co.) so, and then…
ཨོ་ཙ་ ōts ཨའུ་ཙམ་ āutsam (L)	(part.) quite
ཞེ་པོ་ཅིག་ shepoci'	(adv.) very, extremely
ཤེས་ shēn, shē' (L) མཁྱེན་ khyēn (H)	(v.) [inv., EA] to know
ངོ་ཤེས་ ngo shēn ངོ་མཁྱེན་ ngo khyēn (H) ཞལ་འཚོར་ shä: tshōr (h)	(v.) [inv., EA] to know (someone)
དགོས་ ko', kö' (L)	(v.) [inv., DA] to need (aux.) to have to
སྐུ་མཁྱེན་ kūci	(idiom.) please

Proper nouns

དཔལ་རི་སི་ pāris	Paris

The human body

གཟུགས་པོ་ sukpo སྐུ་གཟུགས་ kūsu' (H)	body
མགོ་ ko དབུ་ ū (H)	head
སྐྲ trā དབུ་སྐྲ་ ūtra (H)	hair
དཔལ་སྐོ་ pā:ko' དཔྲལ་སྐོ་ trā:ko' (L)	forehead
མིག་ mī' སྤྱན་ cān (H)	eye
སྣ་ཁུག་ nāku' སྣ་ nā (L) ཤངས་ shāng' (H)	nose
མཆུ་ཏོ་ chūto	lip
ཨ་མཆོག་ āmco' རྣ་བ་ nāwa (L) སྙན་མཆོག་ nyānco' (H)	ear
ཁ་ khā ཞལ་ shä: (H)	mouth
ལྕེ་ cē ལྗགས་ ca'(H)	tongue
གདོང་tong ཞལ་རས་ shä:rä' (H)	face
སོ་ sō ཚེམས་ tsēm' (H)	tooth
མིད་པ་ mikpa	throat
ནུ་མ་ numa	breast
བང་ཁོག་ phangko' བྲང་ཁོག་ thrangko'(L)	chest
ལག་པ་ lakpa ཕྱག་ chā' (H)	hand
མཛུག་གུ་ tsuku ཕྱག་མཛུག་ chāktsu'(H)	finger
སྙིང་ nying མགུལ་སྙིང་། kü:nying(H)	heart
གློ་བ་ lōwa	lung
མཆིན་པ་ chīnpa	liver

ཕོ་བ་ phōwa	belly
གྲོད་ཁོག་ thro̱ko' གསོལ་གྲོད་ sȫ:trö' (H)	stomach
སྒལ་པ་ kä̱:pa སྐུ་སྟོད་ kūtö' (H)	back
སྐེད་པ་ kēpa སྐུ་སྐེད་ kūke' (H)	waist
སྟུ་ tū མོ་མཚན་ mo̱tsän (L)	female sex
ལྟིག་པ་ līkpa ཕོ་མཚན་ phōtsän (L)	male sex
རྐང་པ་ kāngpa ཞབས་ sha̱p (H)	leg, foot
ཚིགས་ tshī'	joint
སྤུས་མོ་ pǖmo	knee

༢༢༢

16.3 Remarks འགྲེལ་བཤད།

16.3.1 The modal verb དགོས་ ko̱

The verb དགོས་ ko̱ "to need, to have to" is used both as either the main verb of a sentence or as modal verb. Finally, it is also used as an auxiliary in future tense constructions (see Lesson 23.3.2).

Like many other languages, Tibetan has certain defective (or irregular) modal verbs. This is the case with verb དགོས་ ko̱', insofar as there are certain restrictions about how it can be combined with auxiliaries. As a main verb it means "to need" or "to want", and occurs only with the following auxiliaries.[132]

Egophoric	དགོས་ཡོད་ko̱'-yö' "I need"	neg.: དགོས་མེད་ ko̱'-me'
	དགོས་ko̱' "I want"	neg.: མི་དགོས་mu-ko̱'
Testimonial	དགོས་འདུག ko̱'-tu' "you, he need(s)"	neg.: དགོས་མི་འདུག. ko̱'-mintu'
Assertive	དགོས་རེད་ko̱'-re' "you, he need(s)"	neg.: དགོས་མ་རེད་ko̱'-mare'

The suffix ki may be inserted between the modal and the auxiliary: དགོས་(ཀྱི་)ཡོད། དགོས་(ཀྱི་)འདུག དགོས་(ཀྱི་)རེད། , but it is usually dropped in conversation. As shown above, the verb may occur alone without auxiliary དགོས་ko̱' མི་དགོས་mu-ko̱'[133] and may then be best translated as "I (do not) want", while with the auxiliary it may be translated as "need".

The subject of དགོས་ ko̱' used as a main verb must be in the dative and the object in the absolutive.[134]

132. The various tenses (future, present, past) have to be deduced from the context.

133. The negation is not pronounced mi as expected but mu.

134. In terms of grammatical roles, the beneficiary comes first and the patient second.

Ex.: ངར་ཁ་བཏགས་དགོས་ཡོད། "I need offering-scarves."
ངར་ཇ་མི་དགོས། "I don't want any tea."
ཁོང་ལ་ཆབ་་དགོས་གནང་གི་འདུག "He needs/ wants water (H)."

See also the modal verb འདོད་ "to want, desire" in 26.3.2.

As a modal verb it means "to have to, need" or even "must",[135] and goes with the following auxiliaries:

Future:	Assertive	དགོས་ཀྱི་རེད་ ko̲'-kire'
Present:	Egophoric	དགོས་(ཀྱི་)ཡོད་ ko̲'-(ki)yö'
	Testimonial	དགོས་(ཀྱི་)འདུག ko̲'-(ki)tu'
	Assertive	དགོས་(ཀྱི་)རེད་ ko̲'-(ki)re'
Past (perfective):	Egophoric	དགོས་བྱུང་ ko̲'-cung
	Testimonial	དགོས་བྱུང་སོང་ ko̲'-cungsong
	Assertive	དགོས་བྱུང་པ་རེད་ ko̲'-cungpare'

It is conjugated in the same way as predicative adjectives such as དགའ་པོ་ "like, be fond of". The forms *དགོས་སོང་, *དགོས་བཞག and *དགོས་པ་རེད་ are usually not acceptable.

The subject's case depends on the main verb.

Ex.: རྒྱང་ཤེལ་བསྣམས་དགོས་རེད། "(We) have to take binoculars."
ང་ཁ་བཏགས་ཉོ་དགོས་ཡོད། "I have to buy offering-scarves."
ངས་དངུལ་སྤྲད་དགོས་བྱུང་། "I had to pay (for it)."
ཁོང་རེ་ལིའི་ནང་ལ་ཞབས་དགོས་བྱུང་སོང་། "He had to take the train." (H)

16.3.2 The interrogative pronoun "why".

Tibetan has several expressions that mean "why": ག་རེ་ཡིན་ན་ kha̲re yi̲nna, ག་རེ་བྱས་ནས་ kha̲re chä̲'-nä'.

Ex.: ཁོང་ཞེད་ཀྱི་འདུག་ ག་རེ་ཡིན་ན། "He's afraid; why?"
ང་རྐང་པ་ན་གིས་ ག་རེ་ཡིན་ན། "My leg's hurting; (I wonder) why?"
ག་རེ་བྱས་ནས་ངུ་གི་ཡོད། "Why are you crying?"
ག་རེ་བྱས་ནས་རྡོ་གཞུས་པ། "Why did you throw stones?"

---

135. In Tibetan, unlike European languages, modal verbs such as *thub* "can", *dgos* "need, must", *chog* "may" do not have an epistemic function and may not indicate probability or certainty (as in "he may be there, he must be there, etc."). There is a special set of auxiliaries devoted to this function (see 11.3.1) as well as the modal epistemic verb *srid* "may".

There is also the formulation: V+ ནས་ག་རེ་བྱེད་ག་ -nä kha̱re che̱'-ka or V+ བྱས་ག་རེ་བྱེད་ག་ -cä kha̱re che̱'-ka. It may be translated as "What do you mean by + *gerundive*". It often figures in reproaches:

Ex.: དཀར་ཡོལ་བཅག་ནས་ག་རེ་བྱེད་ག "Why did you break the cup?"
རྡོ་གཞུས་ནས་ག་རེ་བྱེད་ག "Why did you throw stones?"
ལས་ཀ་མ་བྱས་པ་བྱས་ག་རེ་བྱེད་ག "Why didn't you do any work?"

16.4 Exercises སྦྱོང་ཚན།

16.4.1 Translate into English:

༡) ལམ་ཁག་ག་ནས་འགྲོ་དགོས་རེད།
༢) ལ་མཛོ་པོ་ཅིག་རྒྱག་དགོས་རེད།
༣) ག་དུས་ལེན་གར་ཡོང་དགོས་རེད།
༤) དངུལ་སྤྲད་དགོས་མ་རེད།
༥) ཁོང་ལམ་སང་ཕེབས་དགོས་བྱུང་པ་རེད།
༦) པར་ག་ཚོད་རྒྱག་དགོས་རེད།
༧) ཚོགས་འདུར་ང་ཚོ་ཚང་མ་འགྲོ་དགོས་རེད་པས།
༨) ཁྲོམ་ལ་ཕེབས་ནས་ག་རེ་གནང་ག
༩) ང་སྨན་ཁང་ལ་འགྲོ་དགོས་ཡོད།
༡༠) སྤ་སེ་ཉོ་དགོས་མ་རེད་པས།

16.4.2 Translate into Tibetan:

1. "Why do you have to go the bank?" "Because I need a lot of money."
2. Why did he go to India?
3. They need horses.
4. "Do you know Nyima?" "Yes, I know him well."
5. There are a lot of foreigners in the capital.

"In the kitchen"

ཐབ་ཚང་ནང་ལ།

> *Grammar aims* བརྡ་སྤྲོད་རིག་པའི་དམིགས་ཚད།
>
> • Adjectival suffixes.
> • The present continuous V+ པའི་སྐབས་ཡིན་ or རེད་

ཨ༔། དགོན་པའི་ཁྱི་ལ་བརྡུངས་ན་བླ་མའི་ཐུགས་ལ་ཟུག་ཡོང་།།

"If you strike a monastery dog, you'll hurt the lama's heart." (proverb)[136]

CD I • Tr. 45-46

17.1 Dialogue དྲི་བ་དྲིས་ལན།

བཀྲ་ཤིས་ ༔ ཡར་ཕེབས་སྐྱུར་གནང་གོ

མི་ཤེལ་ ༔ ལགས་སོ། གཟིམ་ཁང་སྤྲོ་པོ་ཞེ་དྲགས་འདུག་ག

བཀྲ་ཤིས་ ༔ ཨོ་ཙ་ཡོད།

མི་ཤེལ་ ༔ འདི་ག་རེ་རེད།

བཀྲ་ཤིས་ ༔ འདི་ཐབ་ཚང་རེད། ཁོང་ངའི་སྐྱིད་དམན་རེད།

ཨ་ལྕུག་ ༔ བཀྲ་ཤིས་བདེ་ལེགས།

མི་ཤེལ་ ༔ བཀྲ་ཤིས་བདེ་ལེགས། ཐབ་ཚང་ཡག་པོ་ཅིག་འདུག ཁོང་ག་རེ་གནང་གི་ཡོད་རེད།

བཀྲ་ཤིས་ ༔ ཁོང་གསོལ་ཇ་བཟོ་གི་ཡོད་རེད།

མི་ཤེལ་ ༔ འདི་ག་རེ་རེད།

བཀྲ་ཤིས་ ༔ འདི་མོག་ཀྲུ་རེད།

མི་ཤེལ་ ༔ བུ་མོ་ཆུང་ཆུང་དེ་སུ་རེད།

བཀྲ་ཤིས་ ༔ དེ་ང་གཉིས་ཀྱི་བུ་མོ་ཡིན།

མི་ཤེལ་ ༔ ཨོ། ཐབ་ཀྱི་འཁྲིས་ལ་ཁྱི་ཆུང་ཆུང་ཅིག་འདུག

---

136. The moral of the proverb is that we should look after our friends' friends.

Pronunciation

- ya̱r chīpkyur nāngko
- la̱'-so si̱mkang trōpo she̱tra' tu̱'-a
- ōts yö̱'
- ti̱ kha̱re rä̱'
- ti̱ thāptsang re' khōng ngä̱: kyēmän re̱'
- trāshi te̱le'
- trāshi te̱le' thāptsang ya̱kpo cī' tu̱' khōng kha̱re nāng-kiyo:rä'
- khōng sȫ:ca so̱-kiyo:re'
- ti̱ kha̱re rä̱'
- ti̱ mo̱ktru re̱'
- phu̱mo chūngcung the̱ sū rä̱'
- the̱ nga̱nyi'-ki phu̱mo yi̱n
- o thāp-ki thrī'-la khyī chūngcung cī' tu̱'.

Traditional Tibetan kitchen

Translation

Trashi — Please come in.
Michel — Oh, this room is very nice!
Trashi — It's not bad.
Michel — What is it?
Trashi — It's the kitchen. This is my wife.
The wife — Hello.
Michel — Hello. The kitchen is lovely. What is she making?
Trashi — She's making tea.
Michel — What's this?
Trashi — This is a *momo* steamer.
Michel — Who's that little girl?
Trashi — That's our daughter.
Michel — Oh, there's a little dog next to the stove!

ཀ་ཁ་ག་ང་

17.2 Vocabulary ཚིག་གསར།

སྐྱེད་དམན་ kyēmän	(n.) woman, wife
ཁྱོ་ག་ khyōka	(n.) husband
ཐབ་ཚང་ thāptsang གསོལ་ཐབ་ sȫ:tap (H)	(n.) kitchen
མོག་གྲུ་ mo̱ktru	(n.) steamer
ཇ་དམ་ cha̱tam	(n.) thermos
མདོང་མོ་ to̱ngmo གསོལ་མདོང་ sȫ:tong (H)	(n.) tea churn
ཤེལ་དམ་ shē:tam	(n.) bottle
ཁང་པ་ khāngpa གཟིམ་ཁང་ si̱mkang (H)	(n.) room
ཐབ་ thāp	(n.) stove, oven
གློག་ཐབ་ lōktap	(n.) electric oven, heater
ཉི་འོད་ཀྱི་ཐབ་ nyi̱wö ki thāp	(n.) solar heater
ཧ་ཡང་ hāyang	(n.) aluminium pan
ཚལ་སླང་ tshǟ:lang	(n.) frying pan
ཁོག་མ་ khōkma	(n.) pot
ཐུར་མ་ thūrma	(n.) spoon
གྲི་ thri̱	(n.) knife
ཀང་དྲ་ kāntra	(n.) fork
སྐྱོག་ kyō'	(n.) ladle
ཁོ་རྩེ་ khōtse	(n.) chopsticks
ཁོག་ཏིར་ khōktir	(n.) teapot, kettle
ཁྱི་ khyī	(n.) dog
ཞི་མི་ shi̱mi བྱི་ལ་ chi̱la (L)	(n.) cat
ཁ་ལག་ + བཟོ་ khāla' so̱	(v.) [vol., E] to prepare food
གསལ་པོ་ sǟ:po	(adj.) bright, clear

གཙང་མ་ tsāngma	(adj.) clean
བཙོག་པ་ tsōkpa	(adj.) dirty

Tibetan wildlife

རི་གོང་ rikong རི་བོང་ ripong (L.)	rabbit	ཨ་བྲ་ āpra	pica (tailless mouse-hare)
ཡོས yö'	hare	སྲམ་ sām	otter
ཕྱི་པི་ chīpi ཕྱི་བ་ chīwa (L.)	marmot	ཙི་ཙི་ tsītsi	mouse, rat
ཙི་ཙི་ལྐང་པོ་ tsītsi kangpo	bat		
བྱ་རྒོད་ chakö'	vulture	བྱ་ཁྲུང་ཁྲུང་ chatrungtrung	crane
བྱ་གླག་ chapla'	eagle	ཕིང་ཀྱུར་མ་ pīngkyuma	kite
འབྲོང་ trong	wild yak	རྐྱང་ kyāng	wild ass
གཙོད་ tsö'	antelope	གླ་བ་ lāwa	musk deer
གཉན་ nyān	argali (wild sheep)	གནའ་བ་ nāwa	blue sheep
བ་མེན་ phāmen	takin	རྒོ་བ་ kowa	gazelle
ཤ་བ་ shāwa	deer	ཝ་མོ་ wamo	fox
སྤྱང་ཀི་ cāngki	wolf	དྲེད་མོང་ thremong	brown bear
དོམ་ thom	bear	བྱི་ལ་དོམ་ chilatom	panda
སྤེའུ pīu སྤྲེའུ trēu (L.)	monkey	གཡི་ yī	lynx
སྟག་ tā'	tiger	གཟིག་ si'	leopard
སྦང་ནག་ pangna'	fly	སྦྲང་ནག་ trangna' (L)	fly
སྦང་ནོར་བུ་ pangnorpu	bee	སྦྲང་ནོར་བུ་ trangnorpu(L)	bee
གྲོག་མ་ throkma	ant	སྡོམ་ tom	spider
སྡིག་པ་ར་ཙ་ tikparatsa	scorpion	སྦྲུལ་ trü:	snake
སྦལ་པ་ pä:pa	frog		

༡༧

17.3 Remarks འགྲེལ་བཤད།

17.3.1 Adjectival suffixes

Generally speaking, Tibetan adjectives strongly resemble verbs and may even be "conjugated" with certain auxiliary verbs. Adjectives usually consist of a radical and a suffix, or else a reduplicated radical.

There are a number of suffixes that specify the degree of the adjective: པོ་ -po positive, པ་ pa comparative, ཤོས་ -shö' superlative (see Lessons 21 and 22) and intensive, པ་ལ་ -pala admirative, དྲགས་ -tra' excessive, ཙམ་ -tsam attenuative, ཐག་ཆོད་ thākcö' or སའི་ -sä: intensives, as well as interrogative suffixes: ལོས་-lö' and expressive suffixes (see Lesson 31).

• The long or "positive" form of adjectives

The positive form of adjectives is formed by using པོ་ po, པ་ pa, མོ་ mo, མ་ ma or by doubling up the radical, which represents a long form of the adjective.

The short form is the monosyllabic root of the adjective. In the case of double forms, the short form is the first, unrepeated, syllable, while in the case of adjectives consisting of a radical and a suffix, the latter is simply dropped. An important exception to this rule is the adjective ཆེན་པོ་ chēn+po "big", of which the short form is ཆེ་ chē and not chēn.

Ex.: སྐྱིད་པོ་ kyīppo "pleasant", དཀར་པོ་ kārpo "white", གསལ་པོ་ sā̃:po "clear", མང་པོ་ ma̱ngpo "many", སྟོང་པ་ tōngpa "empty", བཙོག་པ་ tsōkpa "dirty" གཙང་མ་ tsāngma "clean", གསར་པ་ sārpa "new", རྙིང་པ་ nyīngpa "old", མངར་མོ་ ngārmo "sweet", གྲང་མོ་ thra̱ngmo "cold", ཐུང་ཐུང་ thūngtung "short", ཆུང་ཆུང་ chūngcung "small", ལེབ་ལེབ་ le̱plep "flat", སྒོར་སྒོར་ ko̱rkor "round, circular", རིལ་རིལ་ ri̱:ri: "spherical, cylindrical", ཐང་ཐང་ thāngtang "healthy", ཉུང་ཉུང་ nyu̱ngnyung "few", སོབ་སོབ་ sōpsop "soft", ལྷོད་ལྷོད་ lhȭlö' "relaxed", etc.

Certain adjectives are formed by means of an expression comprising a substantive followed by an adjective such as ཚ་པོ་ tshāpo "hot" (often pejorative), ཆེན་པོ་ chēnpo "big", བདེ་པོ་ te̱po "well", དོད་པོ་ thö̱po "shape, appearance", etc.

Ex.: སེམས་བཟང་པོ་ sēm sa̱ngpo "kind", ལག་པ་དམ་པོ་ la̱kpa tha̱mpo "greedy", ཧྲུས་གཏོགས་ཚ་པོ་ chü̱to' tshāpo "curious", གཡོ་སྒྱུས་ཚ་པོ་ yōkyü' tshāpo "hypocritical", ཧམ་པ་ཚ་པོ་ hāmpa tshāpo "arrogant, brutal", ཞེད་སྣང་ཚ་པོ་ she̱nang tshāpo "scary, terrible", ཐག་ཉེ་པོ་ thā' nye̱po "close, near", མངོན་གསལ་དོད་པོ་ ngȭnsä: thö̱po "manifest, obvious", ཏ་བཟོ་དོད་པོ་ tērso thö̱po "superb", གཙང་བྲ་དོད་པོ་ tsāngtra thö̱po "impeccable", བློ་ཁོག་ཆེན་པོ་ lōko' chēnpo "brave", སྐབས་བདེ་པོ་ tāp te̱po "convenient".

• Short forms of adjectives

All adjectival suffixes are attached to the short form of the adjective, which hardly ever appears alone.

Ex.: ཆུང་ཆུང་ chūngcung "small" > ཆུང་བ་ chūngnga "smaller", ཆུང་དྲགས་ chūngtra' "too small", ཆུང་ལོས་ chūnglö' "how small?", ཆུང་ཤོས་ chūngshö' "the smallest", ཆུང་ཙམ་ chūngtsam "a bit small", ཆུང་ང་ལ་ chūng-ngala "how small!", etc.

• Excessive: དྲགས་ -tra' "too"

This suffix is placed directly after the short form of the adjective, and can be translated by "too".

Ex.: ལྗི་པོ་ ci̱po "heavy" > ལྗི་དྲགས་ ci̱tra' "too heavy"
ཉུང་ཉུང་ nyu̱ngnyung "few" > ཉུང་དྲགས་ nyungtra' "too few"
ཆེན་པོ་ chēnpo "big" > ཆེ་དྲགས་ chētra' "too big"

• The interrogative: ལོས་ -lö' "how…"

This suffix is used to ask quantitative questions like "how big?", "how heavy?", etc.).

Ex.: ལྗི་པོ་ cipo "heavy" > ལྗི་ལོས་ cilö' "how heavy?"
ཆེན་པོ་ chēnpo "grand" > ཆེ་ལོས་ chēlö' "how big?"
ཐག་རིང་པོ་ thā' ringpo "far" > ཐག་རིང་ལོས་ thā' ringlö' "how far?"

17.3.2. The present continuous V+ པའི་སྐབ་ཡིན་ or རེད་

The continuous is more restricted than the English progressive, and signifies that the subject is actually in the process of carrying out an activity. (In English, by contrast, we might say "I'm writing a letter" even when we have taken a break from doing so.) The present continuous is formed by taking the past tense form of the main verb and adding སྐབ་ (lit. "on") followed by the appropriate auxiliary.

Ex.: ང་ཡི་གེ་བྲིས་པའི་སྐབ་ཡིན། "I'm (in the process of) writing a letter."
ཁོང་ཕྱག་ལས་གནང་པའི་སྐབ་རེད། "He's (in the middle of) working."

17.4 Exercises སྦྱོང་ཚན།

17.4.1 Translate into English:

༡) འདི་ནས་ལྷ་ས་ཐག་ཉེ་ལོས་འདུག

༢) ཁྲི་ཆུང་ཆུང་འདི་ཡབ་སོ་རེད་པས།

༣) དེབ་འདི་དཀའ་ལས་ཁག་དྲགས་འདུག ངས་ལྟ་ཐུབ་ཀྱི་མི་འདུག

༤) རི་འདི་མཐོ་དྲགས་པ་རེད། ང་རང་ཚོ་འཛེགས་ཐུབ་ཀྱི་མ་རེད།

༥) གསོལ་ཚིགས་ལ་ལྡུགས་ཚ་ཅུང་དྲགས་མི་འདུག་གས།

༦) ཁ་པར་བཏང་ཡག་ལས་སླ་པོ་འདུག

༧) དཔེ་ཆ་འདི་ལྗི་དྲགས་བཞག

༨) འབྲོང་མཐོང་ཡག་ལས་སླ་པོ་མི་འདུག

༩) བྱང་ཐང་ལ་རྐྱང་དང་གཙོད་མང་པོ་ཞེ་དྲགས་ཡོད་རེད།

༡༠) མི་འདི་སྐྱུག་རྫུན་ཚ་པོ་ཡོད་རེད།

17.4.2 Translate into Tibetan:

1. The kitchen is very clean.
2. The tea is too hot.
3. The children are very dirty.
4. The car is too small.
5. That mountain over there is very high.
6. This sentence is very clear.
7. How far away is the monastery? You have to walk for four hours.
8. This lesson is too easy. It isn't very difficult to learn Tibetan.
9. The knife is too big.
10. It's a very good school.

"How many rooms are there?"

ཁང་མིག་ག་ཚོད་ཡོད་རེད།

Grammar aims བརྡ་སྤྲོད་རིག་པའི་དམིགས་ཚད།

- The nominalizer ས་ sā.
- The auxiliaries of probability:
  – མིན་འགྲོ mä̲ntro ཡིན་འགྲོ yi̲ntro.
- Adverbial constructions with བྱས་ chä̲'.

CD I • Tr. 47-48

18.1 Dialogue དྲི་བ་དྲིས་ལན།

མི་ཤེལ་ཿ འདའི་(འདིར་)ག་རེ་རེད། ཉལ་ཁང་མན་འགྲོ (མིན་འགྲོ)

བཀྲ་ཤིས་ཿ འདི་ ང་ གཉིས་ ཀྱི་ ཉལ་ ཁང་ ཡིན། ད་དེ་ནས། འདི་ སྤུ་ གུ་ ཚོའི་ (ཕྲུ་ གུ་ ཚོའི་) ཉལ་ ས་ རེད། འདི་ ཁྲུས་ ཁང་ རེད། འདི་ མཆོད་ ཁང་ རེད། ད་ དེ་ ནས། འདའི་ ཁང་ པ་ སྟོང་ པ་ ཅིག་ ཡོད། ཁྱེད་ རང་ དོ་ དགོངས་ འདའི་ གཟིམ་ན་འགྲིག་གི་རེད། བྲེལ་བ་མེད་ན་ཉི་མ་ཁ་ཤས་བཞུགས།

མི་ཤེལ་ཿ ལགས་ ཐུགས་ ཆེ་ གནང་། བྲེལ་ བ་ ཞེ་ དྲགས་ མེད། ཉི་ མ་ གཉིས་ གསུམ་ བསྡད་ (སྡོད་) ཀྱི་ ཡིན། འདི་ ཚོམ་ ཆེན་ རེད་ པས།

བཀྲ་ཤིས་ཿ ལགས་རེད།

མི་ཤེལ་ཿ སྡོམ་པས་ཁང་མིག་ག་ཚོད་ཡོད་རེད།

བཀྲ་ཤིས་ཿ ཁང་མིག་དྲུག་ཡོད། ད་ཕར་ཕེབས། གསོལ་ཇ་མཆོད། སྡོད་སྡོད་བྱས་བཞུགས་དོ།

Pronunciation

- tä: khare rä', nyä:kang män-tro

- ti nganyi'-ki nyä:kang yin tha thenä' ti pūkutsö: nyä:-sa re' ti thrūkang re'. ti chōkang re'. tha thenä' tä: khāngpa tōngpa cī' yö'. khyērang thokong tä: sim-na tri'-kire'. thrella me'-na nyima khāshä' shu'

- la' thūkce nāng thrella shetra' me' ; nyima nyī' sūm tä'-kiyin. ti tshōmcen re'-pä'

- la' re'

- tompä' khāngmi' khatsö' yo:rä'

- khāngmi' thru' yö', tha phār phēp sō:ca chō'; lhōlö'-chä' shu'-to.

Translation

Michel — What's this? Maybe it's a bedroom.

Trashi — It's our bedroom. That's the room where the children sleep. That's the bathroom. That's the shrine room. Then there's an empty room. You can sleep here tonight. If you're not in a hurry, stay a few days.

Michel — Yes, thank you. I'm not in a great hurry. I'll stay for two or three days. Is this the living room?

Trashi — Yes.

Michel — How many rooms are there altogether?

Trashi — There are six rooms. Come in. Have some tea. Let's sit here quietly.

ཀ་ཁ་ག་ང་

18.2 Vocabulary ཚིག་གསར།

ཉལ་ཁང་ nyä:kang གཟིམ་ཁང་ simkang (H)	(n.) bedroom
ཉལ་ས་ nyä:sa གཟིམ་ས་ simsa (H)	(n.) sleeping place, bedroom
ཉལ་ཁྲི་ nyä:tri གཟིམ་ཁྲི་ simtri (H)	(n.) bed
ཁྲི་ thrī བཞུགས་ཁྲི་ shuktri (H)	(n.) throne
ཉལ་ཆས་ nyä:cä'	(n.) sheet, bedclothes
བཙུག་ཁྲུ་ tshūktru གཟིམ་ཁྲུ་ simtru (H)	(n.) big woollen blanket
སྔས་མགོ་ ngāko	(n.) pillow
ཁྲུས་ཁང་ thrukang	(n.) bathroom
གསང་སྤྱོད་ sāngcö' གཟིམ་སྤྱོད་ simcö' (H)	(n.) toilet
ཁང་མིག་ khāngmi'	(n.) room
ཚོམ་ཆེན་ tshōmcen	(n.) living room
མཆོད་ཤོམས་ chōshom	(n.) altar
མཆོད་ཁང་ chōkang	(n.) shrine room, chapel
ཞོགས་ཀས་ shokkä' ཞོགས་པ་ shokpa (L)	(n.) morning
དགོངས་དག་ kongta'	(n.) evening
དོ་དགོངས་ thokong	(n.) this evening
མདང་དགོང་ tangkong	(n.) last evening

ཁ་སང་ khāsang ཁ་སེང་ khāseng (L)	(n.) a few days ago
སང་དགོང་ sāngkong	(n.) tomorrow evening
སང་ཞོགས་ sāngsho'	(n.) tomorrow morning
ཁེ་ཉིན་ཀ་ khēnyinka	(n.) the day before yesterday
གནངས་ཉིན་ཀ་ nāngnyinka	(n.) the day after tomorrow
གཞེས་ཉིན་ she̱nyin	(n.) in three days
ད་ལོ་ tha̱lo	(n.) this year
དུས་སང་ thü̱sang	(n.) next year
ཟླ་ཉིན། ta̱nyin ན་ནིང་ naning(L)	(n.) last year
སྟོང་པ་ tōngpa	(adj.) empty
གང་ kha̱ng	(adj.) full
དམ་པོ་ tha̱mpo	(adj.) tight
སློད་སློད་ lhȫlö	(adj.) relaxed, calm
སྡོམ་པས་ to̱mpä'	(adv.) altogether, in total
འཁྲུ་ thrū (1)/ བཀྲུས་ trǖ' (2,3)	(v.) [vol., EA] wash
གཟུགས་པོ་ + བཀྲུས་ su̱kpo trǖ'	(v.) [vol., E] to have a wash
སྐུ་གཟུགས་ + བཞེས་ kūsu' sī: (H)	(v.) [vol., E] to have a wash

18.3 Remarks འགྲེལ་བཤད།

18.3.1 The nominalizer ས་ sā

Lesson 11 introduced nominalizers that transform a verb (or an entire clause) into a noun phrase. Like other nominalizers, this one can form nominal clauses as well as relative clauses (see Lesson 26).

The verb to which the suffix -sa is attached appears in the present-future stem form, but it may be used in the context of the past, present or future.

Ex.: ཞུ་ས་ shu̱-sa but not * ཞུས་ས་shü̱'-sa
ཟ་ས་ sa̱-sa but not * བཟས་ས་ sä̱'-sa
བལྟ་ས་ tā-sa but not * བལྟས་ས་ tǟ'-sa

The nominalizer -sa relates to the **location** or the **goal** of the verbal action.[137]

Ex.: འབྲི་ས་ "the place where one writes, or upon which one writes", ཕུལ་ས་(འབུལ་ས་) "the place where one makes an offering, the person to whom one makes an offering", ཞུ་ས་ "the person to whom one speaks, the place where one speaks", ཉལ་ས་ the place where one sleeps", འགྲོ་ས་ "the place towards which one goes, the trail".

137. In other words, the suffix indicates locative adverbials and indirect objects.

Formulations with -sa are very common in Tibetan, and may sometimes be translated by nouns in European languages.

Ex.: འདིར་བསྡད་ས་(སྡོད་ས་) འདུག་གས། tä: tä'-sa tu'-kä' "Is there a room here?"
སྣུམ་བླུག་ས་ག་པར་འདུག nūm lūk-sa khapar tu' "Where's the gas station?"
པྷ་སེ་ཉོ་ས་ཕ་གིར་འདུག pāse nyo-sa phākä: tu' "The ticket office is over there."
འདི་ཇ་འཐུང་ས་རེད་པས། ti cha thūng-sa re'-pä' "Is that a teashop?" or "Is that a teacup?"

In these examples, the four substantives "room", "gas station", "ticket office" and "teacup" would be translated literally as "sitting place", "gasoline pouring place", "ticket buying place" and "tea drinking place".

The nominalizer -sa provides no clues about the tense-aspect of the event, which has to be deduced from the context.

18.3.2 Auxiliaries of probability

We have already met some epistemic auxiliaries in Lesson 11. They imply that the speaker regards his or her assertion as a probability, not a certainty.

The auxiliaries ཡིན་འགྲོ yintro, ཡོད་འགྲོ yötro, are based on the verbs ཡིན་ yin and ཡོད་ yö', which correspond respectively to essential and existential formulations. They are used either as copulas (linking verbs) or as auxiliaries and occur in the same position as ཡིན་ yin and ཡོད་ yö', (see Table 6 in Appendix 6).

They may be translated in English by the adverb "probably". Their negative counterpart མེད་འགྲོ་ metro, མིན་འགྲོ mäntro[138], express a similar meaning with a slightly weaker probability[139], but they occur more frequently than the positive auxiliaries.

Ex.: ཉལ་ཁང་མན་འགྲོ (མིན་འགྲོ) nyä:kang mäntro
"That's maybe the bedroom."

ཉལ་ཁང་ཡིན་འགྲོ nyä:kang yintro
"That's probably the bedroom. It must be the bedroom."

ལུག་ཤ་ཉོ་ས་ཡོད་འགྲོ luksha nyo-sa yö'-tro
"There's probably a place to buy mutton."

གསོལ་མར་ཉུང་དྲག་པ་མེད་འགྲོ sō:mar nyung-tra'-pa metro
"Maybe there isn't enough butter."

ཁོང་ཇ་ཁང་ལ་ཕེབས་པ་མིན་འགྲོ khōng chakang-la phēp-pa mäntro
"He may have gone to the teashop."

138. With a rising intonation.

139. In English it corresponds rather to "maybe" than to "probably", but the meaning also depends on the intonation.

ཕྱག་དཔེ་འདི་རྒན་ལགས་ལ་མེད་འགྲོ   chā'pe ti̲ kä̲nla'-la me̲tro
"The teacher may have this book *(pecha)*"

Note: The negative forms མེད་འགྲོ་ me̲tro and མིན་འགྲོ་ mä̲ntro are usually used in a positive sense, as the above examples indicate. However, exceptionally, with a falling intonation, they may also express a negative judgement corresponding to "probably not", in which case they are similar to མེད་པ་འདྲ་ me-patra and མིན་པ་འདྲ་ mä̲npatra are (see Lesson 11).

Ex.: ཕྱག་དཔེ་འདི་རྒན་ལགས་ལ་མེད་འགྲོ   chā'pe ti̲ kä̲nla'-la me̲tro
"The teacher probably doesn't have this book *(pecha)*."

18.3.3 Adverbs with བྱས་ chä̲'

Adjectives can be transformed into adverbs by the addition of the suffix chä̲', which is derived from the verb "to do", as the following example shows:

སྐྱིད་པོ་ kyīppo "pleasant" > སྐྱིད་པོ་བྱས་ kyīppo-chä' "pleasantly".

Ex.: ཉོད་ཉོད་བྱས་བཞུགས་དོ། "Let's sit here quietly."

18.4 Exercises སྦྱོང་ཚན།

18.4.1 Insert the appropriate nominalizer: ས་, རྒྱུ་ *or* ཡག་:

༡) ཁྱེད་རང་ལས་ཀ་བྱེད་(   )ག་པར་འདུག
༢) ཁོང་ལ་སྐད་ཆ་འདྲི་(   )མང་པོ་འདུག་གས།
༣) བོད་ཡིག་སློབ་སྦྱོང་བྱེད་(   )གལ་ཆེན་པོ་རེད།
༤) རྟ་རྒྱུག་(   )དེ་ག་པར་འདུག
༥) འདིར་འཁྱུང་(   )ག་རེ་ཡོད་རེད།

18.4.2 Insert the appropriate auxiliary ཡིན་འགྲོ *or* ཡོད་འགྲོ:

༡) ཁོང་ནང་ལ་བཞུགས་མི་འདུག ལས་ཁུངས་ལ་ཕེབས་པ་(   )།
༢) ཁྱེད་རང་ལ་སྨྱུ་གུ་ཡོད་པས། ང་ལ་མེད། ཁོང་ལ་(   )།
༣) བཀྲ་ཤིས་ལགས་གུང་ལོ་༤༥ཙམ་(   )།
༤) ཟླ་བ་ཚང་ལ་དགའ་པོ་(   )།

18.4.3 Translate into English:

༡) གྲོང་གསེབ་འདིའི་ནང་ལ་ཚོང་ཁང་གཅིག་ཡོད་འགྲོ

༢) ཁོང་རྣམ་ཀུན་ལས་ཀར་འགྲོ་གི་ཡོད་འགྲོ

༣) ཁོང་ནང་ལ་བསྡད་མེད་པ་མིན་འགྲོ

༤) ཁོང་གི་ནང་ལ་ཞི་མི་ཡོད་འགྲོ

༥) ཁོང་ད་ལྷ་གཟིམ་ཤག་ལ་བཞུགས་་ཡོད་འགྲོ

༦) སྒྲོལ་མ་ལགས་སློ་བཟང་ལགས་ཀྱི་གྲོགས་མོ་རེད་པས།མིན་འགྲོ་ངས་གསལ་པོ་ཤེས་ཀྱི་མེད།

༧) རྡོ་རྗེ་ལགས་དེ་རིང་ཕྱུག་ལས་ལ་ཕེབས་མི་འདུག

༨) ཁོང་སྟུང་པ་མིན་འགྲོ

༩) གསོལ་ཇ་འདི་ཡག་པོ་བྱུང་མི་འདུག

18.5 Civilization རིགས་གཞུང་།

Tibetan carpets

In Tibetan cultural areas, as in most Central Asia, carpets are one of the first items of furniture a family would try to get after settling in. Bed carpets, called ཁ་གདན་ *khabdän,* cover the beds where Tibetans sleep or sit (often cross-legged) during the day.[140] Usually there is also a carpet-covered cushion as a back-rest.[141] Floor rugs called ས་གདན་ *sabdän*, though rarer, may still be found. Besides the ubiquitous bed-carpets, Tibetans traditionally weave specially shaped saddle-carpets; pillar carpets (very good examples in some palaces of the Norbulingkha, in Samding Monastery, Nagartse, Lhokha); monastery assembly-hall carpets called ཚོགས་གདན་ *tshogdän*, long and narrow to accommodate a row of monks; and ཁྲི་གདན་ *thridän*, throne-fitting seat-and-back carpets for the highest lamas.

The history of Tibetan rugs is very patchy, because very few antique items have made it to modern times. During the period of the Empire, between the eighth and ninth centuries, Tibetans controlled the Silk Road and were thus exposed to Turkish, Persian, and Chinese cultures.

Despite these influences, Tibetan carpets have retained their distinctive features. First the Tibetan knot (referred to as the Senna loop), is different from the two most widely-used knots, the Turkish and Persian. Patterns and colours are also very different and have a characteristic and unmistakable Tibetan personality. There is usually no border on Tibetan carpets, and the central design is simple compared to the complex motifs of Persian carpets. Patterns are much less

---

140. The commonest size is 175 cm x 85 cm (approximately 6 x 3 ft.).

141. These measure approximately 67cm x 45 cm, 2 x 1.5 ft.

stylized and include motifs that are indigenous (the eight auspicious signs, the dorje, snow lions, clouds, etc.), Chinese-inspired (dragons, phoenixes, bats, peonies) or Turkmeni-inspired ("gul" or stylized flower). "Tiger carpets" are very specific to Tibet; once probably power symbols, they imitate tiger skins, either displaying head and limbs or else merely reproducing the stripes.

Tibetan carpet weaving has undergone several innovations since the 1960's, when it became one of the main occupations for Tibetan refugees in Nepal. Tibetans had never woven carpets for export markets, and they had now to adapt to Western tastes. In the mid-1980s, the authorities of the Tibet Autonomous Region and Prefectures started to promote carpet weaving as one of the rare industries that did not require energy or major investment, and for which raw material was locally available. The main production centers are in Lhasa, Gyantse, and Zhikatse. Tibetan wool is valued as one of the best in the world for its high lanoline content. Weaving was primarily an activity of women and a cottage industry, but large factories of more than twenty looms now occupy a major share of the market.

Don't step on a carpet depicting a religious character, or even the Potala, a very common motif on tourist souvenirs – Tibetans would not appreciate it! Use it as a wall hanging or buy flowery carpets instead.

"The post office"

སྦྲག་ཁང་།

Grammar aims བརྡ་སྤྲོད་རིག་པའི་དམིགས་ཚད།

- Imperative markers.
- The modal verb ཆོག་ chō' "to be allowed; may".

CD I • Tr. 49-50

19.1 Dialogue དྲི་བ་དྲིས་ལན།

མི་ཞིག་ ཿ	བློ་ བཟང་ ལགས། འདའི་ (འདིར་) སྦྲག་ ཁང་ ཡོད་ རེད་ པས། ང་ ཡི་ གེ་ ཁ་ ཤས་ བཏང་ (གཏོང་) དགོས་ ཡོད།
བློ་བཟང་ ཿ	འདའི་ སྦྲག་ ཁང་ ཡོད་ རེད། ང་ གཉིས་ ད་ ལྟ་ ལྷན་ རྒྱས་ ཕེབས་ དོ། སྦྲག་ འཛིན་ སྒྲུར་ གནང་ ཡོད་ པས།
མི་ཞིག་ ཿ	སྦྲག་འཛིན་སྒྲུར་ཡོད། ཡིག་སྐོགས་ནང་ལ་པར་བླུག་ན་འགྲིག་གི་རེད་པས།
བློ་བཟང་ ཿ	འགྲིག་གི་རེད།
མི་ཞིག་ ཿ	དེའི་ཞོར་ལ་ཇོ་ཁང་དང་ཁྲོམ་ལ་ཕེབས་ན།
བློ་བཟང་ ཿ	འོ་ཡོང་ང་།
མི་ཞིག་ ཿ	ཇོ་ཁང་ལ་ཐད་(ཐེག་)ན་ཁ་བཏགས་དང་མཆོད་མེ་བསྣམས་དགོས་རེད།
བློ་བཟང་ ཿ	ཁ་བཏགས་ཁྲོམ་ནས་ཉོས་ཆོག་གི་རེད།
མི་ཞིག་ ཿ	འོ་ན་ཕེབས་དོ།
བློ་བཟང་ ཿ	ཁ་བཏགས་རེ་རེར་ག་ཚོད་རེད།
ཁ་བཏགས་འཚོང་མཁན་ ཿ	ཁ་བཏགས་ག་རེ་གཟིགས་ག
བློ་བཟང་ ཿ	ཨ་ཤེ་ཧྲོ་གི་ཡིན།
ཁ་བཏགས་འཚོང་མཁན་ ཿ	ཨ་ཤེ་རེ་རེར་སྒོར་མོ་བཞི་རེད།

Pronunciation

- lōpsang la' tä̱: tra̱kang yo̱:re'-pä' nga̱ yi̱ke khāshä' tāng ko̱-yö'

- tä̱: tra̱kang yo̱:re' nga̱nyi' tha̱nta lhā̃nkyä' phēp-to tra̱ntsin ca̱r nāng-yö'-pä'

- tra̱ntsin ca̱r-yö'. yi̱ko' na̱ng-la pār lū'-na tri̱'-kire'-pä'.

- tri̱'-kire'

- the̱: sho̱r-la chö̱:kang-tang thrōm-la phēp-na

- o yo̱ng-nga

- chö̱:kang-la thā̃'-na khāta'-tang chō̃me' nām' ko̱-re'

- khāta' thrōm-nä' nyö̱' chō'-kire'

- o̱na phēp-to

- khāta' re̱rer kha̱tsö' rä̱'

- khāta' kha̱re si̱'-ka

- āshi nyo̱-kiyin

- āshi re̱rer ko̱rmo shi̱ re̱'

Translation

Michel	—	Lobzang, is there a post office here? I have to send some letters.
Lobzang	—	Yes, there is a post office. Let's go together. Have you already stuck the stamps on?
Michel	—	Yes, I've stuck the stamps on. Can we put photos in the envelope?
Lobzang	—	Yes, it's possible.
Michel	—	Yes, and what about making a round of the Jhokang and the market on the way?
Lobzang	—	All right.
Michel	—	If we go to the Jhokhang, we have to take offering scarves (*khatak*) and butter for the lamps.
Lobzang	—	We can buy the *khatak* in the market.
Michel	—	Fine, let's go.
Lobzang	—	How much does each *khatak* cost?
The *khatak* vendor	—	Which *khatak* do you want to buy?
Lobzang	—	I'd like to buy a top-quality *khatak* (*ashi*).
The *khatak* vendor	—	*Ashi khatak* cost four *gormo* each.

ཀ་ཁ་ག་ང་

19.2 Vocabulary ཚིག་གསར།

དཀོན་གཉེར་ kö̱nnyer	(n.) temple caretaker
སྒོ་སྲུང་ ko̱sung	(n.) caretaker
སྦྲག་འཛིན་ tra̱ngtsin	(n.) stamp
ཡིག་སྒྲོགས་ yi̱ko'	(n.) envelope

པ་སི་ pās	(n.) ticket
ཁ་བཏགས་ khāta' མཇལ་དར་ cä:tar (H)	(n.) *khatak*, silk scarf
ཁྲོམ་ thrōm	(n.) market
ཨ་ཤེ་ āshi	(n.) superior quality *khatak*
རེ་རེ་ rere	(adj.) each
མར་ mar གསོལ་མར་ sō:mar (H)	(n.) butter
མར་མེ་ marme མཆོད་མེ་ chōme	(n.) butter lamp
དེའི་ཞོར་ལ་ the: shor-la	(n.) by/on the way
ཁ་པར་ + བཏང་ khāpar tāng	(v.) [vol., ED] to telephone
ཞལ་པར་ + ཕུལ་ shä:par phū: (h)	(v.) [vol., ED] to telephone
ཞལ་པར་ + གནང་ shä:par nāng (H)	(v.) [vol., ED] to telephone
འབྱོར་ cor	(v.) [inv., DA] to receive
ཁྱེར་ khyēr བསྣམས་ nām' (H)	(v.) [vol., EA] to take, take away
སྦྱར་ car	(v.) [vol., EA] to stick
ཐད་ thā' ཐེག་ thē' (L)	(v.) [vol., A] to go
བླུག་ lū'	(v.) [vol., EA] to pour, put.

19.3 Remarks འགྲེལ་བཤད།

19.3.1 Imperative markers

We have already seen (in Lesson 10) that some volitional verbs have an imperative form.

Ex.: ཉན་ nyän > ཉོན་ nyön "Listen"   ཟ་ sa > ཟོ་ so "Eat"
ལང་ lang > ལོངས་ long "Get up"   ཡོང་ yong > ཤོག་ shō' "Come"

These forms are not used for the negative imperative, which instead takes the present-future form.

Ex.: མ་ཉན། ma nyän "Don't listen", མ་ཟ། ma sa "Don't eat", མ་ཡོང་། ma yong "Don't come".

However, there are many verbs that have no special form to denote the imperative. In such cases, the verb may be used by itself.

Ex.: གསོལ་ཇ་མཆོད། sō:ca chō' "Have some tea", ཕར་ཕེབས། phār phē' "Go over there".

In most cases, the imperative (command) and optative (wish) moods are formed by using particles.

The main particles are: དོ་ -to, དང་ -ta, ཨ་ -a, ཤིག་ -shi, ཤོག་ - sho' and the construction རོགས་གནང་ ro'nang.

• The particle ཏོ་ -to

This particle is used to form the first person plural imperative: the exhortative.

Ex.: ཕེབས་ ཏོ། phēp-to "Let's go.", བཞུགས་ཏོ། shu̱'-to "Let's sit down."

Apart from –to, which is used to form the first person imperative, the other markers all indicate the second person singular or plural imperative, and differ from one another only in terms of nuance or register.

• The expression རོགས་གནང་ ro'nang

This is the most polite form in which to phrase a command or a request. It is used only with honorifics, and takes the present-future (not the imperative) form of the verb.

Ex.:	ཕེབས་རོགས་གནང་།	phēp-ro'nang	"Please go" or "Please come"
	གསུངས་རོགས་གནང་།	sūng-ro'nang	"Please say"
	བཞུགས་རོགས་གནང་།	shu̱'-ro'nang	"Please stay"
	མཆོད་རོགས་གནང་།	chō̄'-ro'nang	"Please eat"
	བཀག་རོགས་གནང་།	kā'-ro'nang	"Please stop" (the car, the dog, etc.)
	ཞུ་རོགས་གནང་།	shu̱-ro'nang	"Please ask."

Note: There is also the non-honorific version རོགས་བྱེད་ ro'ce'.

• The particles དང་ -tang and ཤིག་ -shi'

These very common particles have exactly the same meaning as the expressions described above, but are less formal. In conversation they are pronounced respectively -ta and -sh. They may be used with both honorific and non-honorific forms.

Ex.: གསུངས་དང་། sūng-ta "Say it", ཕེབས་དང་། phē'-ta "Go", ཕེབས་ཤིག phē'-sh "Go", བཞུགས་ཤིག shu̱'-sh "Sit down", བཞུགས་དང་། shu̱'-ta "Sit down", ཟོ་དང་། so̱-ta "Eat", ཉོན་དང་། nyo̱n-ta "Listen", ལབ་དང་། la̱p-ta "Speak", ལྟོས་ཤིག tō̄'-sh "Look".

• The particle ཨ་ -a

This particle, too, is very common, and may also be used with both honorific and ordinary forms. It conveys a sense of urgency or danger, or implies a greater degree of coercion.

Ex.:	སེམས་ཁྲལ་མ་བྱེད་ཨ།	sēmträ: ma̱ che̱'-a	"Don't worry!"
	གཟབ་གཟབ་གནང་ཨ།	sāpsap nāng-a	"Be careful!"
	མ་ལབ་ཨ།	ma̱ la̱p-a	"Just don't talk!"

• The particle ཤོག་ - sho'

This form, which is less common, is also used with both honorific and non-honorific formulations. It conveys immediacy, and implies that the person addressed is hesitant to do what he or she is being told. It may be translated by "Go on!"

Ex.: གསུངས་ཤོག sūng'-sho' "Go on, say it!"
ཕེབས་ཤོག phē'-sho' "Come here, will you!"
ཉོས་ཤོག nyö̱'-sho' "Go on, buy it!"

• The expression པར་བྱེད་ -par che̱'

We have seen above (8.3) that non-volitional verbs cannot take an imperative. However, the verb may be followed by the expression -par che̱' which means "to see to it that".

Ex.: མ་བརྗེད་པར་བྱེད་ཨ། ma̱ ce̱'-par che̱'-a "Don't forget!" (see to it that you don't forget)
ཕྲུ་གུ་མ་ཤོར་པར་བྱེད་ད། pūku ma shōr-pa che̱'-ta "Don't lose the child!"

19.3.2 The modal verb ཆོག་ *chō' "to be allowed, may, can"*

Like other modal verbs, this one goes after the main verb and before the auxiliary. The tense of the main verb may be the present-future or the past – either will do. The verb ཆོག་ chō' is used mainly in with the future auxiliaries: ཆོག་གི་རེད་ chō'-kire' for future and present situations. However, other auxiliaries are sometimes used: ཆོག་གི་འདུག་ chō'-kitu' (testimonial present), ཆོག་གི་ཡོད་རེད་ chō'-kiyo:re' (assertive present). The combinations ཆོག་པ་རེད་ chō'-pare', ཆོག་སོང་ chō'-song, and ཆོག་བཞག་ chō'-sha' are sometimes used in the past, but of course the modal verb ཆོག་ chō' never occurs with intentional egophoric auxiliaries *ཆོག་པ་ཡིན་ chō'-payin' or *ཆོག་གི་ཡིན་ chō'-kiyin.

The verb ཆོག་ chō' has two meanings: The first, and more usual meaning, is "to be allowed", "may"; secondly, it can also have the meaning "to be able, can" in which case it can be replaced by ཐུབ་ thūp.

Ex.: ཁ་བཏགས་ཁྲོམ་ནས་ཉོས་ཆོག་གི་རེད། khāta' thrōm-nä' nyö̱' chō'-kire'
"We can buy khatak in the market."

ལྷ་ཁང་ནང་ལ་པར་བརྒྱབ་ཆོག་གི་རེད་པས། lhākang na̱ng-la pār kya̱p chō'-kire'-pä'
"Are we allowed to take photos inside the temple?"

19.4 Exercises སྦྱོང་ཚན།

19.4.1 Translate into Tibetan:

1. Let's go and eat in a Tibetan restaurant!
2. The post office is going to close soon.
3. That's where we bought some thangka.
4. Don't smoke in front of elderly people!
5. Are we allowed to go to that area?
6. Can I make a phone call? (lit. if I telephone will that be all right?)
7. It is not permitted to read this book.

19.4.2 Complete the sentences with the appropriate modal verb: ཆོག་ or ཐུབ་.

༡) དཔེ་མཛོད་ཁང་ནང་ལ་ཐ་མག་འཐེན་(   )གི་མ་རེད།

༢) རྨོ་ལགས་འདི་འགྲོ་(   )གི་མི་འདུག

༣) ཡིག་སྐོགས་ནང་ལ་པར་བླུག་(   )གི་རེད།

༤) རྒྱ་གར་དང་བལ་ཡུལ་ལ་གླང་ཤ་བཟས་(   )གི་མ་རེད།

༥) ཁ་ལག་མང་དྲགས་བཞག ང་ཟ་(   )གི་མ་རེད།

19.4.3 Translate into English:

༡) འདི་ནས་ཁ་པར་བཏང་ཆོག་གི་རེད།

༢) བོད་ནས་རྒྱ་གར་ལ་ཕྱིན་ཆོག་གི་རེད་པས།

༣) འཕྲོང་བསད་ཆོག་གི་མ་རེད།

༤) ཆུ་འདི་འཐུང་ཆོག་གི་མ་རེད།

༥) དགོན་པའི་ནང་ལ་བསྡད་ཆོག་གི་རེད་པས།

༦) ཚིག་འདི་ལབ་ཆོག་གི་མ་རེད།

"Asking the way"

ལམ་ཁག་འདྲི་བ།

Grammar aims བརྗོད་སྒྲོད་རིག་པའི་དམིགས་ཚད།

- The nominalizer མཁན་ khān.

CD I • Tr. 51 

20.1 Dialogue དྲི་བ་དྲིས་ལན།

བསྟན་འཛིན་ཿ ཨ་ལྕུག་ལགས། གཙུག་ལག་ཁང་ལ་འགྲོ་ས་ག་ནས་རེད།

ཨ་ལྕུ་ཅིག་ཿ འདི་ནས་མར་ཤར་ཀྱག་ཕེབས། མ་གིར་ལམ་ཁག་བཞི་མདོ་ཁ་ལ་སླེབས་སོང་ན་བྱང་ངོས་ལ་ཕེབས་དགོས་
རེད། དེ་ནས་མི་ལ་དྲིས་གནང་ན་མིས་ལམ་ཁག་བསྟན་གི་རེད།

བསྟན་འཛིན་ཿ ལེ་སེ། (ལགས་སོ་) ཐུགས་རྗེ་ཆེ།

བསྟན་འཛིན་ཿ ཀན་ལགས། གཙུག་ལག་ཁང་ལ་འགྲོ་ས་འདི་ནས་རེད་པས།

ཕྲུ་ག་ཅིག་ཿ རེད་རེད། འདི་ནས་ཡར་ཤར་ཀྱག་ཕེབས་ད། བར་སྐོར་ནང་ལ་སླེབས་གི་རེད། བར་སྐོར་ནང་
ལ་བསླེབས་ན་གཙུག་ལག་ཁང་ག་པར་རེད་ཟེ་དྲིས་གནང་དང་། མིས་བསྟན་གྱི་རེད།

བསྟན་འཛིན་ཿ ཐུགས་རྗེ་ཆེ།

བསྟན་འཛིན་ཿ སྐུ་ཞོག་(སྐུ་ཞབས་)གཙུག་ལག་ཁང་ག་པར་རེད།

གྲྭ་པ་ཅིག་ཿ ཕར་ཙམ་དྭགས་རེད། (ཕར་ཙམ་དེ་གར་རེད་) ང་ཡའི་འགྲོ་མཁན་ཡིན། མཉམ་པོ་ཕེབས་དོ།

Pronunciation

- āca'-la' tsūklakang-la tro̲-sa khanä' rä' ?
- ti-nä' ma̲r shārkya phēp. ma̲kir la̲mka shi̲mtoka-la lēp-song-na cha̲ngngö'-la phēp ko̲-re' the̲nä' mi̲-la tri̲ nang-na mi̲' la̲mka tā̄n-kire'
- lase thūkce nāng. kä̲nla' tsūklakang-la tro̲-sa ti̲-nä' re̲'-pä' ?
- re̲' re̲' ti̲-nä' ya̲r sha̲rkya phēp-ta. pha̲rkor na̲ng-la lēp-kire'. pha̲rkor na̲ng-la lēp-na tsūklakang kha̲par re̲'-s tri̲nang-ta. mi̲' tā̄n-kire'
- thūkce chē.
- kūsho', tsūklakang kha̲par rä̲' ?
- phāts tha̲kar re̲'. nga̲ yä: tro̲-ngän yi̲n nyāmpo phēp-to

Translation

Tändzin	—	Excuse me Madam, which is the way to the Jhokhang?
A woman	—	This way, straight! When you reach the crossroads, you have to go north. Then if you ask the way, people will show you.
Tändzin	—	Fine, thank you.
Tändzin	—	Sir, the Jhokhang Temple, is it this way?
A man	—	Yes, yes. Go straight along here. You'll get to the Bharkor (the circumambulation route around the great temple). When you get to the Bharkor, ask where the great temple is. People will show you.
Tändzin	—	Thank you.
Tändzin	—	Your reverence, where is the great temple?
A monk	—	It's just over there. I'm going there too. Let's go together.

ཀ་ཁ་ག་ང་

20.2 Vocabulary ཚིག་གསར།

ཤར་རྐྱུག་ shārkya'	(adj., adv.) direct, straight
ཡ་གིར་ ya̱kä:, yakir (L)	(n.) up there
མ་གིར་ ma̱kä, makir (L)	(n.) down there
བཞི་མདོ་ཁ་ shi̱mtoka	(n.) crossroads
ནུབ་ nu̱p	(n.) west
ལྷོ་ lhō	(n.) south
ཤར་ shār	(n.) east
བྱང་ cha̱ng	(n.) north
ནུབ་ཕྱོགས་ nu̱pco'	(n.) western
ལྷོ་ཕྱོགས་ lhōco'	(n.) southern
ཤར་ཕྱོགས་ shārco'	(n.) eastern
བྱང་ཕྱོགས་ cha̱ngco'	(n.) northern
བྱང་ངོས་ cha̱ngngö'	(n.) northwards
ཕར་ཙམ་ད་གར་ phā:ts tha̱kar	(n.) just there
མཁན་ khā̈n, -ngän	(n.) *nominalizer*
སྐད་ཆ་ kā̈ca བཀའ་མོལ་ kāmö: (H)	(n.) speech
འདྲི་བ་ tri̱wa བཀའ་འདྲི་ kāntri (H)	(n.) question
སྐད་ཆ་ + དྲིས་ kā̈ca thri̱'	(v.) [vol., ED] to ask
བཀའ་འདྲི་ + གནང་ kāntri nāng (H)	(v.) [vol., ED] to ask
བཀའ་འདྲི་ + ཞུ་ kāntri shu̱ (h)	(v.) [vol., ED] to ask
སྐད་ཆ་ + བཤད་ kā̈ca shā̈'	(v.) [vol., ED] to converse, discuss
བཀའ་མོལ་ + ཞུ་ kāmö: shu̱ (h)	(v.) [vol., ED] to converse, discuss
བཀའ་མོལ་ + གནང་ kāmö: nāng (H)	(v.) [vol., ED] to converse, discuss

ལབ་ lap (v.) [vol., EDA] to say
གསུངས་ sūng' (H) (v.) [vol., EDA] to say

Proper nouns

གཙུག་ལག་ཁང་ tsūklakang Jhokhang (other name of the great temple of Lhasa)
བར་སྐོར་ pharkor Bharkor (section of Lhasa around the Jhokhang)

20.3 Remarks འགྲེལ་བཤད།

20.3.1 The nominalizer མཁན་ khān / -ngän

In a more formal register, this nominalizer is pronounced -(n)khān,[142] whereas in conversation it is usually pronounced as ངན་-ngän, and even ཉན་-nyän. The verb to which it is attached takes the present-future.

Ex.: ཞུ་མཁན་ shu-ngän, *but not* * ཞུས་མཁན་ shü'-ngän
ཟ་མཁན་ sa-ngän, *but not* *བཟས་མཁན་ sä'-ngän
ལྟ་མཁན་ tā-ngän, *but not* *བལྟས་མཁན་ tā'-ngän

Like other nominalizers, it can form nominal clauses as well as relative clauses (see Lesson 26). This nominalizer prototypically indicates the **agent** of the verbal action, but also extends to the subject of transitive verbs and even (in most cases) to the subject of intransitive verbs.

Ex.: འབྲི་མཁན་ tri-ngän "the person who writes, the writer", ཞུ་མཁན་shu-ngän "the person who is speaking, the speaker", ཟ་མཁན་ sa-ngän "the person who is eating", ཚོང་མཁན་ tshōng-ngän "the person who is selling, the vendor", རྨི་ལམ་བཏང་མཁན་ mīlam tāng-ngän "the dreamer", ཉལ་མཁན་ nyä:-ngän "the person who is sleeping, the sleeper".

Formulations with -ngän may sometimes be translated by terms for agents in European languages. In English, the suffix *–er* or the name of a profession often best conveys the sense of this nominalizer.

Ex.: ཁོང་བག་ལེབ་བཟོ་མཁན་རེད།
khōng phaklep so-ngän re'
"He's a baker." (lit. he's a bread-maker)

142. The nasal that is noted here, "(n)" (see Appendix 1, section 1), is a velar nasal (a homorganic nasal of the following consonant). It is the one that appears most frequently, except when the verb ends in the consonant p. This nasal, which is preserved in Tibetan spelling, is the source of two current pronunciations: ngän (a velar nasal) and nyän (a palatal nasal). As far as the written form is concerned, the traditional spelling *mkhan* will be retained, since *nyan* and *ngan* never appear in writing.

ང་རང་ཚོའི་གྲོགས་པོ་རྒྱ་མི་དེ་གློག་བརྙན་བཟོ་མཁན་རེད།

nga̱rangtsö: thro̱kpo kya̱mi the̱ lōknyän so̱-ngän re̱'

"Our Chinese friend is a film-maker."

ཐ་མག་འཐེན་མཁན་འདི་སུ་རེད།

thāma' thēn-ngän ti̱ sū rä̱'

"Who's the person who's smoking?" or "Who's the smoker?"

མོ་ཊ་ནག་པོ་ཡོད་མཁན་དེ་རྫོང་དཔོན་གཅིག་རེད།

mo̱tra na̱kpo yö̱'-ngän the̱ tso̱ngpön cī' re̱'

"The person who has the black car is the mayor of a district", or "The owner of the black car is…"

In certain cases, verbs that are nominalized with -ngän are practically the same as conjugated verbs. For example, the sentence: ང་ཡའི་(ཡང་)འགྲོ་མཁན་ཡིན། nga̱ yä: tro̱-ngän yin "I'm also going", which literally means: "I'm also a goer" is similar to: ང་ཡའི་(ཡང་)འགྲོ་གི་ཡིན། nga̱ yä: tro̱-kiyin *idem.*

• Remarks on the tense of nominalized verbs.

The nominalizer -ngän, as we have seen, marks the subject of both transitive and intransitive verbs. In the former case, the tense-aspect of the verb is unspecified, and must be deduced from the context. Thus the sentence "Who is the person who is smoking (or who smokes)" could just as well be translated by the imperfective past as "Who is the person who was smoking? (or who used to smoke?)" or the past perfective, "Who is the person who (has) smoked."

By contrast, when the nominalizer is used with an intransitive verb, it indicates the **present** or the **future** (or else the imperfective past). To indicate the past (perfective) corresponding to the English perfect or preterite, Tibetan uses another nominalizer: པ་-pa.

Ex.:	འགྲོ་མཁན་	tro̱-ngän	"the person who is going, goes, will go, was going"
	བསྡད་མཁན་	tä̱'-ngän	"the person who is staying, who stays, will stay, was staying"
	ཕྱིན་པ་	chīn-pa	"the person who went, has gone"
	བསྡད་པ་	tä̱'-pa	"the person who stayed, has stayed"

20.4 Exercises སྦྱོང་ཚན།

20.4.1 Translate into English:

༡) རྐན་ལགས་བར་སྐོར་ནང་ལ་འགྲོ་ས་འདི་ནས་རེད་པས། —— རེད་རེད། འདི་ནས་ཕར་ཕེབས་ནས་གློག་བརྙན་ཁང་ཡོད་ས་འདི་ནས་གཡོན་ངོས་ལ་ཕེབས་ན་སླེབས་ཀྱི་རེད།

༢) ཨ་ལྕག་ལགས། སྨན་རྩིས་ཁང་ག་པར་ཡོད་རེད། —— གཙུག་ལག་ཁང་གི་མདུན་ནས་མར་ཙམ་ཕེབས་ན་ལྷ་ས་གློག་བརྙན་ཁང་ཡོད་རེད། ལྷ་ས་གློག་བརྙན་ཁང་སྨན་རྩིས་ཁང་ཁ་སྤྱོད་ལ་ཡོད་རེད།

༣) དེང་སང་ཡང་དེ་འདྲས་བྱེད་མཁན་ཡོད་རེད་པས།

༤) ཁ་པར་ལེན་མཁན་མི་འདུག

༥) ཞབས་བྲོ་རྒྱག་མཁན་ཚོས་སྐོར་སྐོར་བྱེད་ཀྱི་ཡོད་རེད།

20.4.2 Translate into Tibetan:

1. Who is the person who's talking to Tshering?
2. In Tibet, there are not many people who drive cars.
3. I know the person who works in the library.
4. Are there people whom we can ask?
5. This is the place where books are kept.

20.4.3 Complete the following sentences with the appropriate nominalizer: ས་ ཡག་ མཁན་.

༡) མོ་ཏ་བཏང་ ( ) སུ་རེད།

༢) སློབ་སྦྱོང་གནང་ ( ) ག་པར་རེད།

༣) ཁ་བཏགས་ཚོང་ ( ) དེ་ལ་སྐད་ཆ་དྲིས་ད།

༤) ཕྱུག་ལས་གནང་ ( ) གཞི་ག་རྩེ་རེད་པས།

༥) དེ་རིང་ཁ་ལག་བཟོ་ ( ) སུ་རེད།

༦) ཁྱེད་རང་ལ་ཅ་ལག་འཚོང་ ( ) ཡོད་པས།

"Tibetan tea or sweet tea?"

བོད་ཇ་ཡང་ན་ཇ་མངར་མོ།

Grammar aims བརྡ་སྤྲོད་རིག་པའི་དམིགས་ཚད།

- Superlative constructions.
- Comparative constructions of equality.
- The construction མ་གཏོགས mato' "except", "unless".

CD I • Tr. 52 

21.1 Dialogue དྲི་བ་དྲིས་ལན།

གླུ་བཟང་ ༔	མི་ཞེལ་ལགས། ང་གཉིས་སྟུན་ལ་(སྔོན་ལ་)ཇ་ཁང་ལ་མཚོད་མཇལ་ལ་ཅིག་ཕེབས། དེ་ནས་ཁྲོམ་ལ་ཅིག་ཕེབས་གས།
མི་ཞེལ་ ༔	སྟུན་ལ་གསོལ་ཇ་གཅིག་མཆོད་གས།
གླུ་བཟང་ ༔	འོ་ཡོང་ང་། མ་གིར་ཟ་ཁང་ཡོད་རེད། དེར་གསོལ་ཇ་བོད་ཇ་དང་ཇ་མངར་མོ་གཉིས་ཀ་ཡོད་རེད།
མི་ཞེལ་ ༔	ཇ་ཞིམ་པོ་འདུག
གླུ་བཟང་ ༔	ད་ཕེབས་དང་། ཇོ་ཁང་གི་གཟིམ་སྒོ་ཕྱི་ཡོད་རེད། མགྱོགས་པོ་ཕྱིན་ན་མ་གཏོགས་མི་མང་པོ་ཞེ་དྲགས་ཡོང་གི་རེད།
མི་ཞེལ་ ༔	ལགས་སོ། ལམ་ཁག་ག་ནས་ཕེབས་ག
གླུ་བཟང་ ༔	ལམ་ཁག་ཐག་ཉེ་ཤོས་འདི་ནས་རེད། ང་ཚོ་འདི་ནས་ཕེབས་དང་།
མི་ཞེལ་ ༔	ཨ་ལའི། ཇོ་ཁང་རྩེ་པོ་བྲང་ནང་བཞིན་མཐོ་པོ་རང་མི་འདུག
གླུ་བཟང་ ༔	ཇོ་ཁང་གཟིམ་སྒོ་ཕྱེ་པ་དག་རེད། ང་རང་ཚོ་སྟུན་ལ་ཇོ་བོ་མཇལ། དེ་ནས་ཐོག་ཀར་ཕེབས་ན་ལྷ་སའི་གྲོང་ཁྱེར་གྱི་གཡས་གཡོན་ཁག་གཅིག་གཟིགས་ཀྱི་རེད།
མི་ཞེལ་ ༔	མཆོད་ཁང་ནང་ལ་ག་རེ་ཕུལ་དགོས་རེད།
གླུ་བཟང་ ༔	མཆོད་མེ་དང་ཁ་བཏགས་ཕུལ་དགོས་རེད།

Translation

Lobzang — Michel, let's go to the Jhokhang first. After that would you like to go to the market?
Michel — Would you like to have some tea first?
Lobzang — Sure. There's a restaurant down there. They have both Tibetan tea and sweet tea there.
Michel — The tea's delicious!
Lobzang — Let's go! The temple doors have been opened. If we don't go there quickly there'll be a lot of people (lit. a lot of people will come).
Michel — Fine. Which way is it?
Lobzang — The shortest route is through here. Let's go that way.
Michel — Oh! The Jhokhang really isn't as high as the Potala.
Lobzang — The doors have just opened. Let's go first and pray in front of the Lord (lit. meet the Lord). After that, if we climb up onto the roof, we'll see a part of the area of Lhasa city.
Michel — What should we offer insidc the chapels?
Lobzang — Butter for the lamps, and *khatak*.

ཀ་ཁ་ག་ང་

21.2 Vocabulary ཚིག་གསར།

ཇ་མངར་མོ་ cha̠ ngārmo	(n.) sweet milk tea
བོད་ཇ་ phö̠ca	(n.) Tibetan tea
ཇ་སྲུབ་མ་ cha̠ sūpma / sü̠ma	(n.) Tibetan tea (lit. "churned tea")
ཇ་ཐང་ cha̠tang	(n.) black tea
འོ་ཇ་ o̠ca	(n.) salted milk tea
འོ་མ་ o̠ma ཆབ་ཞོ་ chāpsho (H)	(n.) milk
ཚྭ་ tshā ཟྭགས་ཚྭ་ ca̠ktsa	(n.) salt
ཨ་རག་ āra' བཞེས་རག(H)	(n.) alcohol
བྷི་རག་ pi̠ra'	(n.) beer
གཅིག་ cī'	(n.) a little, once
གཞུག་ལ་ shu̠'-la	(post., co.) after
རྗེས་ལ་ ce̠'-la	(post., co.) after
མ་གཏོགས་ ma̠to'	(n.) except, unless
གཉིས་ཀ་ nyīka གཉིས་ཆ་ nyīca	(n.) both
ནང་བཞིན་ na̠ngshin	(n.) like
རང་ ra̠ng	(adv.) really
ཁག་ khā'	(n.) sort, kind
གཡས་གཡོན་ yä̠'yön	(n.) to left and right, around
ཐོག་ཀ་ thōkka	(n.) roof
མཆོད་མཇལ་ལ་ཕེབས་ chō̃ncä:-la phe'	(idiom.) to go to the temple
ཡང་ན་ ya̠ngna འམ་ ām (L)	(co.) or

མངར་མོ་ ngārmo	(adj.) sweet
སྐྱུར་མོ་ kyūrmo	(adj.) sour
ཁ་ཏིག་ khāti'	(adj.) bitter
ཚྭ་ཡོད་པ་ tshā yö̲pa	(adj.) salty
ཚྭ་ཁུ་ tshāku	(adj.) (too) salty

21.3 Remarks འགྲེལ་བཤད།

21.3.1 Superlative constructions

These are formed with the superlative form of the adjective. Remember that the latter consists of adding the suffix ཤོས་ -shö' to the short form of the adjective. In the case of relative superlative constructions, the comparison must be introduced by means of the adverb ནང་ནས་ na̲ngnä' "among, out of", preceded by the genitive.

Ex.: ཇོ་མོ་གླང་མ་ནི་འཛམ་གླིང་ཐོག་གི་རི་མཐོ་ཤོས་རེད།

"Jhomolangma is the highest mountain in the world."

དགོན་པའི་ནང་ནས་འབྲས་སྤུངས་ཆེ་ཤོས་རེད།

"Dräpung is the biggest of the monasteries."

དེབ་འདི་ཡག་ཤོས་རེད།

"This book is the best."

བོད་ཀྱི་ཆུ་རིང་ཤོས་ཡར་ཀླུང་གཙང་པོ་རེད།

"The Brahmaputra is the longest river in Tibet."

བོད་ཀྱི་དགོན་པ་རྙིང་ཤོས་བསམ་ཡས་རེད།

"Samyä is the oldest monastery in Tibet."

མི་ཚེ་གཅིག་གི་ནང་ནས་དེ་རིང་སྐྱིད་ཤོས་རེད།

"Today is the finest day of my life."

མེ་ཏོག་དེ་ཚོའི་ནང་ནས་འདི་སྙིང་རྗེ་ཤོས་རེད།

"This is the most beautiful of these flowers."

21.3.2 Comparative constructions of equality

These constructions require the use of ནང་བཞིན་ na̲ngshin "like", "as much as", "as", which goes after the term being compared.

Ex.: ཇོ་ཁང་རྩེ་པོ་བྲང་ནང་བཞིན་མཐོ་པོ་མི་འདུག "The Jhokhang isn't as high as the Potala."

བུ་མོ་འདི་ཨ་མ་ནང་བཞིན་མཛེས་པོ་འདུག "This girl is as beautiful as her mother."

21.3.3 Constructions with མ་གཏོགས་ mato' *"except", "unless", "apart from", "only".*

The expression mato' may be used after a noun. In conversation, the expression མ་བཞིན mashin also occurs with a similar meaning.

Ex.: ཙམ་པ་མ་གཏོགས་གཞན་དག་ཟ་ཡག་ཡོད་མ་རེད། "There's nothing else to eat apart from tsampa."
ས་ཁུལ་འདིར་འབྲོག་པ་ཁ་ཤས་མ་གཏོགས་མི་འདུག "There are only some nomads in this region."
བསྡད་ས་གཅིག་མ་གཏོགས་མི་འདུག "There's only one place."
ངའི་སེམས་ནང་ལ་རང་མ་བཞིན་མེད། "There's nobody but you in my heart."

The expression mato' may also be used after a verb, to produce the following construction:

V(past) + ན་མ་གཏོགས་ na mato'

Ex.: མགྱོགས་པོ་ཐད་ན་མ་གཏོགས་གནམ་གྲུ་རྗེས་ཟིན་གྱི་མ་རེད།
"If you don't hurry, you won't catch the plane."
ཁྱེད་རང་གཟབ་གཟབ་བྱས་ན་མ་གཏོགས་ཅ་ལག་བརླགས་འགྲོ་གི་རེད།
"Be careful or you'll lose your things."
ཁོང་ཚོར་ལག་འཁྱེར་ཡོད་ན་མ་གཏོགས་ཐེབས་ཚོག་གི་མ་རེད།
"They'll only be able to go if they have permits."

21.4 Exercises སྦྱོང་ཚན།

21.4.1 Translate into English:

༡) བོད་ནི་འཛམ་གླིང་ཐོག་ལ་ས་མཐོ་ཤོས་རེད།

༢) ཁྱེད་ཚོའི་འཛིན་གྲྭའི་ནང་ལ་སློབ་གྲྭ་བ་ཡག་ཤོས་སུ་རེད།

༣) སློབ་གྲྭ་ཆེན་མོར་འགྲོ་ཐུབ་མཁན་ཁ་ཤས་མ་གཏོགས་ཡོད་མ་རེད།

༤) ང་རང་ཚོའི་འཛིན་གྲྭའི་ནང་ལ་སློབ་ཕྲུག་ཡག་ཤོས་ཁོང་རེད།

༥) ཞྭ་མོ་འདི་ང་ལ་ཆེ་དྲགས་བཞག

༦) ལུང་པ་འདི་སྐྱིད་ཤོས་རེད།

༧) གྲྭ་པ་མང་ཤོས་འབྲས་སྤུངས་དགོན་པ་རེད།

༨) ཇ་ལ་ཙི་ནི་མང་དྲགས་བཞག

༩) ཁྱེད་རང་མགྱོགས་པོ་ཐེབས་ན་མ་གཏོགས་རེ་ལི་རྗེས་ཟིན་གྱི་མ་རེད།

༡༠) ཁོ་རང་ལ་དགོས་ཡག་མ་གཏོགས་ལྟ་གི་མ་རེད།

21.4.2 Translate into Tibetan:

1. Are there many people who offer butter and khatak?
2. Which way does one go to get to Nepal?
3. Tibetans are the greatest consumers of butter in the world!
4. The horses of Kham are the finest.
5. Lhasa is Tibet's biggest city.
6. Where's the nearest hospital?
7. In the countryside, they drink only Tibetan tea.
8. We ought to hurry or it will be closed.

21.5 Civilization རིག་གཞུང་།

Tibetan tea

The first step in making Tibetan tea (also called butter tea or churned tea) is to prepare plain green tea. There are two ways of doing this. In towns, people usually boil the tea-leaves three times. After each occasion the tea is strained and stored in a container. The concentrate may be kept for several days, and when required a ladleful of it is poured into boiling water. The other method, which is more typical of rural areas, consists of making a fresh brew on each occasion. In either case, the next step consists of pouring the tea into a churn, adding some salt, a large quantity of butter and perhaps some milk. The mixture is churned briskly and the final product served hot. Contrary to common supposition, Tibetans prefer not to use rancid butter to make the tea, and will only use it in the absence of fresh butter.

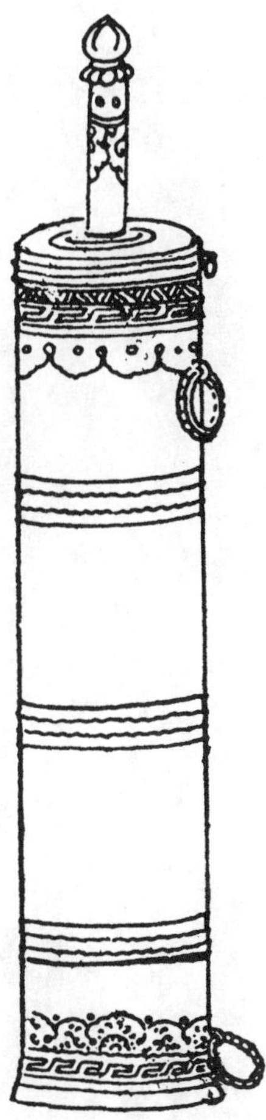

Tibetan churn

For anyone who is unfamiliar with it, this beverage is more like soup than tea. The drink is ideal on the high Tibetan plateau and in the Himalaya, because it is both very warming and has a high nutritional content.

Other kinds of tea are also to be found in Tibet: sweet milk tea, of Indian provenance, is drunk mainly in cities, while salted milk tea is drunk principally by herders in Amdo. Finally, it may be noted that Tibetans don't drink only tea! They also appreciate *chang,* a mildly (and sometimes very) alcoholic barley-based beer. The commonest variety is mild, whitish-coloured and quite thick, with a taste and alcohol content somewhat reminiscent of cider. Fermented barley is also sometimes distilled to make the stronger *arak.*

"The Bharkor"

བར་སྐོར།

Grammar aims བརྡ་སྤྲོད་རིག་པའི་དམིགས་ཚད།

- Comparative constructions of superiority.
- The enumerative connective བྱས་ chä̲'.

༄༅། ལྷ་སའི་རྒད་མོས་ལྷ་སའི་ཇོ་བོ་མ་མཇལ།།
"The old lady of Lhasa never goes to see the Lhasa Buddha." (proverb)

CD I • Tr. 53 

22.1a Dialogue དྲི་བ་དྲིས་ལན།

མི་ཤེལ་ ༔ ཉིན་ལྟར་མཆོད་མཇལ་ཞུ་མཁན་མི་མང་པོ་འདི་འདུས་ཡོད་རེད་པས།

བློ་བཟང་ ༔ ཡོད་ད་ཡོད། ཆོས་བཟང་དུས་བཟང་ལ་འདི་ལས་མང་གི་རེད། མཆོད་མཇལ་ཞུ་མཁན་ནང་ལ་མངའ་རིས་དང་གཙང་དང་ སྟོ་ཁ་དང་ མོན་པ་དང་ དྭགས་པོ་དང་ ཀོང་པོ་ཨ་ནི་ཁམས་དང་ཨ་མདོ་དང་ནག་ཆུ་ཅི་དག་ག་ས་ག་ནས་གནས་སྐོར་བ་མང་པོ་སླེབས་བཞག

མི་ཤེལ་ ༔ ད་ལྷ་བར་སྐོར་གཅིག་བསྐོར་ན།

བློ་བཟང་ ༔ ཏག་ཏག་རེད། ད་ཆུ་ཚོད་བཅུ་གཉིས་ཟིན་བཞག ཞལ་ལག་ཅིག་མཆོད་དོ།

མི་ཤེལ་ ༔ ཉི་མ་ཚ་པོ་ཞེ་དྲགས་འདུག ཞྭ་མོ་ཅིག་ཉོ་གི་ཡིན། ཞྭ་མོ་དཀར་པོ་འདའི་(འདིར)གོང་ག་ཚོད་རེད།

ཞྭ་མོ་ཚོང་མཁན་ ༔ འདི་ལ་སྒོར་མོ་ཉི་ཤུ་རེད།

མི་ཤེལ་ ༔ འོ་ཐུགས་རྗེ་ཆེ།

བློ་བཟང་ ༔ ཨ་ལྕག་ལགས། དེ་རིང་ང་གསོལ་ཚིགས་སྐབས་བདེ་ཅིག་ཞུ་གི་ཡིན།

ཟ་ཁང་གི་ཞབས་ཞུ་བ་ ༔ ང་ཚོའི་འདའི་བཞེས་སྒོ་བྱས། ཤ་འབྲས་བྱས། བཞེས་ཐུག་བྱས། ཨ་ནི་བཞེས་ཚལ་ག་རེ་དགོས་ནའི་(ན་འང་)བཀའ་མངགས་གནང་ན་བཟོ་གི་ཡོད།

བློ་བཟང་ ༔ འོ་ན་བཞེས་སྒོ་བྱས། སོན་ལ་ཕྱུག དེ་ནས་གསོལ་ཇ་མངར་མོ་གནང་རོགས་གནང་།

ཟ་ཁང་གི་ཞབས་ཞུ་བ་ ༔ ལོ་ལགས་སོ།

བློ་བཟང་ ༔ དེ་རིང་ཁ་ལག་མང་ཙང་ཏག་ཏག་བྱུང་།

མི་ཤེལ་ ༔ ད་ལྷ་ཆུ་ཚོད་གཉིས་དང་ཕྱེད་ཀ་རེད། སྤྱིད་ཆུའི་འགྲམ་ལ་འཆམ་འཆམ་གཅིག་ལ་འགྲོ།

བློ་བཟང་ ༔ ད་དངུལ་རྩིས་རྒྱག་དགོས། ཨ་ལྕག་ལགས། གསོལ་ཚིགས་ལ་ག་ཚོད་རེད།

ཟ་ཁང་གི་ཞབས་ཞུ་བ་ ༔ སྒོར་མོ་སུམ་ཅུ་རེད།

མི་ཤེལ་ ༔ གོང་ཁེ་པོ་ཞེ་དྲགས་རེད།

Translation

Michel	—	Are there this many worshippers every day?
Lobzang	—	Certainly! On holy days there are even more than this! Among the worshippers there are many pilgrims from all over – Ngari, Tsang, Lhokha, the Mön region, Kongpo, Dhagpo, Kham, Amdo, Nagchu and so on.
Michel	—	What if we make a circuit of the Bharkor?
Lobzang	—	Good idea (quite so). It's after midday. Let's have lunch.
Michel	—	The sun's very hot! I'm going to buy a hat. How much is this white hat? (lit. what is the price).
Hat seller	—	Twenty *gormo*.
Michel	—	Oh, thanks!
Lobzang	—	Madam, we'll have something simple today.
Waitress	—	We've got *momos*, meat stew (with rice and potatoes), noodle soup, and I can make you whatever vegetables you'd like to order.
Lobzang	—	Fine, so [we'd like] *momos* and sour pink radish; then please give us some sweet milk tea.
Waitress	—	Very good.
Lobzang	—	This is just the right amount of food today.
Michel	—	It's half past two. What about taking a walk along the River of Happiness?
Lobzang	—	We ought to settle up (do the accounts). How much was the food?
Waitress	—	Thirty *gormo*.
Michel	—	That's very cheap!

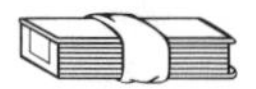

CD I • Tr. 54 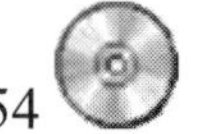

22.1b Text རྩོམ་ཡིག

རྒྱ་ཐང་གི་དཔའ་བོ།

༄༅།། རྒྱ་ཐང་སྐད་ལ་འབྲུ་བསེ་ཞེ་པད་གོག་ཅིག་ཡོད་རེད། ཁོས། རྒྱ་ཐང་འདིའི་སྐད་ལ་ང་ལས་སྟོབས་ཆེ་བ་སུ་ཡོད་རེད་ཟེ་ཡང་ཡང་བཤད་ཀྱི་ཡོད་རེད། ཉི་མ་ཅིག་འབྲུ་གྲོག་མ་ཅིག་གིས། སྟོབས་ཆེན་ལགས། ཁྱེད་རང་ལས་སྟོབས་ཆེ་བ་སེམས་ཅན་གཡག་ཟེར་མཁན་ཅིག་འདུག་ཟེ་ལབ་པ་རེད། བསེ་ཞེ་པད་གོག་གིས། གཡག་ཟེར་མཁན་འདི་ག་པར་འདུག ང་རང་ཁོ་དང་གཅིག་འཛིང་གི་ཡིན་ཟེ་བཤད་པ་རེད། དེ་ནས་ཁོས་གྲོག་མ་དང་མཉམ་དུ་གཡག་ཡོད་ས་དེར་སླེབས་ནས་གྲོག་མ་དེས། གཡག་ཕ་གིར་འདུག ནག་པོ་ཆེན་པོ་དེ་གཡག་རེད་ཟེ་ལབ་པ་རེད། བསེ་ཞེ་པད་གོག་གིས་མགོ་ཡར་བཀྱག་ནས་ཕ་གིར་རི་མ་རེད་པས་ཟེ་ལབ་པ་རེད། དེ་ནས་གཡག་དེ་ཚུར་ཡོང་ནས་བསེ་ཞེ་པད་གོག་ལ་རྫོག་རྫིས་ཏིག་ཙ་(ཏོག་ཙམ་)ཐེབས་པ་རེད། བསེ་ཞེ་པད་གོག་ཞེད་ཐག་ཆོད་ནས་ཁོ་རང་གི་བསྡད་སར་ལོག་ཕྱིན་པ་རེད། གཡག་གིས་བརྫིས་ཙང་གཟུགས་པོའི་ཕྱི་ལྤགས་ཏིག་ཙ་(ཏོག་ཙམ་)རལ་ཡོད་རེད། དྲི་མ་ཡའི་(ཡང་)ཁ་གི་ཡོད་རེད། འབྲུ་ཆུང་ཆུང་དེ་ཚོས། ཨ་ཕོ་སྟོབས་ཆེན་ལགས། ཁྱེད་རང་ག་རེ་གནང་སོང་ཟེ་དྲིས་པ་རེད། ཁོས་ང་དེ་རིང་གཡག་དང་འཛིང་ནས་པགས་ཚག་དེ་ཡའི་ཏིག་ཙ་(ཏོག་ཙམ་)རལ་སོང་། ཚུལ་ཁྲིམས་ཀྱི་དྲི་མ་ཡའི་ཏིག་ཙ་(ཏོག་ཙམ་) དོན་སོང་ཟེ་ལབ་པ་རེད།།

Translation

"The hero of the grassland"

[Once upon a time] on the grasslands, there was a beetle. He would always ask, "On these grasslands, is there anybody stronger than me?". One day, an ant told him, "Oh, big boy, there is an animal called the yak who is stronger than you." The beetle then asked, "Where is the one called the yak? I am going to fight a little with him!". So he went with the ant to the place where the yak was staying. The ant said, "The yak is over there. That big black thing is the yak." The beetle raised his head and asked, "isn't it a mountain?". A little while later, the yak came toward them and slightly crushed the beetle. He got extremely scared and came back home. Since the yak had stepped on him, the carapace on his body was a little torn, and he exuded a bad smell. The other bugs asked him "Hey, big boy, what happened to you?". He answered, "Today, I went to fight with the yak and my *pagtsak* (sheepskin coat) got a bit torn. And what's more, I'm emitting the odor of sanctity."

ཀ་ཁ་ག་ང་

22.2 Vocabulary ཚིག་གསར།

འཆམ་འཆམ་ chāmcam	(n.) stroll
སྐོར་ར་ kōrra སྐོར་བ་ kōrwa (L)	(n.) tour, circuit
གནས་སྐོར་བ་ nǟkorra (L)	(n.) pilgrim
གོང་ kho̲ng	(n.) price
མང་ཉུང་ ma̲ngnyung	(n.) quantity
ཉིན་རྟར་ nyi̲ntar	(n.) every day
ཉིན་རྟར་རེ་བཞིན་ nyi̲ntar re̲shin	(n.) every day
ལོ་རྟར་རེ་བཞིན་ lo̲tar re̲shin	(n.) every year
གནམ་གཤིས་ nāmshi'	(n.) weather, climate
སྟོབས་ tōp	(n.) strength
སེམས་ཅན་ sēmcän	(n.) "sentient beings", animals
དཔའ་བོ་ pāwo	(n.) hero
གསོལ་ཚིགས་ sȫ:tsi' (H)	(n.) meal
འགྲམ་ tra̲m	(n.) by, edge, bank
ཚལ་ tshǟ: བཞེས་ཚལ་ she̲tsä: (H)	(n.) vegetable
སོན་ལ་ཕུག་ sȫnlapu'	(n.) sour pink radish
བསེ་ལེ་པད་གོག་ sēlepäko'	(n.) beetle
རྩ་ཐང་ tsātang	(n.) grassland
ཕྱི་ལྤགས་ chīpa'	(n.) shell
པགས་པ་ pākpa	(n.) skin
པགས་ཚག་ pāktsa'	(n.) sheepskin clothing

ཅི་དག་ cīta'	(part.) et cetera
ཏིག་ཙ་ tē(t)s ཏོག་ཙམ་ tōktsam	(adv.) a little
ཏག་ཏག་ tākta'	(adj.) precisely
སྟབས་བདེ་པོ་ tāp tepo	(adj.) simple, convenient
གོང་ཆེན་པོ་ khong chēnpo	(adj.) expensive
གོང་ཁེ་པོ་ khong khēpo	(adj.) cheap
ཚ་པོ་ tshāpo	(adj.) hot
གྲང་མོ་ thrangmo	(adj.) cold
འཁྱག་ khyā' སྐུ་བསིལ་ kū sī: (H)	(v.) [inv. A] to feel cold
བརྔོས་ ngö'	(v.) [vol., EA] to fry
མངགས་ ngā'	(v.) [vol., EDA] to order
བཀའ་མངགས་ + གནང་ kānga' nāng (H)	(v.) [vol., EDA] order
བཀྲགས་ trā' བསྲེགས་ sē' (L)	(v.) [vol., EA] to grill
བཙོས་ tsö'	(v.) [vol., EA] to cook, boil
རྩིས་ + རྒྱག་ tsī' kya'	(v.) [vol., EA] to count, calculate
སྐོར་ར་ + རྒྱག་ kōrra kya'	(v.) [vol., ED] to make a circuit
འཛིང་ tsing	(v.) [vol., EA] to fight
རྫིས་ tsi'	(v.) [vol., ED] to crush
རལ་ rä:	(v.) [inv., A] to tear, be torn
དོན་ thön	(v.) [vol., A] to go out
ཐོན་ thön	(v.) – [inv., A] to go out – [vol., A] to depart, produce
ཚེས་བཟང་དུས་བཟང་ tshēsang thusang	(idiom.) auspicious day

Proper nouns : Regions of Tibet

ཁམས་ khām'	Kham	མོན་པ་ mönpa	Mön
ཨ་མདོ་ āmto	Amdo	དྭགས་པོ་ thakpo	Dhagpo
མངའ་རིས་ ngāri	Ngari	ཀོང་པོ་ kōngpo	Kongpo
གཙང་ tsāng	Tsang	ནག་ཆུ་ nakcu	Nagchu
ལྷོ་ཁ་ lhōka	Lhokha		

༢༢

22.3 Remarks འགྲེལ་བཤད།

22.3.1 Comparative constructions of superiority

Comparative constructions are formed by taking the comparative (short) form of an adjective and adding the suffix པ་ pa. The standard of comparison is followed by ལས་ -lä'. The markers -lä' and -nä' are the two forms of the ablative that are used in Literary Tibetan, but in the spoken language it is only -nä' that denotes the ablative, whereas -lä' is reserved for comparative constructions.

Ex.: འདི་ལས་མང་ང་(མང་བ་) འདུག "There is more than that."
ཆང་ཕྱི་རག་ལས་ཞིམ་པ། "Chang is better than beer."
དེབ་དེ་འདི་ལས་ཡག་ག (ཡག་པ།) "That book is better than this one."
གཡག་མཛོ་ལས་ཆེ་བ་འདུག་གས། "Are yaks bigger than dzo?"
གཡག་མཛོ་ལས་ཆེ་བ། "Yaks are bigger than dzo!"

The auxiliary འདུག་ is optional in declarative comparative sentences, whereas it is obligatory in negative and interrogative sentences.

Note that the position of the item being compared is not fixed; it may also come first: ཕྱི་རག་ལས་ཆང་ཞིམ་པ། "Compared with beer, *chang* is better."

When the adjective is an attribute of the subject, another construction is also commonly used: the short form of the adjective is followed by the auxiliary གི་རེད། -kire'.

Ex.: འདི་ལས་མང་གི་རེད། "There is more than this."
ཆང་ཕྱི་རག་ལས་ཞིམ་གྱི་རེད། "Chang is better than beer."
གཡག་མཛོ་ལས་ཆེ་གི་རེད། "Yaks are bigger than dzo."
ལྷ་ས་པེ་ཅིང་ལས་བསིལ་གི་རེད། "It's colder in Lhasa than in Peking."
སྣ་ལོ་བཞོན་ན་ཡག་གི་རེད། "It's better to ride a nalo (gentle, hornless yak)."
གནམ་གྲུའི་ནང་ལ་བཏང་ན་གོང་ཆེ་གི་མ་རེད་པས། "Won't it cost more to send it by air?"

• Tibetan has no special constructions for marking comparatives of inferiority. "Less than" is expressed simply reversing the order of comparison or by using an opposite adjective.

For example, to translate the expression "He is less poor than I am", Tibetan would say:

ང་ཁོང་ལས་སྐྱོ་གི་རེད། "I'm poorer than him."

or

ཁོང་ང་ལས་ཕྱུག་གི་རེད། "He's richer than me."

or according to the context

ཁོང་ང་ལས་སྐྱོ་བ་ཡོད་མ་རེད་ "He isn't poorer than me."

The comparative and superlative forms of adjectives

Positive		Comparative		Superlative	
གསར་པ་	"new"	གསར་ར་	གསར་བ་(L)[143]	གསར་ཤོས་	
སྡུག་ཅག་	"bad"	སྡུག་ག་	སྡུག་པ་ (L)	སྡུག་ཤོས་	
མང་པོ་	"many"	མང་ང་	མང་བ་ (L)	མང་ཤོས་	
ཉུང་ཉུང་	"few"	ཉུང་ང་	ཉུང་བ་ (L)	ཉུང་ཤོས་	
རིང་པོ་	"long"	རིང་ང་	རིང་བ་ (L)	རིང་ཤོས་	
ཆུང་ཆུང་	"small"	ཆུང་ང་	ཆུང་བ་(L)	ཆུང་ཤོས་	
ཆེན་པོ་	"big"	ཆེ་བ་		ཆེ་ཤོས་	
སྐྱིད་པོ་	"pleasant"	སྐྱིད་པ་		སྐྱིབ་ཤོས་	སྐྱིད་ཤོས་(L)
གསལ་པོ་	"clear"	གསལ་ར་	གསལ་བ་ (L)	གསལ་ཤོས་	
རྒན་འཁོགས་	"elderly"	རྒན་པ་		རྒན་ཤོས་	
མངར་མོ་	"sweet"	མངར་ར་	མངར་བ་(L)	མངར་ཤོས་	
བསིལ་པོ་	"cool"	བསིལ་ར་	བསིལ་བ་(L)	བསིལ་ཤོས་	

• The construction ལས་ lä' + V: "more than"

The marker lä' may also precede a verb, in which case it is translated as "more than".

Ex.: སྐར་མ་ཉི་ཤུ་ཙམ་ལས་འགོར་གྱི་མ་རེད།

"That won't take more than twenty minutes."

དེ་དུས་ཁོང་དགུང་ལོ་བརྒྱད་ལས་ཕེབས་ཡོད་མ་རེད།

"At that time he wasn't more than eight years old."

22.3.2 The enumerative connective བྱས་ chä̱'

When objects are being enumerated, the connective བྱས་ chä̱', derived from the verb "to do", is commonly interposed between the items in the series.

Ex.: སྤགས་བྱས། ལུག་ཤ་བཙོས་པ་བྱས། དེ་ནས་ཞོ་བྱུང་ན་འགྲིག་གི་མིན་འགྲོ།

"Kneaded tsampa, boiled mutton; then with some yogurt, that should be enough."

ཤ་འབྲས་གཅིག་བྱས། བཞེས་ཐུག་གཅིག་བྱས། ཨ་ཅི་མོག་མོག་གནང་རོགས་གནང་།

"Please give us one stew, one soup, and some momo."

143. The rule concerning changes in the pronunciation of the suffix in the spoken language is explained in section 1.1 of Appendix 1.

22.4 Exercises སྦྱོང་ཚན།

22.4.1 Translate into English:

༡) བསྟན་འཛིན་ལགས་ང་ལས་ཆེ་གི་རེད།

༢) ང་རང་ཚོའི་ནང་ནས་ཇོ་རྗེ་སྤྲོ་ལོ་མཁས་ཤོས་རེད།

༣) ཇ་ལས་ཆང་ཞིམ་གྱི་རེད།

༤) གཞི་ག་རྩེ་ལས་ལྷ་ས་མི་མང་གི་རེད།

༥) ཁོང་ང་ལས་ལོ་ཆུང་གི་རེད།

༦) སྟོད་ཐུང་འདི་ཁྱེད་རང་ལ་ཆུང་དྲགས་འདུག་གས། ཆུང་དྲགས་མི་འདུག་ ཏག་ཏག་འདུག

༧) མ་བྱུན་འདི་གཉིས་ནང་ནས་རྒན་པ་ཡག་ག་ཡོད།

༨) ཨེམ་ཆི་ལས་ཀའི་ནང་ནས་ཡག་ཤོས་ཅིག་རེད།

22.4.2 Translate into Tibetan:

1. He’s made a trip around the world.
2. Have you ever made the circumambulation of Kailash?
3. We’d like some stew, some momo and one soup.
4. The black hat is nicer than the green hat.
5. This car is bigger than Lobzang’s.
6. Tändzin is stronger than Nyima.
7. These pilgrims come from all over Tibet.
8. Sheep are cheaper than yaks.
9. Cars are very expensive in China.
10. Butter isn’t cheap in Tibet.

22.4.3 Conjugate the verbs པར་རྒྱག ལས་ཀ་བྱེད། རྩིས་རྒྱག ཁ་པར་བཏང་། *in all the tense-aspects and moods that you know (same as Exercise 14.4.2, but adding the experiential auxiliary:* བཏང་(གཏོང་) མྱོང་། རྒྱག་མྱོང་། བྱེད་མྱོང་།*).*

"Shopping"

ཉོ་ཆ་རྒྱག་པ།

Grammar aims བརྡ་སྤྲོད་རིག་པའི་དམིགས་ཚད།

- The suffix ཙམ་ -tsam.
- The allocentric future with དགོས་ k̲o, ཆོག་ chō' or ཡོང་ y̲ong.

༄། འདྲ་པོ་འདྲ་པོ་ལྷ་སའི་ཁྲོམ་ལ་ཡོད།།

"There are things like these in Lhasa market!"

(proverb)

CD I • Tr. 55

23.1 Dialogue དྲི་བ་དྲིས་ལན།

བློ་བཟང་ ཿ ཨ་ལྕུག་ལགས། ཀུ་ཤུར་ག་ཚོད་རེད།

ཚོང་མཁན་ ཿ ཀུ་ཤུ་རྒྱ་མར་སྒོར་མོ་བཞི་རེད། ག་ཚོད་གཟིགས་ག

བློ་བཟང་ ཿ རྒྱ་མ་གང་ཉོ་གི་ཡིན།

ཚོང་མཁན་ ཿ རྒྱ་མ་དོ་གཟིགས་ན་རྒྱ་མ་རེ་རེར་སྒོར་མོ་གསུམ་གསུམ་ལ་ཕུལ་ཆོག

བློ་བཟང་ ཿ འོ་ཡོང་ང་། རྒྱ་མ་དོ་ཉོ་གི་ཡིན།

ཚོང་མཁན་ ཿ ལགས་སོ། རྒྱ་མ་དོ་ཀེར་ཀེར་ཡོད།

བློ་བཟང་ ཿ འདའི་(འདིར་) སྒོར་མོ་དུག་ཏག་ཏག་ཡོད།

ཚོང་མཁན་ ཿ གཞན་དག་གཟིགས་ཀྱི་མིན་པས། བཞེས་ཁམ་གཟིགས། ཡག་པོ་ཞི་དྲག་ཡོད།

བློ་བཟང་ ཿ ག་ཚོད་རེད།

ཚོང་མཁན་ ཿ མང་ཙ་(མང་ཙམ་) གཟིགས་ན་གོང་ཁེ་ཙ་ལ་ཕུལ་ཆོག

བློ་བཟང་ ཿ ག་ཚོད།

ཚོང་མཁན་ ཿ རྒྱ་མར་སྒོར་མོ་བཞི་བཞི་གནང་།

བློ་བཟང་ ཿ རྒྱ་མར་སྒོར་མོ་གསུམ་གསུམ་ལ་བསྒྱུན་ན་རྒྱ་མ་དོ་ཉོ་གི་ཡིན།

ཚོང་མཁན་ ཿ ལགས་སོ། ད་ཕུལ་ཆོག

Translation

Lobzang — Madam, how much do apples cost?
Vendor — Four *gormo* a pound. How many will you buy?
Lobzang — I'll buy a pound.
Vendor — If you buy two pounds, I'll give them to you for three *gormo* a pound.
Lobzang — Fine, I'll take two pounds.
Vendor — Well then, here's exactly (lit. I have [the scale] upright on) two pounds.
Lobzang — Here's six *gormo* precisely.
Vendor — Aren't you going to buy something else? Buy some peaches; I have some very nice ones.
Lobzang — How much?
Vendor — If you buy quite a few I'll give you a better price.
Lobzang — How much?
Vendor — Four *gormo* a pound.
Lobzang — If you make it three *gormo* a pound I'll buy two pounds.
Vendor — All right, I'll give them to you [for that].

ཀ་ཁ་ག་ང་

23.2 Vocabulary ཚིག་གསར།

ཀུ་ཤུ་ kūshu བཞེས་ཤུ་ she̱shu (H)	(n.) apple
ཁམ་བུ་ khāmpu བཞེས་ཁམ་ she̱kam (H)	(n.) peach
མངའ་རིས་ཁམས་བུ་ ngāri khāmpu	(n.) apricot
རྒུན་འབྲུམ་ kü̱ntrum	(n.) grape
སྟར་ཁ་ tārka	(n.) nut
ཀེ་ར་ kēra	(n.) banana
ཚ་ལུ་མ་ tshāluma	(n.) orange
སེ་འབྲུ sēntru	(n.) rose-hips; pomegranate
ཞིང་ཏོག་ shīngto'	(n.) fruit
ཏོ་མ་ཏོ་ trōmatro	(n.) tomato
གྲོ་མ་ thro̱ma	(n.) potentilla tubers
ཞོག་ཁོག་ sho̱ko' བཞེས་ཞོག་ she̱sho' (H)	(n.) potato
སོ་ལོ་སྔོན་པོ་ sōlo ngȫnpo	(n.) capsicum, green pepper
ལ་ཕུག་ la̱pu'	(n.) radish
ཚག་ཤ་ tshāksha	(n.) yak meat
ལུག་ཤ་ lu̱ksha	(n.) mutton
གླང་ཤ་ lāngsha	(n.) beef
བྱ་ཤ་ cha̱sha	(n.) chicken (meat)
ཕག་ཤ་ phāksha	(n.) pork
ཉ་ཤ་ nya̱sha	(n.) fish (to eat)
དུག་སློག་ thu̱klo' ནམ་བཟའ་ na̱msa	(n.) cothing
གོས་ཐུང་ khö̱tung	(n.) trousers, pants
ཕྱུ་པ་ chūpa	(n.) traditional robe

སྟོད་ཐུང་ tötung སྐུ་སྟོད་ kūtö' (H)	(n.) shirt
འོག་འཇུག་ o̱'ncu' སྐུ་འཇུག་ kūncu'	(n.) ladies' blouse
ལྷམ་གོ་ (l)hāmko ཞབས་ཕྱུགས་ sha̱pca'	(n.) boot
འཇུར་ཏ་ cu̱rta	(n.) shoe
ཚེ་རིང་སྐྱིན་ཁེབས་ tshēring kīnkor/kīnkep	(n.) tall, fur-rimmed Tibetan hat
ཝ་ཞྭ་ wa̱sha	(n.) foxfur hat
སྐེ་རགས་ kēra'	(n.) belt
རྒྱ་མ་ kya̱ma	(n.) pound, 500 g, hand-held scale
དོ་ tho̱	(class.) two units
ཀེར་ཀེར་ kērker	(n.) upright
བཞི་བཞི་ shi̱ shi̱	(n.) four each
ཆོག་ chō'	(aux.) *future*
ཉོ་ཆ་ + རྒྱག་ nyo̱pca kya̱'	(v.) [vol., E] to do the shopping

༡༢༣

23.3 Remarks འགྲེལ་བཤད།

23.3.1 The suffix ཙམ་ -tsam

This suffix, which we have already encountered, may be used with adjectives (in their short form) as well as with substantives, numbers and verbs. In the conversational register, the suffix ཙམ་-tsam is usually pronounced ཙ་-ts. Its meaning varies according to context:

• After an adjective, it means "a little", or "a little more".

Ex.: མང་ཙམ་ "a little more", གོང་ཁེ་ཙམ་ "a little cheaper", མགྱོགས་ཙམ་ "a little faster", དམར་ཙམ་ "a little red", ལྷག་ཙམ་ "a few more", སྔ་ཙམ་ "a little earlier (or early)".

• After a number, it means "about".

Ex.: མི་བརྒྱ་ཙམ་ "about 100 people", སྒོར་མོ་འབུམ་གཉིས་ཙམ་ "about two hundred thousand gormo (yuan)", སྐར་མ་བཅོ་ལྔ་ཙམ་ "about a quarter of an hour".

• After a noun, a verb or a nominalized verb, depending on context this suffix may mean "only", "simply", "mere", "just", "almost".

Ex.: མིང་ཙམ། "only the name, purely nominal"
ཁོང་ཕེབས་པ་ཙམ་གྱིས་རྙོག་ཁྲ་བཟོས་སོང་། "The mere fact that he came created problems."
ལག་པ་ཐུག་པ་ཙམ་གྱིས་ན་ཚ་གཏང་གིས། "Just touching it with my hand makes it hurt."
ཁོ་རང་མ་ཤི་ཙམ་བརྡུངས་པ་རེད། "He was beaten almost to death."
མགོ་ནས་རྐང་པར་མ་སླེབས་ཙམ་བར་དུ། "Almost from head to foot."

• The suffix also appears in certain adverbial formulations such as: ཨའོ་ཙ་ ōts "quite, not bad", ཕར་ཙ་ད་གར་ phā:ts tha̱kar "just there".

23.3.2 The allocentric future: དགོས་ ko̱, *ཆོག་ chō'* or *ཡོང་ yo̱ng*

The "allocentric" future implies that the speaker intends to perform the action on behalf of his interlocutor. It can be used only in *the first person* singular (and occasionally plural) with volitional verbs. In this context the verbs དགོས་ ko̱ and ཆོག་ chō' have practically the same meaning. The form chō' is used in a rather more formal register.

• With this type of future, the verb stem must be in the past tense.

Ex.: ངས་ཞུས་ཆོག "I'll tell him (for you)." *but not* * ངས་ཞུ་ཆོག
ངས་བཟོས་དགོས། "I'll make it (for you)." *but not* * ངས་བཟོ་དགོས།
ངས་རྩམ་པ་ཉོས་དགོས། "I'll buy some tsampa (for you)."
ངས་ཡི་གེ་འདི་ལམ་སང་སྦྲག་ཁང་ལ་སྐྱུག་དགོས། "I'll post this letter (for you) straight away."
ངས་ཕུལ་ཆོག "I'll give it to you" = ངས་ ཕུལ་དགོས། *idem*.

• If the subject is stated, it must be in the ergative even if it is used with intransitive volitional verbs:

Ex.: ངས་ཕྱིན་དགོས། "I'll go there (for you)." *but not* * ང་ཕྱིན་དགོས།
ངས་ཡོང་དགོས། "I'll come (for you)." *but not* * ང་ཡོང་དགོས།
ངས་བསྡད་དགོས། "I'll stay (for you)." *but not* * ང་བསྡད་དགོས།

• The auxiliary yo̱ng is used when the action implies movement: ངས་ཉོས་ཡོང་། "I'll go and buy it" is therefore equivalent to ངས་ཉོ་གར་ཕྱིན་དགོས།.

23.4 Exercises སྦྱོང་ཚན།

23.4.1 Translate into English:

༡) མོ་ཏ་ངས་བཏང་དགོས།

༢) ཨ་ལྦ་ངས་བཤུས་དགོས།

༣) ཇོ་ངས་ལེན་(བླང་)དགོས།

༤) ཁྱེད་རང་ཕྱག་ལས་འདི་གནང་མ་ཐུབ་ན་ངས་ཕྱག་རོགས་ཞུས་དགོས།

༥) ཁྱེད་རང་ཚོ་དགའ་པོ་ཡོད་ན་ངས་གཞས་བཏང་དགོས།

༦) ངས་རྩམ་པ་ཏོག་ཙམ་ཕུལ་ཆོག སྒོར་མོ་ཉི་བརྒྱ་ཏག་ཏག་ཡོད།

23.4.2 Translate into Tibetan:

1. Sit down, I'll do it!
2. How many pounds do you want?
3. I'd like a pound of peaches.
4. There are many kinds of apples in Tibet.
5. The Tibetans number about six million.
6. Can you drive a little faster?
7. You have to walk about a quarter of an hour from here.

"The picnic"

གླིང་ཀ་གཏོང་བ།

> *Grammar aims* བརྡ་སྤྲོད་རིག་པའི་དམིགས་ཚད།
>
> - Temporal connectives of simultaneity:
>   དུས་ -tü̱' "when, at the time when",
>   སྐབས་ལ་ kāp-la "at the time when",
>   རིང་ལ་ ri̱ng-la "during, while", etc.
> - The future as a habitual or generic.

ཕ་རིའི་ལྕི་བ་མེད་པ། ཚུར་རི་སླེ་པོ་མེད་པ།

"On the other side of the hill there's no yak dung, on this side, there's no basket."

(proverb)

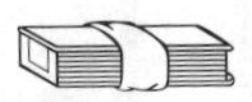

 CD I • Tr. 56

24.1a

Text རྩོམ་ཡིག

༄། དབྱིད་ཀ་ཤར་དུས་ལྷ་ས་བ་མང་པོ་སྐྱིད་ཆུའི་གྲམ་ལ་འགྲོ་གི་རེད། ཁ་ཤས་ཀྱིས་དུང་འཁྲུ་(དྲིག་འཁྲུ་) རྒྱག་གི་རེད། ཁ་ཤས་ཀྱིས་གླིང་ཀ་བཏང་གི་རེད། བོད་པའི་ལུགས་སྲོལ་ལ་གླིང་ཀ་བཏང་(གཏོང་) དུས་རྩེད་མོ་རྩེ་གི་རེད། གཞས་རྣམ་ཐར་བཏང་གི་རེད། ཤོ་རྒྱག་གི་རེད། སྟགས་དང་ཤ་སྐམ་པོ། ཡ་ཞི་ཤ་བག་ལེབ། ཡ་ཞི་མོག་མོག་ཡ་ཞི་བག་ཚ་མར་ཁུ་ཅི་དག་ཟ་གི་རེད། འདི་འདྲས་བྱས་སྐྱིད་པོ་ཞེ་དྲགས་བཏང་གི་རེད།།

CD I • Tr. 57

Dialogue དྲི་བ་དྲིས་ལན།

སྒྲོལ་དཀར་ ཿ བློ་བཟང་། ཡ་ཁ། ང་གཉིས་ཉིན་གུང་ཁ་ལག་འདའི་(འདིར་)བཟས་ནའི་འགྲིག་གི་ཡོད་པ་འདུག

བློ་བཟང་ ཿ སང་ཉིན་གནམ་གཤིས་ཡག་པོ་ཡོང་གི་རེད། ཁ་ལག་འདའི་ཟ་དོ།

སྒྲོལ་དཀར་ ཿ འོ་ན། ག་རེ་མཆོད་ག

བློ་བཟང་ ཿ སྟགས་དང་། ལུག་ཤ་བཙོས་པ་བྱས། དེ་ནས་ཚོ་བྱུང་ན་འགྲིག་གི་མན་འགྲོ།

སྒྲོལ་དཀར་ ཿ ད་ག་རང་། ལུག་ཤ་ཟམ་པའི་འཁྲིས་ལ་ཇོ་ས་ཡོད་འགྲོ།

Translation

When the spring comes, a lot of Lhasans go to the banks of the River of Happiness. Some wash clothes, other picnic. According to Tibetan custom, people play games, sing opera songs, play dice, eat *tsampa* dough and dried meat, bread with meat stuffing, *momos* or *bhagtshamarkhu*, and so on. This is how people spend their time pleasantly.

Drölkar — Lobzang, what a pity, we could surely have had lunch here.
Lobzang — Tomorrow the weather will be fine. Let's come and eat here!
Drölkar — But what would you like to eat?
Lobzang — Tsampa dough and boiled mutton. And with some yogurt, that should be enough.
Drölkar — Absolutely. There must be a place where we can buy some mutton near the bridge.

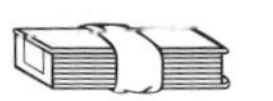

CD I • Tr. 58

24.1b Text ཚིག་ཡིག

ཤིན་ཆུང་དང་ཆུ་བན་གྱི་སྒྲུང་།

༄༅།། སྔན་མ་ཤིན་ཆུང་ཅིག་ཡོད་རེད། ཉི་མ་ཅིག་ཁོང་ཆུ་ལེན་གར་འགྲོ་དུས་གཟབ་གཟབ་མ་བྱས་ཙང་ལམ་ཁག་ལ་འདྲེད་ཧྲར་ཤོར་ནས་ཆུ་བན་ཆག་པ་རེད། ཁོང་གི་སེམས་ལ་ཤག་ལ་ལོག་ཕྱིན་པ་ཡིན་ན་ཆུ་བན་མེད་ཙང་རྒན་ལགས་ཀྱིས་བཀའ་བསྐྱོན་གནང་གི་རེད། ག་རེ་བྱེད་དགོས་ཡིན་ན་བསམས་ནས་སེམས་ཁྲལ་ཆེན་པོ་བྱུང་པ་རེད། དེ་ནས་ཁོང་གིས་ཐབས་ཤེས་ཅིག་དྲན་བྱུས་ཤག་ལ་ལོག་ནས་རྒན་ལགས་ལ། རྒན་ལགས།བུམ་པ་དངོས་པོ་རེད། རྟག་པ་རེད་ཟེ་བཀའ་འདྲི་ཞུས་ནས་རྒན་ལགས་ཀྱིས་བུམ་པ་དངོས་པོ་རེད་ཟེ་གསུངས་པ་རེད། ཡང་ཤིན་ཆུང་གིས། རྒན་ལགས་བུམ་པ་འཇིག་རྒྱུ་ཡོད་རེད་པས་ཟེ་བཀའ་འདྲི་ཞུས་པས། རྒན་ལགས་ཀྱིས། གླུགས་པ་རང་རེད། བུམ་པ་དངོས་པོ་ཡིན་པས་འཇིག་རྒྱུ་ལོས་ཡོད་ཟེ་གསུངས་པ་རེད། ཤིན་ཆུང་གིས། རྒན་ལགས་ད་རང་ང་རང་ཚོའི་ཆུ་བན་དེ་ཆག་སོང་ཟེ་ཞུས་པ་རེད། རྒན་ལགས་ཀྱིས་ལན་ག་གའི་(གང་ཡང་)མ་གསུངས་པ་རེད།།

Translation

"The story of the little monk and the water pot"

Once, there was a little monk. One day, while he was fetching water, he was not careful and slipped on the road, breaking the water jug. He thought that if he were to return to his cell, since he had no more jug, the master would scold him. He was very worried and thought about what he should do. Then he remembered a way and returned to the cell. He asked the master: is a vase an object [an impermanent compound form] or is it permanent? The master answered: it is an object. Then the little monk asked if the vase could be destroyed. The master answered "Completely stupid! Since the vase is an object, it can certainly be destroyed. The little monk said, "Master, this morning I broke our water jug (lit.: our water jug was broken)." The master had no answer to that.

ཀ་ཁ་ག་ང་

24.2 Vocabulary ཚིག་གསར།

ལྷ་ས་བ་ lhāsawa — (n.) Lhasan, inhabitant of Lhasa
དྲེག་པ་ thra̲kpa/ thre̲kpa — (n.) dirt
དྲང་འཁྲུ་ thra̲ngtru   དྲེག་འཁྲུ་ thre̲ktru (L) — (n.) washing (clothes)
དཔྱིད་ཀ་ cīka — (n.) spring
དབྱར་ཀ་ yārka — (n.) summer
དགུན་ཀ་ kü̲nka — (n.) winter
སྟོན་ཀ་ tȫnka — (n.) autumn
ནམ་དུས་ na̲mtü' — (n.) season
ད་རང་ tha̲rang — (n.) this morning
སྤགས་ pā' — (n.) tsampa dough
ཞོ་ sho̲   གསོལ་ཞོ་ sȫ:sho (H) — (n.) yogurt
ལུགས་སྲོལ་ lu̲ksö: — (n.) tradition, custom
ཤ་སྐམ་པོ་ shā kāmpo — (n.) dried meat
བག་ཙ་མར་ཁུ་ pha̲ktsamarku — (n.) *bhaktsamarku*, food made of flour, cheese, melted butter and molasses
ཉིན་གུང་ nyi̲nkung — (n.) midday
ཟམ་པ་ sa̲mpa — (n.) bridge
བུམ་པ་ phu̲mpa — (n.) vase
ཆུ་བན་ chūpän — (n.) pan, pot, water vessel
ཤག་ shā' — (n.) cell (monk)
རྣམ་ཐར་ nāmtar — (n.) biography, hagiography, operatic libretto
ཅི་དག་ cīta'   སོགས་ sō' (L) — (n.) et cetera
སེ་ར་ sēra — (n.) hail
ཆར་པ་ chārpa — (n.) rain
གངས་ kha̲ng' — (n.) snow
ཡིན་ཆུང་ īncung — (n.) young monk
བྱས་ chä̲' — (co.) *punctuates a series*
དུས་ thü̲' — (co) when
དྲེག་འཁྲུ་ + རྒྱག་ thra̲ngtru kya̲' — (v.) [vol., E] to wash clothes
འགམས་ ka̲m — (v.) [vol., EA] to eat powdered food (*tsampa*, etc.)
བལྡགས་ ta̲' — (v.) [vol., EA] to lick; to eat (yogurt)
གཞས་ + བཏང་ shä̲' tāng — (v.) [vol., E] to sing
སྐྱིད་པོ་ + བཏང་ kyīppo tāng — (v.) [vol., E] to have a pleasant time
ཤར་ shār — (v.) [inv., A] to rise, to appear

འདྲེད་རྡར་ + ཤོར་ tre̱tar shōr	(v.) [inv., A] to slide, slip
སེམས་ཁྲལ་ + བྱེད་ sēmträ: che̱'	(v.) [vol., E] to be worried
གཟབ་གཟབ་ + བྱེད་ s̱apsap che̱'	(v.) [vol., A] to be careful
ལོག་ lo̱'	(v.) [vol., A] to turn back
ཤོ་ + རྒྱག་ shō kyā'	(v.) [vol., E] to play dice
རྩེད་མོ་ + རྩེ་ tsēmo tsē	(v.) [vol., E] to have fun, joke
རྩེ་ tsē	(v.) [vol., EA] to play
སེ་ར་ + བཏང་ sēra tang	(v.) [inv., A] to hail
ཆར་པ་ + བཏང་ chārpa tang	(v.) [inv., A] to hail
གངས་ + བཏང་ khang̱' tang	(v.) [inv., A] to snow
གཤེ་གཤེ་ + བཏང་ shēshe tāng	(v.) [vol., EA] to tell off, reprimand
བཀའ་ + བསྐྱོན་ (H) kā kyōn	(v.) [vol., EA] to reprimand
གླིང་ག་ + བཏང་ līngka tāng	(v.) [vol., E] to picnic

24.3 Remarks འགྲེལ་བཤད།

24.3.1 Temporal connectives

"Subordinating conjunctions" or "temporal connectives" are usually attached directly to the verb or to its nominalized form. Each connective takes the present-future or past form of the verb.

• The connectives དུས་ thü̱'/-tü' "when, while", ཞུལ་རིང་ཀར་ - shū̃:ringka "during".

These connectives go directly after the verb. They are always associated with the present-future form.

Ex.: གླིང་ག་བཏང་(གཏོང་)དུས་རྩེད་མོ་རྩེ་གི་རེད།

"When they picnic, they have fun."

ཁོ་རང་རྒྱ་ནག་ལ་བསྡད་(སྡོད་)དུས་ཁྱིའི་ཤ་བཟས་པ་རེད།

"While he was living in China, he ate dog-meat."

ཐུབ་བསྟན་ལགས་པེ་ཅིང་ལ་བཞུགས་དུས་རྒྱ་མིའི་གསོ་བ་རིག་པ་ལ་སློབ་གཉེར་གནང་པ་རེད།

"While he was living in Peking, Thubtän studied Chinese medicine."

མོག་མོག་བཟོ་ཤུལ་རིང་ཀར་སྐད་ཆ་མང་པོ་བཤད་སོང་།

"They talked a lot while they were making momos."

ཞིང་ཏོག་ཉོ་ཤུལ་རིང་ཀར་ཏང་ག་རིལ་ཀྲུ་མ་ལ་ཤོར་སོང་།

"Our bicycle was stolen while we were buying fruit."

• The connectives སྐབས་ལ་ kāp-la "at the time, when, while", རིང་ལ་ ri̱ng-la "while", ཞོར་ལ་ sho̱r-la "on the occasion of, by/on the way".

These are always associated with the past form of the verb. The verb that precedes these connectives must be nominalized by the suffix -pa and followed by the genitive case.

Ex.: ང་རྒྱ་གར་ལ་ཡོད་པའི་སྐབས་ལ་གནས་མཇལ་ལ་མང་པོ་ཕྱིན་པ་ཡིན།

"While I was in India I went on a lot of pilgrimages."

ངས་པར་ཆས་ཉོས་པའི་སྐབས་ལ་ཡག་ཉེས་སྐད་ཆ་དྲིས་པ་ཡིན།

"When I bought the camera, I asked about its quality."

ཁོང་བོད་ལ་ཕེབས་པའི་ཉོར་ལ་བལ་ཡུལ་ལ་ཕེབས་སོང་།

"He passed through Nepal on his way to Tibet."

ཁོང་ཕྱག་ལས་གནང་པའི་རིང་ལ་རླུང་འཕྲིན་སྐད་ཆེན་པོ་བཏང་(གཏོང་)རྒྱུ་ཡོད་མ་རེད།

"We shouldn't have the radio on too loudly while he's working."

24.3.2 The auxiliary of general or habitual truth: གི་རེད་ -kire'

Tibetan very commonly uses the future to indicate a habitual action or process. It is only from the context that we can determine whether it signifies the future or the generic present (also called 'gnomic').

Ex.: འབྲས་གར་དང་རྒྱ་ནག་ལ་འབྲས་བཏབ་ཀྱི་རེད།

"Rice is grown (lit. will be grown) in India and China."

བོད་ལ་མང་ཆེ་བ་བྱ་གཏོར་རྒྱག་གི་རེད།

"In Tibet, most people practise (lit. will practise) sky burial."

ཁ་ཤས་ཀྱིས་གླིང་ག་བཏང་གི་རེད།

"Some people have (lit. will have) picnics."

དཔྱིད་ཀ་ཤར་དུས་ལྷ་ས་བ་མང་པོ་སྐྱིད་ཆུའི་འགྲམ་ལ་འགྲོ་གི་རེད།

"When the spring comes, a lot of people go (lit. will go) to the banks of the Kyichu River."

24.4 Exercises སྦྱོང་ཚན།

24.4.1 Translate the following recipe for bhagtshamarkhu*:*

༄། བག་ཚ་མར་ཁུ་ནི་བོད་རིགས་ཀྱི་ཁ་ལག་ཅིག་རེད། གྲོ་ཞིབ་བརྫིས་ནས་ཛོག་ཛོག་ཆུང་ཆུང་སྲན་མ་ལས་ཆེ་ཙམ་བཟོས་ནས་ཆུ་ཁོལ་ནས་བཙོས་པའི་རྗེས་ལ་ཆུའི་ནང་ནས་ཚུར་བཏོན་ནས་དེའི་ནང་ལ་མར་ཁུ་དང་། བུ་རམ། ཕྱུར་ཞིབ་བརྒྱབ་ན་བག་ཚ་མར་ཁུ་ཆགས་པ་རེད།

24.4.2 Tell the story in 24.1b *in your own words and answer the following questions:*

༡) ཨིན་ཙུང་ག་རེ་བྱེད་གར་ཕྱིན་པ་རེད།

༢) ཨིན་ཙུང་ག་རེ་བྱས་ནས་ཞེད་པ་རེད།

༣) ཨིན་ཙུང་གིས་ཐབས་ཤེས་ག་རེ་དྲན་པ་རེད།

༤) མི་རྟག་པ་ཟེར་ཡག་དེ་ག་རེ་རེད།

༥) ཀན་ལགས་ཀྱིས་གཞི་གཞི་བཏང་གནང་སོང་ངས།

24.4.3 Translate into English:

༡) བོད་ལ་དགེ་འདུན་པས་གསོལ་ཀྲུམ་མཆོད་ཀྱི་རེད་པས།

༢) དགུན་ཁར་གླིང་ག་བཏང་གི་རེད་པས།

༣) ཁ་ལག་ཟ་དུས་སྐད་ཆ་མང་པོ་བཤད་ཀྱི་མ་རེད།

༤) ད་ལོ་ཆར་པ་མང་པོ་བཏང་སོང་།

༥) བོད་ལ་སེ་ར་ཡང་སེ་བཏང་གི་རེད།

24.4.4 Translate into Tibetan:

1. Tibetans like to picnic in spring and summer.
2. The weather's very nice today; let's go to the river-bank.
3. When they play, they drink a lot of chang.
4. It's going to snow tomorrow.
5. When it rains, the roads are not good.
6. It isn't cold in Lhasa in autumn.

"The picnic"

(continued)

སྔ་མའི་འཕྲོས།

Grammar aims བརྡ་སྤྲོད་རིག་པའི་དམིགས་ཚད།

- The nominalizer པ་ -pa.
- The topicalizer ནི་ -ni.

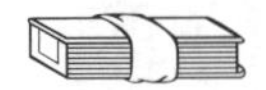

CD I • Tr. 59

25.1 Text རྩོམ་ཡིག

༄།། དེའི་སང་ཉིན་ཁོང་ཚོས་ཤ་དང་། ཤོ་ཉོས་པ་རེད། དེ་ནས་ཟམ་པའི་སྐད་ནས་ཕར་སྐྱིད་ཆུའི་ཕར་ཕྱོགས་ལ་ཕྱིན་པ་རེད།

CD I • Tr. 60

Dialogue དྲི་བ་དྲིས་ལན།

བློ་བཟང་ ཿ ཁའི་ ས་ (ཁ་ ས་)དུས་ ཆེན་ ཡིན་ ཙང་ དར་ ལྕོགས་ གསར་ པ་ ཚོན་ མདོག་ འདྲ་ མི་ འདྲ་ མང་ པོ་ འཛིན་ བཞག བྱས་ཙང་འཇའ་ ཟུག་ པ་ ནང་ བཞིན་ འདུག བསང་ མང་ པོ་ བཏང་ བཞག ཤུལ་ག་ས་ག་ ལ་ བསྡད་ བཞག

སྒྲོལ་དཀར་ ཿ དེ་རིང་འདའི་(འདིར་)ཡོང་པ་ཡག་པོ་བྱུང་བཞག

བློ་བཟང་ ཿ གདན་གཅིག་འདའི་རྒྱབ། གདན་ཅིག་ཕར་ཕྱོགས་ནས་བརྒྱབ་ན་བསྡད་ས་(སྡོད་ས་)ག་ཡངས་པོ་ཡོང་ང་།

སྒྲོལ་དཀར་ ཿ ཡ་ཁ། ཅོག་ཙེ་མི་འདུག

བློ་བཟང་ ཿ གའི་(གང་ཡང་)བྱེད་ཀྱི་མ་རེད། པ་གིར་ཇོ་གྲུ་བཞི་ཡག་པོ་གཅིག་འདུག ཅོག་ཙེ་བྱས་ན།

སྒྲོལ་དཀར་ ཿ འོ་ཏག་ཏག་རེད། ངས་ཞེན་(ལྷང་)དགོས།

བློ་བཟང་ ཿ ཛ་དམ་ཡོད་ཙང་མེ་ནི་བཏང་(གཏོང་)དགོས་མེད། ད་སྔོད་སྔོད་བྱས་ཞུགས་ཤིག

Translation

The following day, they bought some meat and yogurt, and then crossed the bridge to the opposite bank of the River of Happiness.

Lobzang — Because there was a festival yesterday, a lot of new prayer-flags of different colours have been hung up. That's why it's as if there were a rainbow. A lot of fumigation (with aromatic plants) has been performed – the leftovers are all over the place.
Drölkar — It's good that we came here today.
Lobzang — Put one rug here, and if you put one on the other side, there'll be plenty of room to sit down.
Drölkar — Oh, we haven't got a table!
Lobzang — That doesn't matter. There's a nice square stone over there – what if we use that as a table?
Drölkar — Good idea. Let me go and fetch it.
Lobzang — Since we have a thermos, we don't need to light a fire. Now, let's relax.

ཀ་ཁ་ག་ང་

25.2 Vocabulary ཚིག་གསར།

ཅི་དག་ cīta' — (n.) et cetera
དེའི་སང་ཉིན་ the̱: sāngnyin — (n.) the following day
དུས་ཆེན་ thü̱cen — (n.) festival
དར་ལྕོགས་ tha̱rco' — (n.) prayer flag
རླུང་རྟ་ lūngta — (n.) "wind horse"
ཚོན་མདོག་ tshȫnto' — (n.) colour
འཇའ་ ca̱ — (n.) rainbow
གདན་ tä̱n བཞུགས་གདན་ shu̱ktän (H) — (n.) rug, carpet
མེ་ me̱ ཞུགས་མེ་ shu̱kme (H) — (n.) fire
ཤུལ་ shǖ: — (n.) remains, leftovers, traces
རྡོ་ to̱ — (n.) stone, rock
གྲུ་བཞི་ thru̱pshi — (n.) square
ནི་ ni̱ — (part.) *topicalizer*
གུ་ཡངས་པོ་ khu̱ ya̱ngpo — (adj.) wide, spacious
དོག་པོ་ tho̱kpo — (adj.) narrow
ག་ས་ག་ལ་ kha̱sa kha̱la — (adv.) everywhere
གའི་ khä̱: གང་ཡང་ kha̱ngyang (L) — (adv.) nothing
བསང་ + བཏང་ sāng tāng — (v.) [vol., E] to perform fumigations
མེ་ + བཏང་ me̱ tāng — (v.) [vol., E] to light a fire
ཟུག་ su̱' — (v.) [inv., A] to be attached, planted (Here used metaphorically about the rainbow)
འཐེན་ thēn — (v.) [vol., EA] to pull, draw, drag

ཁའི་བྱེད་ཀྱི་མ་རེད་ khä̲: che̲'-kimare'	(idiom.) It doesn't matter, no problem
ཁའི་གནང་གི་མ་རེད་ khä̲: nāng-kimare' (H)	(idiom.) It doesn't matter, no problem

25.3 Remarks འགྲེལ་བཤད།

25.3.1 The nominalizer པ་ -pa

Historically speaking, of the nominalizing suffixes (see 11.4, 18.4 and 20.4), the suffix -pa occupies an essential place to the extent that it is the basic marker of nominalization in Literary Tibetan. In Standard Spoken Tibetan, however, it has far fewer functions.

In Literary Tibetan, the suffix པ་ -pa sometime appears in the variant form:[144] བ་ -wa.

• After the consonants ག་ ད་ ན་ བ་ མ་ ས་ ད་དྲག་ པ་ > པ་

• After vowels and the consonants ང་ འ་ ར་ ལ་ > བ་

In the spoken language, this rule is not followed, and the form -pa is used in all contexts.[145]

In colloquial speech, the suffix *འཀྱོག་ -nkyo' sometimes replaces -pa, but this suffix is never written, and has no known spelling.

The suffix -pa is associated only with the past tense form of the verb, and refers to a past perfective action.

Ex.: ཞུས་པ་ but not * ཞུ་པ་, བཟས་པ་ but not * ཟ་པ་.

A nominalized verb may be followed by a demonstrative, an indefinite article or other determinants such as any substantive.

Ex.: གསུངས་པ་དེ་ཚོ། "Those that [you] mentioned."

The suffix -པ་pa has two essential functions[146]:

• It denotes prototypically the **grammatical patient** of the verbal action in the perfective past. That is, it refers to the direct object when it is used with a transitive verb or the subject when it is used with an intransitive verb. [147] It may be translated in English by using a relative clause or a past participle (for more details about the relative clause, see Lesson 26).

---

144. But be careful! This modification applies only to verb suffixes, and not to suffixes with other functions such as noun or adjective suffixes. Thus Standard Tibetan says *khang-pa* "house" and *stong-pa* "empty", not *khang-ba* and *stong-ba*.

145. Some speakers do, however, follow the rule. In this case, they apply the phonological rule of omitting the bilabial /w/ described in section 1.1 of Appendix 1: nang-wa > nang-nga, phül-wa > phül-la, tshar-wa > tshar-ra.

146. In the same way as the nominalizer ཡག་ya', see Lesson 11.

147. From a syntactic point of view, the nominalized verb functions here as a head noun or as a modifier of the head noun.

Ex.: བཟོས་པ་དེ་ "that which has been built"
དཀྲུས་པ་ "that which has been washed"
ཡོང་པ་ "[the person] who came"
ཉལ་པ་ "[the person] who went to bed"
བྲིས་པ་ "that which has been written"
བསྡད་པ་ "[the person] who lived, sat"
ངུས་པ་ "[the person] who cried"

However, it also extends to the subject of transitive benefactive verbs: ཡོད་པ་ "[the person] who has", ཐོབ་པ་ "[the person] who has obtained".

• The suffix -pa may also be neutral and nominalize **the entire clause.**

In this case, the suffix is not oriented towards any grammatical role and nominalizes the entire clause. From a syntactic point of view, the nominalized verb functions as a head noun and may be translated in English by a verb in the infinitive, an *-ing* clause, a *that* clause or even by a noun.

Ex.: ཡང་དང་པོ་ཐོབ་པ་དེར་ང་དགའ་པོ་བྱུང་
"The fact that she took first place made me happy."
བོད་སྐད་ཤེས་པ་དེ་གལ་ཆེན་པོ་རེད་
"It's very important to know Tibetan." or "Knowledge of Tibetan is very important."
མགོ་ལ་སྐྲ་འཛུག་ཐུབ་པ་དཔེ་རང་རེད།
"To be able to plant hair on the head is incredible!"

It is only from the context that we can distinguish between the two functions described above, as the following examples show:

Ex.: ད་གིན་ཡོང་པ་དེ་སུ་རེད། "Who's the person who came a short while ago?"
དེ་རིང་འདིར་ཡོང་པ་ཡག་པོ་བྱུང་བཞག "It was a good thing/ idea [for us] *to come here today!*"

What is being nominalized in the first case is the verb "to come" modifying the head noun "this one", and in the second the clause "we came here today".

25.3.2 The topicalizer ནི་ -ni

This particle is very common in Literary Tibetan, but less so in the spoken language. It is used to emphasize a group of words preceding it, or else it "thematizes" something – that is, it introduces the topic that is about to be developed. In English, when the thematization concerns the object, the marker ནི་ -ni may be rendered by moving the object to the beginning of the sentence and emphasizing it with some expression such as "as for" or "regarding". Sometimes it may even be left untranslated.

Ex.: པང་གདན་ནི་སྐྱེད་དམན་ཚང་མས་གོན་གྱི་རེད། "As for aprons, all women wear them."
མེ་ནི་བཏང་(གཏོང་)དགོས་མེད། "As for a fire, we don't need to light one."

25.4 Exercises སྦྱོང་ཚན།

25.4.1 Choose the appropriate nominalizer པ་ -pa or ཡག་ -ya':

༡) གོས་ཐུང་འཁྲུ་ ( ) འདི་ག་པར་འདུག

༢) ཁ་ལག་བཟོས་ ( ) དེ་ཞིམ་པོ་འདུག

༣) རས་ཉོས་ ( ) དེ་འདི་རེད།

༤) ཁ་ལག་ཟ་ ( ) དེ་སུས་བཟོས་པ་རེད།

༥) ཁའི་ས་ཕྱིན་ ( ) དེ་ཡག་པོ་བྱུང་བཞག

25.4.2 Translate into English:

༡) ང་ནི་ཁྱོན་ནས་འགྲོ་གི་མིན།

༢) ཁྱེད་རང་ལ་དུས་ཚོད་ནི་འདུག གོ་སྐབས་ནི་འདུག དངུལ་ནི་འདུག ད་ཁྱེད་རང་ལ་གཞན་དག་ག་རེ་དགོས་ཀྱི་འདུག

༣) ངས་ནི་མ་བྱས། ཁོང་གིས་ནི་བྱས་མ་སོང་། ད་སུས་བྱས་པ་རེད།

༤) ཞལ་པར་གནང་པ་ཡག་པོ་ཞེ་དྲགས་བྱུང་།

25.4.3 Translate into Tibetan:

1. The song he sang is very lovely.
2. Did you read the letter that she wrote?
3. It was a mistake to have spoken about it.
4. There are prayer flags on the houses.
5. Where are they going to picnic?
6. Many fumigation rituals (lit. much fumigation) are performed during festivals.

25.5 Civilization རིག་གཞུང་།

• Picnics

Picnics practically have the status of a national sport in Tibet. As soon as the weather begins to warm up in the first few days of spring, Tibetans like to go picnicking or camping – perhaps returning to the lifestyle of their nomadic ancestors. Picnics may last several days. For such occasions people take food supplies and flasks of tea, rugs, a stove, a table and a tent – not forgetting, of course, various games and musical instruments. Favorite picnic spots are grassy streambanks under willow trees. In Lhasa, during the summer Zhotön festival, the offices are closed and many civil servants join the crowds to picnic in the gardens of the Norbu Lingkha, the summer residence of the Dalai Lamas.

• *Fumigation offerings*

Tibetans often perform fumigation rituals to divinities and to the Buddhas. This involves burning branches of juniper or other aromatic plants. Censers for this purpose are located on rooftops, near monasteries and on mountain passes.

"Pilgrimage in Lhoka"

ལྷོ་གནས་ཀྱི་སྐོར།

Grammar aims བརྡ་སྤྲོད་རིག་པའི་དམིགས་ཚད།

- Relative clauses.
- The modal verb འདོད "to want".

CD I • Tr. 61

26.1 Dialogue དྲི་བ་དྲིས་ལན།

༄།། བོད་པ་གཅིག་དང་ཨ་མེ་རི་ཀའི་མི་གཉིས་བོད་ཀྱི་གནས་མཇལ་སྐོར་ལ་བཀའ་མོལ་གནང་བ།

ལྷ་བཟང་ ༔ ཁྱེད་རང་ཚོ་བོད་ལ་ཕེབས་འདོད་ཡོད་པས།
འཛིམ་ ༔ ང་བོད་ལ་འགྲོ་འདོད་ཆེན་པོ་ཡོད།
ཨེ་རིག་ ༔ ང་ཡའི་འགྲོ་སྙིང་འདོད་གིས་(གི་འདུག) ཡིན་ནའི་(ཡིན་ནའང་) ཆོག་མཆན་རག་ཁག་པོ་རེད།
ལྷ་བཟང་ ༔ གལ་སྲིད་བོད་ལ་ཐེངས་གཅིག་ཕེབས་ཐུབ་ན་ལྷོ་ཁར་གནས་མཇལ་ལ་ཕེབས་དགོས་རེད།
འཛིམ་ ༔ ལྷོ་ཁར་གནས་མཇལ་རྒྱུ་མང་པོ་ཡོད་རེད་པས།
ལྷ་བཟང་ ༔ མང་པོ་ཞེ་དྲགས་ཡོད་རེད། བོད་ཀྱི་མཁར་གྱི་ཐོག་མ་ཡུམ་བུ་བླ་སྒང་ཡོད་རེད། བོད་ཀྱི་དགོན་པ་སྔོན་ཤོས་བསམ་ཡས་ཡའི་(ཀྱང་)ལྷོ་ཁར་ཡོད་རེད།
ཨེ་རིག ༔ དེ་ཚོ་བརྒྱབ་ནས་ལོ་ག་ཚོད་ཕྱིན་ཡོད་རེད།
ལྷ་བཟང་ ༔ བསམ་ཡས་ལ་ཆ་བཞག་ན་ལོ་ཆིག་སྟོང་ཉིས་བརྒྱ་ལྷག་ཙ་(ལྷག་ཙམ་) ཕྱིན་པ་དང་ཡུམ་བུ་བླ་སྒང་ལ་ཆ་བཞག་ན་ལོ་ཉིས་སྟོང་ལྷག་ཙ་ཕྱིན་པ་རེད།
འཛིམ་ ༔ དེ་མིན་པ་ཡོད་རེད་པས།
ལྷ་བཟང་ ༔ ད་དུང་འཕྱོངས་རྒྱས་ལ་བོད་ཀྱི་རྒྱལ་པོའི་བང་སོ་དང་རི་བོ་བདེ་ཆེན་ཟེར་མཁན་(ཟེར་བའི་) དགོན་པ་ཆེན་པོ་ཅིག་དང་། གྲ་ཕྱི་ལ་སྨིན་སྒྲོལ་གླིང་ཟེར་མཁན་(ཟེར་བའི་) དགོན་པ་ཆེན་པོ་ཅིག་ཡོད་རེད། དེ་མིན་ག་ས་ག་ལ་དགོན་པ་མང་པོ་ཞེ་དྲག་ཡོད་རེད། ཡིན་ནའི། ཚང་མ་ངས་ཤེས་ཀྱི་མེད།།

Translation

A Tibetan and two Americans are discussing pilgrimage in Tibet.

Lobzang — Do you want to go to Tibet?
Jim — Yes, I want very much to go to Tibet.
Eric — I also want to go, but it's difficult to get permission.
Lobzang — If you are able to go to Tibet one day, you should do the Lhokha pilgrimages.
Jim — Are there lots of pilgrimage places to visit in Lhokha?
Lobzang — There are very many indeed. There's the first castle of Tibet, Yumbulagang. Tibet's oldest monastery, Samyä, is also in Lhokha.
Eric — How long is it since they were built?
Lobzang — In the case of Samyä, for example, over 1,200 years. As forYumbulagang castle, more than two thousand years.
Jim — What else is there?
Lobzang — In addition to those, in Chonggyä there are the tombs of the Tibetan kings, as well as the great monastery called "Riwodechen". In Dhrachi, there's also a big monastery called "Mindröling". Apart from that, there are plenty of monasteries everywhere, but I don't know them all.

ཀ་ཁ་ག་ང་

26.2 Vocabulary ཚིག་གསར།

འདོད་པ་ tö̲pa ཐུགས་འདོད་ thū'ntö' (H)	(n.) desire, wish
ཆོག་མཆན་ chōkcän	(n.) permit, permission
ཐེངས་མ་ thēngma	(n.) time, occasion
ཐོག་མ་ thōkma	(n.) first
བང་སོ་ pha̲ngso	(n.) tomb
མཁར་ khār	(n.) castle
རྒྱལ་པོ་ kyä̲:po	(n.) king
དེ་མིན་པ་ the̲ mi̲npa	(adv.) apart from that
སྙིང་འདོད་ nyīngtö' ཐུགས་འདོད་ thū'ntö' (H)	(v.) [mod] to wish, want
འདོད་ tö̲'	(v.) [mod] to want
རག་ ra̲'	(v.) [inv., DA] to get, obtain
ལ་ཆ་བཞག་ན་ la chā sha̲'-na	(idiom.) for example

Proper nouns

གྲྭ་ཕྱི་ thra̲ci	Dhrachi
སྨིན་གྲོལ་གླིང་ mi̲ntröling	Mindröling
རི་བོ་བདེ་ཆེན་ ri̲wo te̲cen	Riwodechen
འཕྱོངས་རྒྱས་ chōngkyä'	Chonggyä
བསམ་ཡས་ sāmyä'	Samyä
ཡུམ་བུ་བླ་སྒང་ yu̲mpulakang	Yumbulagang

Religions and ideologies

ཆོས་ལུགས་ chȫlu'	religion
ཁ་ཆེ་ khāce	Muslim
ཡེ་ཤུ་ ye̱shu	Christian
ཧིན་དུ་ hīntu	Hindu
ཕྱི་པ་ chīpa	Hindu
ནང་པ་ na̱ngpa	Buddhist
ཆོས་ chȫ'	Dharma
ནང་པའི་ཆོས་ na̱ngpä: chȫ'	Buddhism, Dharma
ནང་པ་སངས་རྒྱས་པའི་ཆོས་ na̱ngpa sāngkyäpä: chȫ'	Buddhism
ཐེག་པ་ཆེན་པོ་ thēkpa chēnpo	Mahāyāna Buddhism
ཐེག་པ་ཆུང་ངུ་ thēkpa chūnngu	Hinayāna Buddhism
རྡོ་རྗེ་ཐེག་པ་ to̱rce thēkpa	Vajrayāna Buddhism
བོན་ phö̱n	*Bön*, one of the religions of Tibet[148]
བོན་པོ་ phö̱npo	*Bönpo*, follower of *Bön*
ཆབ་སྲིད་ chāpsi'	politics
གུང་ཁྲན་རིང་ལུགས་ khu̱ngträn ri̱nglu'	communism
སྤྱི་ཚོགས་རིང་ལུགས་ cītso' ri̱nglu'	socialism
གུང་ཁྲན་ཏང་ khu̱ngträntang	communist party
རིག་གནས་གསར་བརྗེ་ ri̱knä' sārce	Cultural Revolution
མ་རྩའི་རིང་ལུགས་ ma̱tsä: ri̱nglu'	capitalism

26.3 Grammar remarks འགྲེལ་བཤད།

26.3.1 Relative clauses

As a general rule, we can agree with the observation by the linguist Émile Benvéniste that "however [a relative clause] may be attached to its head noun […] it acts like a 'determinate syntactic adjective'".

Tibetan forms relative clauses by nominalizing the verb. Thus, instead of relative pronouns such as we use in English, Tibetan uses nominalizers (see Lessons 11, 18, 20 and 25) that follow the verb of the relative clause. Relative clauses are formed by using the following nominalizers: པ་ pa;[149] ཡག་ ya'; རྒྱུ་ kyu; མཁན་ kän; ས་ sa.

---

148. According to Tibetan, *Bön* was the pre-Buddhist religion of the country. In Western writings it is still sometimes erroneously identified with shamanism.

149. Remember that the marker nkyo' is also used instead of pa in colloquial language.

The construction of relative clauses is a rather complicated matter in Standard Tibetan grammar, insofar as the nominalizer that is used depends not only on the function of the head noun with respect to the verb of the relative clause (subject, object, indirect object, instrument, etc.), but also on the tense[150] and, in some cases, even the class of the verb.

The following table offers a summary of the uses of nominalizers that operate as "relative pronouns."

"Relative pronouns"

Functions of the head noun	Nominalizers ("relative pronouns")
Subject of an intransitive verb: "who, which"	མཁན་ -ngän (present, future) པ་-pa (past) རྒྱུ་ -kyu Δ (future)[151]
Subject of a transitive verb: "who, which"	མཁན་ -ngän (all tenses) པ་-pa Δ[152]
Direct object: "that, whom" or adverbial complement of tense: "when"	ཡག་ -ya' (present, future) པ་ -pa (past) རྒྱུ་ -kyu Δ (future)
Indirect object: "to whom, to which" or place "where"	ས་ -sa (all tenses) པ་ -pa Δ[153] (past)
Adverbial: instrument, cause or manner: "with which, whom"	ཡག་ -ya' (all tenses)
N.B.: The triangle in this case denotes forms that occur only rarely.	

In Standard Tibetan, relative clauses usually go before the head noun. Thus the nominalizer is generally (though not always) followed by the genitive, which connects the relative clause to its head noun. This being said, it does sometimes happen that relative clauses go after the head noun, as in the case of European languages, and in such cases the genitive is not used. The demonstrative adjective དེ་ the̱ often follows the noun phrase, consisting of the head noun plus the relative.

Structure of preceding relative clause**:**

[SN + SV + *nominalizer* + *genitive*] + "head noun" + dem.

150. That is, both tense and aspect. Remember that the term "present" actually refers to the imperfective present and past, and that the term "past" denotes the perfective past (see Lesson 10).

151. This nominalizer, which is used only in the future, is often also used to indicate a necessity or an obligation.

152. For this function, the nominalizer is used only with benefactive verbs (see Lesson 10) in the past tense.

153. This nominalizer is used only with the perfective past when it denotes an adverb of place.

Structure of following relative clause:

[SN] + "head noun" + [SV+ *nominalizer*] + dem.

Examples of preceding relative clauses:

ཁྱེད་རང་གིས་ཉོས་པའི་སྟོད་ཐུང་གསར་པ་དེ་ག་པར་འདུག "Where's the new shirt that you bought?"
སྐད་གྲགས་ཡོད་པའི་རི་དེ་ཚོ་བོད་ལ་ཡོད་རེད། "Those mountains that are famous are in Tibet."

Examples of following relative clauses:

ཁྱེད་རང་གིས་སྟོད་ཐུང་གསར་པ་ཉོས་པ་དེ་ག་པར་འདུག "Where's the new shirt that you bought?"
རི་སྐད་གྲགས་ཡོད་པ་དེ་ཚོ་བོད་ལ་ཡོད་རེད། "Those mountains that are famous are in Tibet."

Following relative clauses are also referred to as "head-internal", because the head noun appears inside the clause. If the verb comes after the head noun (in the example cited above, ཉོས nyö̱', "to buy", comes after the head noun སྟོད་ཐུང་ tȫtung "shirt"), the latter can precede the subject of the relative clause, and the head noun is embedded within the relative clause (as in the example ཁྱེད་རང་གིས་སྟོད་ཐུང་གསར་པ་ཉོས་པ་དེ་ག་པར་འདུག where སྟོད་ཐུང་ tȫtung "shirt" is preceded by the subject ཁྱེད་རང་གིས་ khyērang-ki' "you", which belongs to the relative, not the main, clause, "where is the new shirt?").

It should be noted that in most cases the verb in the relative clause stands by itself, without an auxiliary, followed by the nominalizer. In certain rare instances, however, auxiliaries may be used to indicate the tense-aspect of the relative clause, in which case they must be followed by the nominalizer pa.

Ex.: V+བཞིན་པ་ shin-pa present progressive,
V+ གིན་བསྡད་པ་ kin tä̱'-pa present progressive, V+ཡོད་པ་ yö̱'-pa perfect.

Below are some illustrations of the different functions of the head noun. The nominalizers have been selected in accordance with the rules laid out above in the table.

• Subject (intransitive): "who, which"

In this case the nominalizer depends on the tense-aspect. For the present, the future and the imperfective past, the nominalizer མཁན་-ngän is used, whereas for the perfective, it is the form པ་ -pa that is used.

Ex.: ཕྱི་རྒྱལ་ལ་འགྲོ་མཁན་གྱི་དགེ་རྒན་དེ་སུ་རེད།
"Who is the teacher who is going abroad?"
ཕྱི་རྒྱལ་ལ་ཕྱིན་པའི་དགེ་རྒན་དེ་སུ་རེད།
"Who is the teacher who went abroad?"
དེ་དུས་ཕྱི་རྒྱལ་ལ་འགྲོ་མཁན་གྱི་དགེ་རྒན་དེ་སུ་རེད།
"Who is the teacher who went (or used to go) abroad at that time?"

དེ་ཚོ་བོད་ནས་ཐོན་པའི་ས་གདན་རེད།

"Those are carpets that have been produced in [lit. have come out of] Tibet."

ཕྱི་རྒྱལ་ལ་འགྲོ་རྒྱུའི་དགེ་རྒན་དེ་སུ་རེད།

"Who is the teacher who will be going to Tibet?"

• Subject (transitive): "who, which"

The subject of a transitive verb can always be marked by the nominalizer -ngän irrespective of the tense-aspect. However, in the case of benefactive verbs in the past tense, the nominalizer -pa is usually used.

Ex.: ཡི་གེ་ཤེས་མཁན་གྱི་འབྲོག་པ་ཉུང་ཉུང་རེད།

"Nomads who are literate are few."

ཁ་སང་སྒྲ་སྙན་བཏང་མཁན་གྱི་ཁམས་པ་དེ་ངོ་ཤེས་ཀྱི་ཡོད་པས།

"Do you know the Khampa who played the lute yesterday?"

འགྲན་སྡུར་ནང་ལ་ཨང་དང་པོ་ཐོབ་པའི་སློབ་གྲྭ་བ་དེ་ངའི་ཕ་ཡུལ་གཅིག་པ་རེད།

"The student who took first place in the competition is from the same village as I am."

• Direct object: "whom, that, which"

In this case the nominalizer depends on the tense-aspect. For the present, the future and the imperfective, the nominalizer ya' is used, whereas the perfective past uses the nominalizer pa.

Ex.: ཁྱེད་རང་གིས་བཟོས་པའི་ཁ་ལག་ཞིམ་པོ་ཞེ་དྲག་འདུག

"The food that you have made is very good."

ཁོང་གིས་ཞོན་ཡག་གི་རྟ་དེ་མགྱོགས་པོ་ཞེ་དྲགས་འདུག་ག

"The horse that he is riding is very fast."

ངས་ད་ལྟ་ཀློག་ཡག་གི་དེབ་དེ་སྙན་པོ་ཞེ་པོ་ཅིག་འདུག

"The book that I'm reading now is very interesting."

• Adverbial complement of tense "when"

Ex.: ཁོང་ཕེབས་པའི་ཉི་མ་(ཉིན་མོ་) དེ་ངས་དྲན་གྱིས།

"I remember the day when he came."

ཁོང་ཕེབས་ཡག་གི་དུས་ཚོད་གཏན་འཁེལ་མ་སོང་།

"The time at which he is to come hasn't been confirmed."

• Indirect object (in the dative) and adverbials of place: "to whom", "to which", "that", "where".

With adverbs of place, the tense-aspect of the relative clause may be specified. *Sa* is used to indicate the present, future and imperfective past (the "imperfect"), whereas pa is used for the perfective past. On the other hand, this distinction is not usually made with indirect objects or goals, and only the nominalizer sa is used, irrespective of the tense-aspect.

Ex.: དུག་སློག་བླུག་སའི་སྒམ་འདི་ག་པར་འདུག

"Where is the trunk where the clothes are kept?"

དུག་སློག་བླུག་པའི་སྒམ་འདི་ག་པར་འདུག

"Where is the trunk where the clothes were put?"

སྒང་ལ་བརྙན་འཕྲིན་བཞག་ཡོད་པའི་ལྕོག་ཙེ་ཚུར་ཁྱེར་ཤོག་ད།

"Bring the table on which the television was placed."

སྒང་ལ་བརྙན་འཕྲིན་བཞག་སའི་ལྕོག་ཙེ་ཚུར་ཁྱེར་ཤོག་ད།

"Bring the table on which the television is kept."

སྔོན་མ་ང་ཚོ་རྟག་པར་འགྲོ་སའི་ཟ་ཁང་དེ་དེང་སང་བསྡད་མི་འདུག

"The restaurant where we used to go before doesn't exist any more."

ཁོང་དགའ་སའི་བུ་མོ་དེ་ཆང་ས་བརྒྱབ་ཚར་བཞག

"The girl he loved is already married."

• Instrument, cause and purpose: "with which", "for which".

In order to situate a head noun in an instrumental, causal or purpose clause, the nominalizer ya' is used irrespective of the tense-aspect. It should be noted that the head noun is marked in the same way whether it is a direct object or an instrument (or cause, etc.). The head noun may be taken as an instrument only if the verb is preceded by the direct object. Compare the following:

ངས་བཏུབ་ཡག་གི་ཤ་དེ་སུས་ཉོས་པ་རེད། "Who bought the meat that I'm cutting?"

ཤ་བཏུབ་ཡག་གི་གྲི་འདི་རྣོ་པོ་མི་འདུག "The knife for cutting meat isn't sharp."

The following examples illustrate the instrumental and causal functions:

ནག་པང་ཕྱིས་ཡག་གི་རས་དེ་ག་པར་འདུག "Where's the cloth for wiping the blackboard?"

ང་ཚོ་ཚོགས་འདུ་འཚོགས་ཡག་གི་རྒྱུ་མཚན་འདི་རེད། "This is the reason why we're holding a meeting."

When the head noun of the relative clause denotes the substance of which the object is made, ya' may be replaced by the nominalizer kyu̲: "with, of which", "for."

Ex.: སྒྲ་སྙན་བཟོ་རྒྱུའི་ཤིང་དེ་སྐམ་པོ་རེད།

"The wood for making the lute [of which the lute is made] is dry."

ཕྱུ་པ་བཟོ་རྒྱུའི་སྣམ་བུ་ག་ནས་རག་གི་རེད། "Where can we get the cloth for making the chuba?"

མོག་མོག་བཟོ་ཡག་གི་ཤ་འདི་དཔེ་ཞིམ་པོ་འདུག "This meat for making momos is excellent."

26.3.2 The modal verb འདོད་ *tö̱'*

This verb, which means "to want", requires the main verb to be in the present-future.

It appears only as a modal verb (and not as a main verb), and may be combined with the following auxiliaries. It functions in a similar way to the verb དགོས་ "need."

- in the present: འདོད་ ཡོད་ (ego.), འདོད་འདུག་ or འདོད་ཡོད་རེད་
- in the past: འདོད་བྱུང་ (ego.), འདོད་བྱུང་སོང་ or འདོད་བྱུང་བ་རེད་
- in the future: འདོད་གྱི་ རེད་

The perfective past auxiliaries སོང་, པ་རེད་, བཞག་ may not directly follow the verb འདོད་

*འདོད་སོང་ *འདོད་པ་རེད་ *འདོད་བཞག་

Ex.: ང་གངས་ཏི་སེར་འགྲོ་འདོད་ཡོད། "I want to go to Kailash."
ཁྱེད་རང་ཚོ་བོད་ལ་ཕེབས་འདོད་ཡོད་པས། "Would you like to go to Tibet?"

However, the verb སྙིང་འདོད་ and its honorific form ཐུགས་འདོད་ have a regular conjugation.

—་ཏ་ཀ་ཀ་

26.4 Exercises སྦྱོང་ཚན།

26.4.1 Translate into English:

༡) ལམ་ཁག་བཟོ་མཁན་གྱི་བཟོ་པ་ཚང་མ་བལ་པོ་རེད་བཞག

༢) མོ་ཏ་ཡོད་པའི་མི་ཅིག་གིས་ང་པར་སྐྱེལ་ཐུབ་ཀྱི་རེད་པས།

༣) ཛ་སྤྱུབ་མ་ཟེར་ཡག་དེའི་ནང་ལ་ཚྭ་དང་མར་རྒྱག་གི་ཡོད་རེད།

༤) ངས་ད་ལྟ་ཀློག་བཞིན་པའི་དེབ་དེ་སྙན་པོ་ཞེ་པོ་ཅིག་འདུག

༥) ཁོང་གིས་རྒྱག་བཞིན་པའི་ཁང་པ་དེ་མཐོང་བྱུང་ངས།

༦) ཡི་གེ་འབྲི་སའི་ཤོག་གུ་བཙོང་ཡག་ཡོད་པས།

༧) ཡི་གེ་བྲིས་པའི་ཤོག་གུ་ཚུར་གཡར་རོགས་གནང་།

༨) ཁོང་གིས་ཁ་པར་བཏང་སའི་སྐྱིད་དམན་དེ་མགྲོན་ཁང་གི་བདག་པོ་རེད།

༩) འཕྱོངས་རྒྱས་ཟེར་མཁན་་ལུང་པ་འདི་བོད་ཀྱི་ལོ་རྒྱུས་ནང་ལ་གལ་ཆེན་པོ་ཞེ་དྲགས་རེད།

༡༠) ལྷ་སར་འགྲོ་ཡག་གི་དུས་ཚོད་ག་དུས་ཡག་ག་རེད།

༡༡) ལྷ་ལུང་དཔལ་གྱི་རྡོ་རྗེ་ཟེར་མཁན་གྲྭ་པ་དེས་མདའ་བརྒྱབ་བྱས་གླང་དར་མ་བསད་པ་རེད།

26.4.2 Translate into Tibetan:

1. How many monasteries were destroyed?
2. Where is the first fortress of Tibet?

3. Have you visited the tombs of the Tibetan kings?
4. How long is it since Samyä was built?
5. Where are the books you bought?
6. I know the Khampa to whom he sold his car.
7. The momos you've made are excellent.

6.4.3 Create relative clauses according to the following example:

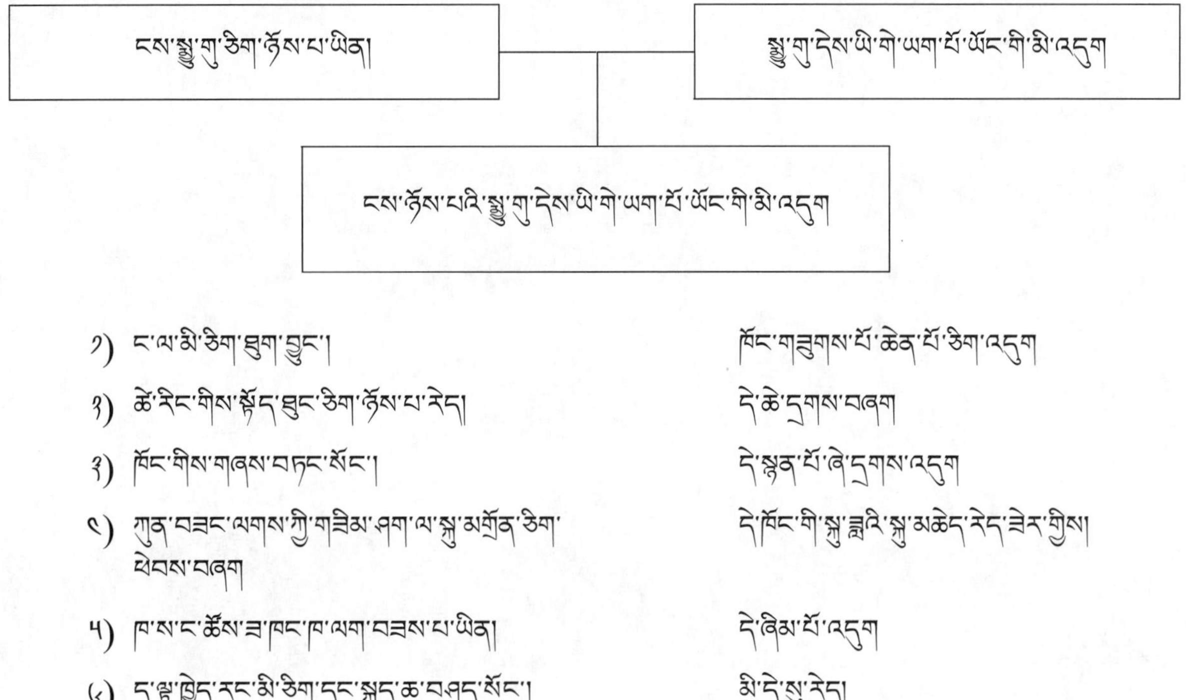

༡) ང་ལ་མི་ཅིག་ཐུག་བྱུང་།	ཁོང་གཟུགས་པོ་ཆེན་པོ་ཅིག་འདུག
༢) ཚེ་རིང་གིས་སྟོད་ཐུང་ཅིག་ཉོས་པ་རེད།	དེ་ཆེ་དྲགས་བཞག
༣) ཁོང་གིས་གཞས་བཏང་སོང་།	དེ་སྙན་པོ་ཞེ་དྲགས་འདུག
༤) ཀུན་བཟང་ལགས་ཀྱི་གཟིམ་ཤག་ལ་སྐུ་མགྲོན་ཅིག་ཕེབས་བཞག	དེ་ཁོང་གི་སྐུ་ཟླའི་སྐུ་མཆེད་རེད་ཟེར་གྱིས།
༥) ཁ་སང་ང་ཚོས་ཟ་ཁང་ཁ་ལག་བཟས་པ་ཡིན།	དེ་ཞིམ་པོ་འདུག
༦) ད་ལྟ་ཁྱེད་རང་མི་ཅིག་དང་སྐད་ཆ་བཤད་སོང་།	མི་དེ་སུ་རེད།

"Visiting the temple"

མཆོད་མཇལ་གྱི་སྐོར།

Grammar aims བརྡ་སྤྲོད་རིག་པའི་དམིགས་ཚད།

- The modal auxiliaries of past and present:
  past: རྒྱུ་བྱུང་ kyu̲ chu̲ng, རྒྱུ་བྱུང་སོང་ kyu̲ chu̲ngsong,
  ཡག་བྱུང་ ya̲' chu̲ng, ཡག་བྱུང་སོང་ ya̲' chu̲ngsong.
  present: རྒྱུ་ཡོད་མ་རེད་ kyu̲ yo̲:mare', རྒྱུ་མི་འདུག་ kyu̲ mi̲ntu'.

ཨོཾ་མ་ཎི་པདྨེ་ཧཱུྃ་

Mantra of Avalokiteśvara

CD I • Tr. 62

27.1 Dialogue དྲི་བ་དྲིས་ལན།

བློ་བཟང་ ༔ ང་ཤོག་ཡོང་དུས་ཁྱེད་རང་མི་འདུག ག་པར་ཐེབ་པ།
སྒྲོལ་མ་ ༔ ང་ཚོགས་གས་(ཚོགས་པ་) མཆོད་མཇལ་ལ་ཕྱིན་པ་ཡིན།
བློ་བཟང་ ༔ མཆོད་ཐེག་བཀོན་པས།
སྒྲོལ་མ་ ༔ ལྷ་ཁང་ཚང་མའི་ནང་ལ་མཆོད་ཐེག་བརྒྱབ་པ་ཡིན། ཇོ་བོའི་སྐུ་མདུན་ལ་གསེར་ཀུང་གཅིག་བརྗེས་པ་ཡིན།
བློ་བཟང་ ༔ གསེར་སྐྱེམས་ཕུལ་(འབུལ་) རྒྱུ་བྱུང་མེད་འགྲོ།
སྒྲོལ་མ་ ༔ དཔལ་ལྡན་ལྷ་མོའི་སྐུ་མདུན་ལ་ལྷགས་སྐྱེམས་ཕུལ་པ་ཡིན།
བློ་བཟང་ ༔ སྣན་ཞལ་བསྣམས་པས།
སྒྲོལ་མ་ ༔ སྣན་ཞལ་ཁྱེར་རྒྱུ་བརྗེད་བཞག ཡིན་ནའི་(ཡིན་ནའང་) གཙུག་ལག་ཁང་གི་འགྲམ་ནས་ཉོས་བྱུས། ཇོ་བོ་ལ་
སྣན་ཞལ་ཕུལ་ནས་སྨོན་ལམ་ཡག་པོ་གཅིག་བརྒྱབ་པ་ཡིན།

Translation

Lobzang — When I came back you weren't there. Where did you go?
Drölma — This morning I went to the temple.
Lobzang — Did you make liquid butter offerings (in the butter lamps)?
Drölma — I made liquid butter offerings in the butter lamps of all the temples. In front of the Lord Jhowo I filled (lit. changed) a golden vessel.
Lobzang — You must have had an opportunity to make a *chang* offering.
Drölma — In front of the image of Pändän Lhamo, I made a *chang* offering.
Lobzang — Did you take some *khatak?*
Drölma — I forgot to take *khatak.* But I bought some in front of the great temple, and after offering a silk scarf I did indeed pray in front of the Lord.

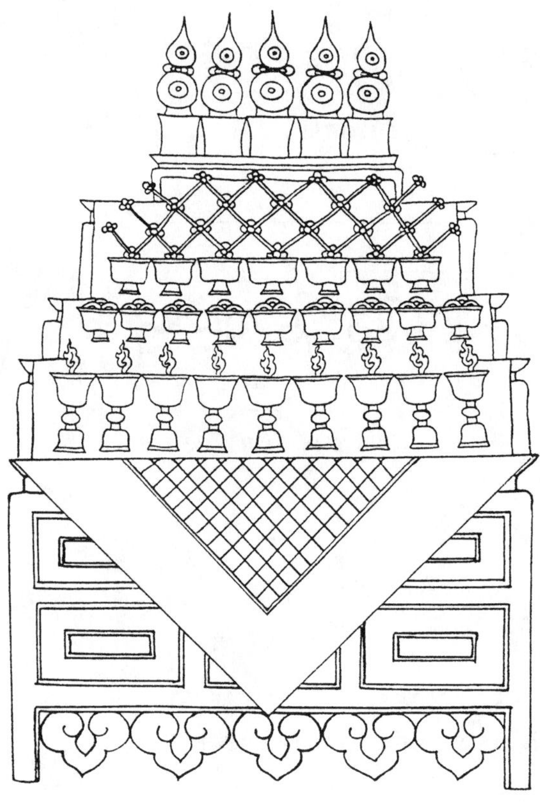

The "five kinds of offerings" to the Triple Gem

ཀ་ཁ་ག་ང་

27.2 Vocabulary ཚིག་གསར།

སྙན་ཤལ་ nyānshä: (H) (n.) *khatak* (for statues)
གསེར་སྐྱེམས་ sērkyem' ཕྱགས་སྐྱེམས་ ca'kyem'(H) (n.) alcohol offering
གསེར་ཀུང་ sērkung (n.) golden butter lamp

སྔགས་པ་ ngākpa	(n.) tantric priest
ལྷ་བཟོ་བ་ lhāpsowa	(n.) sculptor
ལྷ་བྲིས་པ་ lhāpripa	(n.) *thangka* painter
སྟོབས་ལྡན་ tōmtän	(n.) corpse-cutter
སྦྱིན་བདག་ ci̱nta'	(n.) patron, benefactor
སྐུ་མདུན་ kūntün (H)	(n.) presence, title of the Dalai Lama
ལྷ་ lhā	(n.) god, divinity
ལྷ་མོ་ lhāmo	(n.) goddess
མཁའ་འགྲོ་ khāntro	(n.) *ḍaka* (male celestial being)
མཁའ་འགྲོ་མ་ khāntroma	(n.) *ḍākinī* (female celestial being)
བརྗེས་ ce̱'	(v.) [vol., EA] to change
སྨོན་ལམ་ + རྒྱག་ mō̄nlam kya̱'	(v.) [vol., E] to pray
མཆོད་ཁྱིག་ + རྒྱག་ chō̄ti' kya̱'	(v.) [vol., E] to make liquid butter offerings
བྱས། cä̱'	(co.) connective similar to ནས། See Lesson 34

Proper nouns

ཇོ་བོ་ cho̱wo	The Lord, Buddha image in the Jhokhang
ཇོ་ཁང་ chö̱:kang, cho̱kang (L)	The Jhokhang, the main temple in Lhasa where the Lord Buddha's statue is found
དཔལ་ལྡན་ལྷ་མོ་ pā̄ntän lhāmo	The goddess Pändän Lhamo

Names of commonly represented buddhas, bodhisattvas, gods and saints

ཤཱཀྱ་ཐུབ་པ་ shākya thūppa	The Buddha Śākyamuni
རྡོ་རྗེ་འཆང་ to̱rce chāng	Vajradhara
ཀུན་ཏུ་བཟང་པོ་ kūntu sa̱ngpo	Samantabhadra
སངས་རྒྱས་སྨན་བླ་ sāngkyä' mā̄nla	Bhaiṣajyaguru (Medicine Buddha)
འོད་དཔག་མེད་ ö̱pame'	Amitābha
བྱམས་པ་ cha̱mpa	Maitreya
རྡོ་རྗེ་སེམས་དཔའ་ to̱rce sēmpa	Vajrasattva
ཕྱག་ན་རྡོ་རྗེ་ chā'na to̱rce	Vajrapāṇi
འཇམ་དཔལ་དབྱངས་ ca̱mpä: yāng'	Mañjuśrī
སྤྱན་རས་གཟིགས་ cā̄nräsi'	Avalokiteśvara
སྒྲོལ་དཀར་ trö̱:kar	White Tara
གུ་རུ་རིན་པོ་ཆེ་ ku̱ru ri̱npoce	Padmasambhava
མི་ལ་རས་པ་ mi̱laräpa	Milaräpa
ཇོ་བོ་ཨ་ཏི་ཤ་ cho̱wo ātisha	Atīśa
རྗེ་ཙོང་ཁ་པ་ ce̱ tsōngkapa	Tsongkhapa
ནག་པོ་ཆེན་པོ་ na̱kpo chēnpo	Mahākāla

Names of Tibetan Buddhist sects

ཉིང་མ་པ་ nyīngmapa	Nyingmapa
བཀའ་བརྒྱུད་པ་ kākyüpa	Kagyüpa
ས་སྐྱ་པ་ sākyapa	Sakyapa
དགེ་ལུགས་པ་ ke̱lukpa	Gelugpa

༢༧༣

27.3 Remarks འགྲེལ་བཤད།

The past and present modal auxiliaries.

The suffixes ཀྱུ་-kyu and ཡག་-ya' are combined with the auxiliaries བྱུང་and ཡོད་མ་རེད་ to make the following auxiliaries:

- Past: ཀྱུ་བྱུང་ kyu̱ chu̱ng, ཀྱུ་བྱུང་སོང་ kyu̱ chu̱ngsong,
  ཡག་བྱུང་ ya̱' chu̱ng, ཡག་བྱུང་སོང་ ya̱' chu̱ngsong.
- Present: ཀྱུ་ཡོད་མ་རེད་ kyu̱ yo̱:mare', ཀྱུ་མི་འདུག་ kyu̱ mi̱ntu'.

As we shall see below (Lesson 28), they may also be combined with the copulas ཡིན་and རེད་ to form future modal auxiliaries.

All these auxiliaries have a modal sense, and may be translated in English by the modal verbs "to be able to", "to have to."

27.3.1 The auxiliaries ཀྱུ་བྱུང་ kyu̱ chu̱ng *and* ཡག་བྱུང་ ya̱' chu̱ng

These mean, "to have had the opportunity to", and "to have been able to." The preceding verb must be in the present-future.

Ex.:	ཁ་བཏགས་ཕུལ་ཀྱུ་(འབུལ་ཀྱུ་) མ་བྱུང་།	"I didn't get a chance to offer a khatak."
	ཁོང་ལ་དཀའ་མོལ་ཞུ་ཀྱུ་བྱུང་སོང་ངས།	"Was he able to talk to her?"
	ལྟ་སྐོར་བྱེད་ཡག་བྱུང་།	"I was able to do some sightseeing."
	གནས་མཇལ་ལ་འགྲོ་ཀྱུ་བྱུང་ངས་།	"Have you been able to make a pilgrimage?"
	གཉིད་ཉལ་ཀྱུ་མ་བྱུང་།	"I was unable to go to sleep."

27.3 The auxiliary ཀྱུ་ཡོད་མ་རེད་ -kyu̱ yo̱:mare', ཀྱུ་མི་འདུག་ -kyu̱ mi̱ntu'.

This auxiliary, which is always in the negative, means "to ought not." The preceding verb goes in the present-future.

Ex.: སི་པན་མང་པོ་ཟ་རྒྱུ་ཡོད་མ་རེད། — "You shouldn't eat a lot of chili!"
འདི་འདྲས་ལབ་རྒྱུ་ཡོད་མ་རེད། — "You ought not to speak in that way!"
ཁྱེད་རང་སེམས་ཁྲལ་འདི་འདྲས་བྱེད་རྒྱུ་མི་འདུག — "You shouldn't worry so!"

27.4 Exercises སྦྱོང་ཚན།

27.4.1 Translate into Tibetan:

1. Have you had a chance to go to Bhutan?
2. Because I went to Lhasa, I had an opportunity to see the Potala.
3. He had the opportunity to go to the USA.
4. One should not sit on a book.
5. One should not kill insects.
6. One should not drink a lot of tea.

27.4.2 Translate into English

༡) ཕྱུག་རིས་བཏང་གནང་ཡག་ཁ་ཤས་འདུག
༢) མོ་ཏའི་ནང་ལ་གླུག་ཡག་ཙ་ལག་མང་པོ་ཡོད་པས།
༣) ཁྱེད་རང་ལ་ཕྱུག་དངུལ་གཡར་གནང་རྒྱུ་ཡོད་པས།
༤) ཁོང་ཚོར་བོད་པའི་ས་གདན་འཚོང་རྒྱུ་ཡོད་རེད་པས།
༥) ཁོང་ལ་བཀའ་མོལ་ཞུ་རྒྱུ་བྱུང་།
༦) བཀྲ་ཤིས་ལགས་ལ་ཞལ་པར་གནང་རྒྱུ་བྱུང་ངས།
༧) ཁོང་ཚོགས་འདུ་འདི་ལ་ཕེབས་རྒྱུ་མི་འདུག
༨) ན་དུས་ཚང་འཐུང་རྒྱུ་ཡོད་མ་རེད།
༩) ཨ་གསར་བྱེད་རྒྱུ་ཡོད་མ་རེད།
༡༠) སྐྱུག་རྫུན་བཤད་རྒྱུ་ཡོད་མ་རེད།

27.5 Civilization རིག་གཞུང་།

The religions of Tibet

Although religion occupies an important place in Tibetan life, it should not be thought that all Tibetans are religious. Some people, influenced by Western thought or Communism, are either agnostics or atheists. Nevertheless, to understand certain aspects of Tibetan culture and society some knowledge of *Bön*[154] (*bon*) and Buddhism is essential.

---

154. The term Bön is pronounced phö̱n. When the word occurs in an English text, according to our roman transcription, it should thus be rendered as Bhön, however, the traditional form Bön is retained here. see Appendix 7).

• The *Bön* religion.

According to the *Bön* tradition, Mt. Tise (*gangs-ti-se*), called Kailash in the Hindu tradition, is regarded as the center of the world or the "navel of the earth" (*sa'i lte-ba*). This sacred mountain is situated in western Tibet, in the region of Ngari (*mnga'-ris*). The kingdom of Zhangzhung (*zhang-zhung*), which was annexed at the beginning of the seventh century by the emperor Songtsän Gampo (*srong-btsan sgam-po*), had its main center in the area of Tise, like the mythical land of Ölmo Lungring (*'ol-mo lung-ring*). This was the birthplace of Tönpa Shenrap Miwo (*ston-pa gshen-rab mi-bo*), "the Excellent Shen, the Teacher, the Leader of Men", the founder of the *Bön* religion. It remains an open question whether this figure is historical or mythic, but in any event his name appears in numerous hagiographical texts and recitations, the oldest of which date back to the eleventh century. *Bönpo* teachings are concerned mainly with the origin of the world, as well as the appearance of living beings. They also deal with rituals of everyday life and the transition to the next life. The *Bönpo* teachings offer a vision of a purely Tibetan world and genuinely indigenous concepts, and are in this respect distinct from Tibetan Buddhism, which is of Indian origin. In the course of its evolution, the *Bön* religion adopted the concepts of *karma* and rebirth, which it borrowed from Buddhism, and organized its teachings according to a model known as "the nine ways of *Bön*" (*bon theg pa rim dgu*). From the time of its introduction into Tibet in the middle of the eighth century, Buddhism took pains to suppress *Bönpo* beliefs. Gradually but inexorably, the Tibetan people were converted to Buddhism. However, the process of conversion was not complete. In many parts of the country, including Central Tibet[155], there are still *Bönpo* temples and monasteries. Most of these were destroyed before and during the Cultural Revolution, but some have been restored since 1980.

In the *Bönpo* communities that are scattered throughout Tibet, particular importance is accorded to rituals for mountain gods, whose origins go back to the myth of the first king, the founder of the Tibetan nation.

The *Bön* religion has undergone many influences, and has adopted numerous ideas from Tibetan Buddhism, to the extent that the great Gelugpa scholar Thuukän Chökyi Nyima (*thu'u bkwan chos-kyi nyi-ma,* 1723-1802) declared that it was not possible to make a clear distinction between the two religions. By contrast, the eminent British scholar David Snellgrove maintains that the *Bön* religion is the true religion of Tibet, since it has rejected nothing but has enriched itself through the acquisition of new elements.

• Buddhism

In its tantric form ("Vajrayāna"), Buddhism is a non-theistic religious philosophy (denying the existence of a creator God) that stresses the impermanence of the world and advocates belief in the law of cause and effect (*karma*) as well as reincarnation or rebirth. The purpose of the

155. It is often claimed that *Bönpo* monasteries are to be found only in the border areas of Tibet.

Buddha's teaching, his "Dharma", is the recognition of the ultimate nature of the mind, and liberation from negative passions and emotions that constantly obscure our mental state. The methods used include reflection, introspection, meditation, prayer, the use of *mantra* (sacred formulae), ritual objects and *mudra* (symbolic gestures), as well as the practice of various yogas and psycho-physiological exercises.

There are four main schools of Tibetan Buddhism: the Nyingmapa (*rnying-ma-pa*), the Kagyüpa (*bka'-brgyud-pa*), the Sakyapa (*sa-skya-pa*) and the Gelugpa (*dge-lugs-pa*). These four differ from one another largely with respect to the rituals they perform and the emphasis they place on certain practices, but they all subscribe to the same fundamental tenets.

The Tibetan form of the Dharma has certainly been influenced by *Bönpo* thought and ritual, something that explains its originality and uniqueness.

The monasteries of these different schools are populated by monks and nuns who have taken a range of vows, including those of chastity and abstinence from alcohol and other intoxicants. All the schools with the exception of the Gelugpa have a tradition of married priests. Revered teachers, whether married or celibate, who teach the Dharma are classified as lamas.

The successive lives of a great master constitute a lineage of the transmission of teachings. All the sects of Tibetan Buddhism have such lineages. Traditionally, following the death of such a teacher, qualified lamas search for the reincarnation of the master in the form of a young child. These reincarnations are known as *trülku* (*sprul-sku*), "emanation body". Venerated high masters of a lineage are given the title of *rinpoche,* which literally means "precious".

Daily religious practices, pilgrimages, circumambulation of sacred mountains and religious festivals constantly illustrate the remarkable religious conviction of ordinary Tibetans. Some practitioners even go so far as to *prostrate themselves* over the course of thousands of kilometers to visit the statue of the Buddha Sakyamuni located in the great temple of Lhasa.

Most of the six thousand monasteries and temples that existed before 1959 were destroyed either before or during the Cultural Revolution. However, since the beginning of the 1980s, many of the ruined buildings have been restored.

Apart from Buddhists and *Bönpo*, mention should be made of a small minority of Tibetan Muslims, comprising two quite distinct communities: the *Khache* (*kha-che*), originally from Kashmir, and the *Horpaling* (*hor-pa-ling*), who are of Chinese origin. The introduction of Islam dates to the eighteenth century, and there are two mosques in the old sector of Lhasa.

Lesson 28 སློབ་ཚན་ ༢༨

"The car has broken down"

མོ་ཊ་སྐྱོན་ཤོར་བ།

Grammar aims བརྡ་སྤྲོད་རིག་པའི་དམིགས་ཚད།

- The future modal auxiliaries:
  རྒྱུ་ཡིན་ kyu̲yin, རྒྱུ་རེད་ kyu̲re',
  ཡག་ཡིན་ -ya̲yin, ཡག་རེད་ ya̲re'.
- The auxiliaries of probability: པ་འདུག་ patu', པ་ཡོད་ payö'.
- The factitive construction: V+རུ་+འཇུག་.
- The construction: Adj (short form) +རུ་འགྲོ་ -ru tro̲ / རུ་བཏང་ -ru tāng

༄༅། ཁོང་ཁྲོ་ལྟ་བུའི་སྡུག་བསྔལ་མེད། བཟོད་པ་ལྟ་བུའི་བདེ་བ་མེད།།

"There is no suffering like anger, no happiness like patience." *(proverb)*

CD I • Tr. 63

28.1a Dialogue དྲི་བ་དྲིས་ལན།

རྡོ་རྗེ་ ༔ ག་རེ་བྱུས་སོང་།
བློ་བཟང་ ༔ མོ་ཊ་སྐྱོན་ཤོར་སོང་།
རྡོ་རྗེ་ ༔ ད་ག་རེ་བྱེད་དགོས་རེད།
བློ་བཟང་ ༔ སྟན་ལ་གཅིག་ལྟ་གི་ཡིན།
རྡོ་རྗེ་ ༔ སྐྱོན་ག་པར་ཤོར་འདུག
བློ་བཟང་ ༔ ཧ་གོ་གི་མི་འདུག
རྡོ་རྗེ་ ༔ སྣུམ་རྫོགས་པ་མན་འགྲོ (མིན་འགྲོ)
བློ་བཟང་ ༔ མ་རེད། སྣུམ་ཞེ་དྲགས་འདུག
རྡོ་རྗེ་ ༔ ད་བཟོ་ཐུབ་ཀྱི་རེད་པས།
བློ་བཟང་ ༔ སྐྱོན་མ་བརྙེད་ན་བཟོ་ཐུབ་ཀྱི་མ་རེད།
རྡོ་རྗེ་ ༔ ད་ག་རང་དྲག
བློ་བཟང་ ༔ གའི་(གང་ཡང་) བྱེད་ཀྱི་མ་རེད། བཟོ་མ་ཐུབ་ན་དོ་དགོངས་འགྲོག་པའི་འཁྲིས་ལ་གནས་ཚང་གཡར་རྒྱུ་རེད།

Translation

Dorje	—	What's happening? (What has happened?)
Lobzang	—	The car has broken down.
Dorje	—	What should we do now?
Lobzang	—	I'll take a look first.
Dorje	—	Where's the problem?
Lobzang	—	I don't know.
Dorje	—	Perhaps we've run out of petrol.
Lobzang	—	No, there's plenty of petrol.
Dorje	—	Are we going to be able to fix it?
Lobzang	—	If we can't find the problem, we can't fix it.
Dorje	—	What a drag!
Lobzang	—	It doesn't matter. If we can't fix it this evening, we can stay with the nomads.

CD I • Tr. 64 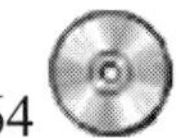

28.1b Text རྩོམ་ཡིག

ཉི་ཆོས་བཟང་པོའི་སྒྲུང་།

༄༅།། སྣེ་གདོང་རྒྱལ་པོ་ཟེར་མཁན་གྱི་(ཟེར་བའི་)རྒྱལ་པོ་ངན་པ་ཅིག་ཡོད་རེད། དེ་ལ་ཉི་ཆོས་བཟང་པོ་ཟེར་མཁན་གྱི་(ཟེར་བའི་)བློན་པོ་རིག་པ་ཅན་ཅིག་ཡོད་རེད། ལོ་གསར་རན་པའི་སྐབས་ལ་ཉི་ཆོས་བཟང་པོས་བློན་པོ་གཞན་དག་རྣམས་ལ་ངས་ལོ་གསར་ཚེས་གཅིག་གི་ཉི་མ་རྒྱལ་པོ་ཁྱི་སྐད་བརྒྱབ་ཏུ་(དུ་)འཇུག་གི་ཡིན་ཟེ་བཤད་པ་རེད། བློན་པོ་དེ་ཚོས། རྒྱལ་པོས་ཚེས་གཅིག་ལ་ཁྱི་སྐད་རྒྱག་སྲིད་ཀྱི་མ་རེད་ཟེ་ལབ་པ་རེད། ལོ་གསར་ཚེས་གཅིག་གི་ཞོགས་གས་(ཞོགས་པ་)ཉི་ཆོས་བཟང་པོས་རྒྱལ་པོ་རིན་པོ་ཆེ། ང་ཚོའི་ཕོ་བྲང་གི་ཉེ་འགྲམ་ལ་འདོགས་ཁྱི་ཆེན་པོ་ཅིག་འཚོང་མཁན་འདུག ཁྱིའི་སྐད་ཡག་ག་ལ། དཔེ་རང་རེད། ཙིག ཙིག ཙིག ཟེར་གྱི་འདུག དེ་སྤུས་གཟིགས་གནང་ནས་ཕོ་བྲང་རྒྱལ་སྒོའི་འགྲམ་ལ་བཏགས་པ་ཡིན་ན་རྔམ་ཟིལ་ཆེན་པོ་ཡོང་པ་འདུག་ཟེ་ཞུས་པ་རེད། རྒྱལ་པོས་ལྐུགས་པ་རང་རེད། ཁྱི་སྐད་དེ་འདྲས་ལ་ཧྲིག་པོ་ཟེར་གྱི་མ་རེད་ཟེར་ལབ་པ་དང་། ཉི་ཆོས་བཟང་པོས་རྒྱལ་པོ་ཁྱི་སྐད་ཡག་ཤོས་ག་འདྲས་ཅིག་དགོས་རེད་ཟེ་བཤད་པ་རེད། དེ་ནས་རྒྱལ་པོ་ཁྲིའི་སྒང་ལ་པུས་མོ་བཙུགས་ལག་པ་གཉིས་ཅོག་ཙེའི་སྟེང་ལ་བཞག་ནས། འབུང་འབུང་འབུང་ཁྱི་སྐད་ཧྲིག་པོ་ཟེར་ན་འདི་འདྲས་ཅིག་དགོས་རེད་ཟེ་ལབ་པ་རེད།།

Translation

"The story of Nyichö Zangpo"

[Once upon a time] there was an evil king called the King of Nedong. He had a clever minister called Nyichö Zangpo. Once, when they were about to celebrate the new year, he told the other ministers that he would be able to make the king bark on New Year's Eve. The ministers answered that it was impossible that the King would bark. On the first day of the new year, in the morning, Nyichö Zangpo [went to the king] and said, "Your Majesty [Precious King], at the doors of the palace somebody is selling a watchdog. This dog has an extraordinary bark, *tsik, tsik, tsik*. If we purchased it and chained it to the doors of the palace, it would be most impressive." The king answered, "Stupid! Such a bark is not impressive!" Then kneeling on the throne and placing his hands on the table, the king said: "*Boong, boong, boong* – now *that* is what an impressive bark should be like."

ཀ་ཁ་ག་ང་

28.2 Vocabulary ཚིག་གསར།

སྐྱོན་ kyȫn	(n.) breakdown, problem fault
སྣུམ་ nūm གཟིམ་སྣུམ་ si̱mnum (H)	(n.) oil, petrol
ཏོ་སྣུམ་ to̱num	(n.) petrol, gasoline
གནས་ཚང་ nǟtsang	(n.) lodging, hospitality
བློན་པོ་ lȫnpo	(n.) minister
ཁྲི་ thrī	(n.) throne
ལོ་གསར་ lo̱sar	(n.) new year
ངན་པ་ ngä̱npa	(adj.) wicked
ལྐུགས་པ་ kūkpa	(adj.) dumb, stupid
ཛིག་པོ་ tsi̱kpo	(adj.) rich, impressive
སྤྱང་པོ་ cāngpo	(adj.) intelligent, clever
རིག་པ་ཅན་ ri̱kpacän	(adj.) intelligent
རྔམ་ཟིལ་ཆེན་པོ་ ngāmsi: chēnpo	(adj.) splendid, magnificent
གང་དྲག་ kha̱ngtra'	(idiom.) what a shame! what a drag!
བྱེད་ che̱' (1) བྱས་ chä̱' (2)	(v.) [inv., A] to happen
ཉམས་གསོ་ + བྱེད་ nya̱mso che̱'	(v.) [vol., EA] to repair, restore
གནས་ཚང་ + གཡར་ nǟtsang yār	(v.) [vol., E] to find lodging
སྐད་ + རྒྱག་ kǟ' kya̱'	(v.) [vol., E] to shout
སྤུས་གཟིགས་གནང་ pǖsi' nāng (H)	(v.) [vol., E] to obtain, buy
བརྙེད་ nyē'	(v.) [inv., DA] to find
བཙལ་ tsǟ:	(v.) [vol., EA] to look for
རྫོགས་ tso̱'	(v.) [inv., A] to be finished, to run out
ཧ་ + གོ་ hā kho̱ མཁྱེན་ khyēn (H)	(v.) [inv., EA] to understand
ཤོར་ shōr	(v.) [inv., (E)A] – to escape, let go – *verbalizer*
བཏགས་ tā'	(v.) [vol., EA] to tie, fix
རན་ rä̱n	(v.) [inv., A] to be time
བཅུག་ cū'	(v.) [vol., EA] to have done, to put

28.3 Remarks འགྲེལ་བཤད།

28.3.1 The future modal auxiliaries:

རྒྱུ་ཡིན་ kyuyin, རྒྱུ་རེད་ kyure', ཡག་ཡིན་ ya'yin, ཡག་རེད་ -ya're'

These indicate the future, and are practically the same as -kiyin, -kire', but with more of a sense of obligation. The forms -kyuyin and -ya'yin are egophoric, whereas -kyure' and -ya're' are neutral. The verb that precedes the auxiliary should be in the present-future.

Ex.: དུས་སང་སློབ་གྲྭ་གསར་པ་རྒྱག་རྒྱུ་རེད། "Next year, we have to build a new school."
གནས་ཚང་གཡར་རྒྱུ་རེད། "We have to find accommodation."
ལམ་སེང་ཕེབས་ཡག་ཡིན་པས། "Do you have to leave immediately?"

In certain contexts, the forms རྒྱུ་ཡིན་ kyuyin and རྒྱུ་རེད་ kyure' may also imply that something that ought to have been done already has yet to be accomplished. In this case, it may be translated by "hasn't yet done X" or "has still to do X." The verb preceding the auxiliary must be in the present-future.

Ex.: ང་ཁ་ལག་ཟ་རྒྱུ་ཡིན། "I haven't eaten yet." (I'm about to eat.)
ཁོང་ཨ་ཅེ་ལྷ་མོ་ལྟ་རྒྱུ་རེད། "He has yet to go to the opera."
ཁྱེད་རང་སྦྲག་ཁང་ལ་ཕེབས་རྒྱུ་རེད། "You still have to go to the post office."
ང་དེ་རིང་གི་ཚགས་པར་ལྟ་རྒྱུ་ཡིན། "I haven't yet read today's newpaper."

Note: The suffixes རྒྱུ་ kyu and ཡག་ ya' are usually interchangeable, but not in all cases. The differences between them may be summarized here. A distinction must be made between their function as nominalizing suffixes and as auxiliaries.

Nominalizing suffixes:

- the patient: རྒྱུ་ kyu (future) and ཡག་ ya' (present or future)
- the instrument: ཡག་ ya' but not * རྒྱུ་ kyu
- the substance: རྒྱུ་ kyu and ཡག་ ya'

The auxiliaries:

- "one should not": རྒྱུ་ཡོད་མ་རེད། kyuyomare' but not *ཡག་ཡོད་མ་རེད། ya'yomare'
- "not yet": རྒྱུ་རེད། kyure' but not *ཡག་རེད། ya' re'
- the imminent future: རྒྱུ་རེད། kyure' and ཡག་རེད། ya' re'
- "to have had the opportunity": རྒྱུ་བྱུང་སོང་ kyu chungsong and ཡག་བྱུང་སོང་ ya' chungsong[156].

156. In all four cases, the corresponding egophoric forms may also be used.

28.3.2 The auxiliaries of probability པ་འདུག་ patu', པ་ཡོད་ payö'

These two auxiliaries express a high degree of certainty and relate to a future event.

The speaker makes an inference from available evidence or from previous knowledge.

These auxiliaries may be translated by "undoubtedly" or "surely", or by some such expression as "I think that." The form པ་འདུག་ patu' is neutral, whereas པ་ཡོད་ payö' is egophoric, and implies an event about which the speaker is privy to certain information. The auxiliary may be translated in English by "from what I know", or "I know that in principle…."

Ex.: ཁོས་གནམ་གྲུ་རྗེས་ཟིན་པ་འདུག

"He'll certainly arrive in time for his flight."

ཨེམ་ཆི་ཅིག་བསྟེན་དགོས་བྱེད་པ་འདུག

"It would surely be better to visit a doctor."

དོ་དགོང་ས་ཆར་པ་བཏང་པ་འདུག་གས།

"Do you think it will rain this evening?"

དོ་དགོང་ས་ཆར་པ་བཏང་པ་འདུག

"It's probably going to rain this evening."

ཁོང་སང་ཉིན་ཚོགས་འདུར་ཕེབས་པ་ཡོད།

"I know he should be coming to the meeting tomorrow."

28.3.3 The factitive construction

A verb is said to be "factitive" when its agent causes an action to be performed by another agent, or has the subject perform the action. In English, the factitive is often expressed by the auxiliary "to have" or "to make" (someone do something). The Tibetan factitive construction may also be translated by "to let" (someone do something).

The usual factitive construction is: V + རུ་ + འཇུག་ ru̱ cu̱'.

A factitive transformation is made by placing after the verb the suffix ru̱, which corresponds to one of the (literary) forms of the oblique, followed by the verb འཇུག་ cu̱', the past tense of which is བཅུག་ cū'. In Literary Tibetan, the form of the oblique is modified according to the last letter of the preceding verb. In the spoken language, however, the particle may often be omitted altogether in the construction.

Ex.: སྐད་བརྒྱབ་[རུ་]འཇུག་ "to make shout", སྐད་བརྒྱབ་ཏུ་འཇུག་ "to make shout" (L)

མོ་རང་གིས་ང་ལས་ཀ་བྱེད་[རུ་]འཇུག་གི་མི་འདུག "She doesn't let me work."

ངས་ཁོང་ཡི་གེ་འབྲི་[རུ་]བཅུག་པ་ཡིན། "I made him write a letter."

28.3.4 The construction: Adj (short form) + རུ་འགྲོ་ -ru tro̲ / རུ་བཏང་ -ru tāng

This construction is used to form verbs from adjectives as follows:

ཆེན་པོ་	ཆེ་རུ་འགྲོ་	ཆེ་རུ་བཏང་
chēnpo	chē-ru tro̲	chē-ru tāng
"big"	"to grow, get bigger"	"to make bigger"
ཡག་པོ་	ཡག་རུ་འགྲོ་	ཡག་རུ་བཏང་
ya̲kpo	ya̲'-ru tro̲	ya̲'-ru tāng
"good"	"to get better"	"to improve, make better"

The past form of རུ་འགྲོ་ -ru tro̲ is རུ་ཕྱིན་ -ru chīn.

In Literary Tibetan, the form that the oblique follows the usual rules.

Ex.: ཡག་ཏུ་བཏང་ ya̲k-tu tāng (L)

རིང་པོ་ ri̲ngpo "long"	>	རིང་རུ་གཏང་ ri̲ngru tāng "to lengthen" རིང་དུ་བཏང་ ri̲ng-tu tāng (L)
ཐུང་ཐུང་ thūngtung "short"	>	ཐུང་རུ་བཏང་ thūng-ru tāng "to shorten" ཐུང་དུ་བཏང་ thūng-tu tāng (L)
མགྱོགས་པོ་ kyo̲kpo "fast"	>	མགྱོགས་རུ་བཏང་ kyo̲'ru tāng "to accelerate" མགྱོགས་སུ་བཏང་ kyo̲ksu tāng (L)
མཐོ་པོ་ thōpo "high"	>	མཐོ་རུ་བཏང་ thōru tāng "to make higher"

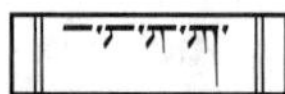

28.4 Exercises སྦྱོང་ཚན།

28.4.1 Translate into Tibetan:

1. He made me work a lot.
2. I have yet to send the letter.
3. We're going to build a school.
4. He hasn't yet repaired the car.
5. We'll soon be crossing the pass.
6. We shouldn't make them wait too long.

28.4.2 Tell the story in 28.1b *in your own words and answer the following questions:*

༡) བློན་པོ་ཚོས་ག་རེ་བསམས་པ་རེད།

༢) བློན་པོ་རིག་པ་ཅན་གྱི་མཚན་ལ་ག་རེ་ཞུ་གི་ཡོད་རེད།

༣) ཉི་ཚོས་བཟང་པོས་རྒྱལ་པོ་ལ་ག་རེ་གནང་དུ་བཅུག་པ་རེད།

28.4.3 Translate into English:

༡) ངས་ཁོང་ལས་ཀ་བྱེད་དུ་བཅུག་པ་ཡིན།

༢) ངས་སྟོད་ཐུང་འདི་ཚོ་ཚེམ་བུ་རྒྱག་དུ་བཅུག་པ་ཡིན།

༣) ཁོང་ཚོས་ང་ཚང་ཞེ་དྲགས་འཐུང་བཅུག་བྱུང་།

༤) ང་ཚོས་ཁོང་སྐྱུག་འཇུག་གི་ཡིན།

༥) ནད་པ་ཚོ་ངལ་གསོ་ཡག་པོ་རྒྱག་དུ་འཇུག་དགོས་རེད།

༦) ཁོང་གིས་ང་ཚོར་སྐད་ཆ་བཤད་དུ་མ་བཅུག་པ་རེད།

༧) ཁའི་ས་གནམ་ཤིས་གྲང་དུ་ཕྱིན་སོང་།

༨) ལྷ་སར་མི་འབོར་ལོ་ལྟར་རེ་བཞིན་ཆེ་དུ་འགྲོ་གི་ཡོད་རེད།

༩) སློབ་གྲྭར་འགྲོ་མཁན་གྱི་ཕྲུ་གུ་མང་དུ་ཕྱིན་པ་རེད།

༡༠) དེང་སང་འཛམ་གླིང་ལ་གནས་ཚུལ་སྡུག་དུ་སྡུག་དུ་འགྲོ་གི་འདུག་ག

"The car has broken down"
(continued)

མོ་ཊ་སྐྱོན་ཤོར་བ།

སྔ་མའི་འཕྲོས།

Grammar aims བརྡ་སྤྲོད་རིག་པའི་དམིགས་ཚད།

- The present gerundive:
  - V(past) + ནས་ nä'.
  - V(pres.) + གིན་ kin + V(pres.) + གིན་ kin.
- The auxiliaries of probability: ཨ་ཡོད་ ā yö', ཨ་ཡིན་ ā yin, ཨ་ཡོང་ ā yong.

CD I • Tr. 65

29.1 Dialogue དྲི་བ་དྲིས་ལན།

རྡོ་རྗེ་ ཿ ཐག་ཉེ་སར་འཕྲུག་པ་ཨ་(ཨེ་)ཡོད།

བློ་བཟང་ ཿ ཡོད་ད་ཡོད། ཕ་གིར་ལུག་རྫི་ཅིག་འདུག དེར་སྐད་ཆ་དྲིས་དང་།

རྡོ་རྗེ་ ཿ ཡའ། ཨ་ལུག་ཁམས་བཟང་།

ལུག་རྫི་ ཿ ཡའ། ཀུན་ཁམས་བཟང་། ཅི་རེད་ཐལ་། (ག་རེ་བྱུས་སོང་།)

རྡོ་རྗེ་ ཿ མོ་ཊ་སྐྱོན་ཤོར་སོང་། དོ་དགོངས་ཐག་ཉེ་ས་གཅིག་ལ་གནས་ཚང་གཡར་ས་ཡོད་རེད་པས།

ལུག་རྫི་ ཿ ཡོད་རེད། ཕ་གིའི་རི་འབུར་ དེའི་རྒྱབ་ལ་འཕྲུག་པ་དུད་ཚང་ཁ་ཤས་ཡོད་རེད། དེར་ཕྱིན་ནས་གནས་ཚང་གཡར་རོགས་ཟེར་ན་གཡར་གྱི་རེད།

རྡོ་རྗེ་ ཿ གོམ་པ་བརྒྱབ་ནས་ཕྱིན་ན་ག་ཚོད་འགོར་གྱི་རེད།

ལུག་རྫི་ ཿ ཐག་ཉེ་པོ་རེད། མགྱོགས་པོ་ཕྱིན་ན་སྐར་མ་ཉི་ཤུ་ལས་འགོར་གྱི་མ་རེད།

བློ་བཟང་ ཿ ད་དོ་དགོངས་འཕྲུག་པའི་རྩ་ལ་འགྲོ་རྒྱུ་རེད།

རྡོ་རྗེ་ ཿ མོ་ཊ་སྒོ་ཡག་པོ་བརྒྱབ་ན་མ་གཏོགས།

བློ་བཟང་ ཿ གའི་(གང་ཡང་) བྱེད་ཀྱི་མ་རེད། འདིའི་ཁུལ་ལ་འཕྲུག་པ་མ་གཏོགས་ཡོད་མ་རེད།

རྡོ་རྗེ་ ཿ ཡིན་ནའི་(ཡིན་ནའང་) མོ་ཊ་འགྲོ་མཁན་ཡོང་གི་རེད།

བློ་བཟང་ ཿ འོང་རེད།

རྡོ་རྗེ་ ཿ ད་འགྲོ།

Translation

Dorje — I doubt that there are any nomads near here.
Lobzang — Yes there are. There's a shepherdess over there. Ask her.
Dorje — How do you do, Miss?
Shepherdess — Fine, thank you Sir. What's happened? [Nomad dialect]
Dorje — The car has broken down. Is there a place nearby where we can spend the night?
Shepherdess — Yes, behind this hill there are several nomad tents (lit. hearths). If you go there and ask for lodging they'll put you up.
Dorje — How long will it take on foot?
Shepherdess — It's very close. If you walk quickly it won't take you more than twenty minutes.
Lobzang — So, this evening we're going to have to stay with (lit. go to) the nomads.
Dorje — Lock the car door properly, otherwise…!
Lobzang — It doesn't matter. There are only nomads in this area.
Dorje — But there are people who come through here in cars.
Lobzang — Ah, right!
Dorje — Let's go!

ཀ་ཁ་ག་ང་

29.2 Vocabulary ཚིག་གསར།

ཙ་ལ་ tsā-la	(post.) at (the house of), near
ནས་ nä'	(co.) *gerundive*
ཨ་པོ་ āpo	(n.) nomad man
རི་འབུར་ r̲inpur	(n.) hill
སྤང་རི་ pāngri	(n.) alpine pasture
བྲག་རི་ thra̲kri	(n.) rocky mountain
གངས་རི་ kha̲ngri	(n.) snow mountain
རྫ་རི་ tsa̲ri	(n.) slate mountain
ལ་ la̲	(n.) pass
དུད་ཚང་ thü̲tsang	(n.) household, family
ས་མ་འབྲོག་ sāmatro'	(n.) semi-cultivator, semi-pastoralist
ལུག་རྫི་ lu̲ktsi	(n.) shepherd, shepherdess
གོམ་པ་ + རྒྱག་ kho̲mpa kya̲'	(v.) [vol., E] to walk
འགོར་ ko̲r	(v.) [inv., A] to last, take (time)
ལ་ + རྒྱག་ la̲ kya̲'	(v.) [vol., E] to cross a pass
ཨེ་ཡོད་ ā yö̲'	(aux.) *dubitative*
ཅི་རེད་ཐལ་ cī re̲'-te[157]	(idiom., dial.) what's up?, what happened?
ཁམས་བཟང་ khāmsang	(idiom.) [nomad greeting] (lit. is your health good?)

157. In this Hor dialect as well as in most Kham dialects, the verb *red* /re̲'/ has a lexical meaning: "to happen". It might be the origin of the auxiliary *red* used in Standard Tibetan.

༣༣༣

29.3 Remarks འགྲེལ་བཤད།

29.3.1 The present gerundive V+ ནས་-nä'

As we have already seen, the particle -nä' has several functions with respect to case and conjunction. It is also used in forming the present gerundive of verbs (of whatever class), especially verbs of motion and stative verbs.

Ex.: གོམ་པ་བརྒྱབ་ནས་ཡོང་པ་ཡིན། "I came on foot (came walking)."
རྟ་ཞོན་ནས་ཕྱིན་སོང་། "He went by horse (went riding a horse)."
རྟ་རྒྱུག་ནས་མེ་མདའ་བརྒྱབ་དགོས་རེད། "You have to shoot as you gallop."

The construction of the present gerundive with ནས་-nä' is ambiguous, insofar as it can also be understood as a past gerundive, implying that the two actions are consecutive. Thus the last example may also be translated as "You have to shoot after you've galloped." Only the context will reveal whether the tense is past or present.

29.3.2 The construction V + གིན་-kin + V + གིན་ -kin

The construction V + གིན་-kin + V + གིན་ -kin conveys the sense of a present gerundive, that is, two actions that are taking place simultaneously.

Ex.: གཞས་བཏང་གིན་གཏང་གིན་(གཏོང་གིན་གཏོང་གིན་)སོ་སོའི་ནང་ལ་ལོག་འགྲོ་གི་རེད།
"They'll go back home singing."

ལམ་ཁག་འགྲོ་གིན་འགྲོ་གིན་ཁ་ལག་བཟའ་ཡག་དེ་ཡག་པོ་ཡོད་མ་རེད།
"It isn't good to eat while you're walking."

29.3.3 The auxiliaries of probability ཨ་ཡོད་ā yö̱', ཨ་ཡིན་ā yi̱n, ཨ་ཡོང་ ā yo̱ng

These commonly-used auxiliaries (and copulas) indicate that the speaker has serious doubts about what he or she is asserting. These three auxiliaries consist of the interrogative particle ཨ ā (or ཨེ་ ē in Literary Tibetan) and the copulas yö̱', yi̱n, or yo̱ng (cf. the examples below).

Ex.: ཐག་ཉེ་སར་འབྲོག་པ་ཨ་ཡོད། "I doubt that there are nomads near here."
ཇ་སྐོལ་ལོང་ད་ཨ་ཡོང་། "I doubt if there'll be time to make tea."
ཨེམ་ཆི་ཅིག་རག་ཨ་ཡོང་། "I doubt that we'll find a doctor."

–་ར་ཀ་ཀ་

29.4 Exercises སྦྱོང་ཚན།

29.4.1 Translate into English:

༡) ཁོང་བོད་པ་ཡ་ཡིན།

༢) ཁོང་རྣམ་ཚོ་བོད་ལ་ཕེབས་ཀྱི་ཡ་ཡོད།

༣) ང་འགྲོ་དགོས་ཡ་ཡོད།

༤) རླུང་འཕྲིན་ཉན་གྱིན་ཉན་གྱིན་གཉིད་ཁུག་བཞག

༥) བོད་ལ་ཞིང་པ་ཚོས་ཞིང་ཁའི་ནང་ལ་ལས་ཀ་བྱེད་ཀྱིན་བྱེད་ཀྱིན་གཞས་བཏང་གི་ཡོད་རེད།

29.4.2 Translate into Tibetan:

1. A lot of people smoke while they eat.
2. I doubt if there's a solution.
3. They recite prayers as they go around the temple.
4. Nyima falls asleep watching television.
5. I doubt if he's at home.

29.4.3 Modify the following sentences using the construction with ཀིན་-kin:

༡) ཁོང་བརྙན་འཕྲིན་བལྟས་པའི་སྐབས་ལ་ཁ་ལག་ཟ་གི་འདུག

༢) བདེ་སྐྱིད་ལམ་ཁག་ལ་ཕྱིན་པའི་སྐབས་ལ་གཞས་བཏང་གི་འདུག

༣) ཁོང་གིས་ལས་ཀ་བྱེད་དུས་ཁ་འདོན་སྐྱོར་གྱི་འདུག

༤) རྒྱ་གར་བ་ཚོས་ཁ་ལག་ཟ་དུས་ཆུ་འཐུང་གི་འདུག

༥) འོང་སྐོར་ལ་རྟ་རྒྱུག་ནས་མདའ་རྒྱག་གི་འདུག

༦) བསྟན་འཛིན་ཡི་གེ་འབྲི་དུས་ཐ་མག་འཐེན་གྱི་འདུག

"Approaching the tents"

སྦྲ་གུར་གྱི་ཉེ་འདབས་ལ་སླེབས་པ།

Grammar aims བརྡ་སྤྲོད་རིག་པའི་དམིགས་ཚད།

- The adverbializer ཟེ་:
  - ག་འདྲས་ kha̲nträ' and ག་འདྲས་ཟེ་ kha̲nträs "how."
  - འདི་འདྲས་ ti̲nträ' and འདི་འདྲས་ཟེ་ ti̲nträs "thus."
  - ད་ག་ tha̲ka "the very" and ད་ག་ཟེ་ tha̲kas "just like that."
- The modal expression: "to have no choice."
  - མ་ma̲ + V + རང་ ra̲ng+ V.
  - མ་ma̲ + V + ཀ་མེད་ kāme' + V.

Song གླུ། ༔ གངས་ཏི་སེ། "Mount Kailash" CD I • Tr. 66

CD I • Tr. 67

30.1 Dialogue དྲི་བ་དྲིས་ལན།

རྡོ་རྗེ་ ༔ ཨོ། གཟབ་གཟབ་གནང་ཨ། སྔོན་ལ་འདི་ནས་སྐད་བཏང་ན་མ་གཏོགས་ཤར་ཀྱག་ཕྱིན་ན་ཁྱིས་སོ་
ཀྱག་གྱི་རེད་ད།

བློ་བཟང་ ༔ ཨ་ཚོ། ཁྱི་བཀག་རོགས་གནང་།

འབྲོག་མོ་ ༔ ཀན། ཁྱི་བཀག་འོང་།(ཡོད།) ཡར་ཤོག་ད།

རྡོ་རྗེ་ ༔ ཡའ་ ཨ་མ་ཁམས་བཟང་། ཨ་ཚོ་ཁམས་བཟང་།

འབྲོག་མོ་ ༔ ཀན་ལགས་གཉིས་ཁམས་བཟང་། སྦ་གུར་(སྦྲ་གུར་)ནང་ལ་ཡར་ཕེབས།

གཉིས་ཀ་ ༔ ཐུགས་རྗེ་ཆེ།

འབྲོག་མོ་ ༔ ཡའ་ཀན་འོ་མ་བཞེས།

རྡོ་རྗེ་ ༔ ཐུགས་རྗེ་ཆེ།

འབྲོག་མོ་ ༔ ཁྱེད་གཉིས་ག་ནས་ཕེབས་པ།

རྡོ་རྗེ་ ༔ ང་གཉིས་ལྷ་ས་ནས་ཡོང་པ་ཡིན།

འབྲོག་མོ་ ༔ ག་པར་ཕེབས་མཁན་ཡིན།

བློ་བཟང་ཿ ནག་ཆུ་ལ་འགྲོ་མཁན་ཡིན། མོ་ཊ་སྐྱོན་ཤོར་ནས་བཟོ་ཐུབ་མ་བྱུང་། དོ་དགོངས་འདའི་(འདིར་)གནས་ཚང་གཡར་རོགས་ཟེར་གར་ཡོང་པ་ཡིན།

འབྲོག་མོ་ཿ ཡིན་ད་ཡིན་(ཡིན་དང་ཡིན་)འགྲིག་གི་རེད།

རྡོ་རྗེ་ཿ ཐུགས་ཆེ་གནང་། ད་ལོ་དཀར་ཆུ་ ག་འདྲས་འདུག

འབྲོག་མོ་ཿ ཡག་པོ་གདའ།(འདུག)[158]

བློ་བཟང་ཿ འབྲི་གཡག་ག་ཚོད་ཡོད།

འབྲོག་མོ་ཿ གཡག་བརྒྱད་བཅུ་དང་། འབྲི་ལྔ་བཅུ་འོད།

རྡོ་རྗེ་ཿ འབྲི་ཚང་མ་བཞོ་ཡག་ཡོད་རེད་པས།

འབྲོག་མོ་ཿ མང་ཆེ་བ་བཞོ་ཡག་འོད་ལེ་རེད།(ཡོད་རེད།)

རྡོ་རྗེ་ཿ ར་ལུག་ཡོད་པས།

འབྲོག་མོ་ཿ ར་དགུ་བཅུ་དང་ལུག་བརྒྱད་བཅུ་ཙ་འོད།(ཡོད།)

བློ་བཟང་ཿ འདི་སྡོད་པ་(སྡུད་པ་) རེད་པས། ག་འདྲས་ཟེ་རྒྱུག་དགོས་རེད།

འབྲོག་མོ་ཿ ཨོ་ཁོ་སླེབས་སོང་། འདི་ངའི་བུ་རེད། ཁོང་ཀུན་བློ་བཟང་དང་ཀུན་རྡོ་རྗེ་རེད། ལྷ་ས་ནས་འོང་ལེ་རེད། (ཡོང་པ་རེད།)

བློ་བཟང་ཿ ཁམས་བཟང་།

བུ་ཿ ཀུན་ཁམས་བཟང་།

བློ་བཟང་ཿ ག་པར་ཕྱིན་པ།

བུ་ཿ ལུང་པའི་ཕུ་ལ་སེར་ཤ་སྒྲུག་གར་ཕྱིན་པ་ཡིན།

བློ་བཟང་ཿ ད་རེས་ངར་སེར་ཤ་ཏིག་ཙ་(ཏོག་ཙམ་)བཙོང་ན་འགྲིག་གི་རེད་པས།

བུ་ཿ ཡིན་ད་ཡིན།

Translation

Dorje — Be careful, if we go straight from here without calling out, the dogs will bite us!

Lobzang — Hello, Shepherd! Tie up (lit. stop) your dogs, please!

A nomad woman comes out of the tent…

The nomad — I've tied up the dogs, sir. Come in!

Dorje — How do you do, *ama* and *apo*?

The nomad — How do you do, gentlemen? Come into the tent.

Dorje and Lobzang — Thanks.

The nomad — Have some milk.

Dorje — Thanks.

The nomad — Where do you come from? (lit. where have you come from?)

Dorje — We've come from Lhasa.

The nomad — Where are you headed?

Lobzang — We're going to Nagchu, but the car broke down and we couldn't fix it. We came to ask if you could put us up for the night.

The nomad — Of course we can. That's fine.

---

158. The auxiliaries *gda'* as well as *le-red* and *'od-le-red,* which appear below, are used in the Nagchu area. These variants give some idea of the reality of communication in the Tibetan region, which comprises many dialects and varieties. However, these dialectal expressions don't hamper communication, because the nomad woman otherwise uses Standard Tibetan to express herself. In Tibetan, changes in verb auxiliaries are the most obvious indicator of dialectal differences (see Tournadre, 2001).

Dorje	—	Thank you. How is the dairy production this year?
The nomad	—	It's good.
Lobzang	—	How many yaks and *dri* [yak-cows] have you got?
The nomad	—	Eighty yaks and fifty *dri*.
Dorje	—	Do all the *dri* give good milk?
The nomad	—	Yes, most of them give good milk.
Dorje	—	Have you got goats and sheep?
The nomad	—	I've got ninety goats and about eighty sheep.
Lobzang	—	This is a bellows, isn't it? How do you use it?

The nomad's son suddenly appears…

The nomad	—	Ah, he's arrived. This is my son. These are Mr. Lobzang and Mr. Dorje. They've come from Lhasa.
Lobzang	—	Hello.
The son	—	Hello gentlemen.
Lobzang	—	Where did you go?
The son	—	I went to the top of the valley to collect mushrooms.
Lobzang	—	Could you sell me a few mushrooms?
The son	—	Certainly!

ཀ་ཁ་ག་ང་

30.2 Vocabulary ཚིག་གསར།

སེར་ཤ་ sērsha	(n.) yellow mushroom (*armillaria luteovirens*)
ཤ་མོ་ shāmo	(n.) mushroom
སྦིད་པ་ pi̱pa སྦུད་པ་ pü̱pa(L)	(n.) bellows
སྦ་གུར་ pa̱kur སྦྲ་གུར་ tra̱kur (L)	(n.) nomad black tent
སྦ་ pa̱ སྦྲ་ tra̱ (L)	(n.) nomad black tent
འབྲི་ tri̱	(n.) female yak
དཀར་ཆུ་ kārcu	(n.) the three dairy products (milk, yogurt and butter)
ལུང་པའི་ཕུ་ lu̱ngpä: phū	(n.) upper end of a valley
ལུང་པའི་མདའ་ lu̱ngpä: ta̱	(n.) lower end of a valley
ཕུ་ phū	(n.) breath
ཨམ་ཕག་ āmpa' ཨམ་ཕྲག་ āmtra' (L)	(n.) pocket of a *chuba*
ཨུར་རྡོ་ u̱rto	(n.) slingshot
མེ་ལོང་ me̱long	(n.) mirror. Also denotes a silver or bronze disk bearing astrological signs
ཆབ་སྐེད་ chāpke'	(n.) belt decorated with carved silver motifs
ཀློ་ཟུང་ lōsung	(n.) metal ornament of double-diamond shape, hung from the belt
བཞོ་འགེལ་ sho̱nki:	(n.) ornament shaped like in inverted "Y" (used for hanging the milk pot)

ཁབ་ཤུབ་ khāpshup — (n.) hussif (sheath containing needles and thread)

མེ་ལྕགས་ me̲ca' — (n.) flint and steel

ལེ་རེད་ -lere' (dial.) = པ་རེད་ -pare' — (aux.) assertive past

གདའ་ ta̲ (dial.) = འདུག tu̲' — (aux.) there is, to have (testimonial)

འོད་ལེ་རེད་ ōlere' (dial.) = ཡོད་རེད་ yo̲re' — (aux.) there is, to have (assertive)

བཀག་ kā' — (v.) [vol., EA] to stop, block

ཚོང་ + རྒྱག་ tshōng kya̲' — (v.) [vol., E] to do business

ཕུ་ + རྒྱག་ phū kya̲' — (v.) [vol., ED] to blow

གཟབ་གཟབ་ + གནང་ sāpsap nāng — (v.) [vol., ED] to be careful

སོ་ + རྒྱག་ sō kya̲' — (v.) [vol., EA] to bite

སྒྲུག་ tru̲' — (v.) [vol., EA] to collect

འོང་ o̲ng (dial.) = ཡོང་ yo̲ng — (v.) [vol., A] to come

སྐད་ + བཏང་ kä' tāng གསུང་ + གནང་ sūng nāng (H) — (v.) [vol., EA] to call

30.3 Remarks འགྲེལ་བཤད།

30.3.1 The adverbs ག་འདྲས་ཟེ་ kha̲nträs *and* ག་འདྲས་ kha̲nträ' *"how."*

- The literary form of ག་འདྲས་ kha̲nträ' is གང་འདྲ་.

The suffix ཟེ་ s of the words ག་འདྲས་ཟེ་ kha̲nträs, ད་ག་ཟེ་ tha̲kas, འདི་འདྲས་ཟེ་ ti̲nträs is sometimes also spelled སེ་[159] ག་འདྲས་སེ་, ད་ག་སེ་, འདི་འདྲས་སེ་.

- The form kha̲nträ' is associated with nouns and adjectives.

Ex.: དེང་སང་ཁྱེད་རང་སྐུ་གཟུགས་ག་འདྲས་འདུག — "How's your health these days?"

ད་ལོ་དཀར་ཆུ་ ག་འདྲས་འདུག — "How's the dairy production this year?"

ལྟོས་དང་། ཁོང་མགྱོགས་པོ་ག་འདྲས་འགྲོ་གི་འདུག — "Look! How quickly he's walking!"

- The form kha̲nträs is associated with verbs. This adverbial form makes it possible to ask about the way in which an action is performed.

Ex.: ག་འདྲས་ཟེ་རྒྱག་དགོས་རེད། — "How should it be done?"

ཁོང་བོད་ནས་ག་འདྲས་ཟེ་ཕེབས་པ་རེད། — "How did he come from Tibet?"

---

159. The first spelling is preferred for etymological reasons: the "s" is in fact derived from the verb *zer,* "to say".

30.3.2 འདི་འདྲས་ ṯinträ *and* འདི་འདྲས་ཟེ་ ṯinträs

The forms ṯinträ and ṯinträs may both be translated by "like this" or "thus." They differ in the same way as the pronouns kha̱nträs and kha̱nträ'. The form འདུག་ཟེ་ tu̱s is sometimes used instead of ṯinträs.

Ex.: སྐྲ་སྤུ་ལུ་འདི་འདྲས་སྙིང་རྗེ་པོ་རེད་པ། "Curly hair like that is nice, isn't it?"
འདུག་ཟེ་རྒྱག་དགོས་རེད། "It should be done like this."
ཁོང་གིས་ཡི་གེ་འདི་འདྲས་ཟེ་འབྲི་གི་འདུག "He writes like this."

30.3.3 ད་ག་ tha̱ka*,* ད་ག་རང་ tha̱ka ra̱ng*,* ད་ག་ཟེ་ tha̱kas

The forms tha̱ka "the very, just" and tha̱ka ra̱ng "the very same" are spelled respectively དེ་ག་ the̱ka, དེ་ག་རང་ the̱ka ra̱ng in Literary Tibetan. The difference between these and tha̱kas "just like that" is the same as that between the sets discussed above

Ex.: ང་ཞུ་ཡག་ད་ག་རང་རེད། "That's just what I say."
ང་ཁྱེད་རང་རྩ་ལ་ད་ག་ཟེ་སྐད་ཆ་བཤད་གར་ཡོང་གི་ཡིན། "I'll drop by your place just to have a chat."

30.3.4 The modal expression: "to have no choice"

The constructions མ་ ma̱ + V + རང་ ra̱ng + V and མ་ ma̱ + V ཀ་མེད་ kāme' mean that the subject has to perform an action and has no choice in the matter (deontic modality). They are commonly used in Spoken Tibetan. Both may be followed by the verb རེད་ re̱'.

Ex.: ང་རང་གཟུགས་པོ་ཡག་པོ་མེད་ཙང་དགོངས་པ་མ་ཞུ་རང་ཞུ་རེད།
"Since I'm not well, I have no option but to leave."
མོ་ཊ་སྐྱོན་ཤོར་ཙང་འབྲོག་པའི་རྩ་ལ་མ་ཕྱིན་རང་ཕྱིན།
"Since the car broke down, we had no choice but to visit the nomads."

30.4 Exercises སྦྱོང་ཚན།

30.4.1 Translate into English:

༡) སྨན་འདི་ཚོ་ག་འདྲས་ཟེ་ཟ་དགོས་རེད།

༢) ཁོང་གིས་བྲིས་པའི་དེབ་དེ་ག་འདྲས་འདུག

༣) འདི་འདྲས་ཟེ་རྒྱག་དགོས་རེད།

༤) ཅ་ལག་འདི་འདྲས་སུ་གང་ལ་ཡོད་མ་རེད།

༥) དུས་ཆེན་སྐབས་ལ་ཆང་མང་པོ་མ་འཐུང་རང་འཐུང་རེད།

༦) གཟའ་སྤེན་པའི་དགོང་དྲོ་ཚང་ཀ་ཞེ་དྲགས་ཡོད་ཙང་།

༧) བབས་ཚུགས་གཅིག་གོམ་པ་བརྒྱབ་ནས་མ་འགྲོ་རང་འགྲོ་རེད།

༨) སང་ཞོགས་ཆུ་ཚོད་བདུན་པར་འཚོགས་འདུ་ཡོད་ཙང་སྔ་པོ་ནས་མ་ལངས་རང་ལངས་རེད།

༩) ཇ་སྣུམ་དེ་ཁ་ཏིག་ཞེ་དྲགས་འདུགཡིན་ནའི། མ་འཐུང་ཀ་མེད་རེད།

30.4.2 Rewrite the sentences according to the example provided:

ཇ་མེད་ཙང་ཆུ་བཏུངས་པ་ཡིན། > ཆུ་མ་བཏུངས་རང་བཏུངས་རེད།

༡) བདེ་སྐྱིད་ལ་ཁང་པ་མེད་ཙང་། ཨ་ཁུའི་རྩ་ལ་བསྡད་པ་རེད།

༢) ང་ཁ་ལག་བཟོ་ཤེས་ཀྱི་མེད་ཙང་། ཟ་ཁང་ལ་བཟས་པ་ཡིན།

༣) ཁོང་གིས་ལས་ཀ་ཡག་པོ་མ་བྱུས་ཙང་འགོ་འཁྲིད་ཀྱིས་གཤེ་གཤེ་བཏང་པ་རེད།

༤) ཚང་མ་ཡུ་ཚུགས་བརྒྱབ་ཙང་། ངས་གཞས་བཏང་པ་ཡིན།

30.4.3 Translate into Tibetan:

1. We have to do this work.
2. We have to go to this kind of meeting.
3. I have to stay at home all day.
4. Dorje couldn't fix the car, and they had to lodge with nomads.
5. They produce diary items and hides.
6. In your place, who takes care of milking the *dri*?
7. Is this how you work the bellows?

"The Nomad Way of Life"

འབྲོག་པའི་འཚོ་བའི་བསྐོར།

Grammar aims བརྡ་སྤྲོད་རིག་པའི་དམིགས་ཚད།

- The constructions V+ དགོས་བྱུང་ k̲ocung and V+ དང་+V "of course".
- The echo question: ཨས་ ä'.
- Expressive adjectives.

CD I • Tr. 68

31.1 Dialogue དྲི་བ་དྲིས་ལན།

སྒྲོལ་མ་ཿ ཕྱག་ཕེབས་གནང་བྱུང་། སྐུ་ལས་ཁག་བྱུང་ངས།
བློ་བཟང་ཿ ཡའོ་ཙ་བྱུང་།
སྒྲོལ་མ་ཿ ད་རེས་ཉི་མ་མང་པོ་འགོར་གནང་ཡག་ག་རེ་བྱས་སོང་།
བློ་བཟང་ཿ མོ་ཏ་སྐྱོན་ཤོར་སོང་། སེམས་ཁྲལ་བྱུང་ངས།
སྒྲོལ་མ་ཿ ཡོང་དགོས་བྱུང་། ཨ་ནི།
བློ་བཟང་ཿ དགོང་དག་གཅིག་འབྲོག་པའི་ནང་ལ་གནས་ཚང་གཡར་ནས་བསྡད་པ་ཡིན།
སྒྲོལ་མ་ཿ ཕྲ་གུར་(སྦྲ་གུར་)ནང་ལ་ཨས།
བློ་བཟང་ཿ ཡིན་དགོས་བྱུང་། ཕྲ་གུར་ཆེན་པོ་ཞེ་པོ་ཅིག་(ཞིག་)འདུག སྔོ་ཡར་འཛུལ་དུས་ཀར་རྒྱུག་(ཀ་རྒྱུག་) གཅིག་ལ་གདོང་མོ་རག་ཤན་གཅིག་བཏགས་བཞག་བཞག ཕྲ་གུར་གྱི་དཀྱིལ་དེར་ཐབ་ཆེན་པོ་གཅིག་འདུག དེའི་ནང་ལ་མེ་དམར་ལྷབ་ལྷབ་འབར་གིས་(འབར་གི་འདུག) ང་ཚོ་ཕྲ་གུར་ནང་ལ་སླེབས་པ་དག ཚ་སོབ་སོབ་བྱས་བྱུང་། ཕྲ་གུར་གྱི་མཐར་ལྕུགས་སྒམ་དང་། འབྲུ་དོ་པོ་བརྩིགས་བཞག་བཞག ཕྲ་གུར་གྱི་སྤྲུག་དེར་མཆོད་ཤོམ་ཅིག་འདུག དེའི་གཤམ་དེར་འཕོལ་གདན་ཆ་གཉིས་བརྒྱབ་བཞག་བཞག དེའི་སྟེང་ལ་ཁ་གདན་བྱ་འབྲུག་ཆ་ཅིག་(ཞིག་)བརྒྱབ་བཞག རྫོ་རྗེ་ང་གཉིས་དེའི་སྟེང་ལ་བཞག་བྱུང་།འབྲོག་མོ་སྙེར་བཟོ་དོད་པོ་ཅིག་འདུག མགོ་ནས་རྟིང་པར་མ་སླེབས་ཙ་བར་དུ་དངུལ་དང་གཡུ། བྱུ་རུ་ཅི་དག་མང་པོ་བཏགས་བཞག གོམ་པ་རྒྱག་དུས་ཤི་ལིག་ཤི་ལིགཟེར་གྱིས་(ཟེར་གྱི་འདུག) པགས་ཚགས་ཀྱི་གོང་གཤམ་དང་ཕུ་དུང་ཅི་དག་ལ་གོ་སྣམ་དམར་པོ་དང་ལྷང་ཁྲའི་མཐའ་རྒྱན་བཏང་ནས་དངོས་འབྲེལ་འཇའ་ཟླུག་པ་ནང་བཞིན་སྙིང་རྗེ་པོ་ཅིག་(ཞིག་)འདུག
སྒྲོལ་མ་ཿ ཡང་འབྲོག་མོར་སེམས་པ་ཤོར་པ་འདྲ།
བློ་བཟང་ཿ ཡང་མིག་སེར་ལང་པ་འདྲ།
མཉམ་དུ་ཿ ཧ་ཧ་ཧ།

Translation

Drölma — Welcome! Are you tired?
Lobzang — Yes, fairly.
Drölma — This time it took you several days. What happened?
Lobzang — The car broke down. Were you worried?
Drölma — Of course I was. And so?
Lobzang — One night we had to stay with some nomads.
Drölma — In a tent?
Lobzang — Of course! The tent was really big! As we went in there was a churn, with hoops of brass, tied to the tentpole. In the middle of the tent there was a big stove, with a nice fire blazing inside. As soon as we arrived inside the tent, there was a pleasant warmth. Inside the rim of the tent there were metal trunks and piled-up sacks of grain. At the far end of the tent there was an altar. At the foot of the altar were two pairs of mattresses, and on top they'd put a couple of rugs with designs of birds and dragons. That's where they put Dorje and me (for the night). The nomad woman looked really impressive. From head to foot she was covered in silver, turquoise, coral and that sort of thing. When she walked, she went *jingle jingle.* The hems of her sheepskin *chuba* and her sleeves were edged with green and red silk borders – as lovely as a rainbow.
Drölma — So, it looks as if you've fallen in love with a nomad!
Lobzang — And it looks as if you're jealous!
Drölma — Ha, ha, ha!

ཀ་ཁ་ག་ང་

31.2 Vocabulary ཚིག་གསར།

སྦུག་ pu̱'	(n.) innermost part
དགུན་ས་ kü̱nsa	(n.) winter camp
དབྱར་ས་ yārsa	(n.) summer camp
འཚོ་བ་ tshōwa	(n.) living
གཤམ་ shām	(n.) below, further down
ཨས ǟ'	(part.) *questions that echo what's just been said*
རྟིང་པ་ tīngpa	(n.) heel
གོང་གཤམ་ kho̱ngsham	(n.) garment edge, hem
ཡིན་དགོས་བྱུང་ yi̱nkocung	(n.) of course
ཆ་ chā	(n.) pair
ད་རེས་ tha̱re	(n.) this time
གདོང་མོ་རག་ཤན་ to̱ngmo ra̱kshän	(n.) brass-hooped churn
མཐའ་ thā	(n.) edge, rim
ལྕགས་སྒམ་ cākkam	(n.) metal trunk

འབྲུ་ tru̲	(n.) grain
དོ་པོ་ tho̲po	(n.) sack
ཀ་རྒྱུག་ kārkyu'	(n.) post, pole
ཁ་གདན་ khāptän	(n.) rug for mattresses
ས་གདན་ sāptän	(n.) floor rug
འབོལ་གདན་ pö̲:tän	(n.) flat square mattress
བྱ་འབྲུག་ cha̲ntru'	(n.) pattern with birds and dragons
སྟེར་བཟོ་དོད་པོ་ tērso thö̲po སྟ་བཟོ་དོད་པོ་ tāso thö̲po (L.)	(adj.) superb, magnificent
བྱུ་རུ་ chi̲ru, chu̲ru	(n.) coral
གཡུ་ yū	(n.) turquoise
སྤོས་ཤེལ་ pōshe:	(n.) amber
གཟི་ si̲	(n.) *zi*, onyx or agate ornament with spots or lines
དཀྱིལ་ kī:	(n.) centre
ཕུ་དུང་ phūtung	(n.) sleeve
འགོ་སྣམ་ ko̲nam	(n.) felt.
དམར་ལྷབ་ལྷབ་ mār lhāplap	(adj.) glowing, blazing
ཚ་སོབ་སོབ་ tshā sōpsop	(adj.) nice and warm
དངོས་འབྲེལ་ ngōntre:	(adv.) really, truly
མིག་སེར་ + ལང་ mi̲kser la̲ng	(v.) [inv., AD] to be jealous
འདོད་ཆགས་ + ལང་ tö̲ca' la̲ng	(v.) [inv., AD] to feel desire
སེམས་པ་ + ཤོར་ sēmpa shōr	(v.) [inv., AD] to fall in love
དཀའ་ལས་ + ཁག་ kālä' khā' སྐུ་ལས་ + ཁག་ kūlä' khā' (H)	(v.) [inv., A] to be tired
འབར་ pa̲r	(v.) [inv., A] to catch fire, burn
བརྩིགས་ tsī'	(v.) [vol., EA] to pile up
འཛུལ་ tsü̲:	(v.) [vol., A] to enter
ཕིད་ phī' ཕུད་ phū' (L)	(v.) [vol., EA] to take off
ཤི་ལིག་ཤི་ལིག་ shīlik shīli'	(idiom.) *onomatopoeia*
མགོ་ནས་རྟིང་པར་ ko̲nä' tīngpar	(idiom.) from head to foot

༣༡༣

31.3 Remarks འགྲེལ་བཤད།

31.3.1 The construction V+ དགོས་བྱུང་ ko̲cung *"of course"*

There are two main ways of conveying the idea of "of course". We've already seen the very common construction ཡིན་དང་ཡིན་ yi̲n-ta yi̲n. Sometimes a verb other than yi̲n may be used in the same construction: V+ ta +V. The same idea may be conveyed by using ko̲cung in association with a verb in the present-future.

Ex.: ངས་ཕྱུག་སྨྱུག་འདི་བེད་སྤྱོད་བྱས་ན་འགྲིག་གི་རེད་པས།

"May I use this pen?"

ཡིན་དང་ཡིན།ཁེད་སྦྱོད་གནང་རོགས་གནང་།

"Sure, go ahead."

ཁྱེད་རང་སློབ་སྦྱོང་ཧུར་བརྩོན་ཞེ་དྲགས་བྱེད་ཀྱི་འདུག་ག

"My, you study very enthusiastically!"

བྱེད་དགོས་བྱུང་། སློབ་སྦྱོང་བྱེད་ཡག་དེ་གལ་ཆེན་པོ་རེད་པ།

"Studying is certainly very important."

ནོར་གྱི་འདུག་ན་ཡོ་བསྲང་གནང་རོགས་གནང་།

"If I make a mistake, please correct me."

ལགས་སེ་ཞུ་དང་ཞུ།

"Certainly I will."

དེ་ལ་རྩམ་པ་རྒྱ་མ་བདུན་ཅུ་ཙམ་དགོས་ཀྱི་ཡོད་འགྲོ།

"Don't you need 70 pounds of tsampa for that?"

དགོས་དང་དགོས།

"Of course you do!"

31.3.2 The echo question ཨས ä'

When someone hasn't heard what the speaker has said, or wishes to make him repeat it, he can use the particle ä', which raises a question about the preceding word. In a similar situation English would use interrogative pronouns.

Ex.:	སྦྲ་གུར་ནང་ལ་ཨས། ཡིན་དགོས་བྱུང་།	"In the tent? — Sure!"
	ཞལ་པར་སླེབས་སོང་། ཕེབས་རོགས་གནང་། སུ། ང་ཨས།	"There's a phone call, come! — Who? Me?"

31.3.3 Expressive adjectives and adverbs

A) Trisyllabic expressions

The short form of certain adjectives is associated with repeated syllables with an expressive meaning. This formulation is used especially with adjectives of colour.[160]

Ex.:	འཇམ་ཐིང་ཐིང་	ca̱m thīnting	"quite calm",
	སྔོ་ཐིང་ཐིང་	ngō thīngting	"bright blue or green" (the grassland, the sky),
	དམར་ཐིང་ཐིང་	mār thīngting	"bright red" (blood),

160. In Dzongkha, the national language of Bhutan, most adjectives are formed on this pattern.

དམར་ལྷབ་ལྷབ་	mār lhāplap	"blazing, burning red" (fire),
ཚ་སོབ་སོབ་	tshā sōpsop	"warm as toast" (pleasant heat),
གྲང་སིལ་སིལ་	thra̲ng sī:si:	"biting cold"
གཙང་ཧྲིལ་ཧྲིལ་	tsāng rhī:ri:	"clean as a whistle".

There is another commonly-used adjectival construction:

Adj (long) + Adj (short) + རྐྱང་ kyāng, which is used to form expressive constructions implying "completely" or "entirely".

Ex.:	གསར་པ་གསར་རྐྱང་	sārpa sārkyang	"completely new",
	ཚ་པོ་ཚ་རྐྱང་	tshāpo tshākyang	"really hot",
	དཀར་པོ་དཀར་རྐྱང་	kārpo kārkyang	"pure white",
	ལྐུགས་པ་ལྐུགས་རྐྱང་	kūkpa kūkkyang	"utterly stupid".

B) Quadrisyllabic expressions

Tibetan contains a number of adjectival and adverbial expressions consisting of four syllables.[161] The general pattern is that the first syllable is phonologically associated with the third, whereas the second is linked to the fourth, according to the pattern: XYX'Y.

Here are a few very common expressions:

གང་བྱུང་མང་བྱུང་ kha̲ngcung ma̲ngcung "anyhow"

ཐ་རེ་ཐོ་རེ་ thāre thōre "scatty, piecemeal"

ཚ་གེ་ཚི་གེ་ tshāke tshīke "nervous, shaky"

ཚབ་བེ་ཚུབ་བེ་ tshāppe tshūppe "hastily"

ཛ་རེ་ཛོ་རེ་ tsha̲re tsho̲re "messy"

31.4 Exercises སྦྱོང་ཚན།

31.4.1 Translate into English:

༡) བྱང་ཐང་སྟོང་པ་སྟོང་རྐྱང་རེད་པས།

༢) སྐད་ཆ་འདི་འདྲས་ལབ་ན་ལྐུགས་པ་ལྐུགས་རྐྱང་རེད།

༣) ཐབ་ཚང་གཙང་མ་གཙང་རྐྱང་རེད་བཞག

༤) མོ་རང་གི་གདོང་པ་དམར་པོ་དམར་རྐྱང་ཆགས་བཞག

161. As a general rule, idiomatic expressions of four syllables are very common (see Sangye T. Naga and Tsepak Rigzin, *Tibetan Quadrisyllabics, Phrases and Idioms*, New Delhi, LTWA, 1994).

༥) ཁོང་གང་བྱུང་མང་བྱུང་བྱེད་ཀྱིས།

༦) གྲོང་ཁྱེར་ཆེན་པོའི་ནང་ལ་མི་མང་པོ་ཚ་གེ་ཚོ་གེ་བྱེད་ཀྱི་ཡོད་རེད།

༧) ཉི་མ་ཚ་དུས་བོད་པ་ཚོས་ཕུ་ཐུང་གཡས་པ་ཕུད་ཀྱི་རེད།

31.4.2 Translate into Tibetan:

1. Nyima must have fallen in love.
2. Don't worry, I shan't come back too late.
3. Pema always wears an old sheepskin coat.
4. Tibetans often don't wear (take off) the right sleeve.
5. Where's Trashi's tent? — Trashi's tent? It's over there.
6. Do drogpa get up early? — They certainly do get up early!
7. In cities, people wear Western clothing.

31.4.3 Translate the expression "of course" in the mini-dialogues below according to the example given:

ཁོང་ལ་གཟིམ་ཤག་ཡག་པོ་ཅིག་འདུག (ཡོད་དགོས་བྱུང་)ཁོང་ཚོང་པ་ཆེན་པོ་ཅིག་རེད།

༡) རྡོ་རྗེ་ཤ་སྐམ་པོ་ཞེ་དྲགས་ཆགས་བཞག (   ) ཁོང་ན་པ་རེད།

༢) དེ་རིང་ཁྱེད་རང་གིས་ཞལ་ལག་མང་པོ་མཆོད་སོང་། (   ) ཁྱེད་རང་གིས་ཞལ་ལག་ཞིམ་པོ་ཞེ་དྲགས་བཟོས་གནང་བཞག

༣) གློག་བརྙན་དེར་མི་མང་པོས་དགའ་པོ་བྱེད་ཀྱི་འདུག་ག (   ) གློག་བརྙན་དེ་སྐད་གྲགས་ཆེན་པོ་རེད།

༤) བོད་ལ་དགུན་ཁ་མི་མང་པོ་པགས་ཚོགས་གོན་གྱི་འདུག (   ) བོད་ལ་གནམ་གཤིས་གྲང་མོ་ཡོད་རེད།

31.5 Civilization རིག་གཞུང་།

The drogpa.

Nomadic herders or *drogpa* traditionally live in big, black yak-hair tents called "*ba*". Although they are transhumant, they usually remain within a well-defined territory. Every *drogpa* family has a fixed abode, corresponding to a winter camp. This camp, usually situated at the lower end of a valley, is usually home to the older family members who no longer follow the young people on the annual circuit. In spring, the nomads move up to higher altitudes and set up summer camps.

The main activity consists of rearing yaks, sheep and goats. Wealthier nomads may also have several horses. They produce butter, cream, cheese and yogurt, and sell hides and wool. Certain *drogpa* families, the *tshapa,* organize caravans to collect salt from the great salt lakes in the north and west of the country. The salt is then carried on the backs of sheep or yaks to farming communities, where it is sold or bartered for *tsampa* or other commodities. Since the late 1980s, the *drogpa* have become increasingly sedentarised, and are tending more to live in stone or mud-brick houses, which have the advantage of being relatively warmer, more weatherproof and less smoky. In many parts of Tibet, however, tents are still the year-round accommodation for nomads.

A group of herders

"City life"

གྲོང་ཁྱེར་གྱི་འཚོ་བ་སྐྱེལ་སྟངས།

Grammar aims བརྗོད་སྒྲོད་རིག་པའི་དམིགས་ཚད།

- The nominalizer སྟངས་ -tang' : "the way of doing X".
- Indirect questions.
- The secondary verb ལོང་ long "to have the time".

༄༅།། ཟ་སྟངས་སྡོད་སྟངས་འགྲོ་སྟངས་གསུམ་དྲིན་ཅན་ཕ་མའི་བསླབ་བྱ་ཡིན།།

"Our way of eating, sitting and behaving is the education we receive from our loving parents."

(proverb)

CD I • Tr. 69

32.1 Dialogue དྲི་བ་དྲིས་ལན།

བུ་ཿ ཨ་མ་ལགས།

ཨ་མ་ཿ ཨ། སླབ་གྲྭ་(སློབ་གྲྭ་)གྲོལ་སོང་ངས་།

བུ་ཿ གྲོལ་སོང་། ཚ་ལུ་མའི་ཁུ་བ་ཡོད་པས།

ཨ་མ་ཿ ཡོད་རེད། འཁྱག་སྒམ་ནང་ལ་རྫོས་དང་། ཕོད་ཐུང་བཅོག་པ་དེ་དེར་མ་བཞག ཁྲུས་སྒམ་ནང་ལ་བླུག་ཞིག

བུ་ཿ ཨོ། པཱ་ལགས། ཆུ་ཚོད་དྲུག་པར་བརྙན་འཕྲིན་ནང་ལ་ འཛམ་གླིང་དྲ་བའི་སྤོ་ལོའི་འགྲན་བསྡུར་བསྟན་གྱི་རེད།

པ་ཕ་ཿ ཐད་ཀར་ཡོང་གི་རེད་པས།

བུ་ཿ རེད། སྲུང་སྐར་འཕྲིན་སྐྱེལ་ནས་ཐད་ཀར་བསྟན་གྱི་རེད།

པ་ཕ་ཿ མཐའ་མའི་མགྲན་སྡུར་རེད་པས།

བུ་ཿ རེད། ཡང་དང་པོ་སུ་ཡིན་མིན་ དེ་རིང་ཧ་གོ་གི་རེད།

པ་ཕ་ཿ ཡིན་ནའི་(ཡིན་ནའང་) ལྟ་ལོང་མེད། ད་ལྟ་ཚོགས་འདུར་འགྲོ་དགོས་རེད། སྒྲོལ་མ་ལགས་ངའི་མོ་ཏའི་ལྡེ་མིག་གཟིགས་བྱུང་ངས།

ཨ་མ་ཿ སྒྲ་ཕབ་འཁོར་ལོའི་སྒང་ལ་འདུག

Translation

Son	—	Mother.
Mother	—	School's over?
Son	—	Yes. Is there some orange juice?
Mother	—	Yes. Look in the fridge. Don't leave your dirty shirt here. Put it in the washing machine.
Son	—	Father, there's the tennis world cup on television at six o'clock.
Father	—	Is it live?
Son	—	Yes, it's being broadcast live by satellite.
Father	—	Is it the final?
Son	—	Yes. Today we're going to know who the champion is.
Father	—	But I haven't got time to watch. I have to go to a meeting. Drölma, have you got my car keys?
Drölma	—	They're on the tape recorder.

ཀ་ཁ་ག་ང་

32.2 Vocabulary ཚིག་གསར།

འཚོ་བ་སྐྱེལ་སྟངས་ tshōwa kyē:-tang'	(n.) lifestyle
སྟངས་ tāng'	(n.) way of, *nominalizer*
སྒྲ་ཕབ་འཁོར་ལོ་ tra̱pap khōrlo	(n.) tape recorder
ཚོགས་འདུ་ tshōntu	(n.) meeting
ཚོགས་པ་ tshōkpa	(n.) group, party
བརྙན་འཕྲིན་ nyā̈ntrin	(n.) television
རླུང་འཕྲིན་ lūngtrin	(n.) radio
ཁུ་བ་ khūwa	(n.) juice, clear soup
འཁྱག་སྒམ་ khyākkam	(n.) refrigerator
འགྲན་སྡུར་ trä̱ntur	(n.) competition
མཐའ་མའི་མགྲན་སྡུར་ thāmä: trä̱ntur	(n.) final
སྲུང་སྐར་ sūngkar	(n.) satellite
ཁྲུས་སྒམ་ thrǖkam	(n.) washing machine
དྲ་བའི་སྤོ་ལོ་ thra̱wä: pōlo	(n.) tennis
ཕིང་ཕང་སྤོ་ལོ་ phīngpang pōlo	(n.) table tennis
བསིལ་དྲའི་སྤོ་ལོ་ sī:trä: pōlo	(n.) basketball
དྲ་བ་ thra̱wa	(n.) net
ཐད་ཀར་ thā̈kar	(n.) direct
ཨང་དང་པོ་ āng tha̱ngpo	(n.) number one, champion
འཕྲུལ་འཁོར་ thrǖ:nkor	(n.) machine
གློག་ཀླད་འཕྲུལ་འཁོར་ lōklä' thrǖnkor	(n.) computer
ལྕགས་པར་ cākpar	(n.) typewriter
སྐམ་གློག་ kāmlo'	(n.) generator
རྒྱང་ཤེལ་ kya̱ngshe:	(n.) binoculars

རྩིས་པ་ tsīpa	(n.) accountant
ཚན་རིག་པ་ tshān̄rikpa	(n.) scientist
མགོ་འཁྲིད་ ko̱tri དབུ་འཁྲིད་ ūtri (H)	(n.) manager, leader
བཟོ་པ་ so̱pa	(n.) worker
མགར་བ་ ka̱rra	(n.) blacksmith
ཆེ་མོ་བ་ chēmowa	(n.) headmaster
རྡོ་བཟོ་བ་ to̱psowa	(n.) mason
གསར་འགྱུར་འགོད་མཁན་ sā:ngkyur ko̱ngkän	(n.) journalist
གྲོལ་ thro̱:	(v.) [inv., A] to finish
འཕྲིན་སྐྱེལ་ thrīn kyē:	(v.) [vol., E] to broadcast
ལོང་ lo̱ng	(v. mod.) to have time
རན་ ra̱n	(v. mod.) to be time (to)

32.3 Remarks འགྲེལ་བཤད།

32.3.1 The nominalizer སྟངས་ tāng' / -tang

Like other nominalizers, this one is directly suffixed to the verb, which goes in the present-future.

Ex.: ལབ་སྟངས་ "way of speaking", འབྲི་སྟངས་ "way of writing", ཟ་སྟངས་ "way of eating", ལྟ་སྟངས་ "way of looking, considering".

The following forms, in which the verb is in the past, are incorrect:
*བྲིས་སྟངས་ *བཟས་སྟངས་ *བལྟས་སྟངས་

This nominalizer shows the way in which the action designated by the verb is performed.

Ex.: དེང་སང་བོད་ཀྱི་ཁང་པ་རྒྱག་སྟངས་སྔོན་མ་དང་གཅིག་པ་མ་རེད།
"The way they build houses in Tibet today is not as it was in the past."
བུ་དང་བུ་མོའི་ཕྱུ་པ་གོན་སྟངས་ཡོགས་ག་རེད།
"The way men and women wear the chuba is different."

The nominalizer may also be translated by a noun.

Ex.: འཚོ་བ་སྐྱེལ་སྟངས་ the lifestyle (lit.: the way of leading one's life),
གཏོར་མ་བཟོ་སྟངས་ the production of tormas.

32.3.2 Indirect questions.

In order to form nominal interrogative clauses, one uses alternative constructions made of positive and negative copulas: ཡིན་མིན་ yin-män ཡོད་མེད་ yö'-me'

And after the main verb, the following auxiliaries:

- Future: V+ གི་ ཡིན་མིན་ -kiyi̱nmin,
- Present: V+ གི་ཡོད་མེད་ ki-yö̱me'
- Past: V+ ཡོད་མེད་ yö̱me'.[162]

These constructions are translated by clauses formed with "if" or "whether" or by interrogative pronouns "what", "who", etc.

Ex.:	ཨང་དང་པོ་སུ་ཡིན་མིན་ དེ་རིང་ཧ་གོ་གི་རེད།	"Today we'll know who the champion is."
	ཁོང་ལ་རླུང་འཕྲིན་ཡོད་མེད་ངས་ཤེས་ཀྱི་མེད།	"I don't know if he has a radio."
	ཁོང་ཚོ་ཡེབས་ཀྱི་ཡོད་མེད་མཁྱེན་བྱུང་ངས།	"Do you know whether they're coming?"
	རྒྱ་གར་ལ་ཡེབས་ཡོད་མེད་ཁོང་ལ་དཀའ་འདྲི་གནང་དང་།	"Ask him if they've gone to India."
	སྒམ་ནང་ལ་ག་རེ་ཡོད་མེད་ངས་ཤེས་ཀྱི་མེད།	"I don't know what's in the box."
	ཁོང་བོད་པ་ཡིན་མིན་ངས་ཧ་གོ་གི་མེད།	"I don't know if he is Tibetan."

32.3.3 The secondary verbs ལོང་ lo̱ng *"to have time", and* རན་ rä̱n *"to be time"*

The verbs lo̱ng and rä̱n are "secondary verbs" (see Lesson 11) that take the same place as modal verbs. The main verb, which precedes them, should be in the present-future and not the past. In the present, the verb lo̱ng is followed by the egophoric auxiliary ཡོད་ or the constative auxiliary འདུག. In the past, the verb lo̱ng is followed by the auxiliary བྱུང་ (egophoric) or བྱུང་སོང་ (constative), in the future by the auxiliary ཡོང་.

The verb རན་ rä̱n is generally used in the past with the following past auxiliaries: རན་སོང་ or རན་བཞག and རན་པ་རེད། and sometimes in the present: རན་གྱི་འདུག

Ex.:	ང་ལ་ཇ་འཐུང་ལོང་མེད།	"I haven't got time to drink tea."
	ཡི་གེ་འདི་ཀློག་ལོང་ཡོད་པས།	"Have you got time to read this letter?"
	ཇ་སྐོལ་ལོང་ད་ཡ་ཡོང་།	"You probably haven't got time to make tea."
	ང་ལས་ཁུངས་ལ་འགྲོ་རན་སོང་།	"It's time I went to the office."

162. The perfective form V + *pa-yin* + *min* is not used.

32.4 Exercises སྦྱོང་ཚན།

32.4.1 Translate into Tibetan:

1. I don't know if they have TV.
2. Do you know if they've gone to Peking?
3. They asked us if a lot of yaks had died.
4. I asked him if he'd ever been on a pilgrimage.
5. They don't like the way you talk.
6. Generally, they haven't got the same way of working as we have.
7. Could you look in the fridge to see if there's any orange juice?

32.4.2 Translate into English:

༡) ལྷ་སར་འགྲོ་མཁན་གྱི་མོ་ཊ་ཡོད་མེད་སྐད་ཆ་དྲིས་པ་ཡིན།

༢) ཁོང་གི་སེམས་ནང་ལ་ག་རེ་བསམ་གྱི་ཡོད་མེད་ངས་གསལ་པོར་ཤེས་ཀྱི་མེད།

༣) ང་ཚོ་སློབ་གྲྭར་འགྲོ་རན་བཞག

༤) དགོང་དྲོའི་གསོལ་ཚིགས་མཆོད་རན་འདུག་གས།

༥) ཁོང་གི་བཀའ་མོལ་གནང་སྟངས་ཁྱད་མཚར་པོ་འདུག

༦) ཁོང་གི་མོ་ཊ་བཏང་(གཏོང་)སྟངས་ཉེན་ཁ་ཆེན་པོ་འདུག

༧) འཛིན་གྲྭ་ག་ཚད་སླེབས་ཡོད་མེད་ང་ལ་གསུང་རོགས་གནང་།

༨) བུ་ཁྱོད་རང་ཨ་མ་ལགས་ཐད་ཀྱི་ཡོད་མེད་བཀའ་འདྲི་ཞུས་ཤོག

༩) ཉི་མའི་སྐད་ཆ་བཤད་སྟངས་དེར་ང་དོགས་པ་ཟ་གི་འདུག

༡༠) ཁ་ལག་བཟོ་སྟངས་ཤེས་ཀྱི་མི་འདུག

༡༡) ཁོང་ཚོའི་བསམ་བློ་བཏང་སྟངས་ཡག་པོ་མི་འདུག་གས།

༡༢) ཁོང་ནང་ལ་ཕེབས་ཡོད་མེད་ཏ་གོ་མ་བྱུང་།

༡༣) མི་དེ་གྲྭ་པ་ཡིན་མིན་ཤེས་ཀྱི་མེད།

༡༤) ཁོང་གི་སྐུ་ཟླ་ཡོད་མེད་ཤེས་མ་བྱུང་།

"The harvest festival"

འོང་སྐོར།

Grammar aims བརྡ་སྤྲོད་རིག་པའི་དམིགས་ཚད།

- Omitting the verbal auxiliary.
- Expressive particles.
- Self-corrective and mnemic particles.

༄༅།། རྟ་ཕོ་ལ་རྒྱུག་ཤེད་ཡོད་ན་བྱང་ཐང་སྟོང་པ་རེད།།

"If the stallion is strong, the whole Northern Plateau is empty."

(proverb)

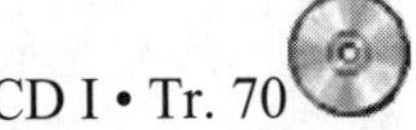

CD I • Tr. 70

33.1 Dialogue དྲི་བ་དྲིས་ལན།

དཔལ་འབྱོར་ཿ ཨོ། བློ་བཟང་ལགས། ཁའི་ས་ཁའི་ཉིན་ (ཁ་སང་ཁ་ཉིན་) ཁྱེད་རང་བཞུགས་མི་འདུག ག་པར་ཕེབས་པ།

བློ་བཟང་ཿ ཆུ་ཤུར་འོང་སྐོར་ལ་ཕྱིན་པ་ཡིན།

དཔལ་འབྱོར་ཿ ཨ་ལའི། ཆུ་ཤུར་འོང་སྐོར་འཁྲུག་པོ་ཞེ་དྲགས་ཡོད་པ་འདྲ།

བློ་བཟང་ཿ དཔེ་རང་རེད།

དཔལ་འབྱོར་ཿ རྟ་རྒྱུག་གི་རེད་པས།

བློ་བཟང་ཿ རྟ་རྒྱུག་གི་རེད། ད་དུང་། ས་ཤུར་གྱི་གཡོན་ཕྱོགས་ལ་འབེན་གསུམ་འབབ་འཁྲིག (འབྲང་འཁྲིག) ནས་བཙུགས་ཡོད་རེད། རྟ་རྒྱུག་ནས་འབེན་གཅིག་ལ་གདུང་བཙུགས་གཅིག་ལ་མདའ་བརྒྱབ་གཅིག་ལ་མེ་མདའ་བརྒྱབ་དགོས་རེད།

དཔལ་འབྱོར་ཿ གསུམ་ཀར་བྱེད་ཐུབ་མཁན་འདུག་གས།

བློ་བཟང་ཿ མང་པོ་འདུག

དཔལ་འབྱོར་ཿ འོང་སྐོར་ལ་ཆོས་པོ་ཏི་སྐལ་པར་ཁྱེར་བྱས་འོང་གར་སྐོར་ར་ (སྐོར་བ་) རྒྱུག་གི་རེད་ཟེར་གྱིས་ (ཟེར་གྱི་འདུག) རེད་པས།

བློ་བཟང་ཿ རེད། སྐུ་གསུང་ཐུགས་རྟེན་མང་པོ་གདན་འདྲེན་ཞུས་ནས་འོང་གར་སྐོར་ར་རྒྱུག་གི་རེད།

Threshing and winnowing

Translation

Pänjor — Oh! Lobzang, you haven't been around recently. Where did you go?
Lobzang — I went to the Chushur harvest festival.
Pänjor — The Chushur harvest festival must be lively!
Lobzang — It's amazing!
Pänjor — Are there horse races?
Lobzang — Yes, and what's more, to the left of the racecourse they'd set up three targets in a row. At a full gallop the riders have to stick a spear in the first, shoot an arrow into the second and fire at the third with a gun!
Pänjor — Are there many people who manage all three?
Lobzang — Yes, plenty!
Pänjor — Apparently they walk around the fields carrying religious books on their backs. Is that true?
Lobzang — Yes, they bring (lit. invite) a lot of supports of [the Buddha's] body, speech and mind and circumambulate the cultivated area.

ཀ་ཁ་ག་ང་

33.2 Vocabulary ཚིག་གསར།

འོང་སྐོར་ o̲ngkor — (n.) *ongkor*. harvest festival
འོང་ག་ o̲ngka — (n.) village fields
འཁྲུག་པོ་ thrūkpo — (n.) lively, animated
རྟ་རྒྱུག་ tā(p)kyu' — (n.) horse race

འབེན་ pe̲n	(n.) target
འཕང་འགྲིག་ pa̲ngtri' འཕྲང་འགྲིག་ tra̲ngtri'(L)	(n.) line, row, queue
གདུང་ tu̲ng	(n.) spear
ས་ཤུར་ sāshur	(n.) course, pitch
གསུམ་ཀ་ sūmka	(n.) all three
དཔལ་འབྱོར་ pǟncor	(n.) wealth, economy
པོ་ཏི་ pōti	(n.) volume (book)
རྟེན་ tēn	(n.) support, base
སྐུ་གསུང་ཐུགས་ kū,sūng thū'	(n.) body, speech and mind
སྐུ་རྟེན་ kūrtēn	(n.) "body support" (*thangka*, statue, etc.)
གསུང་རྟེན་ sūngten	(n.) "speech support" (scripture)
ཐུགས་རྟེན་ thūkten	(n.) "mind support" (stupa)
ཁ་ས་ཁ་ཉིན་ khǟsa khǟnyin	(adv.) recently, in recent days
རྒྱུག་ kyu̲'	(v.) [vol., E] to run
སྐད་ + བཏང་ kǟ' tāng	(v.) [vol., EA] to invite
གདན་འདྲེན་ + ཞུ་ tä̲ntren shu̲ (h)	(v.) [vol., EA] to invite
བཙུགས་ tsū'	(v.) [vol., EA] to plant, insert, begin
མདའ་ + རྒྱག་ ta̲ kya̲'	(v.) [vol., ED] to shoot arrows
མེ་མདའ་+ རྒྱག་ me̲nta kya̲'	(v.) [vol., ED] to fire a gun
དཔེ་རང་རེད་ pē ra̲ng re̲'	(idiom.) it's amazing!

Proper nouns

ཆུ་ཤུར་ chūshur	Chushur (village near Lhasa)
དཔལ་འབྱོར་ pǟncor	Pänjor
བྱང་ཐང་ cha̲ngtang	Jhangthang (Northern Plateau)

33.3 Remarks འགྲེལ་བཤད།

33.3.1 Omitting the verbal auxiliary

As a general rule, the verb in the main clause requires an auxiliary. However, as we have already seen, the verb in subordinate clauses is usually followed directly by the *subordinator* or connective. Moreover, auxiliaries are not used in cases where a series of actions is being enumerated. An example of this is given in the dialogue for this lesson.

Ex.: འབེན་གཅིག་ལ་གདུང་བཙུགས། གཅིག་ལ་མདའ་བརྒྱབ། གཅིག་ལ་མེ་མདའ་བརྒྱབ་དགོས་རེད།

"(The riders) have to stick a spear into the first target, shoot an arrow into the second, and fire a gun at the third!"

In this example, the verbs མདའ་བརྒྱབ ta̲ kya̲p "to shoot an arrow" and གདུང་བཙུགས tu̲ng tsū' "to plant a spear" are not followed by auxiliaries. Only the last verb in the list has an auxiliary.

33.3.2 Expressive particles

We have already encountered a number of expressive particles. These are common in both Standard and Literary Tibetan. Some go at the beginning of a sentence and some at the end, after the verb.

Of those that go at the beginning, the commonest are: ཨོ་ ō "Oh!" ཨ་ལའི་ ālä: "Well, well", ཨ་ཙི་ ātsi "Rats! Darn! Bugger!" ཨ་རོ་ āro "Ow!", ཨ་ཅུ་ ācu "Oo, that's cold!", ཨ་ཚ་ ātsa "Ouch, that's hot!", ཨ་ཁ་ ākha "What a shame!", ཨ་མ་ āma "Oh Lordy (lit. O mother)!"

The particles that appear most frequently at the end of a sentence are: ད་-ta and པ་pa (and their variants ག་-ka, ང་-nga).

• ད་-ta often implies that the speaker is not in agreement with the person to whom he's speaking, or is emphasizing the surprising or threatening nature of the situation in question.

Ex.: འདི་དཔེ་རང་རེད་ད། "It's pretty amazing, huh?"
ཀུ་མ་ཤོར་གྱི་རེད་ད། "But you'll be robbed!"
ཉེན་ཁ་ཡོད་རེད་ད། "But there is some danger!"
རྟ་ཤོར་སོང་ད། "Watch out, the horse has escaped!"

• པ་pa and its variants ག་-ka, ང་-nga are subject to the same modifications[163] as the interrogative particles པས་-pä', གས་-kä', ངས་ -ngä' (see Lesson 2). Using these implies that the speaker is trying to elicit agreement with what he is saying, and they correspond to tag questions. The may therefore be translated in English by "isn't that so?" or "don't you think?" or conveyed by the intonation.

Ex.: ཁྱེད་རང་གི་ཕྲུ་གུ་ཆེན་པོ་ཆགས་འདུག་ག "My God, how your child has grown!"
ད་ལྟ་ཕྱི་པོ་རེད་པ། "It's late now, isn't it?"
སྐྱིད་པོ་བྱུང་སོང་ང་། "It was very pleasant! Eh?"
ངས་ཁྱེད་རང་ལ་ཞུས་བྱུང་ང་། "I told you, didn't I?"
ཁྱེད་རང་སློབ་སྦྱོང་ཧུར་བརྩོན་ཞེ་དྲགས་བྱེད་ཀྱི་འདུག་ག "You study really hard, don't you?"

33.3.3 The "self-corrective" auxiliaries ཡིན་པ་རེད་, ཡོད་པ་རེད་ *and* ཡོད་པ་ཡིན་པ་རེད་

Lesson 6 introduced auxiliaries (or copulas) corresponding to the English verbs "to be" and "to have". Apart from these, there are so-called "self-corrective" auxiliaries (or copulas) that are used much more rarely. They imply that the speaker has just realized that he was mistaken or that he was hitherto unaware of what he is asserting. Statements using these auxiliaries often begin with ཨ་ལའི་ ālä: "Well, well! Oh, I see!"

As in the case of other mediatory auxiliaries and copulas, a distinction may be made between "essential" and "existential".

• The "self-corrective" essential verb ཡིན་པ་རེད་ y̲i̲npare'.

---

163. However in the allegro speech, they are all pronounced /wa/.

This is used instead of the auxiliary (or copula) re'.

Ex.: ཐུབ་བསྟན་ཡིན་པ་རེད། thūptän y̱inpare' "Ah, it's Thubtän!" [I hadn't realized]
འབྲོག་པ་ཡིན་པ་རེད། tro̱kpa y̱inpare' "Oh, it's a nomad." [I hadn't thought so]
ཨ་ལའི་སྨྱོན་པ་ཡིན་པ་རེད། ālä: nyōnpa y̱inpare' "So, he's crazy!" [I didn't know that]

• The "self-corrective" existential verbs: ཡོད་པ་རེད་ yö̱pare'[164], ཡོད་པ་ཡིན་པ་རེད yö̱payinpare'.

These are used instead of the coplas tu̱' and yo̱:re'. There is a subtle difference between the two. The verb yö̱payinpare' is generally used following a modification or rectification made by the speaker's interlocutor, whereas yö̱pare' is used after the speaker has just corrected himself or herself.

Ex.: ཁོང་རྒྱ་ནག་ལ་ཡོད་པ་ཡིན་པ་རེད། "Ah, I didn't know he was in China!"
སྒྲོལ་དཀར་ལ་སྤུ་གུ་གཉིས་ཡོད་པ་ཡིན་པ་རེད། "So, Drölkar has two children!"
ཨ་ལའི། ཚེ་རིང་ལ་མོ་ཊ་ཡོད་པ་རེད། "Well well, so Tshering has a car!"

33.3.4 The "mnemic" auxiliary ཡིན་པ་ཡོད་ y̱inpayö'

Using this auxiliary implies that the speaker has only a vague recollection of what he is saying. It may be translated by "I seem to remember that…" or "I vaguely remember that…".

Ex.: བོད་ཀྱི་འོང་སྐོར་བཏང་ཡག་དེ་ཟླ་བ་བརྒྱད་པའི་ནང་ལ་ཡིན་པ་ཡོད།
"[I seem to remember that] the harvest festival takes place in August."
སློབ་གྲྭ་ཆེན་མོའི་ནང་ལ་དབྱར་ཁའི་གུང་སེང་གཟའ་འཁོར་བདུན་ཡིན་པ་ཡོད།
"[I vaguely recall that] the university summer vacation lasts seven weeks."

33.4 Exercises སྦྱོང་ཚན།

33.4.1 Translate into English:

༡) ཨ་ལའི། ལྷ་སའི་དབྱར་ཁའི་གནམ་གཤིས་ཚ་གྲང་སྙོམ་པོ་ཡོད་པ་རེད།

༢) ང་ཚོའི་འཛིན་གྲྭར་སློབ་གྲྭ་བ་ཉི་ཤུ་རྩ་ལྔ་ཡོད་པ་རེད།

༣) བསོད་ནམས་ལགས་གུང་སང་མ་གཏོགས་བརྙན་འཕྲིན་གཟིགས་ལོང་ཡོད་མ་རེད།

༤) མདང་དགོང་ང་ཚོས་གློག་བརྙན་ལྟ་ལོང་མ་བྱུང་།

༥) ཁྱེད་རང་ཕེབས་རན་སོང་ན་ང་ལ་གསུངས་རོགས་གནང་། ངས་ཕར་བསྐྱལ་དགོས།

༦) ཀུན་ནོར་བུ་ལགས་བཞུགས་མི་འདུག ཚོགས་འདུར་ཐད་པ་ཡིན་པ་རེད།

164. This form should not be confused with its literary homonym, which has the same meaning as yo̱:re'.

33.4.2 Translate into Tibetan:

1. I seem to remember that New Year is on February 20th this year.
2. Ah, so there was a harvest festival at Chushur!
3. Fancy that, he's a government official!
4. When is the horse race?
5. During the harvest festival, people have fun and drink chang.

33.4.3 Answer the following questions:

༡) སྐུ་གསུང་ཐུགས་རྟེན་ཟེར་ཡག་དེ་ག་རེ་རེད།

༢) སྤྱིར་བཏང་བོད་ལ་འོང་སྐོར་ག་དུས་བཏང་གི་རེད།

༣) འབྲོག་པའི་ས་ཁུལ་ལ་འོང་སྐོར་བཏང་ཡག་ལུགས་སྲོལ་ཡོད་རེད་པས།

༤) བོད་ཀྱི་དུས་ཆེན་གཙོ་བོ་ག་རེ་ག་རེ་ཡོད་རེད།

༥) བོད་ཟླ་ལྔ་པའི་ཚེས་བཅོ་ལྔའི་ཉིན་ག་དུས་ཆེན་ག་རེ་བཏང་གི་རེད།

33.5 Civilization རིག་གཞུང་།

Traditional festivals.

Traditionally, there are a number of festivals in the course of the Tibetan year. Their dates are fixed according to the lunar calendar. Some of these occasions are purely local, and may be specific to a particular monastery, valley or region.

Broadly speaking, there are two main types of celebration: folk-festivals, that follow the rhythm of the agricultural or nomadic cycle, and Buddhist or *Bönpo* religious ceremonies. In actual fact the distinction between the two is not always very clear, to the extent that popular celebrations often have a religious component.

Folk festivals include the New Year ལོ་གསར་ lo̱sar. There are in fact different celebrations depending on the areas:

"The Kongpo New Year" ཀོང་པོ་ལོ་གསར་ kōngpo lo̱sar on the first day of ***the tenth month*** of the lunar calendar in the Kongpo area (usually in November). The Impatients' New Year" རྟོགས་ལྡ་ལོ་གསར་ tō'la lo̱sar on the first day of the ***eleventh month*** (usually in December) is known to exist in Tsang. The "Agrarian New Year" སོ་ནམ་ལོ་གསར་ sōnam lo̱sar falls on the first day of the ***twelfth month*** (usually in January).

"The Royal New Year Festival" རྒྱལ་པོའི་ལོ་གསར་ kyä:pö: losar falls on the first day of ***the first month***, which usually takes place in February. The occasion is celebrated by nearly all Tibetans.

The harvest festival, called འོང་སྐོར་ ongkor, which is held around the end of August or the beginning of September, as well as the རྟ་རྒྱུག་ tākyu' "horse races" of the *drogpa*.

These *ongkor* festivals provide an occasion for a range of activities: horse races, yak races, archery, target shooting, wrestling, singing, music, folk dancing as well as a variety of games. The national drink, *chang*, inevitably flows freely on these occasions.

As for Lhasa, mention should be made of the "great ablution", སྐར་མ་སྡོལ་པ་ kārma tōpa (festival of the *sdol-pa* constellation) which takes place in September.

— The following are the main Buddhist festivals and commemorations:

- "The Great Prayer" or སྨོན་ལམ་ཆེན་མོ་ mōnlam chēnmo, which is held on the fourth day of the ***first month*** (usually in February).
- "The Full Moon Offering" or བཅོ་ལྔ་མཆོད་པ་ chōnga chöpa, which is held on the fifteenth day (the full moon) of the ***first month***. Huge statues of buddhas, bodhisattvas and various effigies made of butter used to be presented on the Bharkor.
- "The Great Offering" or ཚོགས་མཆོད་ཆེན་མོ། tshōkcö' chēnmo, which is held on the twenty-first day of the ***second month*** of the lunar calendar (usually in March). It commemorates the death of the Great Fifth Dalai Lama. Its founder was the regent Sanggyä Gyatso.
- "The Buddha's Parinirvana", corresponding to the ས་ག་ཟླ་བ་ sāka tawa festival, which falls on the full moon of the ***fourth month***.
- "The General Fumigation for the World" or འཛམ་གླིང་སྤྱི་བསང་ tsamling cisang at the full moon of the ***fifth month***.
- "The Fourth Day of the ***Sixth Month***" or དྲུག་པ་ཚེས་བཞི་ thrukpa tshē' shi, which commemorates the day on which the Buddha first taught the Four Noble Truths.
- "The Yogurt Festival" or ཞོ་སྟོན་ shotön, on the thirtieth day of the ***sixth month*** at Dräpung, and then at the Norbu lingka on the first day of the seventh month.
- The commemoration of the "Descent from Paradise", or ལྷ་བབས་དུས་ཆེན་ lhāpap thücen, on the twenty-second day of the ***ninth month***.
- The festival of the goddess Pändän Lhamo དཔལ་ལྷའི་རི་ཁྲོད། pālä: ritrö', on the full moon of the ***tenth month***.
- The festival of the Gandän Ngamchö (commemoration of Lord Tsongkhapa's death) དགའ་ལྡན་ལྔ་མཆོད་(རྗེ་ཙོང་ཁ་པའི་གཤེགས་མཆོད་) kantän ngāmchö, on the twenty fifth day of the ***tenth month***. On this occasion butter lamps are place on the roofs and in the windows of houses and monasteries. In pastoralists' areas, people make a special soup called ལྔམ་ཐུག་ *Ngam-thuk* and offer butter lamps in memory of the cattle that have been slaughtered.

- In addition to the above, within the Tibetan lunar calendar the days of the new moon (the first day of each month), the first quarter (the eighth) and full moon (the fifteenth) are regarded as being particularly auspicious and are marked by special and more intensive religious performances.

In Bhutan and Tibet, so-called ཚེས་བཅུ་ tshē' cū ("Tenth Day") rituals are held in *dzong* and monasteries on different days. In Bhutan, the most important are those of Paro and Thimpu.

"A visit to the doctor"

ཨེམ་ཆི་བསྟེན་པ།

Grammar aims བརྡ་སྤྲོད་རིག་པའི་དམིགས་ཚད།

- The connective "before": མ་ + V + གོང་ལ་ / ma̲ + V(past) + kho̲ng-la.
- The connective "after": V + པའི་རྗེས་ལ་ V(past) + pä: ce̲'-la.
- The connective "after": V + པའི་གཞུག་ལ་ V(past) + pä: shu̲'-la.
- The connective བྱས་ chä̲' "after".

༄། ཆུ་ཐོན་ནས་ཟམ་པ་བརྗེད། ནད་དྲག་ནས་ཨེམ་ཆི་བརྗེད།།

"When you cross the river, you forget the bridge; and when you get better, you forget the doctor."

(proverb)

CD I • Tr. 71

34.1 Dialogue དྲི་བ་དྲིས་ལན།

སྨན་པ་ ༔ ཁྱེད་རང་ག་རེ་སྙུང་གི་འདུག

ནད་པ་ ༔ ང་མགོ་དང་ རྐང་ལག་གི་ཚིགས་གཞི་ག་ས་ག་ལ་ན་གིས། (ན་གི་འདུག)

སྨན་པ་ ༔ ཞལ་ལག་གྱི་བྲོ་བ་སྔར་རྒྱུན་ནང་བཞིན་འདུག་གས།

ནད་པ་ ༔ མི་འདུག ཟོ་ཆས་ལ་བྲོ་བ་མེད་པ་དང་། ཏིག་ཙ་(ཏོག་ཙམ་)བཟས་པ་ད་གར་སྐྱུག་མེར་ལང་གིས།

སྨན་པ་ ༔ ཞལ་གདངས་གནང་ད་(དང་)། ལྡགས་མར་རྐྱངས་གནང་ད། ཨོ། མགུལ་སྙུང་གི་མི་འདུག་གས།

ནད་པ་ ༔ ཟོ་ཆས་མིག་དུས་(མིད་དུས་) མིད་པ་ཏིག་ཙ་ན་གིས།

སྨན་པ་ ༔ ཕྱག་ བསྟན་ རོགས་ གནང་ད། ངས་ ཕྱག་ རྩ་ གཅིག་ ལྟ་ གི་ ཡིན། ཁྱེད་ རང་ མགུལ་ ཆམ་ བཞེས་ པ་ རེད། ཉི་མ་གསུམ་གྱི་གསོལ་སྨན་ཡོད། འདི་ཚོ་བཞེས་ན་ག་ཏན་ག་ཏན་དྲངས་གི་རེད།

ནད་པ་ ༔ ཨེམ་ཆི་ལགས། སྨན་འདི་ཚོ་ག་འདྲས་ཟེ་ཟ་དགོས་རེད།

སྨན་པ་ ༔ རིལ་ བུ་ དམར་ པོ་ འདི་ ཞོགས་ གས་ (ཞོགས་ པ་)ཞལ་ ལག་ རྗེས་ ལ་ རིལ་ བུ་ གསུམ་ ཆུ་ ཁོལ་ དྲོད་ འཇམ་ གྱིས་ བཞེས་ རྒྱུ་ དང་། དགོངས་ དྲོ་ མ་ གཟིམ་ གོང་ ལ་ ཐང་ འདི་ ཕྱིར་ ནས་ མཆོད་ བྱས་ གཟིམ་ ཆས་ དྲོ་ པོ་ བཞེས་ ནས་ གཟིམ་ བྱས་ ཧྲལ་ནག་དོན་པ་གནང་དགོས་རེད།

ནད་པ་ ༔ ཐུགས་ཆེ་གནང་། བཞུགས་གདན་འཇགས་གོ

སྨན་པ་ ༔ ག་ལེར་ཕེབས།

Translation

Doctor	—	What seems to be the problem? (lit. with what are you ill?)
Patient	—	My head and the joints of all my limbs are hurting.
Doctor	—	Does your food taste as it usually does?
Patient	—	No, food has no taste. Right after I eat, I feel sick.
Doctor	—	Open your mouth and put out your tongue. Is your throat sore?
Patient	—	When I swallow anything, my throat hurts a little.
Doctor	—	Show me your arm. I'm just going to take your pulse. You've caught a cold. Here's some medicine for three days. If you take it, you'll certainly get better.
Patient	—	How should I take these medicines, doctor?
Doctor	—	You should take three of these red pills after breakfast in lukewarm boiled water. In the evening, before going to bed, you should make a decoction with this pill. Then after you've gone to bed, you should cover yourself with a warm blanket in order to sweat.
Patient	—	Thank you, goodbye.
Doctor	—	Goodbye.

ཀ་ཁ་ག་ང་

34.2 Vocabulary ཚིག་གསར།

ནད་པ་ nä̱pa	(n.) patient
ནམ་རྒྱུན ṉamkyün སྔར་རྒྱུན་ ng̱arkyu̱n	(n.) usual, customary
ལྟོ་ཆས་ tō(p)cä'	(n.) food
རྐང་ལག་ kāngla'	(n.) limb
ཚིགས་གཞི་ tshīkshi	(n.) joint
ཐང་ thāng	(n.) pill for decoctions
རྔུལ་ནག་ ngǖ:na'	(n.) sweat
རིལ་བུ་ ri̱:pu	(n.) pill
རྩ་སྨན་ tsāmän	(n.) medicinal herb
གསོ་བ་རིག་པ་ sōwa ri̱kpa	(n.) medicine
རྩ་ tsā ཕྱག་རྩ་ chāktsa (H)	(n.) pulse, vein, nerve
གསེར་ཁབ་ sērkap	(n.) "golden needle", a type of acupuncture
མེ་བཙའ་ me̱tsa	(n.) moxibustion
སྨན་པ་ mā̈npa	(n.) doctor, physician
གཏན་གཏན་ tā̈ntän	(adv.) certainly, surely
གཞི་ནས་ shi̱nä'	(adv.) only now, from now on
དྲོད་འཇམ་ thrö̱ncam	(adj.) warm
ན་ na̱ སྙུང་ nyūng (H)	(v.) [inv., A] ill (to be)
སྐྱུག་མེར་ + ལང་ kyūkmer la̱ng	(v.) [inv., A] to feel ill
སྐྱུག་པ་ + ཤོར་ kyūkpa shōr	(v.) [inv., A] to vomit
ཁ་ + གདངས་ khā ta̱ng	(v.) [vol., E] to open one's mouth
ཞལ་གདངས་ + གནང་ shä̱:tang nāng (H)	(v.) [vol., E] to open one's mouth

ཆམ་པ་ + རྒྱག་ chāmpa kya̲' (v.) [inv., E] to catch cold
མགུལ་ཆམ་ + བཞེས་ kü̲:cam she̲' (H) (v.) [inv., E] to catch cold
རྟག་དཔྱད་ + བྱེད་ tākcä' che̲' (v.) [vol., E] to examine
ཞིབ་འཇུག་ + བྱེད་ shi̲mcu' che̲' (v.) [vol., E] to do research
ཁྱིར་ ti̲r (v.) [vol., EA] to make a decoction
མིད་ mī' (v.) [vol., EA] to swallow
དྲག thra̲' དྭངས་' tha̲ng' (H) (v.) [inv., A] to get better, recover

34.3 Remarks འགྲེལ་བཤད།

34.3.1 The connective གོང་ལ kho̲ng-la "before"

This connective is associated with the verb in the past tense form. The verb itself must be preceded by a negation.[165]

Ex.: ང་མ་ཕྱིན་གོང་ལ་ལས་ཀ་འདི་ཡིན་གཅིག་མིན་གཅིག་ཚར་དགོས་རེད།
"I really must finish this work before going."
ཁྱེད་རང་མ་གཟིམ་'གོང་ལ་རིལ་བུ་གསུམ་མཆོད་དགོས་རེད།
"You should take three pills before sleeping."

34.3.2 The connectives རྗེས་ལ་ ce̲'-la "after" and གཞུག་ལ་ shu̲'-la "after"

These connectives accompany the verb in the past tense. Moreover, the verb is nominalized with the suffix པ་ -pa and takes the genitive case.

Ex.: ཁོང་ཚོས་དཀའ་མོལ་གནང་པའི་རྗེས་ལ་ཐག་གཅོད་གནང་པ་རེད།
"After holding a discussion, they reached a decision."
དེབ་འདི་བལྟས་པའི་གཞུག་ལ་གནས་ཚུལ་གཞི་ནས་ཧ་གོ་པ་རེད།
"After reading this book, he understood the situation."

34.3.3 The connective བྱས་ chä̲'

This has the same meaning as the ablative ནས -nä' in its connective function (that is, when -nä' is used after a verb). This usage exists only in the spoken language.

Ex.: ཁྱེད་རང་གཟིམ་བྱས་རྔུལ་ནག་འདོན་པ་གནང་དགོས་རེད།
"After you go to bed, you have to sweat."
ཁ་ལག་རྒྱས་པོ་ཞེ་དྲགས་བཟས་བྱས་གཞས་རྣམ་ཐར་བཏང་བྱས་བསྡད་ཀྱི་རེད།
"When they've eaten well, they sit and sing Tibetan operatic songs."

165. The connective "before" is associated with the negation in various languages. This is the case for example in Literary French: "avant que + *negation*".

34.4 Exercises སྦྱོང་ཚན།

34.4.1 Translate into Tibetan:

1. How long have you been ill?
2. I often have headaches.
3. After taking the medicine, he sweated heavily.
4. May I take (lit. look at) your pulse?
5. How should these pills be taken?
6. When she sees raw meat, she feels ill.
7. One should not drink tea before going to bed.

34.4.2 Translate into English:

༡) ཁོང་ཆམ་པ་བརྒྱབ་ཙང་ཡོང་ཐུབ་ཀྱི་མ་རེད།

༢) ངས་དངུལ་གཡར་ནས་སྠག་སྠག་ཉོས་པ་ཡིན།

༣) གསོལ་ཇ་མ་མཆོད་གོང་ལ་ཇ་དམ་དཀྲུག་དཀྲུག་བཏང་རོགས་གནང་།

༤) ཁོང་ཚོ་གཞིས་ཀ་རྩེ་ལ་མ་ཕེབས་གོང་ལ་ང་ཚོས་དགའ་སྟོན་ཞུ་དགོས་ཡོད།

༥) སློབ་གྲྭ་བ་ཚོས་ གྲོང་གསེབ་མ་ཕྱིན་གོང་ལ་ཉོ་ཆ་མང་པོ་བརྒྱབ་སོང་།

༦) ཡི་གེ་མ་བྲིས་གོང་ལ་བསམ་བློ་ཡག་པོ་བཏང་དགོས་རེད།

༧) ང་ཚོ་རི་དེའི་སྐད་ལ་ཉིན་གུང་ཞལ་ལག་བསྣམས་བྱུས་ཕེབས་གས།

༨) ང་ཆམ་པ་བརྒྱབ་ཙང་གྲོ་བ་ཤོར་བཞག

34.4.3 Answer the following questions:

༡) བོད་སྨན་ག་རེས་བཟོ་གི་རེད།

༢) བོད་ཀྱི་གསོ་བ་རིག་པའི་ནང་ལ་སྨན་པས་ནད་པ་ལ་ག་འདྲས་ཟེ་བརྟག་དཔྱད་བྱེད་ཀྱི་རེད།

༣) བོད་སྨན་རིགས་ག་རེ་ག་རེ་ཡོད་རེད།

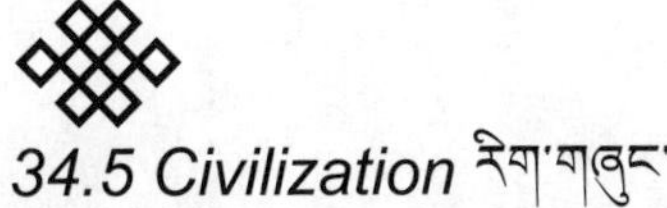

34.5 Civilization རིག་གཞུང་།

Tibetan medicine.

This is a traditional medical system based on plants, minerals and certain animal products. Diagnosis is performed by examining the patient's pulse and, less commonly, his or her urine. Before and during the examination the doctor asks the patient questions that reveal aspects of temperament, daily habits, and living conditions. Medicinal herbs (*tsamän* རྩ་སྨན་) are gathered at specific times of year, and are subjected to meticulous processing. The compound treatments are in the form of pills, decoctions and powders. Tibetan doctors also practice moxibustion (*metsa* མེ་བཙའ་), a form of acupuncture (*serkhap* གསེར་ཁབ་), as well as massage.

The essentials of Tibetan medicine are contained in a treatise entitled "Gyüzhi" (རྒྱུད་བཞི་) and its numerous commentaries. Tibetan medicine works slowly, but is reputed to be particularly effective in the treatment of certain conditions such as hepatitis, ulcers, chest complaints and cerebral congestion.

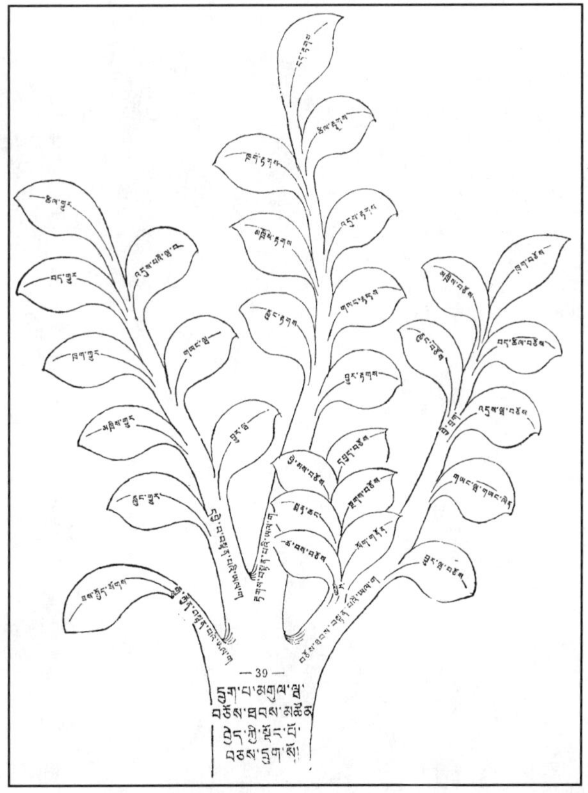

Medical diagram for treating goiters

"Illness"

ན་ཚའི་སྐོར།

> *Grammar aims* བརྡ་སྤྲོད་རིག་པའི་དམིགས་ཚད།
>
> • Causative and resultative verb pairs.

CD II • Tr. 1

35.1a Dialogue དྲི་བ་དྲིས་ལན།

རྡོ་རྗེ་ ༔ ཆུ་ཚན་ལ་ཕྱིན་ནས་ངའི་གྲུམ་བུའི་ན་ཚ་དེ་བསླང་སོང་སྟེ་ད་དྲག་ངེ་བསྟན་གིས། ཡིན་ནའི། ཨེམ་ཆི་ཅིག་བསྟེན་དགོས་བྱེད་པ་(བྱེད་པ་འདུག) དྭགས་པོའི་བརྒྱུད་འདོ་པར་(འདི་པར་)ཨེམ་ཆི་གཅིག་རག་ཨ་ཡོང་། འདོ་པར་མེད་ནའི་(ནའང་) རྩེ་ཐང་ལ་གཏན་གཏན་ཡོད་ཀྱི་རེད།

སྒྲོལ་བཟང་ ༔ ཡོད་ད་ཡོད། དེར་མི་དམངས་སྨན་ཁང་དང་སྒེར་གྱི་སྨན་ཁང་གཉིས་ཀ་ཡོད་རེད། ང་གཉིས་མོ་ཏ་གཅིག་སྒྲུག་ན་ཡག་ག་མི་ཡོང་ངས།

རྡོ་རྗེ་ ༔ ད་ག་རང་རེད། ཟམ་པ་དེ་ཕར་དོན། ཤིང་སྡོང་པ་གིའི་འོག་ལ་བཞུགས་དོ། མོ་ཏ་ཅིག་མ་སླེབས་བར་དུ་ཇ་གཅིག་བསྐོལ་ག

སྒྲོལ་བཟང་ ༔ ཨཙུ། ཇ་སྐོལ་ལོང་ད་ཨ་ཡོང་།

རྡོ་རྗེ་ ༔ ཨོའོ། པ་ནས་ཚུར་མོ་ཏ་ཅིག་ཡོང་གིས(ཡོང་གི་འདུག)

སྒྲོལ་བཟང་ ༔ ཨ་ལྕག་ལགས། ང་གཉིས་རྩེ་ཐང་བར་དུ་འཁྱིད་གནང་ཐུབ་པ་འདུག་གས། ངའི་རོགས་པ་འདི་ཏིག་ཙ་(ཏོག་ཙམ་)བདེ་པོ་རང་མི་འདུག

ཁ་ལོ་པ་ ༔ འོང་འགྲིག་གི་རེད། བདེ་པོ་མེད་ན་མོ་ཏའི་ནང་ལ་ཡར་ཤོག དོ་དགོང་རྩེ་ཐང་ལ་འབྱོར་གྱི་རེད།

Translation

Dorje — I went to the hot springs, and that gave me another bout of rheumatism. It seems to be getting better now. Still, I'd better see a doctor, although there isn't likely to be one in this part of Dhagpo. Even if there isn't one here, there's bound to be one in Tsethang.

Lobzang — Oh, for sure. Tsethang has both a public and a private hospital. Perhaps we should wait for a car.

Lobzang — Good idea. Let's cross the bridge and sit under that tree. We can make some tea before a car comes.

Lobzang — Oh, I doubt that there'll be time to make tea!

Dorje — Hey, there's a car coming this way.

Lobzang — Excuse me Miss, could you give us a lift to Tsethang? My friend isn't very well.

The driver — Sure. If you're not feeling well, come on into the car. We'll be in Tsethang this evening.

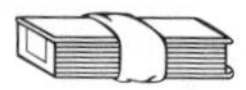

CD II • Tr. 2

35.1b Text རྩོམ་ཡིག

ཨ་ཁུ་སྟོན་པའི་སྒྲུང་།

༄། ཨ་ཁུ་སྟོན་པའི་ལུང་པའི་ནང་ལ་མི་ཚང་ཕྱུག་པོ་ཅིག་ཡོད་པ་དང་། དེའི་པ་ཕའི་མགོ་ལ་སྐྲ་ཡོད་མ་རེད། ཨ་ཁུ་སྟོན་པས་ཁོ་ལ་མགོ་སྐོར་ཅིག་བཏང་དགོས་བསམ་ནས་ཉིན་ལྟར་མི་ཚང་དེའི་སྒོ་འགྲམ་ནས་ལུང་པའི་མདའ་ལ་འགྲོ་ཁག་བྱེད་ཀྱི་ཡོད་རེད། ཉི་མ་ཅིག་ཕྱུག་པོ་དེས་ཨ་ཁུར་ལྷ་ཡེ་ཨ་ཁུ། ཁྱེད་རང་ཉིན་ལྟར་རེ་བཞིན་ལུང་པའི་མདའ་ལ་ག་རེ་གནང་གར་ཕེབས་ཀྱི་ཡོད་ཟེ་དྲིས་པ་རེད། ཨ་ཁུས་ལུང་པའི་མདའ་ལ་གླད་དམར་ར་(སྤྱི་ཐེར་)མང་པོ་ཅིག་འདུག ངས་ཉི་མ་ཁ་ཤས་སྐྲ་བཙུག་ནའི། ད་དུང་བཙུགས་ཚར་མ་སོང་ཟེ་ལབ་པ་རེད། མི་དེའི་སེམས་ལ་མགོ་ལ་སྐྲ་འཛུགས་རྒྱུ་ཡོད་པ་དེ་རིང་མ་གཏོགས་གོ་མ་མྱོང་། ཨ་ཁུ་སྟོན་པ་རིག་པ་ཅན་རང་རེད། མགོ་ལ་སྐྲ་འཛུག་ཐུབ་པ་དཔེ་རང་རེད། ད་ཡག་པོ་བྱུང་བསམ་ནས་ཨ་ཁུ་སྐུ་མཁྱེན་ང་ལ་ཡའི་སྐྲ་འཛུགས་རོགས་གནང་ཟེ་བཤད་ནས་ཨ་ཁུས་ལགས་སོ་ཞུ་དང་ཞུ། ངས་གནང་ཉིན་ཀར་ཞོགས་གས་བཅར་ཆོག་ཟེ་ལབ་པ་རེད། ཉི་མ་གཉིས་རྗེས་ལ་ཨ་ཁུས་ཁོང་ཚོའི་ནང་ལ་ཕྱིན་ནས་མི་ཚང་དེས་ཨ་ཁུར་གསོལ་སྟོན་ཟབ་རྒྱས་ཞུས། ཨ་ཁུས་ཁ་ལག་བཟས་ཚར་པའི་རྗེས་ལ། ཡབ་ཆེན་དགུ་བཞེལ་གནང་རོགས་གནང་། དེ་ཤུལ་ལ་ངས་སྟུང་བུ་འདི་སྟོ་པོ་ཅིག་བསྟར་གྱི་ཡིན་ཟེ་བཤད་ནས་སྟུང་བུ་འཕོམ་པོ་ཅིག་བཏོན་ནས་བསྟར་པ་རེད། པ་ཕས་ཨ་ཁུ། སྟུང་བུ་བསྟར་ནས་ག་རེ་གནང་ག་ཟེ་དྲིས་པ་དང་། ཨ་ཁུས་སྟུང་བུ་རེ་རེ་བཙུག་པའི་ཤུལ་ལ་སྐྲ་ཀང་རེ་རེ་བཙུག་དགོས་རེད་ཟེ་བཤད་པ་རེད། པ་ཕ་དེ་ཞེད་ཐག་ཆོད་བྱུས་ཨ་ཁུ་ལགས། དེ་འདྲས་ཟེ་བཙུགས་ན་མི་ཤི་གི་མ་རེད་པས་ཟེ་ལབ་པ་རེད། ཨ་ཁུས། ཁ་ཤས་ཤི་པ་ཡའི་(ཡང)ཡོང་གིས།(ཡོང་གི་འདུག) ཁ་ཤས་དྲག་པ་ཡའི་ཡོང་གིས། ཁ་ཤས་སྐྲ་འཛུགས་མི་དགོས་པ་གནང་རོགས་གནང་ཟེ་མར་ཀྲོག་ཕུལ་ནས་དགོངས་པ་ཞུ་མཁན་ཡའི་ཡོང་གིས་ཟེ་བཤད་པ་རེད། མི་ཚང་དེའི་པ་ཕས། ད་ང་ཡའི་མར་ཀྲོག་ཕུལ་ནས་དགོངས་པ་ཞུ་རྒྱུ་རང་ཡིན་ཟེ་བཤད་ནས་ཨ་ཁུ་ལ་མར་ཀྲོག་ཅིག་སྤྲད་པ་དང་། ཨ་ཁུས་དེ་ཁྱེར་ནས་ནང་ལ་ལོག་ཕྱིན་པ་རེད།།

Translation

"A story of *Akhu Tönpa*"

In Akhu Tönpa's valley there was a rich family. The father of this family was bald. Akhu Tönpa thought of a way to fool him. Every day he would pass in front of this family's door on his way to the lower end of the valley. One day the rich man asked him, "Hey, Akhu, why do you go to the lower end of the valley every day?" Akhu anwered, "There are a lot of bald people in the lower end of the valley. I have been planting hair on their heads for a few days, but I haven't finished yet." The rich man thought, "Until today, I've never heard about planting hair on heads. Akhu Tönpa is really clever. It is extraordinary to be able to plant hair. Well that is great!" Then, he asked: "Akhu, please could you plant hair on my head too?" Akhu answered, "Sure I will! I'll come the day after tomorow." Two days later, Akhu went to their house and the family served him an excellent meal. After he had eaten, Akhu told the father, "Father, please wash your head while I sharpen the awl." Then he pulled out a big awl and began to grind it. The father asked Akhu, "Why are you sharpening the awl?" "I plant one hair in each of the spots where I stick the awl in," he replied. The father got terribly frightened and asked, "If you stick the awl in like that, don't people die?" "Well some die, some recover and some abandon the idea and offer me (as compensation) a pat of butter." The father of this family said, "I am also going to offer you a pat of butter." He gave a pat of butter to Akhu, who took it back home with him.

ཀ་ཁ་ག་ང་

35.2 Vocabulary ཚིག་གསར།

ཁ་ལོ་པ་ khālopa	(n.) driver
མི་དམངས་ mi̱mang	(n., adj.) people, public
སྒེར་ ke̱r	(n.) private
གཞུང་ shu̱ng	(n.) government
སྲིད་གཞུང་ sīshung	(n.) government
འདོ་པར་ to̱par འདི་པར་ ti̱par (L)	(n.) over there
ཆུ་ཚན་ chūtsän	(n.) hot spring
ཁྲག་ཤེད་ thrākshe'	(n.) blood pressure
ན་ཚ་ na̱tsa སྙུང་གཞི་ nyūngshi (H)	(n.) illness
ཤིང་སྡོང་ shīngtong	(n.) tree
སྙུང་གུ་ nyūngku སྙུང་བུ་ nyūngpu (L)	(n.) awl
ཀླད་དམར་ར་ lǟmarra སྤྱི་ཐེར་ cīter (L)	(n.) bald
མར་གྲོག་ ma̱r trō'	(n.) pat of butter
གྲུམ་བུའི་ན་ཚ་ thru̱mpü: na̱tsa	(n.) rheumatism, arthritis
སྙིང་གི་ན་ཚ་ nyīng-ki na̱tsa	(n.) heart disease
གློ་ནད་ lōnä'	(n.) lung disease, pneumonia
མཆིན་པའི་ན་ཚ་ chīnpä: na̱tsa	(n.) liver disease, hepatitis
མཛེས་ནད་ tse̱nä'	(n.) leprosy
གྲིབ་ thri̱p	(n.) cerebral stroke

ལ་དུག་ la̲tu'	(n.) mountain sickness
རོགས་པ་ ro̲kpa	(n.) friend, companion
ན་ཚ་བཏང་ na̲tsa tāng	(v.) [inv., AD] to hurt
སྙུང་གཞི་བཏང་གནང་ nyūngshi tāngnang	(v.) [inv., AD] to hurt
སྒུག་ ku̲' ཕེབས་སྒུག་གནང་ phē'ku' nāng (H)	(v.) [vol., EA] to wait
འཁྲིད་ thrī' འཁྲིད་གནང་ thrī'-nang (H)	(v.) [vol., EA] to drive, lead
བསླང་ lāng	(v.) [vol., EA] to raise, cause (*caus.*)
བསྟེན་ tēn	(v.) [vol., EA] to consult, visit
བསྐོལ་ kȫ:	(v.) [vol., EA] to boil (*caus.*)
འཁོལ། khȫ:	(v.) [inv., A] to boil (*res.*)
འཁྲོད་ thrȫ'	(v.) [inv., A] to get used to, to endure
དྲག་ངོ་བསྟན་ thra̲'ngo tā̈n	(idiom.) to show signs of getting better

Proper nouns

རྩེ་ཐང་ tsētang	Tsethang (town)
ཨ་ཁུ་སྟོན་པ་ āku tȫnpa	Akhu Tönpa (folktale character)

35.3 Remarks འགྲེལ་བཤད།

35.3.1 Causative and resultative verbs

There is an ancient morphogical verb opposition in Tibetan which corresponds to a causative derivation. This morphological opposition has generated verb pairs: a causative verb, both transitive and volitional, is derived[166] from a basic verb which is usually both intransitive and non-volitional. This basic verb stem is referred to here as the resultative form.

The two verbs that comprise each pair are phonetically very close, and in most cases their pronunciation differs only in terms of *tone* or *aspiration.*

The causative derivation is essential in many Tibet-Burman languages as well as in Classical Tibetan (with over 200 verb pairs) and in some archaic dialects of Amdo, but in Central Tibetan and in the Standard Spoken language, it applies only to a few dozen verbs.

Ex.: བཅག་ cā' "to break" (caus.), ཆག་ chā' "to break" (res.); སྙལ་ nyā̈' "to lay" (caus.), ཉལ་nyä̲: "to lie" (res.); བཀག་ kā' "to stop" (caus.), འགག་ ka̲' "to stop" (res.); བསླངས་ lāng' "to raise" (caus.), ལང་ la̲ng "to rise" (res.); གཏོར་tōr "to scatter" (caus.), འཐོར་ thōr, "to scatter, be scattered" (res.); སྐོལ་ kȫ: "to boil" (caus.), འཁོལ་khȫ: "to boil" (res.); སྐོར་ kōr "to stir,

166. Many of the causative verbs were formed by a morpheme "s" attached to the verb. This is still visible in the Tibetan orthography: *'khol* (resultative) > *skol* (causative), *nyal* (res.) > *snyal* (caus.), *lang* (res.) > *slang* (caus.), *'khor* (res.) > *skor* (caus.), etc.

turn" (caus.), འཁོར་ khōr "to stir, turn" (res.); བཏོན་ tōn "to take out" (caus.), ཐོན་ thö̲n "to go out" (res.); ཕབ་ phāp "to bring down, take down" (caus.), འབབ་ pa̲p "to descend, get down" (res.); སྒྲོལ་ trö̲: "to free" (caus.), གྲོལ་ thrö̲: "to be freed" (res.); དབྲལ་rǟ: "to tear" (caus.), རལ་ rä̲: "to tear" (res.); བཅད་ cǟ' "to cut" (caus.), ཆད་chǟ' "to be cut" (res.), etc.

Compared to the basic resultative stem, the causative always has an additional argument corresponding to an **intentional agent** performing the action.

If the resultative is intransitive, the causative is transitive.

If the resultative is transitive, the causative is ditransitive (see the examples below)

It emerges from the above that all the **causative verbs are transitive and volitional** since they imply an agent is intentionally performing an action on an object or a patient. Resultative verbs are usually intransitive and non-volitional.

Ex.: ཐག་པ་ཆད་སོང་། resultative: "The rope broke."
[the rope got cut by itself, without any intentional cause]
ཁོང་གིས་ཐག་པ་བཅད་སོང་།causative: "He cut the rope."
[an agent cut the rope intentionally]
ཤེལ་སྒོ་ཆག་བཞག resultative: "The pane broke."
[the pane broke by itself, without any intentional cause]
ཕྲུ་གུ་ཚོས་ཤེལ་སྒོ་བཅག་སོང་།causative: "The children broke the pane."
[the children intentionally broke the pane]
མ་ཎི་འཁོར་བསྡད་བཞག resultative: "The prayer wheel is still spinning."
[Nobody is now making it spin, it spins by itself]
རྨོ་ལགས་ཀྱིས་མ་ཎི་བསྐོར་སོང་ resultative: "The old lady has turned the prayer wheel."
[An agent has intentionally turned the wheel]
ཡི་གེ་རལ་བཞག resultative: "The letter is torn."
ཁོང་གིས་ཡི་གེ་དབྲལ་པ་རེད། causative: "He tore the letter (intentionally)."

Certain resultative intransitive verbs may, in some cases, allow the use of an unintentional agent.

Ex.: ཁོང་གིས་ཡི་གེ་རལ་བཞག "He tore [res.] the letter (unintentionally)."
ཕྲུ་གུ་ཚོས་ཤེལ་སྒོ་ཆག་བཞག "The children broke [res.] the pane (unintentionally)."

However, this construction is rather rare in Standard Spoken Tibetan. Some speakers prefer to use other constructions such as the sentence below which has a similar meaning:

ཕྲུ་གུ་ཚོས་གཟབ་གཟབ་མ་བྱས་ཙང་ཤེལ་སྒོ་ཆག་བཞག

"Because the children were not careful, the pane broke."

The resultative verbs include a few intransitive volitional and transitive volitional forms. In such cases, the corresponding causative verbs have a supplementary actant that itself acts on another agent.

Ex.: ཕྲུ་གུ་ཁོ་རང་གིས་ཕྱུ་པ་གོན་པ་རེད།

"The child herself put on [res.] her chuba."

ཨ་མས་ཕྲུ་གུ་ལ་ཕྱུ་པ་སྐོན་པ་རེད།

"The mother put the chuba on [caus.] the child."[167] (ditransitive)

རྒན་ལགས་ལང་ཐུབ་ཀྱི་མི་འདུག

"Thc old lady can't get up [res.]."

ངས་རྒན་ལགས་བསླངས་པ་ཡིན།

"I helped the old lady to get up [caus.]."

Causative and resultative verbs can appear in the same sentence. The causative puts emphasis on **the cause of the process and the effort of the agent** in performing the action, while the resultative verb is concerned only with **the result or the consequence** of that action. Such constructions may therefore be translated by using the verbs "to succeed", "to manage", "can" or other modal expressions.

These constructions which frequently occur in the literary language also appear in the spoken language.

Ex.: བསྔགས་པས་ཆར་པ་ཕབ་ནས་དངོས་ནས་བབས་སོང་ང་།

"After the ngagpa had (performed a ritual to) make rain fall, rain did indeed fall!"

རས་འདི་དཔེ་གྲོག་མཐྲགས་པོ་འདུག   ག་ཚོད་དྲལ་ནའི་རལ་གྱི་མི་འདུག

"This cloth is very strong, I can't tear it!" (lit. however much I [try to] tear it it won't tear)

The following examples are taken from literary texts:

མ་བྲིས་སེམསཀྱི་རི་མོ་སུབ་ཀྱང་ཟུབ་རྒྱུ་མི་འདུག

"Even if one rubs, one cannot rub out the undrawn lines on the heart." [caus.: སུབ་ res.: ཟུབ་]

ནང་རང་སེམས་བཟུང་བས་མ་ཟིན་ན་ཕྱི་གཞན་ལུས་བཟུང་བསཅི་ལ་ཕན

"If you try to control your own mind inside and you don't succeed, then what's the use of catching somebody else's body outside." [caus.: བཟུང་res.: ཟིན་]

---

167. The verb *skon* belongs to the literary or formal register. In the conversational language, the verb *g.yogs* is used instead.

ཁོང་གི་མན་ཌལ་གྱི་སྟེང་ན་གཡུ་ཞིག ཡོད་པ་བྱི་བ་ཞིག་གིས་བཏེག་པས་མ་ཐེག་པ་ལ།

"[Once], he [saw] a mouse trying to move a turquoise that was on his mandala. But the mouse could not lift the jewel on its own, so…" [caus.: བཏེག་ res.: ཐེག་]

35.4 Exercises སྦྱོང་ཚན།

35.4.1 Tell the story of Akhu Tönpa in your own words.

35.4.2 Translate into English.

༡) བོད་ལ་མི་ཚང་མས་བྱ་གཏོར་བྱེད་ཀྱི་རེད་པས།

༢) ཁྲག་ཤེད་མཐོ་ཙམ་འདུག དེ་ས་མཐོ་པོ་སླེབས་ནས་ས་ཆུ་མ་འཁྱོད་ཙང་བྱུས་པ་རེད།

༣) ངས་ཇ་བསྐོལ་ནའི་ད་དུང་འཁོལ་མ་སོང་།

༤) དགོང་དག་གཉིད་ཁུག་གི་མི་འདུག ཁ་ལག་ཡའི་ཞེ་དྲགས་ཟ་ཐུབ་ཀྱི་མི་འདུག

༥) ང་ཚོས་ཤིང་དེ་བཅད་ནའི་ ཆོད་མ་སོང་།

35.4.3 Choose the causative or resultative verb according to the context.

བཅག་ ཆག་ བཀག་ འགག་ སྐོལ་ འཁོལ་ གཏོར་ འཐོར་ སྐོར་ འཁོར་ བཅད་ ཆད་ བཏོན་ དོན་

༡) ལྕགས་པ་བརྒྱབ་ནས་ཤེལ་སྒོ་ (   ) སོང་།

༢) མིད་པ་ (   ) ནས་སྐད་ཆ་བཤད་ཐུབ་ཀྱི་མི་འདུག

༣) ཁོང་གིས་ཆུ་ (   ) ནས་ཇ་བཟོས་སོང་།

༤) ཁོང་གིས་ང་ལ་རྐང་བརྫུག་ནས་་ཆུ་ (   ) བྱུང་།

༥) རྫོ་ལགས་ཀྱིས་ མ་ཇི་ (   ) གྱི་འདུག

༦) ཁོང་གིས་གྲི་བཞུས་ནས་ཐག་པ་ (   ) སོང་།

༧) སྣམ་གྱི་ནང་ནས་ཅ་ལག་ (   ) པ་ཡིན།

35.5 Civilization རིག་གཞུང་།

Sky burials

Several types of funeral are practiced in the Land of Snows. The preservation of remains (*mardung* དམར་གདུང་) was traditionally practiced in the case of kings and high lamas. A thousand years ago interment seems to have been quite widespread, and archaeological research in various parts of Tibet has indeed revealed many burial sites and stone tombs.

In modern times, burial is still performed in certain rare cases, especially if the cause of death is a contagious disease, or in the case of possession by "demonic powers" before death, or in the case of infants. Dead bodies may even sometimes be cast into rivers (*chusham* ཆུ་གཤམས་) and "offered" to the fish. Cremation (*jinsek* སྦྱིན་སྲེག་) is practiced in areas where wood is abundant. When it is not the case, cremation is practiced only for high lamas and officials. The type of funeral that is selected frequently depends on astrological calculations.

The commonest form of funeral throughout Central Tibet, however, is sky burial or *jhator* (བྱ་གཏོར་), literally "scattering to the birds". The dead body is hacked up by a corpse-cutter or *tomdän* (རྟོགས་ལྡན་) who summons the vultures to feast on the remains when he has done his work. The dismemberment is usually attended by a lama or monk, who recites prayers for the deceased. Close relatives generally do not attend the occasion, since the process can obviously be quite an ordeal to watch. Sky burial is well adapted to both the environment and culture of Tibet. The dearth of wood and the fact that the ground is frozen hard for much of the year present difficulties for cremation and interment. Another advantage of dismemberment is that the body disappears quickly – in about half an hour – into the Tibetan sky, whereas burial involves slow decomposition and being eaten by worms and insects. Traditionally, bodies should be disposed of as soon as possible after death to prevent the *namshe* (རྣམ་ཤེས་), the consciousness, of the deceased from returning and trying to reinvest its mortal remains.

"The Tibetan New Year"

ལོ་གསར།

> *Grammar aims* བརྡ་སྤྲོད་རིག་པའི་དམིགས་ཚད།
>
> - The nominalizer སྲོལ་ sȫ:.
> - The aspectual auxiliary ཚར tshār "to finish".
> - The purposive connective ཆེད་དུ་ chētu "in order to".

༄། བཀྲ་ཤིས་བདེ་ལེགས་ཕུན་སུམ་ཚོགས། ཨ་མ་བག་གྲོ་སྐུ་ཁམས་བཟང་། གཏན་དུ་བདེ་བ་ཐོབ་པར་ཤོག

"Best wishes for good fortune, may Mother have good health and happiness."

(New Year's greeting)

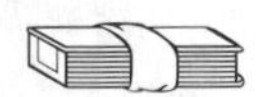

CD II • Tr. 3

36.1a Text རྩོམ་ཡིག

༄།། སྔོན་མ་བོད་ལ་ལོ་གསར་གི་གོང་ལ་དུས་ཆེན་ཅིག་ཡོད་རེད། དེའི་མིང་ལ་དགུ་གཏོར་ཟེར་གྱི་ཡོད་རེད། དུས་ཆེན་དེ་བོད་ཟླ་བཅུ་གཉིས་པའི་ཚེས་ཉི་ཤུ་དགུ་ལ་འཁེལ་གྱི་ཡོད་རེད། དེའི་ཉི་མ་ཉིན་གང་འཚམ་དང་གཏོར་རྒྱག་རྒྱག་གི་ཡོད་རེད། གཏོར་རྒྱག་ནི་ལོ་རྙིང་པའི་གེགས་དཔང་བར་ཆད་སེལ་ཡག་གི་(སེལ་བའི་)ཆེད་དུ་རེད། ད་ག་ནང་བཞིན་ཁྱིམ་ཚང་ནང་ལ་ཡའི་(ཡང་)དགུ་ཐུག་འཐུང་གི་རེད། དགུ་ཐུག་ནང་ལ་སྲན་མ་དང་རྡོ་དང་ཁམ་བུ་དང་སི་པན་དང་བལ་ལ་སོགས་པ་བླུག་གི་རེད། གལ་སྲིད་མི་ཅིག་གི་ཐུག་པའི་ནང་ལ་སི་པན་དོན་པ་ཡིན་ན་དེ་ཁ་ཚ་པོ་ཡོད་པའི་རྟགས་རེད་ཟེར་ཡག་དང་། གལ་སྲིད་ཁམ་བུ་དོན་པ་ཡིན་ན་མི་དེ་ལོ་གསར་པའི་ནང་ལ་ཁམས་བཟང་པོ་ཡོང་ཡག་གི་(ཡོང་བའི་)རྟགས་རེད་ཟེར་སྲོལ་ཡོད་རེད།

སྔོན་མ་ལོ་གསར་གྱི་ཉི་མ་དང་པོ་དེར་ཞོགས་གས་(ཞོགས་པ་)སྔ་པོ་ནས་མི་ཚང་སོ་སོའི་སྒོ་འགྲམ་ལ་འབྲས་དཀར་གྱིས་འབག་དང་བེར་རྒྱག་ཅི་དག་ལ་བཤད་པ་རྒྱག་གི་རེད། དེ་ལ་རྟེན་འབྲེལ་བཟང་པོ་རྩི་གི་རེད་ འབྲས་དཀར་ཟེར་ཡག་(ཟེར་བ་)དེ་ནི་བོད་ཀྱི་སྒྱུ་རྩལ་འཁྲབ་སྟོན་གྱི་རྣམ་གྲངས་གཅིག་རེད། ཞོགས་གས་སྔ་པོ་ནས་ཆང་བསྐོལ་བཏུངས། དེ་ནས་ཕྱེ་མར་དང་ཁ་ཟས་བཀྲུག་གི་རེད། ལོ་གསར་ཉི་མ་གཉིས་པ། ཡང་ན་ཉི་མ་གསུམ་པ་ལ་ཐོག་ཀར་དར་ལྕོག་བཙུག་གི་རེད། དེ་ནས་བསང་བཏང་('གཏོང་')གི་རེད།

CD II • Tr. 4 

36.1b Dialogue དྲི་བ་དྲིས་ལན།

བུ་མོ་ ཿ བཀྲ་ཤིས་བདེ་ལེགས་སྐུ་ཁམས་བཟང་།

ཕ་པ་ ཿ ཨ་མས་ཁྱོད་རང་ལ་ཉལ་སའི་ནང་ལ་བསྐོལ་ལྡན་བཀུགས་བྱུང་ངས།

བུ་མོ་ ཿ བཀོལ་ལྡན་ཞིམ་པོ་དང་ཚ་པོ་ཅིག་གནང་བྱུང་། ད་དུང་ད་ལོ་བཀོལ་ལྡན་ནང་ལ་་བུ་རམ་དང་ཕྱུར་ར་ཞེ་དྲགས་བསྐྱོན་བཞག

ཕ་པ་ ཿ གཟབ་སྦྲོས་མ་བཏང་གོང་ལ་ཁྲུས་བརྒྱབ་པས།

བུ་མོ་ ཿ ཁྲུས་བརྒྱབ་ཚར།

ཕ་པ་ ཿ ད་ཁྱོད་རང་ཕྱིན་ཆོག་ཆོག་ཡིན་པས།

བུ་མོ་ ཿ ལགས་ཡིན།

ཕ་པ་ ཿ ད་བྱུས་ན་ཚོམས་ཆེན་ལ་བཞུགས་གྲལ་བཏང་(གཏོང་)གར་འགྲོ།

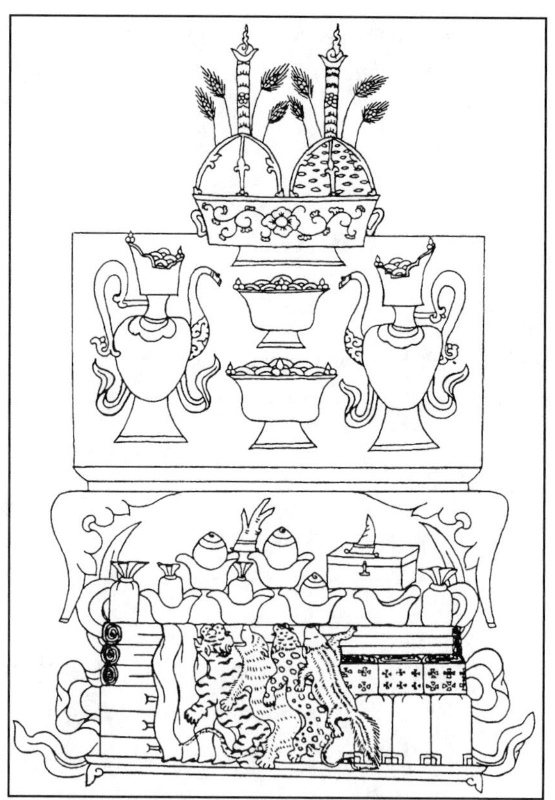

Auspicious Offering

Translation

In the past, in Tibet, there used to be a festival, [just] before the New Year. It was called *Gutor*. This festival was celebrated on the twenty-ninth day of the twelfth month. Throughout the day *cham* [monastic dance] was performed and *torma* were burned. The destruction of the *torma* was aimed at neutralizing the negative karma and the obstacles of the old year. Within families [on the occasion of the *Gutor*], people always drink "soup of nine ingredients". In the soup, they put [inside the dumplings] peas, pebbles, wool, peaches and chili, among other things. It is traditionally said that if you find a chili in the soup, it's a sign that you have a sharp tongue. If you find a peach, it shows that you will enjoy good health in the coming year.

In the past, early in the morning on the first day of the year, the character called *dräkar* would come to the doors of houses and say things about his mask and staff. This was considered to be auspicious. *Dräkar* is a feature of Tibetan dramatic art.

Early on [New Year's] morning, people drink hot *chang,* then make offerings of *tsampa*-and-butter dough and fried pastry. On the second or third day of the New Year they raise prayer flags on the roof and make fumigation offerings [by burning juniper].

Daughter — Best wishes for the New Year and good health!
Father — Did your mother bring you hot *köndän* in bed?
Daughter — She brought me a nice hot *köndän*. What's more, this year she put plenty of cheese and molasses in the *köndän.*
Father — Did you wash before putting on your nice clothes?
Daughter — Yes, I had a wash!
Father — So are you ready to go?
Daughter — Yes.
Father — Well then, let's go and sit in the living room [for the ceremony].

ཀ་ཁ་ག་ང་

36.2 Vocabulary ཚིག་གསར།

དགུ་གཏོར་ ku̲tor — (n.) ceremony of the last day of the year
སྒྱུ་རྩལ་ kyü̲tsä: — (n.) art
གྲོ་སོ་ཕྱེ་མར་ thro̲so chēmar — (n.) arrangement of flour and butter for the New Year
གཏོར་མ་ tōrma — (n.) model, of varying size and complexity, usually made of dough decorated with coloured butter, used in several propitiatory or exorcistic rituals
འབྲས་སིལ་ trä̲si: — (n.) dish of sweetened rice with potentilla tubers
རྟེན་འབྲེལ་ tēmtre: — (n.) karmic interdependence; propitious concatenation of events; ceremony related to this
རྟགས་ tā' — (n.) sign, mark, symbol
ལུག་མགོ་ lu̲'nko — (n.) sheep head, New Year's dish
འཆམས་ chām' — (n.) monastic ritual dance
གེགས་དབང་ khe̲'wang — (n.) calamity, obstacle

བར་ཆད་ pha̲rcä'	(n.) obstacle, obstruction
དགུ་ཐུག་ ku̲tu'	(n.) soup of nine ingredients
བསྐོལ་ལྡན་ kȫntän	(n.) *köndän*, soup based on *chang*
སྲན་མ་ trā̈nma	(n.) peas and other pulses
སི་པན་ sīpän ལྗགས་སྤོད་ (H) ca̲kpö'	(n.) chili
བལ་ phä̲:	(n.) wool
ཕུ་རམ་ phu̲ram	(n.) molasses
ཁ་ཚ་པོ་ khā tshāpo ཞལ་ཚ་པོ་ shä̲: tshāpo (H)	(n.) spicy; fig. sharp-tongued
འབག་ pa̲' ཞལ་འབག་ shä̲pa' (H)	(n.) mask
བེར་རྒྱུག་ phe̲rkyu'	(n.) staff, stick
ཕྱེ་མར་ chēmar	(n.) flour and butter dough
ཁ་ཟས་ khāpsä' ཞལ་ཟས་ shä̲psä' (H)	(n.) fried pastry
ཉི་མ་ཉིན་གང་ nyi̲ma nyi̲nkang	(n.) the whole day
འབྲས་དཀར་ trä̲:kar	(n.) *dräkar*, masked character, symbol of good fortune
ཆོག་ཆོག་ + རེད་ chōco' re̲'	(v.) to be ready
འཁེལ་ khē:	(v.) [inv., A] to coincide, happen
གཟབ་སྒྲོས་ + སྤས་ sa̲ptrö' pā̈' + སྤྲས་ trā̈' (L)	(v.) [vol., E] to put on festive clothes
གཟབ་སྒྲོས་ + བཏང་ sāptrö': tāng	(v.) [vol., E] to put on festive clothes
སེལ་ sē:	(v.) [vol., EA] to clear, eliminate
ཁྲུས་ + རྒྱག་ thrṻ' kya̲'	(v.) [vol., E] to wash
ཞལ་འཁྲུས་ + གནང་ shä̲trü' nāng (H)	(v.) [vol., E] to wash
བཞུགས་གྲལ་ + བཏང་ shu̲kträ: tāng	(v.) [vol., E] to be seated
གཏོར་རྒྱག་ + རྒྱག་ tōrkya' kya̲'	(v.) [vol., E] to destroy *torma*
བཤད་པ་ + རྒྱག shā̈pa kya̲' (H)	(v.) [vol., ED] to make a speech (about)

36.3 Remarks འགྲེལ་བཤད།

36.3.1 The nominalizer སྲོལ་ SN:

Like other nominalizers, this one is attached directly to the verb, which takes the present-future form.

Ex.: འདི་འདྲས་ཟེར་སྲོལ་ཡོད་རེད།

"This is what we usually say."

ཆང་འབུལ་དུས་གཞས་འདི་འདྲས་གཏོང་སྲོལ་ཡོད་རེད།

"When we make a chang offering, this is how we usually sing."

རྟ་དང་བོང་བུ་ཚོང་རྒྱག་པ་ཟེར་སྲོལ་ཡོད་རེད།

"As they say, 'to exchange a horse for a donkey'." (i.e., to make a bad deal)

36.3.2 The secondary verb ཚར་ tshār "to finish"

The verb ཚར་ tshār belongs to the category of secondary verbs, which occupy the same syntactic position as the modal verbs (after the main verb and before the auxiliary). Apart from its usual meaning of "to finish", it may also have the adverbial meaning of "already" or "completely", according to context. When it is used in the first person, the verb may be used without an auxiliary.

Ex.: ཁྲུས་བརྒྱབ་ཚར། "(I've) already washed."
ཁྲུས་བརྒྱབ་ཚར་སོང་། "(He's) already washed."
དེ་ནས་ན་ཚ་དྲག་ཚར་བཞག "Then (he) was completely cured."
ཁྱེད་རང་དངོས་ནས་སྨྱོ་ཚར་འདུག་གས། "Have you really gone completely crazy?"

Note: Depending on the context, the adverb "already" may be translated by the auxiliary nyo̱ng[168] ("to have experienced") or by the auxiliary tshār ("to finish"):

Ex.: ཕྱིན་ཚར། "I've already been there" (just a while ago, so I don't need to go again).
འགྲོ་མྱོང་། "I've already been there" (to India – it's something I've experienced).

36.3.3 The connective ཆེད་དུ་ chētu "in order to"

This connective is used after nominalized verbs to form purpose clauses. It is an elegant construction that also occurs in Literary Tibetan.

Ex.: བོད་ལ་འགྲོ་ཐུབ་ཡག་གི་ཆེད་དུ་བོད་སྐད་ཡག་པོ་སྦྱང་དགོས་རེད།
"In order to go to Tibet, you should learn Tibetan properly."

གཟུགས་པོ་ཐང་པོ་ཡོང་ཡག་གི་ཆེད་དུ་ནམ་རྒྱུན་ལུས་རྩལ་དང་གཙང་སྦྲ་ཡག་པོ་བྱེད་དགོས་རེད།
"In order to be in good health, you should do take regular exercise and keep clean."

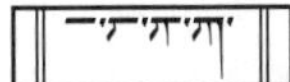

36.4 Exercises སྦྱོང་ཚན།

36.4.1 Translate into Tibetan:

1. He's already gone to the office.
2. The rains have already come this year.
3. Lobzang has already gone to America.
4. Thubtän has finished writing his book.
5. Have you ever drunk köndän?
6. We're about to finish working.

---

168. See 15.3.2.

36.4.2 Translate into English:

༡) ཁོང་ཚོས་ཁང་པ་རྒྱག་ཡག་འགོ་བཙུགས་ཚར་བཞག

༢) ངས་ཁ་ལག་བཟས་ཚར།

༣) ང་གློག་བརྙན་འདི་བལྟས་ཚར། བྱས་ཙང་ཡང་བསྐྱར་ལྟ་གར་འགྲོ་གི་མེད།

༤) ངས་ཁོང་ལ་ད་གིན་ནས་ཞུས་ཚར། ཡིན་ནའི། ཁོང་གིས་དོ་སྣང་གནང་མ་སོང་།

༥) ཁོང་གིས་ཁ་ལག་བཟོ་ཡག་གི་ཆེད་དུ་ཚག་ཤ་དང་ཚལ་ཉོ་གར་ཕྱིན་སོང་།

༦) དགུ་ཐུག་ གི་ ཐུག་ རིལ་ ནང་ ལ་ ག་ རེ་ བླུག་ གི་ རེད་ ཟེར་ ན། ཐུ་རམ་ ཁམ་བུ། བལ། ཤོག་གུ སི་པན། ཚྭ། སོལ་བ། སྨན་མ། རིལ་མ་ ལྡེ་བ་ ཉི་མ་དང་ཟླ་བའི་རྟགས་ལ་སོགས་པ་བླུག་གི་རེད།

36.4.3 Answer the following questions:

༡) དགུ་གཏོར་ཟེར་ཡག་དེ་ག་རེ་རེད།

༢) དགུ་ཐུག་ག་དུས་འཐུང་གི་རེད།

༣) སྐོལ་ལྷན་ཟེར་ཡག་དེ་ག་འདྲས་ཟེ་བཟོ་དགོས་རེད།

༤) ལོ་གསར་ཉི་མ་གཉིས་པ་ཡང་ན་ཉི་མ་གསུམ་པ་ལ་ཁང་པའི་ཐོག་ཀར་ག་རེ་བྱེད་ཀྱི་རེད།

"The Great Prayer and the Full Moon Offering"

སྨོན་ལམ་ཆེན་མོ་དང་བཅོ་ལྔ་མཆོད་པ།

Grammar aims བརྡ་སྤྲོད་རིག་པའི་དམིགས་ཚད།

- The construction V+ པ་མ་ཟད་ "not only", "but"

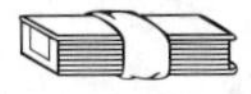

CD II • Tr. 5

37.1 Text རྩོམ་ཡིག

༄། ལྷ་སའི་སྨོན་ལམ་དུས་ཆེན་ནི་ཤར་ཙོང་ཁ་པ་བློ་བཟང་གྲགས་པས་སྤྱི་ལོ་ཆིག་སྟོང་བཞི་བརྒྱ་བཅུ་མེད་དགུའི་ལོ་ལ་གསར་འཛུགས་གནང་པ་རེད། ལོ་རེའི་བོད་ཟླ་དང་པོའི་ཚེས་བཞི་ནས་ཚེས་བཅོ་བརྒྱད་བར་དུ་འཚོག་གི་ཡོད་རེད། ཆིག་སྟོང་དགུ་བརྒྱ་ལྔ་བཅུ་ལྔ་དགུ་བར་དུ་དགེ་འདུན་པ་ཉིས་ཁྲི་ལྷག་ཙམ་འཛོམས་ཀྱི་ཡོད་རེད། དེའི་རིང་ལ་བོད་གཞུང་ནས་དགེ་འདུན་པ་ཚོར་བཞེས་ཐུག་དང་། གསོལ་ཇ་ནར་གཏོང་ཕུལ་(འབུལ་)གྱི་ཡོད་པ་མ་ཟད། འགྱུར་ལྡན་དད་ཅན་ཁག་ནས་ཡའི་(ཀྱང་)གསོལ་ཇ་དང་། བཞེས་ཐུག་སྐུ་འགྱེད་ཅི་དག་ཕུལ་(འབུལ་)མཁན་མང་པོ་ཡོད་རེད། སྨོན་ལམ་ཚུགས་ཤུལ་རིང་གར་(ཡུན་རིང་) ལྷ་སའི་ཁྲིམས་འཛིན་གྱི་དབང་ཆ་ཆ་ཚང་འབྲས་སྤུངས་ཚོགས་ཆེན་ཞལ་ངོ་ལ་ཡོད་རེད། སྨོན་ལམ་སྐབས་སེ་འབྲས་དགའ་གསུམ་གྱི་དགེ་འདུན་གཞུང་བཀའ་པོད་ལྔ་ལ་སློབ་གཉེར་གནང་མཁན་ཚོས་ལྷ་རམས་པ་ཟེར་ཡག་(ཟེར་བའི་)དགེ་བཤེས་ཀྱི་དམ་བཅའ་བཞག་གི་རེད། དེ་ནི་དཔེ་ཆ་བཀླགས་པའི་རྒྱུག་སྤྲོད་བྱེད་སྟངས་ཤིག་རེད། དམ་བཅའ་བཞག་པའི་རྗེས་ལ་ཁོང་ཚོར་དགེ་བཤེས་ལྷ་རམས་པའི་མཚན་ཐོབ་གྱི་རེད། དེ་ནི་རྒྱལ་དབང་སྐུ་ཕྲེང་ལྔ་པས་གཏན་འབེབས་གནང་པ་གཅིག་རེད།

ཐུན་མ་བོད་ཟླ་དང་པོའི་ཚེས་བཅོ་ལྔའི་དགོངས་མོ་ལྷ་སའི་བར་སྐོར་ནང་ལ་བཅོ་ལྔ་མཆོད་པ་སྒྲིག་གཤོམ་བྱེད་ཀྱི་རེད། མཆོད་པ་དེ་ཚོ་ནི་ཚོན་ཁྲ་ཡོད་པའི་མར་གྱིས་བཟངས་(བཞེངས་)པ་ཤ་སྟག་རེད། ད་དུང་སངས་རྒྱས་དང་བྱང་ཆུབ་སེམས་དཔའི་སྐུ་འདྲ་སྣ་མིན་སྣ་ཚོགས་དང་། བཀྲ་ཤིས་རྟགས་བརྒྱད། རྒྱལ་སྲིད་སྣ་བདུན། མཐུན་པ་སྤུན་བཞི་ཅི་དག་ཉམས་འགྱུར་སྣ་ཚོགས་ཡོད་པའི་གཟུགས་བརྙན་འདྲ་མིན་འདྲ་ཡོད་རེད། ཁ་ཤས་''གསང་ཐག་བཏང་ནས་འཁྲུལ་སྐྱོད་བྱེད་ཐུབ་ཀྱི་རེད། བྱས་ཙང་དངོས་འབྲེལ་མི་ཚང་མ་ཏ་ལས་ཡག་དང་ཡ་མཚན་སྐྱེ་ཡག་གི་(སྐྱེ་བའི་) སྒྱུ་རྩལ་ཁྱད་པར་དུ་འཕགས་པ་ཡོད་རེད།།

Translation

The Great Prayer Festival of Lhasa was established in 1409 by Tsongkhapa Lobzang Dhragpa. It is celebrated each year from the fourth to the eighteenth of the first month. Until 1959, more than twenty thousand monks used to assemble. During this period, not only did the government offer soup and tea, but many well-to-do devotees also offered the monks soup, tea or money. In the course of the Great Prayer Festival, all the judicial powers of the City of Lhasa were handed over to the proctor who presided over the general assembly of Dräpung monastery. It was during the Great Prayer Festival that the monks who had studied the five basic subjects [in Lhasa] at [one of the] three monastic seats, Dräpung, Sera or Gandän, would take their doctorates in Buddhist sciences. This was an exam that assessed the study of texts. After their defence, they would obtain the title of *geshe lharampa.* This was instituted by the Fifth Dalai Lama.

In the past, at the full moon of the first Tibetan month, "offerings of the fifteenth" day were presented on the Bharkor. These offerings were made entirely of colored butter. They represented the buddhas, bodhisattvas, the eight auspicious signs, the "four harmonious siblings" [the bird, the hare, the monkey and the elephant], the seven emblems of royalty, etc. These various effigies all had different expressions. Some could be controlled by means of hidden threads, and thus made to move. So it was really a particularly refined art that caused general surprise and amazement.

Philosophical debate

ཀ་ཁ་ག་ང་

37.2 Vocabulary ཚིག་གསར།

སྨོན་ལམ་ཆེན་མོ་ mȫnlam chēnmo	(n.) the Great Prayer [Festival]
བཅོ་ལྔ་མཆོད་པ་ cȫnga chȫpa	(n.) fifteenth-day offering
གཟུགས་བརྙན་ su̱knyän	(n.) image, reflection, effigy
ཤ་སྟག་ shāta'	(adv.) only, solely
དགེ་འདུན་ ke̱ntün	(n.) *sangha*
སྐུ་འདྲ་ kūntra	(n.) statue
མཐུན་པ་སྤུན་བཞི་ thǖnpa pǖnshi	(n.) the four harmonious siblings
རྒྱལ་སྲིད་སྣ་བདུན་ kyä̱:si' nātün	(n.) the seven royal emblems
བཀྲ་ཤིས་རྟགས་བརྒྱད་ trāshi' tā' kyä̱'	(n.) the eight auspicious signs
མ་ཟད་ ma̱sä'	(co.) furthermore, not only
འགྱེད་ kye̱' སྐུ་འགྱེད་ kūnkye' (H)	(n.) food or money offered to monks
ཁྱད་པར་དུ་ khyēpartu	(n.) especially
འཕགས་པ་ phākpa	(n.) noble
སྐུད་པ་ kǖpa	(n.) thread
ཉམས་འགྱུར་ nya̱mkyur	(n.) expression, appearance
སྣ་མིན་སྣ་ཚོགས་ nāmin nātso'	(n.) varied, of different kinds
བོད་གཞུང་ phö̱shung	(n.) Tibetan government
འབྱོར་ལྡན་ co̱rtän	(n.) well-off
དད་ཅན་ tä̱cän	(n.) faithful
ཚོན་ཁྲ་ tshȫntra	(n.) multicolored
ལྷ་རམས་པ་ lhārampa	(n.) doctoral title, the most prestigious obtained during the Mönlam
དགེ་བཤེས་ ke̱she'	(n.) doctor of Buddhist science
དབང་ཆ་ wāngca	(n.) power
སྐུ་ཕྲེང་ kūtreng	(n.) lineage of incarnations
སྐུ་ཕྲེང་ལྔ་པ་ kūtreng ngāpa	(n.) the fifth member of an incarnation lineage
ཁྲིམས་འཛིན་ thrīmtsin	(n.) legislative, judiciary
ཚོགས་ཆེན་ tshōkcen	(n.) general assembly
ཞལ་ངོ་ shä̱:ngo	(n.) proctor, disciplinarian; also, lay title in the pre-1959 administration
རྒྱལ་དབང་ kyä̱:wang	(n.) title of the Fifth Dalai Lama and certain high lamas
གཞུང་བཀའ་པོད་ལྔ་ shu̱ng kāpö' ngā	(n.) five basic studies
ཆ་ཚང་ chātsang	(adj.) whole
གསང་བ་ sāngwa	(adj.) secret, hidden
ཞུལ་རིང་གར་ shü̱:ringkar ཡུན་རིང་ yü̱nring (L)	(adv.) during
རྒྱུག་སྤྲོད་བྱེད་ kyu̱ktrö' che̱'	(v.) [vol., E] to take an exam (oral)

ཡིག་ཚད་བཏང་ yiktsä' tāng — (v.) [vol., E] to take an exam (written)
སློབ་གཉེར་ + གནང་ lōpnyer nāng (H) — (v.) [vol., EA] to undertake (religious) studies
གསར་འཛུགས + གནང་ sā:ntsu' nāng (H) — (v.) [vol., EA] to establish, found
འཛོམས་ tsom — (v.) [vol., A] to gather, convene
སྒྲིག་གཤོམ་ + བྱེད་ trikshom che' — (v.) [vol., EA] to present, exhibit
ཡ་མཚན་ + སྐྱེ་ yamtsän kyē — (v.) [inv., AD] to be amazed
ཧ་ལས་ hā lä' — (v.) [inv., AD] to be amazed
དམ་བཅའ་ + བཞག་ tamca sha' — (v.) [vol., EA] to promise, take vows, defend one's thesis
འགུལ་སྐྱོད་ + བྱེད་ kü:kyö' che' — (v.) [inv./vol., A] to move, stir
གསང་སྐུད་ + བཏང་ sāngkü' tāng — (v.) [vol., E] to pull invisible threads
གསང་ཐག་ + བཏང་ sāngta' tāng — (v.) [vol., E] to pull invisible threads
བཞངས་ shāng' བཞེངས་ shēng'(L) — (v.) [vol., EA] to build, raise
ནར་གཏོང་ + ཕུལ། nartong phṻ: — (v.) [vol., EA] to fulfill a need
གཏན་འབེབས་ + གནང་ tā̈npep nāng — (v.) [vol., EA] to fix, settle

Proper nouns

བློ་བཟང་གྲགས་པ་ lōpsang thrakpa — name of Tsongkhapa, founder of the Gelugpa sect

༣༣༢

37.3 Remarks འགྲེལ་བཤད།

37.3.1 The construction V+ པ་མ་ཟད pamasä' *"not only", "but"*

The formulation pamasä' is connected directly to the verb. It consists of the nominalizer pa and the expression masä'.

Ex.: ཁོང་གིས་བོད་ཡིག་དང་རྒྱ་ཡིག་མཁྱེན་པ་མ་ཟད། ད་དུང་དབྱིན་ཇིའི་ཡི་གེ་མཁྱེན་གྱི་འདུག

"He knows not only (written) Tibetan and Chinese, but also English."

དཔལ་འབྱོར་རང་གི་སློབ་སྦྱོང་ལ་བརྩོན་འགྲུས་བྱས་པ་མ་ཟད་མི་གཞན་དག་ལ་ཡའི་རོགས་རམ་བྱེད་ཀྱི་ཡོད་རེད།

"Not only is Pänjor diligent in his own studies, but he also helps others."

37.4 Exercises སྦྱོང་ཚན།

37.4.1 Answer the following questions:

༡) ལྷ་ས་སྨོན་ལམ་ཆེན་མོ་གསར་འཛུགས་གནང་མཁན་སུ་རེད།

༢) དགེ་བཤེས་ལྷ་རམས་པ་ཟེར་ཡག་དེ་ག་རེ་རེད།

༣) བཅོ་ལྔ་མཆོད་པའི་དུས་ཆེན་སྐབས་ལ་མར་གྱིས་བཞངས་(བཞེངས་)པའི་མཆོད་པ་ག་རེ་ག་རེ་ཡོད་རེད།

༤) མཆོད་པ་དེ་ཚོ་ལ་བལྟ་དུས་མི་ཚང་མ་ཏ་ལས་ཡག་དང་ཡ་མཚན་སྐྱེ་ཡག་གི་རྒྱུ་མཚན་ག་རེ་རེད།

༥) བཅོ་ལྔ་མཆོད་པ་ནི་ཆོས་ལུགས་ཀྱི་དུས་ཆེན་རེད་པས།

37.4.2 Translate into English:

༄༅།། དུས་ཆེན་དེའི་སྐབས་ལ་བར་སྐོར་ནང་ལ་མར་གྱིས་བཟོས་པའི་མེ་ཏོག་དང་མི། སྲོག་ཆགས་སྣ་མི་སྣ་ཚོགས་སྙིང་རྗེ་པོ་དེ་འདྲས་མང་པོ་བསྟན་(སྟོན་)གྱི་རེད། བོད་ཟླ་གསུམ་པའི་ནང་ལ་དུས་ཆེན་ཡོད་མ་རེད། བོད་ཟླ་བཞི་པའི་ནང་ལ་ས་ག་ཟླ་བ་བཏང་གི་རེད། ཆོས་པ་བཅོ་ལྔ་སྟོན་པ་སངས་རྒྱས་བཅོམ་ལྡན་འདས་སྐུ་འཁྲུངས་པ་དང་། སངས་རྒྱས་པ། སྐུ་མྱ་ངན་ལས་འདས་པའི་དུས་ཚོད་ཉི་མ་གཅིག་ལ་མཉམ་དུ་འཁེལ་གྱི་ཡོད་རེད། ལོ་གསར་ཚར་ནས་ཟླ་བ་དང་པོའི་ཆོས་པ་བཞི་ནས་སྨོན་ལམ་ཆེན་མོ་འགོ་ཚུགས་ཀྱི་རེད།

37.4.3 Rewrite the sentences according to the example given:

ཁོས་ཀ་མ་ཀུས་པ་དང་མི་ཡང་བསད་པ་རེད། > ཁོས་ཀ་མ་ཀུས་པ་མ་ཟད། ད་དུང་མི་བསད་པ་རེད།

༡) ཚོང་པ་དེས་དགེ་འདུན་ཚོར་གསོལ་ཇ་ཕུལ་པ་དང་ད་དུང་བཞེས་ཐུག་བཏང་པ་རེད།

༢) ངས་གཞས་བཏང་པ་དང་ཞབས་བྲོ་ཡང་བརྒྱབ་པ་ཡིན།

༣) ང་དེ་རིང་མགོ་ན་པ་དང་ད་དུང་རྐང་པ་ཡང་ན་གི་འདུག

༤) བཀྲ་ཤིས་ཐ་མག་འཐེན་པ་དང་ད་དུང་ཆང་འཐུང་གི་འདུག

"The Great Offering"

ཚོགས་མཆོད་ཆེན་མོ།

Grammar aims བརྡ་སྤྲོད་རིག་པའི་དམིགས་ཚད།

- The connective སྟེ་-te "but".
- Rhetorical questions.

CD II • Tr. 6

38.1a Text རྩོམ་ཡིག

༄༅།། ༡༩༥༩ བར་དུ་ལྷ་སར་བོད་ཟླ་གཉིས་པའི་ནང་ལ་ཚོགས་མཆོད་ཆེན་མོ་འཚུག་གི་རེད། དེའི་དམིགས་ཡུལ་ག་རེ་རེད་ཟེར་ན། (གང་ལགས་ཟེར་ན།) གོང་ས་ལྔ་པ་ཆེན་པོའི་དགོངས་རྫོགས་ཀྱི་ཆེད་དུ་རེད། དེ་འཛུགས་མཁན་ནི་སྡེ་སྲིད་སངས་རྒྱས་རྒྱ་མཚོ་རེད། འོ་ན་ག་དུས་བཙུགས་པ་རེད་ཟེར་ན་སྡེ་སྲིད་སངས་རྒྱས་རྒྱ་མཚོས་རྗེ་བོ་བྲང་སྐུར་བཞེངས་གནང་གྲུབ་པའི་རྗེས་ལ་བཙུགས་པ་རེད། དེའི་མདང་སྔ་ནི་སྤྱིར་བཏང་སྨོན་ལམ་ཆེན་མོ་འདྲ་པོ་རེད་དེ། དམིགས་བསལ་གལ་ཆེ་ཤོས་སེར་ཕང་(སེར་ཕྲེང་)ཆེན་མོ་རེད། སེར་ཕང་ལ་རིན་ཆེན་རྒྱན་ཆ་གོན་མཁན་དང་རྒྱལ་སྲིད་སྣ་བདུན་བཀྲ་ཤིས་རྟགས་བརྒྱད་ཅི་དག་མཆོད་རྫས་སྣ་མིན་སྣ་ཚོགས་དགེ་འདུན་པ་མང་པོས་བསྣམས་ནས་འབབ་སྐྱིག་(འབྲང་སྐྱིག་)གི་རེད། དེ་ནས་འདོད་འཇོའི་བ་མོ་དང་དགེ་སློང་ཉི་མ་རིང་པོ་ཅི་དག་ཐེབས་ཀྱི་རེད།

CD II• Tr. 7

38.1b Dialogue དྲི་བ་དྲིས་ལན།

ཆོས་འཕེལ་ཿ ཁྱེད་རང་གིས་ལྷ་སའི་ཚོགས་མཆོད་གཟིགས་མྱོང་ངས།

བདེ་སྐྱིད་ཿ ཁྲོན་ནས་མཐོང་མ་མྱོང་། སེར་ཕང་(སེར་ཕྲེང་)མ་ཡིན་པ་ག་རེ་ག་རེ་མཐོང་ཡག་ཡོད་རེད།

ཆོས་འཕེལ་ཿ གཏོར་རྒྱག་ཡོད་རེད། དེ་ལ་དམིགས་བསལ་གླུད་འགོང་རྒྱལ་པོ་དོན་གྱི་རེད།

བདེ་སྐྱིད་ཿ དེ་ག་འདྲ་ཅིག་ཡོད་རེད།

ཆོས་འཕེལ་ཿ ཁྲུད་མཚར་པོ་ཅིག་ཡོད་རེད། ཁོའི་འགྲམ་པ་གཡས་པ་དེ་དཀར་པོ་དང་གཡོན་མ་དེ་ནག་པོ་བཟོས་ཡོད་རེད།

བདེ་སྐྱིད་ཿ ཨ་ཙི་དེའི་དོན་དག་ག་རེ་ཡིན་པ་ནོ།

Translation

Until 1959, during the second Tibetan month the Great Offering was held in Lhasa. The purpose was to commemorate the death of the (Great) Fifth Dalai Lama. Its founder was the regent Sanggyä Gyatsho. When was the Great Offering created? It was instituted after the regent Sanggyä Gyatsho had rebuilt the Potala Palace. This ceremony was broadly similar to that of the Great Prayer Festival, but the most important thing was the great procession.

During the latter, [one could see] people lining up, dressed in precious robes as well as many monks carrying a variety of offerings, the eight auspicious signs, the royal emblems and so forth. Then came the wish-fulfilling cow and the character of the monk Nyima Ringpo [who moves extremely slowly].

Chömphel — Have you ever taken part in the Great Offering?
Dekyi — I've never taken part. What is there to see apart from the procession?
Chömphel — The immolation of *torma,* for which the scapegoat (*lügong*) appears.
Dekyi — Oh yes, what's he like?
Chömphel — Very strange. His right cheek is painted white and his left cheek black.
Dekyi — Well, well! I wonder what that means?

ཀ་ཁ་ག་ང་

38.2 Vocabulary ཚིག་གསར།

ཚོགས་མཆོད་ཆེན་མོ་ tshōkcö' chēnmo	(n.) Great Offering
གླུད་འགོང་རྒྱལ་པོ་ lūkong kyä̱:po	(n.) King *lügong*, a character who acts as the scapegoat during the ceremony
གླུད་ lū'	(n.) ransom
དགོངས་རྫོགས་ ko̱ngtso'	(n.) death, death anniversary
དམིགས་ཡུལ་ mī'yü:	(n.) goal, aim
དོན་དག་ tho̱nta'	(n.) meaning, significance
གོང་ས་ kho̱ngsa	(n.) superior position, sovereign
གོང་མ་ kho̱ngma	(n.) emperor; title of certain hierarchs in traditional Tibet
	(adj.) superior, preceding
སྡེ་སྲིད་ te̱si'	(n.) regent
མཛད་སྒོ་ tsä̱ko	(n.) ceremony
སེར་ཕང་ sērpang སེར་ཕྲེང་ sērtreng (L)	(n.) procession
འགྲམ་པ་ tra̱mpa	(n.) cheek
མཆོད་རྫས་ chōtsä'	(n.) items of offering
སེར་སྐྱ་ sērkya	(n.) clergy and laity (lit. yellow and grey)
ག་རེ་ག་རེ་ kha̱re kha̱re	(n.) what sort (of)
རྒྱན་ཆ་ kyä̱nca	(n.) ornaments
གལ་ཆེན་པོ་ khä̱: chēnpo	(adj.) important
ཁྱད་མཚར་པོ་ khyāntsarpo	(adj.) strange

དམིགས་བསལ་ mīksä:	(adj.) special
རིན་ཆེན་ ri̱ncen	(adj.) precious
སྤྱིར་བཏང་ cīrtang	(adv.) in general
དགོངས་པ་ + རྫོགས་ ko̱ngpa tso̱'	(v.) [inv., A] to be extinguished, to die, completely to fulfill one's wishes
སྐྱར་བཞེངས་ + གནང་ kyārsheng nāng	(v.) [vol., EA] to reconstruct, renovate
ཡིན་པ་ནོ་ yi̱npano (H.)	(aux.) see རེད་ *red*
ག་རེ་རེད་ཟེར་ན་ kha̱re re̱' se̱r-na	(idiom.) if you ask why, because, since, for
གང་ཡིན་ཟེར་ན་ kha̱ng yi̱n se̱r-na (L)	(idiom.) if you ask why, because, since, for

Proper nouns

དགེ་སློང་ཉི་མ་རིང་པོ་ ke̱long nyi̱ma ri̱ngpo	Gelong Nyima Ringpo
སངས་རྒྱས་རྒྱ་མཚོ་ sāngkyä' kya̱(m)tso	Sanggyä Gyatsho
འདོད་འཇོའི་བ་མོ་ tö̱cö: pha̱mo	"Wish-fulfilling cow"

38.3 Remarks འགྲེལ་བཤད།

38.3.1 The connective སྟེ་ tē/ -te.

In Literary Tibetan, the adversative connective སྟེ་ -te "but" has several variants according to the last letter of the preceding syllable.

- after ག་ ང་ བ་ མ་ འ་ and vowels > སྟེ་ tē
- after ད་ > དེ་ the̱
- after ན་ ར་ ལ་ ས་ ད་དྲག་ > ཏེ་ tē

In speech, the three are all pronounced -te. This particle has a range of functions in Literary Tibetan. In the spoken language, by contrast, it is used only to introduce an opposition between two clauses or a concession, and may be translated by "but" or "although".

The particle -te is used after only certain auxiliaries. It usually appears in the following combinations: ཡོད་དེ་ yö̱'-te, ཡོད་རེད་དེ yo̱:re'-te, འདུག་སྟེ་ tu̱'-te, ཡིན་ཏེ་ yi̱n-te, རེད་དེ་ re̱'-te.

Ex.: འདྲ་པོ་རེད་དེ་གཅིག་པ་རང་མ་རེད། "Even though they're similar, they're not quite identical."
ཁོང་ལ་དངུལ་ཡོད་རེད་དེ། བེད་སྤྱོད་བཏང་གི་ཡོད་མ་རེད། "He has money but he doesn't use it."
སྐད་ཡག་པོ་འདུག་སྟེ་གཞས་བཏང་གི་མི་འདུག "Although she has a nice voice, she doesn't sing."

38.3.2 Rhetorical questions

Rhetorical questions are very commonly used in both Spoken and Literary Tibetan. They entail the speaker asking a question and immediately replying to it himself.

ག་རེ་རེད་ཟེར་ན་ khare re' ser-na "If you ask why" = because.

ག་དུས་རེད་ཟེར་ན་ khatü' re' ser-na "If you ask when" = when.

Ex.: ག་དུས་བཙུགས་པ་རེད་ཟེར་ན་སྡེ་སྲིད་སངས་རྒྱས་རྒྱ་མཚོས་རྩེ་པོ་བྲང་སྐྱར་བཞེངས་གནང་གྲུབ་པའི་རྗེས་ལ་བཙུགས་པ་རེད།

"When was it instituted? It was after the regent had renovated the Potala Palace"

[i.e., it was instituted when the regent had rebuilt the palace]

དེའི་དམིགས་ཡུལ་ག་རེ་རེད་ཟེར་ན། གོང་ས་ལྔ་པ་ཆེན་པོའི་དགོངས་པ་རྫོགས་ཀྱི་ཆེད་དུ་རེད།

"What was its aim? It was to commemorate the death of the Fifth Dalai Lama"

[i.e., its aim was to commemorate the death of the Fifth Dalai Lama]

38.4 Exercises སྦྱོང་ཚན།

38.4.1 Translate into English:

༡) ངས་ཉི་མ་ཁ་ཤས་སྔོན་བཟས་པ་ཡིན་ཏེ་དྲག་མ་སོང་།

༢) ངས་ཡའི་ཐ་མག་བཞག་ཡག་ཐབས་ཤེས་གང་དྲག་བྱས་པ་ཡིན་ཏེ་ད་ལྟ་ཏོག་ཙམ་ཁག་པོ་འདུག

༣) ཐ་མག་འཐེན་བྱས་དངུལ་མང་པོ་འགྲོ་རྒྱག་བཏང་པ་དེ་རང་ཨོ་ཙ་རེད་དེ། གཟུགས་པོ་ལ་དཔེ་མི་སྲིད་པའི་གནོད་པ་ཆེན་པོ་འདུག

༤) ང་ལྷ་སར་མ་ཕྱིན་ཏེ་ལྷ་སའི་སྐོར་ལ་ཞེ་དྲགས་གོ་བྱུང་།

38.4.2 Answer the following questions:

༡) ཚོགས་མཆོད་ཆེན་མོ་འཛུགས་མཁན་སུ་རེད།

༢) གླུད་གོང་རྒྱལ་པོ་ལ་དམིགས་གསལ་ག་རེ་ཡོད་རེད།

༣) གཏོར་རྒྱག་ཟེར་ཡག་དེ་ག་རེ་རེད།

༤) ཕྲ་མོ་ཚོགས་མཆོད་ཆེན་མོ་ག་དུས་འཚུག་གི་རེད།

༥) དེང་སང་དུས་ཆེན་དེ་བཏང་གི་ཡོད་རེད་པས།

38.4.3 Choose the appropriate form of the connective སྟེ་ ste, དེ་ de, or ཏེ་ te:

༡) ང་དངུལ་མང་པོ་མེད་(   )ཁྱེད་རང་ལ་ཏོག་ཙམ་ཕུལ་ཆོག

༢) ཁོང་ལ་ཨ་ཕྲ་གསུམ་འདུག(   )ནང་ལ་གཅིག་ཀྱང་བཞུགས་ཀྱི་མི་འདུག

༣) ངས་ཁ་ལག་བཟས་པ་ཡིན་(   )ད་དུང་ཟ་འདོད་འདུག

༤) ཁོང་ཚོར་ཁང་པ་རྒྱ་ཆེན་པོ་ཡོད་རེད་(   )ད་དུང་ཉོ་གི་ཡིན་ཟེར་གྱི་འདུག

༥) བསྟན་འཛིན་ལགས་ལ་ཕེབས་རོགས་གནང་ཟེ་ཞུས་སོང་(   )དེ་རིང་ཕེབས་མི་འདུག

“The three monastic seats”

གདན་ས་གསུམ།

Grammar aims བརྡ་སྤྲོད་རིག་པའི་དམིགས་ཚད།

- The nominalizer ཚུལ་ tshü̃:
- Modal constructions of the type ཁག་བྱེད་ khā' + che̲'.

CD II • Tr. 8 

39.1 Text རྩོམ་ཡིག

༄།། གདན་ས་ཆེན་པོ་གསུམ་གྱི་ནང་ནས་གཅིག་གི་མིང་ལ་སེ་ར་ཟེར་གྱི་རེད། དེ་ནི་ལྷ་སའི་བྱང་ངོས་ཀྱི་རིའི་གཤམ་ལ་ཡོད་པ་དང་ལྷ་སའི་བར་སྐོར་ནས་སེ་ར་དགོན་པ་བར་དུ་མོ་ཊའི་ནང་ལ་ཕྱིན་ན་སྐར་མ་བཅོ་ལྔ་ཙ་ལ་(ཙམ་ལ་) སླེབས་ཀྱི་རེད། དགོན་པ་དེ་བཞངས་(བཞེངས་)མཁན་གྱི་མཚན་ལ་བྱམས་ཆེན་ཆོས་རྗེ་ཤཱཀྱ་ཡེ་ཤེས་ཞུ་གི་རེད། སེ་ར་དགོན་པ་ལ་དགེ་འདུན་ཞལ་གྲངས་ལྔ་སྟོང་ལྔ་བརྒྱ་ཡོད་རེད་ཟེ་ཟེར་གྱི་ཡོད་རེད་དེ། ཆིག་སྟོང་དགུ་བརྒྱ་ལྔ་བཅུའི་ནང་ལ་བདུན་སྟོང་ཙ་ཡོད་རེད། དགའ་ལྡན་དགོན་པ་ནི་ལྷ་སའི་ཤར་ཕྱོགས་སྟག་རྩེ་རྫོང་གི་ཁོངས་གཏོགས་ལ་དབང་པོ་རི་ཟེར་མཁན་(ཟེར་བའི) རིའི་ལྟེབས་ལ་ཡོད་རེད། དགོན་པ་དེ་ནི་དགེ་ལུགས་པའི་དགོན་པ་ཆེ་ཤོས་ཀྱི་གྲས་གཅིག་རེད། དེ་ནི་རྗེ་ཙོང་ཁ་པ་བློ་བཟང་གྲགས་པས་སྤྱི་ལོ་ཆིག་སྟོང་བཞི་བརྒྱ་བཅུ་མེད་དགུ་ལ་ཕྱག་བཏབ་གནང་པ་རེད།

ལྷ་ས་ནས་སྤྱི་ལེ་གསུམ་བཅུ་ཙམ་ལས་མེད་ནའི་(མེད་ཀྱང་)ལམ་ཁག་ཡག་པོ་རང་མེད་ཙང་མོ་ཊའི་ནང་ལ་ཆུ་ཚོད་གཅིག་དང་ཕྱེད་ཀ་ཙ་འགོར་གྱི་རེད། སྔོན་མའི་བཤད་སྲོལ་(ཤོད་སྲོལ་)ལ་དགའ་ལྡན་ལ་དགེ་འདུན་ཞལ་གྲངས་སུམ་སྟོང་སུམ་བརྒྱ་ཡོད་རེད་ཟེ་བཤད་(ཤོད་)ཀྱི་ཡོད་རེད་དེ། ཆིག་སྟོང་དགུ་བརྒྱ་ལྔ་བཅུའི་ནང་ལ་དགེ་འདུན་ཞལ་གྲངས་ལྔ་སྟོང་ལྷག་ཙ་(ལྷག་ཙམ)ཡོད་རེད།

འབྲས་སྤུངས་དགོན་པ་ཡའི་(ཡང་)དགེ་ལུགས་པའི་དགོན་པ་ཆེན་པོ་གཙོ་བོའི་གྲས་གཅིག་ཡིན་པས་མ་ཚད། བོད་ཀྱི་དགོན་པ་ཆེ་ཤོས་ཡའི་(ཀྱང་)རེད། དེ་ནི་འཇམ་དབྱངས་ཆོས་རྗེ་བཀྲ་ཤིས་དཔལ་ལྡན་ཞུ་མཁན་གཅིག་གིས་ཆིག་སྟོང་བཞི་བརྒྱ་བཅུ་དྲུག་ལོར་བཞངས་(བཞེངས་)པ་དང་། ལྷ་སའི་ནུབ་ཕྱོགས་ལ་དགེ་འཕེལ་དབུ་རྩེ་ཟེར་མཁན་གྱི་(ཟེར་བའི་)རིའི་ལྟེབས་ལ་ཡོད་རེད། ལྷ་སའི་བར་སྐོར་ནས་འབྲས་སྤུངས་བར་དུ་མོ་ཊའི་ནང་ལ་སྐར་མ་ཉི་ཤུ་ཙ་ལས་འགོར་གྱི་མ་རེད། དགོན་པ་དེར་དགེ་འདུན་ཞལ་གྲངས་བདུན་སྟོང་བདུན་བརྒྱ་ཡོད་ཚུལ་བཤད་ཀྱི་ཡོད་རེད་དེ། ཆིག་སྟོང་དགུ་བརྒྱ་ལྔ་བཅུའི་ནང་ལ་དགེ་འདུན་ཁྲི་གཅིག་ཙ་ཡོད་རེད།།

Translation

Of the three monastic seats, one is named Sera. It is located at the foot of a hill to the north of Lhasa. If you travel by car from the Bharkor to Sera, it will take you about fifteen minutes. The founder of this monastery was called Jamchen Chöje Shakya Yeshe. It's generally said that the number of monks was five thousand five hundred, but in the 1950s there were up to seven thousand.

The monastery of Gandän, to the east of Lhasa, stands on the side of a hill called Wangpori, which belongs to Tagtse. It is one of the largest Gelugpa monasteries. It was founded in 1409 by Tsongkhapa Lobzang Dhragpa. Although it is only thirty-odd kilometers from Lhasa, since the road is in poor condition it takes about an hour and a half. According to oral tradition, there used to be three thousand three hundred monks at Gandän, but in the 1950s there were more than five thousand.

Dräpung Monastery is also one of the principal Gelugpa monasteries, and it is moreover the largest monastery in Tibet. It was founded in 1416 by Jamyang Chöje Trashi Pändän. It is located on the slopes of Gemphel Utse hill to the west of Lhasa. From the Bharkor to Dräpung takes no more than twenty minutes by car. It is said that this monastery had seven thousand seven hundred monks, but in the 1950s it actually had around ten thousand.

ཀ་ཁ་ག་ང་

39.2 Vocabulary ཚིག་གསར།

གདན་ས་ tä̱nsa	(n.) monastic seat
རྫོང་ tso̱ng	(n.) fortress, district
ལྡེབས་ te̱p	(n.) side, flank
ཁ་གྲངས་ khātrang ཞལ་གྲངས་ shä̱:trang (H)	(n.) number (of people)
གྲངས་ཀ་ thra̱ngka	(n.) number
མི་རབས་ mi̱rap	(n.) generation
དུས་རབས་ thü̱rap	(n.) century
སྤྱི་ལེ་ cīle	(n.) kilometer
ཚུལ་ tshǖ:	(n.) way, manner
སྲོལ་ sȫ:	(n.) tradition, custom
གྲས་ thrä̱'	(n.) kind, sort, class
ནང་ནས་ na̱ngnä'	(n.) among
ཕྱག་བཏབ་ + གནང་ chāktap nāng (H)	(v.) [vol., EA] to found (a monastery or institution)
ཁོངས་གཏོགས་ khōngto'	(v.) [inv., AD] to belong
གྲངས་ཀ་ + རྒྱག་ thra̱ngka kya̱'	(v.) [vol., EA] to count

Proper nouns

སྟག་རྩེ་ tāktse	Tagtse village
དགེ་འཕེལ་དབུ་རྩེ་ ke̱pe: ūtse	Gemphel Utse hill
བྱམས་ཆེན་ཆོས་རྗེ་ཤཱཀྱ་ཡེ་ཤེས་ cha̱mcen chōce shākya ye̱she'	Jhamchen Chöje Shakya Yeshe

དབང་པོ་རི་	wāngpo ri̱	Wangpori
འཇམ་དབྱངས་ཆོས་རྗེ་བཀྲ་ཤིས་དཔལ་ལྡན་	ca̱myang chȫce trāshi' pā̈ntän	Jamyang Chöje Trashi Pändän

39.3 Remarks འགྲེལ་བཤད།

39.3.1 The nominalizer ཚུལ་tshǖ:

The nominalizer ཚུལ་tshǖ:, derived from a noun "method, way", has a first meaning similar to སྟངས་ tang (see Lesson 32), but occurs mainly in Literary Tibetan or in a formal spoken language. It expresses the way or the manner the verbal action is performed.

Ex.: ཁོང་གིས་བོད་ཤོག་བཟོ་ཚུལ་འགྲེལ་བཤད་བརྒྱབ་པ་རེད།
"He explained how Tibetan paper is made".

The nominalizer ཚུལ་tshǖ:, and its literary homologue ལུགས་lu̱' "manner", has a second meaning when used with reported speech. It indicates that the speaker is not necessarily subscribing to what he or she is reporting. It may be translated by "they say that" or "apparently".

Ex.: དགོན་པ་དེར་དགེ་འདུན་ཞལ་གྲངས་བདུན་སྟོང་བདུན་བརྒྱ་ཡོད་ཚུལ་བཤད་ཀྱི་ཡོད་རེད།
"They say that there used to be seven thousand seven hundred monks in this monastery."

བླ་མ་ཡིན་ཚུལ་བྱས་པ་རེད།
"He claimed to be a lama."

39.3.2 Modal constructions of the type ཁག་བྱེད་ khā'+che̱'

There are three constructions: ཁག་བྱེད་khā'+che̱', ཁུལ་བྱེད khǖ:+che̱', མདོག་(མདོག་) བྱེད། nto̱'(nto')+che̱' that have much the same meaning as the particle tshǖ: that we've just met. They may be translated by "seem" or "claim". In certain contexts, khā'+che̱' also means "to do something beyond one's capability". The constructions khā'+che̱' and nto̱'(nto')+che̱' go directly after the verb, whereas khǖ:+che̱' requires a nominalized verb (V+ pa) followed by the genitive.

Ex.:	ཁོང་གིས་ང་མ་མཐོང་ཁག་བྱེད་ཀྱི་འདུག	"He's pretending he hasn't seen me".
	ང་ཡར་ཕྱིན་པའི་ཁུལ་བྱེད་ཀྱི་ཡིན།	"I'll make out that I've gone up there."
	ཁོ་ན་ཁག་བྱེད་ཀྱི་ཡོད་རེད།	"He's claiming to be ill."
	ཧ་མ་གོ་ན་ཧ་གོ་མདོག་མདོག་མ་བྱེད།	"If you haven't understood, don't pretend you have."

ཡི་གེ་མགྱོགས་པོ་འབྲི་ཁག་བྱས་མང་པོ་ནོར་བཞག
"He wanted to write fast, but he made a lot of mistakes."

སི་པན་ཟ་ཁག་བྱས་པོ་བའི་ན་ཚ་སྡུག་ཏུ་ཕྱིན་སོང་།
"He wanted to eat some chili and his stomach ache got worse."

39.4 Exercises སྦྱོང་ཚན།

39.4.1 Translate into English:

༡) པད་མ་ཡ་མེ་རི་ཀ་ནས་ཚུར་ལོག་ཡོང་ནས་དབྱིན་ཇིའི་སྐད་ཤེས་པའི་ཁྲལ་བྱེད་ཀྱི་འདུག་ག

༢) ཁོས་གྲོགས་པོ་ཡིན་མདོག་མདོག་བྱས་ནས་མགོ་སྐོར་བཏང་པ་རེད།

༣) བསམ་ཡས་དགོན་པ་ནི་ལྷོ་ཁ་ས་ཁུལ་གྲ་ནང་རྫོང་ཡར་ཀླུང་གཙང་པོའི་བྱང་ངོས་ལ་གནས་ཡོད་རེད། གཙུག་ལག་ཁང་དེ་སྤྱི་ལོའི་དུས་རབས་བརྒྱད་པའི་ནང་ལ་བོད་ཀྱི་རྒྱལ་པོ་ཁྲི་སྲོང་ལྡེ་བཙན་གྱི་སྐབས་ལ་བཞེངས་པ་རེད། རིག་གནས་གསར་བརྗེའི་ལོ་བཅུའི་ནང་ལ་སྐྱོན་ཆ་ཆེན་པོ་བྱུང་པ་རེད། ཡིན་ནའི་དེང་སང་རྒྱལ་ཁབ་ནས་ཉམས་གསོ་གནང་ནས་ཡག་པོ་ཆགས་ཡོད་རེད།

39.4.2 Answer the following questions:

༡) གདན་ས་གསུམ་གྱི་མིང་ལ་ག་རེ་ཟེར་གྱི་ཡོད་རེད།

༢) དབང་པོ་རི་དང་དགེ་འཕེལ་དབུ་རྩེ་ག་པར་ཡོད་རེད།

༣) སེ་ར་དགོན་པར་འགྲོ་ཡག་ལ་ཆུ་ཚོད་གཅིག་འགོར་གྱི་རེད་པས།

༤) དེང་སང་དགའ་ལྡན་དགོན་པ་ལ་འགྲོ་སའི་ལམ་ཁག་ཡག་པོ་བཟོས་འདུག་གས།

༥) འབྲས་སྤུངས་དགོན་པ་ནི་ག་དུས་བཞེངས་པ་རེད།

༦) སྔོན་མའི་བཤད་སྲོལ་ལ་(ཤོད་སྲོལ་ལ་)འབྲས་སྤུངས་ལ་དགེ་འདུན་ཞལ་གྲངས་མང་ལོས་ཡོད་རེད། མངོན་སུམ་༡༩༥༩ བར་དུ་ག་ཚོད་ཡོད་རེད།

CD II • Tr. 9-11 

39.5 Civilization རིག་གཞུང་།

བོད་ཀྱི་དམངས་ཁྲོད་ཀྱི་གཏམ་དཔེ་ཁག་ཅིག *Proverbs*

In Tibet, as in many traditional societies, proverbs play an important part in communication, and people cite them whenever the situation is appropriate. Nomads and farmers are especially inclined to use them. In all languages, proverbs generally correspond to an ancient, and even archaic, phase of linguistic usage. In Tibet, proverbs are usually phrased in a register close to that of the literary language. Several collections of proverbs have been published both in Tibet and in the diaspora. Here are some well-known proverbs.

རྨ་ལ་ཕན་ན་ཁྱིའི་ཚིལ་ཡང་རུང་།

"To treat a wound, even dog-fat will do."

སྐྱེ་དུས་ཆགས་པ་མི་དྲན།
ཆགས་དུས་སྐྱེ་བ་མི་དྲན།

"When you're giving birth, you don't think about sex;
when you're having sex, you don't think about giving birth."

རང་གི་གདོང་པར་འབྲོང་རྒྱུག་པ་མ་མཐོང་།
མི་ཡི་གདོང་པར་ཤིག་རྒྱུག་པ་མཐོང་པ།

"You don't see the wild yak moving across your own face,
but you see the louse crawling on someone else's."

སྐྱིད་པོ་རང་གིས་མ་བྱས་ན་སྡུག་པོ་མི་ཡིས་གཏོང་གི་རེད།

"If you don't take care of your own happiness, others will ensure your misery."

ཨ་ཡག་དགོས་ན་ཨ་ཚ་སྐྱོམ།

"To acquire beauty, you have to suffer."

བཟུང་ན་ལག་པ་འཚིག་བཏང་ན་རྫ་མ་ཆག

"Hold on and your hand will burn, let go and the pot will break."

ཁ་བཤད་ཆུ་ཡི་ལྦུ་བ།
ལག་ལེན་གསེར་གྱི་ཐིག་པ།

"Words from the mouth are bubbles,
deeds of the hand are drops of gold."

ཁ་བདེ་པོ་མི་ཡི་དཔོན་པོ་ཡིན།
ལག་བདེ་པོ་མི་ཡི་གཡོག་པོ་ཡིན།

"The man with the clever words is the leader,
the man with clever hands is a slave."

མིའི་རི་མོ་ནང་ལོགས་དང་།
སྟག་གི་རི་མོ་ཕྱི་ལོགས།

"The tiger's stripes are outside,
but a man's stripes are inside."

ཚིག་པ་གཡག་ལ་ཟ།རྡོག་རྒྱག་བེའུ་ལ་གཞུ།

"You get angry with the yak, but it's the calf you kick."

མི་སུམ་ཅུ་སེམས་སུམ་ཅུ།
མཛོ་སུམ་ཅུ་ལ་རྭ་དྲུག་ཅུ།

"Thirty people makes thirty minds,
thirty *dzo* makes sixty horns."

ཤིག་ལ་བརྒྱབ་ཀྱང་གོང་ངའི་ཕྱི་ལོགས་ཙམ།

"When a louse crosses the pass, it's only gone to the other side of the lapel."

རི་མགོ་ཐམས་ཅད་མིག་དང་སྐྱིག་ཁུག་ཐམས་ཅད་ཨམ་མཆོག་རེད།

"All peaks are eyes, and all recesses are ears."

ཞི་མི་མེད་ན་ཙི་ཙི་ལོ་གསར་རེད།

"When the cat's away, it is New Year for the mice."

"Some summer festivals"

དབྱར་ཁའི་སྐབས་ཀྱི་དུས་ཆེན་ཁ་ཤས།

Grammar aims བརྡ་སྤྲོད་རིག་པའི་དམིགས་ཚད།

- The aspectual auxiliary བསྡད་ tä' "to stay".

CD II • Tr. 12-14 

40.1 Text རྩོམ་ཡིག

༄། ས་ག་ཟླ་བ།

བོད་ཟླ་བཞི་པའི་ཚེས་བཅོ་ལྔའི་ཉི་མ་ནི། (ཉིན་མོ་ནི་) སྟོན་པ་སངས་རྒྱས་བཅོམ་ལྡན་འདས་མངོན་པར་རྫོགས་པར་སངས་རྒྱས་པའི་དུས་ཆེན་རེད། ཉི་མ་དེར་ནི་(དེའི་ཉིན་མོ་ནི་) བོད་པ་ཚོས་རང་རང་གི་ལུང་པའི་ནང་ལ་ཡོད་པའི་དགོན་པ་ཁག་ལ་མཆོད་མཇལ་ལ་འགྲོ་གི་ཡོད་རེད། གཙུག་ལག་ཁང་དང་། མཆོད་རྟེན་ཅི་དག་ལ་སྐོར་ར་བརྒྱབ་གར་འགྲོ་གི་རེད།

བོད་མི་མང་པོས་ས་ག་ཟླ་བའི་ཚེས་བཅོ་ལྔ་བར་དུ་དཀར་སྐྱོང་བྱེད་ཀྱི་རེད། ཚེས་པ་བཅོ་ལྔ་ལ་ལྷ་ས་བ་ཚོས་ཚོགས་གས་(ཚོགས་པ་)གཙུག་ལག་ཁང་ལ་མཆོད་མཇལ་ལ་ཕྱིན། དེ་ནས་གླིང་སྐོར་ལ་ཕྱིན། དེ་ནས་དགོང་དྲོ་རྫོང་རྒྱབ་ཀླུ་ཁང་ནང་ལ་སྒྲ་སྙན་དང་པི་ཝང་ལ་སོགས་པ་བཏང་ནས་གཞས་ཞབས་འཁྲོ་བརྒྱབ། དག་ནང་བཞིན་ཀླུ་ཁང་གི་ཆུའི་ནང་ལ་ཀོ་བ་བཏང་ནས་སྐྱིད་པོ་བྱས་བསྡད་(སྡོད་) ཀྱི་རེད།

འཛམ་གླིང་སྤྱི་བསང་།

བོད་ཟླ་ལྔ་པའི་ཚེས་བཅོ་ལྔའི་ཉིན་གར་ལྷ་ས་བ་ཚོས་འཛམ་གླིང་སྤྱི་བསང་ཟེར་མཁན་(ཟེར་བའི་)ལྷ་གསོལ་ཡག་གི་དུས་ཆེན་བཏང་(གཏོང་)གི་རེད། ཉི་མ་དེར་གཟབ་སྤྲོས་བཏང་ནས་བསང་བཏང་པ་དང་། གླིང་གའི་ནང་ལ་གུར་བརྒྱབ། ཆང་བཏུངས། ཁ་ལག་རྒྱས་པོ་ཞི་དྲགས་བཟས་བྱས་ གཞས་རྣམ་ཐར་བཏང་བྱས་བསྡད་ཀྱི་རེད།

དྲུག་པ་ཚེས་བཞི།

བོད་ཟླ་དྲུག་པའི་ཚེས་བཞི་ལ་སྟོན་པ་སངས་རྒྱས་བཅོམ་ལྡན་འདས་ཀྱིས་བདེན་པ་བཞིའི་ཆོས་ཀྱི་འཁོར་ལོ་བསྐོར་བའི་ཉི་མ་(ཉིན་མོ་) དེ་ཡིན་ཙང་། བོད་ཀྱི་ལུང་པ་ག་ས་ག་ལ་མི་ཚང་མས་གཟབ་སྤྲོས་སྤུས་ནས་(སྤྲས་ནས་)དགོན་པ་དང་། ལྷ་ཁང་། གནས་རི། ཅི་དག་ལ་མཆོད་འབུལ་དང་བསྐོར་ར(བསྐོར་བ་)རྒྱག་གར་འགྲོ་གི་རེད། ལྷ་ས་བ་ཚོར་ཆ་བཞག་ན། ལྷ་སའི་གཙུག་ལག་ཁང་དང་སེ་འབྲས་དགའ་གསུམ་ཅི་དག་ལ་མཆོད་མཇལ་དང་བསྐོར་ར་རྒྱག་གར་འགྲོ་གི་རེད།།

Translation

The month of Saka

The full moon (the fifteenth day of the month) of the fourth month is the festival of the illumination of the (teacher) Buddha (the bhagavan). On that day, Tibetans go to the monasteries of their respective regions to pray. They perform circumambulations around temples and stupas. Many Tibetans abstain from eating meat until the fifteenth day of the month. On the morning of the fifteenth, the inhabitants of Lhasa go to the great temple of the Jhokang and then set off on the Lingkor (the circumambulatory route around Lhasa). Eventually, in the evening, in the Lukhang park, behind the Potala, they spend a nice time playing the *piwang* (the two-stringed Tibetan viola) and the *drapnyän* (Tibetan lute), as well as dancing and singing, and taking coracle trips on the Lukhang lake.

The world fumigation

On the fifteenth day of the fifth month, the inhabitants of Lhasa perform the ceremony for the propitiation of the gods known as the "general world fumigation". On that day, people dress in their finest clothing and perform fumigations (by burning juniper). After pitching their tents in the parks, they drink *chang,* eat heartily and sing operatic songs.

The fourth day of the sixth month

Because the fourth day of the sixth month is the day on which the Buddha turned the wheel of the Dharma of the Four [Noble] Truths, in all parts of Tibet people put on their finest clothing and go to monasteries, sanctuaries, holy mountains and so forth to make offerings and perform circumambulations. For example, the people of Lhasa go to the Great Temple as well as to the monasteries of Sera, Gandän and Dräpung to make offerings and perform circumambulations.

ཀ་ཁ་ག་ང་

40.2 Vocabulary ཚིག་གསར།

སྟོན་པ་ tȫnpa	(n.) teacher, guide
སྒྲ་སྙན་ tra̲pnyän	(n.) Tibetan lute
པི་ཝང་ pīwang	(n.) Tibetan viola
ཀོ་བ་ kōwa	(n.) yak-hide, yak-hide boat, coracle
མཆོད་རྟེན་ chȫrten	(n.) stupa
ས་ག་ཟླ་བ་ sāka ta̲wa	(n.) fourth Tibetan month; name of the ceremony held on the fifteenth day of this month
བདེན་པ་ te̲npa	(n.) truth
བདེན་པ་བཞི་ te̲npa shi̲	(n.) The Four [Noble] Truths
མཆོད་འབུལ་ chȫmpu̲:	(n.) offering
ཉིན་ག་ nyi̲nka ཉིན་མོ་ nyi̲nmo (L)	(n.) day
རྒྱས་པོ་ kyä̲po	(adj.) abundant, plentiful
མཆོད་པ་ + ཕུལ། chȫpa phǖ:	(v.) [vol., EA] to make offerings

གུར་ + རྒྱག་ khu̱r kya̱'	(v.) [vol., E] to pitch a tent
དབུ་གུར་ + སྒྲོན་ ūkur trö̱n (H)	(v.) [vol., E] to pitch a tent
ཞབས་འཁྲོ་ + རྒྱག་ sha̱ptro kya̱'	(v.) [vol., E] to dance
ཀོ་བ་ + བཏང་ kōwa tāng	(v.) [vol., E] to paddle a coracle
འཁོར་ལོ་ + བསྐོར་ khōrlo kōr	(v.) [vol., E] to turn the wheel (of the Dharma), *fig.*: to give teachings
མངོན་པར་རྫོགས་ ngōnpar tso̱'	(v.) [inv., A] to achieve, attain to
དཀར་སྐྱོང་ + བྱེད་ kārkyong che̱'	(v.) [vol., E] to abstain from meat
ལྷ་ + གསོལ་ lhā sō:	(v.) [vol., E] offering-ritual for local gods (of mountains, lakes, etc.)

Proper nouns

ཀླུ་ཁང་ lūkang	Temple for serpent spirits; by extension, name of the lake and park around the Lukhang Temple behind the Potala
བཅོམ་ལྡན་འདས་ cōmtäntä'	Bhagavan, epithet (in Sanskrit) of the Buddha
འཛམ་གླིང་སྤྱི་བསངས་ tsa̱mling cīsang	*name of a ceremony*
དྲུག་པ་ཚེས་བཞི་ thru̱kpa tshēshi	*name of a ceremony*

40.3 Remarks འགྲེལ་བཤད།

40.3.1 The aspectual function of བསྡད་ tä̱' "to stay"

The secondary verb བསྡད་ tä̱' "to stay" has an aspectual sense. The main verb, which is followed by བསྡད་ tä̱', must take the past tense. The connective ནས་ nä̱' may optionally be placed between the main verb and the secondary verb: V + (ནས་) བསྡད་ + AUX.

The secondary verb བསྡད་ tä̱' indicates that an action that was begun in the past *is in the process of happening* either in the present or from a past point of reference, or that the state of affairs resulting from this action is still present. The secondary verb may be followed by:

a) perfective auxiliaries བསྡད་པ་ཡིན་ tä̱'-payin (egophoric), བསྡད་པ་རེད་ tä̱'-pare' (assertive), བསྡད་སོང་ tä̱'-song (testimonial).

b) perfect auxiliaries: བསྡད་ཡོད་ tä̱'-yö' (egophoric), བསྡད་ཡོད་རེད་ tä̱'-yo:re' (assertive), བསྡད་བཞག tä̱'-sha' (inferential).

The former constructions (a) may be translated by the perfective, and the latter (b) by the imperfective or the present perfect continuous according to the context. The use of adverbs such as "still" may help to convey the meaning of these constructions.

Ex.: རྡོ་རྗེ་ནང་ལ་ལོག་ཡོང་དུས་ཉི་མས་དེབ་བལྟས་(ནས་)བསྡད་བཞག

"When Dorje got back home, Nyima was still reading a book."

ཁ་ས་ཁྲོམ་ལ་ཐུག་དུས་མོ་རང་གིས་མར་ཉོས་(ནས)་བསྡད་བཞག

"Yesterday, when I met her in the market, she was buying butter."

མོ་རང་ངུས་ནས་བསྡད་པ་རེད།

"She's been crying constantly."

འཛིན་གྲྭའི་ནང་ལ་སྐད་ཆ་བཤད་ནས་བསྡད་པ་རེད།

"He's been talking all the time in class."

The construction may also indicate a resulting state.

ཁོ་རང་ན་བསྡད་བཞག "He's still unwell."
མོ་རང་ལང་བསྡད་བཞག "She's up." (lit. she got up and she's stayed up)
(Compare this with the sentence: མོ་རང་ཡར་ལངས་སོང་། "she got up")

40.4 Exercises སྦྱོང་ཚན།

40.4.1 Translate into English:

༡) མདང་དགོངས་ང་ཉལ་བསྡད་དུས་ཆར་པ་ཆེན་པོ་བབས་སོང་།

༢) ཁོང་ད་ལྟ་བར་དུ་སྨུག་བསྡད་བཞག

༣) ཆུ་ཚོད་བཅུ་པ་ཟིན་པ་ཡོད་ཙང་ཁོང་ཚོ་སླེབས་བསྡད་ཡོད་རེད།

༤) འཛམ་གླིང་སྤྱི་བསངས་ནི་སྔོན་མ་ཆོས་རྒྱལ་ཁྲི་སྲོང་ལྡེ་བཙན་གྱི་སྐབས་ལ་བསམ་ཡས་གཙུག་ལག་ཁང་བཞེངས་དུས་བར་ཆད་མང་པོ་བྱུང་ཙང་སློབ་དཔོན་པདྨ་འབྱུང་གནས་ཀྱིས་བསངས་བཏང་ཡག་དང་མཆོད་པ་ཕུལ་ཡག་རྒྱ་ཆེན་པོ་གནང་ཙང་རྐྱེན་ངན་བར་ཆད་ཚང་མ་མེད་པ་ཆགས་པ་རེད། འདི་དྲན་གསོ་ཞུ་ཡག་གི་དུས་ཆེན་ཅིག་རེད།

40.4.2 Answer the following questions:

༡) སངས་རྒྱས་བཅོམ་ལྡན་འདས་མངོན་པར་རྫོགས་པར་སངས་རྒྱས་པའི་དུས་ཆེན་གྱི་མིང་ལ་ག་རེ་ཟེར་གྱི་ཡོད་རེད།

༢) བོད་ཟླ་དྲུག་པའི་ཚེས་བཞི་ལ་དུས་ཆེན་ག་རེ་ཡོད་རེད།

༣) ཆོས་ཀྱི་འཁོར་ལོ་སྐོར་བ་ཟེར་ཡག་དེ་དོན་དག་ག་རེ་རེད།

༤) བདེན་པ་བཞི་ཟེར་ཡག་དེ་ནི། སྡུག་བསྔལ་གྱི་བདེན་པ། ཀུན་འབྱུང་གྱི་བདེན་པ། འགོག་པའི་བདེན་པ། བདེན་པ་བཞི་པ་ལ་ག་རེ་ཟེར་གྱི་ཡོད་རེད།

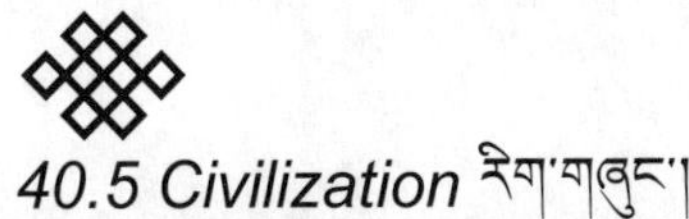

40.5 Civilization རིག་གཞུང་།

ལྡེའུ་ཡི་རྒྱུ་རྩལ། *The art of the riddle: an educational game of the Tibetans.*

The art of the riddle (*deu*, also called *khet* in Amdo) is an important social and cultural phenomenon in Tibetan society, particularly among the *drogpa*. The Tibetans like to practice riddles, especially in the evening before sleeping or early in the morning. In one traditional version of the game, the participants first perform a divination (*mo*) or choose the smallest straw or play "rock-paper-scissors". The winner symbolically becomes the lord of the earth and all that is in it, while the loser becomes the owner of the sky and all it contains. Then the players ask each other riddles, and the loser in each round has to give the winner an object or an animal from his domain.

Usually the riddles are composed in verse and sound like oral poetry. A lot of them concern parts of the body, animals or objects from everyday life in Tibet.

Here are some examples of *deu*:

འབྲོང་མི་འགུལ། རྒྱུ་མ་འགུལ།   ཟེར་བ་དེ་ག་རེ་རེད།

ལན།   སྦྲ་ནག

"What is an immobile wild yak with moving innards?"

Answer: *a nomad tent*

སྤན་འཕྱུངས་འོག་གི་ཞོ་སྐྱལ་བ།   ཟེར་བ་དེ་ག་རེ་རེད།

ལན།   ཀླད་པ།

"What is yogurt fermenting under a bush of penpa grass?"

Answer: *the brain*

དགོན་པ་ཁྲ་རོབ་རོབ་ནང་གི་ཨིན་ཆུང་དམར་རིལ་རིལ།   ཟེར་བ་དེ་ག་རེ་རེད།

ལན།   ཁ།

"What is a glittering monastery with a small red monk in it?"

Answer: *the mouth* (the teeth and the tongue)

© Françoise Robin

Cairn on the banks of the Namtsho Lake.

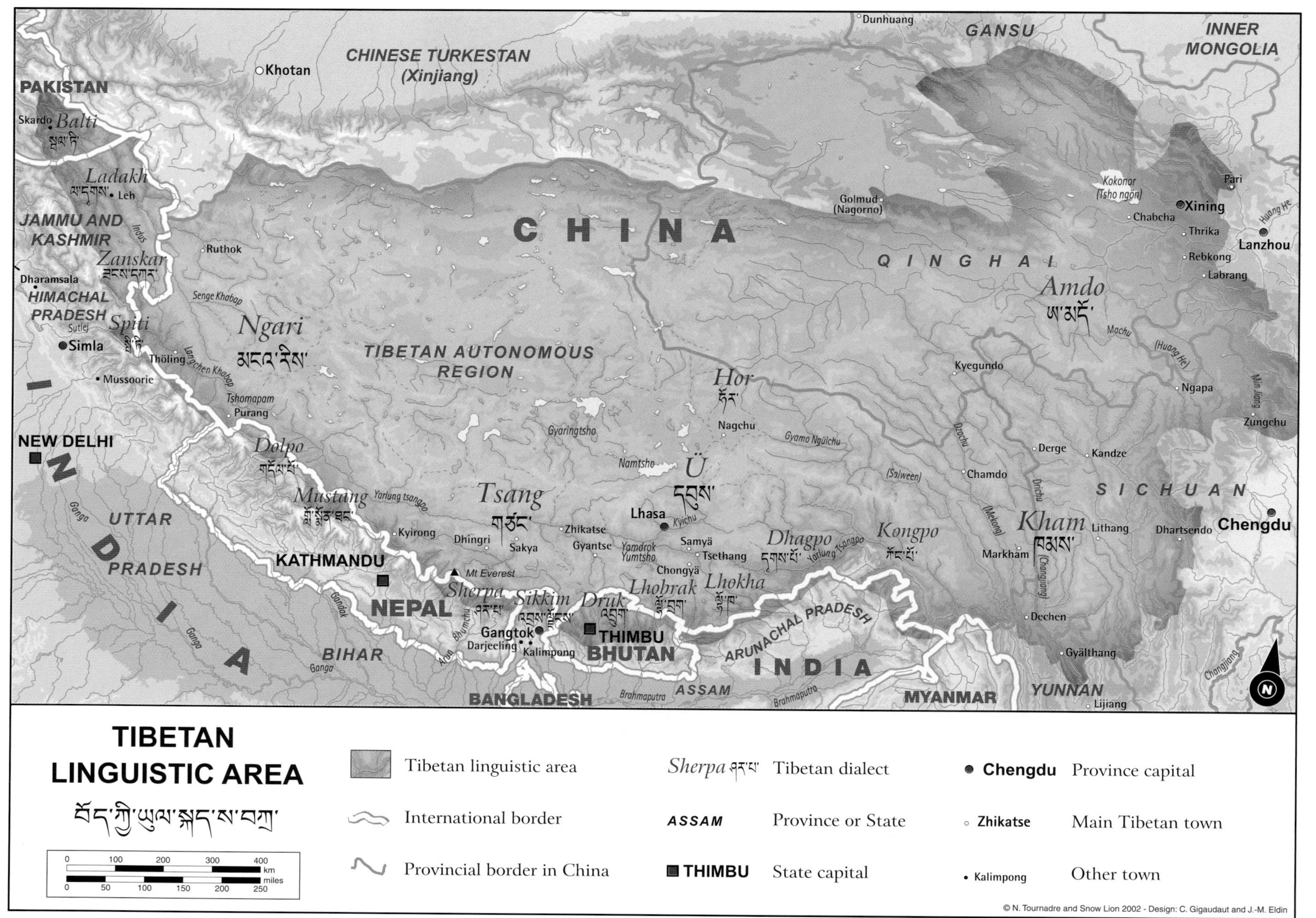
TIBETAN
LINGUISTIC AREA
བོད་ཀྱི་ཡུལ་སྐད་ས་བཀྲ་
km
miles
Tibetan linguistic area
International border
Provincial border in China
Sherpa Tibetan dialect
ASSAM Province or State
THIMBU State capital
Chengdu Province capital
Zhikatse Main Tibetan town
Kalimpong Other town
© N. Tournadre and Snow Lion 2002 - Design: C. Gigaudaut and J.-M. Eldin
CHINESE TURKESTAN (Xinjiang)
GANSU
INNER MONGOLIA
PAKISTAN
JAMMU AND KASHMIR
HIMACHAL PRADESH
CHINA
QINGHAI
TIBETAN AUTONOMOUS REGION
SICHUAN
INDIA
UTTAR PRADESH
BIHAR
NEPAL
BHUTAN
BANGLADESH
ASSAM
ARUNACHAL PRADESH
MYANMAR
YUNNAN
NEW DELHI
KATHMANDU
THIMBU
Khotan
Dunhuang
Golmud (Nagorno)
Kokonor (Tsho ngön)
Pari
Xining
Chabcha
Thrika
Rebkong
Labrang
Lanzhou
Amdo
Machu
(Huang He)
Huang He
Ngapa
Min Jiang
Zungchu
Kyegundo
Derge
Kandze
Chamdo
Dzachu
Drichu
(Mekong)
(Salween)
Kham
Lithang
Dhartsendo
Chengdu
Markham
(Changjiang)
Dechen
Gyälthang
Lijiang
Chongjiang
Skardo
Balti
Ladakh
Leh
Indus
Zanskar
Dharamsala
Sutlej
Spiti
Simla
Thöling
Mussoorie
Ruthok
Senge Khabap
Langchen Khabap
Ngari
Tshomapam
Purang
Dolpo
Mustang
Yarlung tsangpo
Kyirong
Dhingri
Sakya
Tsang
Zhikatse
Gyantse
Yamdrok Yumtsho
Lhasa
Kyichu
Samyä
Tsethang
Chongyä
Gyaringtsho
Namtsho
Ü
Hor
Nagchu
Gyamo Ngülchu
Dhagpo
Kongpo
Lhobrak
Lhokha
Mt Everest
Sherpa
Sikkim
Druk
Gangtok
Darjeeling
Kalimpong
Gandak
Bhumchu
Arun
Ganga
Brahmaputra

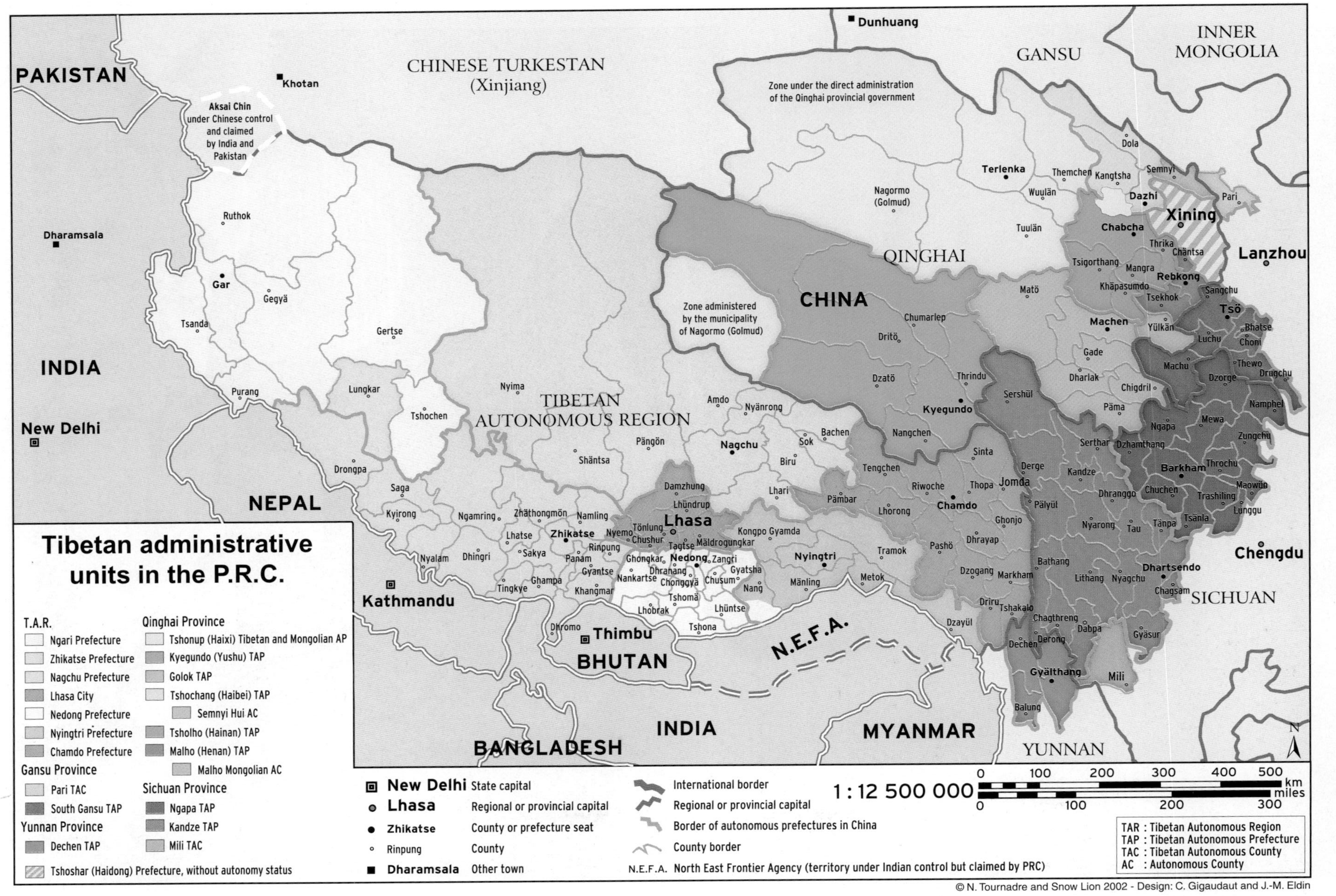

Tibetan administrative units in the P.R.C.
T.A.R.
Ngari Prefecture
Zhikatse Prefecture
Nagchu Prefecture
Lhasa City
Nedong Prefecture
Nyingtri Prefecture
Chamdo Prefecture
Gansu Province
Pari TAC
South Gansu TAP
Yunnan Province
Dechen TAP
Qinghai Province
Tshonup (Haixi) Tibetan and Mongolian AP
Kyegundo (Yushu) TAP
Golok TAP
Tshochang (Haibei) TAP
Semnyi Hui AC
Tsholho (Hainan) TAP
Malho (Henan) TAP
Malho Mongolian AC
Sichuan Province
Ngapa TAP
Kandze TAP
Mili TAC
Tshoshar (Haidong) Prefecture, without autonomy status
New Delhi State capital
Lhasa Regional or provincial capital
Zhikatse County or prefecture seat
Rinpung County
Dharamsala Other town
International border
Regional or provincial capital
Border of autonomous prefectures in China
County border
N.E.F.A. North East Frontier Agency (territory under Indian control but claimed by PRC)
1 : 12 500 000
0 100 200 300 400 500 km
0 100 200 300 miles
TAR : Tibetan Autonomous Region
TAP : Tibetan Autonomous Prefecture
TAC : Tibetan Autonomous County
AC : Autonomous County
PAKISTAN
INDIA
NEPAL
BHUTAN
BANGLADESH
MYANMAR
CHINA
CHINESE TURKESTAN (Xinjiang)
GANSU
INNER MONGOLIA
QINGHAI
SICHUAN
YUNNAN
TIBETAN AUTONOMOUS REGION
N.E.F.A.
Aksai Chin under Chinese control and claimed by India and Pakistan
Zone under the direct administration of the Qinghai provincial government
Zone administered by the municipality of Nagormo (Golmud)
New Delhi
Dharamsala
Khotan
Dunhuang
Kathmandu
Thimbu
Lhasa
Xining
Lanzhou
Chengdu
Ruthok
Gar
Gegyä
Tsanda
Purang
Gertse
Lungkar
Tshochen
Drongpa
Saga
Kyirong
Nyalam
Dhingri
Ngamring
Zhäthongmön
Namling
Lhatse
Zhikatse
Sakya
Tingkye
Ghampa
Panam
Rinpung
Gyantse
Khangmar
Dhromo
Nyima
Shäntsa
Pängön
Damzhung
Lhündrup
Nyemo
Tönlung
Chushur
Tagtse
Mäldrogungkar
Ghongkar
Nedong
Zangri
Dhranang
Nankartse
Chonggyä
Chusum
Gyatsha
Tshomä
Lhobrak
Lhüntse
Tshona
Nang
Kongpo Gyamda
Nyingtri
Mänling
Metok
Tramok
Pashö
Dzayül
Amdo
Nyänrong
Nagchu
Bachen
Sok
Biru
Lhari
Pämbar
Lhorong
Tengchen
Riwoche
Chamdo
Thopa
Jomda
Sinta
Dhrayap
Ghonjo
Dzogang
Markham
Driru
Tshakalo
Nagormo (Golmud)
Terlenka
Themchen
Wuulän
Tuulän
Kangtsha
Dola
Semnyi
Dazhi
Pari
Chabcha
Thrika
Chäntsa
Tsigorthang
Mangra
Rebkong
Khäpasumdo
Tsekhok
Sangchu
Tsö
Bhatse
Choni
Luchu
Yülkän
Matö
Machen
Gade
Dharlak
Chigdril
Päma
Chumarlep
Dritö
Dzatö
Thrindu
Kyegundo
Nangchen
Sershül
Machu
Dzorge
Thewo
Drugchu
Namphel
Mewa
Ngapa
Zungchu
Serthar
Dzhamthang
Barkham
Throchu
Maowün
Chuchen
Trashiling
Lunggu
Tsänla
Tänpa
Tau
Nyarong
Dhranggo
Kandze
Derge
Pälyül
Bathang
Lithang
Nyagchu
Dhartsendo
Chagsam
Chagthreng
Dabpa
Derong
Dechen
Gyäsur
Gyälthang
Mili
Balung
© N. Tournadre and Snow Lion 2002 - Design: C. Gigaudaut and J.-M. Eldin

© Heather Stoddard

Stone lion near the royal tombs in Chonggyä Valley.

© Françoise Robin

Yaks crossing a pass.

© Françoise Robin

Sheep flock on the High Plateau.

© Frédérique d'Aragon

Ploughing in Central Tibet.

Resting on the grassland.

© Françoise Robin

Ngagpa gathering in Amdo.

© Françoise Robin

Chörten overlooking a village in Ngapa area.

© Karen Léotoing

Zhikatse city.

© Françoise Robin

Samyä Monastery.

© Karen Léotoing

Gyantse, as seen from the fortress.

Great *thangka* representing ´S¯akyamuni Buddha.

Torma offering.

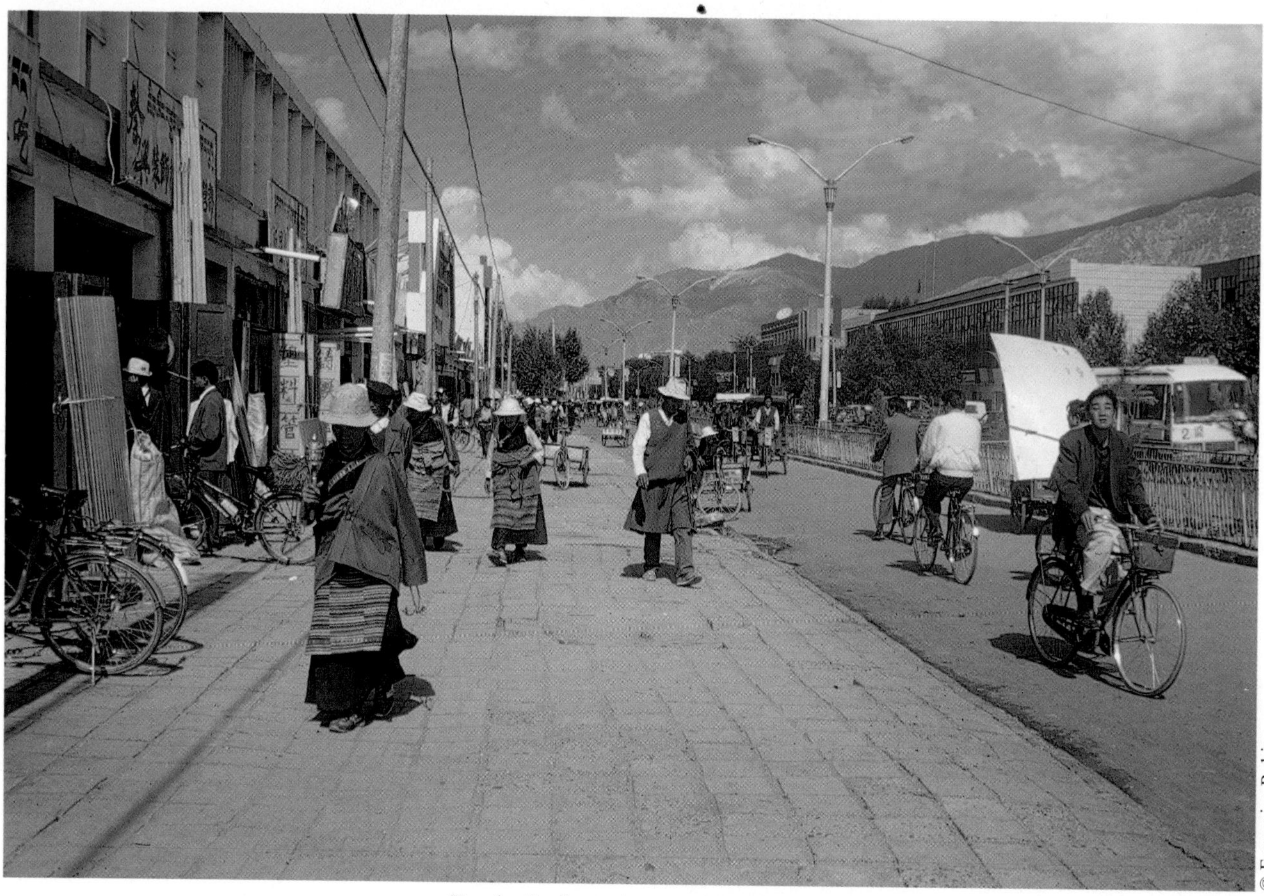

Dzuktrün Lam Avenue in Lhasa.

Dekyi Sharlam Avenue, by the Potala Palace.

"The Yogurt Festival and the Ceremony of Pändän Lhamo"

ཞོ་སྟོན་དང་དཔལ་ལྷའི་རི་ཁྲོད།

Grammar aims བརྡ་སྤྲོད་རིག་པའི་དམིགས་ཚད།

- The directional auxiliaries ཡོང་ yo̱ng and འགྲོ་ tro̱.
- Nominal clauses.
- The construction གང་ khang + Adj / V / doubled Adv.

Traditional music in the Norbu lingkha gardens
(recorded during the Yogurt Festival in 1996)

CD II • Tr. 15 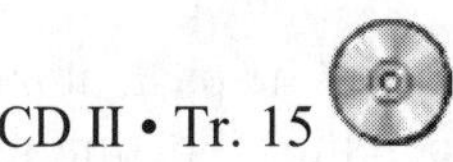

CD II • Tr. 16-17 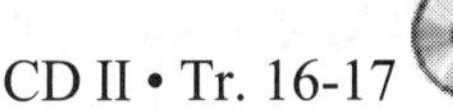

41.1 Text རྩོམ་ཡིག

ༀ། ཞོ་སྟོན།

ཞོ་སྟོན་ཟེར་ཡག་དེ་ནི་(ཟེར་བ་དེ་ནི་) ཟླ་བ་དྲུག་པའི་ཚེས་པ་ ༣༠ ་ཉིན་གར་འབྲས་སྤུངས་ལ་སྐྱོར་མོ་ལུང་བ་དང་། ཟུང་པ་བ། རྒྱང་དཀར་བ་ཅི་དག་གི་ལྷ་མོ་བ་ཚོས་ལྷ་མོ་གཟིགས་འབུལ་ཞུ་གི་ཡོད་རེད། བོད་ཟླ་བདུན་པའི་ཚེས་གཅིག་གི་ཉིན་ནས་ཚེས་པ་བཞི་བར་དུ་ནོར་བུ་གླིང་ཁར་ལྷ་མོ་ཚོགས་པ་རེ་རེ་ནས་ཉི་མ་རེ་རེ་རེ་མོས་བྱས་ནས་ཉིན་འཁྱོངས་ལྷ་མོའི་འཁྲབ་གཞུང་རེ་རེ་འཁྲབ་ཀྱི་རེད།

སྔོན་མ་དགོངས་དྲོ་ལྷ་མོ་འཁྲབ་ཚར་པའི་སྐབས་ལ་དམག་སྒར་ཁག་གི་དམག་མིའི་ཏུ་སྒྲིགས་ཀྱིས་གུས་བཀུས་ཞུ་གི་རེད། ལྷ་མོ་ཚོགས་པ་དེ་ཚོས་ཚེས་ཕ་ནས་བཟུངས་ཉི་མ་ཁ་ཤས་ལྷ་སའི་སྐུ་དྲག་ཆེ་ཁག་གི་གཟིམ་ཤག་ལ་ལྷ་མོ་འཁྲབ་ཀྱི་རེད། ཞོ་སྟོན་ཟེར་ཡག་(ཟེར་བ་)ནི་དང་པོ་འབྲས་སྤུངས་ལ་ཞོའི་སྟོན་མོ་བཏང་སྲོལ་(གཏོང་སྲོལ) བྱུང་བ་ནས་འགོ་བཙུགས་པ་རེད། ཞོ་སྟོན་རིང་གར་ལྷ་ས་བ་མང་ཆེ་བ་གཟབ་འཚེར་གང་ཡག་ཡག་གོན། ཁ་ལག་དང་ཇ་ཆང་ཁྱེར་ནས་ནོར་བུ་གླིང་གར་ལྷ་མོ་ལྟ་གར་འགྲོ་གི་རེད། དགོངས་དག་ཉི་མ་བཞུད་དུས་གཞས་རྣམ་ཐར་བཏང་གིན་བཏང་གིན་སོ་སོའི་ནང་ལ་ལོག་འགྲོ་གི་རེད།

དཔལ་ལྷའི་རི་ཁྲོད།

དཔལ་ལྷའི་རི་ཁྲོད་ཟེར་ཡག་ནི་(ཟེར་བ་ནི་)སྔོན་མ་ལྷ་སར་བོད་ཟླ་བཅུ་པའི་ཚེས་བཅོ་ལྔའི་ཉིན་གར་དཔལ་ལྡན་ལྷ་མོ་བར་སྐོར་ནང་ལ་གདན་འདྲེན་ཞུས་ནས་བར་སྐོར་སྟོ་ཕྱོགས་རབ་གསལ་སྒང་ལམ་ནས་ཞལ་ལྟོར་གཟིགས་ནས་གྲིབ་རྗོང་བཙན་དང་ཞལ་འཛོམས་གནང་གི་རེད། ཉི་མ་དེ་(དེའི་ཉིན་མོ་) ལྷ་ས་བ་ཚོས་གསོལ་ཚོགས་རྒྱས་པོ་བཟོས་ནས་ལྷ་ས་ཞོལ་ས་ཁྲུལ་ནས་དཔལ་ལྡན་ལྷ་མོ་མཇལ་གར་(མཇལ་བར་) ཕེབས་མཁན་ཚོར་སྣེ་ལེན་ཞུ་གི་རེད། ཡང་དགའ་ལྡན་ལྷ་མཆོད་ཀྱི་དགོངས་དྲོ་ཞོལ་པ་ཚོས་ལྷ་སའི་དཀྱིལ་ལ་བཞུགས་མཁན་ཚོར་སྣེ་ལེན་རྒྱས་པོ་ཞུ་གི་རེད། དེ་འདྲས་ཡིན་ཙང་། ལྷ་ས་བ་དཔལ་ལྷའི་རི་ཁྲོད་དང་ཞོལ་པ་དགའ་ལྡན་ལྷ་མཆོད་ཟེར་ཡག་གི་བཤད་སྲོལ་(ཤོད་སྲོལ་)ཡོད་རེད། ཟླ་བ་བཅུ་པའི་ཚེས་ཤར་ནས་ཚེས་བཅོ་ལྔ་བར་ལ་སྤུ་གུ་ཚོར་དགའ་པོ་ཉེ་པོ་དང་སྤུན་རྒྱུག་ཚོས་ཇན་པ་ཉོ་ཡག་(ཉོ་བྱེད་)་དངུལ་སྤྲེར་ཡག་གི་(སྤྲེར་བའི) ལུགས་སྲོལ་ཡོད་རེད། བྱིས་ཅང་སྤུ་གུ་ཚོས་དུས་ཚོད་དེ་སྐབས་ཙ་(སྐབས་ཙམ)ཤར་ན་བསམ་ནས་རེ་བ་བྱས་ནས་སྐུག་བསྡད་ཀྱི་ཡོད་རེད།

Translation

The Yogurt Festival

The Yogurt Festival begins on the thirtieth day of the sixth month in Dräpung Monastery, where the opera troupes of Kyormolungwa, Chungbawa and Gyangkara hold performances throughout the day. This goes on from the first to the fourth of the seventh month in the Norbu lingkha gardens, where opera troupes every day take turns to present an item from the Tibetan opera for a full day. In the past, in the evening when the operatic excerpt was over, the battalions of certain army regiments would hold a parade, and for several days beginning on the fifth, the opera troupes would perform in the houses of certain high noble families. The Zhotön Festival was first cerebrated at Dräpung, where there used to be a yogurt banquet. During the festival, the majority of Lhasa's inhabitants would dress in their finest and go to watch the operatic performances, taking with them food, tea and *chang.* At sunset, they would return home singing operatic songs.

The Ceremony of Pändän Lhamo

In the past, at the time of the full moon (the fifteenth) of the tenth Tibetan month, there was the ceremony of the goddess Pändän Lhamo. On that day in Lhasa, the goddess was brought (lit. invited) to the passage of Rabsäl, south of the Bharkor, and from there, facing south, she went to meet the *tsän* (a local divinity) of Dhribdzong. On that day, the inhabitants of the center of Lhasa would prepare an elaborate meal and host the inhabitants of the Zhöl area [at the foot of the Potala] who came to see Pändän Lhamo.

Similarly, on the evening of the [ceremony of] Gandän Ngamchö, the inhabitants of the Zhöl sector would hold a lavish reception for the inhabitants of the central quarter. It is because of this [association between an area and a ceremony] that there are the customary sayings, "Lhasa and Pälhäritrö (name of the ceremony of Pändän Lhamo)" and "Zhöl inhabitants and Gandän Ngamchö". From the beginning of the tenth month up to the fifteenth day, children are traditionally given money for buying sweets by their relatives and others close to them. This is why children eagerly look forward to this day.

ཀ་ཁ་ག་ང་

41.2 Vocabulary ཚིག་གསར།

ལྷ་མོ་བ་ lhāmowa	(n.) operatic performer
ཉིན་འཁྱོངས་ nyīnkyong'	(n.) all day
འཁྲབ་གཞུང་ thrāpshung	(n.) classical operatic piece
དམག་ mā'	(n.) war
དམག་སྒར་ mākkar	(n.) army camp
རུ་སྒྲིགས་ ru̲tri'	(n.) military parade
རྔན་པ་ ngā̄npa	(n.) gift
སྐུ་དྲག་ kūtra'	(n.) aristocrat, noble
སྲང་ལམ་ trānglam, sānglam (L)	(n.) street, alley
བཙན་ tsā̄n	(n.) *tsän* (local warrior-god)

ནས་བཟུང་ näsung'	(adv.) since
ཀིན་ kin	(part.) *gerundive*
རེ་མོས་+བྱེད་ remö' che'	(v.) [vol., E] to take turns
འཁྲབ་ thrāp	(v.) [vol., EA] to act, perform
སྣེ་ལེན་+ཞུ་ nēlen shu	(v.) [vol., EA] to receive, host
གུས་བཏུས་+ཞུ་ khutü' shu	(v.) [vol., ED] to present one's respects
གཟིགས་འབུལ་+ཞུ་ sīkpü: shu (H)	(v.) [vol., EA] to stage a performance

Proper nouns

སྐྱོར་མོ་ལུང་བ་ kyōrmolungwa	Kyormolungwa (opera troupe)
ཅུང་པ་བ་ cūngpawa	Chungbawa (opera troupe)
རྒྱང་མཁར་བ་ kyangkarwa	Gyangkharwa (opera troupe)
ཞོལ་ shö:	area of Lhasa, at the foot of the Potala
རབ་གསལ་ rapsä:	Balcony in front of a window, name of a Lhasa street: Rabsäl Street
དཔལ་ལྷའི་རི་ཁྲོད་ pālä: ritrö'	Ceremony of Pändän Lhamo
དཔལ་ལྷའི་རི་རབ་ pālä: rirap	Ceremony of Pändän Lhamo (alternative name)
དགའ་ལྡན་ལྔ་མཆོད་ kantän ngāmcö'	Ceremony of Gandän Ngamchö, commemoration of Lord Tsongkhapa's death, on the 25th of the tenth month
ཞོ་སྟོན་ shotön	Zhotön, Yogurt Festival

41.3 Remarks འགྲེལ་བཤད།

41.3.1 The directional and aspectual auxiliaries ཡོང་ yong and འགྲོ་ tro

Verbs of movement are often formed by using directional auxiliaries that specify whether an action is coming towards or going away from the speaker (or the point of reference).

Ex.:	ཁོང་མཆོང་ཡོང་གིས།	"He's coming jumping." (he's jumping this way)
	ཁོང་མཆོང་འགྲོ་གིས།	"He's going jumping." (he's jumping away)
	ང་ནང་ལ་ལོག་འགྲོ་གི་ཡིན།	"I'm going back home (away from the interlocutor)."
	ང་ནང་ལ་ལོག་ཡོང་གི་ཡིན།	"I'm coming back home (towards the interlocutor)."

The two auxiliaries may also be used with non-volitional verbs to indicate the beginning of a process (inchoative sense). The auxiliary yong is used with the first person (singular or plural), whereas tro is used with the second and third persons (singular or plural).

Ex.:	ང་གཉིད་ཁུག་ཡོང་གིས།	"I'm starting to fall asleep."
	ཁོང་གཉིད་ཁུག་འགྲོ་གིས།	"He's starting to fall asleep."

ང་འཁྱག་ཡོང་གིས། "I'm starting to feel cold."
ཁོང་འཁྱག་འགྲོ་གིས། "He's starting to feel cold."

41.3.2 Nominal clauses

Like relative clauses, nominal clauses (whether as subject, object or complement) are formed with the use of a nominalizer, but it is important to distinguish between the two types. For this purpose the nominalizers པ་-pa, ཡག་-ya' and རྒྱུ་-kyu are used (see Lessons 11, 25) . They may be followed by the genitive or oblique case (when the function of the clause requires it). The syntactic position of the nominal clause in the sentence depends on its function as subject, object or complement.

Ex.: ཁྱེད་རང་ཕེབས་ཐུབ་པའི་རེ་བ་ཡོད།

"I hope you'll be able to come." (nominal clause = complement of the noun རེ་བ་)

རང་སློབ་སྦྱོང་ཡག་པོ་དང་གཟུགས་པོ་བདེ་ཐང་ཡོང་ཡག་སྨོན་འདུན་ཞུ་རྒྱུ་ཡིན་

"I pray that you should be in good health and that you study well." (nominal clause =object of the verb སྨོན་འདུན་ཞུ་)

བུ་མོ་དེ་མོ་རང་རང་གི་ཨ་ལྕག་ཡིན་པ་ཤེས་པ་རེད།

"She realized that the girl was her own sister." (nominal clause =object of the verb ཤེས་)

ཁོང་གིས་བོད་པ་ཚང་མ་སྐྱོ་པོ་ཡིན་པ་བསམས་པ་རེད་པས།

"Did he think all Tibetans were poor?" (nominal clause =object of the verb བསམ་)

ཁོང་གིས་བོད་པ་ཚང་མ་སྐྱོ་པོ་རེད་བསམས་པ་རེད་པས། *idem.*

41.3.3 The construction ཁང་khang + Adj / V / doubled Adv

This construction appears in several expressions consisting of the pronoun khang "what", "as much" followed by an adjective or, sometimes, a verb or an adverb, usually doubled.

Ex.: ཁང་མགྱོགས་མགྱོགས་ "as quickly as possible", ཁང་ཡག་ཡག "as well as possible", ཁང་མང་མང་ "as many as possible", ཁང་གཟབ་གཟབ་ "as carefully as possible", ཁང་ཡོད་ཡོད་ "as much as possible".

We also find khang in several constructions such as: ཁང་ཐུབ་ཅི་ཐུབ "as much as possible", ཁང་བྱུང་མང་བྱུང་"anyhow, indiscriminately", ཁང་ལ་ཁང་འཚམས་"as appropriate, as convenient,", etc.

41.4 Exercises སྦྱོང་ཚན།

41.4.1 Translate into English:

༡) ཁོས་བཙུན་མོ་ཆུང་བ་ཀླུ་ལྕམ་མཛེས་མ་ཟེར་མཁན་དེ་འཕྲོག་ཕྱིན་པ་རེད།

༢) ཁོང་གིས་ཐུབ་བསྟན་སྨན་ཁང་ལ་ཁྲིད་ཕྱིན་པ་རེད།

༣) སང་ཉིན་ང་ཚུར་ཡོང་དུས་བུ་རྒན་པ་འཁྲིད་ཡོང་གི་ཡིན།

༤) ཁྱེད་རང་གིས་ཕྱུག་ཟླེ་བསྣམས་ཕེབས་པས།

༥) ང་ད་ལྷ་ཞེད་ཡོང་གིས།

༦) བུ་མོ་ཆུང་ཆུང་དེ་ཁྱི་ལ་ཞེད་འགྲོ་གི་འདུག་ག

༧) དགུན་ཁ་སློབ་སྦྱོང་བྱས་པ་དེ་དབྱར་ཁར་བརྗེད་འགྲོ་གི་རེད།

༨) སྐད་ཆ་བཤད་ན་ཁོང་རླུང་ལང་འགྲོ་གི་རེད།

༩) བོད་ཟླ་དྲུག་པའི་ཚེས་པ་༣༠་ལ་ཞོགས་གས་སྔ་པོ་ནས་འབྲས་སྤུངས་ལ་སྟོན་པ་ཤཱཀྱ་ཐུབ་པའི་སྐུ་ཐང་ཆེན་པོ་ཡོད་པ་དེ་བཀྲམ་གྱི་རེད།

༡༠) དཔལ་ལྷའི་རི་ཁྲོད་ཟེར་ཡག་གི་དུས་ཆེན་གྱི་མིང་དེ་ཁ་རྒྱུན་ལ་ཆགས་པ་རེད་མ་གཏོགས་དངོས་ནས་བྱས་ན་དཔལ་ལྷའི་རི་རབ་ཟེར་གྱི་རེད།

41.4.2 Answer the following questions:

༡) ཞོ་སྟོན་ཟེར་ཡག་དེ་ག་དུས་འགོ་ཚུགས་ཀྱི་རེད།

༢) ཞོ་སྟོན་ཉི་མ་ག་ཚོད་བཏང་གི་རེད།

༣) དཔལ་ལྷའི་རི་ཁྲོད་སྐབས་ལ་ལྷ་ས་བ་ཚོས་ག་རེ་བྱེད་ཀྱི་རེད།

༤) ཟླ་བ་བཅུ་པའི་ཚེས་ཤར་ནས་ཚེས་བཅོ་ལྔ་བར་ལ་ཕྲུ་གུ་ཚོས་ག་རེ་སྤྲུག་བརྡད་ཀྱི་རེད།

41.5 Civilization རིག་གཞུང་།

From Classical to Modern Tibetan literature: a long living tradition.

Literary Tibetan has been around for over a thousand years. The earliest texts go back to the seventh century. In terms of its quality, originality, diversity and sheer volume, the classical literature of the Land of Snows ranks among the great literary traditions of Asia. The Sayings of Sakya Pandita (thirteenth century), the songs of Milaräpa (twelfth century) the poems of the Sixth Dalai Lama and the Epic of Gesar of Ling are already a part of the world's literary heritage. Whether written in prose or verse, traditional Tibetan literature covers a wide range of domains, including Buddhism, history, medicine, astrology, grammar and poetry.

Since the beginning of the twentieth century, Tibet has seen the gradual development of a modern literature that follows on directly from this tradition. The landmark figure of Gendün Chömpel, who died in 1950, provides the link between the classical style and the emergence of modern genres. However, it was only at the beginning of the 1980s that Tibet witnessed a real explosion of this new literature. Innovative genres, such as the short story, free verse and even the novel began to appear, while some thirty new literary magazines made a significant contribution to the development of the field.

Contemporary Tibetan writing has been influenced by several currents: classics in Chinese and in European languages, as well as canonical and Classical Tibetan literature, not to mention the oral traditions of the nomads.

Tibetan authors write in Modern Literary Tibetan, a superb language that has remained very close to the classical style, even though it has evolved gradually and been enriched by the adoption of many neologisms.

The last thirty years have seen the publication, in this modern style, of numerous works covering an extraordinary diversity of subjects such as science, politics, economics, astrology, history, Buddhism, medicine, education and literary criticism.

The preferred literary genres are, understandably enough, poetry and short stories, which give the authors an opportunity to deal with Tibetan thought and culture. Fiction is the ideal medium through which to describe the people and the landscape of the high plateau, and to evoke both ancient traditions as well as the upheavals that the society has experienced. The perspectives of these writers on the Tibetan world are entirely new and original.

It will be evident, from a comparison of the following four poems, that Modern Literary Tibetan doesn't represent a break from the classical language. The first poem was written by Sakya Pandita in the thirteenth century; the second and third are attributed to the Sixth Dalai Lama (early seventeenth century), while the last was written in the late twentieth century by Sangda Dorje, one of the authors of this Manual.

མ་དཔྱད་པ་ལས་དོན་གྲུབ་པ།
བྱུང་ཡང་མཛངས་པར་སུ་ཞིག་བསྟེ།
སྲིན་འབུ་དག་གིས་བྲིས་པའི་རྗེས།
ཡི་གེར་བྱུང་ཡང་ཡིག་མཁན་མིན།།

"Those who achieve something
Without reflecting on it cannot be deemed wise;
Though woodworms may leave traces like letters,
They aren't scribes."

བྱ་དེ་ཁྲུང་ཁྲུང་དཀར་མོ།
ང་ལ་གཤོག་སྒལ་གཡར་དང་།
ཐག་རིང་རྒྱང་ལ་མི་འགྲོ
ལི་ཐང་བསྐོར་ནས་སླེབས་ཡོང་།།

"O white crane,
Lend me your wings!
I shan't go far,
I shall visit Lithang and come back."

བྲིས་པའི་ཡི་གེ་ནག་ཆུང་།
ཆུ་དང་ཐིག་པས་བཞིགས་སོང་།
མ་བྲིས་སེམས་ཀྱི་རི་མོ།
བསུབས་ཀྱང་ཟུབ་རྒྱུ་མི་འདུག།

"Little black letters set down in writing
Are washed away by raindrops;
Unwritten lines on the heart
Can never be erased."

རྒྱང་སླུ།

མཚན	མོའི	མགོན	དུ	བསིལ	བའི	ཟེར	བརྒྱ	དཀར
མཚན	མོའི	གཉེན	མཐོང	སྙིང	སྡུག	བཞིན	མཛེས	དྲན
ཉེན	མོ	ནམ	མཁའ	དྭངས	པར	སྤྲིན	དཀར	གྱི
བྲ	ཚོམ	ནམ	མཁའི	ཟླ	བྲལ	རྒྱན	མཛེས	བཞིན
བཀོད	ཚེ	བདག	ཡིད	སློང	དུ	ཁྲིད	སྒྲུ	འཆར
སྙིང	སྡུག	མིག	ཡངས	རྒྱུན	དུ	དྲན	ནས	སྒྲོ
གྱ	མ	མཛེས	སྡུག	བཞིན	རས	ཆ	རྫོགས	ཟླ
མིག	རྒྱན	མ	ཁྲིད	ལང	ཚོའི	དཔལ	རྫོགས	ཞིང
བཞིན	མཛེས	བརྩེ	ཡང	གྲོགས	སྐལ	དམན	པའི	ཟླ

"Song of Separation"

Künkor[169] by Sangda Dorje (1992)

In the vastness of the night sky, the full moon rises,
White and beautiful, a splendid jewel in cloudless space,
A hundred pale cool beams in the sheltering night.
Seeing this nocturnal companion, as beautiful as my beloved,
Brings her to my mind.
When the white clouds are set like jewels in the brightness of the day's sky,
As beautiful as the unrivalled ornaments of heaven,
Your form arises in the vault of my mind.
The enduring memory of your wide eyes, beloved, saddens me.
Ah, beautiful face like the full moon,
Ornament of the eyes, in the splendour of your youth,
Though your dear face shines with love,
I am your wretched companion.

169. *Künkor,* or "magic squares", originally devised by the Fifth Dalai Lama, may be read in any direction. This poem, for example, has to be read along both diagonals and then across, as one would normally read.

Outlines of the Differences between Literary and Spoken Tibetan

The differences between Literary (Modern and Classical) and Spoken Tibetan lie in the lexicon (vocabulary), grammatical words and, to a lesser extent, syntax and pronunciation.

The classical language is characterized by its conciseness and by the corresponding importance of context and cultural background.

A text in the classical style would be shorter than a Standard Tibetan rendering of the same material. The classical, literary language owes its concentrated, terse character to a number of factors:

— Nouns, adjectives and verbs tend to be monosyllabic, whereas the oral language tends to use polysyllabic forms.

— Verbs can function autonomously, whereas oral Tibetan requires the systematic use of auxiliaries.

— Case markers, nominalizers and conjunctions may be left out when the semantic context is clear enough for them to be redundant. Ellipses of this sort are especially common in poetry, to satisfy the demands of the metre.

— Literary Tibetan often foreshortens compound words by omitting syllables.

— Coreferential pronouns and nouns are generally avoided. When there is no ambiguity, the "subject" is introduced only once, and may not reappear in a given passage.

And finally, from a syntactic point of view, the written language is often more flexible than the oral. For example, adjectives and relative constructions may be placed either before or after the noun, whereas in oral Tibetan they almost always follow and precede them respectively.

Anyone who knows colloquial Tibetan can quite easily learn the literary language, and vice versa. The following pages, containing a systematic survey of the main points of difference, are intended to serve as a bridge between the two registers. The lists presented here are by no means exhaustive, but at least they illustrate some of the fundamental differences. For further details about the literary language we would highly recommend *The Classical Tibetan Language* (Beyer, 1992) and, in French, *le Clair Miroir* (Kesang Gyurmé, 1994).

1. Current and literary pronunciation

Literary Tibetan is used by Tibetans of all regions, however different their spoken dialects may be, as well as in Bhutan, Ladakh and the dozen or so ethnically Tibetan enclaves of Nepal such as Khumbu (the Sherpas), Mustang and Dolpo, as well as by speakers of languages other than Tibetan such as the Mongols, Kalmyks, Buryats and, more recently, Western practitioners of Vajrayana Buddhism. Obviously, the pronunciation of Literary Tibetan will vary according to the reader's regional provenance, so that a native of Kham or Amdo, for example, will read a text in very different accent from a Central Tibetan.

In the following pages, examples of Literary Tibetan will be presented in a transcription that corresponds to the reading pronunciation by a speaker of Standard (or Central) Tibetan.

As a general rule, conversational pronunciation of Standard Tibetan is identical with that of Literary Tibetan[170], and follows the conventions for spelling and pronunciation (see Table 10 in Appendix 6). Certain words, however, are pronounced differently in colloquial usage (this pronunciation will be unmarked) and according to literary convention (marked with an L below), as when someone is reading aloud or quoting.

For example, འབྲི *'bri*, "the yak cow", is pronounced /tri̱/ in literary language and /pi̱/ in colloquial usage. Similarly, in the case of the following words: སྦྲ་ནག་*sbra-nag* "nomad tent" /tra̱na'/(L), /pa̱na'/; བཞེངས་*bZhengs* "to get up" (H), "to construct" /she̱ng'/(L), /sha̱ng'/; འཛེགས་ *'dzegs* "to climb" /tse̱'/(L), /tsa̱'/; ཏོག་ཙམ *tog-tsam* "a little" /tōktsam/ (L), /tē(t)s/; བྲིན་ *brin* "to be sellable, to be sold" /thri̱n/ (L), /phi̱m/; ཤེས་ཀྱི་ཡོད་ *shes+ kyi-yod* "I know" /shē'+kiyö'/ (L), /shēn+kiyö'/; རྔ་མོང་ *rnga-mong* "camel" /ngāmong/ (L), /āmong/; སྤྲང་པོ་ *sprang-po* "beggar" /trāngpo/(L), /pāngko/; མི་དགོས་ *mi dgos* "I don't need" /mi̱ kö̱'/ (L), /mu̱ ko̱'/.

These differences may be explained in terms of the simple rules that will be set out below. The rules will make it possible to account for the majority of cases in which colloquial pronunciation differs markedly from the literary form. Colloquial pronunciation is not accommodated by special spelling, except in the case of certain modern writings that try to reproduce vernacular speech.

---

170. There are some minor discrepancies that occur in a very careful literary or reading pronunciation (and in some cases of hypercorrection): The final suffixed letters *g, l, r* are then respectively pronounced as /k, l, r/ (while in normal reading k yields a glottal stop; l and r a lengthening of the preceding vowel.). Initial aspirate consonants in second syllables usually keep their aspiration in careful reading while the aspiration is lost otherwise.

Features of colloquial pronunciation

- "Floating nasals".
- The disappearance of the subscript *r* of a labial. Thus a labial /p/ is pronounced instead of the usual retroflex affricate /tr/.
- The disappearance of the semi-vowel /w/ in the nominal suffixes /wa/ and /wo/.
- The transformation of the labial /p/ into a /k/ when it is preceded by a velar in the nominal and adjectival suffixes /po/, /pa/, /pu/.

The following unusual phenomena may be added to these basic rules:

- The transformation of vowels within certain words.
- The pronunciation of certain consonants that are usually silent.

1.1 The appearance of "floating nasals" within a word

"Floating nasals" do exist in the literary register, but are more characteristic of the spoken language. They are produced when the following letters (and groups of letters) appear at *the beginning of the second syllable*:

The prefixes *'a* འ (a chung) and *m* མ and the majority of combinations involving an *l*: *zl* ཟླ་, *ld* ལྡ་, *lt* ལྟ་, *lj* ལྗ་.

Furthermore, when the letter *l* ལ་ appears at the end of the first syllable it may also produce a nasal.

The prefixes *'a* and *m,* as well as the combinations that can produce a nasal, are called "nasalizers" (marked as ɴ in the transcription). The resulting nasal is the dental n, the labial m or the velar ng, depending on the case. It is generally articulated in the same place (homorganic articulation) as the final consonant of the first syllable (S1) or the first consonant of the second (S2). The following configurations may be encountered:

- /p/ before the nasalizer is pronounced as /m/.

Ex.: ཞབས་འདེགས་zhabs 'degs > sha̱p+ɴte̱' > sha̱mte' "service"
ཞིབ་འཇུག་ zhib 'jug > shīp+ɴcu̱' > shi̱mcu' "research"

- /k/ before the nasalizer is pronounced as /ng/.

Ex.: མིག་འཁྲུལ་ mig-'khrul > mīk+ɴtrǖ: > mīngtrü: "illusion"

- a nasal consonant before the nasalizer remains unchanged.

Ex.: སྔོན་འགྲོ་sngon 'gro > ngȫntro, སྨོན་འདུན་ smon 'dun > mȫntün

- If the nasalizer is preceded by a vowel or a lengthening (due to an *r* or an *l*), a nasal consonant is produced in the place of articulation of the following consonant, that is, the first consonant of the second syllable (S2). The following configurations may be encountered:

— Before /p/, the nasalizer is pronounced /m/.

Ex.: དཔལ་འབར་ dpal-‘bar > pā̃:+ɴpar > pā̃mpar (personal name)
དམའ་འབེབས་ dma‘-‘bebs > mā̃mpep “contempt”

Sometimes, the labial is present in the spelling only in the form of a *b*:

Ex.: ཤ་འབྲས་ sha-‘bras >shāmträ' “meat stew (with rice and potatoes)”

— Before /t/, /ts/ or /c/, the nasalizer is pronounced /n/:

Ex.: དགེ་འདུན་ dge-‘dun > ke̱ntün
མི་འདུག་ mi-‘dug > mi̱ntu'
བོད་ལྗོངས་ bod-ljongs phö̱ncong “Land of Tibet” (i.e., Tibet)

— Before /k/ or /ky/, the nasalizer is pronounced /ng/:

Ex.: དུས་འཁོར་dus-‘khor > thü̱ngkor “wheel of time”
གསར་འགྱུར་ gsar-‘gyur > sāngkyur “news”

However, in cases where the nasal is due to the prefix *m*, it is this sound that is often heard, whatever the following consonant might be: རྒྱུ་མཚན་ *rgyu-mtshan* “reason” /kyu̱mtsän/.

These nasals are described as “floating” inasmuch as they are not entirely obligatory, especially during “precise” reading. By contrast, they are almost always used in the spoken language.

Thus རྒྱ་མཚོ *rgya-mtsho* “ocean” is pronounced /kya̱mtso/ as well as /kya̱tso/, རྒྱུ་མཚན་ *rgyu-mtshan* “reason” as either /kyu̱mtsän/ or /kyu̱tsän/. But སྐུ་ཟླ་ *sku-zla* “spouse” (H) is always pronounced /kūnta/ and not */kūta/. Similarly, རྒྱལ་རྩེ *rgyal-rtse* “Gyantse town” is pronounced /kya̱ntse/ but never */kya̱tse/; དགེ་འདུན་ *dge-‘dun* “sangha” as /ke̱ntün/ but not */ke̱tün/. It may be mentioned in passing that literate Tibetans are not usually aware of the fact that they are pronouncing floating nasals, which are described neither in traditional grammars nor in more recent works.

Ex. with *zl, ld, lt lj* or *l:* བོད་ཟླ་ *bod-zla* /phö̱nta/ “Tibetan month”, ད་ལྟ་ *da-lta* /tha̱nta/ “now”, དཔལ་ལྡན *dpal-ldan* /pā̃ntän/ “Pändän (personal name)” སྟོབས་ལྡན *stobs-ldan* /tōmtän/ “dismemberer” (of corpses), ཡུལ་ལྗོངས་*yul-ljongs* /yü̱ncong/ “landscape”, འབྲས་ལྗོངས་ *‘bras-ljongs* /trä̱ncong/ “Sikkim”, ཡལ་ག་ *yal-ga* /yä̱:ka/ or /yä̱nka/ “branch”, དགའ་ལྡན་ *dga‘-ldan* /ka̱ntän/ “Gandän (name of a major monastery near Lhasa)”.

Ex. with the prefix *'a:* གསོལ་འདེབས་ *gsol-'debs* /sōntep/ "prayer", དུད་འགྲོ་ *dud-'gro* /thṳ̄ntro/ "animal", ཞིབ་འཇུག *zhib-'jug* /shi̱mcu'/ "research", འཐབ་འཛིང་ *'thap-'dzing* /thāmtsing/ "struggle", སྐུ་འབུམ *sku-'bum* /kūmpum/ "Kumbum (major monastery in Amdo, Chin.: "Daer si"), ཡར་འབྲོག་གཡུ་མཚོ་ *yar-'brog g.yu-mtsho* /ya̱:mtro' yūmtso/ "Lake Yamdroyumtsho", བདག་འཛིན *bdag-'dzin* /ta̱ngtsin/ "selfishness" (lit.: "self-grasping"), སྐྱབས་འགྲོ *skyab-'gro* /kyāmtro/ "refuge", ཁ་འདོན *kha-'don* /khāntön/ "to recite prayers", ཞལ་འདེབས་ *zhal-'debs* /sha̱ntep/ "offering, contribution", ཞབས་འདེགས་ *zhabs-'degs* /sha̱mte'/ "service"; རྟེན་འབྲེལ་ *rten-'brel* /tēmtre:/ "auspicious combination of events, ceremony".

Ex. with the prefix m: རྒྱལ་མཚན་ *rgyal-mtshan* /kya̱ntsän/ "banner", སྐུ་མདུན་ *sku-mdun* /kūntün/ "the presence, (title of the Dalaï Lama); ཕྱག་མཛོད་ *phyag-mdzod* /chāngtsö'/ "treasurer", ལྷ་མཛེས་ *lha-mdzes* /lhāntse'/ "beautiful goddess (personal name)", ལོ་མཆོད་ *lo-mchod* /lo̱mcö'/ "first year commemoration of the death of a person".

1.2 Disappearance of the subscript 'r' of the labial 'p' or 'b'.

Fortunately, the number of words that have this double pronunciation is rather limited.

The colloquial pronunciation can be deduced by dropping the subscript *r* of the labial. There is no systematic rule for dropping the subscript *r*, and the optional pronunciation will therefore be flagged on each occasion.

Other examples:

བྲག་ལྷ་ཀླུ་ཕུག་ *brag-lha lu-phug* thra̱lalupu' (L), pha̱lalupu' Bhalaluphuk (name of a temple in Lhasa)

བྲིན་ *brin* thri̱n (L), phi̱m "to be sellable"

འབྲང་སྒྲིག་ *'brang-sgrig* tra̱ngtri'(L), pa̱ngtri' "to form a queue"

སྦྲ་ནག་ *sbra-nag* tra̱na' (L), pa̱na' "nomad tent"

སྦྲ་ནག་ཞོལ་ *sbra-nag-zhol* tra̱nakshö:(L), pa̱nakshö The Banagzhöl section of Lhasa.

སྦྲང་བུ་ *sbrang-bu* tra̱ngpu (L), pa̱ngku "bee"

དུག་སྦྲང་ *dug-sbrang* thu̱ktrang (L), thu̱kpang "mosquito"

སྦྲང་ནག་ *sbrang-nag* tra̱ngna' (L), pa̱ngna' "fly"(But note that སྦྲང་རྩི་ *sbrang-rtsi* "honey" tra̱ngtsi is not pronounced * pa̱ngtsi.)

སྤྲེའུ་ *spri'u* trīu (L), pīu "monkey"

སྤྲེལ་ལད་བཤད་ *sprel-lad bshad* trēlä' shā̱'(L), pē:lä' shā̱' "to lick someone's boots" (lit. to imitate a monkey)

བྲེགས་ *bregs* thre̱'(L) pha̱', "to cut with scissors."

1.3 The modification of the suffixes /wa, wo, pa, po, pu/

The phonetic rules and transformations that will be described here concern only words that have the nominal or adjectival suffixes /wa, wo, pa, po, pu/. The modifications occur only in a conversational or familiar register. They are determined by the last phoneme of the preceding syllable.

—The /w/ of the suffix /wa/ disappears after the consonants /r/, /l/ and /ng/ which are then doubled:[171]

Ex.: མགར་བ་ *mgar-ba* “blacksmith” k̲arwa (L), k̲arra
སྐོར་བ་ *skor-ba* “circuit”, “to go around” kōrwa (L), kōrra
ཐལ་བ་ *thal-ba* “dust” thā̄:wa (L), thā̄lla
བྲེལ་བ་ *brel-ba* “to be busy” thre̲:wa (L), thre̲lla
གསལ་བ་ *gsal-ba* “clearer” sā̄:wa (L), sā̄rra
སྐལ་བ་ *skal-ba* “fortune, lot” kā̄:wa (L), kā̄lla
དམྱལ་བ་ *dmyal-ba* “hell” nyā̄:wa (L), nyā̄lla
མང་བ་ *mang-ba* “majority” ma̲ngwa (L), ma̲ngnga
ཡོང་བ་ *yong-ba* “all right” yo̲ngwa (L), yo̲ngnga
སོལ་བ་ *sol-ba* “charcoal” sō:wa (L), sōlla

Colloquial pronunciation is sometimes reproduced by the spellings used in letter-writing (though never in literary texts): སྐོར་བ་, མང་བ་ and ཡོང་བ་ are accordingly written: སྐོར་ར་ *skor-ra*, མང་ང་ *mang-nga* and ཡོང་ང *yong-nga*.

—The suffixes /wa/ and /wo/ take the form of a lengthening after /a/ and /o/:

Ex.: ལྷ་ས་བ་ *lha-sa-ba* “inhabitant of Lhasa” lhāsawa (L), lhāsa:
སློབ་གྲྭ་བ་ *slob-grwa-ba* “student” lōptrawa (L), lāptra:
ལྟ་བ་ *lta-ba* “vision, theory” tāwa (L), tā:
ངོ་བོ་ *ngo-bo* “essence” ngo̲wo (L), ngo̲:
གཙོ་བོ་ *gtso-bo* “principal, main” tsōwo (L), tsō:

—The suffixes /pa/, /po/, /pu/ are pronounced respectively[172] /ka/, /ko/, ku/:

Ex.: ཤོག་བུ་ *shog-bu* “paper” shōkpu (L), shūkku[173]
བོང་བུ་ *bong-bu* “donkey” pho̲ngpu (L), phu̲ngku
སྦྲང་བུ་ *sbrang-bu* “bee” tra̲ngpu (L), pa̲ngku
ཡག་པོ་ *yag-po* “good” ya̲kpo (L), ya̲kko
ཡག་པ་ *yag-pa* “better” ya̲kpa (L), ya̲kka
ཀོང་པོ་ *kong-po* “Kongpo” (a region in Tibet) kōngpo (L), kōngko
སྤྲང་པོ་ *sprang-po* “beggar” trāngpo (L), pāngko
མགྱོགས་པོ་ *mgyogs-po* “rapid” kyo̲kpo (L), kyo̲kko

---

171. From a strictly phonetic point of view, these doubled consonants are pronounced like simple consonants (like the *ll* in “wallow”).

172. This may be seen as a case of assimilation: when the labial is preceded by a velar (plosive k or nasal ng), the locus of its articulation changes and it becomes a velar.

173. Remember that geminate consonants (kk, pp, etc.) are pronounced as if there were only one consonant. Only the tone is affected.

Colloquial pronunciation may be reflected in informal spelling: thus ཤོག་བུ་ and ཡག་པ་ are sometimes written as ཤོག་གུ་ *shog-gu* and ཡག་ག *yag-ga*.

Note: This pronunciation is not systematic: thus འབྲེལ་བ་ *'brel ba* "relationship" is pronounced /tre̱:wa/ and never *tre̱lla. Furthermore, it applies only in the case of the suffixes *pa, po, pu* and not the combinations of /k+p/ in general. For example, དམག་སྤུངས་ /mākpung/ "army" never becomes *mākkung, and likewise དམག་དཔོན་/mākpön/ "general" is never pronounced *mākön. Similarly, ཐག་པ་ /thākpa/ "rope" never becomes *thākka.

1.4 Modification of the pronunciation of vowels in certain words

In most cases, vowel changes occur in polysyllabic words, and are caused by the influence of other vowels in the same word. There is a sort of vowel harmony at work.[174] The variations are generally restricted to closely-related vowels: e / i, o / u, ü / i.

Changes may also occur within monosyllabic words, in which case it is no longer a question of vowel harmony. There is no way of predicting this sort of pronunciation, but fortunately there are very few examples. Remember that the examples given here do not apply to literary pronunciation.

— The vowel *e* is sometimes pronounced /a/.

Ex.: འཛེགས་ *'dzegs* "to climb" tse̱' (L), tsa̱', ཚེག་ *tsheg* "intersyllabic mark" tshē' (L), tshā', བཞེང་ *bzheng* "to build" (H), she̱ng (L), sha̱ng, བཤེགས་ *bshegs* "to die" (H) shē' (L), shā'

— The vowel *u* (normally pronounced /ü/ in the combinations *ud, un, us*) becomes /i/ in certain words.

Ex.: སྐྱག་རྫུན་ *skyag-rdzun* "lie" kyāktsün (L), kyāktsin, ཕུད་ *phud* "to take off" phǖ' (L), phī', སྡུག་རུས་ *sdug-rus* "resistance" tu̱krü' (L), tu̱kri'.

— The vowel *o* is sometimes pronounced /u/ in certain words:

Ex.: ཤིང་བཟོ་ *shing-bzo* "carpentry" shīngsu, ཤོག་གུ་ *shog-gu* "paper" shūkku, བོང་བུ་ *bong-bu* "donkey" phu̱ngku

On the other hand, it sometimes happens that the vowel *u* is pronounced /o/. Very exceptionally, the variations that are caused by vowel harmony are formalized in the spelling. Thus བཅུ་ *bcu* "ten" is usually pronounced /cū/ both when it stands alone as well as in the compounds བཅུ་གཅིག་ *bcu-gcig* "eleven" /cūci'/, བཅུ་གཉིས་ *bcu-gnyis* "twelve" /cūnyi'/, བཅུ་གསུམ་ *bcu-gsum* "thirteen" /cūksum/, but is pronounced /cō/ or /cō̈/ and is actually written with an *o* in the compounds བཅོ་ལྔ་ *bco-lnga* "fifteen" /cō̈nga/ and བཅོ་བརྒྱད་ *bco-brgyad* "eighteen" /cōpkyä'/, since the vowel of the second syllable is more open (a, ä).

174. This phenomenon can also be described as an assimilation of the vowel aperture.

— the vowel *e* is pronounced as /i/ in certain words:

Ex.: ཤེས་རིག་ *shes-rig* "culture" shīri'

And finally, there are occasional exceptions such as: ལྕི་བ་ *lci-ba* "dung" cīwa (L), cōwa.

1.5 Special pronunciation of the rhyme 'ab(s)'

In certain colloquial words, the suffixes *ab* and *abs* are pronounced /o/ (sometimes followed by a lengthening). Here are some examples:

དགའ་རབ་ *dga'-rab* ka̲rap (L), ka̲ro "quite a few", སྐུ་ཞབས་ *sku-zhabs* kūshap (L), kūsho "sir", གྲབས་ *grabs* thra̲p (L), tro̲: "to be about to"

1.6 Special pronunciation of certain consonants

In certain rare cases, the consonant /p/ figures in a word even when its presence isn't justified by the spelling.

Ex.: བཟོ་ལྟ་ *bzo-lta* so̲pta: "shape", ཁ་ཟས་ *kha-zas* /khāpsä'/ "fried pastry", རྨ་བྱ་ *rma-bya* /māpca/ "peacock", སྒྲ་སྙན་ *sgra-snyan* /tra̲pnyän/ "Tibetan lute", etc.

On the other hand, the consonants /ng/ and /n/ are sometimes pronounced /m/ at the end of certain words: སྒྲུང་*sgrung* tru̲ng (L), tru̲m "story, tale", ཟིན་*zin* si̲n (L), si̲m "to seize, grasp", བྲིན་ *brin* tri̲n (L), phi̲m "to be sold", མཆོང་*mchong* chōng (L), chōm "to jump", ཤོང*shong* shōng (L), shūm "to fit", མནན་*mnan* nǟn (L), nǟm (or even lǟm) "to press down".

2. The lexicon

2.1 Differences in the vocabulary

The lexicon is one of the fields in which there are major discernable differences between Literary and Spoken Tibetan, even if the basic vocabulary is the same in both registers.

It should not be supposed, however, that there is a clear distinction between the two: some literate Tibetans may use in their daily language words that are more characteristic of the literary register, while certain journals and texts may use colloquial terminology.

In the lists of examples, the words marked with an (L) appear only in literary language. In the subsequent examples, words to the left of the "equals" sign (=) correspond to Literary Tibetan, while those to the right belong to the colloquial register. The few words that are not used in the literary language are marked with the sign (*L).

— Verbs:

Ex.: བྱོན་ = ཕེབས་ "to arrive" (H), རིག་= མཐོང་ "to see", མཛད་/ བགྱིད་ = གནང་ "to do" (H), སྨྲས་/ བརྗོད་ = ལབ་ "to speak", ལྕེབ་= མཆོངས་ "to jump"/ རང་ཤི་བརྒྱབ་ "to commit suicide",

སྐྱོད་/ མཆི་= འགྲོ་ "to go", སྩོལ་= གནང་ "to give" (H), སྙམ་= བསམ་ "to think", མངའ་/ མཆིས་ = ཡོད་ "to be, to exist", བཀྲེས་= གྲོད་ཁོག་ལྟོགས་ "to be hungry", མགུ་= འདོད་པ་ཁེངས་ "to be satisfied"/དགའ "to be happy, to rejoice", འཇིག་/ སྐྲག་= ཞེད་ "to be afraid", བསྐམ་= འདོད་ "to desire", རྒ་ = རྒན་འཁོག་ཆགས་"to age, grow old", བལྟམས་= ཁྲུངས་ "to be born" (H), གསོལ་བ་བཏབ་ = སྨོན་ལམ་རྒྱག་ "to pray", etc.

— Nouns:

Ex.: བཞིན་རས་= ཞལ་རས་ "face" (H) / གདོང་པ་; བྱིས་པ་ / ཕྲུ་གུ་ = ཕུ་གུ (*L) "child", རྣ་བ་ = ཨམ་མཆོག་(*L) "ear", བཤེས་གཉེན་ = དགེ་རྒན་ "teacher" or གྲོགས་པོ་ "friend", བློ་/ ཡིད་ = སེམས་ "mind", སྐུ་ན་= ལོ་ "age", སྐྱེ་བོ་= མི་ "human being", གླེན་པོ་ = གླུགས་པ་ "idiot", ཉིན་= ཉི་མ་ "day", ནགས་ཚལ་ = ཤིང་ནགས་ "forest", ལུས་ = གཟུགས་པོ་ "body", མེ་ལོང་= ཤེལ་སྒོ་ "mirror", ཟས་= ཁ་ལག་ "food", གོས་ = དུག་སློག་(*L) "clothing", ནད་= ན་ཚ་ "illness", etc.

— Adjectives:

Ex.: ལེགས་ = ཡག་པོ་ "good", མྱུར་= མགྱོགས་པོ་ "quick", ཡིད་དུ་འོང་བ་ = སེམས་ལ་འགྲོ་པོ་/ མཛེས་པོ་ "beautiful", ཁྱད་དུ་བྱུང་བ་/ མཆོག་ = རྩེ་གྲ་"excellent, extraordinary"

— Adverbs:

Ex.: ཤིན་ཏུ་ = ཞེ་དྲགས་ "very", ལྟ་བུ་ = ནང་བཞིན་ "like, as", ཀུན་/ ཐམས་ཅད་/ མ་ལུས་/ ཇི་སྙེད་ = ཚང་མ་/ གང་ག་ "all", དུ་མ་ = མང་པོ་ "many", ལ་ལ་/ འགའ་ཞིག་/ ཁ་ཅིག་ = ཁ་ཤས་ "some", འབའ་ཞིག་/ ཁོ་ན་ = རྐྱང་རྐྱང་/ གཅིག་པུ་ "only, solely", དེ་མ་ཐག་= ལམ་སང་ "immediately", ཕྲན་བུ་/ ཅུང་ཟད་ = ཏོག་ཙམ་ "a little", ནངས་པར་ = སང་ཉིན་ "tomorrow"

2.2 Verbalizers

In the spoken language, many verbs consist of a noun followed by a verbalizer (see Lesson 14.). The most frequently encountered verbalizers are རྒྱག་ ***rgyag*** "to make", བྱེད་ ***byed*** "to do", བཏང་ ***btang*** "to send". The noun that precedes the verbalizer is often disyllabic, and is sometimes made up of verb roots that function as autonomous verbs in the written language. In the spoken language, verbs can be monosyllabic, disyllabic or trisyllabic.

In Literary Tibetan, verbalizers are not used and verbs are usually monosyllabic or sometimes disyllabic:

Ex.: སློབ་ "to learn" (L), སྦྱོང་ "to study" (L) = སློབ་སྦྱོང་བྱེད་ "to study"
བརྟག་ "to examine" (L), དཔྱད་ "to research" (L) = བརྟག་དཔྱད་བྱེད་ "to examine"
ངལ་གསོས་ "to rest" (L) = ངལ་གསོ་རྒྱག་ "to rest"
མགོ་སྐོར་ "to trick" (L) = མགོ་སྐོར་བཏང་ "to trick"
མགོ་འཁོར་ "to be tricked" (L) = མགོ་སྐོར་ཐེབས་ "to be tricked"
ཁྲོ་ "to get angry" (L) = ཁོང་ཁྲོ་ལང་ "to get angry"

2.3 Nominal and adjectival suffixes

In Literary Tibetan, substantives and adjectives are usually made up of a monosyllabic root without a suffix, whereas the spoken language uses suffixes such as ***pa, po, ma, etc***. But the reverse is also true: in a few cases literary words have a suffix that is absent in the spoken language.

— Nouns:

Ex.: སྣ་ = སྣ་གུག་ (*L) "nose", ལམ་= ལམ་ཁག་(*L) "road, way", སྤྲིན་ = སྤྲིན་པ་ "cloud", ལག་ = ལག་པ་ "hand", དྲི་ = དྲི་མ་ "smell", དགོན་= དགོན་པ་ "monastery", རི་བོ་= རི་ "mountain", ཆུ་བོ་= ཆུ་ (ཆེན་པོ་) "river".

— Adjectives:

Ex.: ནག་ = ནག་པོ་ "black", དཀར་ = དཀར་པོ་ "white", མཛེས་ = མཛེས་པོ་ "beautiful", ཞིམ་ = ཞིམ་པོ་ "delicious", ཆེ་= ཆེན་པོ་"big", རྒན་ = རྒན་པ་ / རྒན་འཁོག་ "old", སླ་ = ལས་སླ་པོ་ "easy".

2.4 Semantic evolution

There are some words that have the same form in Literary and Spoken Tibetan, but have acquired a different meaning. Many of the words listed below are derived from the vocabulary of the Dharma, but have lost their meaning in the spoken language.

— Verbs:

Ex.: བསྒྲུབས་ trup "to realize, achieve (L), to sell", for example ལྷ་བསྒྲུབས་lhā trup**:** "to realize or invoke a god" (L), ཅ་ལག་བསྒྲུབས་ cāla' trup "to sell things".

— Adjectives:

Ex.: བྱང་ཆུབ་ changcup "bodhi= enlightenment (L)", བྱང་ཆུབ་པ་ changcuppa "expert".

— Nouns:

Ex.: དམ་ཚིག་ thamtsi' "samaya, initiatic bond" (L), "happy coincidence".
བསོད་བདེ་ sōta "merit and happiness derived from virtue" (L), "luck".
སེམས་ཅན་ sēmcän "sentient being (human or animal)" (L), "animal". In Labrang, in Amdo, this word has come to mean "all".
ང་རྒྱལ་ngarkyä: "pride" (L), "agressivity, pride".

2.5 Abbreviations

Abbreviations are very common in Literary Tibetan. They are of two kinds: phonic and graphic. The former usually occur only in the case of quadrisyllabic expressions, and consist of omitting the second and fourth syllables.

Ex.: བྱང་སེམས་ changsem = བྱང་ཆུབ་སེམས་དཔའ་ changcup sēmpa "bodhisattva", དེ་གཤེགས་ theshe' = དེ་བཞིན་གཤེགས་པ་theshin shēkpa "Tathagata", ཐེག་ཆེན་ thēkcen= ཐེག་པ་ཆེན་པོ་ thēkpa chēnpo "Mahayana", ཕྱག་རྡོར་ chāktor Chakdor= ཕྱག་ན་རྡོ་རྗེ་ chākna torce "the bodhisattva Vajrapani (or Chaknadorje)", དགེ་སློབ་ kelop = དགེ་རྒན་དང་སློབ་མ་ kekän-tang lōpma "master and disciple(s)", ཞིང་འབྲོག་ shi̱ngtrok = ཞིང་པ་དང་འབྲོག་པ་ shi̱ngpa-tang tro̱kpa "farmers and nomads".

The same principle applies in the spoken language for abridging personal names of four syllables:

Ex.: ཚེ་རྡོར་ tshētor Tshedor = ཚེ་རིང་རྡོ་རྗེ་ tshēring to̱rce Tshering Dorje, བཀྲ་དཔལ་ trāpä: Trapäl = བཀྲ་ཤིས་དཔལ་ལྡན་ trāshi' pāntän Trashi Pändän, ཆོས་རྒྱམ་ ' chōkyam Chögyam = ཆོས་ ཀྱི་ རྒྱ་ མཚོ་ chō-kyi kya(m)tsho Chökyi Gyatsho (or Gyamtsho), བསོད་སྒྲོན་ sōtrön Södrön = བསོད་ནམས་སྒྲོལ་མ་ sönam trö:ma Sönam Drölma.

Note: In some cases, a resyllabification occurs whereby the prefixed or the superscribed letter of the following syllable is interpreted as the final of the preceding syllable. The written orthography records this phenomenon. For example, the last letter in Chögyam, or Tshedor belongs in fact to the fourth syllable (that has been omitted), respectively *mtsho* and *rje*.

Graphic abbreviations consist of using special signs to replace a group of letters. The following are the commonest:

— The circle °, written above a letter, replaces the suffix *m*.

Ex.: ལཾ = ལམ་

— The ཊ་ *Ta* (reversed t) substitutes for the suffix གས་ *gs*.

Ex.: ལཊ = ལགས་; ལེཊ་ = ལེགས་

— There are also abbreviations in which two syllables are graphically compacted into a single syllable,

Ex.: བོུ = བུ་མོ་ "girl"; ཚོུད་ = ཆུ་ཚོད "hour"; བཀྲིས་བདེ་ལེཊ་ = བཀྲ་ཤིས་བདེ་ལེགས་ "best wishes".

2.6 Punctuation

Literary Tibetan has no punctuation in the European sense of the term: there are no syntactic signs to mark off groups of words, clauses, enumerations, etc. However, there are a number of signs to indicate breathers and pauses in the text, although their use is neither systematic or obligatory.

Of all the symbols used in Tibetan, the closest to the European notion of punctuation is the simple bar | called རྐྱང་ཤད་ ***rkyang-shad*** or ཚེག་རིང་ ***tsheg-ring.*** It goes directly after the last letter of a word, in the place of the intersyllabic dot. There are two exceptions to this rule: the simple bar is not used after the letter ག་ *g,* when the latter carries no subscript or superscript: ག།*;* and after the letter ང་*nga*, an intersyllabic dot is placed before the ***rkyang-shad*** to avoid confusion with the letter ག།: ང་།[175]

This punctuation bar may be used to mark the end of a clause, to make it easier to break up a sentence and to emphasize the rhythm of the statements by marking pauses. It may also occur after individual words, especially in the case of lists. It may also go after case markers ***(Ø, gis, nas, la, du, las, etc.),*** conjunctions (***zhing, dang, nas, ste, la***, etc.) and verbs, as well as after the final particle འོ་ (***'o***). The ***rkyang-shad*** may be represented in European languages by a comma, a semicolon, a colon, a question mark or a period. Note that the simple bar is used at the end of each line in poetic verse.

In Literary Tibetan, many of the tasks that European languages assign to punctuation are fulfilled by grammatical particles. Thus འོ་ ***'o*** (and its variants) signify a period or the end of reported speech, བཅས་ ***bcas*** concludes a list and ཅེས་ ***ces*** closes reported speech. One meaning of the particle སྟེ་ ***ste*** is comparable to the function of the semicolon. And finally, depending on the context, the particle འམ་ ***'am*** may correspond to a question mark, a colon or a comma.

Apart from the single bar ། ***(rkyang-shad),*** Tibetan literature also uses the following symbols:

The sign ༄༅ called ཡིག་མགོ་ ***yig-mgo*** or དབུ་འཁྱུད་ ***dbu-'khyud***, which marks the beginning of a text or of a page. However, other indicators of new chapters may appear on the top left-hand corner of a page. The ***swasti*** precedes texts concerned with ethics, the stem and the lotus denote official correspondence, while the jewel introduces chapters that deal with religion.

— The double bar །། called ཉིས་ཤད་ ***nyis-shad*** usually marks the end of a section, and may be rendered by a full stop. In verse texts, the double bar is always written at the end of each verse.

— Two double bars །། །། calledབཞི་ཤད་ ***bzhi-shad*** mark the end of a chapter or an entire work.

— The "serpentine" ༈ called སྦྲུལ་ཤད་ ***sbrul-shad*** marks a separation between two chapters.

— The bar ༑ called རིན་ཆེན་སྤུངས་ཤད་ ***rin-chen spungs-shad*** which is surmounted by one, two or three small dots, appears on the left of a folio when the line begins with a single syllable, to signify the end of the preceding sentence.

— The sign ༔ called གཏེར་ཤད་ ***gter-shad*** takes the form of two circles placed one on top of the other, and separated by a horizontal line. This sign is used instead of the simple bar in ***terma*** or "treasure-texts" which are traditionally held to have been concealed by Padmasambhava ***(guru rin-po-che)*** and subsequently brought to light by "treasure-revealers" གཏེར་སྟོན་ ***gter-ston***.

— A sequence of intersyllabic dots, signifying that the scribe has made a mistake (the dots fill the space occupied by the erased letters) or that there was no room to write the syllables before the end of a line.

---

175. For examples, see the poems quoted in Lesson 41, section 5).

A few other punctuation marks may be added to this list:

— The ཀུ་རུ་ཁ་ ***ku-ru-kha*** or X (cross), which stands for omitted material that is frequently repeated within the text (in the case of prayers, for example).

— A little circle written beneath a syllable, which is intended to attract the reader's attention to the word in question. It corresponds to underlining in European languages.

— Sentences written in letters smaller than those of the main text, corresponding to notes on the original work that have been added by the author or a later commentator.

— Inverted commas and, more rarely, question marks, which are sometimes used in modern writings.

3. Grammatical words and syntax

Certain grammatical words have a completely different form in oral and written Tibetan, although they perform identical functions. In certain cases, however, there are significant syntactic differences. The main differences are summarized below, in relation to the following: nouns, particles, cases, syntax of adjectives, the noun clause, verbal inflection, auxiliaries, reported speech markers and nominalizers.

3.1 Pronouns

Classical Tibetan contains numerous pronominal forms that are not used in the spoken language. In the following lists, the forms that are followed by "L" are literary, whereas the unmarked forms are used in both the spoken and literary registers.

• *Personal pronouns*

The plural of these pronouns is formed by adding one of the following markers: ཚོ་-tso, རྣམས་ nam, ཅག་ -ca', ཅག་རྣམས་ -ca'nam. In some cases, the reflexive རང་ ra̱ng, "same", may be added to the pronoun without changing its meaning.

— First person singular (I):

ང་ nga̱, བདག་ ta̱' (L), ངེད་ nge̱' (L, el.), ངོས་ngö̱' (L, el.), ཕྲན་ thrǟn (L, h), གུས་པ khü̱pa (L, h, masc.), གུས་མོ་ khü̱mo (L, h, fem.), ཁོ་བོ་ khōwo (L, masc.), ཁོ་མོ་ khōmo (L, fem.), རང་ཉིད་ ra̱ngnyi', ཨུ་གུ u̱ku. (L, arch.).

— First person plural (we):

ང་ཚོ་ nga̱tso, བདག་ཅག་ ta̱'ca' (L), བདག་ཅག་རྣམས་ ta̱'ca'nam (L), ངེད་རྣམས་ nge̱nam, ངེད་ཅག་རྣམས་ nge̱ca'nam (L), ངོས་ཅག་ ngö̱ca' (L), ཕྲན་ཚོ་ thrǟntso (L), རང་ཅག་ ra̱ngca' (L, incl.), ཁོ་བོ་ཅག་ khōwoca' (L, excl.), རང་རེ་ ra̱ngre (L), ཨུ་ཅག་ u̱ca' (L, arch.).

—Second person singular (you):

ཁྱོད་ khyö', ཁྱོད་རང་ khyörang, ཁྱེད་ khyē' (H), ཁྱེད་རང་ khyērang (H), ཉིད་ nyi' (L, el.), ཉིད་རང་ nyirang (L, el.), སྐུ་ཉིད་ kūnyi' (L, H).

—Second person plural (you):

ཁྱོད་ཚོ་ khyötso, ཁྱོད་རང་ཚོ་ khyörangtso, ཁྱེད་ནམ་ཚོ་ khyēnamtso (H), ཉིད་ཚོ་ nyitso (L, el.).

—Third person singular (he, she):

ཁོང་ khōng (H), ཁོ་ khō (masc.), ཁོ་རང་ khōrang (masc.), ཁོ་པ་ khōpa (L, masc.), མོ་ mo (fem.), མོ་རང་ mōrang (fem.).

—Third person plural (they):

ཁོང་ཚོ་ khōngtso (H), ཁོ་ཚོ་ khōtso, ཁོང་ནམ་ཚོ་ khōngnamtso (HH), ཁོ་རང་ཚོ་ khōrangtso.

• *Interrogative pronouns*

The main difference between the two registers lies in the modification, in Spoken Tibetan, of གང་ khang to ག kha. Moreover, the morpheme ག has replaced other classical pronouns such as as ཅི་ cī, ཇི་ chi, དུ་ thu and ནམ་ nam.

Literary	Standard Spoken	
སུ་ sū	སུ་ sū	"who"
གང་ khang	ག་རེ་ khare	"what"
ཅི་ cī	ག་རེ་ khare	"what"
གང་གི khangki	ག་གི khaki	"which"
གང་འདྲ་ khangtra	ག་འདྲས་(ཟེ་) khanträ(s)	"how"
གང་འདྲ་ཞིག་ khangtra shik	ག་འདྲས་ཅིག khanträci'	"what sort"
ཇི་འདྲ་ chintra	ག་འདྲས་(ཟེ་) khanträ(s)	"how"
ཇི་ལྟར་ chitar	ག་འདྲས་(ཟེ་) khanträ(s)	"how"
ཇི་ཞིག་ chishi'	ག་འདྲས་(ཟེ་) khanträ(s)	"how"
ཇི་ཙམ་ chitsam	ག་ཚོད་ khatsö'/ khatsä'	"how many"
དུ་ thu	ག་ཚོད་ khatsö'	"how many"
ནམ་ nam	ག་དུས་ khatü'	"when"
གང་དུ་ khangtu	ག་པར་ khapar	"where"
གང་ན་ khangna	ག་པར་ khapar	"where"
ག་རུ་ karu	ག་པར་ khapar	"where"
གང་ནས་ khangnä'	ག་ནས་ khanä'	"from where"
ཅི་ཕྱིར་ cīcir	ག་རེ་བྱས་ནས་ khare chänä'	"why"
གང་གི་དོན་དུ་ khang-ki thön-tu	ག་རེ་དོན་དག་ལ་ khare thönta'-la	"why"
གང་ཡིན་ནམ་ khang yin nam	ག་རེ་ཡིན་ན་ khare yinna	"why"

• ***Indefinite pronouns***

སུས་ཀྱང་ sü̱'-kyang	སུས+ནའི་ [ནའང] sǖ'+V+nä:	"whoever"
སུ་ཡང་ sūyang +NEG	སུ་གང་ sū kha̱ng+NEG	"nobody"
སུ་ཞིག་ sūshi'	སུ་ཡིན་ནའི་ sū yi̱nnä:	"someone, anyone"
ནམ་ཡང་ nàmyang	ག་དུས་+ནའི་ kha̱tü'+V+nä:	"at any time, always"
ནམ་ཡང་ na̱myang+NEG	ག་དུས་+ནའི་ kha̱tü'+V+nä:+NEG	"never"
ཇི་ཙམ་ཡང་ chi̱tsam yang	ག་ཚོད་+ནའི་ kha̱tsö'+V+nä:	"however many"
གང་ཡང་ kha̱ngyang	ག་རེ་+ནའི་ khàre+V+nä:	"whatever"
གང་ཡང་ kha̱ngyang	གའི་ khæ: (*L)	"something"
གང་ཞིག་ kha̱ngshi'	ཅིག་ cī'	"something (in particular)"
གང་ཡང་ kha̱ngyang+NEG	ག་གའི་ kha̱ khä̱:+NEG (*L)	"nothing"
ཅི་ཡང་ cīyang	ག་རེ་+ནའི་ kha̱re+V+nä:	"anything"
ཅི་ཡང་ cīyang +NEG	ཅི་ཡའི་ cīyä:+NEG	"nothing"
གང་དུ་ཡང་ kha̱ngtuyang	ག་པར་+ནའི་ kha̱par+V+nä:	"anywhere, everywhere"
གང་སར་ kha̱ng	ག་ས་ག་ལ་ kha̱sa kha̱la	"everywhere"
གང་དུ་ཡང་ kha̱ngtuyang	ག་ས་ག་ལ་ kha̱sa kha̱la	"everywhere"

• Remember that ཡང་ ya̱ng is pronounced ཡའི་ yä̱: in speech. The same rule applies in compounds containing this adverb: ནའང་ -naang = ནའི་ nä: (*L), ལ་ཡང་ -layang = ལའི་ -lä: (*L), ཅི་ཡང་ cīyang = ཅི་ཡའི་ cīyä: (*L), etc.

3.2 Particles, connectives and postpositions

• ***Interrogative particles***

The interrogative particles གས་ -kä', བས་ -pä', ངས་ -ngä' are not used in Literary Tibetan. Instead, we find the morpheme འམ་-am and its variants (see Table 9, in Appendix 6), or the morpheme ཨེ་ -e. Note that the interrogative particle ཨེ་ is placed before the verb, unlike the other interrogative particles, which go afterwards. In the spoken language, ཨ་ a which is related to ཨེ་ e has a distinct meaning indicating doubt (not a question).

• ***Articles and number markers***

The marker of the definite plural ཚོ་ tshō is used in both Spoken and Literary Tibetan. There are, however, two other markers, དག་ tha̱' and རྣམས་ nām', that occur in the Literary language (and in some dialects) are hardly ever used in Standard Spoken Tibetan. The indefinite singular marker ཅིག་cī', is used in both registers, but is spelled in three ways in the literary language: ཞིག་ shi̱', ཤིག་ shī', ཅིག་ cī', depending on the last letter of the preceding word (see Lesson 6).

• *The postpositions*

While some postpositions are specific to the literary language, most occur in both registers.

སྟེང་/ ཐོག་(L) = སྟང་ "on, on top of", མཇུག་ (L) = རྗེས་ "after", ཁྲོད་/ གསེབ་(L) = དཀྱིལ་/ དབུས་ "among, in the middle", མཐིལ་(L) = དབུས་ "in the centre", etc.

Postpositions are used in the same way in both registers:

Noun + (gen.) + Post + (obl./abl.)

The syntax of postpositions is more varied in literary than in Spoken Tibetan. For example, the use of the genitive before the proposition and the case marker after it are both optional in Literary Tibetan. Thus there are four possible structures, as the following examples illustrate.

བོད་ཀྱི་ནང་དུ་ཡི་གེ་འབྲི་སྟངས་བཞི་ཡོད་པ་རེད།	"There are four styles of writing in Tibet."
བོད་ནང་དུ་ཡི་གེ་འབྲི་སྟངས་བཞི་ཡོད་པ་རེད།	*idem*
བོད་ཀྱི་ནང་ཡི་གེ་འབྲི་སྟངས་བཞི་ཡོད་པ་རེད།	*idem*
བོད་ནང་ཡི་གེ་འབྲི་སྟངས་བཞི་ཡོད་པ་རེད།	*idem*
བྲག་གི་ཐོག་དུ་མ་ཎི་རྐོ།	"to carve a *mani* on a rock"
བྲག་ཐོག་དུ་མ་ཎི་རྐོ།	*idem*
བྲག་གི་ཐོག་མ་ཎི་རྐོ།	*idem*
བྲག་ཐོག་མ་ཎི་རྐོ།	*idem*

• *Connectives*

Connectives (coordinating and subordinating conjunctions) constitute a category in which there are major divergences from the spoken language. In the following table, the left-hand column corresponds to the literary language.

V+ ཅིང་/V+ སྟེ་/ V+ ལ་	= V+ པ་དང་	"and"
V+ པས་	= V+ ཙང་	"because, as, since"
V+ པར་བརྟེན་/ V+ སྐབས་ / V+ གཞིས་	= V+ ཙང་	"because, as, since"
V+ ཕྱིར་དུ་/ V+ སླད་དུ་	= V+ ཡག་ལ་ (*L)	"to, in order to"
V+ པས་	= V+ ནས་	"then, and, after"
V+ པ་དང་	= V+ པ་དག (*L)	"as soon as"
V+པའི་ ཚེ་/ V+ པའི་ན	= V+པའི་སྐབས་ལ/V+དུས	"when"

3.3 Forms and functions of case markers in Literary Tibetan

The case system in Literary Tibetan is more complex than that of the spoken language. All the cases used in Spoken Tibetan also occur in the literary register, but their forms and functions are more numerous in the latter. The aim here is not to provide a detailed description of cases in Literary Tibetan, only to set out the main differences from the case system of the spoken language. Apart from their case functions when they are associated with nouns, all case markers[176] have a connective function when they are linked to verbs. Literary Tibetan has the following six cases (see Lesson 4):

གིས khi̱'[177]: agentive	གི་ khi̱: genitive	ལ་ la̱ / དུ་ thu̱, / ན་ na̱: oblique
ནས་ nä̱' / ལས་ lä̱': ablative	དང་ tha̱ng: associative	Ø: absolutive

• ***Agentive:***

The form that this case takes depends on the last letter of the preceding syllable: གིས ***(gis)*** khi̱', གྱིས ***(gyis)*** khyi̱', ཀྱིས ***(kyis)*** kyī', ས ***(s)*** -', ཡིས ***(yis)*** yi̱' and the archaic form འིས ***('i)*** -' (see Lesson 8.4). The case functions of this marker are practically identical in the two registers. The agentive indicates the agent, the instrument, the cause and the manner, and forms adverbs.

The applications listed below are limited to the literary language.

The marker khi̱' is sometimes used as a connective by being directly appended to a verb. The translation will vary according to context: "and", "after", "because"…

Ex.: ཁོང་གཉིས་ཕྱིར་ལོག་གིས་ཆུ་ཚོད་གཅིག་སོང་རྗེས་ཡང་བསྐྱར་ཡོང་།

khōng nyī' chīr lo̱'-ki' chūtsö' cī' sōng ce̱' ya̱ngkyar yo̱ng

"The two of them went back **and** returned an hour later."

In Literary Tibetan, the agentive marker is often associated with the nominalizer པ་ pā (or its variant -wa̱): པས་-pä'. This marker also operates as a connective, and depending on the context may be translated as "and", "after", "because, since". It generally introduces comparative clauses (rather like the ablative ***las***).

Ex.: མིག་གི་དབང་པོ་ཉམས་པས་ཐག་རིང་དང་ཆུང་བའི་གཟུགས་མི་མཐོང་།

mī'-ki wāngpo nya̱m'-pä' thā' ri̱ng-tang chūngwä: su̱' mi̱ thōng

"**Because** the sense of sight has been impaired, far-off and small shapes are not seen."

བཅོམ་ལྡན་འདས་ཀྱི་དྲུང་དུ་ཕྱིན་པས་ཁྱོད་ཀྱིས་ལྟ་ཡུལ་མཐོང་ངམ་གསུངས།

---

176. Most case markers have the same spelling and pronunciation as certain nouns and verbs, a fact that beginners especially may find confusing. Here is a list of homonyms that that the reader would do well to be aware of:

gyis: ergative-instrumental case or imperative of the classical verb "to do", *la:* oblique case and also "mountain pass", *su*: oblique case (L) and "who?", *ru*: oblique case (L) and "brigade, section", *du*: oblique case (L) and contracted form of *du-ma* "many" (L), *las*: ablative case and "karma, action", *nas*: ablative case (variant) and "barley", *na*: locative case (L) and conjunction "if" and "to be ill".

177. When they are unstressed, these case markers are pronounced respectively: ki', -ki, -la, -tu, -na, -nä', -lä', -tang. Remember that when the case markers are unstressed, they carry no tone and are unaspirated.

"He went before the Bhagavana **and** (the latter) said (to him), 'Have you seen the divine realm?'"

མཆིལ་བའི་ཞ་ལ་ཆགས་པ་ཡིས་ཉ་རྣམས་དེ་མ་ཐག་ཏུ་གསོད།

"**Because of** their desire for bait, fish are immediately killed."

རང་གི་ལུས་འདི་རྣག་ཁྲག་ཆུ་སེར་གྱི་རྐྱལ་པ་ཡིན་པས་གཅེས་པར་མ་འཛིན།

"**Because** your body is a bag of pus, blood and lymph, don't become attached to it."

རྒྱབ་མདུན་གང་ནས་བལྟས་ཀྱང་ཀུན་བས་མཛེས།

"Whether you see her from behind or from in front, she is lovelier than anyone."

ཀློག་པ་བས་ཀྱང་ཏིང་ངེ་འཛིན་བསྒོམ་པ།

"**Rather than** reading, (it would be better to) practice samadhi meditation."

• ***The genitive***

The form of this case, too, varies according to the last letter of the preceding syllable: གི ***(gi)*** khi̱, གྱི ***(gyi)*** khyi̱, ཀྱི ***(kyi)*** kyī, ཡི ***(yi)*** yi̱, འི ***('i)*** (see Lesson 5.4). The case functions of this marker are the same in both registers. The genitive marks the complement of the noun, and forms relative and nominal clauses. In Literary Tibetan, however, the marker ***gi*** may also serve as a connective meaning "but", "while" or "whereas" when it comes directly after a verb.

Ex.: མཁས་པ་རང་གིས་དཔྱད་ཤེས་ཀྱི། བླུན་པོ་གྲགས་པའི་རྗེས་སུ་འབྲང་།

khā̄pa ra̱ng-ki' cā̄' shē'-ki lū̄npo thra̱kpä: ce̱'-su tra̱ng

"The wise know (the truth) by examining themselves, while fools follow rumour."

གཅིག་ལ་ཕན་པར་འགྱུར་བ་ཡི། བྱ་བ་གཞན་ལ་གནོད་པ་སྲིད།
ཟླ་བ་ཤར་ན་ཀུ་མུ་ད། ཁ་འབྱེད་འགྱུར་གྱི་པད་མ་ཟུམ།

"An action that is beneficial for one person may be harmful for another; when the moon rises the water lily opens, whereas the lotus closes."

• ***The oblique***

Of the various cases, it is the oblique that exhibits the greatest differences across the two registers. It has more forms in Literary Tibetan, and the way in which it functions is more complex than in the spoken language. Traditionally referred to as *la-don* "meaning of *la*"[178], the

178. There are three major problems with the way in which the *la-don* is traditionally presented in the Tibetan grammars: the three particles *la, du* and *na* are equivalent in the case of only one function (the locative without movement), but they differ *in all other respects.* Secondly, the grammatical analysis is based on the Sanskrit case models: accusative (*las-su bya ba*), dative (*dgos ched*) and locative (*gnas gzhi*). The *gnas gzhi* is subdivided into *dngos po'i bdag po ston pa*, the possessive case, *dngos po'i gnas gzhi ston pa*, the case of object location (the locative proper), *tshe skabs la 'jug pa,* the case of temporal location, and *de nyid la 'jug pa*, the case of object incorporation.

And finally, of the seven forms, some are actually variants of the same particle (for example *su, ru, du, tu*), whereas others correspond to quite different particles (for example *na* and *la*). This Manual will not adopt the traditional presentation, since it is too complex and is based on Sanskrit syntax, which is quite unrelated to that of Tibetan.

Mention may be made of one highly unusual feature of the oblique case in Literary Tibetan: it may follow other cases,

oblique actually subsumes three distinct markers: the markers ལ་ la̲ (and its variant ར་-*r*), དུ་ thu̲ (and its variants རུ་ ru̲, ཏུ་tū, སུ་ sū) and finally ན་na̲; a total of seven forms that are used as follows:

- after any ending (vowel or consonant): > ལ་ ***la*** la̲
- after any ending (vowel or consonant): > ན་ ***na*** na̲
- after vowels and འ *'a*: > ར་ ***r***[179] r
  > རུ་ ***ru*** ru̲
- after ང *nga,* ད *da,* ན *na,* མ *ma,* ར *ra,* ལ *la*: > དུ་ ***du*** thu̲
- after ས *sa:* > སུ་ ***su*** sū
- after ག *sa* བ *ba* (and after the second suffix *da*): > ཏུ་***tu*** tū

All these particles may function as the locative (without movement).

Thus any word that ends in a consonant may be followed by one of three possible particles signifying the locative.

Ex.: བོད་དུ་ phö̲'-tu = བོད་ལ་ phö̲'-la = བོད་ན་ phö̲'-na = "in Tibet", སེམས་སུ་ sēm'-su = སེམས་ན་ sēm'-na = སེམས་ལ་ sēm'-la "in the mind", ཤག་ཏུ་ = ཤག་ན་ = ཤག་ལ་ "in the (monastic) cell".

When a word ends in a vowel, there is the additional possibility of using the marker ***r*** instead of ***la.***

Ex.: ལྷ་ས་རུ་ = ལྷ་ས་ན་ = ལྷ་སར་= ལྷ་ས་ལ་ "in Lhasa"
ནམ་མཁའ་རུ་ = ནམ་མཁའ་ན་= ནམ་མཁར་= ནམ་མཁའ་ལ་ "in the sky"

However, each of the three markers has other specific functions that may be summarized briefly:

The marker la̲ (and its variant -r) take on the case functions of the locative (with or without movement) and dative. It also functions as adverbial suffix and marker of ***object incorporation***. The latter serves to express the outcome or the effect of a transformation produced by the verbal action[180]. All these different meanings may be translated into English by "to", "in" or "at", or may remain untranslated as the examples below illustrate.

Ex. of locative:

རྒྱ་གར་ལ་འགྲོ་ kya̲kar-la tro̲ "to go to India"
རྡོ་རྗེ་གླིང་ལ་སྡོད་ "to live in Darjeeling"

---

notably the agentive and the ablative, in formulations such as: *de-ba+s+na* and *nas+su.*

179. In the case of a final *'a*, the latter is replaced by the case marker *r*.

180. From a syntactic point of view, the case marker usually integrates or incorporates the object into the verb and thus creates a compound verb. This function of object incorporation is called *de-nyid* in traditional grammars.

Ex. of dative:

བྱིས་པ་དག་ལ་སྒྲུང་བཤད་ chi̱pa-ta'-la tru̱ng shā̈' "to tell a story to the children"

བྱིས་པ་རྩེད་མོ་ལ་དགའ། "The children like the game" (lit. they have pleasure in the game)

Ex. of object incorporation:

སོལ་བར་གཏོང་ sō̈lwar tōng "to turn into charcoal, to carbonize"

Ex. of adverb:

མགྱོགས་པོར་ kyo̱kpor "quickly, at speed"

The marker la̱ also has connective functions, and may serve as a connective. It can therefore be translated by "and" or "at the time". It may also be used to form purpose clauses.

In the latter case, the marker la̱ is often associated with the nominalizer པ་ -pā (or its variant -wa̱): པར་-par, in which case it it attached directly to the verb.

Ex.: ཤོག་ལ་ལྟོས་ཞིག shō'-la tō̈' shī' "Come **and** look", གསལ་ལ་ཟླུམ་པའི་ཟླ་བ་ "the bright [and] round moon", བོད་སྨན་སློབ་པར་གཏོང་ "to send [someone] **to** study Tibetan medicine", ཆང་ཉོར་(ཉོ་བར་) ཕྱིན་ "to go **to** buy chang".

And finally, the marker la̱ serves as an expressive particle when it is placed after an adjective at the end of a phrase.

Ex.: སྐྱིད་པ་ལ་ kyīpa-la "How pleasant!", སྙིང་རྗེ་བ་ལ་ "How pretty!"

— The marker thu̱ (and its variants sū, ru̱, tū) has locative (with or without movement) case functions. It also functions as adverbial suffix and marker of object incorporation.

Ex. of locative:

གཡོན་དུ་ yō̈n-tu "on/ to the left"

གཡས་སུ་ yā̈'-su "on/ to the right"

རྒྱ་གར་དུ་འགྲོ་ kya̱kar-tu tro̱ "to go to India"

རྡོ་རྗེ་གླིང་དུ་སྡོད་ "to live in Darjeeling"

དུས་སུ་ "at the time"

ལག་ཏུ་ཕྲེང་བ་ "a rosary in the hand"

ཕ་ཡུལ་རྒྱབ་ཏུ་བསྐྱུར་ "to leave one's native land behind"

Ex. of object incorporation:

དཔལ་དུ་འབར་ "to be resplendent" (lit. to blaze in glory)

ཐུང་དུ་གཏོང་ "to shorten" (lit. "to send to short")

Ex. of adverb:

ལྷག་པར་དུ་ "particularly"

ངེས་པར་དུ་ "absolutely"

Note that the marker thu̱ (and its variants), as well as the marker -la are associated with the adverb ཇེ་ "even more" which is used only in the literary language. In the spoken language, the oblique case དུ་ (or rather its variant ཅ་, see Lesson 28.3.4) alone conveys this meaning.

Ex.: ཇེ་མང་དུ་འཕེལ་ "to increase even more"

བདག་འཛིན་ཉོན་མོངས་རྣམ་རྟོག་སོགས་ཇེ་ཆུང་ཇེ་ཆུང་ལ་སོང་

"Selfishness, negative emotions, discursive thought and so on decrease even further."

The marker thu̱ has connective functions when it is followed by a verb. It is also used to form purpose clauses.

Ex.: བོད་སྨན་སློབ་ཏུ་གཏོང་ phö̱' mā̃n lōp-tu tōng "to send [someone] **to** learn Tibetan medicine"

— The marker na̱ has locative (without movement) case functions.

Ex.: ལག་ན་ la̱'-na "in the hand", ས་མཚམས་ན་ sāntsām'-na "at the border"

And finally, apart from its meaning of "if"[181] (as in Spoken Tibetan), it may also mean "when".

Ex.: མེ་ཡོད་ན་དུ་བ་འབྱུང་། me̱ yö̱'-na thu̱wa cu̱ng "If there's fire, there's smoke."
ས་བོན་བཏབ་ན་འབྲས་བུ་སྐྱེ། "If you plant a seed, a fruit will grow."
ནད་མེད་ན་སྨན་པ་ཅིའི་ཕྱིར་བསྟེན། "If there's no illness, why consult a doctor?"
རྒྱ་མཚོ་མཐོང་བ་ན་ཁྲོན་པའི་སྦལ་པ་བརྒྱལ་ནས་མགོ་གས་ཏེ་ཤི་སྐད།
kya̱tso thōngwa-na thrō̃npä: pä̱:pa kyä̱:-nä' ko̱ khä̱'-te shī kā̃'
"It is said that, when it saw the ocean, the frog in the well fainted, its head burst and it died."

• *The ablative*

Apart from the particle ནས་-nä', Literary Tibetan also uses the marker ལས་-lä' to express spatial provenance. The difference between the two is so subtle as to be nonexistent in certain cases. At an abstract level, -lä' may be said to signify a consubstantial origin whereas nä' implies that an object and its source are ontologically different. Another way of expressing the difference would be to say that for -nä' the original space is closed or delimited, whereas for -lä' the space is conceived as open and unbounded.[182]

Concretely, -lä' is used in principle to denote the material that something is made of, or consubstantial provenance, or the source of a quotation, whereas -nä' refers to spatial or temporal origin.

---

181. The marker *na* is almost always associated with the past form of the verb (when there is such a form) or the auxiliary. There are, however, some exceptions to this rule, especially in the case of negation.

182. As suggested by Beyer (1992).

Ex.: གསེར་ལས་བུམ་པ་བྱས་ sēr-lä' phu̱mpa chä̱' "to make a vase out of gold", ཤིང་ལས་ཁང་པ་གྲུབ་ "to build a house out of wood", དངུལ་ལས་རྡོ་རྗེ་གྲུབ་ "to make a *vajra* out of silver", འོ་མ་ལས་མར་བླངས་ "to make butter from milk", ཉི་མ་ལས་འོད་འཕྲོས་ "light emitted by the sun", པདྨ་བཀའ་ཐང་ལས་ "according to the *Padma bka'-thang*", རི་རྩེ་ནས་བབས་ ri̱ tsē-nä' pha̱p "to come down from the mountain-top", ཤར་ཕྱོགས་ནས་འོང་ "come from the east", ཟླ་བ་བཅུ་པ་ནས་འགོ་ཚུགས་ "beginning in the tenth month", དགྲ་བོའི་ལག་ནས་ཐར་ "escaped from enemy hands".

• *The associative*

Whereas this case[183] is not used much in Spoken Tibetan, it is very common in the literary language. The associative དང་ -tang goes with a small class of verbs and adjectives, some of which occur quite frequently:

Ex.: ལྡན་ ta̱n "to possess", བཅས་ cā̈' "to possess", འགལ་ ka̱l "to infringe, to go **against"**, མཚུངས་ thsūng' "comparable **with**", མཇལ་ cä̱: "to meet"(H), ཐུག་ thū' "to meet", མཐུན་ thǖn "to be in agreement (**with**)", སྟུན་ tǖn "to agree, harmonize", འཐབ་ thāp "to fight **with**", ཐག་ཉེ་ thā' nye̱ "to be close (**to**)", འགྲོགས་ tro̱' "to be associated **with,** accompanied **by**", སྒྲགས་ tra̱' "to tie", སྦྱར་ ca̱r "to stick", ལྷན་ lhā̈n "to be together", མཉམ་པོ nyāmpo "to be (**with**)", འདྲེ་ tre̱ "to mingle (**with**)", སྦྲེལ་ tre̱: "to connect, attach", སྡེབ་ te̱p "to join", དམག་བརྒྱབ་ mā' kya̱p "to make war (**on/against**)", བྲལ་ thrä̱: "to be separated (**from**), deprived (**of**)"

Ex.: ནང་པ་དང་ལྟ་བ་མི་མཐུན་པའི་དུས་ཞིག་ཡོང་། na̱ngpa-tang tāwa mi thǖn-pä: thu̱' shī' yo̱ng
"A time will come when there will be a philosophical position hostile to Buddhism."
མི་བཟང་པོ་དང་ཐུག "to meet an excellent person"
ཁྲིམས་དང་འགལ་བ། "to break the law"
ང་ཨ་མ་དང་ཡུད་ཙམ་ཞིག་ཕྲད། "I shall meet my mother (if only) for an instant."
ལྷ་མིན་ལྷ་རྣམས་དང་འཐབ་ཏུ་འགྲོ། "The titans are going to make war on the gods."

As in Spoken Tibetan, the marker may also function as a coordinating conjunction, "and" (see 9.3). It also acts as an imperative marker (see 19.3). In Literary Tibetan, it is also used to introduce temporal clauses: "as soon as, when".

Ex.: ཉི་མ་ཤར་བ་དང་ཕྱིན་པ། "They set off as soon as the sun rose."

---

183. S. Beyer (1992) has proposed that *dang* be treated as a case, but he provides no arguments for his analysis, which is not supported by Tibetan grammars. However, the suggestion is a good one, and a number of arguments may be cited in support. *Dang* cannot be preceded or followed by any other case markers. In other dialects, such as Ladakhi, *dang* marks the instrumental and the associative. In Central Tibetan, *dang* may be replaced by other cases such as the oblique or the absolutive. Like all the other case markers, the absolutive, the genitive, the agentive, the ablative and the oblique, the associative marker has two kinds of functions: case-related and connective. It should also be noted that in Amdo, the usual marker that corresponds to the Central Tibetan *dang* is *la,* which is also a case marker.

This being said, there are two features that give the associative a special character: first, contrary to other case markers, *dang* usually goes before the main verb, with which it has a close relation; and secondly, there are relatively few verbs that can take this marker, so that the case function of *dang* is rather rare.

3.4 The predicative function of adjectives

In Spoken Tibetan, when adjectives take on a "verbal" (or predicative) function and appear at the end of the sentence, they must be ***followed by a copula*** or an auxiliary (except in certain comparative constructions, see Lesson 17.3). In Literary Tibetan, however, adjectives that function as predicates are often treated autonomously, with neither copula nor auxiliary.

Ex.: འདི་ཤིན་ཏུ་མཛེས། t̲i̲ shīntu tse̲' "This is really lovely!"
དལ་འབྱོར་རིན་ཆེན་འདི་ཐོབ་དཀའ། tha̲ncor ri̲ncen t̲i̲ thōp kā
"This precious human body is hard to get."
ཡོན་ཏན་ཆུང་རྣམས་ང་རྒྱལ་ཆེ། "Those with few qualities are full of pride."
གནོད་ལན་ཀུན་གྱིས་སླབ་པར་སླ། "Anyone can easily take revenge."

3.5 Nominal sentences and the concluding particle.

In Literary Tibetan we sometimes find nominal sentences, that is, sentences with no verb (and no adjective with a verb function). These sentences usually end in a noun, but they may also end in some formulation other than a verb (such as a pronoun or an adverb). In most cases, these nominal sentences end in the concluding particle ***'o*** or one of its variants (see Table 9 in Appendix 6).

Ex.: བླ་མ་རྣམས་ཀྱིས་སོ། lāma-nam-kyi'-so "(It was) by the lamas."
སྐྱོ་སྐྱོ་སེམས་པ་སྐྱོའོ། kyō kyō sēmpa kyō: "Sad, sad, my heart (is so) sad."
འདི་ནི་སྡུག་བསྔལ་ལོ། t̲i̲-ni tu̲'ngä:-lo "This (is) suffering."

3.6 Verb inflection

In Literary Tibetan, verb stems are often inflected according to the three tenses and the imperative mood: a maximum of ***four forms.*** These are traditionally referred to as དུས་ད་ལྟ་བ་ *dus da-lta-ba* "present", དུས་མ་འོངས་པ་ *dus ma-'ongs-pa* "future", དུས་འདས་པ་ *dus 'das-pa* "past" and སྐུལ་ཚིག་ *skul-tshig* "imperative". In Literary Tibetan, not all verbs have four forms; some are either invariable or have only two or three forms.

This Manual has retained the traditional terminology for the three tenses: past, present and future. However it is more accurate to speak of aspects (or tense-aspect). The present "tense" is an imperfective aspect, since it may in fact be used not only in the present but also in the imperfective past. For example, in the following sentence:

གཅུང་དགའ་བོ་རབ་བྱུང་ཡང་བསླབས་པ་ལ་མི་སློབ། "Though Nanda became a monk, he wouldn't learn the precepts." [literally: he does not learn the precepts]

Although the verb stem སློབ is in the "present" (and not the past བསླབས་), it conveys the meaning of the imperfective ***past***. Note also the use of the imperfective negation མི་ (and not the "past" མ་).

The traditional designation “past” is technically speaking as inappropriate as “present”. What we are actually dealing with is the perfective aspect: this “past” tense is in fact also used for the perfective future. For example in the sentence:

གཅུང་དགའ་བོ་ལྷ་ཡུལ་དུ་སྐྱེས་ནས་བདེ་བ་མྱོངས་ཏེ། དགེ་འབྲས་ཟད་པ་དང་འདིར་སྐྱེ་བ་ཡིན། “Nanda *will be born* in paradise and will enjoy happiness, [then] when his merit runs out, he will be reborn here.” [literally: once he has been born in the divine realms and has enjoyed happiness]

In the first clause, the verb སྐྱེས is in the “past” (and not the future སྐྱེ་) but it denotes a perfective *future*.

It should be remembered that the number of distinct verb stems has been considerably reduced in the spoken language, and the role of inflection has been largely supplanted by auxiliary verbs. Furthermore, the majority of verbs in the spoken language consist of an invariable noun and a verbalizer.

There are two main reasons for the reduction in the number of inflections in Spoken Tibetan:

a) Certain forms have either become outmoded or completely obsolete.

b) There is a high degree of homophony. In the course of the phonological evolution of Central Tibetan, many verbs with different prefixes (or suffixes, etc.) have come to be pronounced identically. The distinctions that have been retained in writing have disappeared in the spoken language.

The table below provides several examples of comparisons between written and colloquial forms. The first line (in italics) below the Tibetan presents the spelling (and therefore the archaic pronunciation), while the second shows the Standard Tibetan pronunciation. There are also some examples (in brackets) of the literary pronunciation, but these have generally lost their currency in the spoken language.

present-future	**past**	**imperative**	
སྐོར་/བསྐོར *skor / bskor* kōr	བསྐོར་ *bskor* kōr	སྐོར་ *skor* kōr	“to turn”
གཏོང་/ གཏང་ *gtong /gtang* (tōng)/ tāng	བཏང་ *btang* tāng	ཐོངས་ *thongs* (thōng) tāng	“to send”
འགོག་/ དགག་ *‘gog / dgag* (ko̱’/ka̱’) kā’	བཀག་ *bkag* kā’	ཁོག་ *khog* (khō’) kā’	“to stop”
འཆོར་ *‘chor* (chōr)shōr	ཤོར་ *shor* shōr	Ø	“to escape”

ཟོ་/བཟོ་	བཟོས་	བཟོས་	
zo / bzo	*bzos*	*bzos*	"to make"
so̱	sö̱'	sö̱'	
བྱེད་/བྱ་	བྱས	བྱོས	
byed/ bya	*byas*	*byos*	"to do"
che̱'/ (cha̱)	chä̱'	(chö̱') che̱'	
རྒྱག་/བརྒྱག་	བརྒྱབ་	རྒྱོབ་	
rgyag / brgyag	*brgyab*	*rgyob*	"to construct"
kya̱'	kya̱p	kyop/ kya̱p	
ལྟ་/བལྟ་	བལྟས་	ལྟོས་	
lta / blta	*bltas*	*ltos*	"to look"
tā	tǟ'	tȫ'	
ཟ་/ བཟའ་	བཟས་	ཟོ་	
za / bza'	*bzas*	*zo*	"to eat"
sa̱	sä̱'	so̱	
འབུལ་/ དབུལ་	ཕུལ་	ཕུལ་	
'bul / dbul	*phul*	*phul*	"to offer" (h)
(pü̱:/ ǖ:)phǖ:	phǖ:	phǖ:	

The disappearance of certain verb forms in the oral register and the fact that there are so many homophones present certain problems when writing in a converstional or vernacular – rather than a literary – style. The tense of a given form may be radically different in oral and Literary Tibetan. Verb stems corresponding to the literary past tense are used for the present-future in the oral register (since this is the only form that is used in speech, e.g., *bkag* "to stop"). Correspondence between literary and oral forms is a complex matter. In the case of modern texts of this kind, readers should take care to identify the tense of the verb from the auxiliaries ***and not from the inflection*** of the main verb.

On the other hand, Literary Tibetan contains a large number of "causative/resultative" verb pairs. Compared to the basic resultative stem, the causative has always an additional argument corresponding to an intentional agent performing the action. All the causative verbs are transitive and volitional, while resultative verbs are usually intransitive and non-volitional. When occuring in the same sentence, the causative form points to the effort of the agent, whereas the resultative form essentially shows the result of the action (see Lesson 35.3). In written Tibetan, the causative verb often carries a superscript ***s***. In the spoken language, causatives are often distinguishable from their resultative form by tone and aspiration, but in many cases this opposition, too, has disappeared.

Ex.:	causative		resultative	
	སྐོར་ ***bskor***	"to turn"	འཁོར་ ***'khor***	"to circulate"
	/kōr/		/khōr/	
	བཅག་ ***bcag***	"to break"	ཆག་ ***chag***	"to be broken"
	/cā'/		/chā'/	
	བསྒྲིགས་ ***bsgrigs***	"to arrange"	འགྲིག་ ***'grig***	"to be arranged, be enough"
	/tri̱'/		/tri̱'/	
	བསྒུལ་ ***bsgul***	"to cause to move"	འགུལ་ ***'gul***	"to move, be moved"
	/kü̱:/		/kü̱:/	

3.7 Forms and functions of copulas and auxiliaries

In the literary register, copulas are not indispensable (as they are in Spoken Tibetan), but they do occur quite frequently. For the verb "to be" we find the forms: ཡིན་ yi̱n, ལགས་ la̱', and རེད་ re̱' (especially in Modern Literary Tibetan), and for the verbs "to have" or "to exist" we find འདུག་ tu̱', ཡོད་ yö̱', གདའ་ ta̱, སྣང་ nāng, མཆིས་ chī', and ཡོད་པ་རེད་ yö̱pare' (especially in Modern Literary Tibetan). The copulas ཡིན་ yi̱n and ཡོད་ yö̱', which are also used in Spoken Tibetan, are not restricted to the first person (they are not egophoric).

Ex.: གསུམ་གྱི་ལྟབ་གཉིས་ནི་དྲུག་ཡིན། sūm-kyi ta̱p nyī' thru̱' yi̱n "Two threes are six."
ནམ་མཁར་ཉི་ཟླ་སྐར་གསུམ་ཡོད། na̱mkar nyi̱ ta̱ kār sūm yö̱'
"In the sky there are three [celestial bodies], the sun, the moon and the stars."

Final auxiliary verbs[184] represent another area in which there are major differences between the two registers. It should be noted that final auxiliaries are not essential in Literary Tibetan, whereas they are in the spoken language. In the latter (as we have seen above), the auxiliaries provide supplementary information about tense, aspect and mood, but in Literary Tibetan they are also combined with inflection of the main verb.

While verbs may figure as autonomous entities in Classical Tibetan, auxiliaries are sometimes used – even in the most ancient texts, such as the Dunhuang manuscripts. Some auxiliaries are in fact composed of a suffix followed by the auxiliary verb proper, whereas others are directly attached to the verb. Suffixes include mainly the following particles and nominalizers: པ་ pā, པར་ pār, གི་ khi̱, གིན་ khi̱n, བཞིན་ shi̱n, ཞིང་ shi̱ng (and its two variants ཅིང་ cīng, ཤིང་ shīng), ཀྱུ་ kyu̱, མཁན་ khǟn. All auxiliary verbs may also operate autonomously. Here is a list of the main auxiliaries, with the meanings they have as autonomous verbs: བྱེད་ che̱' "to do", མཛད་ tsä̱' "to do"(H), བགྱིད kyi̱' "to do"(H), འགྱུར་ kyu̱r "to change",སོང་ sōng "to go", བྱུང་ chu̱ng "to happen", བསྡད་ tä̱' "to stay", ཡོད་ yö̱' "to exist, to have", འདུག་ tu̱' "to be [seated], to have", གདའ་ta̱ "to exist", སྣང་ nāng "to appear", ཡིན་ yi̱n "to be", ལགས་ la̱' "to be", ཟིན་ si̱n "to finish".

184. These auxiliaries appear only at the end of main clauses, and never after the verbs of subsidiary clauses.

The choice of auxiliary depends on the historical period of the literature in question, and varies also from one region and author to another, but they are of basically two kinds: those that are used in classical literature, and appear frequently in canonical texts translated from Sanskrit, and those that appear particularly in certain *namthar* (hagiographies). However, the two styles often *occur together* within a text.

• Classical style:

tense	causative auxiliaries	resultative auxiliaries
past	V (past) + པར་བྱས་ -par chä'	V (past) + པར་གྱུར་-par kyur
present (imperfective)	V (pres.) + པར་བྱེད་ -par che'	V (pres.) + པར་འགྱུར་ -par kyur
future	V (pres. / fut.) + པར་བྱ་ -par cha	V (pres. / fut.) + པར་འགྱུར་ -par kyur

These auxiliaries, which occur frequently in Classical Tibetan, mark the tense and aspect of the verb; this feature is particularly useful in cases where the verb is invariable. They also specify whether we are dealing with a causative or resultative act (or process).

The causative auxiliaries generally emphasize the agent's effort to perform an action (without anticipating the result). They may be used either with volitional (or "controllable") or non-volitional ("non-controllable") verbs.

• When they are associated with ***volitional*** verbs, causative auxiliaries indicate that the action is intentionally performed by the agent, and emphasize the process or, when they are combined with the future tense, the volition or obligation of the agent.

Ex.: རྒྱལ་པོས་སྙིང་རྗེས་སྐྱོང་བར་བྱེད། "The king rules with compassion."
སྡིག་པ་སྤང་བར་བྱ། "One should make an effort to desist from sinful acts."
ཉ་པས་ཟས་ཀྱིས་ཁ་ཕྲིད་ནས་ཉ་རྣམས་གསོད་པར་བྱེད།
"The fisherman kills fish by attracting them with bait."

• In association with ***non-volitional*** verbs, auxiliaries acquire a factitive or causative meaning. The agent is then the cause of, or the party responsible for, the transformation that something or someone undergoes. It may accordingly be translated by "to see to it that" or "to make sure that".

Ex.: བྱིས་པ་ལ་སློབ་གསོ་ཐེབས་པར་བྱེད་དགོས།
"One ought to see to it that children receive an education."
རང་གི་སྔོན་བྱས་ཀྱི་ལས་ངན་སྨིན་པ་ཤེས་པར་བྱས་ནས་བཟོད་བསྲན་བསྐྱེད་དགོས།
"We should make sure that we are aware of the negative karma of past deeds and endure (their consequences)."

Resultative auxiliaries generally emphasize the result of the action. They are usually used in connection with ***non-volitional*** verbs, but may also figure with volitional verbs.

• In association with non-volitional verbs, the resultative auxiliary confirms that the action or process is unintentional. Resultative auxiliaries are also useful to indicate the tense of the verb when it is invariable.

Ex.: དེ་ནས་རྒྱལ་པོའི་ཕོ་བྲང་མཐོང་བར་གྱུར། "I saw the king's palace from there."
མཐར་འཆི་བར་འགྱུར་རོ། "[We]'ll die in the end."
ན་བའི་བུ་ལ་ཁྱད་པར་དུ། མ་ནི་གདུང་བ་སྐྱེ་བར་འགྱུར། "A mother is especially saddened for a sick son."

• When they are associated with ***volitional*** verbs, they specify that only the object or the result of the action, independent of the agent's volition, are to be taken into account (the agent may be absent). In European languages, these formulations are often translated by the passive.[185]

Ex.: མཆོད་པར་འགྱུར་བའི་ངེས་པ་མེད། "It's not certain that offerings will be made."
བསགས་པའི་ནོར་ནི་སྦྲང་རྩི་ལྟར་ནམ་ཞིག་གཞན་གྱིས་སྤྱོད་པར་འགྱུར།
"The wealth we have accumulated will one day be enjoyed by others, like honey."

• The *namthar* style and Modern Literary Tibetan both use auxiliaries that are formally identical to those of the spoken language, but they function differently from their oral homologues.

Namthar style

tense	auxiliaries
past	V (past)+ སོང་ sōng (distancing), V (past)+ བྱུང་ chu̱ng (nearing) V (past)+ པ་ཡིན་ -pa yi̱n, V (past)+ ཡོད་ yö̱', V (past)+ འདུག་ tu̱'
present	V (pres.)+ གི་འདུག་ -ki tu̱', V (pres.)+ གི་ཡོད་ -ki yö̱', V (pres.)+ གི་ཡོད་པ་རེད་ -ki yö̱pare̱', V (pres.)+ བཞིན་འདུག་ -shi̱n tu̱', V (pres.)+ བཞིན་ཡོད་ -shi̱n yö̱', V (pres.)+ ཅིང་འདུག་ -cīng tu̱', V (pres.)+ ཅིང་ཡོད་ -cīng yö̱', V (pres.)+ གིན་འདུག་ -kin tu̱', V (pres.)+ གིན་ཡོད་ -kin yö̱'.
future	V (pres. / fut.)+ རྒྱུ་ཡིན་ -kyu̱ yi̱n, V (pres. / fut.)+ པ་ཡིན་ -pa yi̱n

The verbal system used in *namthar* will not be described in detail here (see *le Clair Miroir,* Kesang Gyurmé, 1994). It should, however, be pointed out that, unlike their homologues in the

185. In canonical literature, these auxiliaries translate the Sanskrit passive voice.

spoken language, these auxiliaries do not convey evidential moods[186] (or “mediatory” moods): they provide only information relating to tense and aspect. Even in Modern Literary Tibetan, with the exception of writings that reproduce the spoken language, the distinction between the first person (egophoric) and the others is generally not relevant, nor is that between intentional and unintentional, as the following sentence shows:

Ex.: དྭངས་གསལ་སེམས་ཀྱི་མེ་ལོང་གཙང་མ་ལ། འཆི་བདག་རྒྱལ་པོའི་ཁ་རླངས་ཕོག་པ་ཡིན།
tha̱ngsā̈: sēm’-kyi me̱long tsāngma-la chī̄ta’ kyä̱:po khālang phō’-pa yi̱n
“The pure mirror of the clear mind is touched by the breath of the Lord of the Dead.”

In this example, the auxiliary payin is used with a non-volitional verb phōk “to be touched” in the third person. In Spoken Tibetan, this auxiliary is always used in association with the first person of a volitional verb.

Finally, it should be noted that there is a difference with regard to negation. In Literary Tibetan, the use of the particles of negation ma̱ and mi̱ depends on tense-aspect and mood: mi̱ is used with the present (or the imperfective past, which is similar to the present), whereas ma̱ is used with the past (perfective) and the imperative (the negative form of the imperative is similar to the present). The rule may be summarized as follows:

མི་ mi̱	>	present or future
མ་ ma̱	>	past or imperative

Ex.: འགྲོ་མ་ཐུབ། tro̱ ma̱ thūp “(He) could not go.”
འགྲོ་མི་ཐུབ། tro̱ mi̱ thūp “(He) can not go.”
སྨན་པ་དང་མོ་མ་རྣམས་ཀྱིས་ཀྱང་མི་འཚོ་བར་ལུང་བསྟན་ཞིང་ཐོར།
mā̈npa-tang mo̱ma-nam’-kyi’ kyāng mi̱ tshō-war lu̱ng tā̈n-shing pho̱r
“The physicians and the diviners prophesied that he would not survive, and abandoned him.”

Here the use of the negation mi̱ reveals that we are dealing with the future (from the point of view of the past).

This rule doesn’t apply in the spoken language, since མ་ ma̱ and མི་ mi̱ don’t depend on tense but on the type of auxiliary that is used (cf. འདུག tu̱’ > མི་འདུག mi̱ntu’ and ཡོད་རེད་ yo̱:re’ > ཡོད་མ་རེད་ yo̱:mare’).

186. It should be remembered that the originality of the system of final auxiliary verbs in Spoken Tibetan lies not only in the indications of tense and aspect that they provide, but also in various “mediatory” moods (see Lesson 5.4) that specify the source of information used by the speaker to characterize a statement: egophoric, assertive, testimonial and inferential.

3.8 Reported speech

In the classical language and in modern literary texts, reported speech is usually marked by the syllable ཞེས་ she̲' at the end of a quotation, or by its variant form ཅེས་cē' (the variant ཤེས་shē' is archaic).[187] It functions like its oral homologue ཟེ་ -s and comes immediately before the verb of speech. Although this marker is usually used for direct speech, it may also be used to introduce reported speech. There is no structural (or syntactic) difference between the two types of speech. The ways in which reported speech is introduced vary in Classical Tibetan and, apart from she̲', there are several other ways of ending a quotation, although these are used less frequently. The commonest are as follows:

Opening

- speaker + གིས་-ki'
- speaker + ན་རེ་ na̲re
- title (of the cited text) + ལས་ -lä'
- (speaker +) འདི་སྐད་དོ་ ti̲ kā̃'-to, *or* འདི་སྐད་ཅེས་སོ་ ti̲ kā̃'cē'-so, speaker + གི་ཞལ་ནས་ -ki shä̲:-nä'

(lit. from the mouth of)

The explicative conjunction སྟེ་tē and the conclusive particle འོ་ -o and their variants (see Table 9 in Appendix 6) are often used to indicate the closing of a citation.

Closing

- ཞེས་+ གསུང་ she̲' + sūng[188]
- (བ)ར་+གསུང་ (wa)r + sūng
- ལུགས་+ གསུང་ lu̲' + sūng
- ཚུལ་གསུང་ tshǖ: + sūng

Sometimes the end of a reported statement is marked by the verb of speech alone.

There are also a number of forms signifying hearsay, such as: སྐད་ kā̃', གྲགས་ thra̲', etc.

Ex.: ང་ཤི་དུར་ཁུང་ནས་བལྟའོ་ཞེས་གསུངས།
nga̲ shī thu̲rkung-nä' tāo she̲' sūng'
"'I shall watch [you] from the hole in my tomb,' he said."

ཁྱོད་ཚོ་བོད་དུ་རོགས་རམ་ཆེད་ཡོང་ཚུལ་བརྗོད།
khyȫtso phö̲'-tu ro̲kram chē' yo̲ng tshǖ: cö̲'
"You say that you've come to Tibet to help [us]."

---

187. Concerning the use of variants, see Table 9 in Appendix 6.

188. The verb *gsung,* "to say, speak, teach", is used here as an example, and may be replaced by any verb signifying speech or thought.

འགའ་ཤས་ནས་སྟོང་ཕྲག་སུམ་ཅུ་སྐོར་ཡོད་ལུགས་གླེང་།

ka̱shä’-nä’ tōngtra’ sūmcu kōr yö̱’ lu̱’ lēng

“Some said there were around thirty thousand of them.”

འདོད་པ་ཕུང་ཁྲོལ་ཀུན་གྱི་རྩ་བ་ཞེས། རྒྱལ་བའི་དབང་པོས་ཀིམ་པའི་འབྲས་འདྲར་གསུང་།

tö̱pa phūngtrö: kün-ki tsāwa she̱’ kyä̱:wä: wāngpö’ kīmpä: trä̱’ tra̱+r sūng

“Desire is the source of all ills. The Victorious One taught that it is like the fruit of the kimpa tree [beautiful in appearance, but terribly bitter].”

ཞེན་ལོག་སྒོམ་གྱི་རྐང་པར་གསུངས།

she̱nlo’ ko̱m-ki kāngpa+r sung’

“It is taught that detachment constitutes the legs of meditation.”

ཕྱི་བ་ན་རེ། ངས་ནི་ཡེངས་མེད་ཏིང་འཛིན་བསྒོམ།……ཟེར་ནས་མིག་ཟིམ་ཟིམ་བྱེད་སྐད།

chīwa na̱re ngä̱’-ni ye̱ng me̱’ tīngtsin ko̱m… se̱r-nä’ mī’ si̱msim che̱’ kā’

“The marmot said, ‘I practice samadhi meditation without distraction,’ and then, it is said, he winked his eyes.”

བླ་མའི་ཞལ་ནས་དེ་ག་རང་ཟེར།

lāmä: shä̱:-nä’ the̱ka ra̱ng se̱r

“The lama said, ‘That is exactly it.’”

3.9 Relative clauses and nominalization

There are major divergences between the literary and spoken registers in this domain. In either case, relative clauses are formed with the use of nominalizers, but the markers for nominalizing verbs have different forms and functions (for oral Tibetan, see Lesson 26).

The universal marker of nominalization in Tibetan is པ་ pā / བ་ wa̱. However, the following markers are also found: བྱེད་ che̱’, བྱ་ cha̱, རྒྱུ་ kyu̱, ཡུལ་ yü̱l, ས་ sā, མཁན་ khān, མི་ mi̱. Apart from these common nominalizers, there are also markers that convey a complete meaning: སོལ་ sō: “custom, usage”, སྟངས་ tāng’ “way, manner”, འཕྲོ་ thrō “sequel, continuation” and འོ་ཅོག་ o̱cok, དགུ་ ku̱, ཚད་ tshā’ which mean “all, altogether”.[189] The markers ཅན་ cān and ལྡན་ tä̱n are also used to form relative clauses, but they differ from the others insofar as they function, by themselves, as nominalized possessive verbs.

As in the case of their oral homologues, all the nominalizers with the exception of -pa depend on the function of the head noun (antecedent) and, in certain cases, on the tense of the relative clause. Relative clauses usually go before the head noun, but occasionally appear after. In the former case, they are usually (though not always) linked to the noun that they modify by means of a genitive. Finally, in Classical Tibetan, we sometimes find (associated with the nomi-

---

189. These three nominalizers have been described by Stephan Beyer (1992).

nalizer) a true relative pronoun: ཁང་ kha̲ng (see the example with pa). The following table summarizes the uses of the commonest forms.

Nominalizing	Suffix function of the head noun	Verb form	Possible translations
པ་ pa / བ wa	subject, object, etc. (by default)	compatible with all tenses	"who", "what", "to whom", "where", "whose", etc.
བྱེད་ che̲'	instrument, cause or manner	present	"with which", "which"
རྒྱུ་ kyu̲	object subject (intransitive)	future	"that"
བྱ་ cha̲	object subject (intransitive)	future	"that"
ཡུལ་ yü̲: / ས་ sā	indirect object or place adverbial	future or present	"where", "to whom", "to which", etc.
མཁན་ khã̄n / མི་ mi̲	subject	present	"who"

The nominalizers may be briefly described and illustrated:

• པ་ pa / བ wa

The marker -pa or its variant -wa[190] is by far the commonest. It is much more widely used in Literary than in Spoken Tibetan. The function of the head noun must be determined by default. From the syntactic functions that feature in the relative clause, we can use a process of elimination to identify the head noun's function, which may be: subject, object, adverbials indicating time, place, instrument or manner, or noun complement, etc.

Ex.: ལུག་རྣམས་ཆུ་ལོག་གིས་ཁྱེར་བའི་རྫི་བོ། lu̲'-nam chūlo'-ki' khyēr-wä: tsi̲wo

"The shepherd whose sheep were carried away by the current…"

བུ་གཅིག་པུ་ཤི་བའི་མ་བཞིན་དུ། phu̲ cīkpu shī-wä: ma̲ shi̲ntu

"Like a mother whose only son has died…"

ཆོས་ཐོབ་པའི་མི་ལུས་ཞིག chȫ' thōp-pä: mi̲ lü̲'-shi'

"A human body that has received Dharma instruction…"

བུ་སྐྱེ་པའི་ཉི་མ་དེ། phu̲ kyē-pä: nyi̲ma the̲

"The day when the boy was born…"

ནད་གསོ་བར་བྱེད་པའི་གཉེན་པོ། nä̲' sō-war che̲'-pä: nyēnpo

"The antidote that cures illnesses…"

ཁམས་ལ་གནོད་པའི་ཟས། khām'-la nȫ'-pä: sä̲'

"Food that injures the health…"

190. See Table 9 in Appendix 6.

གང་ལ་སྙིང་སྟོབས་མཆོག་མངའ་བའི་རྣལ་འབྱོར་པ་དེ། kha̱ng-la nyīngtop chō' ngāwä: nāncorpa the̱

"That *yogin* who possesses remarkable courage…"

• བྱེད་ che̱'

This marker, which is derived from the present of the verb "to do", is used with a head noun that takes the function of an instrument of cause or manner.

Ex.: དཀྲུག་བྱེད་ཀྱི་དབྱུག་པ། trū' che̱'-kyi yūkpa "the stick that's used for stirring"

ནད་གསོ་བྱེད་ཀྱི་གཉེན་པོ། nä̱' sō che'-kyi nyēnpo "the antidote that cures illnesses"

• རྒྱུ་ kyu̱

This particle, which is essentially a part of speech derived from the noun meaning "cause", is used with a head noun that operates as an object or else as the subject of an intransitive verb. It often carries the modal meaning "to have to".

Ex.: རྒྱ་གར་ནས་འབྱོར་རྒྱུའི་བླ་མ་རྣམས་འབྲས་སྤུངས་ལ་བཞུགས་ཀྱི་རེད།

"The lamas who are to come from India will reside at Dräpung."

གང་བསྐྱབས་པར་བྱ་རྒྱུའི་སེམས་ཅན་ལས་ངན་དེ་ལ་སྙིང་རྗེ་(བསྐྱེད་དགོས)།

"(One should generate) compassion for living beings with bad karma that are to be protected."

• བྱ་ cha̱

This marker, which corresponds to the future of the verb "to do", functions in a similar way to kyu̱ but is used only in Literary Tibetan.

Ex.: གང་ལ་བསྟེན་བྱའི་བླ་མ་དེ་ཡོན་ཏན་འདི་དག་ཚང་བ་ངེས་པར་དགོས།

"The lama whom we follow must certainly have all these qualities."

གདུལ་བྱའི་ཡུལ། tü̱: chä̱: yü̱:

"The land or beings that must be subdued…"

• ཡུལ་ yü̱l, ས་ sā

Both these markers, which mean "place", are used when the head noun assumes the function of an indirect object or a place adverbial. In the spoken language, only sā is used to form relative clauses.

Ex.: ཚོང་པ་རྣམས་ཀྱིས་དད་གུས་བྱ་ཡུལ་ཞིག་ཀྱང་ཡིན། tshōngpa-nam'-kyi' thä̱kü' cha̱ yü̱: shi̱' kyāng yi̱n

"He was also a man who was greatly revered by the merchants."

ཞེ་སྡང་སྐྱེ་ཡུལ་མེད་ན་བཟོད་པ་སུ་ལ་བསྒོམ།

"If there is no one against whom one feels anger, with whom should one practice patience!"

སྦྱིན་པ་གཏང་བྱའི་ཡུལ་དབུལ་པོ། c̲inpa tāng chä̲' yü̲: ǖ:po

"Beggars to whom one should give alms…"

སྣུམ་འཚོང་ས་ཞིག་ཏུ་ཕྱིན། nūm tshōng sā shi̲'-tu chīn

"He went to a place that sold oil."

སྐྱབས་ཡུལ་རྣམས་ལས་བྱིན་རླབས་བདུད་རྩིའི་རྒྱུན་དཀར་གསལ་འོད་ཟེར་རྣམ་པར་དཔག་མེད་བྱུང་།

kyāp yü̲:-nam'-lä' chi̲nlap tü̲tsi: kyü̲n kār sǟ: ö̲ser nāmpar pākme' chu̲ng

"From [the Buddhas] in whom we have taken refuge there came forth an immeasurable white stream of nectar in the form of rays of clear light."

• མཁན་ khǟn/ མི་ mi̲

The use of khǟn is much more limited than in the spoken language. It can only modify head nouns that correspond semantically to "agents". The marker mi̲ has a function similar to that of khǟn, but it is used only in Literary Tibetan.

Ex.: ལས་ནི་ཀུན་བྱེད་རི་མོ་མཁན་དང་འདྲ། lä̲'-ni kūn che̲' ri̲mo khǟn-tang tra̲

"Karma is like a draughtsman who can design anything."

རྒྱ་གླིང་གཏོང་མཁན་གྱི་གྲྭ་པ། kya̲ling tōng khǟn-kyi thra̲pa

"The monk who's playing the shawm."

ཨ་རོག་ཟེར་མི་ཕོ་རོག་ཡིན། āro' se̲r-mi̲ phōro' yi̲n

"The one who calls me an old friend is the crow."

• ཅན་ cǟn, ལྡན་ tä̲n

The markers cǟn and tä̲n usually function like nominalized possessive verbs similar to yö̲'-pa "who has, endowed with". Their meaning is very similar and they are often interchangeable.

Ex.: ཡོན་ཏན་ཅན་ yö̲ntän cǟn = ཡོན་ཏན་ལྡན་ yö̲ntän tä̲n "one endowed with qualities"
མཛོ་ར་ཅན་ tso̲ ra̲ cǟn "a *dzo* with horns"
གསར་ཤོག་ཤོག་ངོ་བཅུ་གཉིས་ཅན་ sārsho' shōngo cūnyi' cǟn "a newspaper with twelve pages"
གསེར་གྱི་པད་མ་ཅན་ sēr-kyi pǟma cǟn "the one with the golden lotus"
གསེར་ལྡན་གྱི་རི་བོ་ sēr tä̲n-kyi ri̲wo "a mountain that harbours gold"

Conclusion

A brief examination of any Tibetan text is enough to reveal whether the work in question belongs to the classical or modern genre, or if it is intended to represent the standard, Central Tibetan spoken language. There are three main criteria that make it possible to make an immediate identification of the style or register:

- case markers,
- auxiliaries,
- the type of connectives.

Any sentence must necessarily contain at least one of these categories. A sound knowledge of the essential differences between the spoken and the literary languages will make it possible to shift from one to the other without any difficulty.

The Elements of Phonology

There are 28 consonontal phonemes (including the glottals, which tend sometimes to disappear and to be pronounced instead as a tone).

Table 1.1

The consonants

	Labials	Dentals	Retroflexes	Palatals	Velars	Glottals
Plosives	p	t	tr	ky	k	’
aspirates	ph	th	thr	khy	kh	
Affricates		ts		c		
aspirates		tsh		ch		
Fricatives		s	r	sh		
aspirates			rh			h
Lateral		l				
aspirates		lh				
Nasals	m	n		ny	ng	
Glides	w			y		

The standard syllable has the form Consonant-Vowel-Consonant (CVC), but it is also possible to find CV and, more rarely, VC and even V.

• **As initial consonants** in a syllable, any of the consonantal phonemes may appear: the plosives /p, t, tr, ky, k/ and their corresponding aspirates /ph, th, thr, khy, kh/; the affricates: /ts, c/ and their corresponding aspirates /tsh, ch/; the fricatives /s, sh, h/ and the retroflex or vibrant fricative /r/ and its aspirate homologue /rh/; the nasals /n, m, ny, ng/; the lateral /l/ and the corresponding aspirate /lh/, and the glides /y, w/.

• **As final consonants,** we find only the plosives /p, k/[191] / and /'/ (the glottal stop), the nasals /n, m, ng/, the liquid /l/ (exclusively in elegant speech) and /r/.

---

191. At the end of a word, k almost always takes the form of a glottal stop.

The relatively small number of final consonants relative to initial consonants is a common feature of the languages of this region.

We may also note that, in Standard Spoken Tibetan, consonant clusters such as *spr, skr, sk, lt, bsk,* etc. do not occur, contrary to the case of Old Tibetan. However, these clusters are preserved in modern spelling.

The description of sounds in polysyllabic words needs to be further refined by taking into consideration not only the initial consonants (Ci) and final consonants (Cf) of the word, but also the final consonant of the first syllable and the first consonant of the second syllable.

Table 1.2

Consonant distribution within a word

Initial consonant of word	Final consonant of interior syllable	Initial consonant of interior syllable	Final consonant of word
k, kh, c, ch, ky, khy, t, th tr, thr, p, ph m, n, ng, ny, r, l, s, sh, y, w	k, p, m, n, ng,(r), (l)	k, ky, c, t, tr, ts, p, m, n, ng, ny, r, l, sh, s, y, w	k, ‘, p, m, n, ng, (r), (l)

It will be seen from this table that the distribution of consonants isn't the same in the four positions. The main difference is that whereas there are no aspirated consonants at the beginning of the internal syllable(s) of a word, they do occur at the beginning of the word itself. However, in order to explain the significant phonetic variations that are found in Tibetan, we also need to examine the intrasyllabic positions, i.e., the beginning and end of the internal syllable (see below for the various pronunciations of the phoneme k).

Table 1.3

The vowels

	Front		Central	Back
	unrounded	rounded		
Close (or high)	i	ü [y]		u
Half-close	e	ö [ø]		o
Half-open	ä [ɛ]			
Open (or low)			a	

There are eight vowel phonemes: /a, ä, e, o, ö, u, ü, i/.

In addition to the five alphabetical vowels, there are three others /ä, ö, ü/ (*umlaut*) that are produced by the addition, in the written language, of the consonants *l*, *s*, *d* and *n*[192] which are themselves no longer pronounced. The three new vowels are a result of the evolution of the system.[193]

One of the problems with Tibetan phonology is the number of variants for each sound according to the context. To produce the right sound it is therefore important to know if it occurs at the beginning, the interior or the end of a word. In addition to the transcription used in this book, presented between oblique strokes, the pronunciation will also be given, in square brackets, in International Phonetic Alphabet (IPA).

One of the phonological features of Standard Tibetan is the absence of a clear opposition between voiced and voiceless consonants. *In a high tone,* all consonants are voiceless, whereas in a low tone we find slightly aspirated voiced consonants as well as partial or complete voicing. Sounds that are midway between being voiced and voiceless are rare in European languages, and therefore require special attention.

The pronunciation of consonants[194]

Certain phonemes are pronounced differently according to context. Phonetic variations depend not only on preceding and following consonants, but also on vowels. The variants and the different contexts in which they occur need not be memorized, since the differences in pronunciation are minimal, and not distinctive. Moreover, they are most easily learned by progressive usage.[195] We do, however, recommend that you make use of the CD, where all the following examples are recorded.[196]

---

192. That is, the coronals. The *n* and the *l* are still partially pronounced.

193. Phonetically, there are actually twelve oral (i.e., non-nasal) vowels with their respective nasal forms, but only the phonemes of the eight vowels listed above play a distinctive role. The vowels are dependent on the context in which they appear, and may not be used in creating oppositions.

194. The order in which these will be presented is as follows:

— Plosives (unaspirated and aspirated): velars, palatals, retroflexes, dentals and labials.

— Affricates (unaspirated and aspirated): palatals, dentals.

— Palatal fricatives, retroflexes and dentals.

— Laterals (unaspirated and aspirated).

— Glides y and w.

195. Ignoring the variants may result in a slight accent, but doesn't impair communication. For example, the phoneme k (see below) may be pronounced [k] wherever it may appear within a word as long as tonal differences are observed.

196. In the recording, the examples often reflect a reading pronunciation. As a consequence, initial aspirate consonants in second syllables often keep their aspiration.

CD II • Tr. 18 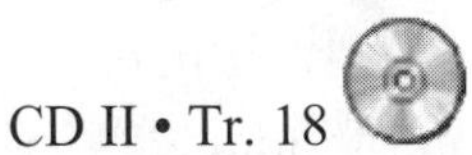

• /k/ may be pronounced in different ways according to the context: [k], [g̣], [ʔ] or [ɣ] or [ŋ].[197]

— The voiceless velar plosive [k] appears *at the beginning of high-tone words*:

Ex.: སྐུ་/kū/ "body" (H), རྐང་པ་/kāngpa/ "leg, foot", སྐོར་བ་/kōrra/ "circuit", སྐར་མ་/kārma/ "star", ཀ་བ་/kāwa/ "pillar", ཀུན་སློང་/kūnlong/ "motivation", རྐུ་མ་/kūma/ "thief", ཀོ་བ་/kōwa/ "leather", ཀུན་བཟང་/kūnsang/ personal name, དཀོན་པོ་/kōnpo/ "rare"

similarly at the beginning of an internal syllable, notably after /p/:

Ex.: སློབ་ཁང་/lōpkang/ "classroom", ཕེབས་འཁོར་/phēpkor/ "car"

[k] appears at *the end of internal syllables* before the consonants /p, t, tr, ts, c, s/ and before the consonants /l,sh/, especially if, in the last two cases, it is preceded by a vowel (i, e).[198]

Ex.: ལྐུགས་པ་/kūkpa/ "idiot", ཐུག་པ་/thūkpa/ "noodles" or "noodle soup", གློག་པར་/lōkpar/ "X-ray", ཚགས་པར་/tshākpar/ "newspaper", དྲག་པོ་/thra̱kpo/ "violent, fierce", ཚོགས་པ་/tshōkpa/ "group", ལྕགས་པར་/cākpar/ "typewriter", རོགས་པ་/ro̱kpa/ "companion", ཡག་པོ་/ya̱kpo/ "good", ལྐུགས་བརྡ་/kūkta/ "sign language", རྙོག་དྲ་/nyōktra/ "problems, complications", ཐུགས་ཁྲལ་/thūkträ:/ "anxiety" (H), རྫོགས་ཆེན་/tso̱kcen/ "Great Perfection", ལུགས་སྲོལ་/lu̱ksö:/ "custom, habit", པགས་ཚག་/pāktsa'/ "sheepskin clothing", བཅུ་གསུམ་/cūksum/ "thirteen", མིག་ཤེལ་/mīkshe:/ "spectacles"

— The partially voiced velar plosive [g̣] appears *at the beginning of low-tone words* (in this case, it is often pronounced as a clearly-voiced [g]):

Ex.: དགའ་པོ་/ka̱po/ "to like", དགུ་/ku̱/ "nine", སྒོར་མོ་/ko̱rmo/ "coin, money", དགའ་རོགས་/ka̱ro'/ "sweetheart", དགོན་པ་/ko̱mpa/ "monastery", སྒམ་/ka̱m/ "box", དགེ་ལེགས་/ke̱le'/ Gelek (personal name),མགོན་པོ་/kö̱npo/ "protector", དགའ་ལྡན་/ka̱ntän/ "Gandän" or "Tushita" (Skt.), name of a major monastery, དགེ་འདུན་/ke̱ntün/ "sangha", དགུང་ལོ་/ku̱nglo/ "age", མགོ་/ko̱/ "head", མགུར་/ku̱r/ "religious song"

It also appears *at the beginning of an interior syllable* after /k, ng, n, m, (r), (l)/ and vowels, as well as *at the end of interior syllables,* especially before /r, l/:

197. That is, the series of velars: voiceless velar plosive, voiced velar plosive, velar nasal and velar fricative, and the glottal.

198. In a more relaxed register, the sound k almost disappears. Thus one hears the pronunciations: /ya'po/ "good"; /thū'trä:/ "worry".

Ex.: ཡི་གེ་/yi̲ke/ "letter", ཐད་ཀར་/thākar/ "direct", ཐོག་ཁ་/thōkka/ "on top, roof", དམག་སྒར་/mākkar/ "military camp", ཡག་ག་/ya̲kka/ "better", ཐང་ཁུག་/thāngku'/ "pouch for kneading tsampa dough", སྡུག་རུས་/tu̲krü'/ "resistance", སྡིགས་ར་/ti̲kra/ "menace", བྲག་རི་ /thra̲kri/ "craggy mountain", རོགས་རམ་/ro̲kram/ "help", མིག་ར་/mīkra/ "eyebrow", གདམ་ཀ་/ta̲mka/ "choice", ཐིག་ལེ་/thīkle/ "sperm", "essence"

— The velar spirant [ɣ] (similarly pronounced to the French *r*) appears *at the end of interior syllables* before the consonants /l, m, ny, n, ng, sh/, especially if preceded by a posterior vowel /o, u, a/:

Ex.: བག་ལེབ་/pha̲klep/ "bread", ལག་ལེན་/la̲klen/ "practice", གློག་བརྙན་/lōknyän/ "cinema", འོག་མ་/wo̲kma/ "younger sibling", བདག་མེད་/ta̲kme'/ "anatma, selflessness", ལག་ཤུབས་/lākshup/ "glove", མདོག་ཉེས་/to̲knye'/ "ugly", གཡུག་ཤོག་/yūk-sho'/ "forget it, leave it", དག་སྣང་/tha̲knang/ "pure perception", སོག་ལེ་/sōkle/ "saw", ཀྱག་ལང་/kyāklang/ "bad habit"

— The glottal stop [ʔ] appears *at the end of a word:*

In this book, the /k/ is marked by an apostrophe /'/[199] when it is pronounced as a glottal stop or a tone to remind beginners that it shouldn't be pronounced as a true *k*:

Ex.: བཀག་/kā'/ "to stop", མིག་/mī'/ "eye", འདུག་/tu̲'/ "to be", སྲོག་/sō'/ "life-force", བསགས་/sā'/ "to collect", གློག་/lō'/ "electricity", དམག་/mā'/ "war", སྟག་/tā'/ "tiger", ཤག་/shā'/ "monastic cell", ཨ་རག་/āra'/ "alcohol", དུག/thu̲'/ "poison", ལོག/lo̲'/ "to turn back", ལྕགས་/cā'/ "iron"

When the glottal stop appears *at the end of a syllable* before /k, ky, w, y/, it is barely audible.

Ex.: ལག་འཁྱེར་/la̲kkyer/ "permit", ཕྱག་དབང་/chā'wang/ "benediction with the hand", ངག་དབང་/nga̲'wang/ Ngawang (personal name), འཕགས་ཡུལ་/phā'yü:/ "India, the exalted land" (compare with ཕ་ཡུལ་/phāyü:/ "native land"), སོག་ཡུལ་/sō'yü:/ "Mongolia", དམིགས་ཡུལ་/mī'yü:/ "sight" (compare with མི་རྒྱུད་/mi̲kyü'/ "lineage")

— /k/ is also pronounced as a velar nasal [ŋ] corresponding to the sound *ng* of the word *king*.

It appears *at the end of internal syllables* before the consonants /m, ny, n, ng/, especially after a preceding vowel /i, e/.

Ex.: རིག་གནས་/ri̲knä'/ "culture", མིག་དམར་/mīkmar/ Mars, Mikmar (personal name), མིག་སྨན་/mīkmän/ "eye-medicine", འཇིགས་མེད་/ci̲kme'/ Jigme (personal name)

199. Except when it precedes the consonant k, as in /la̲kkyer/ "permit".

• /kh/ is an aspirated *k* [kh].

— The aspirated velar [kh] appears only *at the beginning of a word.*

The pronunciation of the k is accompanied by a marked exhalation in high-tone words. In the case of low tones, the exhalation is weaker:

Ex.: ཁ་/khā/ "mouth", ཁ་པར་/khāpar/ "telephone", ཁུ་བ་/khūwa/ "juice", ཁོ་/khō/ "he", ཁོང་/khōng/ "he, she" (H), གོ་/kho̲/ "to hear", ག་འདྲས་ཟེ་/kha̲nträs/ "how", ག་པར་/kha̲par/ "where", གོང་/kho̲ng/ "price", གུར་/khu̲r/ "canvas tent", གའུ་/kha̲u/ "reliquary"

• The apostrophe ' is pronounced as a glottal stop [ʔ] or sometimes as a falling tone. Historically, this sound corresponds to the disappearance of the final *s* and *d,* which are still written but no longer pronounced. It appears only *at the end of the word*:

Ex.: དུས་ཚོད་/thü̲tsö'/ "time", ཁོང་གིས་/khōng-ki'/ "by him/ her", རྒྱུད་/kyü̲'/ "lineage", ལས་/lä̲'/ "karma", རས་/rä̲'/ "cotton", ལུས་/lü̲'/ "body", བདེ་སྐྱིད་/te̲kyi'/ Dekyi (personal name), བསྡད་ /tä̲'/ "to stay, sit", བཟས་/sä̲'/ "to eat", ཞུས་/shü̲'/ "to say", འོད་/ö̲'/ "light", ལྷོད་ལྷོད་ /lhōlö'/ "relaxed", ལོ་རྒྱུས་/lo̲kyü'/ "history"

• /ky/ is pronounced differently according to context: [c] or [ɟ̣]

— The voiceless palatal plosive [c] appears in writing in the form of a subscript *yod* (y) to *k* or to *g*.

It appears at the beginning of high-toned words:

Ex.: སྐྱོ་པོ་/kyōpo/ "poor", སྐྱེས་/kyē'/ "to be born", རྐྱང་/kyāng/ "wild ass", སྐྱུར་མོ་/kyūrmo/ "sour", སྐྱོན་/kyȫn/ "fault, mistake"

It appears at the beginning of the interior syllable after *p*:

Ex.: ཞབས་ཀྱུ་/sha̲pkyu/ (name of the vowel U), སྐྱབས་སྐྱོར་/kyāpkyor/ "support"

— The corresponding voiced palatal plosive [ɟ̣] is often pronounced between the voiceless [c] and the voiced [ɟ].

This sound appears *at the beginning of* low-toned words (in this case, it is often clearly voiced).

Ex.: རྒྱ་གར་/kya̲kar/ "India", རྒྱ་ནག་/kya̲na'/ "China", བརྒྱད་/kyä̲'/ "eight", རྒྱབ་/kya̲p/ "back, rear", མགྱོགས་པོ་/kyo̲kpo/ "quickly", རྒྱལ་ཁབ་/kyä̲:kap/ "state, nation", རྒྱལ་པོ་/kyä̲:po/ "king"

It appears at the beginning of the interior syllable after vowels and the consonants /m, n, ng, k, r l/:

Ex.: སངས་རྒྱས་/sāngkyä'/ "Buddha", རྟ་རྒྱུག་/tākyu'/ "horse race", རྡོག་རྒྱག་གཞུས་/to̲ngkya shü̲'/ "to kick", རིགས་རྒྱུད་/ri̲kkyü'/ "lineage", མིག་སྒྱུ་/mīkkyu/ "mirage", ལོ་རྒྱུས་/lo̲kyü/ "history".

• /khy/ is pronounced like the palatal plosive, but aspirated [c h].

The pronunciation is accompanied by a marked aspiration in the case of high tones, but the aspiration is less marked with low tones.

— This sound appears only *at the beginning of words*:

Ex.: ཁྱེད་རང་/khyērang/ "you" (H), འཁྱག་/khyā'/ "to be cold", ཁྱི་/khyī/ "dog", མཁྱེན་/khyēn/ "to know" (H), གྱོང་/khyo̲ng/ "loss", གྱེན་/khye̲n/ "uphill".

• /tr/ is pronounced differently according to the context: [ʈ] or [ɖ]:

— [ʈ] is a retroflex plosive (slightly affricate), that is, a sound produced by the tip of the tongue being turned back and touching the upper gums. The voiceless retroflex plosive [ʈ] appears *at the beginning of high-tone words.*

Ex.: སྐྲ་/trā/ "hair", སྤྲིན་པ་/trīnpa/ "cloud", སྤྲོ་པོ་/trōpo/, "pleasant, fun", སྒྲུན་/trǖn/ "to construct", སྤྲུལ་སྐུ་/trǖ:ku/, "reincarnate lama"

It also appears at the beginning of internal syllables after /p, k/:

Ex.: སློབ་གྲྭ་/lāptra/ "school", ཐུགས་ཁྲལ་/thūkträ:/ "anxiety" (H), ས་བཀྲ་/sāptra/ "map"

— The partially voiced retroflex plosive [ɖ̥] appears *at the beginning of low-toned words* (in which case it may be a clearly-voiced [ɖ]):

Ex.: འགྲོ་/tro̲/ "to go", འདྲ་པོ་/tra̲po/ "similar", འབྲས་/trä̲'/ "rice", འབྲས་བུ་/trä̲pu/ "result", དགྲ་བོ་/tra̲wo/ "enemy", སྦྲུལ་/trü̲:/ "snake", སྒྲུང་/tru̲m/ "story", འགྲིག་/tri̲'/ "to be appropriate"

It also appears *at the beginning of an internal syllable* after vowels or the consonants /m, n, ng, r, l/:

Ex.: ག་འདྲས་ཟེ་/kha̲nträs/ "how", ཤ་འབྲས་/shāmträ'/ "rice and meat stew", ལམ་འགྲོ་/la̲mtro/ "luck", མཁའ་འགྲོ་མ་/khāntroma/ "dakini, goddess", སྐུ་འདྲ་/kūntra/ "statue", སྐུ་དྲག་/kūtra'/ "aristocrat"

• /thr/ is pronounced as a retroflex /tr/ but aspirated [ʈ h]. The pronunciation of the retroflex is accompanied by a marked exhalation in the case of high tones. With low tones the exhalation is light or altogether absent.

The aspirated retroflex plosive appears only *at the beginning of words*:

Ex.: ཁྲག་/thrā'/ "blood", འཁྲུག་པ་/thrūkpa/ "dispute", ཕྲེང་བ་/thrēngnga/ "rosary", མཁྲེགས་པོ་/thrākpo/ "hard, stubborn", འཁྲུངས་ཡུལ་/thrūngyü:/ "birthplace", ཁྲོམ་/thrōm/ "market", གྲངས་ཀ་/thra̲ngka/ "number", དྲང་པོ་/thra̲ngpo/ "honest", དྲག་པོ་/thra̲kpo/ "violent", གྲང་མོ་/thra̲ngmo/ "cold", དྲུག་པ་/thru̲kpa/ "sixth", འཕྲུལ་འཁོར་/thrǖnkor/ "machine"

• /t/ is pronounced differently according to the context: [t] or [d̥].

— The voiceless dental plosive [t] appears *at the beginning of high-toned words*:

Ex.: རྟ་/tā/ “horse”, གཏོར་མ་/tōrma/ “torma”, བཏང་/tāng/ “to send”, སྟོབས་ཤུགས་ /tōpshu'/ “strength”, རྟག་པར་/tākpar/ “always”, སྟོང་པ་/tōngpa/ “empty”

At the beginning of an internal syllable after /k, p/:

Ex.: ཐོབ་ཐང་/thōptang/ “right, share”, ཟོ་ལྟ་ /so̱pta/ “shape”, སྲོག་ཐོག་བཏང་/sōkto tāng/ “to execute”, ཞབས་དག་/sha̱pta'/ “cheers! (down in one)”

— The partially-voiced dental plosive [ḍ] appears *at the beginning of low-toned words* (in which case it is often pronounced as a clearly-voiced [d]):

Ex.: རྡོ་རིང་/to̱ring/ “stele, stone pillar”, འདུག་/tu̱'/ “there is”, བདུན་ /tü̱n/ “seven”, མདངས་/ta̱ng'/ “tune”, མདའ་/ta̱/ “arrow”, རྡོ་/to̱/ “stone”, རྡོ་རྗེ/to̱rce/ “dorje, diamond”, སྡོམ་/to̱m/ “spider”

— It appears *at the beginning of internal syllables* after /m, n, ng, r, l/:

Ex.: མེ་མདའ་/me̱nta/ “gun”, གསོལ་འདེབས་/sȫntep/ “prayer”, ནང་དོན་/na̱ngtön/ “meaning, content”, ཏན་ཏན་/tā̃ntän/ “certain, sure”, སྐུ་ཟླ་/kūnta/ “spouse”, ཤིང་སྡོང་/shīngtong/ “tree”

• /th/ is pronounced like *t* but aspirated [t h]. The pronunciation of the *t* is accompanied by marked exhalation in the case of high tones. With low tones the exhalation is light.

— [t h] appears only at the beginning of a word:

Ex.: མཐོ་པོ་/thōpo/ “high”, མཐའ་མ་/thāma/, “last”, ཐུར་/thūr/ “downward slope”, ཐ་མག་ /thāma'/ “tobacco, cigarette”, ཐོམས་/thōm/ “to be confused”, ཐུགས་/thū'/ “mind, heart” (H), དང་པོ་ /tha̱ngpo/ “first”, དོམ་/tho̱m/ “bear”, དོན་དག་/thö̱nta'/ “meaning”

• /p/ is also pronounced differently according to context: [p] or [ḅ].

— The voiceless bilabial plosive [p] appears *at the beginning of high-toned words*:

Ex.: པར་/pār/ “photo”, པིར་/pīr/ “paintbrush”, པདྨ་/pā̃ma/ “lotus”, སྤུ་/pū/ “fur”, སྤོ་ལགས་/pōla'/ “grandfather”, སྤང་རི་/pāngri/ “alpine pasture”, སྤོ་ལོ་/pōlo/ “ball”

— [p] also appears at the beginning of internal syllables after /k/:

Ex.: ཡག་པོ་/ya̱kpo/ “good”, ཐུག་པ་/thūkpa/ “noodles, noodle soup”, བཙོག་པ་/tsōkpa/ “dirty”, ལྕགས་པར་/cākpar/ “typewriter”, རོགས་པ་/ro̱kpa/ “companion”

It appears *at the end of an internal syllable* before the consonants /p, t, tr, ts, c, s, sh/:

Ex.: ས་གདན་/sāptän/ “rug”, ཐབ་ཚང་/thāptsang/ “kitchen”, ཁེ་བཟང་/khēpsang/ “profit”, བསླབ་བྱ་ /lāpca/ “advice”, བློ་བཟང་/lōsang/ Lobzang (personal name), ཨབ་སོག་/āpso/ “Lhasa apso”(dog), ཐབས་ཤེས་/thāpshe'/ “means”

— The semi-voiced bilabial plosive [b̥] appears *at the beginning of words* (in which case it may be fully voiced as [b]):

Ex.: འབུ་/pu̲/ "insect, bug", འབའ་ཆ་/pa̲ca/ "musical instrument", འབུམ་/pu̲m/ "hundred thousand", རྦ་རླབས་/pa̲lap/ "wave", སྦྲ་ནག་/pa̲na'/ "nomad tent"

It appears *at the beginning of internal syllables* after the consonants /p, m, ng, n, r, l/ and vowels:

Ex.: ལྔ་པ་/ngāpa/ "fifth", ཚེས་པ་/tshēpa/ "date", རྒྱལ་པོ་/kyä̲:po/ "king", རྟ་པ་/tāpa/ "rider", བསླབ་པ་/lāppa/ "teaching", གསར་པ་/sārpa/ "new"

— Note that when people are speaking quickly, a *b* between two vowels may be pronounced as a labiodental spirant [β] similar to a Spanish *v* as in *voz*: [ŋaβa], [sarβa].

— And finally, the phoneme /p/ may also be pronounced as a glottal [ʔ] at the end of a word (see above). This is characteristic of rapid speech, but the [p] may reappear when people are speaking more carefully.

Ex.: ཕེབས་ phē' = phēp "come, go" (H), སླེབས་ lē' = lēp "to arrive"

• /ph/ is pronounced *p* but aspirated [ph]. The pronunciation of the *p* is accompanied by a marked exhalation. In the case of high tones the aspiration is strong, but is weak with low tones.

— [ph] appears only at the beginning of a word:

Ex.: ཕར་/phār/ "over there", "thither", ཕ་མ་/phāma/ "parents", ཕུ་/phū/ "upper part of a valley", བུ་/phu̲/ "son", བལ་/phä̲:/ "wool", བ་ཕྱུགས་/pha̲cu'/ "cow"

• /c/ is pronounced differently according to context: [tɕ] or [dʑ].

— The voiceless affricate palatal [tɕ] appears *at the beginning of high-toned words*:

Ex.: ལྕི་བ་/cōwa/ "dung", གཅིག་/cī'/ "one", ཅ་ལག་/cāla'/ "thing, item", བཅུ་/cū/ "ten"

It also appears at the beginning of an internal syllable after /p, k/:

Ex.: བསླབས་ བྱ་ /lāpca/ "advice", སྲོག་ཆགས་/sōkca'/ "creature, sentient being", བརྟག་དཔྱད་/tākcä'/ "analysis", སློབ་སྦྱོང་/lōpcong/ "study", ནུབ་ཕྱོགས་/nu̲pco'/ "west", ནུབ་བྱང་/nu̲pcang/ "north west"

— The partially voiced affricate palatal [d̥ʑ] appears *at the beginning of low-toned words* (in which case it may be clearly voiced as [dʑ]):

Ex.: འཇའ་/ca̲/ "rainbow", འཇིག་རྟེན་/ci̲kten/ "world", འཇམ་པོ་/ca̲mpo/ "gentle", མཇལ་/cä̲:/ "to meet" (H), བརྗེད་/ce̲'/ "to forget"

It also appears *at the beginning of internal syllables after* the consonants /m, n, ng, r, l/ and vowels:

Ex.: ཨ་ལྕག་/āca/ "elder sister", གསོལ་ཇ་/sȫ:ca/ "tea", གསར་བརྗེ་/sārce/ "revolution", ཨ་ཅོར་/ācor/ "towel"

• /ch/ is pronounced [t ç h].

— This is an voiceless affricate palatal pronounced like a /c/ but aspirated. In the case of high-toned words the aspiration is strong, but is weaker or may even be absent altogether with low tones.

— This sound appears only *at the beginning of* words:

Ex.: ཆུ་/chū/ "water", ཇ་/cha̱/ "tea", ཆ་/chā/ "pair", ཆང་/chāng/ "chang, Tibetan beer", ཆེན་པོ་ /chēnpo/ "big", ཆུང་ཆུང་/chūncung/ "small", ཆོས་/chȫ'/ "dharma", བྱང་/cha̱ng/ "north", བྱམས་པོ་/cha̱mpo/ "affection, love", བྱང་ཆུབ་སེམས་དཔའ་/cha̱ngcup sēmpa/ "bodhisattva"

• /ts/ is pronounced differently according to the context: [t s] or [d ẓ].

— The voiceless affricate dental [t s] appears at the beginning of high-toned words:

Ex.: རྩེ་/tsē/ "peak", རྩ་/tsā/ "vein", གཙོ་བོ་/tsōwo/ "principal", རྩམ་པ་/tsāmpa/ "ground roasted barley", བཙོན་པ་/tsȫnpa/ "prisoner", རྩེ་མོ་/tsēmo/ "game"

It also appears *at the beginning of internal syllables* after the consonants [p] and [k]:

Ex.: སྟག་ཚང་/tāktsang/ "tiger's lair" (place name), སྟག་རྩེ་/tāktse/ place name, ཐབ་ཚང་/thāptsang/ "kitchen", སྣག་ཚ་/nāktsa/ "ink", སློབ་ཚན་/lōptsän/ "lesson"

— The partially-voiced affricate dental [d ẓ] appears *at the beginning of low-toned words* (in which case it may be pronounced as a clearly voiced [d z]):

Ex.: ཛོགས་/tso̱'/ "to be finished, to run out", འཛམ་གླིང་/tsa̱mling/ "world, earth", མཛེས་པོ་/tse̱po/ "beautiful", འཛིན་གྲྭ་/tsi̱ntra/ "class" (place name), མཛོ་ /tso̱/ "dzo, yak-cow crossbreed"

It also appears *at the beginning of internal syllables* after the /m, n, ng, r, l/ and vowels:

Ex.: རང་བཙན་ /ra̱ngtsän/ "independence", ས་མཚམས་/sāntsam/ "border", སྦྲང་རྩི་/tra̱ngtsi/ "honey", བསྟན་འཛིན་/tǟntsin/ "one who possesses teachings" (personal name)

• /tsh/ is pronounced [t s h]:

— This is an voiceless affricate palatal pronounced like /ts/ but aspirated. The aspiration is marked in the case of high-toned words, but light with low-toned words.

— This sound appears only *at the beginning of words*.

Ex.: ཚྭ་/tshā/ "salt", མཚོ་/tshō/ "lake", ཚུར་/tshūr/ "this way, hither", ཚོར་སྣང་/tshōrnang/ "reaction", ཚེ་/tshē/ "life", ཚོང་པ་/tshōngpa/ "merchant, businessman", ཛ་དྲག་/tshatra/ "urgent", ཛོར་པོ་/tshorpo/ "dirty".

• /sh/ is pronounced [ç] .

— The voiceless palatal fricative [ç] appears *at the beginning of words* (before both high and low tones) as well as *at the beginning of internal syllables*:

Ex.: ཤ་/shā/ "meat", ཤོར་/shōr/ "to lose, let go", ཞོར་/shor/ "moment, occasion", ཤིང་ཏོག་/shīngto'/ "fruit", ཤ་མོ་/shāmo/ "mushroom", ཞྭ་མོ་/shamo/ "hat", ཞིང་ཁ་/shingka/ "field", ཤག་/shā'/ "monk's cell"

• /r/ is pronounced differently according to context: [r], [ɹ] or a lengthening of the vowel [ː].

— /r/ has two free variants: [r] and [ɹ]. These two free variants appear *at the beginning of words and of internal syllables*:

Ex.: ར་/ra/ "goat", རི་/ri/ "mountain", རོ་/ro/ "corpse", རང་ /rang/ "self", གངས་རི་/khangri/ "snow-mountain", ཁོ་རང་/khōrang/ "he", རི་མོ་/ rimo/ "drawing"

— The lengthening of the preceding vowel [ː] occurs only when the *r* is *at the end of the word or syllable,* rather as in the case of English (as opposed to American) pronunciation, in which the final *r* disappears.

Ex.: མར་/mar/ "butter", མི་འབོར་/ mimbor/ "population", མོར་/mor/ "to her", གསར་པ་/sārpa/ "new", དཔེར་ན་/pērna/ "for example"

Note that in fastidious pronunciation the final *r* may reappear – as indeed it sometimes does in English.

• /rh/ is pronounced [ʂ]:

— The sibilant retroflex fricative [ʂ] represents the voiceless and slightly aspirated equivalent of the /r/. This sound appears only *at the beginning of high-toned words,* and appears only in a few rare words and expressions.

Ex.: ཧྲང་ཧྲང་/rhāngrang/ "solitary", ཧྲིལ་པོ་/rhī:po/ "complete", ཧྲག་ཧྲག་ /rha'ra'/ "the best quality", མིག་ཧྲིག་ཧྲིག་/mī' rhī'rhi'/ "squinting", ཧྲོབ་ཧྲོབ་/rhōprop/ "rough, boorish"

• /s/ is pronounced as a dental fricative [s]:

It is pronounced similarly to the English *s* in "sit" or "summer".

It appears *at the beginning of words and of internal syllables:*

Ex.: ས་/sā/ "earth, ground", སོ་/sō/ "tooth", ཟ་/sa̱/ "to eat", བཟོ་/so̱/ "to make", ལྷ་ས་/lhāsa/ "Lhasa", གསུངས་/sūng'/ "to say", འགྲོ་སོང་/tro̱song/ "expenditure", དེང་སང་/the̱nsang/ "these days", ཁ་ས་/khā̱sa/ "yesterday"

• /l/ is pronounced in two different ways depending on the context: [l] or a lengthening of the vowel.

— The dental lateral [l] appears *at the beginning of a word or of an internal syllable:*

Ex.: ལ་/la̱/ "mountain pass", པ་ལགས་/pāla'/ "father" (H), ལང་/la̱ng/ "to arise", ལོ་/lo̱/ "year", མི་ལ་རས་པ་/mi̱laräpa/ "Milaräpa", ཨ་ལོང་/ālong/ "earring"

— [ː] corresponds to a lengthening of the preceding vowel when *l* figures at the end of a word or syllable. In a case of a more literary pronunciation, the *l* reappears. In this book the position is marked with a lengthening [ː] rather than an /l/ to remind beginners not to pronounce a true *l*.

Ex.: བལ་/phä̱:/ "wool", གལ་ཆེན་པོ་/khä̱: chēnpo/ "important", བལ་ཡུལ་/phä̱:yü:/ "Nepal" (lit. "Wool country"). These same words may also be pronounced respectively: phä̱l "wool", khä̱l chēnpo "important", phä̱lyül "Nepal"

• /lh/ is pronounced as an aspirated voiceless lateral [l̥h].

— [l̥h] appears *only at the beginning of words*. The normal *l* is pronounced with a strong aspiration:

Ex.: ལྷ་/lhā/ "divinity", ལྷོ་/lhō/ "south", ལྷོད་ལྷོད་/lhōlö'/ "relaxed", ལྷང་ལྷང་/lhānglang/ "clear (sound, etc.)", ལྷུང་/lhūng/ "to fall"

• /h/ is pronounced as an voiceless glottal fricative [h] which usually appears only *at the beginning of a high-tone word*:

Ex.: ཧམ་པ་/hāmpa/ "brutal, insolent, barbarous", ཧ་ལས་/hā lä̱'/ "to be amazed", ཧ་གོ་/hā kho̱/ "to understand", ཧོན་ཐོར་/hōn thōr/ "to be astonished", ཧ་ཅང་/hācang/ "excessively".

• /m/ is pronounced as a nasal bilabial [m].

— It occurs *at the beginning and end of words and of internal syllables:*[200]

200. In certain rare cases the aspirated voiceless form [hm̊] also occurs, but this is very uncommon, and insofar as it is not opposed to the voiced form (except perhaps for three or four words in the dialects of some speakers), it is phonologically negligible. Examples are [m̥ha] "negation" (when it precedes a high-tone aspirated consonant) and [ŋhøʔ] "to be well fried". By contrast, aspirated nasals are both common and relevant in other Tibetan dialects and in Burmese.

Ex.: རྨོ་ལགས་/mōla'/ "old lady, grandmother", སྨན་/mān/ "medicine", ཐམ་པ་/thāmpa/ "multiple of ten", ལམ་ཁག་/lamka'/ "road", ཕ་ལམ་/phālam/ "diamond", མར་/mar/ "butter", མི་/mi/ "man", རོགས་རམ་/rokram/ "help"

• /n/ is pronounced: [n].

— The dental nasal [n] appears at the beginning of words, at the beginning of syllables and also at the end of syllables before the dentals /t/ and /tr/:

Ex.: ནང་པ་/nangpa/ "Buddhist", ནུས་པ་/nüpa/ "courage, strength", ག་འདྲས་ཟེ་/khanträs/ "how", དོན་དག་/thönta'/ "meaning", དོ་སྣང་/thonang/ "interest", སྣུམ་/nūm/ "oil", ནམ་མཁའ་/nāmka/ "sky", ནད་པ་/näpa/ "ill"

— But /n/ is also pronounced [m], [ñ] and [ŋ] *within words, depending on the following consonant.* The labial consonant [m] appears before the labial consonant [p], the velar nasal *ng* [ŋ] appears before the velar consonant /k/, and the nasal palatal *ny* [ñ] appears before the palatal consonant /ky/. These fluctuations between nasals are similar to the negative prefix which is pronounced *in* before *t* and *im* before *p* (as in "interminable", "impossible", etc.). Contrary to the case of Tibetan, however, this difference is now represented in spelling.

Ex.: སྟོན་པ་/tõnpa/ "teacher, guide" is often pronounced: tõmpa, རིན་པོ་ཆེ་/rinpo chē/: rimpo chē "precious one, term of address for high-ranking incarnate lamas", ཕྱིན་པ་རེད་/chīn-pare'/: chīm-pare'[201] "(he) went" སྤུན་སྐྱ་ /pīnkya'/: pīñkya' "sibling, relative", དགུན་ཁ་/künka/: küngka "winter"

— [~] corresponds to a nasalization of the preceding vowel, and appears only with an *n* at the end of a word, although this often remains barely audible.

Ex.: ལན་/län/ "reply", གདན་/tän/ "cushion", རྟེན་/tēn/ "support", བོན་/phön/ "the Bön religion", བདུན་/tün/ "seven", ཡིན་/yin/ "I am"

• /ny/ is pronounced as a palatal nasal [ñ]. It appears *at the beginning of a word or a syllable.*

Ex.: ཉ་/nya/ "fish", ཉུང་ཉུང་/nyungnyung/ "few", ཉམས་མྱོང་/nyamnyong/ "experience", སྙིང་/nyīng/ "heart", ཉོན་མོངས་/nyönmong/ "negative emotions", ཉམས་ལེན་/nyamlen/ "practice"

• /ng/ is pronounced as [ŋ] or as a nasalization according to context:

---

201. The pronunciation of the phoneme n as [m] before a labial is very common, and may be illustrated by the following anecdote: /könpa/ is almost always pronounced [gompa], to the extent that certain Tibetans who are not particularly adept at spelling tend to write it as *sgompa* (*sgom* means "meditation"). The popular variant [gompa] is now so widely used that the word has come to acquire two pronunciations, a more "correct" /könpa/ and a vernacular /kompa/ (with a loss of the umlaut on the ö). This phenomenon also applies to nasals in the case of conjugated verbs. For example, /chin-pare'/ is often pronounced chimpare'. In this case, too, the dental nasal reappears in more "refined" speech.

— The velar nasal [ŋ] corresponding to the sound *ng* in "king", appears *at the beginning of a word or of an internal syllable*, or *at the end of a word or syllable* /ng/. It nasalizes the preceding syllable: V nasal + /ng/:

Ex.: སྔ་པོ་/ngāpo/ "soon", ང་/nga̲/ "I", དངུལ་/ngǖ:/ "silver, money", བཏང་/tāng/ "to send", ལང་/la̲ng/ "to arise", སང་ཉིན་/sāngnyin/ "tomorrow", སྡུག་བསྔལ་/tu̲'ngä:/ "suffering, misery"

• /w/ is prononounced as a bilabial glide [w]. It appears *at the beginning of words* and *at the beginning of internal syllables.*

Ex.: དབང་/wāng/ "power", ངག་དབང་/nga̲'wang/ "power of speech" (personal name), ཟླ་བ་/ta̲wa/ "moon", དྲི་བ་/thri̲wa/ "question", ཝ་མོ་/wa̲mo/ "fox", ཨ་ཝ་/āwa/ "child" (H)

• /y/ is pronounced as a palatal glide [j] or yod. It appears *at the beginning of words* and *at the beginning of internal syllables*:

Ex.: ཡག་པོ་/ya̲kpo/ "good", ཡོན་ཏན་/yö̲ntän/ "quality", ས་ཡ་/sāya/ "million", དབྱར་ཁ་/ya̲rka/ "summer", ཡུམ་/yu̲m/ "mother", ཕ་ཡུལ་/phāyü:/ "native land", ཧ་ཡང་/hāyang/ "aluminum".

The pronunciation of vowels

The 8 Tibetan vowels /a, e, ä, o, ö, u, ü, i/ do not pose any special problems for speakers of French or German. For English speakers, however, the oppositions /e, ä/, /o, ö/, /u, ü/ require careful attention . The only rather surprising feature is the variability of certain vowels depending on the context in which they appear. The nasal consonants /n, ng/ produce nasal vowels, but these are not distinctive. Thus Tibetan is ill-equipped to distinguish between pairs such as the French "main" and "mène".

• /a/ is pronounced as an open central vowel [a] and sometimes as a schwa [ə].

— [a] usually appears in all positions except atonal suffixes:

Ex.: ཁ་/khā/ "mouth", བླ་མ་/lāma/ "lama, guru", ཨ་མ་/āma/ "mother", རྩམ་པ་/tsāmpa/ "milled roasted barley"

In an atonal position or as a closed syllable (before *p*), /a/ is pronounced [ʌ] or [ə].

Ex.: ཁབ་/khāp/ "needle", ཐབ་/thāp/ "stove"
ཡོང་པ་རེད་/yong-pare'/ is pronounced [j õ ŋ b ə r e ʔ].

• /ä/ is pronounced as a half-open front vowel [ɛ] (corresponding to the *ai* of English *pair*)

Ex. : རས་/rä̲'/ "cotton cloth", ལས་/lä̲'/ "karma", འབྲས་/trä̲'/ "rice", ཉལ་/nyä̲:/ "to sleep", གསལ་པོ་/sǟ:po/ "clear"

• /e/ is pronounced as a half-close front vowel [e] (corresponding to *é* of French *été* or the *ee* of German *See*):

Ex.: རེད་/re̱'/ "to be", ཉེ་པོ་/nye̱po/ "near", མེ་/me̱/ "fire", སེལ་/sē:/ "to clear, remove"

It is also pronounced [ɛ], or *ay* as a closed syllable:

Ex.: སླེབས /lēp/ "to arrive", ཕེབས་/phēp/ "to go, to come" (H), དེང་སང་/the̱ngsang/ "these days"

• /ö/ is pronounced as a half-open front vowel [ø]:

Ex.: བོད་/phö̱'/ "Tibet", དངོས་ནས་/ngȫnä'/ "really", གསོལ་འདེབས་ /sȫntep/ "prayer"

Finally, it should be noted that at the beginning of low-tone words, round vowels are often "labialized" and preceded by the sound [w]. Thus འོད་/ö̱'/ "light" is pronounced wö̱'.

• /o/ is pronounced as a half-closed back vowel [o] corresponding to the *o* of English "go":

Ex.: ལོ་/lo̱/ "year", རྡོ་/to̱/ "stone", ལོ་མ་/lo̱ma/ "leaf", བ་སོ་/phä̱:so/ "ivory"

When the syllable is closed, the sound is generally a more open [ɔ] as in the case of the English "got":

Ex.: འཁོར་བ་/khōrwa/ "samsara, cyclic existence", སོབ་སོབ་/sōpsop/ "soft"

Finally, note that *at the beginning of low-tone words*, the vowel is often preceded by the sound [w]. Thus འོ་མ་/o̱ma/ "milk" is pronounced wo̱ma. In the same way, འོག་མ་/o̱'ma/ "younger sibling" is pronounced wo̱'ma.

• /u/ is pronounced as a closed back vowel [u]:

Ex.: ཀླུ་/lū/ "naga (serpent-spirit)", སྐུ་/kū/ "body", སུ་/sū/ "who", ནུ་མ་/nu̱ma/ "breast"

At the beginning of low-toned words, the vowel is often preceded by the sound [w].

Ex.: འུག་པ་/u̱kpa/: wu̱kpa "owl"

• /ü/ is pronounced as a rounded close front vowel [y]:

Ex.: ཕུལ་/phǖ:/ "to give" (h), དུས་ཚོད་/thü̱tsö'/ "time", ས་ཁུལ་/sākü:/ "region"

• /i/ is pronounced as a closed front vowel [i]:

Ex.: མི་/mi̱/ "man", རིགས་/ri̱'/ "sort, kind", རི་/ri̱/ "mountain", ཞི་བདེ་/shi̱te/ "peace", ཞིམ་པོ་/shi̱mpo/ "delicious"

Conclusions on pronunciation and phonological oppositions

As we have seen, some phonemes vary considerably according to their context. As a general rule, consonants are very clearly pronounced at the beginning of a word, but less so in other positions, especially at the end.

Thus /k/ is pronounced [k] at the beginning of a syllable, but in a final internal position within a word it is often weakened to [ɣ], similar to the French pronunciation of *r*, and at the very end of a word it may even disappear altogether or be transformed into a simple glottal stop [ʔ].

The same observations apply to /p/, which is pronounced [p] at the beginning of a word but often as [β] between vowels, and sometimes may become a glottal stop [ʔ] at the end of a word.

Finally, the phonemes /l/ are /r/ pronounced respectively [l] and [r] at the beginning of a syllable, whereas at the end they are transformed into a lengthening [:] of the vowel.

Remarks on stress

Stress is not particularly marked in Tibetan (see Introduction). It should be noted, however, that in the case of a certain number of words comprising suffixes, nouns and verbs may be distinguished by stress (and tone). Thus in the following examples, each of the two syllables carries equal stress, whereas in the case of the verb – whether in the infinitive or the past participle – the accent falls on the first syllable while the second syllable *pa* is an unstressed suffix. This feature is analogous to the distinction between nominal and verbal forms of homonyms that is made in English: contráct (verb), cóntract (noun); recórd (verb), récord (noun); conflíct (verb), cónflict (noun).

CD II • Tr. 19

རྩིས་པ་/tsīpa/ "astrologer, accountant"	རྩིས་པ་/tsī'-pa/ "to count"
བསམ་པ་: /sāmpa/ "thought"	བསམས་པ་ /sām'-pa/ "to think"
རིག་པ་ /ri̱kpa/ "knowledge"	རིག་པ་ /ri̱'-pa/ "to see, know"
སླབ་པ་ /lāppa/ "teaching"	སླབ་པ་ /lāp-pa/ "to teach, learn"
དཀོད་པ་ /kō̄pa/ "arrangement, disposition"	དཀོད་པ་ /kō̄'-pa/ "to arrange, dispose"
ཆད་པ་ /chā̄pa/ "punishment"	ཆད་པ་ /chā̄'-pa/ "to punish"
རྟོག་པ་ /tōkpa/ "awareness, realization"	རྟོག་པ་ /tō'-pa/ "to understand, realize"
སྦྱིན་པ་ /ci̱npa/ "offering"	སྦྱིན་པ་ /ci̱n-pa/ "to offer"
སྐྱུག་པ་ /kyūkpa/ "vomit"	སྐྱུག་པ་ /kyū'-pa/ "to vomit"

The Honorific Register

As in other Asian languages such as Japanese and Korean, Tibetan has developed an honorific register that make it possible to express social relations through linguistic usage. The honorific should be understood as a sophisticated form of politeness expressed through personal pronouns, names, verbs, auxiliaries and even adjectives and adverbs. The honorific register, called ཞེ་ས་ she̱sa:, is used for people of superior and equal social standing, and even between friends and married couples. The ordinary register, སྐད་དཀྱུས་མ་ kā kyūma, is used for all others, that is, those younger than oneself (although the honorific is sometimes used with certain juniors) and social inferiors.

Students of Tibetan should certainly learn both registers, but if you were to learn only one, the ordinary register would be better for two reasons: some people without much education hardly use the honorific register; and secondly, even if you use honorifics to another person you should always use ordinary terms (in the absence of humilifics) for yourself. And finally the good news: quite a number of words have only one form.

Most nouns, adjectives and adverbs have only one type of honorific.

noun	ordinary	honorific
tea	ཇ་ cha̱	གསོལ་ཇ་ sō:ca
water	ཆུ་ chū	ཆབ་ chāp
book	དེབ་ thēp	ཕྱག་དེབ་ chā'tep

For verbs, however, as well as for pronouns, there are several types of honorific.

— སྤྱིར་བཏང་ཞེ་ས་ cīrtang she̱sa — the **"general honorific"** (H),

— ཞེ་ས་མཐོ་པོ་ she̱sa thōpo — the **"high honorific"** (HH),

— དམའ་ས་བཟུང་བའི་ཞེ་ས་ māsa su̱ngwä: she̱sa — the **"humilific"** (h),

— ཕྱོགས་གཉིས་ཀྱི་ཞེ་ས་ chō' nyī'-ki she̱sa — the **"double honorific"** (hH).

The general and high honorifics correspond to forms of politeness that indicate a respectful attitude towards *the subject of an action.* The high honorific conveys an even more polite and reverential attitude than the general honorific, and is used especially in the case of high lamas and State dignitaries. The humilific[202] is systematically used for the first person as the subject, but more generally to indicate a respectful attitude on the part of the speaker towards the person to whom that action is directed (which, from a syntactic perspective, may comprise various complements: object, indirect object, etc.). It should be emphasized that the honorific is *never used with reference to oneself,* and for the first person the humilific is consequently needed.

Finally, the double honorific denotes that both the subject of the action and the person to whom it is directed are considered by the speaker to merit equal respect. Note that there are only a few high and double honorifics, and they are not often used.

Here is an illustration of the different levels:

verb	humilific (h)	ordinary	honorific (H)
to drink	ཞུས་ shü̱'	འཐུང་ thūng	མཆོད་ chȫ'
to give	ཕུལ་ phǖ:	སྤྲད་ trǟ'	གནང་ nāng
to stay, sit	—	བསྡད་ tä̱'	བཞུགས་ shu̱'
to go	བཅར་ cār	འགྲོ་ tro̱	ཕེབས་ phēp
to speak	བཀའ་མོལ་ཞུས་ kāmö: shü̱'	སྐད་ཆ་བཤད་ kǟca shä'	བཀའ་མོལ་གནང་ kāmö: nāng

Special cases of high and double honorifics:

verb	high honorific (HH)	double honorific (hH)
to give	—	ཕུལ་གནང་ phǖ: nāng
to stay, sit	བཞུགས་གདན་འཛགས་ shu̱'tänca'	—
to go	ཆིབས་སྒྱུར་གནང་ chīpkyur nāng	—
to speak	—	བཀའ་མོལ་ཞུས་གནང་ kāmö: shü̱' nāng

Perfect mastery of honorifics is not easy,[203] but you need not worry too much about this because Tibetans themselves often make mistakes! There is a common expression, "lame honor-

202. This term was coined by S.Beyer (1992).

203. The use of honorific registers may entail true linguistic virtuosity, to the extent that not only pronouns, but also adjectives, adverbs, verbs and auxiliaries should be in honorific form, while the speaker should also diminish himself or herself by using the appropriate humilifics.

ifics" (*zhe-sa rkang-chag*), to signify the fact that some terms in a sentence are honorific whereas others belong to the ordinary level. The misuse of honorifics is a common source of amusement for Tibetans.

The basis for a mastery of the honorific language is a sound knowledge of the pronouns and a few of the main nouns, verbs (especially the main verbs of movement, speech and action) and auxiliaries. The she̱sa vocabulary will gradually increase with usage.

The honorific language is especially used in Standard Tibetan and the dialects of Central Tibet and Tsang, as well as certain outlying regions such as Mustang, in Nepal. It is also very important in Tibetan literature, where it may even play a grammatical role since it can substitute for the subject and other markers of person by establishing the relationship between characters, and hence identify them. Contrary to a widespread belief, the honorific is not altogether absent in the dialects of Kham and Amdo, even though it is much less frequently used than in Central Tibet.

Most honorifics are derivatives of ordinary terms, and relatively few are original. For the most part, nouns are formed by the use of honorific prefixes. There are perhaps just a dozen or so such prefixes, corresponding to honorific terms for body parts: སྐུ་ kū "body", ཕྱག་ chā' "hand", དབུ་ ū "head", སྤྱན་ cā̄n "eyes", ཞལ་ shä̱: "mouth", ཞབས་ sha̱p "leg", ལྗགས་ ca̱' "tongue", ཐུགས་ thū' "mind", བཀའ་ kā "speech", as well as a few prefixes derived from verbs: གསོལ་ sȫ: "to pray", བཞེས་ she̱' "to take", གཟིམ་ si̱m "to sleep", etc.

Each prefix is associated with a very wide semantic field related to its original meaning. Thus the prefix kū often appears in words denoting not only body parts but also physical activities, bodily representations, kinship ties, clothing, belongings, social ranks, certain illnesses and so on. For example: སྐུ་ཁྲག་ kūtra' "blood", སྐུ་སྟོད་ kūtö' "shirt", སྐུ་ཆས་kūcä' "possessions", སྐུ་བརྙན་ kūnyän "statue", སྐུ་མགྲོན་ kūntrön "guest", etc.

Verbs fall into two categories:

— a) verbs consisting of a noun and a verbalizer (these constitute the majority).

— b) simple verbs.

In the first case, the honorific is obtained by putting the noun that precedes the verb in the honorific (according to the principle outlined above) and then replacing the verbalizer by its honorific (or humilific) homologue. Here are some verbs with common honorific verbalizers:

གནང་nāng honorific for བྱེད་che̱' "to do" *(verbalizer)* and སྤྲད་trā̄' "to give"

བསྐྱོན་kyȫn honorific for བརྒྱབ་kya̱p "to do, to make" *(verbalizer)*

བཏང་གནང་tāng nāng honorific for བཏང་tāng "to send" *(verbalizer)*

བཞེས་she̱' honorific for ལེན་le̱n to take, ཟ་sa̱ "to eat", འཐུང་thūng "to drink"

ཞུས་shü̱' humilific for ཟ་sa̱ "to eat", འཐུང་thūng "to drink",ལེན་le̱n "to take", བཤད་shā̄' "to say"

ཕུལ་phǖ: humilific for སྤྲོད་trǟ' "to give"

བཞེངས་sha̱ng' honorific for ལངས་la̱ng' "to rise" *(verbalizer)*

Ex.: ལས་ཀ་བྱེད་lä̱ka che̱' "to work" > ཕྱག་ལས་གནང་chā'lä' nāng(H)
ཇ་འཐུང་cha̱ thūng "to drink tea" > གསོལ་ཇ་མཆོད་sȫ:ca chȫ' (H) or གསོལ་ཇ་ཞུས་sȫ:ca shü̱' (h)
མེ་བཏང་ me̱ tāng "to set fire" > ཞུགས་མེ་བཏང་གནང་ shu̱kme tāng nāng (H)
དཔར་བརྒྱབ་ pār kya̱p "to photograph" > སྐུ་དཔར་བསྐྱོན་ kūpar kyȫn

In the case of certain simple verbs, the honorific entails a different lexical root.

Ex.: འགྲོ་tro̱ "to go" > ཕེབས་phēp (H), མཐོང་thōng "to see" > གཟིགས་si̱' (H)

Note that there are only a few adjectives and adverbs that have a true honorific form. In such cases, the honorific has a different root from the ordinary term.

Ex.: སྐྱིད་པོ་kyīppo "happy, pleasant", ཞིམ་པོ་shi̱mpo "delicious" > སྤྲོ་པོ་trōpo (H)
མཉམ་དུ་nyāmtu "together" > ལྷན་རྒྱས་lhǟnkyä' (H)
མགྱོགས་པོ་kyo̱kpo"fast, quickly" > སྐྱོལ་པོ་tsö:po (H, rare)

In a few rare cases, the honorific form of the adjective is formed by using a suffix གནང་པོ་ pronounced གནང་གོ་ na̱ngko.

Ex.: འཇོལ་པོ་ "soft". འཇོལ་གནང་གོ་
མགོ་ཆོད་པོ་ "capable" དབུ་ཆོད་གནང་གོ་
དབེན་པོ་ "quiet, calm" དབེན་གནང་གོ་

Finally, it should be emphasized that respect is shown not only by using terminology but through a wide repertoire of appropriate gestures. Even nowadays, in many rural areas, people greet visitors by protruding their tongues, joining their hands and bowing slightly. The guest of honor always goes first and takes the highest seat, usually located in the innermost part of the room. He always receives the choicest food, served with deferential gestures in a quiet voice, and so on.

Loans from Other Languages

For a long period of their history (from the 8th to the 13th centuries) the Tibetans were assiduously engaged in translation, mainly from Sanskrit, with the primary aim of acquiring and spreading Buddhist teachings.

The skill and precision of the Tibetan translators, or *lotsawa,* were such that Tibetan texts may reliably be used to retranslate into Sanskrit works that were lost at the time of the Muslim invasions of India. For several years now, a team of translators in Varanasi (Benares) has been working on the reproduction of Sanskrit works from Tibetan versions.

Over the course of time, Tibetan, like any other language, has enriched its vocabulary through lexical borrowings. The main sources have been Sanskrit, Mongolian, Uighur and Ancient Chinese, with more recent recourse to English, Hindi and Modern Chinese (*putonghua*).[204] It is likely that other languages such as Zhangzhung (part of which later became the kingdom of Guge), Tangut (*mi-nyag*) and other Himalayan languages such as Kinnauri also contributed to Tibetan vocabulary.

Whatever the case, it is a striking fact that Tibetan actually contains very few pure loans (also called "transfers"),[205] and has tended to prefer calques (loan translations). This process consists of coining neologisms using Tibetan roots conveying the semantic content of compound

204. For further details see Beyer (1992:138 -145)

205. Here is Beyer's definition of "transfer" (1992:139): "One type of borrowing is the process we will call transfer, whereby a foreign word or phrase is simply incorporated wholesale into the lexicon, with more or less adaptation to native phonology and orthography." Transfers are rare in Tibetan, except in technical domains such as medicine, which contain a relatively larger proportion of Sanskrit and Chinese words.

words from other languages, such as Sanskrit, Chinese and so on. The vocabulary that has been borrowed extends almost exclusively to *nouns,* and includes almost no verbs or adjectives.

Unlike the majority of other literary Asian languages (Chinese, Japanese, Thai, Burmese, etc.), Tibetan has calqued or translated, rather than borrowed, the essential vocabulary of Buddhism.

Ex.: Buddha = སངས་རྒྱས་ sāngkyä'; bodhisattva = བྱང་ཆུབ་སེམས་དཔའ་ cha̱ngcup sēmpa; karma = ལས་ lä̱', etc.

Even the names of Hindu divinities have been "translated":

Ex.: "Indra" = བརྒྱ་བྱིན་ kya̱cin; "Brahmā" = ཚངས་པ་ tshāngpa; "Śiva" = དབང་ཕྱུག་ wāngcu', etc.

The Tibetan *lotsawa* sometimes preferred to calque glosses or definitions of certain words, rather than the words themselves (see below). We refer to this type of loan as *indirect calques*.

Here are some examples of transfers, calques, and mixed forms.

Transfers

• From Sanskrit

པདྨ་ pāma (*pad-ma*) "lotus" < *padma*; སེངྒེ་ sēngke "lion" < *simha*; བྱི་ལ་ chīla (*byi-la*) "cat" < *bila* (*prakrit*) < *biDala*; མ་ཎི་ ma̱ni "jewel" < *maNi*; ཙན་དན་ tsāntän "sandalwood" < *candana*[206] ; མུ་ཏིག་ mu̱ti' < *muktika*; གུ་རུ་ ku̱ru "master", < *guru;* པོ་ཏི་ pōti "volume, book"< *pustika*; པོ་ཏ་ལ་ pōtala "Potala Palace"< *pota* "boat", etc.

• From Ancient or Old Chinese

ཇ་ cha̱ "tea" < *jha*[207]; ཏོང་ཙེ་ tho̱ngtse "money" (archaic)< **dhung-tsi*; ཅོག་ཙེ་ cōktse "table" < *coksi* "table" (Mod. Ch. *zhuozi*)

• From Mongolian

བ་དུར་ pha̱tur *ba-dur* "warrior" < *baɣatur*; ཐ་མག་ thāma' "tobacco" < *thama*, etc.

• From Uighur

ཐམ་ག་ thāmka "seal" < *thamɣa* "mark, label"; དར་ tha̱r "silk" < *torɣu*; པག་ཤི་ pākshi[208] "master" < *bakshi*; ཨེམ་ཆི་ ēmci "doctor" < *ɛmci*, etc.

---

206. One of the rare loan words borrowed by both European languages and Tibetan is the word *sandal* in *sandalwood* and the Tibetan word *tsan-dan* which have the same Sanskrit origin. See Beyer (1992:142).

207. Which is also the origin of the Arabic *ʃaj* ("shay"), Turkish *çaj* ("chay"), Russian *čaj* ("chay"), Portuguese *cha*, English *tea*, and French *thé*.

208. As seen, for example, in the name Kar-ma pag-shi, which was the title of a master of the Karmapa school.

• From Persian

གུར་གུམ་ khu̱rkum "saffron" < kurkum; དེབ་ཐེར་ the̱pter "annals, document" < *dɛbtɛr*; ཁོ་ཐ་ kho̱ta "God", "Allah" for Tibetan Muslims < *xoda*.

• From Latin (via Persian)

གེ་སར་khe̱sar (*hero of the Tibetan epic*)[209] < Caesar, *kaisar*, *tzar*;

• From Arabic

ཨ་རག་ ara' "alcohol" < *ʔarak* "toddy, palm sap"; ཕྱུ་པ་ chūpa "gown" < *juba* (Turkish) <jabba.[210]

• From Modern Chinese (*putonghua*)

ཏན་ཧྲི་ tānshi "television" < *dianshi*; ཀུང་ལི་kūngle "kilometer" < *gongli*; ཙེ་དན་tsētän "audio cassette"< *caidan*; ཀྲུང་གོ་trūngko "China" < *zhongguo*; ཀུང་ཀུང་ཆིའི་ཁྲེ་ kūngkung chī:tre "bus" < *gonggong qiche*; ཡོའོ་ཕྱོའོ་yo̱:pio: "postage stamp" < *you piao*, etc.

• From English

སྤ་སི་pās "ticket" < *pass*; ཏི་ཀ་སི་tīkasi "postage stamp" < *ticket*; པེ་སེ་ཀོབ་pēsekop "cinema" (obsolete) < *bioscope*; རི་ལི་ri̱li "train" < *rail*; མོ་ཊ་mo̱tra "car" < *motor*; འབའ་སི་pa̱s "bus" < *bus*, etc.

• From Hindi

པུ་ར་ pūra "all" < *pura*; cīni "sugar" < *cini*; ཀ་རི་ ka̱ri "car" < *ghari*; རྐང་ཀ་རིལ་ kāngkari: "bicycle" < *ghari* "car, vehicle" and *rkang* (Tib. = foot, leg)

Calques (direct and indirect)

• From Sanskrit

སངས་རྒྱས་sāngkyä' "Buddha" ~ *buddha* "the awakened one" (< *sangs* "awakened" and *rgyas* "expanded". Beyer (1992:143-144) gives the following commentary: "Tibetan *sangs-rgyas* [has been coined] on the basis of two different Sanskrit etymological glosses:[…] He is like a man who has awakened (prabuddha) because his sleep of delusion has vanished and […] He is Buddha because his mind (buddhi) has opened up like a lotus that has expanded (vibuddha)."

---

209. The epic of Gesar is the great epic of Central Asia, considerably exceeding in length others such as Gilgamesh.

210. According to M. Fasmer's etymological dictionary (*Etimologičeskij slovar' russkogo jazyka*, Moskva 1986) the French word *jupe* "skirt" is also derived from the Arabic *jabba.* Thus the French word *jupe* and the Tibetan *chuba* share a common origin.

བྱང་ཆུབ་སེམས་དཔའ་ cha̱ngcup sēmpa “*bodhisattva*” (< *byang* “has purified faults”, *chub* “has assimilated [all] knowledge”, *sems* “mind” and *dpa‘* “hero” = hero of the mind who has purified his faults and has assimilated all knowledge).

ལས་ lä̱' “karma, action” ~ *karma*

སྟོང་པ་ཉིད་ tōngpanyi' “the void” ~ *shunyata*

ལེགས་སྦྱར་ le̱kcar “Sanskrit” ~ *sam-skrit* “well-composed (language)” (<*legs* = “excellent” and *sbyar* = “put together, composed”)

འཁོར་བ་ khōrwa “transmigration, *samsara*” (<*‘khor* = “to circle”, *‘khor-ba* = “the round, the cycle [of existence]”)

མྱ་ངན་ལས་འདས་པ་ nya̱ngänlä' tä̱pa “*nirvana*” (lit. “passed beyond suffering”) ~ *nir-vana* “blown out, extinguished”

ཉོན་མོངས་ nyö̱nmong “negative emotions” ~ *kleśa* “torment”

གྲུབ་ཐོབ་ཆེན་པོ་ thru̱ptop chēnpo “Mahasiddha” ~ *maha-siddha* “masters with great accomplishments” (<*grub* “accomplishment”, *thob* “to obtain”, *chen-po* “big”)

• From Classical Chinese

ཉི་འོག་ nyi̱o' “the world” (lit. that which is beneath the sun) ~ *tian xia* (nyi = *tian* “day” and ‘og = *xia* “under”)

གསེར་ཡིག་ sēryi' “golden letter, letter from a high dignitary” < *jin-zi* (gser = *jin* “gold” and yig = *zi* “character”)

• From Modern Chinese

མེ་འཁོར་ me̱kor “train” ~ *huo che* (*me* = *huo* “fire” and *‘khor* = *che* “car”)

གློག་བརྙན་ lō'nyän “cinema” ~ *dianyin* (*glog* = *dian* “electric”, *brnyan* = *yin* “image”)

གློག་ཀླད་འཕྲུལ་འཁོར་ lō'lä' thrūngkor “computer” ~ dian nao (*glog* = *dian* “electric” and *klad* = *nao* “brain” + *‘phrul ‘khor* “machine”)

རྡོ་སྣུམ་ to̱num “petrol, gasoline” < *shi you* (*rdo*= *shi* “stone” and *snum* = *you* “oil”, cf. Latin *petra+oleum* > petrol)

Mixed forms

In the same way as certain English words are composed of a Greek root combined with a Latin root (e.g., “television”) Tibetan sometimes unites two different origins within a single word. Here are two examples:

འཛམ་བུ་གླིང་ tsa̱mpuling “the world” < *jambu-dvipa* (Skt.) “name of one of the seven continents around Mt Meru” and *gling* (Tib.) “island” (*dvipa* in Sanskrit).

པཎ་ཆེན་ pāncen “title of the lama of Trashi Lhünpo”, abbreviation of *pan-Di-ta chen-po* < *pandita* (Skt.) and *chen-po* (Tib.) “great”

Neologisms

Modern Tibetan has produced a large number of neologisms to translate scientific or technical terms. Dictionaries of university-level mathematics, physics and chemistry, as well as a large number of popular works have also been published. Unfortunately, since these books are not very widely distributed, the majority of Tibetans use loanwords (from Chinese or English) according to where they live.

In the case of certain neologisms, it may happen that there are three different terms for the same object: one Literary Tibetan term and two in the spoken language. Of the latter, one is likely to be a Chinese loanword used in the T.A.R. or the Tibetan-speaking Chinese provinces, and the other an English loan used in the diaspora.

We see this in the case of སྦྲག་རྟགས་ tra̲kta’ “stamp” (literary), which is also denoted by the words ཏི་ཀ་སི་ tīkasi (< English) and ཡོའོ་ཕིའོ་ yo̲:pio: (< Chinese). Similarly, སྤྱི་སྤྱོད་རླངས་འཁོར་ cīcö’ lāngkor “bus” (literary) is also called ཀུང་ཀུང་ཆིའི་ཁྲེ་ kūngkung chītre (< Chinese) and འབའ་སི་ pa̲s (< English).

Native neologisms

Some old or new neologisms are purely Tibetan scientific or vernacular inventions. Here are a few examples:

ལྕགས་རྟ་ cākta “bicycle” < “iron horse”; ལྕགས་བྱ་ cākca “airplane” < “iron bird”;

རླུང་འཕྲིན་ lūngtrin “radio” < “air message”; གཟུགས་མཐོང་རླུང་འཕྲིན་ su̲ktong lūngtrin “television” < “form-seeing radio”; etc.

Code switching

Some Tibetans, particularly among the urban young people, tend to make massive borrowing from the dominant surrounding languages (mainly Chinese or English, depending on where they live). This phenomenon has increased in the past two decades. There is also a tendency to switch from Tibetan to Chinese, back and forth within the same conversation. Both the massive borrowings and code switching are often referred to as ར་མ་ལུག་སྐད་ “half-goat-half-sheep language”.

Appendix 5

Compound Words

This appendix will take a brief look at the rich field of lexical compounds, but will not tackle the matter of inflectional morphology or lexical derivations.[211] A great many Tibetan words are in fact compounds which for the most part have a clear enough etymology. The following pages will set out the main rules for the construction of words that are valuable for both the spoken and the written languages.

1. Nominal compounds

There are a number of processes relating to the formation of compound nouns, and these apply also to adjectives and verbs. There are basically four types of formation: synonym compounds, polar compounds, compounds with a determinant, and cumulative or sequential compounds.[212]

1.1 Synonym compounds

• Compounds made up of two synonymous nouns:

དུས་སྐབས་ *dus-skabs* "period" (time-moment), ལུགས་སྲོལ་ *lugs-srol* "tradition" (tradition-custom), རེ་འདུན *re-'dun* "hope" (hope-wish), གླུ་གཞས་ *glu-gzhas* "song" (song-song).

• Compounds consisting of two synonymous verbs:

འཛིན་བཟུང་ *'dzin-bzung* "capture" (seize – hold), མཇལ་ཕྲད་ *mjal-phrad* "encounter" (meet (H) – meet), གསུང་བཤད་ *gsung-bshad* "speech, discourse" (say (H) – say), འཕེལ་རྒྱས་ *'phel-rgyas* "development" (increase – spread), བཀག་འགོག་ *bkag-'gog* "obstruction" (stop [past] – stop [present]), འཛུག་སྐྲུན་ *'dzug-skrun* "construction" (establish – construct).

1.2 Polar compounds

A common principle is to combine polar opposites, especially of adjectives.

• Polar compounds comprising adjectives:

Structure: adj. (positive) – adj. (negative)

ཚ་གྲང་ *tsha-grang* "temperature" (hot-cold), མཐོ་དམན་ *mtho-dman* "height" (high-low), ཆེ་ཆུང་ *che-chung* "size" (big-small), མང་ཉུང་ *mang-nyung* "quantity (much-little), ཡག་ ཉེས་

211. These two domains are actually more relevant to a diachronic perspective or a study of Tibetan etymology, and are not directly useful for learning Modern Spoken Tibetan. For further information, see *le Clair Miroir* by Kesang Gyurmé (1992) or, in English, Stephan Beyer (1992).

212. The terminology concerning compound nouns used in this Manual is based on Goldstein (1983).

yag nyes "quality" (good-bad), བཟང་ངན་ *bzang-ngan* "quality" (excellent-bad), རིང་ ཐུང་ *ring-thung* "length" (long-short), ཉེ་རིང་ *nye-ring* "distance" (near-far), དཀར་ནག་ *dkar-nag* "opposites" (white-black), གསར་རྙིང་ *gsar-rnying* "age" (new-old), སྐྱིད་སྡུག་ *skyid-sdug* "living conditions" (happy-wretched), སྲབ་མཐུག་*srab-mthug* "density" (thin-thick), སྐམ་རློན་ *skam-rlon* "humidity" (dry-wet), དྲག་ཤན་*drag-shan* "power" (strong-weak)

• Polar compounds comprising nouns:

ཕ་མ་*pha-ma* "parents" (mother-father), ཉིན་མཚན་*nyin-mtshan* "day and night" (day-night), གཞུང་སྒེར་*gzhung-sger* "everyone" (government-private), ལྷ་འདྲེ་ *lha-'dre* "gods and demons" (gods-demons), རྒྱུ་འབྲས་*rgyu-'bras* "causality" (cause-result)

• Polar compounds comprising verbs:

ཉོ་ཚོང་ *nyo-tshong* "commerce" (buy-sell), ཐོབ་ཤོར་*thob-shor* "gain and loss" (win-lose), འགྲོ་སྡོད་ *'gro-sdod* "movement" (go-stay), ཡིན་མིན་*yin-min* "truth and falsehood" (be-not be)

1.3 Premodifying compounds

• Structure: noun (modifier) – noun (modified)

གནམ་གྲུ་ *gnam-gru* "airplane" (sky-vessel), ལྷ་ཁང་ *lha-khang* "temple" (god-house), དུས་དེབ་ *dus-deb* "journal" (time-book), ཁང་བདག་ *khang-bdag* "owner" (house-owner), སྙིང་རུས་ *snying-rus* "endurance" (heart-bone), མིག་ལྤགས་ *mig-lpags* "eyelid" (eye-skin), མེ་མདའ་ *me-mda'* "gun" (fire-arrow), མེ་རོ་ *me-ro* "embers" (fire-corpse), ཆུ་མིག་ *chu-mig* "spring" (water-eye), མིག་ཆུ་ *mig-chu* "tear" (eye-water)

Note: The spelling of a lexical morpheme remains the same whatever its position may be within a word, whether as the first or as the second syllable. There are, however, some rare exceptions to this rule. Thus the word for "skin, bark" is spelled པགས་པ་*pags-(pa)* /pākpa/, when it features as the first syllable, as in པགས་ཞྭ་ /pāksha/ "fur hat", whereas it is written as ལྤགས་*lpags* when it occurs as the second syllable, as in ལུག་ལྤགས་*lug-lpags* /lu̱kpa'/ "sheepskin" or སྟག་ལྤགས་*stag-lpags* /tākpa'/ "tiger-skin".

• Structure: adjective (modifier) – noun (modified)

དམ་ཚིག་ *dam-tshig* "samaya, vow" (sacred-word), ཉེ་ལམ་ *nye-lam* "shortcut" (near-road), དབེན་གནས་ *dben-gnas* "hermitage" (lonely-place)

• Structure: adjective (modifier) – verb (modified)

གསར་བརྗེ་ *gsar-brje* "revolution" (new-change), གསར་འཛུགས་ *gsar-'dzugs* "construction" (new-establish), གོང་འཕེལ་ *gong-'phel* "development" (high-increase), ཡར་རྒྱས་ *yar-rgyas* "progress, improvement" (upward-spread)

• Structure: verb (modifier) – noun (modified)

འགྲོ་ལམ་ *'gro-lam* "path" (go-way), སློབ་དེབ་ *slob-deb* "manual" (learn-book), ཚོང་དཔོན་ *tshong-dpon* "merchant" (sell-lord), སྡོད་ཁང་ *sdod-khang* "dwelling" (live-house), སྲུང་སྐར་ *srung-skar* "satellite" (protect-star)

• Structure: noun (modifier) – verb (modified)

བདག་འཛིན་ *bdag-'dzin* "selfishness" (self-hold), སྐྱོན་བརྗོད་ *skyon-brjod* "criticism" (fault-say), གདན་འདྲེན་ *gdan-'dren* "invitation" (carpet-draw), སེམས་གསོ་ *sems-gso* "consolation" (mind-repair), རྐུབ་བཀྱག་ *rkub-bkyag* "chair" (backside-lift), ཆུ་ཁོལ་ *chu-khol* "boiled water" (water-boil), རྫས་འགྱུར་ *rdzas-'gyur* "chemistry" (object-transform), སྐད་བསྒྱུར་ *skad-bsgyur* "interpreter" (language-transform)

1.4 Postmodifying compounds

• Structure: noun (modified) – adjective (modifier)

གླང་ཆེན་ *glang-chen* "elephant" (bull-big), རྡོ་རིང་ *rdo-ring* "stone pillar, standing stone, *doring*" (stone-long), ངོ་ཚ་ *ngo-tsha* "shame" (face-hot), ཚོགས་ཆེན་ *tshogs-chen* "great assembly" (gathering-big), རྫོགས་ཆེན་ *rdzogs-chen* "path of the great perfection" (perfection-great), བྱ་རྒོད་ *bya-rgod* "vulture" (bird-wild), ལམ་རིམ་ *lam-rim* "graduated path" (path-progressive), བློ་བཟང་ *blo-bzang* Lobsang (*personal name*: mind-excellent), ཚེ་རིང་ *tshe-ring* Tshering (*personal name*: life-long)

1.5 Conjunctive compounds

• Structure: noun – noun

This juxtaposed or paratactic structure involves the coordination of nouns without the use of connectives. ཞིང་འབྲོག་ *zhing-'brog* "nomads and farmers", དགེ་སློབ་ *dge-slob* "teachers and students", རྒྱ་བོད་ *rgya-bod* "Chinese and Tibetans" or "China and Tibet" (but in a more ancient context, Indians and Tibetans or India and Tibet

• Sequential verb structure: verb 1 – verb 2

ཉམས་གསོ་ *nyams-gso* "restoration" (ruin-repair), བཅིངས་འགྲོལ་ *bcings 'grol* liberation (bind-free)

2. Verb composition

Compound verbs are essentially of three types: compounds that are difficult to analyse in synchrony; verbs with internal objects, and verbs involving the use of a verbalizer.

2.1 Compounds that are difficult to analyse without a historical perspective

The construction of these verbs is difficult to understand at the present time. The meaning of one of the components taken by itself is no longer comprehensible, or has been partially lost.

ཡིད་ཆེས་ *yid ches* "to have faith", ཧ་ལས་ *ha las* "to be surprised", གཉིད་ཁུག་ *gnyid khug* "to fall asleep", ཧོན་ཐོར་ *hon thor* "to be astonished", etc.

2.2 Verbs with an internal object

These are made up of a verb and an "internal" object formed from the same root as the verb. They are similar to certain English expressions such as "to live life", "to dream a dream", etc. These verbs, which are mainly trisyllabic, are relatively uncommon.

རྩེད་མོ་རྩེ་ *rtsed-mo rtse* "to play", གད་མོ་དགད་ *gad mo dgad* "to laugh", ལྟས་མོ་ལྟ་ *ltas mo tla* "to watch a show", རྐུ་མ་རྐུ་ *rku-ma rku* "to steal", སྐོར་བ་སྐོར་ *skor ba skor* "to circle, circumambulate", དྲི་བ་འདྲི་ *dri ba 'dri* "to ask questions", རྨི་ལམ་རྨི་ *rmi-lam rmi* "to dream" (dial. or L), ཟ་མ་ཟ་ *za ma za* "to eat" (dial. or L)

2.3 Compounds using verbalizers

These verbs, consisting of a "verbalizer" and a noun constitute the majority of verbs in Standard Spoken Tibetan. The noun may be replaced by an adjective, an adverb or an onomatopoeia. Remember that the three main verbalizers are: བྱེད་ *byed* "to do, to act", རྒྱག་ *rgyag* "to make, to do" and བཏང་ *btang* "to send, to do" (and their honorific equivalents, see Lesson 11).

The verbalizer may be preceded by:

• a simple noun

མོ་ཊ་བཏང་ *mo-tra btang* "to drive a car", གཞས་བཏང་ *gzhas btang* "to sing", སྐད་བཏང་ *skad btang* "to call", མེ་བཏང་ *me btang* "to set fire", སྐད་རྒྱག་ *skad rgyag* "to shout"

• an adjective

སྐྱིད་པོ་བཏང་ *skyid-po btang* "to have fun", སྡུག་པོ་བཏང་ *sdug-po btang* "to abuse", དགའ་པོ་བྱེད་ *dga'-po byed* "to like", ཆུང་རུ་བཏང་ *chung ru btang* "to reduce", ཆེ་རུ་བཏང་ *che-ru btang* "to enlarge"

• a noun compound (see section 1 above in this appendix)

སློབ་སྦྱོང་བྱེད་ *slob sbyong byed* "to study", སྒྱུར་བཅོས་བཏང་ *sgyur-bcos btang* "to reform", ཡར་རྒྱས་བཏང་ *yar rgyas btang* "to improve", སེམས་གསོ་བྱེད་ *sems gso byed* "to console", གདན་འདྲེན་ཞུ་ *gdan 'dren zhu* "to invite"

• a doubled form (with a verb, an adverb, an adjective or an onomatopeia)

སྐྱོམ་སྐྱོམ་བྱེད་ *kyom-kyom byed* "to stir a liquid", དཀྲུག་དཀྲུག་བཏང་ *dkrug dkrug btang* "to stir, shake", གཟབ་གཟབ་བྱེད་ *gzab gzab byed* "to be careful", རུག་རུག་བྱེད་ *rug-rug byed* "to gather", ཕུར་ཕུར་བཏང་ *phur-phur btang* "to massage, stroke", ལྷོད་ལྷོད་བྱེད་ *lhod lhod byed* "to relax"

Review Tables

This appendix contains review tables of verb "conjugations", "declensions" and the variant forms of grammatical morphemes.

Table 1: The copulas and their meanings

Copulas	Mediatory moods	Meaning	Translation
ཡོད་ yö̱'	egophoric	existential, expresses possession situative attributive (evaluative)	"to have" ("I have") "to be (somewhere)" ("I am at…") "to be"
འདུག་ tu̱'	testimonial	existential situative expresses possession attributive (evaluative)	"there is, are" "to be (somewhere)" "to have, possess" "to be"
ཡོད་རེད་ yo̱:re'	assertive	existential expresses possession situative attributive (evaluative)	"there is, are" "to have, possess" "to be (somewhere)" "to be"
ཡིན་ yi̱n	egophoric	essential attributive modal	"to be" ("I am") "to be" ("I am") "to be" ("it's according to me")
རེད་ re̱'	assertive	existential attributive inalienable possession	"to be" "to be" "to have, to own"
རེད་བཞག་ re̱'-sha'	revelatory	essential	"to be" ("Why, it's…!)

Table 2: Forms of copulas

affirmative	interrogative (without pronoun)	interrogative (with pronoun)	negative	negative interrogative
ཡིན་ yin	ཡིན་པས་ yin-pä'	ཡིན་།ཡིན་པ་ yin/ yin-pa	མིན་ män	མིན་པས་ män-pä'
རེད་ re'	རེད་པས་ re'-pä'	རེད་ rä'	མ་རེད་ mare'	མ་རེད་པས་ mare'-pä'
ཡོད་ yö'	ཡོད་པས་ yö'-pä'	ཡོད་ yö'	མེད་ me'	མེད་པས་ me'-pä'
འདུག་ tu'	འདུག་གས་ tu'-kä'	འདུག་ to'	མི་འདུག་ mintu'	མི་འདུག་གས་ mintu'-kä'
ཡོད་རེད་ yo:re'	ཡོད་རེད་པས་ yo:re'-pä'	ཡོད་རེད་ yo:re'	ཡོད་མ་རེད་ yo:mare'	ཡོད་མ་རེད་པས་ yo:mare'-pä'

Table 3: The main auxiliaries

FUTURE		
assertive	V(pres.) + གི་རེད་	-kire'
intentional egophoric	V(pres.) + གི་ཡིན་	-kiyin
allocentric intentional egophoric	V(past) + དགོས་	-ko'
allocentric intentional egophoric or imminent danger	V(past) + ཡོང་	-yong
PRESENT (and imperfective past)		
assertive	V(pres.) + གི་ཡོད་རེད་	-kiyo:re'
testimonial	V(pres.) + གི་འདུག་	-kitu'
intentional or habitual egophoric	V(pres.) + གི་ཡོད་	-kiyö'
habitual/ generic assertive	V(pres.) + གི་རེད་	-kire'
PAST (perfective)		
simple perfective		
assertive	V(past) + པ་རེད་	-pare'
testimonial	V(past) + སོང་	-song
receptive egophoric	V(past) + བྱུང་	-cung
intentional egophoric	V(past) + པ་ཡིན་	-payin
experiential egophoric	V(pres.) + མྱོང་	-nyong
perfect		
assertive	V(past) + ཡོད་རེད་	-yo:re'
inferential	V(past) +བཞག་	-sha'
intentional egophoric	V(past) + ཡོད་	-yö'

Table 4: The different mediatory moods according to tense-aspect

tense-aspect	egophoric	testimonial	inferential	assertive
future	གི་ཡིན་ kiyin དགོས་ ko			གི་རེད་ kire'
present (or imperfective past)	གི་ཡོད་ kiyö'	གི་འདུག་ kitu'		གི་ཡོད་རེད་ kiyo:re'
past *simple perfective*	པ་ཡིན་ payin བྱུང་ cung མྱོང་ nyong	སོང་ song		པ་རེད་ pare'
past *perfect*	ཡོད་ yö'		འདུག་ tu' བཞག་ sha'	ཡོད་རེད་ yo:re'

Table 5: Auxiliaries according to tense-aspect

future

affirmative	interrogative (without pronouns)	interrogative (with pronouns)	negative	negative interrogative
གི་ཡིན་ kiyin	གི་ཡིན་པས་ / གས kiyin-pä' / kä'	ག་ ka	གི་མིན་ kimän	གི་མིན་པས་ kimän-pä'
གི་རེད་ kire'	གི་རེད་པས་ kire'-pä'	གི་རེད་ kirä'	གི་མ་རེད་ kimare'	གི་མ་རེད་པས་ kimare'-pä'

present (and imperfective past)

affirmative	interrogative (without pronouns)	interrogative (with pronouns)	negative	negative interrogative
གི་ཡོད་ kiyö'	གི་ཡོད་པས་ kiyö'-pä'	གི་ཡོད་ kiyö'	གི་མེད་ kime'	གི་མེད་པས་ kime'
གི་འདུག་/གིས་ kitu'/ki'	གི་འདུག་གས་ kitu'-kä'	གི་འདུག་ kito'	གི་མི་འདུག་ kimintu'	གི་མི་འདུག་གས་ kimintu'-kä'
གི་ཡོད་རེད་ kiyo:re'	གི་ཡོད་རེད་པས་ kiyo:re'-pä'	གི་ཡོད་རེད་ kiyo:rä'	གི་ཡོད་མ་རེད་ kiyo:mare'	གི་ཡོད་མ་རེད་པས་ kiyo:mare'-pä'

past (perfective)

affirmative	interrogative (without pronouns)	interrogative (with pronouns)	negative	negative interrogative
པ་ཡིན་ payin	པས་ pä'	པ་ pa	མ་ + V ma+V	མ་ + V+པས་ ma+V+pä'
བྱུང་ cung	བྱུང་ངས་ cung-ngä'	བྱུང་ cung	མ་བྱུང་ macung	མ་བྱུང་ངས་ macung-ngä'
སོང་ song	སོང་ངས་ song-ngä'	སོང་ song	མ་སོང་ masong	མ་སོང་ངས་ masong-ngä'
པ་རེད་ pare'	པ་རེད་པས་ pare'-pä'	པ་རེད་ parä'	མ་ + V+པ་རེད་ ma+V+pare'	མ་ + V+པ་རེད་པས ma+V+pare'-pä'
ཡོད་ yö'	ཡོད་པས་ yö'-pä'	ཡོད་ yö'	མེད་ me'	མེད་པས་ me'-pä'
བཞག་ / འདུག་ sha'/tu'	འདུག་གས་ tu'-kä'	འདུག་ to'	མི་འདུག་ mintu'	མི་འདུག་གས་ mintu'-kä'
ཡོད་རེད་ yo:re'	ཡོད་རེད་པས་ yo:re'-pä'	ཡོད་རེད་ yo:rä'	ཡོད་མ་རེད་ yo:mare'	ཡོད་མ་རེད་པས་ yo:mare'-pä'

Table 6: Copulas and auxiliaries of probability

Copulas (positive doubt)			
essential copulas		existential copulas	
ཡིན་པ་འདྲ་	y̲inpatra	ཡོད་པ་འདྲ་	yö̲patra
ཡིན་ཀྱི་རེད་	y̲inkire'	ཡོད་ཀྱི་རེད་	yö̲kire'
མིན་འགྲོ་	mä̲ntro	མེད་འགྲོ་	me̲tro
ཡིན་ས་རེད་	y̲insare'	ཡོད་ས་རེད་	yö̲sare'
མདོག་ཁ་པོ་རེད་	nto̲kkapo re'	མདོག་ཁ་པོ་འདུག་	nto̲kkapo tu̲'
Copulas (negative doubt)			
essential copulas		existential copulas	
ཡིན་འགྲོ་	y̲intro	ཡོད་འགྲོ་	yö̲tro
ཨ་ཡིན་	āyin	ཨ་ཡོད་	āyö'
The main auxiliaries of probability			
Present-future			
V(pres.)	+	གི་ཡིན་པ་འདྲ་	-kiyinpatra
V(pres.)	+	གི་ཡིན་ཀྱི་རེད་	-kiyinkire'
V(pres.)	+	གི་ཡོད་འགྲོ་	-kiyötro
V(pres.)	+	གི་མེད་འགྲོ་	-kimetro
V(past)	+	པ་ཡོད་	-payö'
V(past)	+	པ་འདུག་	-patu'
V(pres.)	+	གི་ཡོད་པ་འདྲ་	-kiyöpatra
V(pres.)	+	གི་ཡོད་ཀྱི་རེད་	-kiyökire'
Past (perfective)			
V(past)	+	པ་འདྲ་	-patra
V(past)	+	ཡོད་ཀྱི་རེད་	-yökire'
V(past)	+	ཡོད་པ་འདྲ་	-yöpatra
V(past)	+	པ་ཡིན་ཀྱི་རེད་	-payinkire'
V(past)	+	ཡོད་ས་རེད་	-yösare'

Table 7: Case markers

• absolutive	གཞུང་	shu̲ng	"the government"
• agentive	གཞུང་གིས་	shu̲ng-ki'	"(by) the government"
• ablative	གཞུང་ནས་	shu̲ng-nä'	"from the government"
• oblique	གཞུང་ལ་	shu̲ng-la	"to/ in the government"
• genitive	གཞུང་གི་	shu̲ng-ki	"of the government"
• associative	གཞུང་དང་	shu̲ng-tang	"with the government"
• absolutive	དགེ་རྒན	ke̲kän	"the teacher"
• agentive	དགེ་རྒན་གྱིས་	ke̲kän-ki'	"(by) the teacher"
• ablative	དགེ་རྒན་ནས་	ke̲kän-nä'	"from the teacher"
• oblique	དགེ་རྒན་ལ་	ke̲kän-la	"to the teacher"
• genitive	དགེ་རྒན་གྱི་	ke̲kän-ki	"of the teacher"
• associative	དགེ་རྒན་དང་	ke̲kän-tang	"with the teacher"
• absolutive	རྒྱལ་ཁབ་	kyä̲:kap	"the State"
• agentive	རྒྱལ་ཁབ་ཀྱིས	kyä̲:kap-ki'	"(by) the State"
• ablative	རྒྱལ་ཁབ་ནས་	kyä̲:kap-nä'	"from the State"
• oblique	རྒྱལ་ཁབ་ལ་	kyä̲:kap-la	"to/ in the State"
• genitive	རྒྱལ་ཁབ་ཀྱི་	kyä̲:kap-ki	"of the State"
• associative	རྒྱལ་ཁབ་དང་	kyä̲:kap-tang	"with the State"
• absolutive	ཉི་མ་	nyi̲ma	"the sun"
• agentive	ཉི་མས	nyi̲mä'	"(by) the sun"
• ablative	ཉི་མ་ནས་	nyi̲ma-nä'	"from the sun"
• oblique	ཉི་མར་	nyi̲mar	"to/ in the sun"
• genitive	ཉི་མའི་	nyi̲mä:	"of the sun"
• associative	ཉི་མ་དང་	nyi̲ma-tang	"with the sun"

Table 8: The cases

Agentive གིས་ *gis*	**Ablative** ནས་ལས་ *nas/las*	**Absolutive** Ø	**Oblique** ལ་ར་ན་དུ་ *la/r/na/du*	**Genitive** གི་ *gi*	**Associative** དང་ *dang*
			Case functions		
agent sensorial experiencer	spatial or temporal origin *nas/*las*[213]	single participant (subject of an intransitive verb)	destination, beneficiary, owner *la/r*	noun complement "of"	prepositional complement "against, with"
instrument/ cause/manner	comparison "more than" *las / *pa-s*	patient (object of a transitive verb)	goal finality *la/ *r /*du*		
comparison "more than" **pa-s*	selection "among" **las /nas*	affective experiencer (subject of an affective verb)	localization *la/ r /*du/ *na*		
adverbial suffix *gis*	adverbial suffix *nas*	duration	*transformation of the object ("into") *la/ r /du*		
emphasis/ focus on the agent	instrument/ manner *nas*		*categorisation of an entity (as, inasmuch as) *la/ r/ du*		
	agent *nas*		Adverbial suffix *r/ du*		
			emphasis/ focus on the patient *la*		
			connective functions		
*causal subordinate *(pa)-s*	causal subordinate *nas*	*coordination (parataxis)	conditional subordinate *na*	relative "who, which" *(pa)-'i / gi*	coordinating conjunction "and"
*subordinate of anteriority ** (pa)-s*	subordinate of anteriority *nas*		purposive subordinate *(yag)-la/ *du/ *pa-r*	nominal clause "that-clause"	temporal subordinate "as soon as"
*coordination *(pa)-s*	subordinate of simultaneity **las/ nas*		* subordinate of simultaneity *la/ pa-r/ (pa)na*	connects the verb and the auxiliary (to the imperfective)	imperative or injunctive marker
	coordination *nas*		*coordination *la*	*adversative conjunction "but"	exclamation
	"rather than" *las*		*connects the verb and the auxiliary V+*(pa)-r* + aux.		
			exclamation *la*		

213. The asterisk indicates forms that occur only in literature. Underlining denotes the commonest functions in Standard Spoken Tibetan. Some cases are preceded by a particle such as *pa* or *yag*.

Table 9: Variant written forms of grammatical cases and morphemes

cases/ suffixes	ག་ *– g*	ང་ *– ng*	ད་ *– d*	ན་ *– n*	བ་ *– b*	མ་ *– m*	འ་ *– ʻa*	ར་ *– r*	ལ་ *– l*	ས་ *– s*	Ø	*da drag*
Oblique case *la-don*	ཏུ་ *tu*	དུ་ *du*	དུ་ *du*	དུ་ *du*	ཏུ་ *tu*	དུ་ *du*	ར་ *r*	དུ་ *du*	དུ་ *du*	སུ་ *su*	ར་ *r*	ཏུ་ *tu*
Genitive case *ʻbrel-sgra*	གི་ *gi*	གི་ *gi*	ཀྱི་ *kyi*	གྱི་ *gyi*	ཀྱི་ *kyi*	གྱི་ *gyi*	འི་ *ʻi*	གྱི་ *gyi*	གྱི་ *gyi*	ཀྱི་ *kyi*	འི་ *ʻi*	ཀྱི་ *kyi*
Agentive case *byed-sgra*	གིས་ *gis*	གིས་ *gis*	ཀྱིས་ *kyis*	གྱིས་ *gyis*	ཀྱིས་ *kyis*	གྱིས་ *gyis*	ས་ *s*	གྱིས་ *gyis*	གྱིས་ *gyis*	ཀྱིས་ *kyis*	ས་ *s*	ཀྱིས་ *kyis*
Adjunctive-adversative conjunction *rgyan-sdud*	ཀྱང་ *kyang*	ཡང་ *yang*	ཀྱང་ *kyang*	ཡང་ *yang*	ཀྱང་ *kyang*	ཡང་ *yang*	ཡང་ *yang*	ཡང་ *yang*	ཡང་ *yang*	ཀྱང་ *kyang*	ཡང་ *yang*	ཀྱང་ *kyang*
Adjunctive-explicative conjunction *lhag-bcas*	སྟེ་ *ste*	སྟེ་ *ste*	དེ་ *de*	ཏེ་ *te*	སྟེ་ *ste*	སྟེ་ *ste*	སྟེ་ *ste*	ཏེ་ *te*	ཏེ་ *te*	ཏེ་ *te*	སྟེ་ *ste*	ཏེ་ *te*
Imperfective suffix	གིན་ *gin*	གིན་ *gin*	ཀྱིན་ *kyin*	གྱིན་ *gyin*	ཀྱིན་ *kyin*	གྱིན་ *gyin*	ཡིན་ *yin*	གྱིན་ *gyin*	གྱིན་ *gyin*	ཀྱིན་ *kyin*	ཡིན་ *yin*	ཀྱིན་ *kyin*
Adjunctive conjunction *cing*	ཅིང་ *cing*	ཞིང་ *zhing*	ཅིང་ *cing*	ཞིང་ *zhing*	ཅིང་ *cing*	ཞིང་ *zhing*	ཞིང་ *zhing*	ཞིང་ *zhing*	ཞིང་ *zhing*	ཤིང་ *shing*	ཞིང་ *zhing*	ཅིང་ *cing*
End of quotation *ces*	ཅེས་ *ces*	ཞེས་ *zhes*	ཅེས་ *ces*	ཞེས་ *zhes*	ཅེས་ *ces*	ཞེས་ *zhes*	ཞེས་ *zhes*	ཞེས་ *zhes*	ཞེས་ *zhes*	ཞེས་ *zhes*	ཞེས་ *zhes*	ཅེས་ *ces*
Indefinite article	ཅིག་ *cig*	ཞིག་ *zhig*	ཅིག་ *cig*	ཞིག་ *zhig*	ཅིག་ *cig*	ཞིག་ *zhig*	ཞིག་ *zhig*	ཞིག་ *zhig*	ཞིག་ *zhig*	ཤིག་ *zhig*	ཞིག་ *zhig*	ཅིག་ *cig*
Disjunctive and interrogative conjunction	གམ་ *gam*	ངམ་ *ngam*	དམ་ *dam*	ན་ *nam*	བམ་ *bam*	མམ་ *mam*	འམ་ *ʻam*	རམ་ *ram*	ལམ་ *lam*	སམ་ *sam*	འམ་ *ʻam*	ཏམ་ *tam*
Final particle *rdzogs-tshig*	གོ་ *go*	ངོ་ *ngo*	དོ་ *do*	ནོ་ *no*	བོ་ *bo*	མོ་ *mo*	འོ་ *ʻo*	རོ་ *ro*	ལོ་ *lo*	སོ་ *so*	འོ *ʻo*	ཏོ *to*
Nominalizer *pa / ba*	པ་ *pa*	བ་ *ba*	པ་ *pa*	པ་ *pa*	པ་ *pa*	པ་ *pa*	བ་ *ba*	བ་ *ba*	བ་ *ba*	པ་ *pa*	བ་ *ba*	པ་ *pa*

Table 10: Correspondences between spelling and pronunciation

Using the table

The table of correspondences between spelling and pronunciation presented below is organized according to a dual alphabetical and phonological principle: on the one hand, the *root letters* are listed in Tibetan alphabetical order, while on the other the combinations of letters that produce the same sound are presented together. Thus the organization of the table makes it possible to be read in two ways. It will tell you the pronunciation of a syllable from its spelling, and also provides the range of possible spellings for an identical pronunciation. The latter feature is particularly useful in view of the large number of homophonic syllables, which are spelled differently but pronounced the same.

On the basis of this list, it will be possible to know the pronunciation of a syllable in both Standard Spoken as well as Literary Tibetan in *nearly all cases.* However, as in the case of European languages, it is not always possible to predict the pronunciation of certain words. With these exceptions there is no exact correspondence between the written and phonetic forms. Remember also that certain words exist only in the spoken language and have no corresponding written form. Phonological transcription is therefore indispensable in these cases.

The following table presents first the Tibetan, then the transliteration in italics, and finally the pronunciation in roman font.

The first part of the table presents the initial consonants of syllables and the second part the codas, that is, the vowels and final consonants of syllables. The initials of syllables often have two pronunciations. The first, which carries a tone, corresponds to the first syllable of a word. The second denotes the pronunciation of syllables within or at the end of a word, and is preceded by a dash. Certain other combinations involve an N, which corresponds to a nasal: m, ng or n. This nasal does not always manifest in speech, although it may do so commonly (see Appendix 1, section 1.1). The particular nasal involved, m, ng or n, is not always predictable, and depends on the words.

Ex.: a-**md**o > āmto "Amdo province", rgya-**mtsh**o > kya̲tso / kya̲mtso "ocean",
sku-**md**un > kūntün "(in) the presence, the Dalai Lama"

The table does not include certain regular variations in pronunciation that occur in the spoken language with respect to the literary pronunciation (see Appendix 1, section 1).

The "sharp" symbol denotes combinations used in words borrowed from foreign languages.

For certain combinations in syllabic rhyme, a second pronunciation, corresponding to a phoneme variant, is presented in parentheses. This variant may be used to reproduce actual pronunciation more closely and to make it easier to learn the proper sound.

Ex.: dm**ag**-mi > mā'mi "soldier" (instead of makmi), gs**ar**-'gyur > sā:ngkyur "news" (instead of sarngkyur), st**ag** > tā' "tiger" (instead of tāk)

The dash after certain combinations means that this pronunciation is used only after another syllable.

Ex.: kha**ms-**pa > khāmpa "inhabitant of Kham", khri**ms-**dpon > thrīmpön "judge"

Finally, remember that the apostrophe after a nasal represents a modulation as opposed to a flat tone, which carries no apostrophe. The historical explanation of this modulation is the presence of the suffix *s* after the nasal. It disappears with polysyllabic words.

Table of correspondences between spelling and pronunciation

The onset of the syllable

spelling	*pronunciation*
• ཀ་ *ka* ཀྭ་ *kwa* དཀ་ *dka* བཀ་ *bka* རྐ་ *rka*	kā, -ka
ལྐ་ *lka* སྐ་ *ska* བརྐ་ *brka* བསྐ་ *bska*	kā, -ka
ཀྱ་ *kya* དཀྱ་ *dkya* བཀྱ་ *bkya* རྐྱ་ *rkya*	kyā, -kya
སྐྱ་ *skya* བསྐྱ་ *bskya* བརྐྱ་ *brkya*	kyā, -kya
ཀྲ་ *kra* དཀྲ་ *dkra* བཀྲ་ *bkra* བསྐྲ་ *bskra* ཊ་ *Ta*	trā, -tra
པྲ་ *pra* སྤྲ་ *spra* དཔྲ་ *dpra*	trā, -tra
ཀླ་ *kla* → ལ་ *la*	
• ཁ་ *kha* ཁྭ་ *khwa*	khā, -ka
མཁ་ *mkha* འཁ་ *'kha*	khā, -Nka
ཁྱ་ *khya*	khyā, -kya
མཁྱ་ *mkhya* འཁྱ་ *'khya*	khyā, -Nkya
ཁྲ་ *khra* ཕྲ་ *phra*	thrā, -tra
མཁྲ་ *mkhra* འཁྲ་ *'khra* འཕྲ་ *'phra*	thrā, -Ntra
• ག་ *ga*	kha̱, -ka
རྒ་ *rga* དགའ་ *dga* བགའ་ *bga'* སྒ་ *sga* བརྒ་ *brga* བསྒ་ *bsga*	ka̱, -ka
འགའ་ *'ga'* མགའ་ *mga'* ལྒ་ *lga*	ka̱, -Nka
གྱ་ *gya*	khya̱, -kya
རྒྱ་ *rgya* དགྱ་ *dgya* བགྱ་ *bgya* བརྒྱ་ *brgya* བསྒྱ་ *bsgya*	kya̱, -Nkya
འགྱ་ *'gya* མགྱ་ *mgya*	kya̱, -Nkya
གྲ་ *gra* གྲྭ་ *grwa* དྲ་ *dra* བྲ་ *bra*	thra̱, -tra
སྒྲ་ *sgra* དགྲ་ *dgra* བགྲ་ *bgra* བསྒྲ་ *bsgra* སྦྲ་ *sbra* ཌ་ *Da*	tra̱, -tra
འགྲ་ *'gra* མགྲ་ *mgra* འབྲ་ *'bra* འདྲ་ *'dra*	tra̱, -Ntra
གླ་ *gla* → ལ་ *la*	

- ང་ *nga* — nga̲, -nga
  དངའ་ *dnga'* མངའ་ *mnga'* — ngā, -nga
  རྔ་ *rnga* བརྔ་ *brnga* བསྔ་ *bsnga,* ལྔ་ *lnga* སྔ་ *snga* — ngā, -nga

- ཅ་ *ca* གཅའ་ *gca'* བཅའ་ *bca'* ལྕ་ *lca* དཔྱ་ *dpya* སྤྱ་ *spya* — cā, -ca

- ཆ་ *cha* ཕྱ་ *phya* — chā, -ca
  མཆའ་ *mcha'* འཆའ་ *'cha'* འཕྱའ་ *'phya'* — chā, -ɴca

- ཇ་ *ja* བྱ་ *bya* — cha̲, -ca
  རྗ་ *rja* བརྗ་ *brja* སྦྱ་ *sbya* — ca̲, -ca
  འཇའ་ *'ja'* མཇའ་ *mja'* ལྗ་ *lja* འབྱ་ *'bya* — ca̲, -ɴca

- ཉ་ *nya* ཉྭ་ *nywa,* མྱ་ *mya* — nya̲, -nya
  རྙ་ *rnya* སྙ་ *snya* བརྙ་ *brnya* བསྙ་ *bsnya* — nyā, -nya
  དམྱ་ *dmya* རྨྱ་ *rmya* སྨྱ་ *smya* མཉ་ *mnya* གཉའ་ *gnya'* — nyā, -nya

- ཏ་ *ta* གཏའ་ *gta'* བཏའ་ *bta'* རྟ་ *rta* སྟ་ *sta* བརྟ་ *brta* བསྟ་ *bsta* — tā, -ta
  ལྟ་ *lta,* བལྟ་ *blta* — tā, -ɴta

- ཐ་ *tha* — thā, -ta
  མཐ་ *mtha* འཐ་ *'tha* — thā, -ɴta

- ད་ *da* དྭ་ *dwa* — tha̲, -ta
  རྡ་ *rda* གདའ་ *gda'* བདའ་ *bda'* སྡ་ *sda* བརྡ་ *brda* བསྡ་ *bsda* — ta̲, -ta
  མདའ་ *mda'* ལྡ་ *lda* འདའ་ *'da'* བལྡ་ *blda* ཟླ་ *zla* བཟླ་ *bzla* — ta̲, -ɴta
  དྲ་ *dra* → གྲ་ *gra*

- ན་ *na* — na̲, -na
  རྣ་ *rna* གནའ་ *gna'* བནའ་ *bna'* སྣ་ *sna* བརྣ་ *brna* — nā, -na
  བསྣ་ *bsna* སྣྲ་ *snra* མནའ་ *mna'* — nā, -na

- པ་ *pa* སྤ་ *spa* ལྤ་ *lpa* དཔ་ *dpa* — pā, -pa
  པྱ་ *pya* → ཅ་ *ca,* པྲ་ *pra* → ཀྲ་ *kra*

- ཕ་ *pha* — phā, -pa
  འཕ་ *'pha* — phā, -ɴpa
  ཕྱ་ *phya* → ཆ་ *cha,* ཕྲ་ *phra* → ཁྲ་ *khra*

• བ་ *ba*	pha̱, -wa
རྦ་ *rba* སྦ་ *sba*	pa̱, -pa
འབའ་ *‘ba‘* ལྦ་ *lba*	pa̱, -ɴpa
བྱ་ *bya* → ཇ་ *ja,* བྲ་ *bra* → གྲ་ *gra,* བླ་ *bla* → ལ་ *la*	
དབྲའ་ *dbra‘* → ར་ *ra,* དབའ་ *dba‘* → ཝ་ *wa,* དབྱའ་ *dbya‘* → ཡ་ *ya*	
• མ་ *ma*	ma̱
རྨ་ *rma* སྨ་ *sma‘* དམའ་ *dma‘* སྨྲ་ *smra*	mā
མྱ་ *mya* → ཉ་ *nya*	
• ཙ་ *tsa* གཙ་ *gtsa* བཙ་ *btsa* རྩ་ *rtsa* སྩ་ *stsa* བརྩ་ *brtsa* བསྩ་ *bstsa* རྩྭ་ *rtswa*	tsā, -tsa
• ཚ་ *tsha* ཚྭ་ *tshwa*	tshā, -tsa
མཚ་ *mtsha* འཚ་ *‘tsha*	tshā, -ɴtsa
• ཛ་ *dza*	tsha̱, -tsa
རྫ་ *rdza* བརྫ་ *brdza*	tsa̱, -tsa
འཛའ་ *‘dza‘* མཛའ་ *mdza‘*	tsa̱, -ɴtsa
• ཝ་ *wa*	wa̱, -wa
དབའ་ *dba‘*	wā, -wa
• ཞ་ *zha* གཞ་ *gzha* བཞ་ *bzha* ཞྭ་ *zhwa*	sha̱, -sha
• ཟ་ *za* གཟ་ *gza* བཟ་ *bza*	sa̱, -sa
ཟླ་ *zla* → ད་ *da*	
• འ་ *‘a*	a̱, -a
• ཡ་ *ya*	ya̱, -ya
གཡ་ *g.ya* དབྱའ་ *dbya‘*	yā, -ya
• ར་ *ra*	ra̱,-ra
དབྲའ་ *dbra‘*	rā, -ra
ཧྲ་ *hra*	rhā, -ra
རླ་ *rla* → ལ་ *la*	
• ལ་ *la* ལྭ་ *lwa*	la̱, -la
རླ་ *rla* ཀླ་ *kla* བཀླ་ *bkla* གླ་ *gla* བླ་ *bla* སླ་ *sla* བསླ་ *bsla*	lā, -la
ལྷ་ *lha*	lhā, -la

- ཤ་ *sha* ཤྭ་ *shwa* གཤའ་ *gsha‘* བཤའ་ *bsha‘* shā, -sha

- ས་ *sa* གསའ་ *gsa‘* བསའ་ *bsa‘* sā, -sa
  སྲ་ *sra* བསྲ་ *bsra* sā, -sa
  སླ་ *sla* → ལ་ *la*

- ཧ་ *ha* ཧྭ་ *hwa* hā, -ha
  ལྷ་ *lha* → ལ་ *la,* ཧྲ་ *hra* → ར་ *ra*
  ཧྱ་ *hya #* hyā
  ཧྥ་ *hpha #* fā

- ཨ་ *a* ā

Syllable rhyme

ཨ་ *a* a

ཨག་ *ag*	ak (a’)	ཨགས་ *ags*	ak (a’)
ཨབ་ *ab*	ap	ཨབས་ *abs*	ap
ཨང་ *ang*	ang	ཨངས་ *angs*	ang’, ang-
ཨམ་ *am*	am	ཨམས *ams*	am’, am-
ཨན་ *an*	än	ཨད་ *ad*	ä’, ä-
ཨས་ *as*	ä’, ä-	ཨའེ་ *a‘e #*	ae
ཨར་ *ar*	ar (a:)	ཨལ་ *al*	ä:
ཨའོ་ *a‘o #*	ao	ཨའུ་ *a‘u*	au
ཨཱ་ *a: #*	a:	ཨའི་ *a‘i*	ä:

ཨི་ *i* i

ཨིག་ *ig*	ik (i’)	ཨིགས་ *igs*	ik (i’)
ཨིབ་ *ib*	ip	ཨིབས་ *ibs*	ip
ཨིང་ *ing*	ing	ཨིངས་ *ings*	ing’, ing-
ཨིམ་ *im*	im	ཨིམས་ *ims*	im’, im-
ཨིན་ *in*	in	ཨིར་ *ir*	ir (i:)
ཨིལ་ *il*	i:	ཨིད་ *id*	i’; i-
ཨིས་ *is*	i’, i-	ཨིའུ་ *i‘u*	iu
ཨིའི་ *i‘i*	i:		

ཨུ་ *u* u

ཨུག་ *ug*	uk (u’)	ཨུགས་ *ugs*	uk (u’)
ཨུབ་ *ub*	up	ཨུབས་ *ubs*	up
ཨུང་ *ung*	ung	ཨུངས་ *ungs*	ung’, ung-
ཨུམ་ *um*	um	ཨུམས་ *ums*	um’, um-
ཨུན་ *un*	ün	ཨུལ་ *ul*	ü:
ཨུར་ *ur*	ur (u:)	ཨུད་ *ud*	ü’, ü-
ཨུས་ *us*	ü’, ü-	ཨུའོ་ *u‘o #*	uo
ཨུའི་ *u‘i*	ü:		

ཨེ་ *e* e

ཨེག་ *eg*	ek (e’)	ཨེགས་ *egs*	ek (e’)
ཨེབ་ *eb*	ep	ཨེབས་ *ebs*	ep
ཨེང་ *eng*	eng	ཨེངས་ *engs*	eng’, eng-
ཨེམ་ *em*	em	ཨེམས་ *ems*	em’, em-
ཨེན་ *en*	en	ཨེར་ *er*	er (e:)
ཨེལ་ *el*	e:	ཨེའུ་ *e‘u*	eu
ཨེའོ་ *e‘o #*	eo	ཨེའི་ *e‘i*	e:
ཨེད་ *ed*	e’, e-	ཨེས་ *es*	e’, e-

ཨོ་ *o* o

ཨོག་ *og*	ok (o’)	ཨོགས་ *ogs*	ok (o’)
ཨོབ་ *ob*	op	ཨོབས་ *obs*	op
ཨོང་ *ong*	ong	ཨོངས་ *ongs*	ong’
ཨོམ་ *om*	om	ཨོམས་ *oms*	om’, om-
ཨོལ་ *ol*	ö:	ཨོན་ *on*	ön
ཨོར་ *or*	or (o:)	ཨོད་ *od*	ö’, ö-
ཨོས་ *os*	ö’, ö-	ཨོའུ་ *o’u*	ou
ཨོའི་ *o‘i*	ö:	ཨོའོ་ *o‘o #*	o:

A Simplified System for Transcribing Tibetan Words

The international Wylie system for the romanized transliteration is widely used by specialists for reproducing the spelling of Tibetan words, but it offers no direct clues about pronunciation. (Remember that pronunciation is very different from spelling.) This Manual has been using a system of phonological transcription that was devised for teaching Tibetan and for use in scholarly works on the language and culture of the country. Its technical character makes it less than ideal for a wider readership, for example in magazine articles, popular books and maps.

There is still no standard system of transcription for publications of this sort. In collected volumes of articles authors often use different ways of transcribing even the same word. Authors often come up with their own conventions without following any explicit principles. For example, the personal name that is spelled *don-grub* is rendered variously as Dondup, Dondrup, Dhondup, Dhundup, Tondup, Tondub, Thöndup, etc. The same is true of the name of Tibet's second city, *gzhis-ka-rtse*, for which the following renderings are in current use: Shigatse, Shikatse, Rigaze, Xigaze, Zhigatse, etc. What is urgently needed is a system for standardising the transcription of Tibetan pronunciation, and this appendix suggests a simplified convention that would enable Tibetan names and most terms to be spelled consistently.

The simplified notation presented here differs from the phonological transcription of the Manual in two main respects:

The absence of special signs for marking tones;

It can be easily and directly deduced from Wylie transliteration.

The convention has been used in this work for presenting Tibetan names in English passages.

Although the simplified transcription doesn't use any diacritics, it gives a fairly clear indication of how words are pronounced in Standard Tibetan, and where tonal distinctions should be made. In most cases there is only one possible unambiguous transcription for a given word if the rules are observed.

The convention is relatively close to English pronunciation: Thus <ch> corresponds to the 'ch' of *chair,* <j> to the 'j' of *jazz,* and <w> to the 'w' of *win.*

Above all, the system suggested below has the advantage of being consistent and based on a simple principle, and hence avoids the idiosyncrasies to be found in much of the secondary literature on Tibet.

a) The general principle

The simplified transcription uses the same correspondences between the Tibetan script and the roman alphabet as the Wylie system of transliteration presented in Table 2 of the Introduction. Only two letters are different: **c > ch** and **'a > a.**

The thirty consonants: transliteration and pronunciation

ཀ *ka*	ཁ *kha*	ག *ga*	ང *nga*
ཅ *ca* > cha	ཆ *cha*	ཇ *ja*	ཉ *nya*
ཏ *ta*	ཐ *tha*	ད *da*	ན *na*
པ *pa*	ཕ *pha*	བ *ba*	མ *ma*
ཙ *tsa*	ཚ *tsha*	ཛ *dza*	ཝ *wa*
ཞ *zha*	ཟ *za*	འ *'a* > a	ཡ *ya*
ར *ra*	ལ *la*	ཤ *sha*	ས *sa*
ཧ *ha*	ཨ *a*		

The four vowels

ཨི *i*	ཨུ *u*	ཨེ *e*	ཨོ *o*

The system proposed here entails dispensing with the letters used by the Wylie system that are no longer pronounced in Standard Tibetan.

This concerns mainly the superscribed consonants *r, l* and *s,* the prefixes *g, d, b, m* and ', and the suffixes *s* and *d.* However, as the examples below will show, some affixed consonants are pronounced. Although the letters *l* and *r* are generally replaced by a lengthening of the preceding vowel, they will be retained here because they are still audible if a reader is enunciating carefully. The elimination of these sounds results in the remaining vowels and consonants being pronounced as they would be in Standard Tibetan. In the following examples, the letters that are actually pronounced are presented in bold type.

Ex.: **lha-sa** > Lhasa, **sa-**s**kya-pa** > Sakyapa, b**lo-bzang** > Lobzang,
r**nying-ma-pa** > Nyingmapa, r**do-rje** > Dorje, d**ge-lugs**-**pa** > Gelugpa,
g**zhi**s-**ka**-r**tse** > Zhikatse, **mar-me** > marme.

b) Special rules

1) The letters *c* and *ch* as used in the Wylie system are both marked as ch.

Ex.: **bcu** > chu, **lce** > che, **rin-chen** b**zang-po** > Rinchen Zangpo, **nag-chu** > Nagchu.

2) When the vowels *a, o, u* are followed by the consonants *d, n, l, s* they acquire an umlaut and become, respectively, ä, ö, ü.

al → äl, ol → öl, ul → ül.

ö corresponds to the sound ö in German *Götter*, or the *eu* in the French word *feu.*

ü corresponds to the sound ü in German *Rücke,* or the *u* of the French word *rue.*

ä corresponds to the sound ä in German *Käse,* or the *ai* in French *aime.*

Ex.: **thub**-bs**tan** > Thubtän, **'jam-dpal-**d**byangs** > Jampälyang, b**ka'**-r**gyud**-**pa** > Kagyüpa, s**rong**-b**tsan** s**gam-po** > Songtsän Gampo, b**sod**-**nam**s > Sönam, bs**tan-'dzin** > Tändzin, **mi-la-ra**s-**pa** > Milaräpa.

3) The suffixes *g* and *b* on the end of a word are devoiced and marked as k and p.

Ex.: **dge-leg**s > Gelek, **kha**-b**tag**s > khatak, b**ka'-shag** > kashak, **thab**s > thap.

4) When the simple consonants (that is, without affixes) *ba* and *bo* appear as the second syllable of a word, they are pronounced wa and wo.

Ex.: **lha-sa-ba** > Lhasawa, **jo-bo** > Jhowo, d**pa'-bo** > pawo.

5) The initial consonant clusters *py, phy* and *by* are pronounced respectively ch, ch and j.

Ex.: s**pyan-ra**s-g**zig** > Chänräzik, s**byin**-b**dag**> Jindak

6) The initial consonant clusters *kr, khr, gr, pr, phr, br,tr, thr, dr*

kr, pr, tr are all pronounced as tr.

khr, phr, thr are all pronounced thr.

gr, br, dr are all pronounced dr.

Ex.: s**grol-ma** > Drölma, r**ten**-'**brel** > tendrel, '**bra**s-s**pung**s > Dräpung, '**phrin**-**la**s > thrinlä

7) When a voiced radical such as *g, j, d, b* or *dz* or a cluster such as *gy* and *by* appears with no prefix, it is voiceless and slightly aspirated, a feature that will be marked by the addition of an h: gh, jh, dh, bh, dzh, ghy, jh.

Ex.: **bar-skor** > Bharkor, **ding-ri** > Dhingri, **jo-mo glang-ma** > Jhomo Langma, **jo-khang** > Jhokhang, **don-grub** > Dhöndrup, **bag-gro** > Bhagdro, **byams-pa** > jhampa, **byang-thang** > Jhangthang. **dra-ba** > dhrawa.

8) The consonant clusters *dbr, dby* and *db*

dbr is pronounced r.

dby is pronounced y.

db is pronounced w.

Ex.: d**bang** > wang, db**ral** > ral, db**yar-kha** > yarkha

c) Exceptional pronunciations

The prefixes *'a* and *m* and the superscript *l* produce a nasal n or m in certain words.

l and ' —> n or m.

m → m

Ex.: **dga'-ldan** > Gandän, dge-**'dun** > Gendün, **a-mdo >** Amdo, r**ta-mgrin** > Tamdrin. **rgyal-rtse** > Gyantse

In a few cases the production of a nasalization by the letters *', l* and *m* results in the disappearance of the preceding consonant.

Ex.: **cha(b)-mdo >** Chamdo, d**pa(l)-ldan** > Pändän, d**pa(l)-'bar** > Pämbar, **ri(g)-'dzin** > Rindzin, s**kya(b)-'gro** > kyamdro.

Finally, in certain words that contain an r affixed to a labial p, ph or b, the r disappears in normal pronunciation.

Ex.: **'bri-ru >** Biru, s**bra-nag-zhol** > Banagzhöl

Prosody and Accentuation in Literary Tibetan

One of the difficulties with the reading of Literary Tibetan is the absence of separation between words. There is no rule that can predict whether a word has one, two or more syllables, but there are important conventions concerning the phrase and clause prosody. It should be emphasized that prosody and accentuation are extremely important for reading Literary Tibetan, whether verse or prose. Even from a grammatical point of view it is essential to make the right pauses and these follow some prosodic rules. If those rules are not applied, the text becomes incomprehensible for the hearer. The traditional Tibetan treaties of grammar and poetry do not provide these rules, probably because there were entirely different from those which applied to Sanskrit. However, when Tibetan scholars read a text,[214] they naturally apply the prosodic and accentuation rules.

• The main rule is that grammatical particles should normally be read together with the preceding word. There should not be **any pause between the word and the following particle,** but **a pause after the particle**. When there is a succession of particles (two or more), they should normally be read without an intervening pause.

In most cases, grammatical particles are not stressed, but when there is a focus, a topicalization or for metric reasons, it is possible to stress the particle.

Here is the list of the main particles affected by the prosodic rule mentioned above:

• the case particles: གིས་ *gis* (or its variants), དུ་ *du* (or its variants), ལ་ *la* (or its variants), ནས་ *nas,* ལས་ *las,* དང་ *dang,* གི་ *gi* (or its variants)

• the quantifiers: དག་ *dag,* ཚོ *tsho,* རྣམས་ *rnams,* ཏོག་ཙོག་ *to-cog* (or its variants), ཙམ་ *tsam,* ཞིག་ *zhig*

• the topicalizer ནི་ *ni*

• the statement particle འོ་ *'o* (or its variants)

---

214. This is true for all types of Literary Tibetan: Classical or Modern, religious or lay.

• the alternative and question particle འམ་ *'am* (or its variants)

• the adjunctive and adversative particle ཡང་ *yang* (or its variants)

• the nominalizers: པ་ *pa* (or *ba*), མཁན་ *mkhan*, ཅན་ *can*, ལྡན་ *ldan*, རྒྱུ་ *rgyu*, སྟངས་ *stangs*, ཚུལ་ *tshul*, ཁུལ་ *khul*, མི་ *mi*, འཕྲོ་ *'phro*

• the connective particles: སྟེ་ *ste*, ཞིང་ *zhing* (and their variants), ན་ *na*, དུས་ *dus*, ཚེ་ *tshe*

These particles generally occur at the end of a phrase or a clause, and are often followed by the clause ending punctuation mark *shad*. Some rare particles, such as the adjunctive particle ཡང་ *yang*, may occur at the beginning of a clause.

Ex.: དེ་ཡང་བླ་མ་དེའི་ཞལ་གསུང་ཐོས་པ་ཙམ་མམ།

de yang bla ma de'i zhal mjal gsung thos ***pa tsam mam***

ཐ་ན་མཚན་ཙམ་ཐོས་པས་ཀྱང་ལུས་བ་སྤུ་ལྡང་བའི་དད་པ་གཡོ་ནུས།

tha na mtshan tsam thos ***pa+s kyang*** *lus ba spu ldang ba'i dad pa g.yo nus /*

"Just meeting that lama or hearing his words, and even just hearing his name, can generate devotion to the extent that the hairs on one's body stand on end."

• When the connective *na* particle conveys the meaning of a hypothesis "if", it should be read with a rising intonation, but when it means "when", as in the following example, it should read with a falling intonation:

རྒྱ་མཚོ་མཐོང་བ་ན་ ཁྲོན་པའི་ སྦལ་བ་བརྒྱལ་ནས་ མགོ་གས་ཏེ་ ཤི་སྐད།

*rgya-tmtsho mthong+****ba+ na*** *khron-pa'i sbal-ba brgyal+nas mgo gas+ te shi skad*

"It is said that, when it saw the ocean, the frog in the well fainted, its head burst and it died."

The Main Symbols of Tibet

Tibetan culture is very rich in symbols. While these symbols usually have a deep meaning, they also have an aesthetic function. Most are related to the philosophic-religious tradition, but some are only found in popular culture. These symbols are to be seen in murals on monastery walls, on *thangka* (Tibetan icons), carpets, and, in a few cases, on the walls and doors of houses, on tents, clothing and jewelry. The following examples are among those which are most likely to be encountered, with a brief description of each.[215]

བཀྲ་ཤིས་རྟགས་བརྒྱད། trāshi' tā' kyä̱'

(Skt.: *aṣṭamaṅgala*).

The Eight Auspicious Signs.

---

215. Although a number of these signs are originally derived from the Indian tradition, the interpretations offered here are primarily Tibetan. Symbols may often have more than one interpretation, even within Tibet. For more information see: Robert Beer, *Encyclopedia of Tibetan Symbols and Motifs* (London: Serindia, 1999); Dagyab Rinpoche, *Buddhist Symbols* (Boston: Wisdom Publication, 1995); Eva Rudy Jansen, *Le Livre du Bouddha, divinité et symboles rituels du bouddhisme* (Diever, Holland: Éditions Binkey Kok, 1990).

འཁོར་ལོ། khōrlo (Skt.: *dharmacakra*)

The wheel

The wheel represents the teaching or the spread of the Dharma, or the pacification of living beings by the Dharma. The eight spokes represent the Noble Eightfold Path. More generally, the wheel stands for royal power.

གདུག། tu̲' (Skt.: *chattra*)

The parasol

It reduces the pain resulting from the heat of negative emotions.

རྒྱལ་མཚན། kya̲ntsän (Skt.: *dhvaja*)

The victory banner

It stands for victory over demons and heretics, and represents the flag of perfect knowledge.

པ་ཏྲ། pātra or དཔལ་བེའུ། pālpiu (Skt.: *śrīvatsa*)

The *patra*

The *patra* symbolizes perfection, fullness and the glory of the five wisdoms. It is sometimes referred to as the "knot of eternity", and is associated with the concept of *tendrel (rten-'brel),* meaning "interdependence". This is one of the fundamental notions of Buddhism in general, insofar as all phenomena are regarded as being interdependent and linked to causes and conditions.

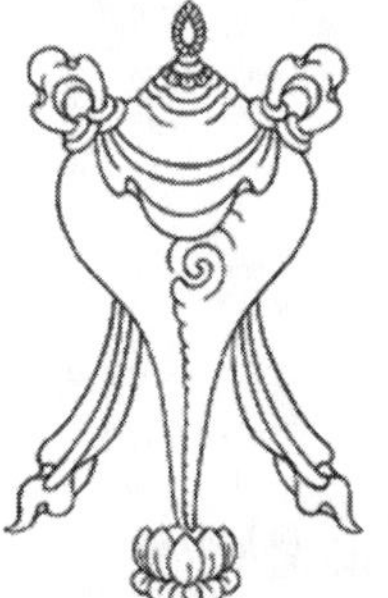

དུང་གཡས་འཁྱིལ། thùngyäkyi: (Skt.: *dakṣiṇāvartaśaṅkha*)

The clockwise-spiralling white conch

It announces in all directions the sweet sound of the Dharma and the glory of all the buddhas.

བུམ་པ། phu̱mpa (Skt.: *kalaśa*)

The vase

It contains the essence of knowledge and of pure merit, and represents the fulfilment of wishes.

པདྨ། pāma (Skt.: *padma*)

The lotus

The lotus stands for the perfectly pure spirit of one who is born in samsara and yet remains detached and untainted by negative emotions and impurities.

གསེར་ཉ། sērnya (Skt.: *suvarṇamatsya*)

The (two) golden fish

A sign of good fortune. According to some interpretations, the two fish symbolize the two sacred Indian rivers of the Ganges and the Yamuna.

རྡོ་རྗེ། to̱rce (Skt.: *vajra*)

The adamantine thunderbolt

This is the central symbol of Tantric Buddhism or Vajrayāna *(rdo-rje theg-pa),* from which the name of the latter is derived. The thunderbolt represents indestructible force and symbolizes the unchanging nature of ultimate Reality (the Void), the permanence of the Buddha-mind and the immutable truth of the Dharma. It also represents the masculine aspect of the path to enlightenment.

རྡོ་རྗེ་རྒྱ་གྲམ། to̱rce kya̱tram (Skt.: *viýśvavajra*)

The "double vajra" or "crossed vajra"

It symbolizes realization linked to the four types of worldly activity. The crossed vajra also represents the seal of the secret or of eternity.

དྲིལ་བུ། thri̱lpu (Skt.: *ghanta*)

The ritual bell

The ritual bell or *drilbu* represents the wisdom of selflessness associated with the feminine principle, whereas the vajra stands for compassion, associated with the male principle.

ནོར་བུ་མེ་འབར། nōrpu me̱mpar (Skt.: *cintamaṇi*)

The blazing jewel or *norbu membar*

Also known as the wish-fulfilling gem.

དགའ་འཁྱིལ། ka̱kyi:

The *gakyil*

This jewel represents the combination of happiness and joy.

རྣམ་བཅུ་དབང་ལྡན། nāmcu wāngtän

The ten letters of the Kālacakra mantra

Namchu wangdän is the symbol of the Kālacakra, the wheel of time, and represents the Kālacakra mantra comprising ten superimposed letters.

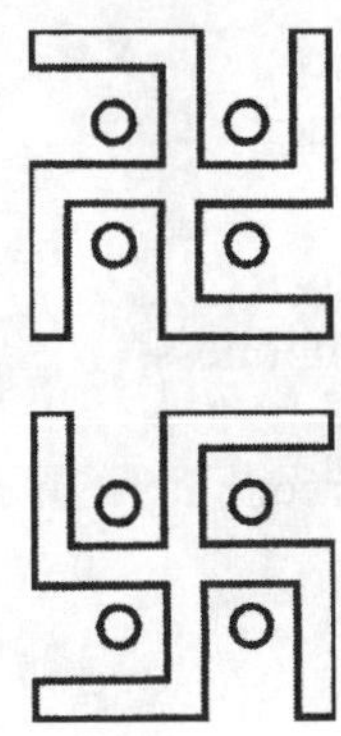

གཡུང་དྲུང་། yūngtrung

The swastika

This is the most important symbol of the Bön religion (the anti-clockwise swastika), but the clockwise variant is also used in Buddhism to denote immutability. The sign sometimes appears on the Buddha's footprints. According to Bön teachings, the origin of the yúngtrung is not Sanskritic, and the symbol is therefore not assimilated to the Indian swastika.

འདོད་ཡོན་ལྔ་། tö̱yön ngā

The objects of the five senses

These are: the mirror, the lute, the conch filled with water, the fruit and the silk scarf. Each represents a sensual pleasure. They may be united in a single compilation, as here, or displayed separately.

རྩེ་གསུམ་། tsēsum (Skt.: *triśula*)

The trident

This symbol is generally to be seen on monastery roofs and as an attribute of certain divinities. It represents the three jewels: the Buddha, the Dharma and the Sangha.

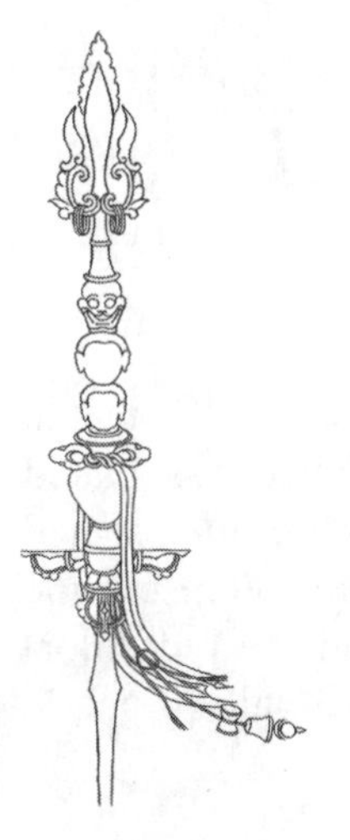

ཁ་ཊྭཾ་ག། khātramka (Skt.: *khatvanga*)

The khatamka

This trident or magic sceptre, usually adorned with a string of skulls, is the attribute of certain divinities. It destroys the three poisons: ignorance, hatred and lust, or else stands for the divinity's consort.

 chōncung nōlma

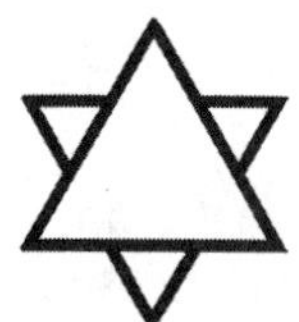

Symbol of the ḍākinī

The three angles of the two triangles represent respectively:
— non-adherence to subject and object, and ultimately emptiness;
— being concept-free and therefore unqualifiable;
— non-attachment to the five aggregates, and hence freedom from desires.

གྲི་གུག། thri̲ku' (Skt.: *kartika*)

The crescent knife, an attribute of the ḍākinī

This symbol represent wisdom, which cuts through the ego.

ཕུར་པ། phūrpa (Skt.: *vajrakilaya*)

The stake of male wrathful divinities

Sometimes referred to as a dagger, it represents the destruction of all conceptualization and of the notion that phenomena have an intrinsic reality. During certain rituals this stake is thrust into an effigy representing demonic forces in order to subdue them.

ཉི་མ། nyi̲ma ཟླ་བ། ta̲wa

Sun and moon

These are often displayed on doors of houses in nearly all Tibetan villages, as well as on flags. They represent abundance (associated with the stars) and happiness. The buddhas and gods are often seated on a solar and/or lunar disk, in which case the latter represent the union of wisdom, the female principle (the sun and the red color) and the means or compassion corresponding to the male principle (the moon and the white color).

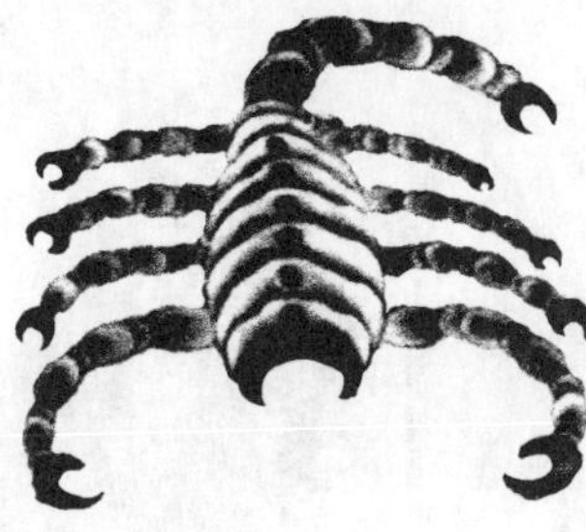

སྡིག་པ་ར་ཙ་ t̲ikparatsa *or* སྡིག་པ་ར་ཉག། t̲ikparanya'

The scorpion

The scorpion often figures on the walls of Tibetan village houses. It is believed to repel evil spirits and to eliminate obstacles.

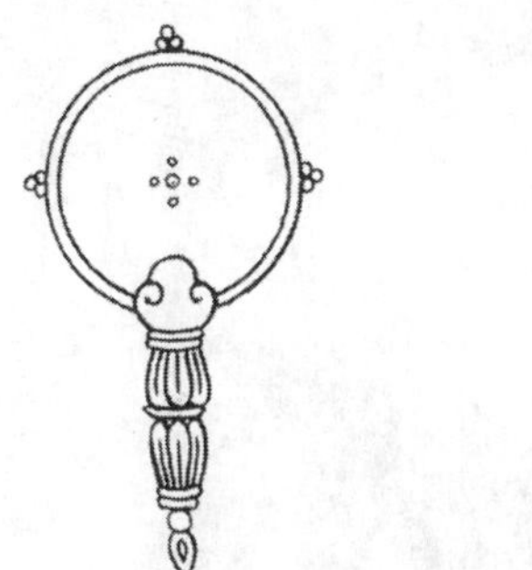

མེ་ལོང་ me̲long (Skt.: *ādarśa*)

The mirror

This is an important symbol, especially in the school of the Great Perfection (Dzogchen). Representing the mind in which all phenomena are reflected, the mirror is associated with wisdom.

མཐུན་པ་སྤུན་བཞི་ thǖnpa pǖn shi̲

The four brothers in harmony

The drawing portrays an elephant, a monkey, a rabbit and a bird. They signify friendship and cooperation, as well as a proper moral and virtuous attitude.

དཀྱིལ་འཁོར་ kyīnkor (Skt.: *maṇḍala*)

The maṇḍala

This is a diagram consisting of concentric circles and squares, symbolising the cosmos (the external mandala) or the human body (the internal mandala). It may be represented in various different ways as a drawing, a thangka, a sculpture or as a composition of colored sand or rice.

བཀྲ་ཤིས་རྫས་བརྒྱད་ trāshi tsä̲' kyä̲'

The eight auspicious materials

The mirror, yoghurt, the durwa grass (Panicum dactylon), the wood apple (Aegle marmelos), the clockwise-spiralling conch, ghiwang pigment (bezoard), vermilion powder and grains of white mustard.

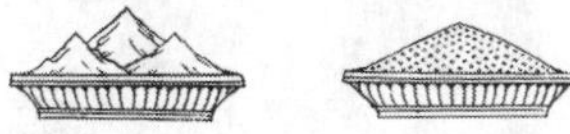

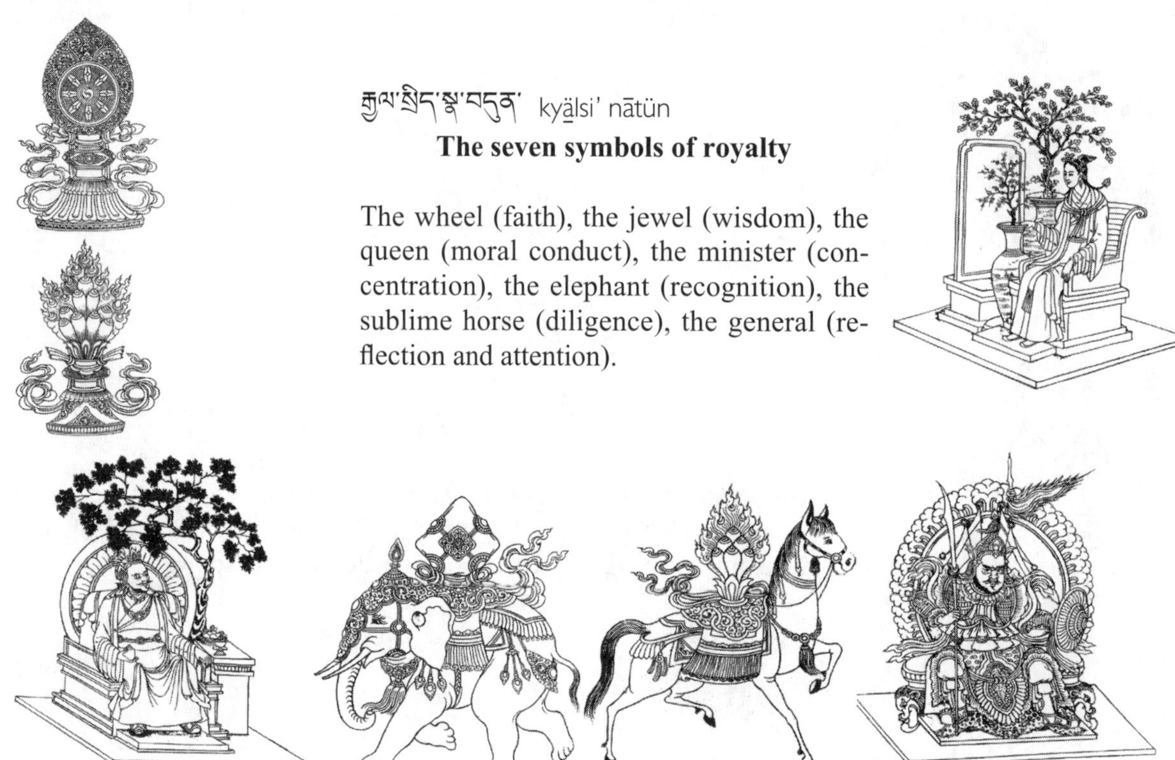

རྒྱལ་སྲིད་སྣ་བདུན་ kyä̱lsi' nātün

The seven symbols of royalty

The wheel (faith), the jewel (wisdom), the queen (moral conduct), the minister (concentration), the elephant (recognition), the sublime horse (diligence), the general (reflection and attention).

རླུང་རྟ་ lūngta

The wind-horse

This term variously denotes a kind of individual energy, a ritual, and also a prayer-flag associated with this ritual. On these flags of different colors, representing the five elements, are printed "wind-horses" and mantra that the wind carries with it in all directions. *Lungta* are generally found on mountain passes as well as on the roofs of houses and monasteries. In the centre of each flag is the "wind-horse", carrying on its back the *cintamani* or "wish-fulfilling gem" (see above), while each of the four corners features one of four protective animals: སྟག་ tā' "tiger", འབྲུག་ tru̱' "dragon", བྱ་ཁྱུང་ cha̱kyung "garuda (mythic eagle)" and སེངྒེ་ sēngke "snow lion". The "wind-horse" or *lungta* symbolizes good fortune. In Spoken Tibetan, "to have *lungta*" means "to be lucky".

Glossary of Linguistic Terms

ablative:
The ablative case indicates spatial or temporal provenance. (see Lesson 9)

absolutive:
The unmarked case: It indicates the grammatical patient, that is, the participant that undergoes the action (in the case of transitive verbs) and the single participant (in the case of intransitive verbs). (see Lesson 4)

affective (verb):
With an affective verb, the subject is in the absolutive case (unmarked case) and the object is in the dative. (see Lesson 9)

agentive:
The agentive denotes the agent of an action (the ergative function) as well as the instrument, the cause of an action and manner in which it is produced (instrumental functions). The agentive may also be designated by the term "ergative-instrumental". (see Lesson 8)

allocentric future:
The allocentric future implies that the speaker intends to perform the action on behalf of an interlocutor. It can be used only in the first person singular (and occasionally plural) with volitional verbs. (see Lesson 23)

anticipatory mood:
In the case of interrogative sentences that directly concern the person being addressed, the questioner must anticipate an answer containing an "I" or a "we" by making advance use of an egophoric auxiliary in the question itself. This "anticipatory mood" is a distinctive feature of Tibetan. It appears not only in Standard Tibetan but in all other Tibetan dialects too, though not in the classical literary language.

aorist (aspect):
The aorist is a perfective aspect of the verb that denotes that an action performed in the past has no bearing on the present. (see Lesson 10)

aspect:
Together with tense, verb aspect is an essential notion for understanding the system of verb "tenses" in the majority of the world's languages. Verb aspect specifies whether an action is completed (perfective) or non-completed (imperfective) with respect to a given reference-point (past, present or future). In Tibetan, the present and the imperfective past are formally identical, whereas the perfective past (the aorist and the perfect) have a completely different form. (see Lesson 10)

assertive (mood):
The assertive mood corresponds to a historical or general truth, or a piece of information that the speaker regards as certain even if he or she may not have verified it directly. The mood is marked by appropriate verb auxiliaries. (see Lessons 5 and 10)

associative:
The associative case conveys the meaning of "with", "against" or "from", but it may also function as the conjunction "and". (see Lesson 9)

causative/resultative verbs:
Causative and resultative verbs are phonetically closely-related pairs. Causative verbs emphasize the cause of a process and the role of the agent in performing an action. Resultative verbs stress the result obtained and the state of the patient or object. All causative verbs are transitive and volitional. Resultative verbs are generally non-volitional and intransitive. (see Lesson 35)

connective:
The connective is a grammatical morpheme that makes it possible to turn two basic sentences into one. It corresponds to both coordinating and subordinating conjunctions of traditional grammar.

directional (auxiliary)**:**
Directional auxiliaries are used with verbs of movement to indicate whether an action is taking place towards or away from the speaker or the point of reference. (see Lesson 41)

egophoric (mood):
The egophoric mood translates a personal knowledge on the part of the speaker, or else an intention on his or her part that is often directly implied in the event that he or she is describing. Egophoric auxiliaries are therefore always associated with an "I" (whether explicit or implicit) in the statement, whatever the function of that "I" may be (subject, object, indirect object or complement). (see Lessons 3 and 10)

ergative:
The ergative and the instrumental cases together provide the two functions of the agentive case. The ergative denotes the agent of the action. In syntactic terms, it denotes the subject of most transitive verbs. (see Lesson 8)

ergative (verb):
With an ergative verb, the subject is in the ergative case and the object is in the absolutive. (see Lesson 8)

essential (stative verb)**:**
Stative verbs or essential copulas denote an essential quality inherent in the person or the thing. The difference between essential and existential verbs is similar to that between the Spanish verbs ser and estar. (see Lesson 6)

evidential mood:
See mediatory mood

existential (stative verb):
Stative verbs or existential copulas express the existence of a phenomenon or a circumstantial characteristic that may often imply a value-judgment on the speaker's part. (see Lesson 6)

experiential (auxiliary):
The use of this auxiliary signifies that the subject has experienced the action at least once in the past. (see Lesson 15)

genitive:
The genitive case denotes the noun complement (see Lesson 4).

inferential (mood):
The inferential mood implies that the speaker is basing what he or she is saying on an inference or a deduction drawn from the traces or results of a past action. The mood is expressed through the appropriate verb auxiliaries. (see Lesson 10)

intentional (auxiliary):
Intentional auxiliaries are compatible only with volitional verbs. They imply that the agent-speaker has voluntarily performed the action. (see Lessons 8 and 10)

mediatory (mood):
Mediatory moods are conveyed by auxiliary verbs (or copulas) and have the role of specifying the source of information that provides the authority for the speaker's statement. There are basically four moods: egophoric, testimonial, assertive and inferential. The information that all these moods convey is certain. (see Lessons 5 and 10)

mnemic (auxiliary):
The use of this type of auxiliary implies that the speaker has only a vague memory of what he or she is saying. (see Lesson 33)

nominalizer:
Nominalizers are suffixes that make it possible to transform a verb or clause into a noun (or a noun phrase). Verbs that have been nominalized in this way operate as nouns or participles, depending on the context. (see Lesson 11)

oblique:
The oblique case indicates the goal (dative function), place or direction (locative function). Thus, the oblique may be referred to as the "dative-locative". (see Lesson 5)

participant:
A participant is a person or thing that is involved in a process to some degree. It is generally a noun, which is directly governed by the verb. Different verbs may have one, two or three participants. Thus the verb "to walk", for example, has just one participant (the one who is walking), the verb "to see" has two (the seer and the seen), and the verb "to give" has three (the giver, the thing given, and the recipient). The same verb may have a different number of participants according to its particular meaning in a given context.

perfect (aspect):
The perfect is a perfective aspect of verbs that specifies that the result of an action performed in the past is still present at the time of utterance. (see Lesson10)

possessive (verb):
With a possessive verb (also called benefactive verb), the subject is in the dative case and the object is in the absolutive (see Lesson 9)

postposition:
postposition: Postpositions are "prepositions" that go after the noun with which they are associated. They have the same function as prepositions (in, on, below, etc.) in European languages. (see Lesson 7)

receptive (auxiliary):
The receptive egophoric auxiliary, which is used only in the past, implies that the subject-speaker of a sentence has undergone the action, has perceived it (involuntarily) or has been its goal. (see Lesson 10)

resultative verb:
See causative verb

secondary verb:
"Secondary" verbs are for the most part modal verbs that go between the main verb and the final auxiliary. (see Lesson 11)

self-corrective (auxiliary):
"Self-corrective" auxiliaries imply that the speaker has just realized that he was mistaken or else that he has just discovered something. (see Lesson 33)

situational grammar:
Tibetan is particularly sensitive to situation and environment, as well as the sources of information on which a speaker's assertions are based. When a statement cannot be immediately associated with a concrete situation of communication, Tibetans tend not to accept it or find it strange. One consequence of this attitude is a reluctance to present verbs in a series of conjugations. The existence of an anticipatory mood and evidential auxiliaries is a manifestation of this situational grammar. The specific function of auxiliaries in dreams or in reported speech also illustrates the importance of pragmatics in this language. (see Lessons 6 and 10)

testimonial (mood):
The testimonial mood specifies that the speaker was himself witness to what he is stating. The testimony is usually visual, but may also be based on hearing or any of the other senses (touch, smell or taste). This mood is marked by appropriate verb auxiliaries. (see Lessons 5 and 10)

topicalizer:
A topicalizer in Tibetan is a particle that makes it possible to emphasize or "topicalize" the group of words that precedes it. (see Lesson 25)

valency (verb):
The verb valency corresponds to the number of participants (or valents) with which a verb is combined. There are basically monovalent (valency of 1), bivalent (valency of 2) and trivalent (valency of 3) verbs. (Tibetan does not have any verb with zero valency). Thus the verb "to walk" is monovalent (the one who is walking), the verb "to see" is bivalent (the seer and the seen), and the verb "to give" is trivalent (the giver, the thing given, and the recipient).

verb types:
From a syntactic perspective, the Tibetan verbs may be divided into the following types: ergative verb, possessive verb (or benefactive verb) and affective verb, according to the various cases the verb governs. (see Lesson 9).

verbalizer:

Verbalizers are verbs that are either intrinsically meaningless or have a general meaning such as "to do" or "to send". A great many verbs in Standard Spoken Tibetan consist of a noun followed by a verbalizer. Thus Tibetan doesn't say "to study" but "to do study". Similarly, for "work", "telephone" and "photograph", the literal translation of the Tibetan constructions would be "to do work", "to send telephone" and "to make photograph".(see Lesson 14)

volitional/non-volitional verb:

Tibetan verbs fall into two basic categories: volitional and non-volitional. The former relate to controllable actions, and are compatible with intentional (and any other) auxiliaries. The latter imply non-controllable processes that do not depend on the subject's volition and cannot be combined with intentional auxiliaries or imperative markers. (see Lesson 8)

English-Tibetan Glossary

དབྱིན་བོད་རྒྱུན་མཁོའི་ཚིག་མཛོད་ཆུང་ངུ་།

A

a short while ago ད་གིན།
a, an ཅིག (ཞིག ཤིག) L
abandon, leave, to བཞག
able, to be ཐུབ།
about, approximately ཙམ།
above all ལྷག་པར་དུ།
abundant, copious རྒྱས་པོ།
accent)-གདངས:
accept, agree, to ཁས་ལེན་ + བྱེད།
accident རྐྱེན་ངན།
accountant, astrologer རྩིས་པ།
accuse unjustly, to མ་ཉེས་ཁ་གཡོགས་ + བྱེད།
accuse, to ནག་ཉེས་ + བཙུགས།
act, deed ལས་ཀ། བྱ་བ། L
act, do, to བྱེད། 1, 3 བྱས། 2
act, to (theatre) འཁྲབ།
actor འཁྲབ་མཁན།
acupuncture གསེར་ཁབ།
address ཁ་བྱང་། ཞལ་བྱང་། H
administration འཛིན་སྐྱོང་།
advise, to བསླབ་བྱ་ + རྒྱག
advise, to བཀའ་སློབ་ + གནང་། H
aeroplane གནམ་གྲུ།
affection (to show) བྱམས་པོ་ + བྱེད།
affectionate བྱམས་པོ།
Africa ཨ་ཧྥི་རི་ཀ།
after རྗེས་ལ། གཞུག་ལ།
age ལོ། དགུང་ལོ། H
agree, arrange, to འགྲིག
agreement, harmony མཐུན་སྒྲིལ།
agriculture ཞིང་ལས། སོ་ནམ།
Ah! I see! ཨ་ལའི།
aim, goal དམིགས་ཡུལ།
air རླུང་།
airport གནམ་གྲུ་འབབ་ཐང་།
alcohol (distilled) ཨ་རག བཞེས་རག H
alive, living གསོན་པོ།
all day ཉི་མ་ཉིན་གང་།
all three གསུམ་ཀ།
all ཚང་མ། སྐྱང་ག
alone གཅིག་པུ། སྐུ་རྐྱང་། H
already ད་ལྟ་ནས།
also ཡའི། ཡང་། L
altar མཆོད་གཤོམ།
altitude sickness ལ་དུག
altitude མཐོ་ཚད།
altogether སྡོམ་པས།
aluminum container ཧ་ཡང་།
always རྟག་པར།
amazed, to be ཧ་ལས།
ཡ་མཚན་ + སྐྱེ།
amazing! (that's) དཔེ་རང་རེད།
ambassador གཞུང་ཚབ།
amber སྤོས་ཤེལ།
Amdo ཨ་མདོ།
America, American ཨ་མེ་རི་ཀ།
American ཨ་མེ་རི་ཀ་བ།
among ནང་ནས།
analyse, to བརྟག་དཔྱད་ + བྱེད།
and དང་།
anger someone, to ཁོང་ཁྲོ་ + བསླང་།
anger ཁོང་ཁྲོ།
angry, to get རླུང་ + ལང་།
angry, to get སྐུ་རླུང་ + བཞེངས། H
angry, to get ཚིག་པ་ + ཟ།
ཁོང་ཁྲོ་ + ལང་།
animal དུད་འགྲོ། སེམས་ཅན།
annihilate, to མེད་པ་ + བཟོ།
ant གྲོག་མ།
antelope གཙོད།
apart from that དེ་མིན་པ།
apple ཀུ་ཤུ། བཞེས་ཤུ། H
apricot མངའ་རིས་ཁམ་བུ།
April ཕྱི་ཟླ་བཞི་པ།
Arabia, Arab ཨ་རབ།
argali, wild sheep གཉན།

aristocrat, noble	སྐུ་དྲག
arithmetic, mathematics	ཨང་རྩིས།
arm	ལག་ ངར།
army	དམག་སྤུངས།
army camp	དམག་སྒར།
around, about	གཡས་གཡོན།
arrive late, to	རྗེས་ལུས་ + ཐེབས།
arrive on time, to	རྗེས་ཟིན།
arrive, reach, to	སླེབས།
arrow	མདའ།
art	སྒྱུ་རྩལ།
article	ཆེད་རྩོམ།
Asia	ཤར་ གླིང་ །
ask, to	བཀའ་འདྲི་ + ཞུས། h
ask, to	བཀའ་འདྲི་ + གནང་། H
ask, to	སྐད་ཆ་+ དྲིས།
asleep, to fall	གཉིད་ཁུག མནལ་ཁུག H
assembly hall	འདུ་ཁང་།
assembly	ཚོགས་ཆེན།
at home	ནང་ལ།
at the home of, near	རྩ་ལ།
attach, tie, to	བཏགས།
August	ཕྱི་ཟླ་བརྒྱད་པ།
aunt (maternal)	སྲུ་མོ།
aunt (paternal)	ཨ་ནེ།
author	རྩོམ་ པ་པོ།
autumn, fall	སྟོན་ཀ།

B

back	སྒལ་པ། སྐུ་སྟོད། H
backside, rump	རྐུབ།
bad, wicked	སྡུག་ཆགས། ངན་པ།
bag	ཁུག་མ། །སྒོ་ཕད།
ball	སྤོ་ལོ།
balloon	གླང་ཕུག
bamboo	སྨྱུག་མ།
banana	ཀེ་ར།
bandit	ཇག་པ།
bank	དངུལ་ཁང་།
bar, pub	ཆང་ཁང་།
barber, hairdresser	སྐྲ་བཞར་ཁང་།
barley	ནས།
base, foundation	གཞི།
basket	སླེ་ པོ།
bathe, wash oneself, to	གཟུགས་པོ་ + བཀྲུས།
bathe, wash oneself, to	སྐུ་གཟུགས་ + བསིལ། H
bathroom, washroom	ཁྲུས་ཁང་།
battery	གློག་རྫས།
be about to, to	འགྲོའོ། གྲབས། L
be, to	རེད། ཡིན།
bean	གྲན་མ། སྲན་མ། L
bear, black	དོམ།
bear, brown	དྲེད་མོང་།
beard	རྒྱ།
bearded	རྒྱ་པོ།
beat, to	བརྡུངས། གཞུས།
beautiful woman	མཛེས་མ།
because, since	ཙང་།
because, since	ག་རེ་རེད་ཟེར་ན།
become, to	ཆགས།
bed	ཉལ་ཁྲི། གཟིམ་ཁྲི། H
bedroom	ཉལ་ཁང་།
	གཟིམ་ཁང་། H
bee	སྦྲང་ནོར་བུ།
beef	གླང་ཤ།
beer	སྦི་རག
before, in the past	གནའ་སྔ་མོ།
before, preceding	སྔན་མ། སྔོན་མ། L
beggar	སྤྲང་གོ སྤྲང་པོ། L
begin (sth.), to	འགོ་བཙུགས།
begin (sth.), to	དབུ་བཙུགས། H
begin, to	འགོ་ཚུགས།
begin, to	ཚུགས།
behind	རྒྱབ།
behind, rear	རྒྱབ་ལོགས།
Beijing	པེ་ཅིན།
believe	ཡིད་ ཆེས་ + བྱེད།

bellows	སྦིད་པ། སྦུད་པ། L
belly	ཕོ་བ།
belong, to	ཁོངས་གཏོགས།
belt	སྐེ་རགས།
bharal, blue sheep	གནའ་བ།
Bharkor	བར་སྐོར།
Bhutan	འབྲུག་ཡུལ།
Bhutanese	འབྲུག་པ།
bicycle	རྐང་ག་རིལ། རྐང་འཁོར། L
big	ཆེན་པོ།
binoculars	རྒྱང་ཤེལ།
biography (of a saint)	རྣམ་ཐར།
bird	བྱིའུ། བྱ།
birthday	སྐྱེས་སྐར། འཁྲུངས་སྐར། H
birthplace	སྐྱེ་ས། འཁྲུངས་ཡུལ། H
bite, to	སོ་ + རྒྱག
bitter	ཁ་ཏིག
black	ནག་པོ།
blacksmith	མགར་བ།
blanket, cover	ཉལ་གཟན། ཀམ་པར་ལི།
blood pressure	ཁྲག་ཤེད།
blood	ཁྲག སྐུ་ཁྲག H
blow, to	ཕུ་ + རྒྱག
blue, green (grass)	སྔོན་པོ།
boat	གྲུ་གཟིངས།
Bodhgaya	རྡོ་རྗེ་གདན།
bodhisattva	བྱང་ཆུབ་སེམས་དཔའ།
body	གཟུགས་པོ།
body	སྐུ་གཟུགས། H
body-cutter	སྟོབས་ལྡན།
boil, to	འཁོལ།
boil, to (cause to)	བསྐོལ།
Bön (religion)	བོན།
bon appétit!	ཞལ་ལག་མཉེས་པོ་གནང་གོ
bone	རུས་ཁོག
Bönpo	བོན་པོ།
book (Western style)	དེབ། ཕྱག་དེབ། H
book, exercise	འབྲི་དེབ།
book, Tibetan pecha	དཔེ་ཆ། ཕྱག་དཔེ། H
bookshop	དཔེ་དེབ་ཚོང་ཁང་།
boot	ལྷམ་གོ། ཞབས་ཕྱུགས། H
border, limit	མཐའ།
bored, to be	ཉོབ།
born, to be	སྐྱེ། འཁྲུངས། H
borrow, to	གཡར།
both	གཉིས་ཀ།
bottle	ཤེལ་དམ།
bottom's up, cheers !	ཞབས་དག
boundary	ས་མཚམས།
bowl (wooden)	ཕོར་པ།
box	སྒམ།
boyfriend, girlfriend	དགའ་རོགས།
branch	ཡལ་ག
brass	རག
brave	བློ་ཁོག་ཆེན་པོ།
bread with meat stuffing	ཤ་བག་ལེབ།
bread	བག་ལེབ། བཞེས་བག H
break down, to	སྐྱོན་ + ཤོར།
break, be broken, to	ཆག
break, to	བཅག
breakdown	སྐྱོན།
breast	ནུ་མ།
breath	ཕུ།
breath	དབུགས་རླུང་།
breathe, to	དབུགས་+ བཏང་།
bride, daughter-in-law	མནའ་མ། བག་མ།
bridge	ཟམ་པ།
bring back, to	ཚུར་ཁྱེར།
bring: *see lead*	
broadcast, transmit, to	འཕྲིན་སྐྱེལ།
bronze	ཁྲོ།
bronze (high-quality)	ལི།
brother, older	ཅོ་ཅོག ཇོ་ལགས། H
brother, younger	འོག་ མ། ཨོ་ལགས། H
brown	རྒྱ་སྨུག
Buddha Śākyamuni	ཤཱཀྱ་ཐུབ་པ།
Buddha	སངས་རྒྱས།

Buddhism	ནང་པའི་ཆོས།
Buddhism, Mahayāna	ཐེག་པ་ཆེན་པོ།
Buddhism, Hinayāna	ཐེག་པ་ཆུང་ངུ།
Buddhism, Vajrayāna	རྡོ་རྗེ་ཐེག་པ།
Buddhist	ནང་པ།
Burma, Myanmar	འབར་མ།
burn, to	ཚིག
burn, to (cause to)	མེ་ཀྲག་ + བཏང་།
burn, to (cause to)	མེ་སྲེག + བཏང་། L
bus, coach	སྤྱི་སྤྱོད་རླངས་འཁོར།
business, to do	ཚོང་ + རྒྱག
business, trade	ཉོ་ཚོང་།
busy, occupied	བྲེལ་བ་ཚ་པོ།
but	ཡིན་ནའི། ཡིན་ན་ཡང་། L
butter	མར། གསོལ་མར། H
butter lamp	མར་མེ། མཆོད་མེ། H
butterfly	ཕྱེ་མ་ལེབ།
build (house) to	རྒྱག 1 བརྒྱབ། 2 རྒྱོབ། 3
buy, to	གཟིགས། H
buy, to	ཉོ། 1 ཉོས། 2, 3

C

calculate, to	རྩིས་རྒྱག
call someone, to	གསུང་ + གནང་། H
call someone, to	སྐད་ + བཏང་།
called, to be	ཟེར། ཞུ། H
calm	སྙོད་སྙོད།
calm, to be	སྙོད་སྙོད་+ བྱེད།
camera	པར་ཆས།
capital city	རྒྱལ་ས།
capital, investment	མ་རྩ།
capitalism	མ་རྩའི་རིང་ལུགས།
car	རླངས་འཁོར། L
car	མོ་ཏ། ཕེབས་ཏོ། H
care (medical)	སྨན་བཅོས།
careful, to be	གཟབ་གཟབ་ + བྱེད།
carpenter	ཤིང་བཟོ་བ།
carpet, floor rug	ས་གདན།
carry, to	ཁྱེར། བསྣམས།
carry, to	བཀུག
cast, throw	གཡུགས།
cat	ཞི་མི། བྱི་ལ། L
catch, hold, to	ཟིམ། ཟིན། L
cause	རྐྱེན། རྒྱུ།
cell (monastic)	ཤག
cemetery	དུར་ཁྲོད།
centre, middle	དཀྱིལ། དབུས།
century	དུས་རབས།
ceremony	མཛད་སྒོ།
certain, some	ཁ་ཤས།
certainly	གཏན་གཏན།
certainly	ཡིན་ད་ཡིན།
certainly, really, exactly	ད་ག་རང་།
chain (iron)	ལྕགས་ཐག
chair	ཀུབ་ཀྱག ཞབས་ཀྱག H
chang, Tibetan beer	ཆང་། མཆོད་ཆང་། H
change (money)	དངུལ་སིལ་མ།
change, alteration	འགྱུར་ལྡོག
change, exchange, to	བརྗེས། བརྗེས་པོ་རྒྱག
change, to	སྒྱུར།
chapel, shrine	མཆོད་ཁང་།
character, temperament	གཤིས་ཀ།
chase, pursue	རྗེས་འདེད་ + བཏང་།
cheap, inexpensive	གོང་ཁེ་པོ།
cheat, deceive, to	མགོ་སྐོར་ + བཏང་།
cheek	འགྲམ་པ།
cheers! bottoms up!	ཞབས་དག
cheese	ཕྱུར་བ། ཞབ་ཕྱུར། H
chemist's shop	སྨན་ཚོང་ཁང་།
chemistry	རྫས་འགྱུར།
cheque	དངུལ་འཛིན།
chest	བང་ཁོག བྲང་ཁོག L
chicken	བྱ།
child	ཕྱུ་གུ ཨ་ལྷ། H ཕྲུ་གུ L
chili	སི་པན། ཟློགས་སྤོད། h
China (P.R.C.)	ཀྲུང་གོ
Chinese (spoken)	རྒྱ་སྐད།

Chinese (written)	རྒྱ་ཡིག
choose, to	གདམ་ཀ་ + རྒྱག
chopstick	ཁོ་ཙེ།
Christian	ཡེ་ཤུ།
churn for tea	མདོང་མོ། གསོལ་མདོང་། H
cigarette, tobacco	ཐ་མག བཞེས་ཐག H
cinema	གློག་བརྙན།
circuit	སྐོར་ར། སྐོར་བ། L
circuit, to make a	སྐོར་ར་ + རྒྱག
circumambulate, to	སྐོར་ར་ + རྒྱག
Civilization, culture	རིག་གཞུང་།
class, course	འཛིན་གྲྭ།
classroom	སློབ་ཁང་།
clean	གཙང་མ།
clear	གཙང་མ། གསལ་པོ།
clear, bright	གསལ་པོ།
clear, to	གཙང་མ་བཟོ།
clever, smart	སྤྲུང་པོ།
climb, to	འཛགས། འཛེགས། L
clock, watch	ཆུ་ཚོད། ཕྱག་ཚོད།
close (door), to	གཟིམ་སྒོ་ + བསྐྱོན། H
close (door), to	སྒོ་ + རྒྱག
close (objects), to	ཁ་ + རྒྱག ཁ་ + བསྐྱོན། H
cloth (cotton)	རས་ཆ།
clothing	དུག་སློག ན་བཟའ། H
cloud	སྤྲིན་པ།
coat	ཀོར། ཕྱུ་པ།
coffee	ཁོ་ཕི།
coincide, fall, to	འཁེལ།
cold	གྲང་མོ།
cold, flu	ཆམ་པ།
cold, to catch	ཆམ་པ་ + རྒྱག
cold, to catch	མགུལ་ཆམ་ + བཞེས། H
cold, to feel	འཁྱག སྐུ་བསིལ། H
collect, save, to	བསགས།
collect, to	སྡུག
college (of monastery)	གྲྭ་ཚང་།
colour	ཚོན་མདོག ཁ་མདོག

comb one's hair, to	རྒྱུག་ཤས་ + རྒྱག
come in!	ཡར་ཤོག ཡར་ཕེབས། H
come, to	ཕེབས། H
come, to	ཡོང་། 1, 2 ཤོག 3
commemorate, to	དྲན་གསོ་ + བྱེད།
commemoration, memorial	དྲན་གསོ།
common, ordinary	ཐུན་མོང་གི
Communism	གུང་ཁྲན་རིང་ལུགས།
Communist Party	གུང་ཁྲན་ཏང་།
companion	རོགས་པ།
compare, to	བསྡུར།
compassion	སྙིང་རྗེ། ཐུགས་རྗེ། H
competition	འགྲན་སྡུར།
complete, accomplish, to	གྲུབ།
complicated	མགོ་རྙོག་པོ།
computer	གློག་ཀླད་འཕྲུལ་འཁོར།
concerning	སྐོར།
conditions	ཆ་རྐྱེན།
conflict	འགལ་ཟླ།
consciousness	འདུ་ཤེས།
consider: *see think, to*	
construct (house, bridge…)	རྒྱག 1 བརྒྱབ། 2 རྒྱོབ། 3
construct (road, object…)	བཟོ། 1 བཟོས། 2,3
construct, build, to	བཞངས། H བཞེངས། HL
consult, to	བསྟེན།
continue, to	མུ་མཐུད།
convenient, simple	སྟབས་བདེ་པོ།
converse, talk, to	བཀའ་མོལ་ + ཞུས། h
converse, talk, to	བཀའ་མོལ་ + གནང་། H
converse, talk, to	སྐད་ཆ་ + བཤད།
cook	མ་བྱན།
cook, to	བཙོས།
copper	ཟངས།
copy, to	ཤུས།
coral	བྱུ་རུ།
corpse, dead body	རོ།
correct, to	ཞུ་དག་ + བཏང་།
cost, to	གནས།
cotton cloth	རས་ཆ།

cotton	རས།
cough, to	གློ་ + རྒྱག
count, calculate, to	རྩིས་ + རྒྱག
count, to	གྲངས་ཀ་ + རྒྱག
country, valley	ལུང་པ།
countryside, village	གྲོང་གསེབ།
courage, bravery	བློ་ཁོག
court, courtyard	སྒོ་ར།
court, tribunal	ཁྲིམས་ཁང་།
cousin, brother	སྤུན་སྐྱ། སྐུ་མཆེད། H
cow	བ་ཕྱུགས།
crag, cliff	བྲག
crane (bird)	བྱ་ཁྲུང་།
create, to	གསར་གཏོད་ + བྱེད།
criticise, to	སྐྱོན་བརྗོད་ + བྱེད།
cross a pass, to	ལ་ + རྒྱག
cross, to	བཅད།
crossing	བཞི་མདོ་ཁ།
crossroads	བཞི་མདོ་ཁ།
crude, boorish	ཧམ་པ་ཚ་པོ།
crudeness, boorishness	ཧམ་པ།
crush, to	རྫིས།
cry, weep, to	ངུ།
cultivated land	ཞིང་ག
Cultural Revolution	རིག་གནས་གསར་བརྗེ།
culture	རིག་གནས། ཤེས་རིག
cup	དཀར་ཡོལ། ཞལ་དཀར། H
curious, inquisitive	ཧུས་གཏོགས་ཚ་པོ།
curtain	ཁྲ་ཡོལ།
customs	འགག་སྒོ།
cut, to	བཅད།
cut, to be	ཆད།

D

dairy products	དཀར་ཆུ།
ḍākinī	མཁའ་འགྲོ་མ།
Dalai Lama	ཏཱ་ལའི་བླ་མ།
Dalai Lama (title)	སྐུ་མདུན།
Dalai Lama (title)	ཡིད་བཞིན་ནོར་བུ།
Dalai Lama (title)	རྒྱལ་བ་རིན་པོ་ཆེ།
damage, loss	སྐྱོན། གྱོང་།
damp, wet	རློན་པ།
dance, to	ཞབས་བྲོ་ + རྒྱག
danger	ཉེན་ཁ།
dare, to	ནུས།
Darjeeling	རྡོ་རྗེ་གླིང་།
date	ཚེས་པ།
daughter, girl	བུ་མོ། སྲས་མོ། H
day	ཉི་མ། ཉིན། L
day after tomorrow	གནངས་ཉིན་ཀ།
day before yesterday	ཁ་ཉིན་ཀ།
day	ཉི་མ། ཉིན་གར།
day, the following	དེའི་སང་ཉིན།
deaf	ཨ་མཆོག་འོན་པ།
debt	བུ་ལོན།
deceitful	གཡོ་སྒྱུ་ཚ་པོ།
deceived, to be	མགོ་སྐོར་ + ཐེབས།
December	ཕྱི་ཟླ་བཅུ་གཉིས་པ།
decide, to	ཐག་བཅད།
deep	གཏིང་ཟབ་པོ།
deer	ཤ་བ།
defecate, to	སྐྱག་པ་ + བཏང་།
defend a thesis	དམ་བཅའ་+ བཞག
defend, protect, to	སྲུང་སྐྱོབ་ + བྱེད།
Delhi	དི་ལི།
delicious	ཞིམ་པོ། སྦྲོ་པོ། H
democracy, democratic	དམངས་གཙོ་རིང་ལུགས།
demolish, to	གཏོར།
depend, to	རག་ལས།
desert (sand)	བྱེ་ཐང་།
deserted land	ས་ཆ་སྟོང་པ།
desire	འདོད་པ།
	ཐུགས་འདོད། H
desire, to feel	འདོད་ཆགས་ + ལང་།
desire, want, to	ཐུགས་འདོད། H
desire, want, to	སྙིང་འདོད།
destroy, demolish	གཏོར་བཤིག་ + རྒྱག

destroy, waste	གཏོར།
detailed, precise	ཞིབ་ཕྲ།
development, progress	གོང་འཕེལ།
Dhagpo	དྭགས་པོ།
Dharamsala	དྷ་རམ་ས་ལ།
Dharma	ཆོས།
Dharma centre	ཆོས་ཚོགས།
dialect	ཡུལ་སྐད།
diamond	ཕ་ལམ།
dictionary	ཚིག་མཛོད།
die, to	ཤི། གྲོངས། H
difference	ཁྱད་པར།
different	མི་ འདྲ་བ།
difficult	དཀའ་ལས་ཁག་པོ།
diligent, earnest	བརྩོན་པོ། ཧུར་བརྩོན།
direction	ཁ་ཕྱོགས།
director, leader	འགོ་ཁྲིད། དབུ་ཁྲིད། H
dirt	དྲག་པ། དྲེག་པ། L
dirty	བཙོག་པ།
disappear, to	མེད་ པ་ཆགས། ཡལ།
disaster, obstacle	གེགས་དབང་།
disciple	སློབ་མ།
discipline, rules	སྒྲིག་ལམ།
disorder, chaos	ཟང་ཟིང་།
distance	རྒྱང་ཐག
distinguish, to	དབྱེ་བ་ + ཕྱེ།
district	རྫོང་།
disturb, to	ཅ་བཤུན་པོ་ + བཟོ།
divide, to	བགོ་ཤ་རྒྱག
do, act, to	བྱེད། 1, 3 བྱས། 2
do, act, to	གནང་། H
doctor, physician	ཨེམ་ཆི། སྨན་པ།
doctrine, vision	ལྟ་བ།
dog	ཁྱི།
doll, puppet	ཨ་ལད་ པད་ གོག
domain, property	གཞིས་ཀ།
done, to have	བཅུག
donkey, ass	ཕོང་གུ། ཕོང་བུ། L
door	སྒོ། གཟིམ་སྒོ། H
dot, intersyllabic	ཚེག
dough of tsampa	ཕྱགས།
down, below	གཤམ།
down there	མ་གིར།
down, to bring	ཕབས།
down, to go	བབས།
downwards	མར།
Dräpung (monastery)	འབྲས་སྤུངས།
drawing	རི་མོ།
dream	རྨི་ལམ། མནལ་ལམ། H
dream, to	རྨི་ལམ་ + བཏང་།
dream, to	མནལ་ལམ་ + བཏང་གནང་། H
dress, wear, to	གོན།
drink, to	འཐུང་། 1 བཏུངས། 2 འཐུངས། 3
drink, to	ཞུ། 1 ཞུས། 2, 3h མཆོད། H
drive (a car), to	མོ་ཊ་ + བཏང་།
driver, pilot	ཁ་ལོ་པ།
drop (of liquid)	ཐིགས་པ།
drugstore	སྨན་ཚོང་ཁང་།
drum	རྔ།
drunk, to be	ར་བཟི།
dry	སྐམ་པོ།
dumb, mute	ལྐུགས་པ།
during, while	ཞུལ་རིང་གར། ཡུན་རིང་། L
dust	ཐལ་ལ། ཐལ་བ། L
dwindle, to	ཉུང་ དུ་འགྲོ

E

each	རེ་རེ།
eagle	བྱ་གླག
ear	ཨ་མཆོག སྙན་མཆོག H
early	སྔ་པོ།
earring	ཨ་ལོང་།
earth, soil, land	ས།
east	ཤར།

eastern	ཤར་ཕྱོགས།
easy	ལས་སླ་པོ།
eat (flour), to	འགམས།
eat	ཁ་ལག་+ ཟ།
eat, to	ཟ། 1 བཟས། 2 ཟོ། 3
eat, to	ཞུ། 1 ཞུས། 2, 3 h མཆོད། H
economy, wealth	དཔལ་འབྱོར།
edge, end	མཐའ།
educate	སློབ་གསོ་+ བཏང་།
education	སློབ་ གསོ།
effort	འབད་བརྩོན།
effort, to make	འབད་བརྩོན་ + བྱེད།
egg	སྒོང་ང་། བཞེས་སྒོང་། H
eight	བརྒྱད།
eighteen	བཅོ་བརྒྱད།
eighty	བརྒྱད་ཅུ།
electricity	གློག
eleven	བཅུ་གཅིག
eliminate, clear	སེལ།
embassy	གཞུང་ཚབ་ཁང་།
emotion (negative)	ཉོན་མོངས།
emperor	གོང་མ།
empty	སྟོང་པ།
enclosure, surrounding wall	ལྕགས་རི།
end	མཐའ་མཇུག
end of month	ཟླ་འཇུག
end, be ended, to	གྲོལ། ཚར།
endure, get used to, to	འཕྲོད།
endure, support, to	སྡུག་རུས་རྒྱག
enemy	དགྲ་བོ།
energy	ནུས་པ།
England, English	དབྱིན་ཇི།
enough, to be	ལྡང་།
enter, to	འཛུལ།
entrust, transmit, to	བསྐུར།
envelope	ཡིག་སྐོགས།
equal	སྙོམ་པོ།
era, time	དུས་ སྐབས།
erase, to	སུབ།
erased, to be	ཟུབ།
error	ནོར་འཁྲུལ།
escape, to	བྲོས།
establish, fix, settle	གཏན་འབེབས་ + གནང་།
establish, set up, to	གསར་འཛུགས་ + གནང་།
et cetera	ཅི་དག སོགས། L
Europe, European	ཡུ་རོབ།
evening	དགོང་དག
evening, this	དོ་དགོང་།
ever, never	ནམ་ཡང་།
Everest, Mount	ཇོ་མོ་གླང་མ།
every day	ཉིན་ལྟར་རེ་བཞིན།
every year	ལོ་ལྟར་རེ་བཞིན།
everywhere	ག་ས་ག་ལ།
exact	ཏག་ཏག
exam, test (oral)	རྒྱུག་སྤྲོད།
exam, test (written)	ཡིག་ཚད།
exam, to take a written	ཡིག་ཚད་ + བཏང་།
exam, to take an oral	རྒྱུག་སྤྲོད་ + བྱེད།
examine, to	བརྟག་དཔྱད་ + བྱེད།
example	དཔེར་བརྗོད།
example, for	དཔེར་ན།
except, save	མ་གཏོགས།
exception	དམིགས་གསལ།
excrement	སྐྱག་པ།
excuse me!	དགོངས་འགལ་མེད་པ་ཅིག
excuse me!	དགོངས་པ་མ་ཚོམས།
exercise	སྦྱོང་ཚན།
exhibit, to	སྒྲིག་གཤོམ་ + བྱེད།
exhibition	འགྲེམ་སྟོན།
existence	འཚོ་བ།
expensive, costly	གོང་ཆེན་པོ།
experience	ཉམས་མྱོང་།
expert, skillful	མཁས་པོ།
explain, to	འགྲེལ་བཤད་ + རྒྱག

express, show, to བསྟན།
expression, appearence ཉམས་འགྱུར།
exterior, outside ཕྱི་ལོགས།
eye མིག སྤྱན། H

F

face གདོང་པ། ཞལ་རས། H
factory བཟོ་གྲྭ
faithful (religion) དད་ཅན།
fake, false རྫུས་མ།
fall in love, to སེམས་པ་ + ཤོར།
fall, fall over, to རིལ།
fall, to ཟག བབས།
fame, glory སྐད་གྲགས།
family མི་ཚང་། ཁྱིམ་ཚང་།
family member ནང་མི།
famous, well known སྐད་གྲགས་ཆེན་པོ།
far, distant ཐག་རིང་པོ།
farmer ཞིང་པ། སོ་ནམ་པ།
farmer ཞིང་པ།
farmer-nomad ས་མ་འབྲོག
fashion དཔེ་གསར།
fast, rapid མགྱོགས་པོ། སྟོལ་པོ། H
fat, stout རྒྱགས་པ།
fat, stout ཤ་ རྒྱགས་ པ།
father པ་ཕ། པ་ལགས། H
father (of someone else) ཡབ། H
fault སྐྱོན།
fear ཞེད་སྣང་།
fear, be afraid, to ཞེད།
February ཕྱི་ཟླ་གཉིས་པ།
feel, to ཚོར།
feeling, sensation ཚོར་སྣང་།
female sex མོ་མཚན།
festival, ceremony དུས་ཆེན།
fever ཚ་བ།
few days ago, a ཁ་སང་། ཁ་སེང་། L
few ཉུང་ཉུང་།
field ཞིང་ཁ།
fifteen བཅོ་ལྔ།
fifty ལྔ་བཅུ།
fight, quarrel, to རྒྱག་རེས་ + ཤོར།
fight, quarrel, to རྒྱག་རེས་ + རྒྱག
fight, to འཛིང་།
figure, number ཨང་གྲངས།
fill, be filled, to ཁངས། ཁེངས། L
film གློག་བརྙན།
find བརྙེད།
fine (powder, etc.), detailed ཞིབ་ཞིབ།
fine! all right! ཡོང་ང་།
finger མཛུབ་གུ། ཕྱག་མཛུབ H
fingernail སེན་མོ། ཕྱག་སེན། H
finish, to ཚར།
fire མེ། ཞུགས་མེ། H
fire (to break out) མེ་ཤོར།
fire, shoot, to མེ་མདའ་ + རྒྱག
fire, to light མེ་ + བཏང་།
fire, to set མེ་རྒྱག
first དང་པོ ཐོག་མ།
fish ཉ།
fish (dish) ཉ་ཤ།
fish, to ཉ་ཟིན།
five ལྔ།
flat ལེབ་ལེབ།
flee, run away བྲོས།
floor, storey ཐོག་ས།
flour གྲོ་ཞིབ། གསོལ་ཞིབ། H
flour of roasted barley རྩམ་པ། གསོལ་ཞིབ། H
flower མེ་ཏོག
flute གླིང་བུ།
fly (insect) སྦང་ནག སྦྲང་ནག L
fly, to འཕུར།
fold, to ལྟེབ་རྩེག་ + རྒྱག
follow, to གཞུག་ལ་ཡོང་།
food ཁ་ལག ཞལ་ལག H
food ཟོ་ཆས།
food, to prepare ཁ་ལག + བཟོ།

foodstuffs	བཟའ་ཆས།
foot, leg	རྐང་པ། ཞབས། h
football	རྐང་རྩེད་སྤོ་ལོ།
forehead	དཔལ་སྒྲོ། དཔྲལ་སྒྲོ། L
foreigner	ཕྱི་རྒྱལ།
forest	ཤིང་ནགས།
forget, to	བརྗེད།
fork	ཀང་དྲ།
fortress	མཁར། རྫོང་།
forty	བཞི་བཅུ།
found (institution)	ཕྱུག་བཏབ་ + གནང་། H
four	བཞི།
Four [Noble] Truths	བདེན་པ་བཞི།
fourteen	བཅུ་བཞི།
fox	ཝ་མོ།
foxfur hat	ཝ་ཞྭ།
France	ཕྲ་རན་སི།
free	རང་དབང་ཡོད་པ།
free, let loose, to	ཤོར།
free, liberate, to	བཅིངས་ བཀྲོལ་ + བཏང་།
freedom, liberty	རང་དབང་།
frequent	ཡང་སེ།
Friday	གཟའ་པ་སངས།
friend	གྲོགས་པོ།
friendly, compatible	མཐུན་པོ།
frog	སྦལ་པ།
front of, in	མདུན།
fruit	ཤིང་ཏོག
fry, to	བརྔོས།
frying pan	ཚལ་སླང་།
full	གང་།
fumigation, to perform	བསང་ + བཏང་།
funds	ཐེབས་རྩ།
funny	དགོད་བྲོ་པོ།
funny, amusing	བསྟན་ བཞིག་ ཚ་པོ།
funny, comical	དགོད་བྲོ་ པོ།
furniture, item of	འཛོན་ཆས།

G

game, toy	རྩེད་མོ།
Gandän (monastery)	དགའ་ལྡན།
garbage, rubbish	གད་སྙིགས།
gasoline, petrol	རྡོ་སྣུམ།
gather, meet, to	འཛོམས།
gather, to	བསྡུ། བསྡུས།
gazelle	རྒོ་བ།
Gelugpa (sect)	དགེ་ལུགས་པ།
generally	སྤྱིར་བཏང་།
generation	མི་རབས།
generator	སྐམ་སློག
gentle	འཇམ་པོ།
geography	ས་ཁམས་རིག་པ།
Germany	འཇར་མན།
geshe	དགེ་བཤེས།
get rid of, to	བསྡུ་གསོག་རྒྱག
gift	རྫན་པ།
gift, to make a	སྐྱེར།
gift, to make a	གསོལ་རས་ + གནང་། H
girlfriend	གྲོགས་མོ།
girlfriend, boyfriend	དགའ་རོགས།
give, offer, to	སྤྲད། ཕུལ། h གནང་། H
glass (drinking)	ཤེ་ལ་སེ།
glass (substance)	ཤེལ་སྒོ།
glasses, spectacles	མིག་ཤེལ། སྤྱན་ཤེལ། H
glove	ལག་ཤུབས།
go back, return, to	ལོག
go out, to	ཐོན། ཐོན། L
go out, to (of fire)	མེ་ཤི།
go, to	འགྲོ 1 ཕྱིན། 2 རྒྱུགས། 3
go, to	ཕེབས། H ཐེག H
goat	ར།
god, divinity	ལྷ།
goddess	ལྷ་མོ།
gold	གསེར།
good, well	ཡག་པོ།
goodbye (to so. departing)	ག་ལེ་ཕེབས། H
goodbye (to so. staying)	ག་ལེ་བཞུགས། H

goods, items	ཚོང་ཟོག
gormo, currency unit	སྒོར་མོ།
government	གཞུང་། སྲིད་གཞུང་།
gown, chuba	ཕྱུ་པ།
grain, seed	འབྲུ།
granddaughter	ཚ་མོ།
grandfather, old man	སྤོ་བོ། སྤོ་ལགས། H
grandmother, old lady	རྨོ་མོ། རྨོ་ལགས། H
grandson	ཚ་བོ།
grasp, seize	འཛུ། 1 བཛུས། 2,3
grass	རྩྭ།
grassland	རྩ་ཐང་།
great temple of Lhasa	གཙུག་ལག་ཁང་།
green (dark)	ལྗང་ཁུ།
grey	སྐྱ་བོ།
groom, son-in-law	མག་པ། སྐུ་བག H
group	ཚོགས་པ།
guardian of temple	དགོན་གཉེར།
guerrilla warfare, to wage	འཇབ་དམག་ + རྒྱག
guest	མགྲོན་པོ། སྐུ་མགྲོན། H
gun	མེ་མདའ།

H

habit, custom	གོམས་གཤིས།
hail	སེ་ར།
hail, to	སེ་ར་ + བཏང་།
hair	སྐྲ། དབུ་སྐྲ། H
hairdresser, barber	སྐྲ་བཞར་ཁང་།
half	ཕྱེད་ཀ།
Han China	རྒྱ་ནག
Han Chinese	རྒྱ་མི།
hand	ལག་པ། ཕྱག H
handsome	མཛེས་པོ།
hang, to	བཀལ།
happen, to	བྱེད། 1, 3 བྱས། 2
happiness	བདེ་བ། བདེ་སྐྱིད།
happy, content	སྐྱིད་པོ།
happy, pleasant	སྐྱིད་པོ།
hard, fierce	དྲག་པོ།
hard, solid	མཁྲགས་པོ།
	མཁྲེགསཔོ། L
hare	ཡོས།
harm	གནོད།
harm, to	གནོད་སྐྱེལ།
harmonious, interesting	སྙན་པོ།
harvest festival	འོང་སྐོར།
harvest	སྟོན་ཐོག
hat	ཞྭ་མོ། དབུ་ཞྭ། H
have to, to	དགོས།
have, to	ཡོད། འདུག ཡོད་རེད།
he	ཁོ།
he, she	ཁོང་། H
head	མགོ དབུ། H
headmaster	ཆེ་མོ་བ།
heal, get better, to	དྲག དྲངས། H
health	སྐུ་ཁམས།
	འཕྲོད་བསྟེན།
healthy	ཐང་པོ།
heap, pile	ཕུང་། ཕུང་གསོགས།
hear, to	གོ གསན། H
heart (anatomical)	སྙིང་། མགུལ་ སྙིང་། H
heart (spiritual)	སྙིང་། ཐུགས། H
heart disease	སྙིང་གི་ན་ཚ།
heat	ཚ་བ། དྲོད།
heat, to	ཚ་པོ་+ བཟོ།
heater	ཐབ།
heavy	ལྗིད་པོ།
heel	རྟིང་པ།
height	མཐོ་ཚད།
helicopter	ཐད་འཕུར་གནམ་གྲུ།
hello, best wishes	བཀྲ་ཤིས་བདེ་ལེགས།
help	རོགས་རམ།
help, to	ཕྱག་ རོགས་ + གནང་། H
help, to	རོགས་རམ་+ བྱེད།
hepatitis	མཆིན་པའི་ན་ཚ།
herd, flock, pack	ཁྱུ།

herder, nomad, drogpa	འབྲོག་པ།
here	འདའི། འདིར། L
hesitate, doubt, to	ཐེ་ཚོམ་ + བྱེད།
hide (of yak); coracle	ཀོ་བ།
hide (oneself), to	གབ།
hide, to	སྦས།
high	མཐོ་པོ། མཐོན་པོ། L
high school: *see school*	
hill	རི་འབུར།
hill, mountain	རི།
Himalaya	ཧི་མ་ལ་ཡ།
Hindi	རྒྱ་གར་སྐད།
Hindu	ཕྱི་པ། ཧིན་དུ།
history	ལོ་རྒྱུས་།
hit, hurt oneself, to	བརྡབས།
hold, to	ཟིམ། ཟིན། L
holiday, vacation	གུང་སང་། གུང་སེང་། L
hollow	ཁོག་ སྟོང་།
homeland	ཕ་ཡུལ།
honest	དྲང་པོ།
hope, to	རེ་ བ་ + བྱེད།
horrible	སྐྱུག་ཆགས་ཞེ་པོ་ཅིག
horse	རྟ། ཆིབས་པ། H
horse race	རྟ་རྒྱུག
hospital	སྨན་ཁང་།
hot spring	ཆུ་ཚན།
hot	ཚ་པོ།
hotel	མགྲོན་ཁང་།
hour, watch, clock	ཆུ་ཚོད། ཕྱག་ཚོད། H
house	ཁང་པ། གཟིམ་ཤག H
household	དུད་ཚང་།
how are you?	སྐུ་དཀྱིལ་གསལ་དྭངས། HH
how are you?	སྐུ་གཟུགས་བདེ་པོ། H
how much? how many?	ག་ཚད། ག་ཚོད། L
how?	ག་འདྲས་ཟེ།
humble	ཞམ་ཆུང་།
hundred million	དུང་ཕྱུར།
hundred thousand	འབུམ།
hundred	བརྒྱ།
hungry, to be	གྲོད་ཁོག་ལྟོགས།
hungry, to be	གསོལ་གྲོད་ + བཀྲེས་གནང་། H
hunt, to	རི་དྭགས་+བཏང་།
hurry, to	མགྱོགས་ པོ་ + བྱེད།
hurt, to	ན་ཚ་ + བཏང་།
hurt, to	སྙུང་གཞི་ + བཏང་གནང་། H
hydroelectric plant	གློག་ཁང་།

I

I	ང་།
ice	ཁྱགས་པ།
idea	བསམ་བློ།
idea, thought	བསམ་བློ། དགོངས་པ། H
idiot	ལྐུགས་པ།
if, in the event that	གལ་སྲིད།
ill, sick	ནད་པ།
ill, to be	ན། སྙུང་། H
illness, disease	ན་ཚ། སྙུང་གཞི། H
illusion	མིག་འཕྲུལ། སྒྱུ་མ།
image, reflection	གཟུགས་བརྙན།
imbecile: *see idiot*	
imitate, to	ལད་མོ་ + བྱེད།
immediately, at once	ལམ་སང་། ལམ་སེང་། L
imperialism	བཙན་རྒྱལ་རིང་ལུགས།
important	གལ་ཆེན་པོ།
impossible	ཡིན་སྲིད་ཀྱི་མ་རེད།
impression, feeling	ཚོར་ སྣང་། བག་ ཆགས་
in	ནང་།
India	རྒྱ་གར།
Indian	རྒྱ་གར་བ།
indicate, to: *see show*	
industry	བཟོ་ལས།
influence	ཤུགས་རྐྱེན།
injection, to administer	ཁབ་ + རྒྱག
ink	སྣག་ཚ། ཕྱག་སྣག H
innermost part	སྦུག
insect, bug	འབུ།
instant, moment	སྐད་ཅིག

instrument (musical)	འབའ་ཆ།
instrument: *see tool*	
intellectual	ཤེས་ཡོན་ཅན།
intelligent	རིག་པ་ཅན།
intelligent, clever	སྤྱང་པོ།
interest, preoccupation	སེམས་ཁུར།
interesting, nice (to hear)	སྙན་པོ།
interior, inside	ནང་ལོགས།
international	རྒྱལ་སྤྱི།
interpreter	སྐད་སྒྱུར། གསུང་སྒྱུར། H
interpreter: *see translator*	
invent: *see create*	
invite, to	གདན་འདྲེན་ + ཞུས། H
invite, to	སྐད་ + བཏང་།
iron	ལྕགས།
island	གླིང་ཕྲན།
Italy	ཨི་ཏ་ལི།

J

jacket, coat	ཀོར།
January	སྤྱི་ཟླ་དང་པོ།
Japan	ཉི་ཧོང་།
jealous	མིག་སེར་ + ལང་།
jewel	དཀོན་མཆོག ནོར་བུ།
Jhangthang	བྱང་ཐང་།
Jhokhang	ཇོ་ཁང་།
joint, articulation	ཚིག་གཞི།
joke, to	བསྟན་ བཞིག་ + བསླད།
joke, to; to have fun	རྩེད་མོ་ + རྩེ།
journal, newspaper	ཚགས་པར།
journalist	གསར་འགྱུར་···· འགོད་མཁན།
joy	དགའ་བ། བདེ་སྐྱིད།
joyful	སྐྱིད་པོ། དགའ་པོ།
judge	ཁྲིམས་དཔོན།
juice, clear soup	ཁུ་བ།
July	སྤྱི་ཟླ་བདུན་པ།
jump, to	མཆོམས། མཆོངས། L
June	སྤྱི་ཟླ་དྲུག་པ།
Jupiter	ཕུར་བུ།
just to there	ཕར་ཙམ་ད་གར།

K

Kagyüpa (sect)	བཀའ་བརྒྱུད་པ།
Kalimpong	ཀ་སློན་ སྤུག
karma	ལས།
Kathmandu	ཡམ་བུ། ཀ་ཏེ་མན་གྲུ།
Kazakh	ཧ་ས་ཁ་པ།
keep, look after, to	ཉར།
kettle, teapot	ཁོག་ཞིར།
key	ལྡེ་མིག ཕྱག་ལྡེ། H
Kham	ཁམས།
khatak, silk scarf	ཁ་བཏགས།
	མཇལ་དར། H
kidney	མཁལ་མ།
kill, to	བསད།
kilogramme	སྤྱིའི་རྒྱ་ མ།
kilometer	སྤྱི་ལེ།
kind, good-hearted	སེམས་བཟང་པོ།
kind, sort	སྣེ་ཁ།
king	རྒྱལ་པོ།
kiss, to	ཁ་སྐྱེལ།
kitchen	ཐབ་ཚང་། གསོལ་ཐབ། H
kite	བྱ་འཕིར།
kite (bird)	ཕིང་ཀྱུར་མ།
knee	པུས་མོ།
knife	གྲི།
knock	གཞུས། བརྡུངས།
knot	མདུད་པ།
know (someone), to	ངོ་ཤེས། ངོ་མཁྱེན། H
	ཞལ་ཚོར། h
know, to	ཤེས། མཁྱེན། H
knowledge, quality	ཡོན་ཏན།
Kongpo	ཀོང་པོ།

L

Ladakh	ལ་དྭགས།
ladder	སྐས་ འཛེགས།
ladle	སྐྱོག
lake	མཚོ།

lama, teacher, master བླ་མ།
lamp ཞུ་མར།
land, earth ས།
Land of Snows, Tibet གངས་ལྗོངས།
landscape, countryside ཡུལ་ལྗོངས།
language, speech, sound སྐད།
last མཐའ་མ།
last, to འགོར།
late ཕྱི་པོ།
late, to be ཕྱི་པོ་བྱེད།
laugh, to གད་མོ་ + བགད།
laugh, to make གད་མོ་ + བསླངས།
laughing, to burst out གད་མོ་ + ཤོར།
laundry, washing, to do དྲིག་འཁྲུ་ + རྒྱག
law, rule ཁྲིམས།
lay down (someone), to བསྙལ།
laziness ལེ་ལོ།
lazy ལེ་ལོ་ཅན།
lead (metal) ཞ་ཉེ།
lead, drive འཁྲིད།
lead, drive, to འཁྲིད། འཁྲིད་གནང་། H
leader, chief འགོ་འཁྲིད། དབུ་འཁྲིད། H
leaf ལོ་མ།
learn, to སྦྱོངས།
leave, abandon, to ལས། ལུས། L
leave, go out, to ཐོན།
leave, put, place, to བཞག
leave, to take དགོངས་པ་ + ཞུ། H
left གཡོན།
leg, foot རྐང་པ། ཞབས། h
legal, judicial ཁྲིམས་འཛིན།
Leh གླེ།
lend, borrow, to གཡར། གཡར་གནང་། H
leopard གཟིག
leprosy མཛེས་ནད།
lesson སློབ་ཚན།
let go, allow to go, to བཏང་།
let go, drop, to ཤོར།

letter, mail ཡི་གེ ཕྱག་བྲིས། H
level (water or fig.) ཆུ་ཚད།
level, rank, order གོ་རིམ།
Lhasa ལྷ་ས།
Lhokha ལྷོ་ཁ།
library དཔེ་མཛོད་ཁང་།
lick, eat (yogurt), to བལྡགས།
lie down, to ཉལ།
lie, falsehood སྐྱག་རྫུན། ཞལ་རྫུན། H
lie, to tell a སྐྱག་རྫུན་ + བཤད།
life མི་ཚེ། སྲོག
lifestyle འཚོ་བ་སྐྱེལ་སྟངས།
light (weight) ཡང་པོ།
light འོད།
light, to སྦར།
like ནང་བཞིན།
like, as དེ་འདྲ།
like, to དགའ་པོ། མཉེས་པོ། H
limb རྐང་ལག
line ཐིག
line, lineage, tantra རྒྱུད།
line, queue འབང་འགྲིག
འབྲང་འགྲིག L
lineage of incarnations སྐུ་ཕྲེང་།
lion སེངྒེ།
lip མཆུ་ཏོ།
liquid རླན་གྱི་རིགས།
list ཐོ། མིང་ཐོ།
listen, to ཉན། གསན། H
lit, to be; to burn འབར།
literature རྩོམ་རིག
little more, a ལྷག་ཙ། ལྷག་ཙམ། L
little, a ཏིག་ཙ། ཏོག་ཙམ། L
little, a ཏོག་ཙམ།
little, a; once གཅིག
live, lead a life, to འཚོ།
live, sit, to བསྡད། བཞུགས། H
lively, agitated འཁྲུག་པོ།

liver	མཆིན་པ།
living room, sitting room	ཚོམས་ཆེན།
lodging, hospitality	གནས་ཚང་།
lodging, to find	གནས་ཚང་ + གཡར།
logic	ཚད་མ་རིག་པ།
long	རིང་པོ།
long (time)	ཡུན་རིང་པོ།
look for, to	བཙལ།
look, to	གཟིགས། H
look, to	ལྟ། 1 བལྟས 2 ལྟོས། 3
lose, to	བརླགས།
loss, damage	གྱོང་།
love	བརྩེ་གདུང་།
love, in: *see fall in love, to*	
love, to	དགའ། མཉེས། H
low	དམའ་པོ།
luck	ལམ་འགྲོ
lucky	བསོད་བདེ་ཆེན་པོ།
lung disease	གློ་ནད།
lung	གློ་བ།
lute, Tibetan	སྒྲ་སྙན།
lynx	གཡི།

M

machine	འཕྲུལ་འཁོར།
mad, crazy	སྨྱོན་པ།
mad, crazy, to be	སྨྱོ།
Madam	ཨ་ལྕག།
magazine, journal	དུས་དེབ།
magnet	ཁབ་ལེན།
Maitreya	བྱམས་པ།
majority, most	མང་ཆེ་བ།
make up one's mind, to	ཐག་ཆོད།
make, prepare, to	བཟོ། 1 བཟོས། 2, 3
male sex	ཕོ་མཚན།
male	ཕོ།
man, human, person	མི།
man, husband	ཁྱོ་ག
manner, way	སྟངས།
mantra	སྔགས།
manual (book)	སློབ་དེབ།
many	མང་པོ།
map	ས་བཀྲ།
March	ཕྱི་ཟླ་གསུམ་པ།
market	ཁྲོམ།
marmot	ཕྱི་པི། ཕྱི་བ། L
marriage	ཆང་ས། འཁྲུང་ས། H
marry, to	ཆང་ས་ + རྒྱག
Mars	མིག་དམར།
mask	འབག ཞལ་འབག H
mason	རྡོ་བཟོ་བ།
master, chief	དཔོན་པོ།
match	མུ་ཟི།
material, substance	རྒྱུ་ཆ།
mathematics	ཨང་རྩིས།
matter, it doesn't	གའི་གནང་གི་མ་རེད། H
matter, it doesn't	གའི་བྱེད་ཀྱི་མ་རེད།
mattress (square, flat)	འབོལ་གདན།
maximum, most	མང་ཤོས།
May	ཕྱི་ཟླ་ལྔ་པ།
meal, food	ཁ་ལག ཞལ་ལག H
meal, food	གསོལ་ཚིགས། H
meaning	དོན་དག
means, method	ཐབས་ཤེས།
measure	ཚད།
measure, to	ཚད་ + རྒྱག
meat	ཤ། གསོལ་ཀྱུམ། H
mechanic	འཕྲུལ་ཆས་བཟོ་པ།
Medicine Buddha	སངས་རྒྱས་སྨན་བླ།
medicine, medical science	གསོ་བ་རིག་པ།
medicine, medication	སྨན། གསོལ་སྨན། H
medium	འབྲིང་ བ།
meet, to	ཐུག མཇལ། H
meeting	ཚོགས་འདུ།
melody, tune	དབྱངས།
member, representative	འཐུས་མི།
memory	དྲན་པ།

merchant, businessman	ཚོང་པ།	
Mercury	ལྷག་པ།	
merit	བསོད་ནམས།	
message, answer	ལན། ཞུགས་ལན།	H
meter	སྨི་ཁྲི།	
method, way	ཐབས་ཤེས།	
midday, noon	ཉིན་གུང་།	
midnight	ནམ་ཕྱེད།	
milk	འོ་མ། ཆབ་འོ།	
million	ས་ཡ།	
mind, spirit	སེམས། ཐུགས།	H
mineral	གཏེར་ཁ།	
minimum, fewest	ཉུང་ཤོས།	
minister	བློན་པོ།	
minute	སྐར་མ།	
mirror	ཤེལ་སྒོ། མེ་ལོང་།	L
misfortune, unhappiness	རྐྱེན་ངན།	
mistaken, to be	ནོར།	
mix, be mixed, to	འདྲེས།	
mix, to	བཀྲེས། བསྲེས།	L
modern	དེང་རབས་ཀྱི།	
molasses	བུ་རམ།	
momo, Tibetan ravioli	མོག་མོག བཞེས་མོག	H
Mön (tribe)	མོན་པ།	
monastery	དགོན་པ།	
monastic dance	འཆམས།	
Monday	གཟའ་ཟླ་བ།	
Mongol	སོག་པོ།	
Mongolia	སོག་ཡུལ།	
monk	གྲྭ་པ། དགེ་འདུན་པ།	H
monkey, ape	སྤེའུ། སྤྲེའུ།	L
Mönlam, Great Prayer	སྨོན་ལམ་ཆེན་མོ།	
month (international)	ཕྱི་ཟླ།	
month (lunar)	བོད་ཟླ།	
month, beginning of	ཟླ་འགོ།	
month	ཟླ་བ།	
moon	ཟླ་བ།	
moreover, furthermore	ད་དུང་།	

morning	ཞོགས་ཀས། ཞོགས་པ།	L
morning, this	ད་རང་།	
mosquito	དུག་སྦང་། དུག་སྦྲང་།	L
mother	ཨ་མ། ཨ་མ་ལགས།	H
mother (of someone else)	ཡུམ།	H
motorcycle	སྟག་སྟག	
mountain sickness	ལ་དུག	
mountain, hill	རི།	
mountain, sacred	གནས་རི།	
mouse, rat	ཙི་ཙི།	
moustache	ཨ་ར།	
mouth	ཁ། ཞལ།	H
move house, to	ཁང་པ་ + སྤོ། 1 སྤོས།	2,3
move, to	འགུལ་སྐྱོད་ + བྱེད།	
moved, to be	སེམས་འགུལ་ཐེབས།	
movie	གློག་བརྙན།	
movie theater	གློག་བརྙན་ཁང་།	
moxibustion	མེ་བཙའ།	
mule	དྲེལ།	
museum	འགྲེམས་སྟོན་ཁང་།	
mushroom	ཤ་མོ།	
music	རོལ་མོ།	
musician	རོལ་ཆ་བཏང་མཁན།	
musk deer	གླ་བ།	
Muslim	ཁ་ཆེ།	
mute, dumb	ལྐུགས་པ།	
mutton	ལུག་ཤ།	

N

naga, serpent-spirit	ཀླུ།	
naked, nude	དམར་ཧྲེང་བ།	
name	མིང་། མཚན།	H
narrow	དོག་པོ།	
national	རྒྱལ་ཡོངས།	
nationality	མི་རིགས།	
native land	ཕ་ཡུལ།	
naturally	རང་བཞིན་གྱིས།	
nature	རང་འབྱུང་ཁམས།	
near	འཁྲིས་ལ།	

near, by	འགྲམ།
near, close	ཐག་ཉེ་པོ།
necessity	དགོས་ མཁོ །
need, to	དགོས།
needle	ཁབ།
neighbour	ཁྱིམ་མཚེས།
neighbourhood, proximity	ཉེ་འདབས།
Nepal	བལ་ཡུལ།
Nepalese	བལ་པོ།
nephew, grandson	ཚ་པོ། སྐུ་ཚ། H
nervous	ཚ་གི་ཚི་གི
net	དྲ་བ།
never, not at all	ཁྱོན་ནས།
New Year	ལོ་གསར།
new	གསར་པ།
news	གསར་འགྱུར།
next	རྗེས་མ།
next, following	རྗེས་མར།
Ngari	མངའ་རིས།
niece, granddaughter	ཚ་མོ། སྐུ་ཚ། H
night	མཚན་མོ།
nine	དགུ
nineteen	བཅུ་དགུ
ninety	དགུ་བཅུ།
noble	འཕགས་པ།
noise	སྐད་ཅོར།
nomad (male)	ཨ་པོ།
nomad, herder, drogpa	འབྲོག་པ།
nomad-farmer	ས་མ་འབྲོག
noodles, noodle soup	ཐུག་པ། བཞེས་ཐུག H
noon, midday	ཉིན་གུང་།
Norbu lingkha	ནོར་བུ་གླིང་ཀ
north	བྱང་།
northern	བྱང་ཕྱོགས།
nose	སྣ་གུག ཤངས། H
not at all	ཁྱོན་ནས།
not bad!	ཨོ་ཙ། ཨའུ་ཙམ། L
nothing	གའི། གང་ཡང་། L
notice, to	དོ་སྣང་བྱུང་།
November	ཕྱི་ཟླ་བཅུ་གཅིག་པ།
novice monk	ཨིན་ཆུང་།
now	ད་ལྟ།
now, so then	ད།
nowadays	དེང་ སང་ །
number	གྲངས་ཀ།
number (of people)	ཁ་གྲངས། ཞལ་གྲངས། H
number one, champion	ཨང་དང་པོ།
number	ཨང་གི
numerous	མང་པོ།
nun	ཨ་ནི། རྗེ་བཙུན་མ། H
nurse	ནད་གཡོག
Nyingmapa (sect)	རྙིང་མ་པ།

O

obey, to	ཁ་ལ་ཉན།
object, thing	དངོས་པོ། ཅ་ ལག
obstacle, obstruction	བར་ཆད།
obtain, acquire	རག ཐོབ།
occasion, opportunity	གོ་སྐབས།
occupation	འབྲེལ་བ།
ocean	རྒྱ་མཚོ།
October	ཕྱི་ཟླ་བཅུ་པ།
offer, give, to	སྤྲད། ཕུལ། h གནང་། H
offering	མཆོད་པ།
offering, item of	མཆོད་རྫས།
offerings, to make	མཆོད་པ་ + འབུལ། h
office, bureau	ལས་ཁུངས།
official, civil servant	ལས་བྱེད་པ།
often	ཡང་སེ།
Oh no! What a shame!	ཨ་ཙི།
oil, petrol, gasoline	སྣུམ། གཟིམ་སྣུམ། H
old (object)	རྙིང་པ།
old, elderly	རྒན་འཁོགས། བགྲེས་སྐྱོང།H
on foot	རྐང་ཐང་།
on the occasion	དེའི་ཞོར་ལ།
on, on top of	སྟེང་།

one	གཅིག
oneself	རང་།
only, solely	ཤ་སྟག
open (door), to	སྒོ་ཕྱེ། གཟིམ་སྒོ་ + ཕྱེ། H
open (objects), to	ཁ་ཕྱེ། ཞལ་ཕྱེ། H
operatic piece	འཁྲབ་གཞུང་།
operation, to undergo	གཤག་གཅོད་ + བྱེད།
opinion	བསམ་ཚུལ།
opponent, adversary	ཁ་གཏད།
opposite	ཕྱོག་ཕྱོགས།
or	ཡང་ན། འམ། l
orange	ཚ་ལུ་མ།
order, command, to	བཀའ་ + བཏང་།
order, to	བཀའ་མངགས་ + གནང་། H
order, to	མངགས།
ordinary	དཀྱུས་མ།
order, command	བཀའ།
organisation	སྒྲིག་འཛུགས།
origin	འབྱུང་ཁུངས།
ornament, jewel	རྒྱན་ཆ།
other	གཞན་དག
otherwise	མ་གཏོགས།
otter	སྲམ།
Ouch, that's cold!	ཨ་ཅུ།
Ouch, that's hot!	ཨ་ཚ།
outside	ཕྱི་ ཕོགས།
oven (electric)	གློག་ཐབ།
Ow! Ouch!	ཨ་རེ།
owner	བདག་པོ།

P

packet, package	འཐུམ་སྒྲིལ།
Padmasambhava	གུ་རུ་རིན་པོ་ཆེ།
page	ཤོག་ལྷེ།
paint a thangka, to	ལྷ་བྲིས་པ།
paint, to	ཚོན་ + བཏང་།
pair	ཆ།
Pakistan	པ་ཀི་སི་ཏན།
palace	ཕོ་བྲང་།
panda	བྱི་ལ་དོམ།
pane of glass	ཤེལ་སྒོ།
pants, trousers	གོས་ཐུང་།
paper	ཤོག་གུ ཕྱག་ཤོག H
paralysed, to be	གཟའ་ + རྒྱག
parasol, umbrella	ཉི་གདུགས།
pardon, forgiveness	དགོངས་དག
parent	ཕ་མ། ཡབ་ཡུམ། h
park	གླིང་ག བཞུགས་གླིང་། H
part	ཆ་ཤས།
particularly	ལྷག་པར་དུ། ཁྱད་པར་དུ།
party (political)	ཏང་།
pass (mountain)	ལ།
passport	ལག་ཁྱེར། ཕྱག་ཁྱེར། H
past	འདས་པ།
pastry, fried	ཁ་ཟས། ཞལ་ཟས། H
pasture, alpine meadow	སྤང་རི།
patience	བཟོད་པ།
patient (to be)	བཟོད་པ་ + སྒོམ།
paw	རྐང་པ།
pay a salary, to	ཕོགས་ + རྒྱག
peace	ཞི་བདེ།
peaceful, tranquil	ཁུ་སིམ་པོ།
peach	ཁམ་བུ། བཞེས་ཁམ། H
peacock	རྨ་བྱ།
pear	ལི།
Peking	པེ་ཅིང་།
pelt, leather coat	པགས་ཚག
pen	སྨྱུ་གུ ཕྱག་སྨྱུག H
people, populace, popular	མི་དམངས།
pepper, capsicum	སེ་ལོ་སྔོན་པོ།
perfect	ཡང་དག་པ།
perfume	ཆུ་དྲི་ཞིམ།
perhaps, maybe	གཅིག་བྱས་ན།
period	དུས་སྐབས།
permission, authority	ཆོག་ཐང་།

permit, allow, to	ཆོག
permit, authorisation	ཆོག་མཆན།
permit, passport	ལག་ཁྱེར། ཕྱག་ཁྱེར། H
Persia, Iran	ཏ་ཟིག
person, human	མི།
person, people, man	མི།
petrol, gasoline	སྣུམ།
pharmacy	སྨན་ཚོང་ཁང་།
photo	པར། སྐུ་པར། H
photograph, to	པར་ + རྒྱག
physics	དངོས་ཁམས་རིག་པ།
pica (tailless mouse-hare)	ཨ་བྲ།
pick, gather, to	བཏོག།
picnic, to	གླིང་ག་ + བཏང་།
piece	དུམ་བུ།
pig	ཕག་ པ།
pile up, to	བརྩིགས།
pilgrim	གནས་སྐོར་བ།
pilgrimage	གནས་མཇལ། ཆོས་མཇལ།
pill	རིལ་བུ།
pillar	ཀ་བ།
pillow	སྔས་མགོ།
pine	ཐང་ཤིང་།
pipe	གང་ཟག
place	ས་ཆ།
place, leave, put, to	བཞག
place, seat, habitation	བསྡད་ས། བཞུགས་ས། H
plan, scheme	འཆར་གཞི།
planet	གཟའ།
plant	རྩི་ཤིང་།
plant, insert, begin, to	བཙུགས།
plant, medicinal	རྩ་སྨན།
plant, to	བཏབ།
plastic (elastic)	འཁྱིག
plastic (hard)	སྲོས་དཀར།
plate	ཐ་པག སྡེར་ཙེ།
play ballgames, to	སྦོ་ལོ་ + རྒྱག
play dice, to	ཤོ་ + རྒྱག

play, have fun, to	རྩེད་མོ་ + རྩེ།
pleasant	སྐྱིད་པོ། སྤྲོ་པོ། H
please	སྐུ་མཁྱེན།
please, like, to	དགའ་པོ་ + ཡོད། / འདུག
pocket (of clothing)	པ་ཀིར།
pocket of chuba	ཨམ་ཕག ཨམ་ཕྲག L
poetry	སྙན་ ངག
point of view	ལྟ་སྟངས།
police	པུ་ལི་སི།
politics	ཆབ་སྲིད། སྲིད་ཇུས།
poor	སྐྱོ་པོ།
population	མི་འབོར།
pork	ཕག་ཤ།
port, harbour	གྲུ་ཁའི་གྲོང་ཁྱེར།
possible, to be	སྲིད། ཐུབ།
post office	སྦྲག་ ཁང་ །
post, pillar	ཀ་བ།
postman	སྦྲག་པ།
pot	ཁོག་མ།
Potala	པོ་ཏ་ལ། རྩེ་པོ་བྲང་།
potato	ཞོག་ཁོག བཞེས་ཞོག H
pound, 500 g	རྒྱ་མ།
pour, put, to	ལྡུག
power	ནུས་པ།
power, might	དབང་ཆ།
practise, apply, to	ལག་ལེན་ + བྱེད།
practise, to	སྦྱོང་བརྡར་ + བྱེད།
practise, to	ཉམས་ལེན་ + བྱེད།
pray, to	ཁ་འདོན་ + བྱེད།
pray, to	སྨོན་ལམ་ + རྒྱག
prayer flag	དར་ལྕོག།
precious	རིན་ཆེན།
Precious One (title)	རིན་པོ་ཆེ།
precise	ཞིབ་ཕྲ།
prefer, to	དགའ་ བ་ + ཡོད། / འདུག
pregnant, to be	གཟུགས་པོ་ + འདུག
prepare, to	གྲ་སྒྲིག་ + བྱེད་།
president	སྲིད་འཛིན།

press, to — མནན།
pretty, sweet, cute — སྙིང་རྗེ་པོ།
prevent, prohibit, to — V+རྒྱུ་མ་བཅུག
price — གོང་།
pride — སྤོབས་པ།
pride, arrogance — ང་རྒྱལ།
priest, tantric — སྔགས་པ།
principal — གཙོ་བོ།
printing press — པར་ཁང་།
prison — བཙོན་ཁང་།
prisoner — བཙོན་པ།
private — སྒེར།
problem — རྙོག་དྲ།
procession — སེར་སྦྲང་། སེར་ཕྲེང་། L
produce, to — ཐོན།
profit — ཁེ་བཟང་།
progress, development — ཡར་རྒྱས།
promise, acceptance — ཁས་ལེན། ཞལ་བཞེས། H
promise, to — དམ་བཅའ་ + བཞག
proof — ར་སྤྲོད།
protest, to — ངོ་རྒོལ་ + བྱེད།
proud, arrogant — ང་རྒྱལ་ཆེ་པོ།
prove, to — ར་སྤྲོད་ + བྱེད།
proverb — གཏམ་དཔེ།
province — ཞིང་ཆེན།
psychology — སེམས་ཁམས་རིག་པ།
public — མི་དམངས།
publicity — ཁྱབ་བསྒྲགས།
pull, draw, drag — འཐེན།
pulse — རྩ། ཕྱག་རྩ། H
punish, to — ཉེས་འཐག་ + བཏང་།
pure — གཙང་མ།
purse — སྤ་ཁུག
push, to — སྤུད་རྒྱག་ + བཏང་།
put out (a fire), to — མེ་བསད།
put, place, leave, to — བཞག

Q

quality, excellence — ཡོན་ཏན།
quantity, amount — མང་ཉུང་།
question — དྲི་བ། བཀའ་འདྲི། H
queue, line — འབང་འགྲིག
འབྲང་འགྲིག L

R

rabbit — རི་གོང་། རི་བོང་། L
race, human race, tribe — མི་རིགས།
radiator — ཚ་སྒྲོག
radio — རླུང་འཕྲིན།
radish — ལ་ཕུག
radish, pink sour — སོན་ལ་ཕུག
rain — ཆར་པ།
rain, to — ཆར་པ་ + བཏང་།
rainbow — འཇའ།
raincoat — ཆར་ཐི།
raise, incite, to — བསླང་།
raisin — རྒུན་འབྲུམ།
range of mountains — རི་རྒྱུད།
rank — རིམ་པ།
rare — དཀོན་པོ།
rat, mouse — ཙི་ཙི།
read (aloud) — ཀློག
ཞྭགས་ཀློག་གནང་། H
read, to — གཟིགས། H
read, to — ལྟ། 1 བལྟས 2 ལྟོས། 3
ready, to be — ཆོག་ཆོག་རེད།
ready, to get, to make — གྲ་སྒྲིག་ + བྱེད།
real — ངོ་མ། མངོན་སུམ།
reason, cause — རྒྱུ་མཚན།
receipt — བྱུང་འཛིན།
receive, get , to — འཁྱོར།
receive, lodge, to — སྣེ་ལེན་ + ཞུ།
recently — ཁ་ས་ཁ་ཉིན།
recently — ཉེ་ཆར།
reception, banquet, party — ཐུགས་སྤྲོ།
recognise, identify — ངོས་འཛིན་ + བྱེད།

red	དམར་པོ།
reflect, think	བསམ་བློ་ + བཏང་།
reflect, think	དགོངས་པ་ + བཞེས། H
reflection, image	གཟུགས་བརྙན།
reform	བསྒྱུར་བཅོས།
refrigerator	འཁྱག་སྒམ།
refugee	སྐྱབས་བཅོལ་བ།
refuse, to	ཁས་ + མ་བླང་།
regent	སྡེ་སྲིད།
region	ས་ཁུལ།
register, catalogue	དཀར་ཆག
regret, to feel	འགྱོད་པ་ + སྐྱེ།
regret, to feel	ཐུགས་འགྱོད་ + གནང་། H
regular	འཆར་ཅན།
relationship, connection	འབྲེལ་བ།
relaxed, calm	ཀློད་ཀློད།
religion	ཆོས་ལུགས།
remain, stay, to	བཞུགས། H
remain, stay, to	བསྡད། 1, 2 སྡོད། 3
remember, recall, to	དྲན།
remind someone, of sth., to	དྲན་གསོ་ + བཏང་།
remove, take off, to	ཕིད། ཕུད། L
renovate, restore, to	བསྐྱར་བཞེངས་ + གནང་།
rent (on house)	ཁང་གླ།
rent, to	གླ།
repeat, say again, to	ཡང་བསྐྱར་བཤད།
replace, to	ཚབ་བྱེད།
	སྐུ་ཚབ་གནང་། H
reply, answer, to	ལན་ + རྒྱག
reply, answer, to	ཞུགས་ལན་ + བསྐྱོན། H
represent, mean, to	རྟགས་མཚོན།
reprimand, chide, to	བཀའ་ + བཀྱོན། H
reprimand, chide, to	གཤེ་གཤེ་ + བཏང་།
republic	སྤྱི་མཐུན་རྒྱལ་ཁབ།
research	ཞིབ་འཇུག
research, to do	ཞིབ་འཇུག་ + བྱེད།
resemble, to	འདྲ་པོ་རེད།

reservoir	ཆུ་རྫིང་།
respect	གུས་ཞབས།
respect, to	གུས་ཞབས་ + བྱེད།
responsibility	ལས་འགན།
rest	ངལ་གསོ།
rest, to	ངལ་གསོ་ + རྒྱག
restaurant	ཟ་ཁང་།
restore, renovate, to	ཉམས་གསོ་ + བྱེད།
result	གྲུབ་འབྲས། འབྲས་བུ།
return, give back, to	ཕར་བསློགས།
	ཚུར་བསློགས།
revenge, to take	དགྲ་ཤ་ + ལེན།
Reverence, Your; Sir	སྐུ་ཞོག H སྐུ་ཞབས། LH
revolt, rebel, to	ངོ་ལོག་ + རྒྱག
revolution	གསར་བརྗེ།
rheumatism, arthritis	གྲུམ་བུའི་ན་ཚ།
rice	འབྲས། ཞེས་འབྲས། H
rich	ཕྱུག་པོ། རྫིག་པོ།
rickshaw	རིག་ཤོག
ride (horse, bike, etc.), to	ཞོན།
right, correct	ཏག་ཏག
right, right-hand	གཡས།
Rinpoche, Precious One	རིན་པོ་ཆེ།
rise, appear, to	ཤར།
river	གཙང་པོ།
road, way, route	ལམ་ཁག ལམ། L
roast, grill, to	བཀྲུགས། བསྲེགས། L
robbed, to be	རྐུ་མ་ + ཤོར།
roof	ཐོག་ཀ།
room (in a house)	ཁང་མིག
room, chamber	ཁང་པ། གཟིམ་ཁང་། H
rosehip	སེ་འབྲུ།
rot, decay	རུལ།
rough, brutal	རྩམ་པ་ཚ་པོ།
round	སྒོར་སྒོར།
row	གྲལ།
rug (for mattresses)	ཁ་གདན།
rug	གདན། བཞུགས་གདན། H

run out, to; to finish	རྫོགས།
run, race, to	རྒྱུག་ཤར་ + སློད།
run, to	རྒྱུག
Russia, Russian	ཨུ་རུ་སུ།

S

sacred	ཙ་ཆེན་པོ།
sad	སེམས་སྐྱོ་པོ།
sailor	གྲུ་གཟིངས་ལས་མི།
Sakyapa (sect)	ས་སྐྱ་པ།
salary	ཕོགས།
salary, to pay	ཕོགས་ + རྒྱག
salt	ཚྭ།
salty	ཚྭ་ཁ།
same way, in the	ད་ག་ནང་བཞིན།
same	གཅིག་པ།
samsara, cycle	འཁོར་བ།
sanctuary, shrine, temple	ལྷ་ཁང་།
sangha	དགེ་འདུན།
satellite	སྲུང་སྐར།
satisfied	འདོད་པ་ + ཁངས / ཁེངས། L
Saturday	གཟའ་སྤེན་པ།
Saturn	སྤེན་པ།
save life, to	སྲོག་བསྐྱབས།
say, to	གསུངས། H
say, to	ལབ།
scholar	མཁས་པ།
school	སླབ་གྲྭ སློབ་གྲྭ L
school (primary)	སློབ་གྲྭ་ཆུང་ཆུང་།
school (secondary)	སློབ་གྲྭ་འབྲིང་བ།
science	ཚན་རིག
scientist	ཚན་རིག་པ།
scorpion	སྡིག་པ་ར་ཙ།
sculptor	ལྷ་བཟོ་བ།
sea: *see ocean*	
seal, sign	རྒྱ།
season	ནམ་དུས།
second (of a series)	གཉིས་པ།
second (time)	སྐར་ཆ།
secret, hidden	གསང་བ།
secretary	དྲུང་ཡིག
security	བདེ་འཇགས། ཉེན་སྲུང་།
see you later	རྗེས་མར་མཇལ་ཡོང་།
see, to	མཐོང་། གཟིགས། H
self	རང་།
selfishness	བདག་ འཛིན།
sell, to	འཚོང་། 1 བཙོང་། 2,3
send, to	བཏང་།
sentence	ཚིག་གྲུབ།
separate (oneself), to	ཁག་ཁག་ + བྱེད།
separate, to	ཁག་ཁག་ + བཟོ།
September	སྤྱི་ཟླ་དགུ་པ།
Sera (monastery)	སེ་ར།
servant	གཡོག་པོ། ཞབས་ཕྱི། H
set fire, to	མེ་རྒྱག
seven	བདུན།
seventeen	བཅུ་བདུན།
seventy	བདུན་ཅུ།
several	ཁ་ཤས།
sew, to	ཕྱག་ཚེམ་ + བསྐྱོན། H
sew, to	ཚེམ་བུ་ + རྒྱག
shadow	གྲིབ་ནག
shame	ངོ་ཚ།
shape	དབྱིབས།
share, to	བགོ་བཤའ་རྒྱག
sharp	རྣོ་པོ།
shave, to	བཞར།
she	མོ།
sheep	ལུག
sheepskin	པགས་ཚགས།
sheet, bedding	ཉལ་ཆས།
shell	ཕྱི་ལྤགས།
shepherd	ལུག་རྫི།
shine, to (of the sun)	ཉི་མ་ + བསྟན།
shirt	སྟོད་ཐུང་། སྐུ་སྟོད། H

shiver, tremble, to	འདར།
shoe	འཛར་ཏ།
shoot arrows, to	མདའ་ + རྒྱག
shop, store	ཚོང་ཁང་།
shopping, to do	ཉོ་ཆ་ + རྒྱག
short (not tall)	གཟུགས་པོ་ཆུང་ཆུང་།
short	ཐུང་ཐུང་།
shout	སྐད་ + རྒྱག
show, performance	ལྟད་མོ། གཟིགས་མོ། H
show, to	བསྟན།
sick, to feel	སྐྱུག་མེར་ + ལང་།
side, direction	ཕྱོགས།
side, slope	ལྡེབས།
sign, indication	མཚོན་རྟགས།
sign, mark	རྟགས།
sign, to	ས་ཡིག་ + རྒྱག
signature	ས་ཡིག
Sikkim	འབྲས་ལྗོངས།
silent, stay to	ཁ་ཁར་བསྡད།
silk vest	འོག་འཇུག སྐུ་འཇུག H
silver	དངུལ། ཕྱག་དངུལ། H
similar	འདྲ་པོ།
simple, convenient	སྟབས་བདེ་པོ།
since	ནས་བཟུང་།
sing (a *lu*), to	གླུ་ + ལེན།
sing, to	གཞས་ + བཏང་།
sister (elder)	ཨ་ལྕག།
sister (younger)	འོག་མ། ཨོ་ལགས། H
sit down, please	བཞུགས་་་
	གདན་འཛགས། HH
sit, to	མར་བཞུགས། H
sit, to	མར་བསྡད།
situation, information	གནས་ཚུལ།
six	དྲུག
sixteen	བཅུ་དྲུག
sixty	དྲུག་ཅུ།
skillful	མཁས་ པོ།
skin, hide	པགས་པ།
skirt	སྨད་གཡོགས།
sleep, lie down, to	ཉལ། གཟིམ། H
sleep, to put to	བསྙལ།
sleeve	ཕུ་དུང་།
slide, slip	འདྲེད་རྡར་ + ཤོར།
slim, thin	ཤ་སྐམ་པོ།
slingshot	ཨུར་རྡོ།
slow	ག་ལེ་ག་ལེ།
slowly, gently	ག་ ལེ་ ག་ ལེ།
small	ཆུང་ཆུང་།
smell	དྲི་མ།
smile, to	ཁ་ཚེག་ཚེག་ + བྱེད།
smile, to	འཛུམ་དམུལ་དམུལ་ + བྱེད།
smoke	དུ་བ།
smoke, to	ཐ་མག་ + འཐེན།
snake	སྦྲུལ།
snow	གངས།
snow, to	གངས་ + བཏང་།
so, and so	བྱས་ན།
so, well	འོ་ན།
so? and then?	ཨ་ནི། དེ་ནས། L
soap	ཡི་རྩི།
socialism	སྤྱི་ཚོགས་རིང་ལུགས།
society	སྤྱི་ཚོགས།
soft	སོབ་སོབ།
soldier	དམག་མི།
solitary	གཅིག་པུ། སྐུ་རྐྱང་། H
some, several	ཁ་ཤས།
someone	ཅིག
something	ཅིག
sometimes	མཚམས་མཚམས།
son, boy	བུ། སྲས། H
sort, kind	ཁག སྣེ་ཁ།
sound	སྒྲ།
soup with noodles	ཐུག་པ།
soup, based on chang	བསྐོལ་ལྡན།
sour	སྐྱུར་མོ།
south	ལྷོ།

south, southern	ལྷོ་ཕྱོགས།
sow	བཏབ།
Spain, Spanish	སེ་པན།
speak, to	ལབ།
special	དམིགས་བསལ།
speech, talk	སྐད་ཆ། བཀའ་མོལ། H
spelling	དག་ཆ།
spicy, hot	ཁ་ཚ་པོ། ཞལ་ཚ་པོ། H
spider	སྡོམ།
spoiled, to be	ཉམས།
sponsor, patron	སྦྱིན་བདག
spoon	ཐུར་མ།
sport	ལུས་རྩལ།
spouse, husband, wife	ཟླ་པོ། སྐུ་ཟླ། H
spread, be spread, to	དར།
spring	དཔྱིད་ཀ།
spy	སོ་པ།
square	གྲུ་བཞི།
stadium	ལུས་རྩལ་ཐང་།
staff, stick	བེར་ཀ
stage a show, to	གཟིགས་འབུལ་ + ཞུས། h
stamp, postal	སྦྲག་འཛིན།
standard, level	ཆུ་ཚད།
star	སྐར་མ།
State, country	རྒྱལ་ཁབ།
station	འབབ་ ཚུགས།
statue	སྐུ་འདྲ།
steal, to	རྐུ་མ་ + རྐུ།
step, pace	གོམ་པ།
stew	ཤ་འབྲས།
stick, to	སྦྱར།
still, further	ད་དུང་།
sting, bite, to	སོ་ + རྒྱག
stomach	གྲོད་ཁོག གསོལ་གྲོད། H
stone, rock	རྡོ།
stop, be blocked, to	འགག
stop, block, to	བཀག
storm	ཐོག་ + རྒྱག
story, tale	སྒྲུང་།
stove, hearth	ཐབ།
straight, direct	ཤར་རྒྱག ཐད་ཀར།
strange, bizarre	ཁྱད་མཚར་པོ།
strange, curious	ཁྱད་མཚར་པོ།
stream, brook	ཆུ།
street, alley	སྲང་ལམ།
strength	སྟོབས། ཤུགས།
stroke, caress, to	ཕུར་ཕུར་ + བྱེད།
stroke, cerebral hemorrhage	གྲིབ།
stroll, walk	འཆམ་འཆམ།
strong	ཤུགས་ཆེན་པོ།
student, pupil	སླབ་གྲྭ་བ། སློབ་གྲྭ་བ། L
student, pupil	སློབ་མ། སློབ་ཕྲུག
study, to	སློབ་སྦྱོང་ + བྱེད།
stūpa	མཆོད་རྟེན།
stupid, dumb	གླུགས་པ།
such, thus, like this	འདི་འདྲས།
suddenly	གློ་བུར་ དུ།
suffering	སྡུག་བསྔལ།
suffice, to	ལྡང་།
suicide, to commit	རང་ཤི་ + རྒྱག
suitcase	ཀོ་སྒམ།
summarize, to	མདོར་བསྡུས།
summer	དབྱར་ཀ
summer camp	དབྱར་ས།
summit, peak	རྩེ།
sun	ཉི་མ།
Sunday	གཟའ་ཉི་མ།
superb, magnificent	སྙེར་བཟོ་དོད་པོ།
superior, preceding	གོང་མ།
support, base	རྟེན།
sure	གཏན་གཏན།
surface	ཁ།
surroundings	ཉེ་སྐོར།
suspect, doubt, to	དོགས་པ་ + ཟ།
suspicion, doubt	དོགས་པ།
sutra	མདོ།

swallow, to	མིད།	
swear, vow, to	མནའ་སྐྱེལ།	
sweat	རྔུལ་ནག	
sweep, to	གད་ + རྒྱག	
sweet	མངར་མོ།	
sweet, candy	བྱི་རིལ།	
swim, to	ཆུ་རྐྱལ་ + རྒྱག	
Switzerland, Swiss	སུད་སི།	
symbol	རྟགས། མཚོན་རྟགས།	
system	ལམ་ལུགས།	
	འགྲོ་ལུགས།	

T

table	ཅོག་ཙེ། གསོལ་ཅོག	H
tail	རྔ་མ། གཞུག་གུ	
take away, to	ཕར་ཁྱེར།	
take out, remove, to	བཏོན།	
take part, to	གཞུགས།	
take, take away, to	ཁྱེར། བསྣམས།	H
take, to	ལེན། བཞེས།	H
tall	གཟུགས་པོ་རིང་པོ།	
tantra	རྒྱུད།	
tantric priest	སྔགས་པ།	
tape recorder	སྒྲ་ཕབ་འཁོར་ལོ།	
target	འབེན།	
taste, savour	བྲོ་བ། ཞྫགས་བྲོ།	H
taste, to	བྲོ་ བ་ལྟ།	
taste, try	མྱོང་།	
tax	ཁྲལ།	
taxi	གླ་བྱེད་མོ་ཊ།	
tea	ཇ། གསོལ་ཇ།	H
tea (plain)	ཇ་ཐང་།	
tea (sweet milky)	ཇ་མངར་མོ།	
tea (Tibetan)	བོད་ཇ། ཇ་སྲུབ་མ།	
teach, to	བསླབས།	
teacher	དགེ་རྒན། རྒན་ལགས།	H
teacher, guide	སྟོན་པ།	
teacher, master	དགེ་རྒན། རྒན་ལགས།	H
team	རུ་ཁག	
teapot, kettle	ཁོག་ཧྲིར།	
tear, to	དྲལ།	
tease, joke, to	འཕྱ་ལས་རྒྱག	
teashop, café	ཇ་ཁང་།	
technology	ལག་རྩལ།	
telegram	ཏར།	
telephone	ཁ་པར། ཞལ་པར།	H
telephone, to	ཁ་པར་ + བཏང་།	
telephone, to	ཞལ་པར་ + གནང་།	H
telephone, to	ཞལ་པར་ + ཕུལ།	h
television	བརྙན་འཕྲིན།	
temperature	ཚ་གྲང་།	
temple, to visit a	མཆོད་མཇལ་ལ་ཕེབས།	
ten	བཅུ།	
ten million	བྱེ་བ།	
ten thousand	ཁྲི།	
tend, treat, to	སྨན་བཅོས་ + བྱེད།	
tense, tight	དམ་པོ།	
tent (cotton)	གུར།	
tent (yak hair)	སྦ་གུར། སྦྲ་གུར།	L
tent, to pitch	གུར་ + རྒྱག	
tepid, warm	དྲོད་འཇམ།	
thank you	ཐུགས་རྗེ་ཆེ།	
thank, to	ཐུགས་རྗེ་ཆེ་ + ཞུ།	
that (one) over there	ཕ་ག	
that	དེ།	
theatre (hall)	ཟློས་གར་ཁང་།	
theatre, drama	ཟློས་གར།	
theory	ལྟ་བ།	
there is, there are, to have	འདུག ཡོད་རེད།	
there, around here, thereabouts	འདོ་པར། འདི་པར།	H
therefore	བྱས་ ཙང་།	
thermos, vacuum flask	ཇ་དམ།	
these	འདི་ཚོ།	
these days	དེང་སང་།	
they	ཁོ་རང་ཚོ།	
they	ཁོང་ཚོ།	H
thick	མཐུག་པོ།	

thick (cylindrical object)	སྦོམ་པོ།
thief, robber	རྐུ་མ་ རྐུན་མ། L
Thimphu	ཐིམ་ཕུ།
thin (cylindrical object)	ཕ་པོ། ཕྲ་པོ། L
thin, fine (cloth),	ཀྲབ་པོ། སྲབ་པོ། L
thin, slim	སྐམ་པོ།
thin, weak (liquids)	སླ་པོ།
thing, belongings	ཅ་ལག སྐུ་ཆས། H
think, reflect, to	བསམ་བློ་ + བཏང་།
think, reflect, to	དགོངས་པ་ + བཞེས། H
think, to	བསམས།
thirsty, to be	ཁ་སྐོམ། ཞལ་སྐོམ། H
thirteen	བཅུ་གསུམ།
thirty	སུམ་ཅུ།
this	འདི།
those (over there)	ཕ་ཚོ།
those two	ཁོང་གཉིས།
those	དེ་ཚོ།
thought, idea	བསམ་བློ། དགོངས་པ། H
thousand	སྟོང་ཕྲག
thread	སྐུད་པ།
threaten	སྡིགས་ར་སྐུལ།
three days's time, in	གཞེས་ཉིན།
three	གསུམ།
threshold, hearth	ཐེམ་པ།
throat	མིད་པ།
throne	ཁྲི། བཞུགས་ཁྲི། H
throw, to	གཡུགས།
thumb	མཐེ་བོ།
thunder, to sound	འབྲུག་སྐད་ + རྒྱག
Thursday	གཟའ་ཕུར་བུ།
Tibet	བོད།
Tibetan	བོད་པ།
Tibetan race	བོད་རིགས།
Tibetan spoken language	བོད་སྐད།
Tibetan written language	བོད་ཡིག
ticket	ཐ་སེ།
tidy up, to	བསྡུ་གསོག་ + རྒྱག

tie up, to	བསྡམ།
tie, attach, to	བཏགས།
tiger	སྟག
time	དུས་ཚོད།
time (to), to be	རན།
time, occasion	ཐེངས་མ།
time, this	ད་རེས།
time, to have	ལོང་།
tired, to be	དཀའ་ལས་ཁག
tired, to be	སྐུ་ལས་ཁག H
tired, worn out, to be	ཐང་ཆད།
tired, worn out, to be	སྐུ་ཐང་མཉེལ། H
to, of, before (time)	ཟིན་པར
tobacco	ཐ་མག བཞེས་ཐག
today	དེ་རིང་།
together	མཉམ་དུ།
toilet, lavatory	གསང་སྤྱོད།
	གཟིམ་སྤྱོད། H
tomato	ཊོ་མ་ཊོ།
tomb, grave	བང་སོ།
tomorrow evening	སང་དགོང་།
tomorrow morning	སང་ཞོགས།
tomorrow	སང་ཉིན།
tongue	ལྕེ། ལྗགས། H
too much	མང་དྲགས།
tool	ལག་ཆ།
tooth	སོ། ཚེམས། H
torma	གཏོར་མ།
torn, to be	རལ།
total	ཁྱོན་བསྡོམས།
touch (accidentally), to	ལག་པ་ + ཐུག
touch, to	ལག་པ་ + འཆངས།
tourism	ཡུལ་སྐོར་སྤྲོ་འཆམ།
tourism, to do	ལྟ་སྐོར་ལ་འགྲོ།
towel	ཨ་ཅོར། ཞལ་ཅོར། H
town	གྲོང་ཁྱེར།
traces, remains	ཤུལ།
tradition, custom	ལུགས་སྲོལ།

trail	ས་ཤུར།
trail, route	ལམ་ཁག ལམ། L
train	རི་ལི། མེ་འཁོར། L
translate, to	སྐད་སྒྱུར་ + བྱེད།
translator, interpreter	སྐད་སྒྱུར། གསུང་སྒྱུར། H
transport	སྐྱེལ་འདྲེན།
transport, to	སྐྱེལ་འདྲེན་ + བྱེད།
travel, to	འགྲུལ་ + རྒྱག
traveller	འགྲུལ་པ།
treasurer	ཕྱག་མཛོད།
tree	ཤིང་སྡོང་།
triangle	ཟུར་གསུམ།
true, actual	ངོ་མ།
true, real	བདེན་པ། ངོ་མ།
truly	དངོས་གནས།
truly, actually	དངོས་འབྲེལ།
trunk, strongbox	ལྕགས་སྒམ།
truth	བདེན་པ།
try, to	ལྟ། གཟིགས། H
tsampa, flour of roast barley	རྩམ་པ། གསོལ་ཞིབ། H
tsän (local warrior-god)	བཙན།
Tsang	གཙང་།
Tuesday	གཟའ་མིག་དམར།
tune, melody	དབྱངས།
turn (sth.), to	སྐོར།
turn, circle, to	འཁོར།
turquoise	གཡུ།
twelve	བཅུ་གཉིས།
twenty	ཉི་ཤུ།
two	གཉིས།
type, kind	རིགས།
type, kind, sort	གྲས།
typewriter	ལྕགས་པར།

U

ugly	མདོག་ཉེས།
Uighur	ཡུ་གུར་རིགས།
umbrella	ཉི་གདུགས།
uncle (maternal)	ཨ་ཞང་།
uncle (paternal)	ཨ་ཁུ།
under, beneath	འོག
undergo, be caught, to	ཐེབས།
undershorts, underpants	ཧབ་པན།
understand, to	ཧ་གོ
understand, to	ཤེས། མཁྱེན། H
unintentional	ཀྲང་བཙུགས་མིན་པ།
unique, extraordinary	ཐུན་མོང་མ་ཡིན་པ།
university	སློབ་གྲྭ་ཆེན་མོ།
united	གཅིག་གྱུར།
up there	ཡ་གིར།
up to, until	བར་དུ།
upwards	ཡར།
urgent matter	བྲེལ་བ། ཐུགས་བྲེལ། H
urgent	ཛ་དྲག་ཆེན་པོ།
urinate	གཅིན་པ་+ བཏང་།
urine	གཅིན་པ།
use, to	བེད་སྤྱོད་ + བྱེད།
useful	ཕན་ཐོགས་ཡོད་པ།
usefulness	ཕན་ཐོགས།
usual(ly)	ཕྱིར་བཏང་།
usual(ly)	ནམ་ རྒྱུན།

V

vajra, dorje	རྡོ་རྗེ།
valley, lower part	ལུང་པའི་མདའ།
valley, upper part of	ལུང་པའི་ཕུ།
value	དགེ་མཚན།
variable	འགྱུར་བ་ཆེན་པོ།
various	འདྲ་མི་འདྲ།
various, diverse	སྣ་མིན་སྣ་ཚོགས།
vase	བུམ་པ།
vegetable	ཚལ། བཞེས་ཚལ། H
vegetable garden	ལྡུམ་ར།
vegetarian, to be	དཀར་སྐྱོང་ + བྱེད།
vein	ཁྲག་རྩ།
vendor, salesperson	ཚོང་མཁན།
Venerable (nun)	ཆོས་ལགས། H
Venus	པ་སངས།

very	ཞེ་དྲགས།
victory	རྒྱལ་ཁ།
village, countryside	གྲོང་གསེབ།
villager	གྲོང་གསེབ་པ།
viol (Tibetan)	པི་ཝང་།
violent	དྲག་པོ།
visit, to	ལྟ་སྐོར་ + བྱེད།
vocabulary, lexicon	ཐ་སྙད་གཏེར་མཛོད།
voice	སྐད། གསུང་སྐད། H
volume (book)	པོ་ཏི།
volunteer, to	དང་བླངས་ + བྱེད།
vomit, to	སྐྱུག་པ་ + ཤོར།
vote, to	འོས་ཤོག་ + བླུག
vulture	བྱ་རྒོད།

W

waist	སྐེད་པ། སྐུ་སྐེད། H
wait, to	སྒུག
	ཕེབས་སྒུག་གནང་། H
wake, to	གཉིད་སད།
walk, stroll	འཆམ་འཆམ།
walk, to	གོམ་པ་ + རྒྱག
walk, to take a	འཆམ་འཆམ་ལ་འགྲོ།
wall	རྩིག་པ།
walnut	སྟར་ཁ།
want, desire, to	འདོད།
war	དམག
war, to wage	དམག་ + རྒྱག
warm	དྲོད་འཇམ།
wash (oneself), to	ཁྲུས་ + རྒྱག
wash (oneself), to	ཞལ་ཁྲུས་ + གནང་། H
wash, to	འཁྲུ། 1 བཀྲུས། 2, 3
washing machine	ཁྲུས་སྒམ།
washing, laundry	དྲང་འཁྲུ། དྲེག་འཁྲུ། L
watch, clock	ཆུ་ཚོད། ཕྱག་ཚོད།
watchman, guard	སྒོ་སྲུང་།
water	ཆུ། ཆབ། H
water for offerings	ཡོན་ཆབ།
way, manner	ཚུལ།
we two	ང་གཉིས།
we	ང་ཚོ།
weak, feeble	གཟུགས་པོ་སྐྱོ་པོ།
wealth, economy	དཔལ་འབྱོར།
wealth, possessions	རྒྱུ་ཅ་ལག རྒྱུ་ནོར།
wealthy	འབྱོར་ལྡན།
weather, climate	གནམ་གཤིས།
Wednesday	གཟའ་ལྷག་པ།
week	བདུན་ཕྲག
weekend	གཟའ་འཛུག
weigh, to	ཡང་ལྗི་བཀྱུགས།
weight	ལྗིད་ཚད།
welcome!	ཕྱག་ཕེབས་གནང་བྱུང་།
welcome, to	དགའ་སུ་ + ཞུ
well, good	ཡག་པོ། བདེ་པོ།
well-mannered	ཡ་རབས།
west	ནུབ།
western	ནུབ་ཕྱོགས།
wet, damp	རློན་ པ།
what a pain! what a shame!	གང་དྲག
what kind of	ག་རེ་ག་རེ།
what, which	ག་རེ།
what?	ག་རེ། ག་གི།
wheat	གྲོ།
wheel	འཁོར་ལོ།
when, time	དུས།
when?	ག་དུས།
where from?	ག་ནས།
where?	ག་པར།
which?	ག་གི
white	དཀར་པོ།
who?	སུ།
whole, entire, complete	ཆ་ཚང་།
why	ག་རེ་ཡིན་ན།
	ག་རེ་བྱས་ནས།
wicked, bad	ངན་པ།
wide, spacious	གུ་ཡངས་པོ།
width, breadth	ཞེང་ག

wild ass རྐྱང་།
will, willpower སྙིང་རུས། འདོད་པ།
willow ལྕང་མ།
win, get, to ཐོབ།
wind ལྷགས་པ།
windhorse རླུང་རྟ།
window སྒེའུ་ཁུང་།
windy, to be ལྷགས་པ་ + རྒྱག
wine རྒུན་འབྲུམ་ཆང་།
winter དགུན་ཀ
winter camp དགུན་ས།
wipe, to ཕྱིས།
wish, longing འདོད་པ། ཐུགས་འདོད། H
with མཉམ་པོ། ལྷན་རྒྱས། H
withdraw, to འཁྲུམ་པ།
within ནང་།
without མེད་པར།
witness དཔང་པོ།
wolf སྤྱང་ཀི།
woman སྐྱེད་དམན།
wood ཤིང་།
wool བལ།
word ཚིག
work ལས་ཀ། ཕྱག་ལས། H
work, to ཕྱག་ལས་ + གནང་། H
work, to ལས་ཀ་ + བྱེད།
worker བཟོ་པ།
world (animate and inanimate) འཇིག་རྟེན།
world (geographic) འཛམ་གླིང་།
worry, anxiety སེམས་ཁྲལ།
ཐུགས་ཁྲལ། H
worry, to སེམས་ཁྲལ་ + བྱེད།
wound, injury རྨ།
write, to འབྲི། 1 བྲིས། 2, 3
writer རྩོམ་པ་པོ།

X

Xining ཟི་ལིང་།

Y

yak གཡག
yak meat ཚག་ཤ།
yak, wild འབྲོང་།
year ལོ།
year (international) སྤྱི་ལོ།
year, last ཟླ་ཉིན། ན་ཉིང་། L
year, next དུས་སང་།
year, this ད་ལོ།
yellow སེར་པོ།
yes རེད། འདུག
yesterday ཁའི་ས། ཁ་ས། L
yesterday evening མདང་དགོང་།
Yi [people] དབྱིས་རིགས།
yogurt ཞོ། གསོལ་ཞོ། H
you [sing.] ཁྱོད། རང་།
you [plur.] ཁྱོད་རང་ཚོ།
ཁྱེད་རང་ཚོ། H
you [plur.] ཁྱེད་རྣམ་ཚོ། HH
you [sing.] ཁྱེད་རང་། H
you two ཁྱེད་རང་གཉིས། H
young གཞོན་གཞོན།
Your Excellency སྐུ་ངོ་།
Yumbulagang ཡུམ་བུ་བླ་སྒང་།

Z

Zangskar ཟངས་དཀར།
zero ཀླད་ཀོར།
Zhikatse གཞིས་ཀ་རྩེ།
zi (ornament) གཟི།

Tibetan-English Glossary

བོད་དབྱིན་རྒྱན་མཁོའི་ཚིག་མཛོད་ཆུང་ངུ།

ཀ། Ka

ཀ་རྒྱུག	(n.) post, pole 31.2
ཀ་བ།	(n.) pillar
ཀ་སློན་སྤུག	(pr. n.) Kalimpong
ཀང་དྲ།	(n.) fork 17.2
ཀམ་པར་ལི།	(n.) blanket
ཀུ་ཤུ། བཞེས་ཤུ། H	(n.) apple 23.2
ཀེ་ར།	(n.) banana 23.2
ཀེར་ཀེར།	(adj.) upright, vertical 23.2
ཀོ་སྒམ།	(n.) suitcase
ཀོ་བ།	(n.) yakhide, hide boat, coracle....................... 40.2
ཀོ་བ་ + བཏང་།	(vol. v.) to paddle .... 40.2 a coracle
ཀོང་པོ།	(pr. n.) Kongpo 22.2
ཀོར།	(n.) coat, jacket
ཀྲན་མ།	see སྲན་མ།
ཀྲབ་པོ།	see སྲབ་པོ
ཀྲུང་གོ	(pr. n.) People's Republic of China................................ 9.2
ཀླད་ཀོར།	(n.) zero
ཀླད་པ།	(n.) brain
ཀླད་དམར་ར།	
སྐྲི་ཐེར། L	(n.) bald 35.2
ཀླུ།	(n.) naga, acquatic serpent-spirit
ཀླུ་ཁང་།	(pr. n.) Lukhang park 40.2
ཀློག	
ཕྱག་ཀློག་གནང་། H	(vol. v.) to read
དཀའ་ལས་ + ཁག	(inv. v.) to be tired 31.2
སྐུ་ལས་ + ཁག H	
དཀའ་ལས་ཁག་པོ།	(adj.) difficult 4.2
དཀར་སྐྱོང་ + བྱེད།	(vol. v.) to be vegetarian.......................... 40.2
དཀར་ཆག	(n.) catalogue, register
དཀར་ཆུ།	(n.) milk products 30.2
དཀར་པོ།	(adj.) white 3.2
དཀར་ཡོལ།	
ཞལ་དཀར། H	(n.) cup 1.2
དཀོན་གཉེར།	(n.) temple janitor 19.2
དཀོན་མཆོག	(n.) jewel
དཀོན་མཆོག་གསུམ།	(idiom.) the Three Jewels
དཀོན་པོ།	(adj.) rare
དཀྱིལ།	(n.) centre, middle 31.2
དཀྱིལ་འཁོར།	(n.) mandala
དཀྱུས་མ།	(adj.) ordinary
དཀྲུག་དཀྲུག་ + བཏང་	(vol. v.) to stir, shake
བཀག	(vol. v.) to stop, block 30.2
བཀའ།	(n.) order, command
བཀའ་ + བསྐྱོན།	(vol. v.) to criticise
གཤེ་གཤེ་ + བཏང་། H	reprimand 24.2
བཀའ་འགྱུར།	(pr. n.) Kangyur (work containing the Buddha' s teachings)
བཀའ་རྒྱུད་པ།	(pr. n.) Kagyüpa (sect) 27.2
བཀའ་མངགས་ + གནང་། H	(vol. v.) to order 22.2
བཀའ་དྲིན།	(n.) kindness
བཀའ་འདྲི་ + གནང་། H	(vol. v.) to ask 20.2
བཀའ་འདྲི་ + ཞུས། h	(vol. v.) to ask 20.2
བཀའ་བློན།	(n.) minister in the Kashak
བཀའ་མོལ་ + གནང་། H	(vol. v.) to converse,talk 20.2
བཀའ་མོལ་ + ཞུས། h	(vol. v.) to converse, talk 20.2
བཀའ་ཤག	(n.) ministerial cabinet, Kashak
བཀའ་སློབ་+གནང་། H	(vol. v.) to advise
བཀལ།	(vol. v.) to hang
བཀོག	(vol. v.) to pluck
བཀུག	(vol. v.) to bring, take..........10.2
བཀྲ་ཤིས་བདེ་ལེགས།	(idiom.) hello, best wishes....3.2
བཀྲ་ཤིས་རྟགས་བརྒྱད།	(idiom.) the eight auspicious signs...................................37.2
བཀྲགས།	see བསྒྲིགས།
བཀྲིས།	see བསྒྲིས།
རྐང་ག་རིལ།	
རྐང་འཁོར། L	(n.) bicycle 12.2
རྐང་ཐང་།	(n.) on foot 16.2
རྐང་པ། ཞབས། H	(n.) foot, leg.........................16.2

རྐང་བརྩུགས་ནས།	(adv.) deliberately
རྐང་བརྩུགས་མིན་པ།	(adv.) unintentionally
རྐང་རྩེད་སྤོ་ལོ།	(n.) football 12.2
རྐང་ལག	(n.) limb 34.2
རྐུ་མ། རྐུན་མ། L	(n.) thief
རྐུ་མ་+ རྐུ།1/ བརྐུས། 2,3	(vol. v.) to rob, steal
རྐུ་མ་+ ཤོར།	(inv. v.) to be robbed
རྐུབ།	(n.) backside, bottom
རྐུབ་ཀྱག ཞབས་ཀྱག H	(n.) chair 2.2
རྐྱང་།	(n.) donkey, ass 17.2
རྐྱེན།	(n.) cause
རྐྱེན་ངན།	(n.) unfortunate accident
ལྐུགས་པ།	(adj.) idiot, mute 28.2
སྐད། གསུང་སྐད། H	(n.) language, speech
	(n.) sound
	(n.) voice
སྐད་ + བཏང་།	(vol. v.) to call 30.2
གསུང་ + གནང་། H	
སྐད་ + བཏང་།	(vol. v.) to invite 33.2
གདན་འདྲེན་ + ཞུས། h	
སྐད་ +རྒྱག	(vol. v.) to shout 28.2
སྐད་ཆ། བཀའ་མོལ། H	(n.) speech, subject 20.2
སྐད་ཆ་ + དྲིས།	(vol. v.) to ask 20.2
སྐད་ཆ་ + བཤད།	(vol. v.) to converse, speak 20.2
སྐད་གྲགས།	(n.) fame, glory
སྐད་གྲགས་ཆེན་པོ།	(adj.) famous, celebrated
སྐད་སྒྱུར་+ བྱེད།	(vol. v.) to translate
སྐད་སྒྱུར། གསུང་སྒྱུར། H	(n.) translator, interpreter
སྐད་ཅིག།	(n.) instant
སྐད་ཅོར།	(n.) noise
སྐམ་སློག	(n.) generator 32.2
སྐམ་པོ།	(n.) dry
སྐར་ཆ།	(n.) second (of time) 12.2
སྐར་མ།	(n.) star, minute 12.2
སྐས་འཛེགས།	(n.) ladder
སྐེ་རགས།	(n.) belt 23.2
སྐེད་པ། སྐུ་སྐེད། H	(n.) waist 16.2
སྐུ། H	(n.) body
སྐུ་དཀྱིལ་གསལ་དྭངས། H	(idiom.) how do you do? 9.2
སྐུ་ཁམས།	(n.) health
སྐུ་ཁམས་བཟང་།	(idiom.) how are you? (lit. "is your health good?") 29.2
སྐུ་མཁྱེན།	(idiom.) please 16.2
སྐུ་ངོ་།	(n.) Your excellency 13.2
སྐུ་མདུན། H	(post.) "in the presence",
	(n.) title of the Dalai Lama 27.2
སྐུ་དྲག	(n.) aristocrat, noble 41.2
སྐུ་འདྲ།	(n.) statue 37.2
སྐུ་ཐང་མཉེལ། H	(inv. v.) to be tired
སྐུ་ཕྲེང་།	(n.) incarnation lineage 37.2
སྐུ་ཞོག H སྐུ་ཞབས། LH	(n.) Sir, Venerable (monk) 2.2
སྐུ་གཟུགས་ + བསིལ། H	(vol. v.) to bathe 18.2
སྐུ་གཟུགས་…	
བདེ་པོ་ཡིན་པས།	(idiom.) how are you? 3.2
སྐུ་ཁྲུང་བཞེངས། H	(inv. v.) to get angry, be annoyed
སྐུད་པ།	(n.) thread 37.2
སྐོར།	(vol. v.) to turn
སྐོར།	(post.) about, concerning 7.2
སྐོར་ར། སྐོར་བ། L	(n.) tour, circuit 22.2
སྐོར་ར་ + རྒྱག	(vol. v.) make a circuit 22.2
སྐྱ་བོ།	(adj.) pale, grey; lay(person)
སྐྱག་པ།	(n.) excrement, shit
སྐྱག་པ་+བཏང་།	(vol. v.) to defecate
སྐྱག་རྫུན།	(n.) lie
སྐྱག་རྫུན་+ བཤད།	(n.) to lie
སྐྱིད་ཆུ།	(pr. n.) Kyichu, "River of Happiness" 15.2
སྐྱིད་པོ་ + བཏང་།	(vol. v.) to have a pleasant time 24.2
སྐྱིད་པོ། སྤྲོ་པོ། H	(adj.) pleasant, gay, happy 8. 2
སྐྱིད་པོ་+བཏང་།	(vol. v.) to have a pleasant time
སྐྱུག་པ་ + ཤོར།	(inv. v.) to vomit 34.2
སྐྱུག་མེར་ + ལང་།	(inv. v.) to feel ill, nauseous 34.2
སྐྱུར་མོ།	(adj.) sour 21.2
སྐྱེ། འཁྲུངས། H	(inv. v.) to be born 7.2
སྐྱེ་སྐར། འཁྲུངས་སྐར། H	(n.) birthday

སྐྱེ་ས། འཁྲུངས་ཡུལ།	H	(n.) birthplace
སྐྱེད་དམན།		(n.) woman, wife
སྐྱེལ་འདྲེན།		(n.) transport
སྐྱེལ་འདྲེན་+བྱེད།		(vol. v.) to transport
སྐྱོག		(n.) ladle 17.2
སྐྱོན།		(n.) fault, defect.................. 28.2
སྐྱོན་བརྗོད་+བྱེད།		(vol. v.) to criticise
སྐྱོན་ཤོར།		(inv. v.) to break down
སྐྱབས་བཅོལ་བ།		(n.) refugee
སྐྲ། དབུ་སྐྲ།	H	(n.) hair (of the head)......... 16.2
སྐྲ་ཁང་།		
སྐྲ་བཞར་ཁང་།	L	(n.) barber's,hairdresser's . 12.2
བསྐྱུར།		(vol. v.) to send, load
བསྐོལ།		(vol. v.) to boil.................... 35.2
བསྐོལ་ཐུན།		(n.) soup made with chang......................... 36.2
བསྐྱར་བཞེངས་ + གནང་།		(vol. v.) to renew 17.2

ཁ་ Kha

ཁ། ཞལ།	H	(n.) mouth.......................... 16.2
		(n.) surface
ཁ་སྐོམ། ཞལ་སྐོམ།	H	(inv. v.) to be thirsty
ཁ་སྐྱེལ།		(vol. v.) to kiss
ཁ་ཁར་བསྡད།		(vol. v.) to be silent
ཁ་གྲངས།		
ཞལ་གྲངས།	H	(n.) number (of people)...... 39.2
ཁ་+རྒྱག ཁ་+བསྒྱུན།	H	(vol. v.) to close (objects) .. 13.2
ཁ་ཆེ།		(n.) Muslim 26.2
ཁ་ཏིག		(adj.) bitter 21.2
ཁ་གཏད།		(n.) opponent, adversary ... 12.2
ཁ་བཏགས།		
མཇལ་དར།	H	(n.) khatak, ceremonial...... 19.2 scarf
ཁ་ + གདངས།		(vol. v.) to open one's mouth................................. 34.2
ཁ་གདན།		(n.) carpet for a mattress .. 31.2
ཁ་མདོག		(n.) colour
ཁ་འདོན་+བྱེད།		(vol. v.) to recite prayers
ཁ་པར་ + བཏང་།		(vol. v.) to telephone 19.2
ཁ་པར། ཞལ་པར།	H	(n.) telephone 3.2
ཁ་ཕྱེ། ཞལ་ཕྱེ།	H	(vol. v.) to open (objects)....13.2
ཁ་ཕྱོགས།		(n.) direction
ཁ་བྲལ།		(v.inv.) to separate
ཁ་བྱང་། ཞལ་བྱང་།	H	(n.) address
ཁ་ཚ་པོ། ཞལ་ཚ་པོ།	H	(n.) spicy (dish), sharp-tongued 36.2
ཁ་ཚོག་ཚོག་+བྱེད།		(vol. v.) to smile
ཁ་ཟས། ཞལ་ཟས།	H	(n.) doughnut 36.2
ཁ་ལ་ + ཉན།		(vol. v.) to obey
ཁ་ལག + བཟོ།		(vol. v.) to prepare a meal 17.2
ཁ་ལག ཞལ་ལག	H	(n.) meal, food 8.2
ཁ་ལོ་པ།		(n.) driver, pilot 13.2
ཁ་ཤས།		(adj.) some, certain, several.................................14.2
ཁ་ས་ཁ་ཉིན།		(adv.) in recent days 33.2
ཁ་སང་། ཁ་སེང་།	L	(adv.) a few days ago 18.2
ཁག		(n.) sort, kind.......................21.2
ཁག་ཁག་+བཟོ།		(vol. v.) to separate
ཁག་ཁག་+བྱེད།		(vol. v.) to separate (oneself from sth. or someone)
ཁང་གླ		(n.) rent (on a house)
ཁང་མིག		(n.) room 18.2
ཁང་པ་+སྤོ། 1		
སྤོས། 2, 3		(vol. v.) to move house
ཁང་པ་+རྒྱག		(vol. v.) to build
ཁང་པ། གཟིམ་ཁང་།	H	(n.) room 17.2
ཁང་པ། གཟིམ་ཤག	H	(n.) house 4.2
ཁངས།		see ཁེངས།
ཁམ་བུ། བཞེས་ཁམ།	H	(n.) peach 23.2
ཁམས།		(n pr.) Kham 22.2
ཁམས་པ།		(n.) Khampa
ཁབ་ལེན།		(n.) magnet
ཁབ།		(n.) needle
ཁབ་རྒྱག		(vol. v.) to administer an injection
ཁའི་ས། ཁ་ས།	L	(adv.) yesterday 7.2
ཁས་མ་བླངས་།		(vol. v.) to refuse

ཁས་ལེན།	
ཞལ་བཞེས། H	(n.) promise, agreement
ཁས་ལེན་བྱེད།	(vol. v.) to agree, accept
ཁུ་བ།	(n.) juice, broth 32.2
ཁུ་སིམ་པོ།	(adj.) tranquil, calm
ཁུག་མ།	(n.) little bag, pouch
ཁེ་ཉིན་ཀ།	(adv.) the day before yesterday 18.2
ཁེ་བཟང་།	(n.) profit
ཁེངས། L ཁངས།	(inv. v.) to be filled
ཁོ།	(pron.) he 2.2
ཁོ་ཙེ།	(n.) chopstick..................... 17.2
ཁོ་རང་ཚོ།	(pron.) they.......................... 2.2
ཁོ་ཧྥི།	(n.) coffee 10.2
ཁོག་སྟོང་།	(adj.) hollow
ཁོག་མ།	(n.) pot 17.2
ཁོག་ཕྱིར།	(n.) teapot, kettle 17.2
ཁོང་། H	(pron.) he, she..................... 2.2
ཁོང་ཁྲོ།	(n.) anger
ཁོང་ཁྲོ་+བསླང་།	(vol. v.) to anger someone
ཁོང་ཁྲོ་+ལང་།	(inv. v.) to get angry
ཁོང་གཉིས།	(pron.) those two................. 3.2
ཁོང་རྣམ་ཚོ། HH	(pron.) they 3.2
ཁོང་ཚོ། H	(pron.) they 2.2
ཁོངས་གཏོགས།	(inv. v.) to belong 39.2
ཁྱགས་པ།	(n.) ice
ཁྱད་པར།	(n.) difference
ཁྱད་པར་དུ།	(adv.) especially 37.2
ཁྱད་མཚར་པོ།	(adj.) strange, bizarre 38.2
ཁྱི།	(n.) dog 17.2
ཁྱིམ་ཚང་།	(n.) family 15.2
ཁྱིམ་མཚེས།	(n.) neighbour 15.2
ཁྱུ།	(n.) flock, herd, pack
ཁྱེད་རྣམ་ཚོ། HH	(pron.) you (pl.) 3.2
ཁྱེད་རང་། H	(pron.) you (sing.)................ 3.2
ཁྱེད་རང་གཉིས། H	(pron.) you two 3.2
ཁྱེད་རང་ཚོ། H	(pron.) you (pl.) 3.2
ཁྱེར། བསྣམས། H	(vol. v.) to take, carry......... 19.2
ཁྱོ་ག	(n.) man, husband 17.2
ཁྱོད་རང་ཚོ།	(pron.) you (pl.) 3.2
ཁྱོད།	(pron.) you (sing.) 3.2
ཁྱོན་བསྡོམས།	(adv.) in total, altogether
ཁྱོན་ནས།	(adv.) certainly not, never, not at all 10.2
ཁྲ་ཡོལ།	(n.) curtain
ཁྲག སྐུ་ཁྲག H	(n.) blood 35.2
ཁྲག་རྩ།	(n.) vein
ཁྲག་ཤེད།	(n.) blood pressure 35.2
ཁྲལ།	(n.) tax, duty
ཁྲི། བཞུགས་ཁྲི། H	(n.) throne 18.2
ཁྲིམས།	(n.) law, rule
ཁྲིམས་དཔོན།	(n.) judge
ཁྲིམས་འཛིན།	(adj.) legal, judicial..............37.2
ཁྲིམས་ཁང་།	(n.) lawcourt........................12.2
ཁྲུས་ཁང་།	(n.) bathroom 18.2
ཁྲུས་ + རྒྱག	(vol. v.) to (have a) wash....36.2
ཁྲུས་སྒམ།	(n.) washing machine 32.2
ཁྲོ།	(n.) bronze
ཁྲོམ།	(n.) market 19.2
མཁའ་འགྲོ་མ།	(n.) ḍākinī 27.2
མཁའ་འགྲོ།	(n.) daka 27.2
མཁར།	(n.) fortress 26.2
མཁལ་མ།	(n.) kidney
མཁས་པ།	(n.) scholar, expert
མཁས་པོ།	(adj.) skilled, learned, expert
མཁྱེན། H	(inv. v.) to know, understand..........................28.2
མཁྲེགས་པོ། L	
མཁྲགས་པོ།	(adj.) hard, solid
འཁུམ།	(inv. v.) to shrink, contract
འཁེལ།	(inv. v.) to coincide, happen 36.2
འཁོར་བ།	(n.) samsara
འཁོར་ལོ།	(n.) wheel
འཁོར་ལོ་ + བསྐོར།	(vol. v.) to turn the wheel, teach the Dharma 40.2
འཁོལ།	(v.inv.) to boil
འཁྱག སྐུ་བསིལ། H	(inv. v.) to feel cold 22.2
འཁྱག་སྒམ།	(n.) refrigerator....................32.2
འཁྲགས་པོ།	see འཁྲེགས་པོ།

འཁྲབ།	(vol. v.) to act........................ 41.2
འཁྲབ་མཁན།	(n.) actor
འཁྲབ་གཞུང་།	(n.) classical opera 41.2
འཁྲིད། འཁྲིད་གནང་། H	(vol. v.) to lead, take 35.2
འཁྲིས།	(post.) by, near 7.2
འཁྲུ། 1 བཀྲུས། 2, 3	(vol. v.) to wash.................. 18.2
འཁྲུག་པོ།	(adj.) lively, animated......... 33.2

ག་ Ga

ག་གི	(interr. pron.) which?............ 8.2
ག་རེ།	(interr. pron.) what? 1.2
ག་དུས།	(interr. pron.) when? 10.2
ག་འདྲས་ཟེ།	(interr. pron.) how? 11.2
ག་ནས།	(interr. pron.) from where?... 9.2
ག་པར།	(interr. pron.) where? 6.2
ག་ཚད། ག་ཚོད། L	(interr. pron.) how many? ... 9.2
ག་ལེ་ག་ལེ།	(adj., adv.) slow, slowly, softly 8.2
ག་ལེ་ཕེབས།	(idiom.) goodbye .... 13.2 (to so. who is leaving)
ག་ལེ་བཞུགས།	(idiom.) goodbye .... 13.2 (to so. who is staying)
ག་རེ་ག་རེ།	(interr. pron.) what, what kind of 38.2
ག་རེ་བྱས་ནས།	(interr. pron.) why ?
ག་རེ་ཡིན་ནམ།	(interr. pron.) why?
ག་རེ་རེད་ཟེར་ན།	(idiom.) because, since, for 38.2
ག་ས་ག་ལ།	(adv.) everywhere 25.2
གང་།	(class.) one unit 10.2
གང་།	(adj.) full, filled.................... 18.2
གང་དྲག	(idiom.) what a shame! how unfortunate! 28.2
གང་ཟག	(n.) pipe
གང་ཡིན་ཟེར་ན།	(idiom.) if you ask why, because, since, for 38.2
གངས།	(n.) snow 24.2
གངས་ལྗོངས།	(n.) Land of Snows, Tibet
གངས་ + བཏང་།	(inv. v.) to snow 24.2
གངས་རི།	(n.) snow mountain 29.2
གད་+རྒྱག	(vol. v.) to sweep
གད་སྙིགས།	(n.) rubbish
གད་མོ་+བགད།	(vol. v.) to laugh
གད་མོ་+ཤོར།	(inv. v.) to laugh, burst out laughing
གད་མོ་+བསླངས།	(vol. v.) to make so. laugh
གབ།	(vol. v.) to hide (oneself)
གའི། གང་ཡང་། L	(adv.) nothing 25.2
གའི་གནང་གི་མ་རེད། H	(idiom.) it doesn't matter, no problem..........................25.2
གའི་བྱེད་ཀྱི་མ་རེད།	(idiom.) it doesn't matter, no problem..........................25.2
གལ་ཆེན་པོ།	(adj.) important 38.2
གལ་སྲིད། H	(co.) if, in the event that......13.2
གུ་ཡངས་པོ།	(adj.) wide, spacious...........25.2
གུ་རུ་རིན་པོ་ཆེ།	(n pr.) Padmasambhava.....27.2
གུང་ཁྲན་རིང་ལུགས།	(n.) Communism 26.2
གུང་ཁྲན་ཏང་།	(n.) Communist Party 26.2
གུང་སང་། གུང་སེང་། L	(n.) vacation 10.2
གུར།	(n.) tent
གུར་ + རྒྱག	(vol. v.) to pitch a tent.........40.2
གུས་ཞབས།	(n.) respect
གུས་ཞབས་བྱེད།	(vol. v.) to respect
གེགས་དབང་།	(n.) disaster, obstacle 36.2
གོ གསན། L	(inv. v.) to hear
གོ་སྐབས།	(n.) chance, opportunity
གོ་རིམ།	(n.) rank, status, level
གོང་།	(n.) price 22.2
གོང་ཁེ་པོ།	(adj.) inexpensive, cheap ..22.2
གོང་ཆེན་པོ།	(adj.) expensive 22.2
གོང་འཕེལ།	(n.) development, improvement, progress
གོང་མ།	(n.) emperor, sovereign......38.2 (adj.) preceding, above
གོང་ས།	(n.) superior position...........38.2
གོང་གཤམ།	(n.) hem..............................31.2
གོན།	(vol. v.) to dress, wear
གོམ་པ།	(n.) step
གོམ་པ་ + རྒྱག	(vol. v.) to walk 29.2

གོམས་གཤིས།	(n.) habit, custom
གོས་ཐུང་།	(n.) trousers, pants............ 23.2
གྱོང་།	(n.) loss, damage
གྲ་སྒྲིག་བྱེད་།	(vol. v.) to prepare
གྲང་མོ།	(adj.) cold 22.2
གྲངས་ཀ།	(n.) number 39.2
གྲངས་ཀ་ + རྒྱག	(vol. v.) to count 39.2
གྲལ།	(n.) row, line
གྲས།	(n.) kind, sort, class........... 39.2
གྲི།	(n.) knife 17.2
གྲིབ།	(n.) cerebral stroke 35.2
གྲིབ་ནག	(n.) shadow
གྲུ་ཁའི་གྲོང་ཁྱེར།	(n.) port, harbour
གྲུ་བཞི།	(n.) square 25.2
གྲུ་གཟིངས།	(n.) boat 13.2
གྲུ་གཟིངས་ལས་མི།	(n.) sailor
གྲུབ།	(inv. v.) to accomplish, achieve
གྲུབ་འབྲས།	(n.) result
གྲུམ་བུའི་ན་ཚ།	(n.) arthritis 35.2
གྲོ།	(n.) wheat
གྲོ་མ།	(n.) potentilla tuber............ 23.2
གྲོ་ཞིབ། གསོལ་ཞིབ། H	(n.) flour
གྲོ་སོ་ཕྱེ་མར།	(n.) display of flour and butter
for	the New Year 36.2
གྲོག་མ།	(n.) ant 17.2
གྲོང་གསེབ།	(n.) village, countryside 15.2
གྲོང་སྲེབ་པ།	(n.) villager
གྲོང་ཁྱེར།	(n.) town, city 12.2
གྲོགས་པོ།	(n.) friend (male) 4.2
གྲོགས་མོ།	(n.) friend (female) 4.2
གྲོངས། H	(inv. v.) to die
གྲོད་ཁོག གསོལ་གྲོད། H	(n.) stomach 16.2
གྲོད་ཁོག་ལྟོགས	(inv. v.) to be hungry
གྲོལ།	(inv. v.) to be over,
	to be released 32.2
གྲྭ་པ། དགེ་འདུན་པ། H	(n.) monk 2.2
གྲྭ་ཚང་།	(n.) monastic college
གླ།	(vol. v.) to rent
གླ་བ།	(n.) musk deer 17.2
གླ་ཁྱེད་མོ་ཊ།	(n.) taxi
གླང་ཤ།	(n.) beef 23.2
གླིང་ཀ་ + བཏང་།	(vol. v.) to picnic 24.2
གླིང་ཀ	
བཞུགས་གླིང་། H	(n.) park 7.2
གླིང་སྐོར།	(n.) circular pilgrimage
	route 7.2
གླིང་ཕྲན།	(n.) island
གླིང་བུ།	(n.) flute
གླུ།	(n.) lu, (slow) song
གླུ་ལེན།	(vol. v.) to sing a *lu*
གླུད།	(n.) ransom 38.2
གླུད་འགོང་རྒྱལ་པོ།	(n.) the lügong king,
	"scapegoat" 38.2
གླེ།	(pr. n.) Leh (capital of
	Ladakh)
གློ་རྒྱག	(inv. v.) to cough
གློ་ཁོག	(n.) courage
གློ་ཁོག་ཆེན་པོ།	(adj.) courageous
གློ་བུར་དུ།	(adv.) abruptly, suddenly
གློ་བ།	(n.) lung...............................16.2
གློག	(n.) electricity
གློག་ཀླད་འཕྲུལ་འཁོར།	(n.) computer 32.2
གློག་ཁང་།	(n.) hydroelectric plant........12.2
གློག་བརྙན།	(n.) film, cinema
གློག་བརྙན་ཁང་།	(n.) movie theater 12.2
གློག་ཐབ།	(n.) oven, stove..................17.2
གླྣེ་ལ་སེ།	(n.) drinking glass
དགའ། མཉེས། H	(inv. v.) to like........................8.2
དགའ་ལྡན།	(pr. n.) Gandän
	Monastery 11.2
དགའ་པོ། མཉེས་པོ། H	(adj.) happy, glad
	(inv. v.) to like, to please 8.2
དགའ་བ། བདེ་སྐྱིད།	(n.) joy, happiness
དགའ་བ་+ཡོད། འདུག	(inv. v.) to prefer
དགའ་བསུ་+ཞུ། h	(vol. v.) to welcome, receive
དགའ་རོགས།	(n.) girlfriend, boyfriend
དགུ	(adj.) nine
དགུ་བཅུ།	(adj.) ninety
དགུ་གཏོར།	(n.) festival for the end
	of the Old Year 36.2

དགུ་ཐུག (n.) soup made with nine ingredients 36.2

དགུན་ཀ (n.) winter 24.2

དགུན་ས། (n.) winter camp 31.2

དགེ་རྒན།

རྒན་ལགས། H (n.) teacher, master 2.2

དགེ་བ། (n.) virtue

དགེ་མཚན། (n.) value

དགེ་འདུན། (n.) sangha 37.2

དགེ་བཤེས། (n.) Doctor of Divinity in Buddhism, geshe 37.2

དགེ་ལུགས་པ། (pr. n.) Gelugpa (sect) 27.2

དགོངས་དག (n.) sorry 3.2

དགོང་དག དགོང་མོ། L (n.) evening 18.2

དགོངས་རྫོགས། (n.) death-anniversary funeral 38.2

དགོངས་པ་ + བཞེས། H (vol. v.) to think, ponder 14.2

དགོངས་པ་ + རྫོགས། H (inv. v.) to die, to fulfill one's wishes completely 38.2

དགོངས་པ་ + ཞུ། h (vol. v.) to take leave........... 8.2

དགོངས་པ་མ་ཚོམས། (idiom.) sorry! .... 8.2 excuse me!

དགོད་བྲོ་པོ (adj.) funny, comical

དགོན་པ། (n.) monastery 11.2

དགོས། (inv. v.) to need
(aux.) to have to 16.2

དགྲ་བོ། (n.) enemy

དགྲ་ཤ་ལེན། (vol. v.) to avenge

བགོ་ཤའ་རྒྱག (vol. v.) to divide, share

མགར་བ། (n.) blacksmith 32.2

མགུལ་ཆམ་ + བཞེས། H (inv. v.) to catch cold.......... 34.2

མགོ། དབུ། H (n.) head 16.2

མགོ་སྐོར་+བཏང་། (vol. v.) to deceive, trick

མགོ་སྐོར་+ཐེབས། (inv. v.) to be tricked, conned

མགོ་ཁྲིད། དབུ་ཁྲིད། H (n.) leader, chief................ 32.2

མགོ་རྙོག་པོ། (adj.) complicated

མགྱོགས་པོ། ཕྱོལ་པོ། H (adj.) fast, quickly 8.2

མགྱོགས་པོ་+ བྱེད། (vol. v.) to hurry

མགྲོན་ཁང་། (n.) hotel 12.2

མགྲོན་པོ། སྐུ་མགྲོན། H (n.) guest

འགག (inv. v.) to be stopped, blocked

འགག་སྒོ། (n.) customs office

འགམས། (vol. v.) to eat "powdered" food (tsampa, etc.) 24.2

འགལ་ཟླ། (n.) conflict

འགུལ་སྐྱོད་ + བྱེད། (inv. v.) to move, stir 37.2

འགོ་སྣམ། (n.) felt 31.2

འགོ་བཙུགས། (vol. v.) to begin 12.2

དབུ་བཙུགས། H

འགོ་ཚུགས། (inv. v.) to begin 12.2

འགོར། (inv. v.) to last 29.2

འགྱིག (n.) plastic (soft)

འགྱུར་ (v.inv.) to change, transform

འགྱུར་ལྡོག (n.) change

འགྱུར་བ་ཆེན་པོ། (adj.) variable

འགྱེད། སྐུ་འགྱེད། H (n.) food offering 37.2

འགྱོད་པ་སྐྱེ། (inv. v.) to regret 12.2

འགྲམ་པ། (n.) cheek 38.2

འགྲན་སྡུར། (n.) competition..................32.2

འགྲམ། (post.) near 22.2

འགྲིག (inv. v.) to be arranged, to be fixed, to be all right....13.2

འགྲུལ་རྒྱག (vol. v.) to travel

འགྲེམ་སྟོན། (n.) exhibition

འགྲེམ་སྟོན་ཁང་། (n.) museum

འགྲོ 1 ཕྱིན།2 རྒྱུགས།3 (vol. v.) to go 4.2

འགྲོ་ལུགས། (n.) system

འགྲོའོ། གྲབས། L (aux.) to be about to, to have just......................... 13.2

རྒན་ལགས། H (n.) Sir (term of address)
(n.) teacher, master 2.2

རྒན་འཁོགས།

བགྲེས་སྒོང་། H (adj.) elderly 6.2

རྒུན་འབྲུམ། (n.) grape 23.2

རྒུན་འབྲུམ་ཆང་། (n.) wine

རྒོ་བ། (n.) gazelle 17.2

རྒྱ། (n.) seal
(n.) beard

རྒྱ་སྐད། (n.) Chinese (language) 9.2

རྒྱ་གར། (pr. n.) India, Indian 5.2

རྒྱ་གར་བ། (pr. n.) Indian 9.2
རྒྱ་ནག (pr. n.) China 5.2
རྒྱ་པོ། (adj.) bearded
རྒྱ་མ། (n.) pound, 500 g................ 23.2
རྒྱ་མི། (pr. n.) Chinese (person) 9.2
རྒྱ་སྨུག (adj.) brown
རྒྱ་མཚོ། (n.) sea, ocean
རྒྱ་ཡིག (n.) Chinese script 5.2
རྒྱག1 བརྒྱབ། 2 རྒྱོབ། 3 (vol. v.) to build
རྒྱག་རེས་རྒྱག (vol. v.) to quarrel
རྒྱག་རེས་ཤོར། (inv. v.) to quarrel
རྒྱང་ཐག (n.) distance
རྒྱང་ཤེལ། (n.) binoculars 32.2
རྒྱན་ཆ། (n.) ornament, jewel........... 38.2
རྒྱབ། (post.) behind 7.2
རྒྱབ་ཕྱོགས། (n.) behind, rear
རྒྱལ་ཁ། (n.) victory
རྒྱལ་ཁབ། (n.) State, country 9.2
རྒྱལ་པོ། (n.) king 26.2
རྒྱལ་མོ། (n.) queen
རྒྱལ་སྤྱི། (adj.) international
རྒྱལ་དབང་། (n.) title of Dalai Lama and certain high officials 37.2
རྒྱལ་ཡོངས་། (adj.) national
རྒྱལ་བ་རིན་པོ་ཆེ། (n.) title of Dalai Lama
རྒྱལ་ས། (n.) capital city.................... 16.2
རྒྱལ་སྲིད་སྣ་བདུན། (idiom.) the seven royal emblems............................ 37.2
རྒྱས་པོ། (adj.) abundant, copious 40.2
རྒྱུ། (n.) primary cause
རྒྱུ་ཅ་ལག (n.) wealth
རྒྱུ་ཆ། (n.) material
རྒྱུ་ནོར། (n.) wealth
རྒྱུ་མཚན། (n.) reason
རྒྱུག (vol. v.) to run 33.2
རྒྱུག་སྤྲོད། (n.) oral exam
རྒྱུག་སྤྲོད་+བྱེད། (vol. v.) to take an exam ... 37.2
རྒྱུག་ཤས་+རྒྱག (v.) to brush/comb one's hair
རྒྱུགས་ཤར་+སྤྲོད། (vol. v.) to run

རྒྱུད། (n.) line, series, chain 13.2
(n.) tantra
སྒང་ཐུག (n.) ball
སྒང་། (post.) on, on top of 7.2
སྒང་ག (adj.) all
སྒམ། (n.) box
སྒལ་པ། སྐུ་སྟོད། H (n.) back 16.2
སྒུག
ཕེབས་སྒུག་གནང་། H (vol. v.) to wait.....................35.2
སྒེའུ་ཁུང་། (n.) window
སྒེར། (adj.) private........................35.2
སྒོ། གཟིམ་སྒོ། H (n.) door 13.2
སྒོ་+རྒྱག
གཟིམ་སྒོ་+བསྐྱོན། H (vol. v.) to shut the door 13.2
སྒོ་+ཕྱེ།
གཟིམ་སྒོ་+ཕྱེ། H (vol. v.) to open the door ...13.2
སྒོ་ར། (n.) courtyard
སྒོ་སྲུང་། (n.) watchman, janitor.........19.2
སྒོང་ང་། བཞེས་སྒོང་། H (n.) egg
སྒོར་སྒོར། (adj.) round
སྒོར་མོ། (n.) *gormo*, unit of currency 14.2
སྒྱུ་རྩལ། (n.) art.................................36.2
སྒྱུར། (vol. v.) to change, transform
(vol. v.) to multiply
སྒྲ། (n.) sound, pronunciation
སྒྲ་གདངས། (n.) accent
སྒྲ་སྙན། (n.) Tibetan lute 40.2
སྒྲ་ཕབ་འཁོར་ལོ། (n.) tape recorder 32.2
སྒྲིག་འཛུགས། (n.) organisation
སྒྲིག་ལམ། (n.) discipline, rules
སྒྲིག་གཤོམ་ + བྱེད། (vol. v.) to exhibit, display ..37.2
སྒྲུག (vol. v.) to gather 30.2
སྒྲུང་། (n.) story, account
སྒྲོལ་མ། (pr. n.) Tara...........................7.2
སྒྲོལ་དཀར། (pr. n.) White Tara 27.2
བརྒྱ། (adj.) hundred
བརྒྱད། (adj.) eight
བརྒྱད་བཅུ། (adj.) eighty
བསྒྱུར་བཅོས། (n.) reform

ང་ Nga

ང།	(pron.) I 3.2
ང་གཉིས།	(pron.) we two 3.2
ང་རྒྱལ།	(n.) pride, arrogance, aggressivity
ང་རྒྱལ་ཚ་པོ།	(adj.) proud, aggressive
ང་ཚོ།	(pron.) we 3.2
ངལ་གསོ།	(n.) rest
ངལ་གསོ་+རྒྱག	(vol. v.) to rest
ངན་པ།	(adj.) bad, wicked.............. 28.2
ངུ།	(vol. v.) to cry, weep
ངོ་རྒོལ་+བྱེད།	(vol. v.) to protest
ངོ་མ། མངོན་སུམ།	(adj.) true, real
ངོ་ཚ།	(n.) shame
ངོ་ལོག་+རྒྱག	(vol. v.) to revolt
ངོ་ཤེས། ངོ་མཁྱེན། H	
ཞལ་ཚོར། h	(inv. v.) to know someone . 16.2
ངོས་འཛིན་+བྱེད།	(vol. v.) to recognise, identify
དངུལ། ཕྱག་དངུལ། H	(n.) money, silver 12.2
དངུལ་ཁང་།	(n.) bank 12.2
དངུལ་འཛིན།	(n.) cheque
དངུལ་སིལ་མ།	(n.) small change
དངོས་ཁམས་རིག་པ།	(n.) physics
དངོས་པོ།	(n.) object
དངོས་འབྲེལ།	(adv.) actually, genuinely... 31.2
དངོས་ནས།	(adv.) really 8.2
མངགས།	(vol. v.) to order, command........................... 22.2
མངའ་རིས།	(pr. n.) Ngari 22.2
མངའ་རིས་ཁམ་བུ།	(n.) apricot 23.2
མངོན་པར་རྫོགས།	(inv. v.) to achieve fulfillment, attain to Buddhahood 40.2
མངར་མོ།	(adj.) sweet 21.2
རྔ།	(n.) drum
རྔ་མ།	(n.) tail
རྔན་པ།	(n.) gift 41.2
རྔམ་བརྗིད་ཆེན་པོ།	(adj.) great, impressive...... 28.2
རྔུལ་ནག	(n.) sweat 34.2
ལྔ།	(adj.) five
ལྔ་བཅུ།	(adj.) fifty
སྔ་པོ།	(adj.) early 17.2
སྔགས།	(n.) mantra
སྔགས་པ།	(n.) tantrist, ngagpa 27.2
སྔན་མ།	see སྔོན་མ: 6.2
སྔར་རྒྱུན། L ནམ་རྒྱུན།	(n.) usually, habitually 34.2
སྔོན་པོ།	(adj.) blue, green (grass) 7.2
སྔོན་མ། L སྔན་མ།	(adj.) before, previously 6.2
སྔས་མགོ།	(n.) pillow 18.2
བརྔོས།	(vol. v.) to fry 22.2

ཅ་ Ca

ཅ་བསྣུན་པོ་+བཟོ།	(vol. v.) to disturb
ཅ་ལག སྐུ་ཆས། H	(n.) thing, object, belongings..........................13.2
ཅི་དག སོགས། L	(part.) et cetera 22.2
ཅིག	(pron.) someone
	(pron.) something 10.2
ཅིག (ཞིག་ཤིག་) L	(art.) a, an 6.2
ཅོ་ཅོག ཇོ་ལགས། H	(n.) elder brother...................6.2
ཅོག་ཙེ། གསོལ་ཅོག H	(n.) table..............................2.2
གཅིག	(adj.) one 6.2
གཅིག་སྒྱུར།	(n.) union
གཅིག་པུ། སྐུ་རྐྱང་། H	(n.) alone, solitary
གཅིག་བྱས་ན།	(adv.) perhaps
གཅིན་པ།	
ཆབ་གསང་། H	(n.) urine
གཅིན་པ་+བཏང་།	(vol. v.) to urinate
གཅུང་པོ། L	(n.) younger brother 6.2
གཅུང་མོ། L	(n.) younger sister 6.2
གཅེན་མོ། L	(n.) elder sister 6.2
གཅེན་པོ། L	(n.) elder brother 6.2
བཅག	(vol. v.) to break
བཅད།	(vol. v.) to cut, cross
བཅུ།	(adj.) ten
བཅུ་དགུ	(adj.) nineteen
བཅུ་གཅིག	(adj.) eleven
བཅུ་གཉིས།	(adj.) twelve
བཅུ་གསུམ།	(adj.) thirteen
བཅུ་དྲུག	(adj.) sixteen

བཅུ་བདུན། (adj.) seventeen
བཅུ་བཞི། (adj.) fourteen
བཅུག (vol. v.) to make/ have someone do sth., to put
བཅིང་བཀྲོལ་+བཏང་། (vol. v.) to free, liberate
བཅོ་བརྒྱད། (n.) eighteen
བཅོ་ལྔ། (n.) fifteen
བཅོམ་ལྡན་འདས། (pr. n.) Bhagavan 40.2
ལྕགས། (n.) iron
ལྕགས་ཐག (n.) chain
ལྕགས་པར། (n.) typewriter 32.2
ལྕགས་རི། (n.) enclosure, perimeter wall
ལྕགས་སྒམ། (n.) trunk, coffer 31.2
ལྕང་མ། (n.) willow
ལྕེ། ལྗགས། H (n.) tongue 16.2

ཆ་ Cha

ཆ། (n.) pair 31.2
ཆ་རྐྱེན། (n.) conditions
ཆ་ཚང་། (adj.) whole 37.2
ཆ་ཤས། (n.) part
ཆག (inv. v.) to break, be broken
ཆགས། (inv. v.) to become 8.2
ཆང་། མཆོད་ཆང་། H (n.) chang, local beer 1.2
ཆང་ཁང་། (n.) bar, tavern 12.2
ཆང་ས། འཁྲུང་ས། H (n.) marriage
ཆང་ས་ + རྒྱག (vol. v.) to marry 14.2
ཆབ་སྲིད། (n.) politics 26.2
ཆད། (inv. v.) to cut
ཆམ་པ། (n.) cold, influenza
ཆམ་པ་ + རྒྱག། (inv. v.) to catch cold 34.2
ཆར་པ། (n.) rain 24.2
ཆར་པ་ + བཏང་། (inv. v.) to rain 24.2
ཆར་ཕྱི། (n.) raincoat
ཆུ། ཆབ། H (n.) water 7.2
ཆུ། (n.) stream, river 15.2
ཆུ་རྐྱལ་+ རྒྱག་པ། (vol. v.) to swim
ཆུ་དྲི་ཞིམ། (n.) perfume
ཆུ་བན། (n.) water pot 24.2

ཆུ་ཚད། (n.) level
ཆུ་ཚན། (n.) hot spring...................... 35.2
ཆུ་ཚོད། ཕྱག་ཚོད། H (n.) hour, watch 12.2
ཆུ་རྫིང་། (n.) cistern, reservoir 7.2
ཆུང་ཆུང་། (adj.) small 3.2
ཆེ་མོ་བ། (n.) headmaster 32.2
ཆེད་རྩོམ། (n.) article (newspaper, etc.)
ཆེན་པོ། (adj.) big 3.2
ཆོག (aux.) future 23.2
(mod. v.) to be allowed
ཆོག་ཆོག + རེད། (v.) to be ready.................... 36.2
ཆོག་མཆན། (n.) permit, authorisation 26.2
ཆོས། (n.) Dharma, religion 26.2
ཆོས་ཚོགས། (n.) Dharma centre
ཆོས་ལགས། H (n.) Venerable (nun) 2.2
ཆོས་ལུགས། (n.) religion, sect 26.2
འཆམ་འཆམ། (n.) walk, stroll
འཆམ་འཆམ་ལ་འགྲོ (vol. v.) to walk, stroll.......... 22.2
འཆམ། (n.) monastic dance 36.2
མཆིན་པ། (n.) liver 16.2
མཆུ་ཏོ། (n.) lip 16.2
མཆོངས། མཆོམས། L (vol. v.) to jump
མཆོད། H (vol. v.) to make offerings
(vol. v.) to eat, drink
མཆོད་ཁང་། (n.) shrine-room, chapel..... 18.2
མཆོད་མཇལ་ལ་ཕེབས། (idiom.) to visit a temple 21.2
མཆོད་རྟེན། (n.) stupa 40.2
མཆོད་ཞིག་ + རྒྱག (vol. v.) to make an offering of liquid butter for votive lamps.................................. 27.2
མཆོད་པ་ + ཕུལ། (vol. v.) to make offerings... 40.2
མཆོད་པ། (n.) offering
མཆོད་འབུལ། (n.) offering 40.2
མཆོད་རྫས། (n.) offerings 38.2
མཆོད་ཤོམས། (n.) altar 18.2
འཆར་ཅན། (adv.) usually, routinely
འཆར་གཞི། (n.) plan, project

ཇ་ Ja

ཇ། གསོལ་ཇ། H	(n.) tea	1.2
ཇ་ཁང་།	(n.) teashop	12.2
ཇ་མངར་མོ།	(n.) sweet milk tea	21.2
ཇ་ཐང་།	(n.) black unsweetened tea	21.2
ཇ་དམ།	(n.) thermos	17.2
ཇ་སྲུབ་མ།	(n.) churned tea	21.2
ཇག་པ།	(n.) bandit	
ཇུས་གཏོགས་ཆེ་པོ།	(adj.) inquisitive, indiscreet	
ཇོ་བོ་ཨ་ཏི་ཤ།	(pr. n.) Atīśa	27.2
ཇོ་བོ།	(n.) Lord (Buddha), statue in the Jhokhang	27.2
ཇོ་ཁང་།	(pr. n.) The Jhokhang (main temple in Lhasa)	11.2
ཇོ་མོ་གླང་མ།	(pr. n.) Mt. Everest	
འཇབ་དམག་རྒྱག	(vol. v.) wage guerilla warfare	
འཇམ་པོ།	(adj.) gentle	
འཇམ་དཔལ་དབྱངས།	(pr. n.) Mañjushri	27.2
འཇར་མན།	(pr. n.) Germany	9.2
འཇའ།	(n.) rainbow	25.2
འཇིག་རྟེན།	(n.) the world	
འཇུ། བཇུས།	(vol. v.) to grasp	
འཇུར་ཏ།	(n.) shoe	23.2
རྗེས་མ།	(adj.) next	3.2
རྗེས་མར།	(adv.) after, later	3.2
རྗེས་མར་མཇལ་ཡོང་།	(idiom.) see you later	3.2
རྗེ་ཙོང་ཁ་པ།	(pr. n.) Tsongkhapa	27.2
རྗེས་འདེད་+བཏང་།	(vol. v.) to chase, pursue	
རྗེས་ལ།	(n.) after	21.2
རྗེས་ལུས་ཐེབས།	(inv. v.) to arrive late	
རྗེས་ཟིན།	(inv. v.) to arrive on time	
ལྗགས་ལན་+བསྐྱོན། H	(vol. v.) to reply	
ལྗང་ཁུ།	(adj.) green	7.2
ལྗིད་པོ།	(adj.) heavy	
ལྗིད་ཚད།	(n.) weight	
བརྗེད།	(inv. v.) to forget	
བརྗེས།	(vol. v.) to change, exchange	27.2
བརྗེས་པོ་+རྒྱག	(vol. v.) to exchange	

ཉ་ Nya

ཉ།	(n.) fish	7.2
ཉ་པ།	(n.) fisherman	7.2
ཉ་ཤ།	(n.) fish (on a plate)	23.2
ཉན། གསན། H	(vol. v.) to listen to	
ཉམ་ཆུང་།	(adj.) humble	
ཉམས།	(inv. v.) to be spoiled	
ཉམས་འགྱུར།	(n). expression, appearance	37.2
ཉམས་མྱོང་།	(n.) experience	
ཉམས་ལེན་+བྱེད།	(vol. v.) to practise	
ཉམས་གསོ་ + བྱེད།	(vol. v.) to repair, renovate	28.2
ཉར།	(vol. v.) to keep	
ཉལ། གཟིམ། H	(vol. v.) to sleep, go to bed	7.2
ཉལ་ཁང་།		
གཟིམ་ཁང་། H	(n.) bedroom	18.2
ཉལ་ཁྲི། གཟིམ་ཁྲི། H	(n.) bed	18.2
ཉལ་ཆས།	(n.) bedclothes	18.2
ཉལ་ཟན།	(n.) blanket, quilt	
ཉི་གདུགས།	(n.) umbrella, parasol	
ཉི་མ།	(n.) sun, a day	1.2
ཉི་མ་བསྣན།	(inv. v.) to shine (of the sun)	
ཉི་མ་ཉིན་གང་།	(idiom.) the whole day	36.2
ཉི་འོད་ཀྱི་ཐབ།	(n.) solar heater	17.2
ཉི་ཤུ།	(adj.) twenty	
ཉི་ཧོང་།	(pr. n.) Japan	9.2
ཉིན་འཁྱོངས།	(adv.) the whole day	41.2
ཉིན་ག ཉིན་མོ། L	(n.) daytime	40.2
ཉིན་གུང་།	(n.) noon, afternoon	24.2
ཉིན་ལྟར་རེ་བཞིན།	(idiom.) each day	22.2
ཉུང་ཉུང་།	(adj., adv.) few	5.2
ཉུང་དུ་འགྲོ།	(v.inv.) to diminish	
ཉུང་ཤོས།	(adj.) minimum	
ཉེ་སྐོར།	(n.) surroundings	11.2
ཉེ་འདབས།	(n.) proximity	11.2
ཉེན་ཁ།	(n.) danger	
ཉེན་ཁ་ཆེ་པོ།	(adj.) dangerous	
ཉེན་སྲུང་།	(n.) safety, security	

ཉེས་ཐག་བཏང་། (vol. v.) to punish

ཉོ། 1ཉོས 2,3 (vol. v.) to buy 12.2

ཉོ་ཆ་ + རྒྱག། (vol. v.) to do the shopping 23.2

ཉོ་ཚོང་། (n.) commerce, business

ཉོན་མོངས། (n.) misery, wretchedness negative emotion

ཉོབ། (inv. v.) to be bored

གཉན། (n.) argali, mountain sheep 17.2

གཉིད་ཁུག (inv. v.) to fall asleep

གཉིད་སད། (inv. v.) to wake up
(vol. v.) to wake up someone

གཉིས། (adj.) two

གཉིས་ཀ། གཉིས་ཆ། (n.) both 21.2

མཉམ་དུ། ལྷན་རྒྱས། H (adv.) together, with 7.2

མཉམ་པོ། (adv.) together, with

རྙིང་པ། (adj.) old (object)................. 4.2

རྙིང་མ་པ། (pr. n.) Nyingmapa (sect)... 27.2

སྙོག་དྲ། (n.) problem

སྙན་ངག (n.) poetry

སྙན་པོ། (adj.) pleasant-sounding, interesting, harmonious 5.2

སྙན་ཤལ། H (n.) khatak (for idols) 27.2

སྙིང་། མགུལ་སྙིང་། H (n.) heart (anatomical) 16.2

སྙིང་། ཐུགས། H (n.) heart (spiritual)

སྙིང་རྗེ། ཐུགས་རྗེ། H (n.) compassion

སྙིང་འདོད།
ཐུགས་འདོད། H (mod. v.) to want, desire 26.2

སྙིང་རྗེ་པོ། (adj.) pretty, sweet 5.2

སྙིང་རུས། (n.) determination, courage

སྣུང་གུ། སྣུང་བུ། L (n.) awl 35.2

སྣུང་གཞི་བཏང་གནང་།H (inv. v.) to hurt, cause pain......................... 35.2

སྙོམ་པོ། (adj.) equal

བརྙན་འཕྲིན། (n.) television..................... 32.2

བརྙེད། (inv. v.) to find 28.2

བསྙལ། (vol. v.) to put (a child to bed)
(vol. v.) to ferment
(vol. v.) to hatch

ཏ་ Ta

ཏ་ཟིག (pr. n.) Persia, Iran, Iranian 9.2

ཏཱ་ལའི་བླ་མ། (n.) Dalai Lama (title)

ཏག་ཏག (adj.) exact 22.2

ཏར། (n.) telegram

ཏོག་ཙམ། L ཏིག་ཙ། (adv.) a little 22.2

ཏོ་མ་ཊོ། (n.) tomato 23.2

གཏན་འབེབས་ + གནང་། (vol. v.) to fix, establish 37.2

གཏན་གཏན། (adj., adv.) certain, sure 34.2

གཏམ་དཔེ། (n.) proverb

གཏིང་ (n.) base, bottom

གཏིང་ཟབ་པོ། (adj.) deep

གཏེར་ཁ། (n.) mine (gold, etc.)

གཏོར། (vol. v.) to destroy, demolish, waste, scatter

གཏོར་མ། (n.) *torma* 36.2

གཏོར་རྒྱག་ + རྒྱག (vol. v.) to destroy *torma* 36.2

བཏགས། (vol. v.) to tie, attach 28.2

བཏང་། (vol. v.) to send,
(vol. v.) to allow to go,
verbalizer 19.2

བཏབ། (vol. v.) to sow, plant

རྟ། ཆིབས་པ། H (n.) horse 5.2

རྟ་རྒྱུག (n.) horse race 33.2

རྟག་པར། (adv.) always

རྟགས། (n.) sign, mark, ... 36.2 symbol

རྟགས་མཚོན། (vol. v.) to represent, symbolise

རྟིང་པ། (n.) heel 31.2

རྟེན། (n.) support, base 33.2

རྟེན་འབྲེལ། (n.) interdependence, ceremony 36.2

ལྟ་བ། (n.) doctrine, theory 12.2

ལྟ། 1 བལྟས 2 ལྟོས། 3 (vol. v.) to look 12.2
(vol. v.) to try
(vol. v.) to read

ལྟ་སྐོར་+བྱེད། (vol. v.) to visit

ལྟ་སྐོར་ལ་འགྲོ།	(vol. v.) to go on a tour
ལྟ་སྟངས།	(n.) point of view
ལྟད་མོ། གཟིགས་མོ། H	(n.) show, spectacle 12.2
ལྟེབ་རྩེག་རྒྱག	(vol. v.) to fold
ལྟོ་ཆས།	(n.) food 34.2
ལྟོ་ཕད།	(n.) bag (for food)
སྟབས་བདེ་པོ།	(adj.) simple, convenient.... 22.2
སྟག	(n.) tiger 17.2
སྟངས།	(n.) way, manner,
	nominalizer 32.2
སྟར་ཁ།	(n.) walnut 23.2
སྟེར། གནང་། H	(vol. v.) to present a gift 8.2
སྟེར་བཟོ་དོད་པོ།	(adj.) superb, magnificent . 31.2
སྟོང་པ།	(adj.) empty 18.2
སྟོང་ཕྲག	(adj.) thousand
སྟོད་ཐུང་། སྐུ་སྟོད། H	(n.) shirt
སྟོན་ཐོག	(n.) harvest
སྟོན་ཀ།	(n.) autumn 24.2
སྟོན་པ།	(n.) guide, master 40.2
སྟོབས།	(n.) power, strength 22.2
སྟོབས་ལྡན།	(n.) corpse-cutter............... 27.2
བརྟག་དཔྱད་ + བྱེད།	(vol. v.) to examine,
	analyse 34.2
བསྟན།	(vol. v.) to show, express... 13.2
བསྟན་འགྱུར།	(pr. n.) Tängyur
བསྟན་བཞིག་ + བསླང་།	(vol. v.) to joke
བསྟན་བཞིག་ཚ་པོ།	(adj.) funny, amusing
བསྟེན།	(vol. v.) to consult 35.2

ཐ་ Tha

ཐ་སྙད་གཏེར་མཛོད།	(n.) vocabulary, lexicon
ཐ་མག བཞེས་ཐག H	(n.) cigarette, tobacco 12.2
ཐ་མག་འཐེན།	(vol. v.) to smoke
ཐ་པག	(n.) plate
ཐག་བཅད།	(vol. v.) to decide
ཐག་ཆོད།	(inv. v.) to resolve, make up one's mind
	(adv.) really, very 10.2
ཐག་ཉེ་པོ།	(adj.) close, near 14.2
ཐག་རིང་པོ།	(adj.) far, distant.................14.2
ཐང་།	(n.) plain, plateau
	(n.) pill for medical concoction..........................34.2
ཐང་ཆད།	(inv. v.) to be tired
ཐང་པོ།	(adj.) healthy
ཐང་ཤིང་།	(n.) pine, conifer
ཐད་ཀར།	(n.) direct, straightforward...................32.2
ཐད་འཕུར་གནམ་གྲུ།	(n.) helicopter 13.2
ཐད། H ཐེག HL	(vol. v.) to go 19.2
ཐབ་ཚང་།	
གསོལ་ཐབ། H	(n.) kitchen 17.2
ཐབ།	(n.) oven, stove, hearth 17.2
ཐབས་ཤེས།	(n.) means, method
ཐལ་ལ། ཐལ་བ། L	(n.) dust
ཐིག	(n.) line
ཐིགས་པ།	(n.) drop
ཐིམ་ཕུ།	(pr. n.) Thimphu
ཐུག མཇལ། H	(inv. v.) to meet....................8.2
ཐུག་པ། བཞེས་ཐུག H	(n.) noodles, noodle soup ...8.2
ཐུགས་འགྱོད་གནང་། H	(inv. v./ vol. v.) to regret
ཐུགས་རྗེ་ཆེ།	(n.) thank you 3.2
ཐུགས་རྗེ་ཆེ་+ཞུ། h	(vol. v.) to thank
ཐུགས་སྒྲོ།	(n.) reception, banquet,party
ཐུང་ཐུང་།	(adj.) short 3.2
ཐུན་མོང་།	(adj.) ordinary
ཐུན་མོང་མ་ཡིན་པ།	(adj.) unique, extraordinary
ཐུབ།	(mod. v.) to be able 11.2
ཐུར་མ།	(n.) spoon 17.2
ཐེ་ཚོམས།	(n.) doubt
ཐེ་ཚོམས་བྱེད།	(vol. v.) to hesitate
ཐེག་པ་ཆེན་པོ།	(n.) Mahayāna Buddhism..........................26.2
ཐེག་པ་ཆུང་ངུ།	(n.) Hīnayāna Buddhism 26.2
ཐེངས་མ	(n.) time, occasion 26.2
ཐེབས།	(inv. v.) to undergo, get hit, get taken, *verbalizer*
ཐེབས་རྩ།	(n.) funds

ཐེམ་པ། (n.) threshold 15.2
ཐོ། (n.) list
ཐོག་ཁ། (n.) roof
ཐོག་+རྒྱག (inv. v.) to have a lightning
ཐོག་མ། (n.) first 26.2
ཐོག་ས། (n.) storey
ཐོན། (inv. v.) to go out, leave 22.2
(vol. v.) to produce
ཐོབ། (inv. v.) to get, obtain, win
ཐོབ་ཐང་། (n.) right, authorisation
མཐའ། (n.) edge, margin, end 31.2
མཐའ་མ། (adj.) last 32.2
མཐུག་པོ། (adj.) thick, dense
མཐུན་སྒྲིལ། (n.) understanding, harmony, accord
མཐུན་པ་སྤུན་བཞི། (idiom.) the four harmonious siblings 37.2
མཐུན་པོ། (adj.) friendly, compatible
མཐུམ་སྒྲིལ། (n.) packet
མཐེ་བོ (n.) thumb
མཐོ་པོ། མཐོན་པོ། L (adj.) high 5.2
མཐོ་ཚད། (n.) altitude, height
མཐོང་། (inv. v.) to see
འཐུང་། 1 བཏུངས། 2 འཐུངས། 3 (vol. v.) to drink 10.2
འཐེན། (vol. v.) to pull, draw 25.2
འཐོར། (inv. v.) to be scattered, splashed

ད་ Da

ད། (adv.) now, so
ད་ག་ནང་བཞིན། (adv.) in the same way 11.2
ད་ག་རང (adv.) absolutely, really...... 13.2
ད་གིན། (adv.) a short while ago
ད་ལྟ། (adv.) now
ད་ལྟ་ནས (adv.) already
ད་དུང་། (adv.) moreover, again 5.2
ད་རང་། (adv.) this morning 24.2
ད་རེས། (adv.) this time 31.2
ད་ལོ། (adv.) this year 18.2
དག་ཆ། (n.) spelling
དང་། (co.) and 5.2
དང་པོ། (adj.) first
དད་པ། (n.) faith 5.2
དམ་བཅའ་ + བཞག (vol. v.) to promise, ... 37.2 to defend one's thesis
དམ་པོ། (adj.) tense, tight 18.2
དར། (inv. v.) to spread
དར་ལྕོག། (n.) prayer flag 25.2
དྭགས་པོ། (pr. n.) Dhagpo 22.2
དུ་བ། (n.) smoke
དུག། (n.) poison
དུག་སྦྲང་། L
དུག་སྦང་། (n.) mosquito 17.2
དུག་སློག ན་བཟའ། H (n.) clothing 23.2
དུང་ཕྱུར། (adj.) a hundred million
དུད་འགྲོ། (n.) animal, beast
དུད་ཚང་། (n.) family, household 29.2
དུམ་བུ། (n.) piece
དུར་ཁྲོད། (n.) cemetery
དུས། (co.) when 24.2
དུས་སྐབས། (n.) period
དུས་ཆེན། (n.) festival 25.2
དུས་དེབ་ (n.) magazine 5.2
དུས་ཚོད། (n.) time, moment 11.2
དུས་རབས། (n.) century 39.2
དུས་སང་། (adv.) next year 18.2
དེ། (dem.) that, *distant dem.* 1.2
དེ་འདྲ། (adv.) like that, such 8.2
དེ་ནས། L ཨ་ནི། (co.) and so? 16.2
དེ་མིན་པ། (adv.) apart from that 26.2
དེ་ཚོ། (dem.) those, *distant dem.* ... 2.2
དེ་རིང་། (adv.) today 8.2
དེང་སང་། (adv.) these days 10.2
(adv.) at present
དེབ། ཕྱག་དེབ། H (n.) book (Western style) 1.2
དེའི་སང་ཉིན། (adv.) the following day 25.2
དེའི་ཚེར་ལ། (co.) on the occasion 19.2
དོ། (class.) two units 23.2

དོ་དགོངས།	(adv.) this (coming) evening 18.2
དོ་སྣང་།	(n.) interest, attention
དོ་སྣང་+བྱེད།	(vol. v.) to be interested, to pay attention, to notice
དོ་པོ།	(n.) bag, pack (on an animal) 31.2
དོག་པོ།	(adj.) narrow 25.2
དོགས་པ།	(n.) suspicion, doubt
དོགས་པ་+ཟ།	(inv. v.) to be suspicious, doubt, distrust
དོན།	(vol. v.) to come out 22.2
དོན་དག	(n.) meaning 38.2
དོམ།	(n.) bear
དྲ་བའི་སྤོ་ལོ།	(n.) tennis 32.2
དྲ་བ།	(n.) net 32.2
དྲག དྭངས། H	(inv. v.) to get better 34.2
དྲག་པ།	see དྲེག་པ།
དྲང་འཁྲུ།	see དྲེག་འཁྲུ།
དྲང་པོ།	(adj.) honest
དྲག་པོ།	(adj.) hard, violent
དྲན།	(inv. v.) to remember, recall
དྲན་གསོ།	(n.) memorial, souvenir
དྲན་གསོ་+བྱེད།	
ཐུགས་དྲན་+གསོ། H	(vol. v.) to commemorate
དྲན་གསོ་+བཏང་།	(vol. v.) to remind so. of sth.
དྲན་པ།	(n.) memory
དྲན་པ་+བསོ།	(inv. v.) to recover one's senses
	(vol. v.) to remind someone
དྲི་བ། བཀའ་འདྲི།H	(n.) question
དྲི་མ།	(n.) smell, odour
དྲིལ་བསྒྲགས།	(n.) propaganda, publicity
དྲུག	(adj.) six
དྲུག་ཅུ།	(adj.) sixty
དྲུང་ཡིག	(n.) secretary 2.2
དྲེག་འཁྲུ། L དྲང་འཁྲུ།	(n.) washing, laundry 24.2
དྲེག་འཁྲུ་ + རྒྱག	(vol. v.) to do laundry 24.2
དྲེག་པ། H དྲག་པ།	(n.) dirt 24.2
དྲེད་མོང་།	(n.) Tibetan brown bear 17.2
དྲེལ།	(n.) mule
དྲོད་འཇམ།	(adj.) warm 34.2
དྭང་བླངས་+བྱེད།	(vol. v.) to volunteer
དྷ་རམ་ས་ལ།	(pr. n.) Dharamsala
གདན།	(n.) rug, low seat, cushion
གདན་ས།	(n.) seat; major monastic centre 39.2
གདམ་ཀ་+རྒྱག	(vol. v.) to choose
གདུང་།	(n.) spear 33.2
གདོང་པ། ཞལ་རས། H	(n.) face 16.2
བདག	(n.) self, I
བདག་པོ།	(n.) owner, lord
བདག་འཛིན།	(n.) selfishness
བདུན།	(adj.) seven
བདུན་ཅུ།	(adj.) seventy
བདུན་ཕྲག	(n.) week 9.2
བདེ་འཇགས།	(n.) safety, security
བདེ་པོ།	(adj.) well, fine 3.2
བདེན་པ།	(n.) truth 40.2
མདའ།	(n.) arrow
མདའ་ + རྒྱག	(vol. v.) to do archery, loose an arrow 33.2
མདང་དགོང་།	(adv.) yesterday evening.... 18.2
མདུད་པ།	(n.) knot
མདུན།	(post.) in front of 7.2
མདོ།	(n.) sutra
མདོང་མོ།	
གསོལ་མདོང་། H	(n.) tea churn 17.2
མདོག་ཉེས།	(adj.) ugly 13.2
མདོར་བསྡུད།	(vol. v.) to summarize, abridge
འདའི། འདིར། L	(adv.) here 10.2
འདར།	(inv. v.) to shake, tremble
འདས་པ།	(n.) the past
འདི།	(dem.) this near *dem.* 1.2
འདི་འདྲ།	(dem.) like this, such
འདི་ཚོ།	(dem.) these near *dem.* 2.2
འདུ་ཁང་།	(n.) assembly hall (in a monastery) 12.2
འདུ་ཤེས།	(n.) consciousness

འདུག	(aux.) there is, to have, to be *(testimonial)* 3.2
འདོ་པར། འདི་པར། H	(adv.) that way, around here 35.2
འདོད།	(mod. v.) to want 26.2
འདོད་ཆགས་ +ལང་།	(inv. v.) to become desirous 31.2
འདོད་པ། ཐུགས་འདོད།	(n.) desire, longing 26.2
འདོད་པ་ཁེངས།	(v.inv.) to be satisfied
འདྲ་པོ།	(adj.) like, resembling, similar
འདྲ་མི་འདྲ།	(adj.) various 9.2
འདྲེད་ཐར་ + ཤོར།	(inv. v.) to slip, slide 24.2
འདྲེས།	(inv. v.) to mix
རྡོ།	(n.) stone 25.2
རྡོ་རྗེ།	(n.) dorje, vajra 3.2
རྡོ་རྗེ་ཐེག་པ།	(n.) Vajrayana Buddhism .. 26.2
རྡོ་རྗེ་གླིང་།	(pr. n.) Darjeeling
རྡོ་རྗེ་གདན།	(pr. n.) Bodhgaya
རྡོ་སྣུམ།	(n.) petrol, gasoline 28.2
རྡོ་བཟོ་པ།	(n.) stonemason 32.2
ལྡང་།	(inv. v.) to be enough
ལྡི་ལི།	(pr. n.) Delhi
ལྡིར།	(vol. v.) to make a decoction34.2
ལྡུམ་ར།	(n.) kitchen garden
ལྡེ་མིག ཕྱག་ལྡེ། H	(n.) key................................. 3.2
ལྡེབས།	(n.) side, surface 39.2
ལྡོག་ཕྱོགས།	(n.) opposite
སྡིག་པ་ར་ཙ།	(n.) scorpion 17.2
སྡིགས་ར་སྐྱུལ།	(vol. v.) to threaten
སྡུག་བསྔལ།	(n.) suffering 4.2
སྡུག་ཆགས།	(adj.) bad, wicked 5.2
སྡུག་ཆགས་ཞེ་པོ་ཅིག	(adj.) horrible
སྡུག་རུས་རྒྱག	(vol. v.) to endure, put up with
སྡེ་སྲིད།	(n.) regent........................... 38.2
སྡེར་ཙེ།	(n.) plate
སྡོམ།	(n.) spider 17.2
སྡོམ་པས།	(adv.) altogether, in sum ... 18.2
བརྡབས།	(inv. v.) to run into, be hit
བརྡུངས།	(vol. v.) to hit, beat
བལྡགས།	(vol. v.) to lick, eat (yogurt) 24.2
བསྡད། 1,2 སྡོད། 3 བསྡད་ས།	(vol. v.) to sit, stay, live.........4.2
བཞུགས་ས། H	(n.) place, seat, dwelling 14.2
བསྡམ།	(vol. v.) to tie, bind
བསྡུ།1 བསྡུས། 2,3	(vol. v.) to collect, gather
བསྡུ་གསོག་རྒྱག	(vol. v.) to put away, get rid of
བསྡུར།	(vol. v.) to compare

ན་ Na

ན། ནམ། L	(part.) final interrogative particle..................................3.2
ན། སྙུང་། H	(inv. v.) to be ill 34.2
ན་ནིང་། L ཟླ་ཉིན།	(adv.) last year
ན་ཚ།	(n.) illness 35.2
ན་ཚ་+བཏང་།	(inv. v.) to hurt, cause pain...........................35.2
ནག་ཉེས་+བཙུགས།	(vol. v.) to accuse
ནག་པོ།	(adj.) black 3.2
ནང་།	(post.) in, inside 7.2
ནང་ནས།	(post.) among 39.2
ནང་པ།	(n.) Buddhist 26.2
ནང་པའི་ཆོས།	(n.) Buddhism, Dharma 26.2
ནང་མི།	(n.) family, family member....6.2
ནང་ལ།	(idiom.) at home 7.2
ནང་བཞིན།	(post.) like, as 21.2
ནང་ལོགས།	(n.) interior, inside 7.2
ནད་པ།	(n.) patient
ནད་གཡོག	(n.) nurse...............................8.2
ནམ་དུས།	(n.) season 24.2
ནམ་ཕྱེད།	(adv.) midnight
ནམ་ཡང་།	(adv.) never
ནས།	(n.) barley
ནས་བཟུང་།	(adv.) since 41.2
ནི།	(part.) thematizer 25.2
ནུ་མ།	(n.) breast 16.2
ནུབ།	(n.) west 20.2
ནུབ་ཕྱོགས།	(n.) west, western 20.2

ནུས། (mod. v.) to dare
ནུས་པ། (n.) power, energy
ནོར། (n.) wealth, yak
ནོར་ (inv. v.) to make a mistake
ནོར་བུ། (n.) jewel
ནོར་འཁྲུལ། (n.) mistake
ནོར་བུ་གླིང་ཁ། (pr. n.) Norbu lingka, summer palace of the Dalai Lama.. 11.2
གནང་། H (vol. v.) to give, offer 8.2
do, act *verbalizer*
གནངས་ཉིན་ཀ། (adv.) day after tomorrow .. 18.2
གནམ་གཤིས། (n.) weather, climate 22.2
གནམ་གྲུ། (n.) aeroplane..................... 13.2
གནམ་གྲུ་འབབ་ཐང་། (n.) airport.......................... 13.2
གནའ་བ། (n.) bharal, blue sheep....... 17.2
གནའ་སྔ་མོ (adv.) once upon a time, long ago
གནས། (inv. v.) to cost, be worth
གནས་སྐོར་བ། (n.) pilgrim 22.2
གནས་མཇལ། (n.) pilgrimage 11.2
གནས་ཚང་། (n.) lodging 28.2
གནས་ཚང་+ གཡར། (vol. v.) to find lodging 28.2
གནས་ཚུལ། (n.) situation, information
གནས་རི། (n.) holy mountain 11.2
གནོད། (n.) harm
གནོད་སྐྱེལ། (vol. v.) to harm
མནན། (vol. v.) to press
མནའ་སྐྱེལ། (vol. v.) to swear an oath
མནའ་མ། བག་མ། (n.) bride 6.2
མནལ་ཁུག H (inv. v.) to fall asleep
མནལ་ལམ་ +བཏང་གནང་། H (inv. v.) to dream
རྣམ་འགྱུར། (n.) attitude
རྣམ་ཐར། (n.) biography, hagiography
(n.) operatic libretto............ 24.2
རྣོ་པོ། (adj.) sharp
སྣ་ཁུག ཤངས། H (n.) nose 16.2
སྣ་མིན་སྣ་ཚོགས། (adj.) various, of different kinds 37.2
སྣག་ཚ། ཕྱག་སྣག H (n.) ink 1.2
སྣུམ། གཟིམ་སྣུམ། H (n.) oil, petrol 28.2
སྣེ་ཁ། (n.) sort, kind..........................8.2
སྣེ་ལེན་+ཞུ། h (vol. v.) to welcome, offer hospitality, lodge 41.2
བསྣམས། H (vol. v.) to take, take away............................19.2

པ་ Pa

པ་ཀི་སི་ཏན། (pr. n.) Pakistan 9.2
པ་ཀེཊ། (n.) pocket (in clothing)
པ་ཕ། པཱ་ལགས། H (n.) father 4.2
པ་སངས། (pr. n.) Venus (planet) 14.2
པགས་པ། (n.) skin, peel 22.2
པགས་ཚག (n.) sheepskin clothing 22.2
པར། སྐུ་པར། H (n.) photograph 6.2
པར་ཁང་ (n.) printing house
པར་ + རྒྱག (vol. v.) to photograph 14.2
པར་ཆས། (n.) camera 6.2
པི་ཝང་། (n.) Tibetan viol...................40.2
པིང་ཀྲུར་མ། (n.) kite (bird) 17.2
པེ་ཅིན། (pr. n.) Peking
པེ་ཤག (n.) money, change
པོ་ཏ་ལ། (pr. n.) Potala
པོ་ཏི། (n.) volume (book) 33.2
པུ་ལི་སི། (n.) police
པུས་མོ། (n.) knee 16.2
དཔང་པོ། (n.) witness
དཔལ་སྒོ། དཔྲལ་སྒོ། L (n.) forehead
དཔལ་ལྡན་ལྷ་མོ། (pr. n.) the goddess Pändän Lhamo 27.2
དཔལ་འབྱོར། (n.) economy, wealth
དཔེ་ཆ། ཕྱག་དཔེ། H (n.) pecha, Tibetan-style book 1.2
དཔེ་དེབ་ཚོང་ཁང་། (n.) bookshop
དཔེ་མཛོད་ཁང་། (n.) library 12.2
དཔེ་རང་རེད། (idiom.) that's amazing! 33.2
དཔེ་གསར། (n.) fashion
དཔེར་ན། (idiom.) for example 16.2
དཔེར་བརྗོད། (n.) example

དཔོན་པོ།	(n.) boss, leader, lord
དཔྱིད་ཀ།	(n.) spring 24.2
སྤ་སེ།	(n.) ticket............................ 19.2
སྤགས།	(n.) tsampa dough............. 24.2
སྤང་གོ	see སྤྲང་པོ། 29.2
སྤང་རི།	(n.) alpine pasture 29.2
སྤི་རག	(n.) beer 21.2
སྤྲིན་པ།	(n.) cloud
སྤུ་གུ	see ཕྲུ་གུ............................... 4.2
སྤུན་སྐྱ། སྐུ་མཆེད། H	(n.) relative, sibling, cousin 6.2
སྤུས་གཟིགས་+གནང་།	(vol. v.) to buy, obtain 28.2
སྤེན་པ།	(pr. n.) Saturn (planet) 14.2
སྤེའུ།	see སྤྲེའུ།
སྤོ་བོ། སྤོ་ལགས། H	(n.) grandfather, elderly man 6.2
སྤོ་ལོ།	(n.) ball 12.2
སྤོ་ལོ་+རྒྱག	(vol. v.) to play ball
སྤོབས་པ།	(n.) pride
སྤོས་དཀར།	(n.) hard plastic
སྤོས་ཤེལ།	(n.) amber 31.2
སྤྱང་ཀི།	(n.) wolf 17.2
སྤྱང་པོ།	(adj.) intelligent, clever 28.2
སྤྱན་རས་གཟིགས།	(pr. n.) Avalokiteśvara ...... 27.2.
སྤྱི་ཁྲེ།	(n.) meter
སྤྱི་མཐུན་རྒྱལ་ཁབ།	(n.) republic
སྤྱི་སྤྱོད་རླང་འཁོར།	(n.) bus 13.2
སྤྱི་ཚོགས།	(n.) society
སྤྱི་ཚོགས་རིང་ལུགས།	(n.) socialism..................... 26.2
སྤྱི་ཟླ།	(n.) month (international calendar) 14.2
སྤྱི་ལེ།	(n.) kilometer..................... 39.2
སྤྱི་ལོ།	(n.) year (international calendar) 14.2
སྤྱིའི་རྒྱ་མ།	(n.) kilogram
སྤྱིར་བཏང་།	(adv.) in general................ 38.2
སྤྲང་པོ།L སྤང་གོ	(n.) beggar 29.2
སྤྲེའུ། L སྤེའུ།	(n.) monkey, ape............... 17.2
ཕ་ Pha	
ཕ་གི	(dem.) that one (over there) *far dem.* 1.2
ཕ་ཚོ།	(dem.) those (over there) *far dem.* 2.2
ཕ་གཅིག་མ་གཅིག	(n.) sibling (same parents) ...6.2
ཕ་པོ།	see ཕྲ་པོ།
ཕ་མ། ཡབ་ཡུམ།H	(n.) parents
ཕ་ཡུལ།	(n.) natal land........................5.2
ཕ་ལམ།	(n.) diamond
ཕག་པ།	(n.) pig 23.2
ཕག་ཤ།	(n.) pork...............................23.2
ཕན་ཐོགས།	(n.) benefit, usefulness
ཕན་ཐོགས་ཡོད་པ།	(adj.) useful
ཕབས།	(vol. v.) to lower, drop, cause to fall
ཕར།	(adv.) away 15.2
ཕར་ཙམ་ད་གར།	(n.) just there.......................20.2
ཕར་བསློགས།	(vol. v.) to give back, return
ཕིང་ཕང་སྤོ་ལོ།	(n.) table tennis...................32.2
ཕིད།	see ཕུད།
ཕུ།	(n.) breath 30.2
ཕུ་ + རྒྱག	(vol. v.) to blow....................30.2
ཕུ་དུང་།	(n.) sleeve 31.2
ཕུང་།	(n.) heap, pile
ཕུད། L ཕིད།	(vol. v.) to take off, dismiss 31.2
ཕུར་ཕུར་+བྱེད།	(vol. v.) to stroke, massage
ཕུར་བུ།	(pr. n.) Jupiter (planet)........14.2
ཕུལ། h	(vol. v.) to give, offer, *verbalizer* 8.2
ཕེབས། H	(vol. v.) to go, come.............4.2
ཕོ།	(n.) male, masculine
ཕོ་བ།	(n.) belly 16.2
ཕོ་བྲང་།	(n.) palace 11.2
ཕོ་མཚན།	(n.) male sex 16.2
ཕོགས།	(n.) salary
ཕོགས་རྒྱག	(vol. v.) to pay a salary
ཕོར་པ།	(n.) wooden bowl 1.2

ཕྱག་བཏབ་+གནང་། H (vol. v.) to found (e.g., a monastery) 39.2

ཕྱག་ཕེབས་གནང་བྱུང་། (idiom.) welcome!................. 4.2

ཕྱག་ཚེམ་བསྐྱོན་པ། H (vol. v.) to sew

ཕྱག་མཛོད། (n.) treasurer

ཕྱག་རོགས་+གནང་། H (vol. v.) to help

ཕྱི་རྒྱལ། (n., adj.) abroad, foreign land.................................... 16.2

ཕྱི་པ། (n.) Hindu........................... 26.2

ཕྱི་པོ། (adj.) late 17.2

ཕྱི་པོ་བྱེད། (inv. v.) to be late

ཕྱི་ལྤགས། (n.) shell, carapace 22.2

ཕྱི་པི། ཕྱི་བ། L (n.) marmot......................... 17.2

ཕྱི་ཕྱོགས། (n.) outside, exterior............. 7.2

ཕྱིས (vol. v.) to wipe

ཕྱུ་པ། (n.) traditional robe, chuba................................. 23.2

ཕྱུག་པོ། (adj.) rich

ཕྱུར་བ། ཞིབ་ཕྱུར། H (n.) cheese

ཕྱེ་མར། (n.) dough of tsampa and butter 36.2

ཕྱེ་མ་ལེབ། (n.) butterfly

ཕྱེད་ཀ། (n.) half 12.2

ཕྱོགས། (n.) direction, side 15.2

ཕྲ་པོ། L ཕ་པོ། (adj.) thin (of cylindrical objects)

ཕྲུ་གུ L ཕྲུ་གུ ཨ་ལྷ། H (n.) child 4.2

འཕགས་པ། (n.) exalted, noble 37.2

འཕུར། L འཕིར། (vol. v.) to fly, glide

འཕྱ་ལས་རྒྱག། (vol. v.) to ridicule, mock

འཕྲིན་སྐྱེལ། (vol. v.) to transmit (by radio) 32.2

འཕྲུལ་འཁོར། (n.) machine, device 32.2

འཕྲུལ་ཆས་བཟོ་པ། (n.) mechanic 32.2

འཕྲོད། (inv. v.) to get used to, put up with.......................... 35.2

འཕྲོད་རྟེན། (n.) hygiene, health

བ Ba

བ་ཕྱུགས། (n.) cow 5.2

བག་ཆགས། (n.) impression, imprint

བག་ལེབ། བཞེས་བག H (n.) bread 8.2

བག་ཚ་མར་ཁུ། (n.) bhagtshamarkhu, (traditional Tibetan dish) 24.2

བང་ཁོག chest

བང་སོ། (n.) tomb.............................26.2

བབས། (vol. v.) to descend, to go down (inv. v.) to fall

བར་སྐོར། (pr. n.) Bharkor (part of Lhasa). 20.2

བར་དུ། (post.) up to, until..................9.2

བར་ཆད། (n.) obstacle, obstruction....36.2

བལ། (n.) wool 36.2

བལ་པོ། (pr. n., adj.) Nepalese 9.2

བལ་ཡུལ། (pr. n.) Nepal.........................9.2

བུ། སྲས། H (n.) son, boy..........................4.2

བུ་མོ། སྲས་མོ། H (n.) girl, daughter 4.2

བུ་རམ། (n.) molasses 36.2

བུ་ལོན། (n.) debt

བུམ་པ། (n.) vase 24.2

བེད་སྤྱོད་+བྱེད། (vol. v.) to use

བེར་ཀ (n.) walking stick 36.2

བོང་གུ see བོང་བུ།

བོང་བུ། L བོང་གུ (n.) donkey............................5.2

བོད། (pr. n.) Tibet 1.2

བོད་སྐད། (n.) Tibetan (oral) 5.2

བོད་ཇ། (n.) Tibetan tea 21.2

བོད་པ། (n., adj.) Tibetan 1.2

བོད་ཟླ། (n.) month (lunar calendar) 14.2

བོད་ཡིག (n.) Tibetan (written) 5.2

བོད་རིགས། (n.) Tibetan (nationality) 5.2

བོན། (n.) Bön 26.2

བོན་པོ། (n.) Bönpo 26.2

བྱ། (n.) bird

བྱ་རྒོད། (n.) vulture............................5.2

བྱ་གླག (n.) eagle............................17.2

བྱ་ཁྲུང་། (n.) crane (bird)...................17.2

བྱ་འཕིར། (n.) kite (plaything)
བྱ་ཤ། (n.) chicken (dish) 23.2
བྱང་། (n.) north 20.2
བྱང་ངོས། (n.) northward 20.2
བྱང་ཆུབ་སེམས་དཔའ། (n.) bodhisattva
བྱང་ཐང་། (pr. n.) Jhangthang, the Northern Plateau.......... 33.2
བྱང་ཕྱོགས། (n.) northern 20.2
བྱམས་པ། (pr. n.) Maitreya................. 27.2
བྱམས་པོ། (adj.) affectionate, gentle
བྱམས་པོ་+བྱེད། (vol. v.) to show affection
བྱས་ན། (co.) and so 12.2
བྱས་ཙང་། (co.) therefore..................... 12.2
བྱིའུ། (n.) small bird, fledgling
བྱི་ལ་དོམ། (n.) panda 17.2
བྱི་རིལ། (n.) sweet, candy
བྱུ་རུ། (n.) coral 31.2
བྱུང་། (inv. v.) to happen, occur
(aux.) receptive 8.2
བྱུང་འཛིན། (n.) receipt, bill
བྱེ་བ། (n.) ten million
བྱེ་མ། (n.) sand
བྱེ་ཐང་། (n.) sand desert
བྱེད། (1,3) བྱས། 2 (vol. v.) to do, act 8.2
(vol. v.) to become
(inv. v.) to happen, *verbalizer*........................... 28.2
བྲག (n.) cliff, crag
བྲག་རི། (n.) rocky mountain 29.2
བྲང་ཁོག L བང་ཁོག (n.) chest 16.2
བྲེལ་བ། ཐུགས་བྲེལ། H (n.) pressing business, hurry 12.2
བྲེལ་བ་ཚ་པོ། (adj.) busy
བྲོ་བ། ལྗགས་བྲོ། H (n.) taste 8.2
བྲོ་བ་ལྟ། (vol. v.) to taste
བྲོས། L བོས། (vol. v.) to escape, flee
བླ་མ། (n.) lama, master................. 2.2
བླུག (vol. v.) to pour, put............ 19.2
བློན་པོ། (n.) minister 28.2
དབང་སྒྱུར་+བྱེད། (vol. v.) to control, dominate

དབང་ཆ། (n.) power............................37.2
དབྲལ། (vol. v.) to tear
དབྱངས། (n.) tune
དབྱར་ཁ། (n.) summer.........................24.2
དབྱར་ས། (n.) summer camp 31.2
དབྱིན་ཇི། (n., adj.) England, English....5.2
དབྱིབས། (n.) shape, form
དབྱིས་རིགས། (pr. n.) Yi (ethnic group)
དབྱེ་བ་ཕྱེ། (vol. v.) to distinguish, differentiate
དབུ་གུར་ + སྒྲོན། (vol. v.) to pitch a tent.........40.2
དབུགས་+བཏང་། (vol. v.) to breathe
དབུགས་རྒྱུང་། (n.) breath
དབུས། (n.) centre, middle
(pr. n.) Central Tibet 11.2
དབུས་གཙང་། (pr. n.) Central and West-central Tibet
འབག ཞལ་འབག H (n.) mask 36.2
འབང་འཁྱིག see འབྲང་འཁྱིག
འབད་བརྩོན། (n.) effort
འབད་བརྩོན་+བྱེད། (vol. v.) to make an effort
འབབ་ཚུགས། (n.) station 13.2
འབའ་ཆ། (n.) musical instrument
འབར་མ། (pr. n.) Burma, Myanmar......9.2
འབར། (inv. v.) to be lit, burn 31.2
འབུ། (n.) insect, worm, bug...........7.2
འབུམ། (adj.) hundred thousand
འབེན། (n.) target 33.2
འབོལ་གདན། (n.) square, flat mattress 31.2
འབྱུང་ཁུངས། (n.) origin, source
འབྱོར། (inv. v.) to receive 19.2
འབྱོར་ལྡན། (n.) well-off, prosperous 37.2
འབྲང་འཁྱིག L
འབང་འཁྱིག (n.) queue, line....................33.2
འབྲས། ཞེས་འབྲས། H (n.) rice 8.2
འབྲས་དཀར། (n.) *dräkar*, operatic character.............................36.2
འབྲས་ལྗོངས། (pr. n.) Sikkim (India) 5.2
འབྲས་སྤུངས། (pr. n.) Dräpung monastery 11.2
འབྲས་བུ། (n.) result, fruit, consequence

འབྲས་སིལ།	(n.) sweet rice with potentilla tubers.................. 36.2
འབྲི།	(n.) yak-cow....................... 30.2
འབྲི། 1བྲིས། 2,3	(vol. v.) to write.................... 8.2
འབྲི་དེབ།	(n.) exercise book 8.2
འབྲིང་བ།	(adj.) middle, medium
འབྲུ།	(n.) grain 31.2
འབྲུག	(n.) dragon
འབྲུག་སྐད།	(n.) thunder
འབྲུག་སྐད་+རྒྱག	(inv. v.) to thunder
འབྲུག་པ།	(pr. n.) Bhutanese 9.2
འབྲུག་ཡུལ།	(pr. n.) Bhutan 5.2
འབྲེལ་བ།	(n.) relationship, connection
འབྲོག་པ།	(n.) nomad, herder 2.2
འབྲོང་།	(n.) wild yak 17.2
སྦ་ཁུག	(n.) purse, pouch
སྦ་གུར།	see སྦྲ་གུར།
སྦག་སྦག	(n.) motorcycle 12.2
སྦང་གུ།	see སྦྲང་བུ།
སྦང་ནག	see སྦྲང་ནག
སྦལ་པ།	(n.) frog.............................. 17.2
སྦས།	(vol. v.) to hide
སྦིད་པ།	see སྦུད་པ།
སྦུག	(n.) innermost part 31.2
སྦུད་རྒྱག་+བཏང་།	(vol. v.) to push
སྦུད་པ། L སྦིད་པ།	(n.) bellows........................ 30.2
སྦོམ་པོ།	(adj.) thick (cylindrical object)
སྦྱངས།	(vol. v.) to learn, study 10.2
སྦྱར།	(vol. v.) to stick 19.2
སྦྱིན་བདག	(n.) sponsor, patron 27.2
སྦྱོང་བརྡར་+བྱེད།	(vol. v.) to practise, train
སྦྱོང་ཚན།	(n.) exercise
སྦྲ་གུར། L སྦ་གུར།	(n.) yak-hair tent................. 30.2
སྦྲག་འཛིན།	(n.) postage stamp 19.2
སྦྲག་ཁང་།	(n.) post office 12.2
སྦྲག་པ།	(n.) postman/ -woman
སྦྲང་ནག L སྦང་ནག	(n.) fly (insect) 17.2
སྦྲང་བུ། L སྦང་གུ	(n.) flying insect................. 17.2
སྦྲང་ནོར་བུ། L སྦང་ནོར་བུ།	(n.) bee
སྦྲད། གནང་། H	(vol. v.) to give, offer, pass...8.2
སྦྲུམ་མ། L	(n.) pregnant woman
སྦྲུལ།	(n.) snake 17.2

མ་ Ma

མ།	(part.) negation 2.2
མ་གིར།	(adv.) down there................20.2
མ་ཉེས་ཁ་གཡོགས་ + བྱེད།	(idiom.) to accuse falsely......3.2
མ་གཏོགས།	(post.) except, otherwise 21.2
མ་འདྲ་བ།	(adj.) different
མ་བྱུན།	(n.) cook 8.2
མ་རྩ།	(n.) capital, investment
མ་རྩ་རིང་ལུགས།	(n.) capitalism 26.2
མ་ཟད།	(post.) apart from, not only...............................37.2
མང་ཆེ་བ།	(n.) majority, most.................5.2
མང་ཉུང་།	(n.) quantity 22.2
མག་པ། སྐུ་བག H	(n.) groom, husband 6.2
མང་དྲགས།	(adv.) too much, too many
མང་པོ།	(adj., adv.) many 5.2
མང་ཤོས།	(adj., adv.) most, maximum..5.2
མན། མིན། L	(aux.) not to be, *egophoric* ...3.2
མར།	(adv.) down, downwards 4.2
མར། གསོལ་མར། H	(n.) butter 19.2
མར་གྲོག	(n.) pat of butter 35.2
མར་བསྡད།	
མར་བཞུགས། H	(vol. v.) to sit down................4.2
མར་མེ། མཆོད་མེ། H	(n.) butter lamp 19.2
མི།	(n.) human being, man, person, people (aux.) *negation*......................3.2
མི་འདུག	(aux.) there is not,. not to have, not to be, *testimonial* 3.2
མི་འབོར།	(n.) population
མི་དམངས།	(n., adj.) populace, the people, public 35.2
མི་ཚང་།	(n.) family 15.2
མི་ཚེ།	(n.) life

མི་ལ་རས་པ།	(pr. n.) Milaräpa.................. 27.2
མི་རབས།	(n.) generation.................... 39.2
མི་རིགས།	(n.) race, nationality, ethnic group
མིག སྤྱན། H	(n.) eye 16.2
མིག མིད།L	(vol. v.) to swallow 34.2
མིག་པ། མིད་པ།L	(n.) throat............................ 16.2
མིག་དམར།	(pr. n.) Mars (planet).......... 14.2
མིག་ཤེལ། སྤྱན་ཤེལ། H	(n.) glasses, spectacles
མིག་སེར་ + ལང་།	(inv. v.) to be jealous.......... 31.2
མིང་། མཚན། H	(n.) name 9.2
མུ་ཟི།	(n.) matches
མུ་མཐུད།	(vol. v.) to continue
མེ། ཞུགས་མེ། H	(n.) fire 25.2
མེ་ཀྲག་བཏང་།	see མེ་སྦྲིག་བཏང་།
མེ་རྒྱག	(vol. v.) to set fire
མེ་ཏོག	(n.) flower 7.2
མེ་ + བཏང་།	(vol. v.) to light a fire 25.2
མེ་མདའ།	(n.) gun
མེ་མདའ་+རྒྱག	(vol. v.) to fire a gun........... 33.2
མེ་བཙའ།	(n.) moxibustion 34.2
མེ་ལོང་། H ཤེལ་སྒོ།	(n.) mirror 30.2
མེ་ཤི།	(inv. v.) to go out (of fire)
མེ་ཤོར།	(inv. v.) to catch fire
མེ་སྦྲིག་+བཏང་།L མེ་ཀྲག་+ བཏང་།	(vol. v.) to burn, set sth. on fire
མེ་ + བསད།	(vol. v.) to put out (a fire)
མེད།	(aux.) not to have, *egophoric*............................. 5.2
མེད་པ་+ཆགས།	(inv. v.) to disappear
མེད་པ་+བཟོ།	(vol. v.) to annihilate
མེད་པར།	(adv.) without
མོ།	(pron.) she........................... 2.2
མོ་ཊ། ཕེབས་ཏོ། H	(n.) car, automobile........... 11.2
མོ་ཊ་བཏང་།	(vol. v.) to drive (a car)
མོ་མཚན།	(n.) female sex 16.2
མོག་མོག བཞེས་མོག H	(n.) momo, Tibetan ravioli.... 8.2
མོག་ཀྲུ།	(n.) steamer....................... 17.2
མོན་པ།	(n.) Mönpa......................... 22.2
མོན་ཡུལ།	(pr. n.) Mönyül (region)
མྱངས།	(inv. v.) to feel, experience
མྱོང་།	(aux.) *experiential*...............15.2
དམག	(n.) war 41.2
དམག་+རྒྱག	(vol. v.) to wage war
དམག་སྒར།	(n.) military camp 41.2
དམག་སྤུངས།	(n.) army
དམག་མི།	(n.) soldier 13.2
དམངས་གཙོ་རིང་ལུགས།	(n.) democracy
དམངས་བཙུགས་སློབ་གྲྭ	(n.) state school 15.2
དམར་པོ།	(adj.) red...............................7.2
དམར་ཧྲེང་བ། L དམར་རང་ང་།	(adj.) naked
དམའ་པོ།	(adj.) low................................5.2
དམིགས་བསལ།	(adj.) special, exceptional (n.) exception 38.2
དམིགས་ཡུལ།	(n.) goal, aim.......................38.2
རྨ།	(n.) wound, injury
རྨ་བྱ།	(n.) peacock 17.2
རྨི་ལམ།	(n.) dream
རྨི་ལམ་+བཏང་།	(inv. v.) to dream
རྨོ་མོ། རྨོ་ལགས། H	(n.) grandmother, 2 elderly woman.........................6.
སྨད་གཡོགས།	(n.) skirt
སྨན། གསོལ་སྨན། H	(n.) medicine 8.2
སྨན་ཁང་།	(n.) hospital 12.2
སྨན་བཅོས།	(n.) medical treatment
སྨན་བཅོས་བྱེད།	(vol. v.) to nurse, treat medically
སྨན་པ།	(n.) doctor, physician 34.2
སྨན་རྩིས་ཁང་།	(pr. n.) Mäntsikhang, traditional hospital in Lhasa.................12.2
སྨན་ཚོང་ཁང་།	(n.) pharmacy, chemist
སྨོན་ལམ་ + རྒྱག	(vol. v.) to pray....................27.2
སྨོན་ལམ་ཆེན་མོ།	(pr. n.) the Great Prayer Festival, Mönlam 37.2
སྨྱུ་གུ ཕྱག་སྨྱུག H	(n.) pen.................................1.2
སྨྱུག་མ།	(n.) bamboo..........................1.2
སྨྱོ།	(inv. v.) to be mad, crazy
སྨྱོན་པ།	(adj.) mad

ཙ Tsa

ཙང་།	(co.) because 11.2
ཙམ།	(part.) about, roughly 9.2
ཙི་ཙི།	(n.) mouse, rat.................. 17.2
ཙི་ཙི་ལྡང་པོ།	(n.) bat 17.2
གཙང་།	(pr. n.) Tsang (region) 22.2
གཙང་པོ།	(n.) river 15.2
གཙོ་བོ།	(adj.) main, principal 11.2
གཙང་མ།	(adj.) clean, clear 17.2
གཙང་མ་ + བཟོ།	(vol. v.) to clean
གཙུག་ལག་ཁང་།	(pr. n.) the main temple of Lhasa, Jhokhang 20.2
གཙོ་འཛིན།	(n.) chief, head, director
གཙོད།	(n.) antelope 17.2
བཙན།	(n.) *tsän* (local warrior-god)....................... 41.2
བཙན་རྒྱལ་རིང་ལུགས།	(n.) imperialism
བཙལ།	(vol. v.) to look for, seek 28.2
བཙུགས།	(vol. v.) to plant, begin 33.2
བཙུག་ཁྲུ། གཟིམ་ཁྲུ། H	(n.) big woollen blanket 18.2
བཙུན་པོ།	(adj.) diligent, hard-working
བཙོག་པ།	(adj.) dirty 17.2
བཙོན་ཁང་།	(n.) prison
བཙོན་པ།	(n.) prisoner
བཙོས།	(vol. v.) to cook, boil........... 22.2
རྩ། ཕྱག་རྩ། H	(n.) pulse 34.2
རྩ་ལ།	(post.) at the home of, close to 29.2
རྩ་ཐང་།	(n.) grassland, steppe........ 22.2
རྩ་སྨན།	(n.) medicinal plant 34.2
རྩམ་པ། གསོལ་ཞིབ། H	(n.) tsampa, roasted barley flour........................... 8.2
རྩི་ཤིང་།	(n.) plant, vegetable
རྩིས་པ།	(n.) accountant, astrologer 32.2
རྩིག་པ།	(n.) wall
རྩིས་ + རྒྱག	(vol. v.) to count, calculate, reckon 22.2
རྩྭ།	(n.) grass
རྩེ།	(n.) peak, summit
རྩེ་པོ་བྲང་།	(pr. n.) "Summit Palace" (synonym of Potala)
རྩེ།	(vol. v.) to play 24.2
རྩེ་ཐང་།	(pr. n.) Tsethang, town 35.2
རྩེད་མོ།	(n.) game, toy
རྩེད་མོ་ + རྩེ།	(vol. v.) to play, joke 24.2
རྩོམ་པ་པོ།	(n) writer, author
རྩོམ་རིག	(n) literature
བརྩེགས།	(vol. v.) to pile up 31.2
བརྩེ་གདུང་།	(n.) love

ཚ Tsha

ཚ་གི་ཚོ་གི	(adj., adv.) nervous
ཚ་གྲང་།	(n.) temperature
ཚ་སྒྲོག	(n.) radiator
ཚ་པོ།	(adj.) hot.............................22.2
ཚ་པོ་ + བཟོ།	(vol. v.) to warm, heat up
ཚ་བོ། སྐུ་ཚ། H	(n.) nephew, grandson 6.2
ཚ་བ།	(n) heat, fever
ཚ་མོ། སྐུ་ཚ། H	(n.) niece, grand-daughter ...6.2
ཚ་ལུ་མ།	(n.) orange 23.2
ཚག་ཤ།	(n.) yak-meat.......................23.2
ཚགས་པར།	(n.) newspaper.....................2.2
ཚང་ཀ།	(n.) queue, line (of people)
ཚང་མ།	(quant.) all 13.2
ཚད།	(n.) measure
ཚད་རྒྱག	(vol. v.) to measure
ཚད་མ་རིག་པ།	(n.) logic
ཚན་རིག	(n.) science
ཚན་རིག་པ།	(n.) scientist........................32.2
ཚབ།	(post.) instead of
ཚབ་ + བྱེད།	
སྐུ་ཚབ་ + གནང་། H	(vol. v.) to replace, substitute
ཚར།	(vol. v.) to finish, end 12.2
ཚལ། བཞེས་ཚལ། H	(n.) vegetable 22.2
ཚལ་སླང་།	(n.) frying pan......................17.2
ཚྭ།	(n.) salt 21.2
ཚྭ་ཁ།	(adj.) salted 21.2
ཚིག	(n.) word 8.2

ཚིག	(inv. v.) to burn
ཚིག་གྲུབ།	(n.) sentence 8.2
ཚིག་པ་ཟ།	(inv. v.) to get angry
ཚིག་མཛོད།	(n.) dictionary 8.2
ཚིགས།	(n.) joint............................... 16.2
ཚུགས།	(inv. v.) to be established, to begin
ཚུར།	(n.) hither, towards oneself 15.2
ཚུར་བསློགས།	(vol. v.) to give back
ཚུལ།	(n.) way, manner 39.2
ཚེ་རིང་སྐྱིན་ཁེབས།	(n.) Tibetan "top-hat" 23.2
ཚེག L ཚག	(n.) intersyllabic point
ཚེམ་བུ་ +རྒྱག	(vol. v.) to sew
ཚེས་པ།	(n.) date 14.2
ཚེས་བཟང་དུས་བཟང་།	(idiom.) auspicious date.... 22.2
ཚོགས་ཆེན།	(n.) general assembly 37.2
ཚོགས་འདུ།	(n.) meeting 32.2
ཚོགས་འདུ་+ཚོགས།	(vol. v.) to hold a meeting
ཚོགས་པ།	(n.) group, party 32.2
ཚོང་ཁང་།	(n.) shop, store 12.2
ཚོང་མཁན	(n.) sales assistant
ཚོང་ + རྒྱག	(vol. v.) to do business 30.2
ཚོང་པ།	(n.) merchant, trader businessman 15.2
ཚོང་ཟོག	(n.) merchandise
ཚོན་ཁྲ།	(adj.) coloured 37.2
ཚོན་+བཏང་།	(vol. v.) to paint
ཚོན་མདོག	(n.) colour 25.2
ཚོམས་ཆེན།	(n.) living room 18.2
ཚོར་སྣང་	(n.) impression, sensation, feeling
མཚན་མོ།	(n.) night
མཚམས་མཚམས།	(adv.) sometimes, on occasion
མཚོ།	(n.) lake
མཚོན་རྟགས	(n.) sign, symbol
འཚོ།	(vol. v.) to live, lead a life
འཚོ་བ།	(n.) existence...................... 31.2
འཚོ་བ་སྐྱེལ་སྟངས།	(n.) way of living 32.2
འཚོང་། 1 བཙོང་། (2,3)	(vol. v.) to sell 12.2
འཚོར།	(inv. v.) to feel

ཛ་ Dza

ཛ་དྲག་ཆེན་པོ།	(adj.) urgent
མཛད་སྒོ།	(n.) ceremony......................38.2
མཛུབ་གུ། ཕྱག་མཛུབ H	(n.) finger............................16.2
མཛེས་མ།	(n.) beautiful woman
མཛེས་ནད།	(n.) leprosy..........................35.2
མཛེས་པོ།	(adj.) beautiful, handsome .13.2
མཛོ་	(n.) dzo, crossbreed of yak and cow..........................5.2
འཛགས།	see འཛེགས།
འཛམ་གླིང	(n.) world (geographical) 1.2
འཛིང་།	(vol. v.) to fight 22.2
འཛིན་སྐྱོང་།	(n.) administration
འཛིན་གྲྭ	(n.) class, course 2.2
འཛིན་ཆས།	(n.) furniture
འཛུམ་དམུལ་དམུལ་ + བྱེད།	(vol. v.) to smile
འཛུལ།	(vol. v.) to enter, go in.........31.2
འཛེགས། L འཛགས།	(vol. v.) to climb...................31.2
འཛོམས།	(vol. v.) to convene 37.2
རྫ་རི།	(n.) slate mountain 29.2
རྫས་འགྱུར།	(n.) chemistry
རྫིག་པོ།	(adj.) rich, impressive 28.2
རྫིས།	(vol. v.) to crush 22.2
རྫུས་མ།	(adj.) artificial, fake
རྫོགས།	(inv. v.) to be finished, be completed 28.2
རྫོང་།	(n.) fortress, county, county headquarters...........39.2

ཝ་ Wa

ཝ་མོ།	(n.) fox.................................17.2
ཝ་ཞྭ།	(n.) foxfur hat 23.2

ཞ་ Zha

ཞ་ཉེ།	(n.) lead
ཞྭ་མོ། དབུ་ཞྭ། H	(n.) hat..................................2.2
ཞབས་དག	(idiom.) cheers! bottoms up!

ཞབས་འཁྲོ་ + རྒྱག།	(vol. v.) to dance 40.2
ཞལ་འཁྲུས་ + གནང་། H	(vol. v.) to have a wash...... 36.2
ཞལ་ངོ།	(n.) disciplinarian,
	military rank (pre-1959) 37.2
ཞལ་གདངས་	(vol. v.) to open one's
+ གནང་། H	mouth................................ 34.2
ཞལ་པར་ + གནང་། H	(vol. v.) to telephone 19.2
ཞལ་པར་ + ཕུལ། H	(vol. v.) to telephone 19.2
ཞལ་ལག་མཉེས་པོ་...	(idiom.) bon appétit!,
གནང་གོ	enjoy your meal!.................. 8.2
ཞི་བདེ།།	(n.) peace
ཞི་མི། བྱི་ལ། L	(n.) cat 17.2
ཞིང་ཁ།	
ཕྱག་འདེབས། H	(n.) field................................ 4.2
ཞིང་ཆེན།	(n.) province
ཞིང་པ།	(n.) farmer............................ 2.2
ཞིང་ལས།	(n.) agriculture 2.2
ཞིབ་འཇུག	(n.) research
ཞིབ་འཇུག་ + བྱེད།	(vol. v.) to do research....... 34.2
ཞིབ་ཕྲ།	(adj.) detailed, precise
ཞིབ་ཞིབ།	(adj.) fine (powder, etc.),
	detailed
ཞིམ་པོ། སྤྲོ་པོ། H	(adj.) delicious...................... 8.2
ཞུ། 1ཞུས། 2,3 h	(vol. v.) to take 8.2
	(vol. v.) to ask, say
	(vol. v.) to eat, drink, *verbalizer*
ཞུ་དག་+བཏང་།	(vol. v.) to correct
ཞུ་མར།	(n.) lamp
ཞེ་དྲགས།	(adv.) very 7.2
ཞེ་པོ་ཅིག	(adv.) very 16.2
ཞེང་ག	(n.) width
ཞེད།	(inv. v.) to fear, be afraid...... 9.2
ཞོ། གསོལ་ཞོ། H	(n.) yogurt........................... 24.2
ཞོག་ཁོག བཞེས་ཞོག H	(n.) potato........................... 23.2
ཞོགས་གས།	
ཞོགས་པ། H	(n.) morning......................... 18.2
ཞོན།	(vol. v.) to ride (a horse,
	bicycle, etc.)
གཞན་དག	(adj.) other........................... 6.2
གཞས་ + བཏང་།	(vol. v.) to sing.................... 24.2
གཞི།	(n.) base, foundation
གཞིས་ཀ	(n.) domain, property
གཞིས་ཀ་རྩེ།	(pr. n.) Zhikatse....................1.2
གཞུག	(vol. v.) to take part
གཞུག་སྒུ	(n.) tail
གཞུག་ལ།	(post.) after.........................21.2
གཞུག་ལ་ཡོང་།	(vol. v.) to follow
གཞུང་།	(n.) government
	(n.) canonical work 35.2
གཞུང་ཚབ།	(n.) ambassador
གཞུང་ཚབ་ཁང་།	(n.) embassy 12.2
གཞུ། 1 གཞུས། 2, 3	(vol. v.) to strike, throw
གཞེས་ཉིན།	(n.) in three days' time........18.2
གཞོན་གཞོན།	(adj.) young 6.2
བཞག	(vol. v.) to put, set,
	leave, abandon 12.2
བཞངས།	see བཞེངས།
བཞར།	(vol. v.) to shave
བཞི།	(adj.) four
བཞི་བཅུ།	(adj.) forty
བཞི་མདོ་ཁ།	(n.) crossing, crossroads ...20.2
བཞུགས། H	(vol. v.) to stay, live...............4.2
བཞུགས་གྲལ་ + བཏང་།	(vol. v.) to take one's
	place..................................36.2
བཞུགས་...	
གདན་འཇགས། HH	(idiom.) please sit down 4.2
བཞེངས། L བཞངས།	(vol. v.) to build, construct ..37.2

ཟ་ Za

ཟ། 1བཟས། 2 ཟོས། 3	(vol. v.) to eat 10.2
ཟ་ཁང་།	(n.) restaurant 12.2
ཟ་པོ།	(adj.) deep
ཟག	(inv. v.) to fall
ཟང་ཟིང་།	(n.) disorder, chaos
ཟངས།	(n.) copper
ཟངས་དཀར།	(pr. n.) Zangskar (India) 5.2
ཟམ་པ།	(n.) bridge...........................24.2
ཟི་ལིང་།	(pr. n.) Xining
ཟིན། L ཟིམ།	(vol. v.) to catch, hold, grasp

ཟིན་པར	(n.) to (telling the time) 12.2
ཟིམ།	see ཟིན།
ཟུག	(inv. v.) to be fixed, planted 25.2
ཟུག+ རྒྱག	(inv. v.) to hurt, be in pain
ཟུབ།	(inv. v.) to be deleted
ཟུར།	(n.) corner, angle
ཟུར་གསུམ།	(n.) triangle
ཟེར། ཞུ། H	(vol. v.) to be called, to say 9.2
ཟླ་ཉིན། ན་ནིང་། L	(n.) last year 18.2
ཟླ་འགོ།	(n.) beginning of the month
ཟླ་འཇུག	(n.) end of the month
ཟླ་བ།	(n.) moon, month................. 1.2
ཟླ་བ་དགུ་པ།	(n.) 9th month..................... 14.2
ཟླ་བ་བརྒྱད་པ།	(n.) 8th month..................... 14.2
ཟླ་བ་ལྔ་པ།	(n.) 5th month..................... 14.2
ཟླ་བ་བཅུ་པ།	(n.) 10th month................... 14.2
ཟླ་བ་བཅུ་གཅིག་པ།	(n.) 11th month................... 14.2
ཟླ་བ་བཅུ་གཉིས་པ།	(n.) 12th month................... 14.2
ཟླ་བ་གཉིས་པ།	(n.) 2nd month 14.2
ཟླ་བ་དང་པོ།	(n.) 1st month..................... 14.2
ཟླ་བ་དྲུག་པ།	(n.) 6th month..................... 14.2
ཟླ་བ་བདུན་པ།	(n.) 7th month..................... 14.2
ཟླ་བ་བཞི་པ།	(n.) 4th month 14.2
ཟླ་བ་གསུམ་པ།	(n.) 3rd month..................... 14.2
ཟླ་པོ། སྐུ་ཟླ། H	(n.) spouse 6.2
ཟློས་གར།	(n.) theatrical performance
ཟློས་གར་ཁང་།	(n.) theater hall 12.2
གཟབ་གཟབ་ + བྱེད།	(vol. v.) to be careful 24.2
གཟའ།	(n.) planet 14.2
གཟའ་རྒྱག	(inv. v.) to be paralyzed
གཟའ་འཇུག	(n.) weekend
གཟའ་ཉི་མ།	(n.) Sunday........................ 14.2
གཟའ་པ་སངས།	(n.) Friday 14.2
གཟའ་སྤེན་པ།	(n.) Saturday 14.2
གཟའ་ཕུར་བུ།	(n.) Thursday 14.2
གཟའ་མིག་དམར།	(n.) Tuesday 14.2
གཟའ་ཟླ་བ།	(n.) Monday....................... 14.2
གཟའ་ལྷག་པ།	(n.) Wednesday 14.2
གཟི།	(n.) zi-stone (ornament)......31.2
གཟིག	(n.) leopard..........................17.2
གཟིགས་འབུལ་+ཞུ། h	(vol. v.) to stage a performance........................41.2
གཟིགས། H	(vol. v.) to buy (vol. v.) to look at (inv. v.) to see 12.2
གཟུགས་བརྙན།	(n.) image, reflection...........37.2
གཟུགས་པོ།	
སྐུ་གཟུགས། H	(n.) body................................3.2
གཟུགས་པོ་ + བཀྲུས།	(vol. v.) to bathe (oneself) .18.2
གཟུགས་པོ་སྐྱོ་པོ།	(adj.) weak
གཟུགས་པོ་ཐུང་ཐུང་།	(adj.) short (stature) 3.2
གཟུགས་པོ་ + འདུག	(inv. v.) to be pregnant
གཟུགས་པོ་རིང་པོ།	(adj.) tall (stature) 3.2
བཟའ་ཆས།	(n.) provisions, victuals
བཟོ། 1བཟོས། 2,3	(vol. v.) to make, construct (roads, objects, etc.), *verbalizer* 8.2
བཟོ་གྲྭ།	(n.) factory
བཟོ་ལྟ།	(n.) shape
བཟོ་པ།	(n.) worker...........................32.2
བཟོ་ལས།	(n.) industry
བཟོད་པ།	(n.) patience
བཟོད་པ་+སྒོམ།	(inv. v.) to be patient

འ་ 'a

འུར་རྡོ།	(n.) slingshot 30.2
འོ་མ། ཆབ་འོ།	(n.) milk 21.2
འོ་ན།	(idiom) well, and so 3.2
འོག	(post.) under, underneath.....7.2
འོག་འཇུག སྐུ་འཇུག H	(n.) woman's blouse 23.2
འོག་མ། ཨོ་ལགས། H	(n.) younger sibling...............6.2
འོང་སྐོར།	(n.) harvest festival 33.2
འོང་ག	(n.) village fields 33.2
འོད།	(n.) light
འོས་ཤོག་བླུག	(vol. v.) to vote

ཡ་ Ya

ཡ་གིར། (adv.) up there 20.2
ཡ་མཚན་ + སྐྱེ། (inv. v.) to be amazed 37.2
ཡ་རབས། (adj.) polite
ཡག་པོ། (adj.) good, well 5.2
ཡང་། L ཡའི་ (co.) also, too 5.2
ཡང་བསྐྱར་+ བཤད། (vol. v.) to repeat
ཡང་དག་པ (adj.) perfect
ཡང་ན། འམ། L (co.) or, or else 21.2
ཡང་ཚི་+བརྒྱུགས། (vol. v.) to weigh
ཡང་པོ། (adj.) light
ཡང་སེ། (adv.) often, frequently
ཡབ། H (n.) father (of so. else) 6.2
ཡམ་བུ། (pr. n.) Kathmandu
ཡའི་ see ཡང་།
ཡར། (adv.) upwards 4.2
ཡར་རྒྱས། (n.) progress
ཡར་ཤོག ཡར་ཕེབས། H (vol. v.) come in! 4.2
ཡར་ཆིབས་སྒྱུར་'''
གནང་གོ HH (idiom.) come in! 10.2
ཡལ་ག (n.) branch
ཡི་གེ ཕྱག་བྲིས། H (n.) letter, mail 5.2
ཡི་རྩི། (n.) soap
ཡིག་སྐོགས། (n.) envelope 19.2
ཡིག་ཚད། (n.) written examination
ཡིག་ཚད་+བཏང་། (vol. v.) to sit an exam 37.2
ཡིད་ཆེས་+བྱེད། (vol. v.) to believe, believe in
ཡིད་བཞིན་ནོར་བུ། (n.) title of the Dalai Lama
ཡིན། (aux.) to be, *egophoric* 3.2
ཡིན་དགོས་བྱུང་། (adv.) of course 31.2
ཡིན་ད་ཡིན།
ཡིན་དང་ཡིན། L (adv.) of course 13.2
ཡིན་ན་ཡང་། L
ཡིན་ནའི། (adv.) but 5.2
ཡིན་ནའི། see ཡིན་ན་ཡང་།
ཡིན་སྲིད་ཀྱི་མ་རེད། (idiom.) impossible
ཡུ་གུར་རིགས། (n.) Uighur
ཡུ་རོབ། (pr. n., adj.) Europe, European 5.2
ཡུམ། H (n.) mother (of so. else) 6.2
ཡུམ་བུ་བླ་སྒང་། (pr. n.) Yumbulakang 26.2
ཡུན་རིང་པོ། (adv.) for a long time
ཡུལ་སྐད། (n.) dialect
ཡུལ་སྐོར་སྤྲོ་འཆམ། (n.) tourism
ཡུལ་ལྗོངས། (n.) countryside, landscape
ཡེ་ཤུ། (n.) Christian 26.2
ཡོང་། 1,2 ཤོག 3 (vol. v.) to come 4.2
ཡོང་ང་། (idiom.) all right, OK 14.2
ཡོད། (aux.) to have, *egophoric* 5.2
ཡོད་མ་རེད། (aux.) there isn't, not to have, *assertive* 5.2
ཡོད་པ་འདྲ། (aux.) there probably is 11.2
ཡོད་རེད། (aux.) there is, to have *assertive* 5.2
ཡོན་ཆབ། (n.) offering-water
ཡོན་ཏན། (n.) quality, excellence
ཡོས (n.) hare 17.2
གཡག (n.) yak 5.2
གཡར། (vol. v.) to lend, borrow 12.2
གཡས། (post.) right (hand) 7.2
གཡས་གཡོན། (post.) around 21.2
གཡི། (n.) lynx 17.2
གཡུ། (n.) turquoise 31.2
གཡུགས། (vol. v.) to throw
གཡོ་སྒྱུ་ཆ་པོ (adj.) hypocrite
གཡོག་པོ།
ཞབས་ཕྱི། H (n.) servant
གཡོན། (post.) left (hand) 7.2

ར་ Ra

ར་བཟི། (inv. v.) to be drunk
ར་སྤྲོད། (n.) proof
ར་སྤྲོད་+ བྱེད། (vol. v.) to prove
ར། (n.) goat 5.2
རག (n.) brass
རག (inv. v.) to obtain, acquire 26.2
རག་ལས། (inv. v.) to depend

རང་།	(pron.) oneself
	(pron.) you 3.2
	(adv.) really 21.2
རང་འབྱུང་ཁམས།	(n.) nature
རང་དབང་།	(n.) freedom
རང་དབང་ཡོད་པ།	(adj.) free
རང་ཤི་རྒྱག	(vol. v.) to commit suicide
རང་བཙན།	(n.) independence
རན།	(mod. v.) to be time to........ 28.2
རལ།	(inv. v.) to be torn 22.2
རས།	(n.) cotton
རས་ཆ།	(n.) cotton cloth
རི།	(n.) hill, mountain 5.2
རི་གོང་། རི་བོང་། L	(n.) rabbit........................... 17.2
རི་རྒྱུད།	(n.) mountain range 13.2
རི་དྭགས།	(n.) game, wild animal
རི་དྭགས་བཏང་།	(vol. v.) to hunt
རི་འབུར།	(n.) hill................................. 29.2
རི་མོ།	(n.) drawing 6.2
རི་ལི། མེ་འཁོར། L	(n.) train 13.2
རིག་གནས།	(n.) culture
རིག་གནས་གསར་བརྗེ།	(n.) Cultural Revolution...... 26.2
རིག་པ་ཅན།	(adj.) intelligent................... 28.2
རིག་གཞུང་།	(n.) culture, civilization
རིག་ཤོག	(n.) rickshaw....................... 14.2
རིགས།	(n.) sort, kind
རིང་པོ།	(adj.) long 3.2
རིན་ཆེན།	(adj.) precious 38.2
རིན་པོ་ཆེ།	(n.) Precious One (title), Rinpoche
རིམ་པ།	(n.) rank, level
རིལ།	(inv. v.) to fall, trip
རིལ་བུ།	(n.) pill................................. 34.2
རུ་ཁག	(n.) team, brigade............... 12.2
རུ་སྒྲིགས།	(n.) military march 41.2
རུ་མ་བཅུག	(vol. v.) to forbid
རུལ།	(inv. v.) to rot, decay
རུས་ཁོག	(n.) bone
རེ་བ།	(n.) hope
རེ་བ་+ བྱེད།	(vol. v.) to hope
རེ་མོས་+བྱེད།	(vol. v.) to take one's turn...41.2
རེ་རེ།	(adj.) each...........................19.2
རེད།	(aux.) to be...........................1.2
རེད་པ།	(aux.) isn't that so? 10.2
རེད་བཞག	(aux.) to be, revelatory 6.2
རོ།	(n.) corpse
རོགས་གནང་། H	(aux.) imperative.................13.2
རོགས་པ།	(n.) companion....................35.2
རོགས་རམ།	(n.) help
རོགས་རམ་+བྱེད།	(vol. v.) to help
རོལ་ཆ་བཏང་མཁན།	(n.) musician
རོལ་མོ།	(n.) music
རླངས་འཁོར། L	(n.) car.................................11.2
རླུང་།	(n.) air
རླུང་རྟ།	(n.) "wind-horse" 25.2
རླུང་འཕྲིན།	(n.) radio.............................32.2
རླུང་ལང་པ།	(inv. v.) to get angry
རླུང་བསླང་པ།	(vol. v.) to make someone angry
རློན་པ།	(adj.) wet, damp
རློན་གྱི་རིགས།	(n.) liquid
བརླགས།	(inv. v.) to lose

ལ་ La

ལ།	(n.) mountain pass..............29.2
ལ་ + རྒྱག	(vol. v.) to cross a pass 29.2
ལ་དུག	(n.) altitude sickness...........35.2
ལ་དྭགས།	(pr. n.) Ladakh 5.2
ལ་ཕུག	(n.) radish............................23.2
ལ་སོགས་པ།	(part.) et cetera 5.2
ལག་ཁྱེར། ཕྱག་ཁྱེར H	(n.) permit, passport 13.2
ལག་ངར།	(n.) arm
ལག་ཆ།	(n.) tool, instrument
ལག་རྟགས།	(n.) gift
ལག་པ། ཕྱག H	(n.) hand..............................16.2
ལག་པ་འཆངས།	(vol. v.) to touch
ལག་རྩལ།	(n.) technology
ལག་ལེན་+བྱེད།	(vol. v.) to put into practice
ལག་ཤུབས།	(n.) glove

ལགས།	(part.) marker of politeness . 1.2
ལད་མོ་+བྱེད།	(vol. v.) to imitate
ལན། ལྷུགས་ལན། H	(n.) reply, message
ལན་རྒྱག	(vol. v.) to reply
ལབ།	(vol. v.) to say, speak......... 20.2
ལམ་ཁག ལམ། L	(n.) road, way, route............ 3.2
ལམ་འགྲོ	(n.) luck, fortune
ལམ་ལུགས།	(n.) system
ལམ་སེང་།	
L ལམ་སང་།	(adv.) immediately, at once
ལས།	(n.) karma
ལས། ལུས། L	(inv. v.) to leave, abandon
ལས་ཀ། ཕྱག་ལས། H	(n.) work, action 10.2
ལས་ཀ + བྱེད།	(vol. v.) to work.................. 10.2
ལས་ཁུངས།	(n.) office
ལས་འགན།	(n.) responsibility
ལས་བྱེད་པ།	(n.) official, civil servant 13.2
ལས་སླ་པོ།	(adj.) easy............................ 4.2
ལི།	(n.) high-quality bronze
	(n.) pear
ལུག	(n.) sheep 5.2
ལུག་རྫི།	(n.) shepherd..................... 29.2
ལུག་ཤ།	(n.) mutton 23.2
ལུགས་སྲོལ།	(n.) tradition, custom.......... 24.2
ལུང་པ།	(n.) valley, land.................... 5.2
ལུང་པའི་མདའ།	(n.) lower part of a valley,
	major valley 30.2
ལུང་པའི་ཕུ།	(n.) upper part of a valley,
	tributary valley.................... 30.2
ལུས། L	(n.) body
ལུས་རྩལ།	(n.) sport
ལུས་རྩལ་ཐང་།	(n.) stadium
ལེ་ལོ།	(n.) laziness
ལེ་ལོ་ཅན།	(n.) lazy
ལེན། བཞེས། H	(vol. v.) to take 10.2
ལེབ་ལེབ།	(adj.) flat
ལོ། དགུང་ལོ། H	(n.) year, age
ལོ་རྒྱུས།	(n.) history
ལོ་ལྟར་རེ་བཞིན།	(n.) each year.................... 22.2
ལོ་མ།	(n.) leaf
ལོ་གསར།	(n.) New Year......................28.2
ལོག	(inv. v.) to return, go back ..24.2
ལོག་དགར།	(adj.) separate, different
ལོང་།	(mod. v.) to have time.........32.2

ཤ་ Sha

ཤ། གསོལ་ཀྲུམ། H	(n.) meat...............................8.2
ཤ་སྐམ་པོ།	(adj.) thin, slim
	(n.) dried meat 24.2
ཤ་རྒྱགས་པ།	(adj.) fat, stout, stocky
ཤ་སྟག	(adv.) only, solely................37.2
ཤ་བ།	(n.) deer..............................17.2
ཤ་བག་ལེབ།	(n.) bread with meat filling....8.2
ཤ་འབྲས།	(n.) rice and meat stew 8.2
ཤ་མོ།	(n.) mushroom 30.2
ཤཱཀྱ་ཐུབ་པ།	(pr. n.) the Buddha
	Śākyamuni 27.2
ཤག	(n.) monk's or nun's cell 24.2
ཤར།	(n.) east..............................20.2
ཤར།	(inv. v.) to rise, appear 24.2
ཤར་གླིང་།	(pr. n.) Asia
ཤར་རྒྱག	(adj., adv.) straight,
	directly................................20.2
ཤར་ཕྱོགས།	(adj.) eastern, oriental 20.2
ཤི། གྲོངས། H	(inv. v.) to die
ཤིང་།	(n.) wood
ཤིང་བཟོ་བ།	(n.) carpenter
ཤིང་ནགས།	(n.) forest
ཤིང་ཏོག	(n.) fruit...............................23.2
ཤིང་སྡོང་།	(n.) tree...............................35.2
ཤུགས།	(n.) strength
ཤུགས་རྐྱེན།	(n.) influence, effect
ཤུགས་ཆེན་པོ།	(adj.) strong
ཤུལ།	(n.) traces, remains
	(n.) ruins.............................25.2
ཤུལ་རིང་གར།	
ཡུན་རིང་། L	(co.) during.........................37.2
ཤུས	(vol. v.) to copy
ཤེལ།	(n.) crystal, glass

ཤེལ་སྒོ།	(n.) window pane, mirror
ཤེལ་དམ།	(n.) bottle 17.2
ཤེས་ཡོན་ཅན།	(n.) intellectual
ཤེས། མཁྱེན། H	(inv. v.) to know, understand 16.2
ཤེས་རིག	(n.) culture
ཤོ་ + རྒྱག	(vol. v.) to play dice........... 24.2
ཤོག་གུ ཕྱག་ཤོག H	(n.) paper............................. 1.2
ཤོག་ལྷེ།	(n.) page
ཤོར།	(inv. v.) to let go, release *verbalizer*........................... 28.2
གཤག་གཅོད་བྱེད།	(vol. v.) to be operated on
གཤམ།	(adv.) below, lower............ 31.2
གཤིས་ཀ།	(n.) character, temperament
གཤེ་གཤེ་བཏང་།	(vol. v.) to reprimand, scold
གཤེགས། HL གཤགས། H	(inv. v.) to die
བཤད།	(vol. v.) to relate, speak, say
བཤད་པ་ + རྒྱག	(vol. v.) to make a speech, explain 36.2

ས་ Sa

ས།	(n.) earth, place *nominalizer*......................... 14.2
ས་བཀྲ།	(n.) map 1.2
ས་སྐྱ་པ།	(pr. n.) Sakyapa (sect) 27.2
ས་ཁམས་རིག་པ།	(n.) geography
ས་ཁུལ།	(n.) region
ས་ག་ཟླ་བ།	(pr. n.) the Fourth Month, a Buddhist festival............. 40.2
ས་ཆ།	(n.) place, location
ས་གདན།	(n.) floor rug....................... 31.2
ས་མ་འབྲོག	(n.) part herder, part farmer......................... 29.2
ས་མཚམས།	(n.) frontier, boundary
ས་ཤུར།	(n.) ditch, trench................ 33.2
ས་ཡ།	(n.) million
ས་ཡིག	(n.) signature
ས་ཡིག་+རྒྱག	(vol. v.) to sign
སང་དགོང་།	(adv.) tomorrow evening.... 18.2
སང་ཉིན།	(adv.) tomorrow.....................8.2
སང་ཞོགས།	(adv.) tomorrow morning.....18.2
སངས་རྒྱས།	(n.) Buddha 27.2
སི་པན། ཞྷགས་སྤོད་ H	(n.) chili, hot spice...............36.2
སུ།	(interr. pron.) who? 2.2
སུད་སི།	(pr. n.) Switzerland, Swiss ...9.2
སུབ།	(vol. v.) to erase
སུམ་ཅུ།	(adj.) thirty
སེ་པན།	(n.) Spain, Spanish...............9.2
སེ་འབྲུ	(n.) berry................................23.2
སེ་ར།	(pr. n.) Sera Monastery 11.2
སེ་ར།	(n.) hail 24.2
སེ་ར་ + བཏང་།	(inv. v.) to hail 24.2
སེང་གེ	(n.) lion
སེན་མོ། ཕྱག་སེན། H	(n.) fingernail
སེམས། ཐུགས། H	(n.) mind, spirit......................3.2
སེམས་སྐྱོ་པོ།	(adj.) sad
སེམས་ཁམས་རིག་པ།	(n.) psychology
སེམས་ཁུར།	(n.) interest, preoccupation
སེམས་ཁྲལ།	(n.) worry, anxiety
སེམས་ཁྲལ་ + བྱེད།	(vol. v.) to worry..................24.2
སེམས་འགུལ།	(n.) emotions
སེམས་ཅན།	(n.) living being, animal 22.2
སེམས་བཟང་པོ།	(adj.) kind-hearted
སེམས་པ་ + ཤོར།	(inv. v.) to fall in love...........31.2
སེར་པོ།	(adj.) yellow...........................7.2
སེར་ཕྲེང་། L	
སེར་ཕང་།	(n.) procession....................38.2
སེར་ཤ།	(n.) variety of mushroom ...30.2
སེལ།	(vol. v.) to purge..................36.2
སོ། ཚེམས། H	(n.) tooth.............................16.2
སོ་ + རྒྱག	(vol. v.) to bite 30.2
སོ་ནམ།	(n.) agriculture
སོ་ནམ་པ།	(n.) farmer
སོ་པ།	(n.) spy
སོ་ལོ་སྔོན་པོ།	(n.) capsicum, green pepper................................23.2
སོག་པོ།	(pr. n.) Mongol 9.2
སོག་ཡུལ།	(pr. n.) Mongolia 9.2
སོན་ལ་ཕུག	(n.) pink radish....................22.2

སོབ་སོབ།	(adj.) soft
སྲང་ལམ།	(n.) street, alley 41.2
སྲབ་པོ།L ཀྲབ་པོ།	(adj.) thin (cloth)
སྲམ། L ཀྲམ།	(n.) otter............................. 17.2
སྲན་མ།L ཀྲན་མ།	(n.) bean 36.2
སྲིད།	(mod. v.) to be possible, be able
སྲིད་འཛིན།	(n.) president
སྲིད་གཞུང་།	(n.) government.................. 35.2
སྲུ་མོ།	(n.) maternal aunt................. 6.2
སྲུང་སྐར།	(n.) satellite......................... 32.2
སྲུང་སྐྱོབ་+བྱེད།	(vol. v.) to defend, protect
སྲོག	(n.) life
སྲོག་བསྐྱབས།	(vol. v.) to save (life)
སླ་པོ།	(adj.) weak, diluted
སླེ་པོ།	(n.) basket
སླབ་གྲྭ	see སློབ་གྲྭ
སླེབས།	(inv. v.) to arrive, reach.................................. 13.2
སློབ་ཁང་།	(n.) classroom
སློབ་གྲྭ L སླབ་གྲྭ	(n.) school............................ 2.2
སློབ་གྲྭ་བ།L སླབ་གྲྭ་བ།	(n.) student, pupil 2.2
སློབ་གྲྭ་འབྲིང་བ།	(n.) secondary school 12.2
སློབ་གྲྭ་ཆེན་མོ།	(n.) university..................... 12.2
སློབ་གྲྭ་ཆུང་ཆུང་།	(n.) primary school 12.2
སློབ་དེབ།	(n.) instruction manual
སློབ་སྦྱོང་ + བྱེད།	(vol. v.) to study................. 10.2
སློབ་མ།	(n.) pupil, disciple
སློབ་ཚན།	(n.) lesson, course 1.2
སློབ་གསོ།	(n.) education
སློབ་བསོ་+བཏང་།	(vol. v.) to educate
གསང་བ།	(adj.) secret, hidden........... 37.2
གསང་སྤྱོད།	
གཟིམ་སྤྱོད། H	(n.) toilet 18.2
གསར་འགྱུར།	(n.) news
གསར་འགྱུར་'''	
འགོད་མཁན།	(n.) journalist 32.2
གསར་བརྗེ།	(n.) revolution
གསར་གཏོད་+བྱེད།	(vol. v.) to create, invent
གསར་པ།	(adj.) new............................. 4.2
གསར་འཛུགས་ + གནང་།	(vol. v.) to establish, found, build 37.2
གསལ་པོ།	(adj.) clear 17.2
གསུངས། H	(vol. v.) to say, speak 20.2
གསུམ།	(adj.) three
གསུམ་ཀ།	(n.) all three........................33.2
གསེར།	(n.) gold
གསེར་སྐྱེམས།	
ཕྱགས་སྐྱེམས། H	(n.) alcohol offering.............27.2
གསེར་ཁབ།	(n.) acupuncture 34.2
གསོ་བ་རིག་པ།	(n.) medicine 34.2
གསོན་པོ།	(adj.) alive
གསོལ་གྲོད'''	
བཀྲེས་གནང་། H	(inv. v.) to be hungry
གསོལ་རས་ + གནང་། H	(vol. v.) to make a gift...........8.2
གསོལ་ཚིགས་བཟོས། H	(vol. v.) to prepare a meal ..41.2
གསོལ་ཚིགས། H	(n.) meal 22.2
བསགས།	(vol. v.) to save, collect
བསད།	(vol. v.) to kill
བསང་ + བཏང་།	(vol. v.) to perform a ritual fumigation 25.2
བསམས།	(inv. v.) to think, consider ...14.2
བསམ་བློ།	
དགོངས་པ། H	(n.) thought, idea 14.2
བསམ་བློ་ + བཏང་།	(vol. v.) to think, ponder......14.2
བསམ་ཚུལ།	(n.) opinion
བསམ་ཡས།	(pr. n.) Samyä 26.2
བསིལ་དྲའི་སྤོ་ལོ།	(n.) basketball 32.2
བསེ་ལེ་པད་གོག	(n.) beetle............................22.2
བསོད་བདེ་ཆེན་པོ།	(adj.) lucky, fortunate
བསོད་ནམས།	(n.) merit
བསོད་པ།	(adj.) really good
བསྲེགས། L བཀྲགས།	(vol. v.) to grill 22.2
བསྲེས། L བཀྲེས།	(vol. v.) to mix
བསླང་།	(vol. v.) to make sth. stand up, raise, erect, incite, provoke 35.2
བསླབས།	(vol. v.) to teach, learn........10.2
བསླབས་བྱ་+རྒྱག	(vol. v.) to advise

ཧ་ Ha

ཧ་ + གོ	(inv. v.) to understand 28.2
ཧ་ཡང་།	(n.) aluminum, aluminum container 17.2
ཧ་+ལས།	(inv. v.) to be amazed 37.2
ཧ་ས་ཁ་པ།	(pr. n.) Kazakh
ཧབ་པན།	(n.) underpants, shorts
ཧམ་པ།	(n.) brutality, savagery
ཧམ་པ་ཚ་པོ།	(adj.) brutal
ཧི་མ་ལ་ཡ།	(pr. n.) Himalaya 13.2
ཧིན་དུ།	(n.) Hindu........................... 26.2
ཧུར་བརྩོན།	(adj.) diligent, earnest
ཧྥ་རན་སི།	(pr. n.) France, French......... 9.2
ལྷ།	(n.) god, divinity................. 27.2
ལྷ་ཁང་།	(n.) temple, chapel, sanctuary........................... 12.2
ལྷ་བྲིས་པ།	(n.) thangka painter........... 27.2
ལྷ་མོ།	(n.) goddess 27.2
	(n.) Tibetan opera 41.2
ལྷ་བཟོ་བ།	(n.) sculptor 27.2
ལྷ་རམས་པ།	(n.) Buddhist Doctor of Divinity (highest rank)........ 37.2
ལྷ་ས།	(pr. n.) Lhasa....................... 1.2
ལྷ་ + གསོལ།	(vol. v.) ritual propitiation of local divinities (of mountains, rivers, etc.)...... 40.2
ལྷག་པ།	(pr. n.) Mercury (planet)..... 14.2
ལྷག་པར་དུ།	(adv.) especially, above all
ལྷག་ཙམ། L ལྷག་ཙ།	(adv.) a little more 15.2
ལྷགས་པ།	(n.) wind............................. 14.2
ལྷགས་པ་རྒྱག	(inv. v.) to be windy
ལྷམ་གོ	
ཞབས་ཕྱུགས། H	(n.) boot............................. 23.2
ལྷོ།	(n.) south 20.2
ལྷོ་ཁ།	(pr. n.) Lhokha................... 22.2
ལྷོ་ཕྱོགས།	(n.) southern...................... 20.2
ལྷོད་ལྷོད།	(adj.) relaxed 18.2
ལྷོད་ལྷོད་+བྱེད།	(vol. v.) to calm down, relax

ཨ་ A

ཨ་ཁུ།	(n.) paternal uncle............... 6.2
ཨ་ཁུ་སྟོན་པ།	(pr. n.) Akhu Tönpa, a folk-hero..........................35.2
ཨ་ཅོར། ཞལ་ཅོར་ H	(n.) towel
ཨ་ལྕག	(n.) elder sister, wife, madam 6.2
ཨ་ཚུ།	(part.) Oh, it's cold!............16.2
ཨ་མཆོག རྣ་བ། L	
སྙན་མཆོག H	(n.) ear...............................16.2
ཨ་མཆོག་འོན་པ།	(adj.) deaf
ཨ་མདོ།	(pr. n.) Amdo......................22.2
ཨ་མདོ་བ།	(pr. n.) Amdowa
ཨ་ནི། དེ་ནས།	(co.) and so? so what?
ཨ་ནེ།	(n.) paternal aunt 6.2
ཨ་ནེ། རྗེ་བཙུན་མ། H	(n.) nun.................................2.2
ཨ་ཧྥེ་རི་ཀ	(n. pr) Africa
ཨ་ཕོ།	(n.) nomad (male)..............29.2
ཨ་བྲ།	(n.) pika (small rodent) 17.2
ཨ་མ། ཨ་མ་ལགས། H	(n.) mother 4.2
ཨ་མ་མ།	(part.) good heavens! 16.2
ཨ་མེ་རི་ཀ།	(pr. n.) America....................5.2
ཨ་མེ་རི་ཀ་བ།	(pr. n.) American
ཨ་ཙི།	(part.) Oh no! Dammit! 16.2
ཨ་ཚ།	(part.) Oh, it's hot!...............16.2
ཨ་ལད་པད་གོག	(n.) doll
ཨ་ལའི།	(idiom.) really! well well! 3.2
ཨ་ལོང་།	(n.) earring
ཨ་ཞང་།	(n.) maternal uncle................6.2
ཨ་ར།	(n.) moustache
ཨ་རག བཞེས་རག H	(n.) alcohol 21.2
ཨ་རབ།	(n.) Arab 9.2
ཨ་རོ།	(part.) Ow! Ouch!................16.2
ཨ་ཤེ།	(n.) high-quality khatak.......19.2
ཨང་གྲངས།	(n.) number, figure
ཨང་རྩིས།	(n.) mathematics,calculation
ཨང་དང་པོ།	(n.) first-class 32.2
ཨམ་ཕག ཨམ་ཕྲག L	(n.) pocket of a chuba.........30.2
ཨས།	(part.) echo question 31.3
ཨི་ཏ་ལི།	(pr. n.) Italy, Italian................9.2
ཨིན་ཆུང་།	(n.) young monk.................24.2
ཨུ་རུ་སུ།	(pr. n.) Russia, Russian........9.2
ཨེམ་ཆི།	(n.) doctor............................8.2
ཨོ་ཙ། ཨཏུ་ཙམ། L	(part.) not bad! 16.2

Bibliography

Manuals, grammars and dictionaries for Literary Tibetan

In English

Beyer, Stephan. 1992. *The Classical Tibetan Language.* Albany: State University of New York Press.

Das, Sarat Chandra. 1979. *Tibetan-English Dictionary*. Kyoto: Rinsen Book Company.

Goldstein, Melvyn C., with Gelek Rimpoche and Lobsang Phuntshog. 1991. *Essentials of Modern Literary Tibetan: A Reading Course and Reference Grammar.* Berkeley: University of California Press.

Roerich, George Nicolas. 1983. *Tibetsko-russko-anglijskij slovar's sanskritskimi paralleljami* (Tibetan-Russian-English dictionary with Sanskrit correspondences). 11 vols. Moskva: Izdatel'stvo Nauka.

In French

Kesang Gyurme (Skal-bzang 'gyur-med). 1994. *Le Clair Miroir.* Translated and annotated by H. Stoddard and N. Tournadre. Revised ed. Villeurbane: Sagesse-Diffusion.

In Tibetan

Bod-rgya tshig-mdzod chen-mo (Large Tibetan-Tibetan-Chinese dictionary). 1985. 3 vols. [2 vol. ed.: Minzu chubanshe, 1993]. Beijing: Mi-rigs dpe-skrun-khang.

Bya-tshig tshig-mdzod (Dictionary of verbs). 1986. Beijing: Mi-rigs dpe-skrun-khang.

Dag-yig gsar-bsgrigs (New Tibetan dictionary). 1979. Xining: Mtsho-ngon mi-rigs dpe-skrun-khang.

Dag-yig ma-nor lam-bzang (Dictionary of homophones). 1958. Beijing: Mi-rigs dpe-skrun-khang.

Kesang Gyurme (Skal-bzang 'gyur-med). 1981. *Bod kyi bdra-sprod rig-pa'i khrid-rgyun rab gsal me-long* (The clear mirror; see above under *Le Clair Miroir*).

Chengdu: Si-khron mi-dmangs dpe-skrun-khang.

Zhe-sa'i tshig-mdzod rab-gsal me-long *(Dictionary of honorific language). 1993.* Beijing: Mi-rigs dpe-skrun-khang.

Manuals, grammars and dictionaries for Standard Spoken Tibetan

In English

Goldstein, Melvyn C. 1978. *Tibetan-English Dictionary of Modern Tibetan.* Bibliotheca Himalayica II/7. Kathmandu: Ratna Pustak Bhandar.

Goldstein, Melvyn C., and Nawang Nornang. 1978. *Modern Spoken Tibetan: Lhasa Dialect.* Bibliotheca Himalayica II/14. Kathmandu: Rata Pustak Bhandar.

Goldstein, Melvyn C., and Ngawangthondup Narkyid. 1986. *English-Tibetan Dictionary of Modern of Tibetan.* Dharamsala: Library of Tibetan Works and Archives.

Goldstein, Melvyn C., ed., T. N. Shelling and J. T. Surkhang, assoc. eds., with Pierre Robillard. 2001. *The New Tibetan-English Dictionary of Modern Tibetan.* Berkeley: University of California Press.

Losang Thonden. 1986. *Modern Tibetan Language.* 2 vols. Dharamsala: Library of Tibetan Works and Archives.

Tashi. 1990. *A Basic Grammar of Modern Spoken Tibetan: A Practical Handbook.* Dharamsala: Library of Tibetan Works and Archives.

Tashi Tsering. 1988. *English-Tibetan-Chinese Dictionary.* Beijing: Mi-rigs dpe-skrun-khang.

In French

Blondeau, Anne-Marie, Ngawang Dakpa, and Fernand Meyer. 2001. *Dictionnaire thématique français-tibétain du tibétain parlé (Language standard).* Vol. 1: *L'homme, anatomie, fonctions motrices et viscerales.* Paris: L'Harmattan.

Tengye and Tensang. 1988. *Manuel de tibétain.* La Rochette, Savoie: Institut Karma Ling.

Tomulic, Rose. 1983. *Manuel de tibétain, parler de Lhassa.* Paris: Éditions Arc-en-ciel.

Tournadre, Nicolas. 1996. *L'Ergativité en tibétain: approche morphosyntaxique de la langue parlée.* Louvain and Paris: Peeters.

In Tibetan

Bod yig brda tshad ldan du sgyur ba'i las don u yon lhan khang gis bsgrigs (Committee for the standardization of the Tibetan language). 1999. *Bod kyi spyi skad skor gyi ched rtsom phyogs bsgrigs* (Collected articles on Standard Spoken Tibetan). Beijing: Mi-rigs dpe-skrun-khang.

In Chinese

Hu, Tan, et al. 1989. *Lasa kouyu duben* (Manual of Lhasa spoken language). Beijing: Minzu chubanshe.

Thub-bstan dbang-po, bsod-stobs lu'u ping fen. 1996. *Lha-sa'i kha-skad sbyong-deb, Lasa kouyu huihua shouce* (Collection of Tibetan texts in the Lhasa spoken dialect on Tibetan civilization). Beijing: Zhongyang minzu daxue chubanshe.

Other references

Manuals, grammars and studies on dialects

Agha, Asif. 1993. *Structural Form and Utterance Context in Lhasa Tibetan: Grammar and Indexicality in a Non-configurational Language.* Monographs in Linguistics and the Philosophy of Language, 2. New York: Peter Lang.

Anila Rinchen Palmo. 1988. *Introduction à la langue tibétaine* (with one cassette). Saint-Léon-sur-Vézère: Éditions Dzambala.

Anila Rinchen Palmo. 1988. *Lire et écrire le tibétain.* Saint-Léon-sur-Vézère: Éditions Dzambala.

Anila Rinchen Palmo. 1992. *Familiarisez-vous avec le tibétain.* Saint-Léon-sur-Vézère: Éditions Dzambala.

Bacot, Jacques. 1948. *Grammaire du tibétain littéraire.* 2 vols. Paris: Librairie d'Amerique et d'Orient.

Bell, Charles. 1996. *Grammar of Colloquial Tibetan.* London: Curzon.

Bielmeier, Roland. 1985. *Das Märchen vom Prinzen Cobzan: Eine tibetische Erzählung aus Baltistan. Text, Übersetzung, Grammatik und westtibetisch vergleichendes Glossar.* Beiträge zur tibetischen Erzählforschung, Bd. 6. Sankt Augustin: VGH Wissenschaftsverlag.

Bielmeier, Roland. 2000. "Syntactic, semantic and pragmatic-epistemic functions of auxiliaries in Western Tibetan." *Linguistics of the Tibeto-Burman Area* 23(2): 79-125.

Cabezón, José Ignacio, and Roger R. Jackson, eds. 1996. *Tibetan Literature: Studies in Genre.* Ithaca: Snow Lion Publications.

Causemann, Margret. 1989. *Dialekt und Erzählungen der Nangchenpas.* Beiträge zur tibetischen Erzählforschung, Bd. 11. Bonn: VGH Wissenschaftsverlag.

Chang, Kun, and Betty Shefts (with the help of Nawang Nornang and Lhadon Karsip). 1964. *A Manual of Standard Tibetan (Lhasa Dialect).* Seattle: University of Washington Press.

David-Neel, Alexandra. "Grammaire du tibétain." Unpublished manuscript. Digne: Fondation David-Neel.

DeLancey, Scott. 1986. "Evidentiality and volitionality in Tibetan." In *Evidentiality: The Linguistic Coding of Epistemology*, edited by Wallace Chafe and Johanna Nichols. Advances in Discourse Processes, 20. Norwood, NJ: Ablex Publishing Corporation.

DeLancey, Scott. 1998. "Semantic Categorization in Tibetan Honorific Nouns." *Anthropological Linguistics* 40: 109-123.

Denwood, Philip. 1999. *Tibetan.* Amsterdam and Philadelphia: John Benjamins Publishing Company.

Desgodins, Auguste. 1899. *Dictionnaire thibétain, latin, français.* Hong Kong: Les missionaires catholiques du Thibet.

Dpal ldan bkra shis, ed. 1999. *Tibetan-English Dictionary.* Gansu: Gansu Nationalities Press.

Driem, George van. 1998. *Dzongkha* (with three CDs). Leiden: Research CNWS, School of Asian, African, and Amerindian Studies.

Foucaux, Philippe Edouard. 1858. *Grammaire de la langue tibétaine.* Paris: Imprimerie impériale.

Geshe Lhundrup Sopa. 1983. *Lectures on Tibetan Religious Culture.* 2 vols. Dharamsala: Library of Tibetan Works and Archives.

Grand-Clément, Sylvie. 1989. *Le Tibétain sur le bout de la langue* (with one audiotape). Éditions Grandclément.

Hahn, Michael. 1994. *Lehrbuch der klassischen tibetischen Schriftsprache.* Swisttal-Odendorf: Indica and Tibetica Verlag.

Haller, Felix. 2000. *Dialekt und Erzählungen von Shigatse.* Beiträge zur tibetischen Erzählforschung, Bd. 13. Bonn: VGH Wissenschaftsverlag.

Haller, Felix. 2000. "Verbal categories of Shigatse Tibetan and Themchen Tibetan." *Linguistics of the Tibeto-Burman Area* 23(2): 175-191.

Hannah, Herbert Bruce. 1973. *A Grammar of the Tibetan Language: Literary and Colloquial.* Delhi: Cosmo Publications.

Häsler, Katrin. 2001. "An empathy-based approach to the description of the verb system of the Dege dialect of Tibetan." *Linguistics of the Tibeto-Burman Area* 24(1): 1-34.

Hein, Veronika. 2001. "The role of the speaker in the verbal system of the Tibetan dialect of Tabo/Spiti." *Linguistics of the Tibeto-Burman Area* 24(1): 35-48.

Hodge, Stephen. 1990. *An Introduction to Classical Tibetan.* Warminster: Aris and Phillips.

Hua, Kang, and Klu 'bum rgyal. 1993. *Bod rgya shan sbyar a mdo'i kha skad tshig mdzod* (Tibetan-Chinese Dictionary of the spoken language of Amdo). Gansu: Minzu chubanshe.

Huber, Brigitte. 2000. "Preliminary report on evidential categories in Lende Tibetan (Kyirong)." *Linguistics of the Tibeto-Burman Area* 23(2): 155-174.

Jäschke, H. A. 1929. *Tibetan Grammar.* Addenda by A. H. Francke, assisted by W. Simon. Berlin-Leipzig: Walter de Gruyter & Co.

Jäschke, H. A. 1971. *Handwörterbuch der tibetischen Sprache.* Osnabrück: Biblio Verlag.

Jäschke, H. A. 1980. *A Tibetan-English Dictionary.* Delhi: Motilal Banarsidass.

Karma Sanguié and Rigpéi Guielmo. 1995. *Le roi de la forêt (poème de mémorisation grammaticale).* Bouddhéité.

Koshal Sanyukta. 1979. *Ladakhi Grammar.* Delhi: Motilal Banarsidass.

Koshal Sanyukta. 1982. *Conversational Ladakhi.* Delhi: Motilal Banarsidass.

Lhamo Pemba. 1996. *Tibetan Proverbs (Bod kyi gtam-dpe).* Dharamsala: Library of Tibetan Works and Archives.

Lalou, Marcelle. 1950. *Manuel élémentaire de Tibétain classique: méthode empirique.* Paris: A. Maisonneuve.

Losang Thonden and Dekyi Thonden. 1993. *Talk Tibetan Today.* Delhi: Jayyed Press.

Magee, William A., and Elizabeth S. Napper; Jeffrey Hopkins, ed. 1993. *Fluent Tibetan.* 3 vols. Ithaca: Snow Lion Publications.

Nagano, Yasuhiko. 1995. *A Morphological Index of Classical Tibetan.* Tokyo: Seishido.

Namgyäl Tshering (Rnam rgyal tshe ring). 2001. *Bod yig brda rnying tshig mdzod* (Dictionary of old terms). Beijing: Krung go'i bod rig-pa dpe-drun-khang.

Norbu Chophel. 1989. *Say It in Tibetan: Conversations in Colloquial Tibetan.* New Delhi: Norbu Chophel.

Parfionovich, I. 1970. *Tibetskij pis'mennyj jazyk.* Moskva: Izdatel'stvo Nauka.

Roerich, George Nicolas. 1933. "The Tibetan Dialect of Lahul." *Journal of the Urusvati Himalayan Research Institute* 3: 83-189.

Roerich, George Nicolas. 1958. *Le parler de l'Amdo. Étude d'un dialecte archaïque du Tibet.* Serie Orientale Roma, 18. Rome: Istituto italiano per il Medio ed Estremo Oriente.

Roerich, George Nicolas, and Lopsang Phuntshok. 1957. *Textbook of Colloquial Tibetan.* Calcutta: Govt. of West Bengal, Education Dept., Education Bureau.

Sandup Tsering and Melvyn C. Goldstein. 1996. *Tibetan Phrasebook.* Lonely Planet Language Survival Kit. Oakland: Lonely Planet Publications.

Sangda Dorje (Gsang-bdag rdo-rje). 1994. *Mig-yid rna ba'i dga' ston legs bshad gter gyi bum bzang* (An excellent vase containing maxims, a feast for the eyes, the mind, and the hearing [a treatise on Tibetan poetry]). Lhasa: Bod-ljongs mi-dmangs dpe-skrun-khang.

Sangye T. Naga (Acharya) and Tsepak Rigzin. 1994. *Tibetan Quadrisyllabics, Phrases and Idioms.* Dharmasala: Library of Tibetan Works and Archives.

Sun, Jackson T. S. 1986. *Aspects of the Phonology of Amdo Tibetan Ndzorge śœme xora Dialect.* Tokyo: Institute for the Study of Languages and Cultures of Asia and Africa, Tokyo University of Foreign Studies.

Tashi. 1993. *Textbook of Modern Colloquial Tibetan Conversations.* Dharamsala: Library of Tibetan Works and Archives.

Thomas, Dominique. 1997. *Les bases essentielles de la grammaire tibétaine.* Saint-Léon-sur-Vézère: Éditions Dzambala.

Tournadre, Nicolas. 1991. "The rhetorical use of the Tibetan ergative." *Linguistics of the Tibeto-Burman Area* 14(1): 93-107.

Tournadre, Nicolas. 1995. "Tibetan Ergativity and the Trajectory Model." *New Horizons in Tibeto-Burman Morphosyntax.* Senri Ethnological Studies, 41. Osaka: National Museum of Ethnology.

Tournadre, Nicolas. 2001. "Final auxiliary verbs in literary Tibetan and in the dialects." *Linguistics of the Tibeto-Burman Area* 24(1): 49-111.

Volkart, Marianne. 2000. "The meaning of the auxiliary morpheme '*dug* in the aspect systems of Central Tibetan dialects." *Linguistics of the Tibeto-Burman Area* 23(2): 127-153.

Wilson, Joe B. 1992. *Translating Buddhism from Tibetan.* Ithaca: Snow Lion Publications.

Yu, Daoquan, et al. 1983. *Zang Han duizhao Lasa kouyu cidian* (Tibetan [Lhasa dialect]-Chinese dictionary). Beijing: Minzu chubanshe.

Works on Tibetan calligraphy

Beer, Robert. 1999. *The Encyclopedia of Tibetan Symbols and Motifs.* London: Serindia Publications.

Dawa Tsering (Zla-wa tshe-ring). 1983. *Mdzes-yig* (Esthetic writing). Chengdu: Si-khron mi-rigs dpe-skrun-khang.

Dawa Tsering (Zla-wa tshe-ring). 1999. *Yig gzugs sna brgya'i phyi mo zhal bshus ma* (A hundred types of calligraphy, the face of writing). Beijing: Mi-rigs dpe-skrun-khang.

Gangs-can bho-ta yig gzugs sna tshogs kyi phyi g.yu-khri'i phyag-'bri zhes bya ba bzhugs so (Collected articles; various original forms of calligraphy from the Land of Snows, cursive writing of the turquoise throne). 1987.

Go-ba dbyig and Hri zhod lis. *Gangs-can mkhas-pa'i phyag bris sna tshogs phyogs bsdud rin chen phreng-ba* (Precious rosary, a collection of calligraphic styles of learned ones from the Land of Snows). 1990. Lanzhou: Gan-su'u mi-rigs dpe-skrun-khang

Yig-gzugs 'bri stangs gsal-ba'i me-long (Clear mirror of calligraphy). 1993. Kunming: Yun-nan mi-rigs dpe-skrun-khang.

Some important websites on Tibetan culture

www.thdl.org [Tibetan and Himalayan Digital Library]

www.asianclassics.org [Asian Classics Input Project]

www.tbrc.org [Tibetan Buddhist Resource Center]